DISCARD

WORTH DOING

WORTH
DOING

∾

Steven G. Smith

STATE UNIVERSITY OF NEW YORK PRESS

Published by
State University of New York Press, Albany

© 2004 State University of New York

For information, address State University of New York Press,
90 State Street, Suite 700, Albany, NY 12207

Production by Diane Ganeles
Marketing by Anne M. Valentine

Library of Congress Cataloging in Publication Data

Smith, Steven G.
    Worth doing / Steven G. Smith.
      p. cm.
    Includes bibliographical references (p.) and index.
    ISBN 0-7914-6105-X (alk. paper) — ISBN 0-7914-6106-8 (pbk. : alk. paper)
    1. Life. 2. Values. I. Title.

  BD435.S723 2004
  121'.8—dc22   2003059029

10 9 8 7 6 5 4 3 2 1

As if you could kill time without injuring eternity.
—Thoreau

Contents

Preface

One day back in the supposedly mercenary 1980s, while listening to a college student explain his choice of job in terms of salary prospects, it hit me that he didn't care about wealth, as such, at all. What he wanted was a rationale that would make sense to the people he had to talk to about his life. He simulated selfishness because he longed for justification. Joining the Peace Corps or dropping out of respectable society to write poetry might have been equally good plans, had he been able to make them work in conversations like the one he was having with me.

Money does have an attribute that makes it a very desirable token in practical justification, something better even than its associations with pleasure and power: its definiteness. The issue here is the articulation of worth. Say that one job starts at $40,000 per year and another at $60,000. Sixty thousand dollars is quite evidently better worth your while. What would be an impressive reason to take the lower-paying job? If you say, "Because I think it will be more fun," can you expect anyone to approve? Under what conditions can you credibly say, "Because it leads to a more meaningful career"? What is the power of the claim, "Because it's what I love"? If, on the other hand, you choose the higher-paying job on the grounds that the pay makes it more definitely worthwhile, can you redeem your choice by showing that it is also humanly and personally *worthy* (that you are not after all taking a "mercenary" course of action in this instance)? Finally, at the highest and haziest end of worth articulation, what reasons for choosing a job can be given in relation to a transworldly point of reference like divine being or nirvana? What might people be talking about with phrases like "faith in work" or "a job for the soul"?

The more one reflects on the logical and experiential diversity of the questions that can be asked concerning worthy and worthwhile actions, the more one desires an overview of them and a fundamental analysis of them. But what would a theory of worth look like? It would be a form of moral philosophy, but it would have to be less abstract than moral philosophy as customarily done; it would have to come to grips with our practical choice-making at the level of "a job like this" and "a game like that," not only at the level of "justice" and "happiness"; it would have to sort through practical alternatives in a relatively permissive and pluralistic way, in the manner of a morally sensitive conversation among friends. In making fuller contact with a rich array of considerations that actually play a commanding role in everyday deliberation, such a theory could have the advantage also of creating a morally interesting and useful portrait of the cultural ethos the theorist inhabits.

"The good life" is, grammatically, an oversimple ideal. True, each of us has just one life to try to live in the best way, yet each of us must speak and think in variously figured domains, responding to deeply different challenges that life presents. There is a work way of working well, a play way of playing well, and so on. We are bound to forget much and become confused often as we move through our various zones of activity. Nothing is more characteristic of everyday life than feeling somewhat distracted and uncertain about the worth of what we are doing. And an agent who overcomes this with single-minded dedication to one kind of action, say one who works hard and wholeheartedly, is thereby placed at greater risk of missing the points of other kinds of action and of living a deformed life as a consequence. Thus an imperative of practical wisdom is to unify our strategies of practical evaluation so that everything we mean to do makes sense in relation to everything else we might mean to do. What sort of unification is called for? I doubt the value of boiling down all our practical standards into generalities about authentic or fulfilling human existence. That can be a way of overlooking all the things that actually matter. The more promising plan, I think, is to bring our ordinary working systems of practical evaluation into perspicuous togetherness with each other, framed but not tyrannized by more general principles, in such a way as to allow them in their reciprocal commentary and pooled suggestiveness to open up morally richer and happier prospects of life. I suggest elements for such a framing in the first and last chapters of this book.

The major domains of worth have not failed to attract a great deal of humanistic attention, including the attention of ethicists. But ethical reflection is typically committed to generalized principles of virtue, obligation, and/or value in such a way that it cannot or will not be guided by the internal goods of the actual practices it is applied to. For example, ethical treatments of issues relating to work, political participation, and sex tend to revolve around some generic conception of human dignity on the assumption that only such a generic conception can provide philosophical or rational leverage on a concrete moral issue; and as these treatments represent only thinly, if at all, the standards of success implied by the distinctive agencies of work, political action, and love, they fail to disclose and assess some of our ideally strongest motivations. (The situation is better in the realm of play, where the clue of playfulness is almost impossible to ignore.) The remedy for this thinness—and also for the haziness of philosophical models of "the good life" as a whole—is an immersion in domain-specific worth evaluations. The philosophical task here, or rather series of tasks, is to elucidate the conceptual forms specific to each domain that allow us to discuss our conduct articulately and responsibly in each domain and to compare and collate our practices across domains. To make a substantial start with this program is the mission of the chapters I have written on play, work, "action" in an eminent sense, love, and the borders of worth.

☙

For their good criticisms and suggestions relating to various parts of this book I'm grateful to Ted Ammon, Fletcher Cox, Richard Freis, David Holley, Bob King, Rick Mallette, Elise Smith, Katy Smith, Matt Smith, Jeff Wattles, Steve Webb, and the SUNY Press readers, and also to Jane Bunker, Bob Ginsberg, Bob McElvaine, and Edith Wyschogrod for help along the way.

Part of chapter 4 appeared as "'The Gates of Greatness Break Open': Religious Understandings of Worth in Action," *Journal of the American Academy of Religion* 70 (June 2002), and an earlier version of part of chapter 6 appeared as "On the Borders of the Worthwhile: Intoxication and Worship," *Journal of Value Inquiry* 30 (June 1996).

Chapter 1

෧ඏ

WORTH THINKING

1.1 Worth questions

"What did you do this afternoon?" a father asks his daughter over supper.

"We had softball," she replies warily.

"You played softball? What about your homework?"

"Dad, this was a scheduled practice. And the tournament's next week."

"Oh. Well—did you work on your fielding?"

Talking about things to do, we regularly signal our intentions with freighted words like "work" and "play." Here the father's purpose in drawing the work-play distinction is to put work before play. We have all grown up learning uses and counteruses for evaluatively charged action terms of this sort. "Work" and "play" are the ones we have heard and used the most, probably, but there are many others. They shape our practical thinking as a trellis shapes a vine.

Are there fixed principles of work and play meaning? The father invokes work in recognition of what seems to him practically necessary. Play, in contrast, is conceived as gratuitous—meaningful in *that* way. The father disapproves of her playing through the afternoon, but he understands why she wanted to. He would gladly play ball if the circumstances seemed right. Nevertheless, he wants his daughter to choose to work for another sort of reason, and he is unsure whether the claims of softball count enough to offset the work need he perceives; this is an apples-and-oranges problem, and it disturbs him not to have a sufficiently clear measure in hand by which to help his daughter's life stay in the right balance.

Suppose that instead of using the shield of a work reason, the daughter goes on the offensive: "I played softball this afternoon because I felt like having some fun." This starts a two-level struggle. The daughter means to assert *happiness* as a *personal* prerogative, that is, she wants it acknowledged that individuals rightly seek happiness as the product always in part of a free personal vibrancy, never solely of a conventional justification. But her way of making this assertion effective is to mobilize a *conception* of how time is spent in a *really worthwhile* manner, a conception that can compete with her father's in a generally intelligible discussion. Everyone sees the good of having fun on occasion. Play is part of everyone's flourishing. Her father can argue that getting on with homework would have been a better investment of afternoon effort because it would have increased available time in the future; she can argue that working all the time would burn her out. Behind their rival prescriptions for a worthwhile afternoon would be rival understandings of how one puts one's whole life into good shape.

A dispute like this confronts us with the problem of what makes for a well-shaped action of people together, as a collective. A third party might say, "Stop! Arguments like this are a waste of time." But they feel that their active disagreement is, for their purposes, worthwhile. They exhibit a moral culture.

It is important to recognize both that they *choose* to have this discussion and that they are *able* to have it. For we can imagine the daughter baldly asserting her independence or the father his authority—either way, someone's positional uniqueness defeating or overriding the fellowship of their jointly assumed question about what is worth doing. Or they might find themselves incapable of the discussion, thwarted by incommensurable differences of perspective, nonnegotiable differences of desire, lack of clear and demonstrable standards of adjudication, or lack of a binding adjudication procedure. All the same, people generally need to have such discussions. That is how they conjure into definite form the meaning of their lives. Aloofness in practical evaluation is hard; total aloofness, impossible.

In the present example, two people do go on. The father resumes:

"I don't know why you waste so much of your time with softball, anyway. You should concentrate more on academics if you want to get into a good college."

"I don't want to be a lawyer or a doctor. I want to play softball as a pro!" (So much for the play defense! Now she's taken over her coach's all-business view. Can an activity be accurately typed in conflicting ways?)

"That's crazy. Even if you could do that, it would be a waste. It's not worthy of you." (She hears in this also: "It's not worthy of *us*." The family restraint is irksome. But where *will* she fit in? How does one earn or assume one's proper share in a larger human enterprise?)

"It's what I like to do. It's what I'm really good at."

"I can understand how you feel that way now. But softball isn't a career."

"You're just saying that because it's nothing like *your* career!"

Why might it be thought that playing softball could or couldn't become a career? How would career plans justify the daughter to her father? If the father is sizing up career prospects unfairly, how could his bias be exposed? Could any other sort of share in social reality count as much as having a recognized career?

᭶

Twenty years later, the daughter has long since given up softball and found rich professional reward in the practice of law. A different problem emerges. She is close to an enviable completeness—family, home, friendships, social connections, and recreational pursuits falling into place as nicely as her work—and yet she experiences a sort of hollowness in everything. Her life is impeccably worthwhile and yet insufficient. "Is this all?" she asks herself.

Friends give her advice: "Have you ever tried hang gliding?" "What are you doing for your creative side?" "Your problem is you're not madly in love." Adventuring, creating, and romance form different categories of worth, at least, than the ones in which she is already a success. She can regain the free vibrancy of happiness-seeking by striking out in new directions. But apart from the value of simple variety, do adventurous, creative, and romantic actions promise significant kinds of benefit that no human agent should be content to miss? The very mention of these practical categories seems to possess some force. How should the lawyer weigh their claims? What other such categories exist? How, if at all, are they subject to reasonable assessment? Can they fit together coherently in a moral ideology?

She discusses her life with a religious counselor, who looks at it from a different angle entirely. The central problem, on this view, is that her dominant practical reference points are selfish and worldly. She cannot expect to find true happiness and peace of mind until she disinvests in all the forms of excellence that have appeared in her calculus so far. She should confide herself to a higher power (characterized as ____) that will enable the untying of those motivational knots and a surpassing of those limited horizons. Once the higher power takes over, all her actions will be essentially different; they will be better than "worthy." Jane finds it hard to fathom the practical meaning of this suggestion, but hard also to dismiss it. Is she really in the neighborhood of some sort of frontier of all worth that she could step across?

☙

The practical uncertainties of everyday worth thinking continually spur us to try to understand its logic better. Some questions that have peeked out in one sketch of a life:

Do we have clear and consistent evaluative conceptions of actions? (The *typing* issue.)

Can we make definite enough comparisons and measurements of worth to make decisions about it? (The *determinacy* issue.)

How do the sense and reality of self depend on worth pursuits? In what sense do I acquire worth? How does my qualification by worth of one sort relate to my qualification by worth of another sort? To what extent does the worth I achieve belong to myself and to what extent to collectives to which I belong? (The *identity* issue.)

What do I owe myself and what do I owe others in the pursuit of worth? (The *ethical* issue, in the more familiar sense.) How is worth negotiated between subjects? How may distorted views of worth be detected and corrected? (Issues of *reasonableness* and *validity*, for normative reflection; descriptively, the *culture* issue.)

Can self-gratification be combined coherently with worth justification? Can my own true desire be to impress others ideally? Can the measured pursuit of satisfaction be reconciled with the free pursuit of gladness and joy? (*Happiness* issues.)

Is it possible to make sense of a radically different approach to personal success, one that proposes a transcendence of ordinary worldly personal existence? (Issues posed typically by *religious* claims.)

1.2 Worth thinking as a moral system

I hypothesize that the prevalence of worth terms like "work" and "play" in our everyday practical discussions manifests the operation of a deeply entrenched, widely ramified, and humanly definitive system of evaluative conceptions. I aim to confirm this hypothesis by displaying a wide and dense array of worth conceptions and an order in their deployment and implications. The system of worth thinking is properly called moral, because it administers our lives with normative force and its implications for any of us matter to all of us. It is inconspicuous in formalized ethics, in spite of its importance in practice, because it is pluralistic and flexible rather than universalistic and ideally compulsory in its application. Also, it is hard for many of us to appreciate insofar as the relentless discussion of justice issues in a liberal, egalitarian society fosters a homogenized conception of goodness and simplistic disjunctions between other-regarding and self-regarding aims. Explicit worth thinking gets shoved aside in the ongoing moral emergency of a justice debate. But it returns whenever we let it, for its theme is the morally *best* state of affairs for each of us.

When we wish to address the social question of how we are faring together, and how each of us is capable of helping or hindering the others in faring well, we hold the focus of formalized public discussion on *value*, the transferable commodity-form of goodness; or on *well-being*, the goodness of a subject's life in the respect in which it may be affected by others' actions; or on *virtue*, an agent's general capacity to act in accordance with agreed moral requirements. In everyday reflective and persuasive discussions, however, our leading interest is most often in an agent's distinctive self-formation and self-expression in making choices that are not only right but the best, the strongest, seen in the context of what everyone else is doing, and accordingly our focus is on *worth*. Thus, whether a war's good results can outweigh its bad results or under what conditions citizens are obliged to participate in war (whether or not they in any sense want to) are familiar ethicists' questions, and important questions for the managers of a war effort; but whether it is sweet and fitting to die for one's country, or in what respects battle is like sport (and whether redeemingly or grotesquely), are questions for worth thinking, vitally important for the participants and hence for the leaders of a war. Worth thinking cultivates fully sufficient, freely adoptable reasons for action as distinct from ideally necessary constraints on action.

More often used and more influential than "right" and "wrong" are our numerous worth-terms for types of practical possibility (sport, for example, or work), types of event (game, career), types of act (helping, dominating), experienced qualities of activity (fun, tedious), and ascribed qualities of activity (noble, sleazy). We use this vocabulary to articulate satisfaction and dissatisfaction with our lives and, indeed, to make our lives knowable at the most elementary level. Our discourse in such terms is cosmogonic in the sense that it generates and sustains a practical human world, a stable order (actually a cluster of orders) in which to navigate and evaluate.[1] The reach of this discourse is, therefore, as wide as the whole human world. No issue of practical evaluation will not be touched by it. The evaluation of artworks, for example, will be affected by evaluation of the personal quality of the play, work, and experiencing of artists; the evaluation of public policy will be affected by evaluation of the leadership of those who propose and direct it; the evaluation of a business will be affected by evaluation of the impressiveness of the owners' ownership, the managers' managing, the producers' producing, and so forth.

Underlying the observable ubiquity and force of worth talk is a principle that I will put forward as a thesis of moral psychology: *worth is what we ordinarily think we mainly want*, what our right hands are reaching for, so to speak. As reasoning, communicative agents in a world, and collectively as a culture, we are worth chasers. By means of worth concepts we represent to ourselves what we mainly want to do, what we would like others to mainly want to do and to accomplish, and what will set the best practical example for others or ourselves. Practical deliberation is complex and often agonizing, because we want to maximize worth not only in objective terms, considering types and degrees of value, but also in terms of agent identity, considering how a realization of worth might enhance an individual or collective portfolio, establishing *how* it is good that *these* agents cooperate in a world. What value and identity actually mean in practice is, in major part, a function of worth seeking; thus the psychological hypothesis implies that worth conceptions can give us access to important aspects of value and identity (and agency, interest, happiness, and cosmology) that would otherwise remain hidden.

A corollary of this psychological claim is that it is false that we mainly seek either happiness, in the sense of having enjoyable experiences, or virtue, in the sense of satisfying the community's generic moral requirements on action. Stringent demands of justice and compassion do make a moral agent consider very seriously whether other subjects are enjoying life; the results of action must not fail the happiness test. Nor are failings in virtue to be condoned. An agent's principal project is not to be happy or virtuous, however, but rather to be *someone*—someone lacking whom the world of human agency would be poorer. And agents are deeply committed to assessing other agents in this light. It is even characteristic of us to get carried away with our worth preoccupations to the point of caring more about player statistics than about the beauty of playing a game, or caring more about the reputations of scientific researchers than the truth of scientific discoveries.

My claim also pulls against the romantic ideal of a self whose independent essence is the supreme reference of aspiration and the supreme test of the relevance of a moral demand. No one can articulate what being true to him- or herself amounts to without abiding by some, at least, of the terms of an interpersonal worth discourse. The wildest romantic protagonists are, after all, worth discussing and perhaps emulating. If one could march to a drummer *purely* one's own, in *no* way intending to impress other agents—if that were psychologically possible—one would become radically alienated from human life. (This point takes nothing away from the various sorts of personal independence and self-optimizing that *are* impressive.) In the perspective of worth thinking, there is not a split between individual and communal value any more than there is between happiness and virtue. Worth terms express an already-negotiated (yet still negotiating) adjustment among the different sites and potentialities of goodness in life.

Our typical difficulty in seeing how worth differences could be resolved (as in the daughter-father story) has a positive significance bearing on the relationship between the worth-seeking individual and the larger worth conversation. Worth prospects are exciting and alluring because they are open to unforeseen personal attunements. In this respect they accommodate me, as a free and complex seeker of identity and happiness; they accommodate you and the others, as my uncoercible partners in life; and they accommodate our collective sense of freedom and growth, as makers of a culture. Moreover, worth ideals relate us to fundamental principles of life that are not directly observed and so are bound to be expressed dubiously and controversially on the surface of practical affairs. (What he thinks of as his work, his answer to necessity, she thinks of as his hobby.)

But although there are permanent grounds of ambiguity, there could be no generally intelligible talk of worth if worth thinking did not possess a considerable degree of objective determinacy. Having drawn us in with its open prospects and intriguing problems, worth thinking must enable us to have a somewhat productive practical discussion. We cannot realize freedom, or encounter each other as other, or explore the foundational structures of our existence, except on certain terms. If we wanted to interpret fun, for instance, as an entirely subjective factor, unaccountable, we would take away the point of much of our fun talk—as in "That was a fun horror movie!" followed by "How can you say that?" So the discourses of worth require objectivity for the sake of both communicability (objectivity as stable information) and communion (objectivity as intersubjectivity). The encouraging implication for a philosophical discourse that would track the discourses of worth is that it can hope to accomplish something intellectually even as it remains convivially open.

Recognizing worth thinking as a moral system is rather like recognizing the earth as a physical system. "System" in this context means only that the phenomena cohere according to principles, not that the phenomena can be deduced from principles. Geological laws are a great help in interpreting what we find on the earth's surface, but knowing them does not remove the necessity of observing the oceans and the continents, the mountains and the basins, and particular mountain features. We can hope to take a well-routed trip through the world of worth thinking, offering looks at a number of major meaning-investments that have been made or that we seem generally to be prepared to make. No world trip is *the* world trip, and yet a good set of observations within a heuristically powerful set of principles can give us essential insights into a world's nature.

1.3 Worthwhileness and worthiness

We most often figure worth in an economic way, implying something spent and something purchased. In whatever is *worthwhile*, there is a satisfactory ratio between what an agent gives and what he or she gets. What an agent has to give is something that can be treated as a practical resource, like time or effort. Asking what is worthwhile for us, we think of ourselves as investing our resources in the things we choose to do. Our quality of life will go up or down as a result. We *acquire* the results of practical self-investment. But whereas the payoff from investing capital resources is that one becomes better or worse *off*, extrinsically advantaged, the payoff from self-investment is that one's personal existence becomes qualitatively better or worse in some measurable way. (Does "having a better life" turn into "being a better person" at any point?)

A daughter argues with her father about softball because her limited time must be spent on one thing or another. But the argument itself might not be worthwhile. One tries to judge the trade-off between the power of argument to improve the participant's lives and its direct negative effect or opportunity cost.

Now consider the decidedly noneconomic character of *worthiness*. To say that an agent or action or thing is worthy is to lift her, him, it, or them out of trade-off calculations and into a realm of goodness that we affirm unconditionally.[2] A worthy deed, for instance, is worth doing no matter what the cost. (This is more clearly affirmable when cost is measured in baser terms; but what about an Antarctic explorer who, in dying gallantly, leaves young orphans?) Regarding persons as worthy, we regard them as having an irrevocable share in what we conceive to be human *reality*, whatever else we feel or know about them. They are among the necessary causes of the personal world that has been made and is yet in the making. Regarding them as worthy, it is impossible not to attend to *who* they are. (Storytelling responds to the mandate of "who"-discernment.) Our starting assumption is that each agent *is* worthy as an indispensable referent of the basic moral thesis that agent diversity is unconditionally and concretely good—and this because each person *can* manifest himself or herself in such a way as to amplify the goodness of human and individual identity. (You already know that you can't have the best world without me, but you know it better if I do something estimable.)

Worthiness is not attached to anyone's while—or rather, worthiness belongs to a person's *whole* while in a completely gathered, conceivably immortal or eternal identity, a strong "who," "*who I really am*," rather than in the temporally dispersed mode that allows living time to be divided into portions, like a day wasted or a year well spent. A worthwhileness judgment assumes an agent, the owner of disposable potentiality, already set up and defined; then a more specific, additional identity—perhaps a professional identity achieved by a certain schooling and practice, like that of a baseball star, or perhaps only the casual identity of a Sunday fisherman who might catch something—can be checked against the ambitions and limitations that belong to the more fundamental identity. But judgments of worthiness pertain directly to fundamental identity. To be a good sport, for example, is a worthy way of being a baseball player, and is conceived as a more fundamental personal goodness shining through a sports identity. An unworthy action ("That was a cheap shot") darkens our vision of affirmable identity or weakens our grip on it.

Worthiness and worthwhileness can run together in such a way that they are hard to disentangle. For example, tool use is typically very worthwhile because it enables us to get more done, and at the same time, and much for that reason, it is a most worthy activity, manifesting a defining human power. We have a fundamentally distinctive position in the world because of our elaborated tool use. We would not have the dignity of the human position without the technical advantage of tools. Yet we don't identify the dignity with the advantage; indeed, it would seem deeply wrong in many situations to expect human beings to prove their worth by setting to work with tools.

More blurring of the worthiness-worthwhileness distinction occurs in the debates between the formalist and consequentialist schools of ethics, as each approach stretches to account for the moral considerations that the other deems central. Contractarians come to speak of elementally worthwhile "primary goods" and utilitarians concern themselves with the worthiness form of "virtues."[3] Attending to the worthiness-worthwhileness relation helps to clarify the structure and sense of these debates.

Ideals of worthiness attempt to express the ultimate standards by which we ask what is to be desired. We should not be able to ask meaningfully whether nobility, for instance, is to be desired; if it isn't, the possibility of asking whether anything is really to be desired seems to collapse. Kant's instructive way of getting at this point was to identify his single principle of worthiness (a principle of ruling one's life by strictly impartial policies) with the *form* of ethical judgment.[4] This form directly characterizes the root cause of moral action—where the agent is coming from, as we say. One does not choose to perform a noble deed because it contains a high score of goodness compared to other sorts of deeds; rather, one embraces and lives *from* nobility as a format related to or constituting an acceptable self-identity.[5]

The *matter* of ethical judgment, the practical object of choice—that is, the envisioned action, including its definitive consequences—is subordinate yet (as Kant recognized) essential in its own way. One cannot realize nobility of character without choosing concrete actions that express nobility. Conveniently, many actions carry prima facie worthwhileness characterizations relating them to standards of worthiness; for instance, charity work counts as worthwhile in a way that is congenial with the worthiness standard of nobility.

Corresponding to these counters of practical worth are pieces of identity with which we install ourselves relatively firmly in the world. By doing something worthwhile, one becomes a more definitely knowable self, an agentic commodity—as a baseball player who bats .300 *is* a good hitter—while the worthy self, as such, is more open to interpretation (Is he really a good sport? Has he been given a fair chance?). The self of worthwhileness is a desirable self, without much question, yet more negotiably so. I'd be very proud to be a .300 hitter against major league pitching, but I am not ashamed not to be this. I may be ashamed if I am *nothing* like this in *any* context, but with respect to any specified worthwhile action I am morally freer than I am with respect to standards of worthiness.

We need schemes of worthwhileness to possess more comfortable, discussable, and manipulable identities. We need ideals of worthiness to address the more threateningly and excitingly open questions about how to live. We need schemes of worthwhileness to implement ideals of worthiness practically, in measures of time; we need ideals of worthiness to prevent schemes of worthwhileness from becoming arbitrary or petty, losing touch with meanings that hold for all time. We need a map of worthwhileness to find our way in a world; we need an understanding of worthiness to assume and sponsor a world.

These two kinds of worth standard both support and destabilize each other. Worthiness ideals cannot be left shapelessly abstract; we want defining phrases and paradigm stories, as (in the case of nobility) a soldier assisting a fallen foe or a wife forgiving her unfaithful husband, so that we know to some extent how to respond to the most deeply open practical questions. Yet we dare not maintain so precise and accessible an understanding of nobility that anyone can come along and acquire merit by going through certain motions. Motivation, essentially invisible, counts for too much. An achievement too little open to question, too little dependent on the good will of the judges, and too little indicative of the agent's freedom would reduce to the winning of a certain game or the doing of a certain job, that is, to a species of worthwhileness at best. Thus, we must be a little evasive in defining the worthy. But we cannot guard against the mercenary threat so zealously that we no longer know how to praise worthiness, for without visible standards our moral community would dissolve.

Worthwhileness would cease to be meaningful if we came to see its negotiable counters as holding no more than revocable exchange value, like paper money. To keep intrinsic worth in worthwhileness, we give a certain reverence to games, jobs, and other conventionally worthwhile acts and experiences. We treat major forms of worthwhileness as unique, never interchangeable, so that it is never the case that by utilitarian calculation I can determine that I might *just as well* play a game as do a job. We think that moral identity is shaped and revealed by one's choices among such options. Whereas the need for tangibleness gives the mercenary a chance to undermine worthiness, the risk we run in respecting the forms of worthwhileness is that a false priest can easily load too much portent into a game or a job, trying to get it accepted as a full realization of unconditionally affirmable life. Balanced worth thinking requires us to restrain our reverence for the worthwhile, just as it asks us to ward off too definite a measurement of the worthy. Given the right interplay of these inhibitions, worthiness and worthwhileness make contact in the positive relationships of implementation (as worthwhile activities like charity work are needed to implement worthy qualities like nobility) and redemption (as worthy qualities like nobility make activities like charity work really meaningful). It follows that my own full practical reality is found neither in my mysterious "deep self" alone, nor in my "shallower" selves of worthwhile endeavor, but in the implementing and redeeming interplay between these two dimensions.[6]

The identity-constituting circuit of worth runs through our *world*, is cosmological as well as anthropological, in ways that are only faintly indicated by virtue ethics. Certainly the subject of virtue must be *in* a world—possessing courage, for example, implies exposure to threats of some sort—and the actual practices of our world put the virtues in strong demand. But a courageous agent, purely as such, does not partake of the substance *of* the world in the way that a "leader" does. An industrious agent, as such, is not concretely estimable in the way that a "real worker" is. A cheerful or inventive agent, as such, may be a good choice to play with, but is not yet understood as actually participating in the articulation of a particular domain of happy possibility in the way that a "real player" is. To approve of someone who "loves appropriately" is not to pick him or her out as a "real lover."[7] Action-centered categories like "leader," "worker," "player," "lover," and so forth reflect how we are embedded in projects of world-building in accordance with the most momentous opportunities that our humanity affords us.

An ethics of human rights or dignity is likely to stress a universal right of individuals not to be unnecessarily hindered from pursuing self-fulfillment. The virtue of such a theory is precisely *not* to prescribe any worth identities.[8] It leaves room for freedom and difference. So long as moral discussion revolves strictly around unconditional obligations and occasions of compulsion, this approach is hard to refute, for moral obligations must be freely and authentically assumed by moral subjects. The protection of human rights is also an attractive public policy inasmuch as it conduces to a more vibrant society, as Mill argued in *On Liberty*. But in its abstractness this ethic does not take up important tasks of moral discernment.

1.4 Worth domains

An agent's worth identity is built up out of citizenships and records kept in different worth countries, each a major domain of practical possibility. (When we speak of a "domain" we take the point of view of the agent who can see the implications of controlling practical principles and act by them, with somewhat predictable effects; we can also take the point of view of an interpreter of the text of practice and speak of worth "genres.") I do often want to offer an overall worth-characterization of a person, as in "Pat's a noble woman," but to explain or verify such a judgment I need a point of reference in a certain context, like Pat's leadership in community service. Having come to know Pat in this way, I am indeed confident that she will conduct herself nobly in any context, but the expectation spreads out unevenly. I suppose that in play, for instance, she would be a good sport; but what would be a case of creating nobly? Nobility can mean something in creation, no doubt, but it's not immediately clear what. At any rate, I have no reason (so far) to think of Pat as playful or creative; if I find that she excels in either of these ways, I have important new worth information about her.

Philosophers studying a generically conceived action-as-such are like physicists studying light-as-such. They know that types of action can exist, but not why the type differences would matter, just as physicists know about wavelength variation in light but not why color, as such, would matter. To a vision psychologist, however, color is a chief object of interest, because colors make a great difference for color perceivers. Species of action likewise make a great difference for practical evaluators, and so an account of worth must be, like vision psychology, prismatic.

Which domains of worth exist, then? And why those? This two-part question could send us astray in any of several ways. We might overoptimistically suppose that worth types can be deduced from the conditions of the possibility of practice in the same rigorous way that syllogistic forms are deduced from the conditions for inference. Or we could give the quest for necessity a naturalistic turn, treating the worth types as neurologically fixed, much as colors are largely determined by the physical structure of our visual nervous system. Or we could claim phenomenological necessity for those forms of practical meaning that we think we can render adequately evident in intuitive research. Or we could construe the subject as completely historical, as though the worth countries we recognize are finite threads in an endless rope of happenstance, as accidental as Yugoslavia.

The color analogy is helpful at this juncture. Blue, yellow, green, and red cannot be deduced from a general principle or placed with intuitive necessity in their actual positions in the visual scheme. Yet colors are not unaccountable. One can reflect on the prospect of color vision for beings like ourselves and see that there *would* be a calm color, something like blue, and an exuberant one, something like yellow, given that we are so much affected by emotions across that range. There would be a deeply encouraging color signifying the presence of our most precious material needs, like green (the oasis). Clearly we need an alarm-color, like red (blood). The something-like-blue demanded by this sort of argument captures the most important part of the meaning of actual blue, a meaning constructed by our talk and practice out of materials furnished by color vision. So the actual colors (in a culturally specified set of colors) do correspond to the basic structure of our relation with the world. They must, because they bear practical meaning.

One limitation of the light analogy is that a person can be totally color-blind and still see things, thanks to differences of brightness, whereas blindness to worth types, if not an outright impossibility, would constitute a grave human impairment. Imagine two individuals wondering together what to do without any cognizance of worth domains. One says, "Let's throw a ball back and forth." The other says, "No, let's sweep the sidewalk." We understand the nouns and verbs of this exchange, but in a more important way it is utterly enigmatic. We cannot sense the meaning of the practical alternatives unless we bring in the valuations and beliefs associated with the domains of work and play.

The light analogy suggests another point: we can see by considering the very idea of color that there must be a limited number of colors that count as primary. If there were a multitude of primary colors, too few of them could hold a proportionally large enough share of all color-meaning to seem as important as we want and need them to be. Similarly, there must be a limited number of main practical issues that we feel to be most important. They should reflect the recognizably largest human patterns of mattering. Among these, there should be a work realm somehow mapping human survival requirements and a play realm corresponding to our spontaneity. So much of the meaning of our lives is a function of our relationships that we should find ourselves also in the domains of "action" in the eminent sense

(helping, fighting, leading) and of love. These four we will explore in subsequent chapters. That they are of the highest significance is attested by the
rich literatures associated with them. They are not the only major worth
types worth exploring, but they make a very full introductory menu.[9]

Each worth color holds a spectrum of its own shades, offering its own
hierarchy and logic of discrimination. In each domain it is possible to
become fully absorbed in the loftier question of the essential worthiness of
the activity and to grapple with the nuts-and-bolts questions of worthwhile
choice of action. Whenever we stop and think evaluatively about what sort
of action to engage in, we stand at the brink of one or more of the worth
domains; whenever we act intelligently, we move with vision and scruple
into one or more of those worlds.

Holding all the worth domains together in a most obvious way is a
single master question, the force of which we are always able to feel: What
is worth doing? We pose this question to express our central concern for the
whole reality and value of our active existence, and we continually pursue
it using cross-domain conceptions like competence, dignity, satisfaction,
and happiness. The regulative ideal of our concern, practical worth, pertains to the real person across worth domains, although it is specified differently in different domains and is not definitely graspable in itself.

The worth domains also *bind each other* into a unity. Each has implications for all the others; each, in expressing hopes for ultimate worthiness and in receiving the implications of the other forms of worth,
becomes a holographic representation of the whole of action. Each can
become the main theme of a popular psychology (where its distinguishing
features will be rubbed off, promoting confusion). Each can generate an
evaluative perspective on everything, an ethos and an ethic. Unlike pure
colors, worth forms can saturate each other or disguise themselves as each
other. Their distinctness is assured only by the stability of our most effective strategies for evaluating practice—a stability that we can confirm by
developing useful, well-differentiated accounts for key terms in their
home contexts.

Play is action in the character of free assumption of possibilities that
present themselves. One can put on a work-self or a love-self in the same
spontaneous, profoundly optional way in which one playfully puts on a
play-self. We would misunderstand work and love if we stressed only their
contrasts with play.

Work centrally represents our liability to be caught by a practical
demand, our having to measure up. Productivity is a preeminent norm of
work but can become an issue even in play and love.

Action in the eminent sense means directing the community of subjects.
But all human activities are in some way undertaken by a community and

in some way affect it. Every activity needs leadership and diplomacy. A sports team needs a captain; lovers need a pact.

Loving is self-giving movement toward another reality seen in the character of an ultimate good. But any activity is perfected in love, as in devoted work or passionate play. A central issue in all our practice is how much we give ourselves to it.

I place these worth domains in a certain order to reflect some larger structures in worth. Play and work are appropriate to discuss first, because they present arresting examples of activity on the lower end of worth, the preworth/worth frontier (in sheer fun and brute labor), where the minimum conditions of worth are at issue (chapters 2 and 3). They also get us off to a fast start in bringing out the systematic character of worth thinking, because many of their principles have already been relatively well articulated in everyday discourse. Action and love, on the other hand, are more centrally concerned with the embedding and reorienting of world and life in human relationships. The moral exigency of relationship issues is supreme.[10] In that sense, we come in these domains to the high end of the worth manifold (chapters 4 and 5). Indeed, love in its self-abnegating aspect bids to leave worth reckoning behind altogether, and so love makes a good transition to consideration of practices the real point of which is to step outside of worth, like intoxication and worship (chapter 6).

1.5 Transworth and religion

We humans want even more than the human: we wish for infinite reality and value to be poured somehow into human vessels, so that we may have a life like that of "the gods . . . in the highest degree blessed and happy" (Aristotle).[11] This lust for worth opens us to the possibility of what I will call transworth. It can lead to a subordination of worth standards to considerations of another sort, or it can lead to a blurring or unraveling of our worth concepts as we try to apply them outside their proper human sphere—to Nature or Being or God, for example. In any case, the system of worth thinking cannot be made safe against transworth simply by counseling sobriety. Basic principles of measurement and justification open the door to it.

Within the system of worth thinking, worthiness judgments are effectively beyond challenge insofar as they express the constitutive rules of the system. The point of having a worthiness concept like dignity lies in being always able to ask whether an act or activity—say, playing softball—is dignified or degrading, and in *not* being able to ask (relevantly) whether dignity is worthwhile or whether a paradigmatic instance of degradation, like rape or torture, is bad. But we do not revere worthiness standards only because they furnish the formal conditions of the possibility of evaluation. Even more importantly, we realize that the jurisdiction in these matters is not our own but is actually and potentially shared with our fellow subjects, and that the shared subjectivity that ideally determines worthiness is a more thoroughly mediated, normatively purer subjectivity than that of worthwhileness judgments. To illustrate: playing softball is standardly granted by Americans to be a fun thing to do. If you report to an American that you have spent a couple of hours playing softball, then, other things being equal, you can expect some sort of affirming response. Even in a pro-softball society, however, subjects differ greatly in their appreciation for the sport. You may not expect that the second person you speak to will grant your having played softball the same degree of worthwhileness that your first respondent granted. In contrast, you may and should expect that any fellow subject will revere human dignity and abhor degradation unconditionally. (The fact that we do have different shades of aversion to rape or torture is not allowed practical meaning.) Our worthiness judgments are required to match, because we construe standards of worthiness as definitive of affirmable human life in general, not just of a particular hue in the human spectrum. They are understood to represent all of us most perfectly. Worthiness judgments are the dimension in worth thinking where we meet the moral authority of public subjectivity most directly.

Granting all that in principle—and ignoring, for now, all the problems that arise in producing and applying worthiness judgments with general acceptance—a question remains about how a moral community can know that their assumptions about human potentiality and well-being are sound. One can admit that measurement would not be possible without a certain yardstick already in use and still ask for a measurement of the yardstick. Measurement involves a relation between an intentionally fixed value and a phenomenon; but any concrete standard of measure itself is a phenomenon and can become the object of a differently articulated interest. The yardstick paradox is that any yardstick awaits measurement by a different yardstick. If drug-related problems make us uncertain of our medical assumptions, for example, we can ask to what extent "health" as medically administered corresponds to real wellness. We can ask if our laws really promote justice. Whether we can answer such a question, at a given juncture, depends on whether we can bring a new measuring conception into focus.

Usually, the regress of measurement demands is cut off when practical interest disappears. I may need to know that a foot of length corresponds to a human foot, but the human foot's length needs no explanation, as it is evidently and inescapably *my* foot. I may, however, become mystified by the size of my foot, and more broadly by the scale of organismal structures in physical nature, and want a measure that relates these phenomena intelligibly to the rest of what occurs on our planet. No obtainable measure can close such questioning once and for all. Resolution comes only in a shift *to a different question,* such as in moving from one measurement issue to another or in moving from a measurement question to a justification question.

The quest for justification is similarly open. How could a moral community know that their relations are perfectly regulated and adequately responsible? A community's awareness is always liable to be changed, as new expressions of personal freedom require renegotiation of forms of togetherness, hidden injustices come to light, or new subjects present themselves. A new way of measuring the intelligence of sentient beings or their capacity for suffering may produce a whole new class of fellow subjects in relationship with whom justification must be sought.

That measurement and justification are pursued on different lines has already become evident in the central bifurcation of worth thinking, according to which worthwhileness judgments are keyed to measurement and worthiness judgments aim for deeper justification. Measurement responds to a requirement for fixing and reconciling the contents of consciousness; justification responds to a requirement for intersubjective concurrence. The measurement issue is shaped by what we happen to be able to think of; the issue of intersubjective concurrence is shaped by the fellow subjects who happen to be around.

Although justification questions always take precedence normatively, either sort of question can be decisive in the configuration of worth thinking. For example: (1) The thesis that a baseball player with a .300 batting average is a good hitter is supportable by measurement up to a point—we can show that a team is likely to win more games for every player who gets hits that often—but if you think "So what?," if you need to be shown that a .300 average really merits respect, you must check with the people who care about baseball performance, for it is their concurring in appreciation of the .300 hitter and your concurring with them that resolves that question. (2) A system for distributing material goods equally to all subjects is demonstrably just when no more mutually agreeable alternative is conceivable, and yet it still may be unclear whether the whole system of consumption is happy or miserable, "worth it" or not, until Buddhist measurements of psychic reality and satisfaction are applied.

Both measurement and justification issues are implicated in the appearance of the putatively transworthy. If we were not aware of the yardstick paradox, we could not recognize the possible meaningfulness of an unfamiliar way of measuring—a claim that the humble are exalted, for instance, or that nonaction is effective action. If we were not ordinarily in search of justified relationship with our fellow human subjects, we would not be liable to be caught up in relationship with an extraordinary Other (like God or the Enlightened Mind) with whom concurrence is sought very differently. Our understanding of the possible meanings of "spiritual" life—a life in direct relation with the ultimate conditions of valid living—is built on our constant contact with these mysteries of measurement and relationship.[12]

Suppose now that an emissary of some transworthy realm comes to the earthly ruler, worth thinking, sees the authority of worthiness standards within worth thinking, and says: "Worthiness! Give yourself up! You know that precisely to the extent that you seek to be unconditionally imperative, you cannot stand to be taken for any kind of specified worthwhileness. In pursuit of a final adjudication of value, all pretentions of merit must be abandoned. The ultimate evaluation of human life cannot be in human hands, anyway; it can be given and articulated only in a larger-than-human perspective. And humans can appropriate such an evaluation only in inmost inwardness, not in the marketplace of interhuman concurrence. This possibility can now become actual, we know, due to _____ [an exemplary event]. In comparison with the now-revealed transworthy [such as enlightenment, or divine love, or an all-darkening horror], one can see that what has passed for worthiness in ordinary talk is but splendid worthlessness."

Notice that this religious argument can trade on an analogy between the position of the transworthy vis-à-vis worth thinking and the position of worthiness vis-à-vis worthwhileness. Worthiness ideals must be as open and deep as possible while still performing their function of guiding conduct. The transworthy trumps them with infinite openness and depth. But because the transworthy also wants to guide conduct and to take practical form in transplaying, transworking, and so forth, worthiness can answer its challenge in this way: "I have already distanced myself from myopic worldly calculations. Endorsing restraint and sacrifice, I rise unmistakably out of the world to a position from which worldly choices can be made with critical discernment. Yet my connection with the world is not broken. Praise and blame on my terms always have palpable reference and practical relevance. Action in worth domains is reliably affirmable. My way sustains personal identity, as it allows each individual to have an intelligible career. Transworth, however, can scarcely be related to human beings at all, for on its so-called path personalities are erased and actions become unpredictable, unrecognizable, and unaccountable. The world is thus betrayed, not redeemed. It is as though, adapting the words of Kant, 'the light dove of worthiness, cleaving the air in her free flight, and feeling its resistance, imagined that its flight would be still easier in empty space,' that is, away from human worth."[13]

The position of worthiness in this exchange has strengths and weaknesses like those of worthwhileness in the internal debate of worth thinking. It is strong in representing the necessity for determination and implementation. It is weak in its clinging to particular forms—a grand vision of humanity and the world, perhaps, but still a particular vision—insofar as this determinacy compromises its mission of addressing the greatest questions about life *in their openness.*

The merely abstract possibility of transworth is evaluatively vacuous, and worthiness has little to fear from it. Even if miracles break out all over, pointing up the questionableness of our yardsticks, they may suggest no criteria of judging other than those already given with worthiness standards, and practical evaluators may shrug them off. The claim of a transworthy *reality*, however, pushing measurement and justification into new forms, can crack the pretended sovereignty of worthiness. Beyond a provocative message, religious movements characteristically present an array of actual better-than-worthy actions performed by their members—actions of radical generosity or fervor, for example, that instantly redefine the boundaries of excellence in human life.

Supposing that the superior demands of transworth can be sustained—supposing, in other words, that this religious sort of life is livable—worthiness ought not to capitulate wholly. It can repeat to the transworthy what it has always been hearing from worthwhileness: "For human beings inhabiting a world, in time, there must be a measuring out and an implementation of the good life. You can strike the pose of unworldly grandeur and purity; you can complain of the distortions of goodness entailed in the very notion of ethics (such as legalism); but if there is to be any sort of coherent practical response to your claim, you must enter into a partnership with moral judgment, and a crucial part of the scaling of your claim to life in the world will be handled by judgments of worthiness and worthwhileness. When we offer on your behalf a 'noble discourse' on 'true satisfaction' and 'true merit,' you will prefer to think of a transcendence of the categories of satisfaction and merit, while we will prefer to think of the coming-to-earth of your goodness and its insertion into human life. We will implement you by providing the attention-commanding language and practical devices of worth; you will redeem us with your cogent handling of the unsurpassable measurement and justification issues that you have forced on our attention."

The practical transworth-worth relationship is a key to the distinctive character of religious morality no less important than religion's special epistemological or cosmological claims. Among the forms this relationship can assume, a striking difference appears between the "salvationist" religion that promises liberation from worth thinking—an exalted reward of love or bliss that completely supersedes our worldly or ego-bound forms of success—and the "worldly" religion that aims to secure the foundations and perfect the guidance of worth thinking. Not that salvationist religion dispenses with worth thinking or that worldly religion uncritically accepts it; it is fairer to say that the one approach inclines more to paradox and tension, while the other is more constructive and harmonizing. This complexity in the transworth-worth relationship is mirrored, in turn, in worthiness-worthwhileness relations: in one worth ethos, *of course* people who want to be noble do charitable work (are they crass?), while in a more disjunctive ethos no one would *ever* perform an act under the description "charitable work" thinking it relevant to true nobility (are they whimsical?).

The explorations of the following chapters will include some probing of transworthy horizons that belong to each worth domain. Although we will turn up a number of clues for a theory of religious morality or, more broadly, of religious meaning, we will not attempt to construct one; our main interest here is in recognizing how worth thinking is exposed to religious challenge and how it can in some ways incite and support religious appeals.

1.6 The ideal of practical lucidity

The drive to get clear on what is worth doing and to be really interested in what is really practically interesting is central in any morally sensitive life. It animates communities as well as individuals, as one can hear in the discourse of leaders and would-be leaders. Listen, for example, to what candidates in a national election say about courses of action that are worthy of the nation or worthwhile for it. Notice how much of the substance of leadership, in general, is the propagation of a vision of what is worth doing for the community that is to be led. We are brought up short when we see that the boldest articulation of what is communally worth doing is found in fascist discourse. (It was the vigorous adducing of this kind of meaning that made Hitler's speeches so effective.) To oppose fascism, one swings toward the liberal position of refusing to impose on others in any avoidable way and the libertarian position of refusing to be imposed on oneself. But then what can draw us from these morally alienated positions back into a collective and comprehensive deliberation on the best practices?

A first answer has already been indicated. We *do not* leave each other alone. Each human life is interwoven with an indefinite number of others through the sort of communication we more or less constantly engage in—declaring intentions to each other on a huge platform of assumed common meaning. To think that the assumed common meanings are only instrumental and "value-neutral," that we are entirely at liberty in relation to them, is unrealistic. Given that we are deep in each other's games, we are better off if we are conscious of what is going on and able to ask explicitly how our lives should be coordinated.

A still more important answer is that we really do want and need what only relationship with others can give. First, our worth ideals need *content*; I cannot gain much understanding of what constitutes success in living if I lack concrete reference points like Muhammad or Mother Teresa or the good person who lives next door.[14] Second, as to the necessary goal of *maximizing* worth, I cannot fail to be interested in every actual or possible incarnation of worth by every other person. Once I admit that my own life is richer because certain real, estimable individuals have lived, I must admit also that my happiness is ultimately affected by the worth status of every agent. Third, as to *validity*, I cannot think of myself or anyone else succeeding if I cannot think that someone else thinks (or should think) the same. I can experience pleasure quite privately—and the sweetest fruits of pleasure may indeed tempt me off onto "disgraceful" paths—but I cannot know or enjoy worth by myself.

Thus, we are all already busy perceiving and trying to justify worth attainments. But why should we ever think that we *can* know what we are about well enough to resolve a given set of practical uncertainties? This question is easier to answer for the familiar sort of "ethics problems" that are created by clashing interests and policies. In those cases the lack of a resolution is a roadblock to coexistence, and any way of treating them that did not yield a resolution would seem pointless. But worth thinking typically operates in a more open practical space where agent freedom is freer, not trapped in a conflict of rival freedoms. Worth advice is friendly; its prospect is mutual gain, seen opportunistically. Should we therefore regard worth thinking as more personal, more inspirational, less reasonable?

Yes and no. I have already pointed out that as a system of evaluation and means of regulating relationships, worth thinking requires considerable objective determinacy. At the very minimum, we must be able to discuss worth judgments with each other just because we must be able to discuss anything with each other. The need is more urgent with matters we care more about. But in those matters we also have a greater need to maintain defenses and escape routes. Our jealousy for our freedom is somewhat at odds with our interest in understanding the structure of practice clearly. We want to be persuaded rather than compelled to our actions. Thus, whatever the results of our inquiry, it will remain true of worth conceptions *normatively* that one has more discretion in their interpretation and use than one can have with the rules that come into play in "ethics problems." The discretion granted is not, however, complete liberty. How could anyone in good conscience refrain from looking to see as much goodness as can be seen on paths that lie ahead? Not to look, not to map, not to infer rules, not to pursue implications on the largest scale would be to abandon one's role in a system of mutual guidance and to forswear the human excellence of knowing. The goal of our exercise need not be to gain the power of imposing a particular set of worth judgments on anyone, even oneself; but it may be to gain the richest possible awareness in order to *teach* someone, even oneself, about the shapes of human fulfillment.[15]

1.7 Human-kind bias as a problem for worth thinking

Any discourse that purports to define the meaning of human life is bound to be haunted by *human-kind bias*. For many people, this kind of bias is not an everyday practical concern. We do readily understand questions about personal bias, since each of us is involved in daily collisions of perspective with other individuals to whom we must adjust. Generally obvious, too, is our daily experience of failure and perishing, of being overmatched by an indifferent cosmos, humanity's limits chafing us in such a way that we are moved to wonder what our humanoid delusions may be. But the possibility of distorted judgment rooted in human-kind differences like sex, race, age, class, and culture is peculiarly invisible to those of us who do not consciously suffer the more debilitating effects of one or another kind of discrimination. Although it is obvious that human-kind differences exist and that they involve differences in judging that matter a great deal, one's *own* way of judging, as far as this difference is concerned, still seems unimpeachable insofar as one believes and feels oneself to be in a natural, nonnegotiable, and nonproblematic place in a human-kinds system. Thus, a woman might say, "That's a man for you," yet feel no obligation to take masculine valuations seriously; an older man might say, "Youth is wasted on the young," but feel no obligation to rouse youthfulness in his own heart; an ethnic group might make it a point of honor to discount another ethnic group's perspective. A well-known problem with the object of human-kinds talk is stereotyping; the correlated problem with the subject is a kind of complacency *in* type. To pretend to solve this problem by adding extra critical cycles to one's own method of reflection would be ludicrous. The best hope, of course, is to place one's thinking in a large conversation with diverse participants.

An account of worth that did not represent human life fairly would fail a rather important test. But consider the biased affiliation of worth with privileged classes. One could predict that any class that sees itself as superior would reserve for itself the activities to which the greatest worth accrues; they would want to manipulate a worth scheme to prop up their social rank or give it meaningful content. This reading of the situation assumes a quasi-objective worth scheme in which the most powerful get to do what any human being would naturally wish to do. But socially accepted worth schemes might always have been tilted or warped already in favor of the special opportunities of the most powerful. The masculine glorification of fighting, for example, has produced not only certain values attaching to war but war itself as a sex-marked institution, which is the presupposition of war's glory. War as a moral thing (a practice in the sense developed by MacIntyre) is a posit of worth thinking that we cannot very well account for if we do not know about a specifically male quest for advantage.[16]

Worth as such, the very ideal, may be sex- and gender-biased. In most human cultures, articulable worth *in general* is affiliated more with males than with females.[17] Men earn prestige or honor in prescribed ways and by definite increments. Thanks to this intelligible structure for achieving identity, males can compete, can have justifiable causes of quarrel, can know when a quarrel is over, and can become famous or contemptible. Women, on the other hand, tend to be valued in a less measured way. They tend to be regarded as outside worth or as infinitely worthy. A person in the female-subject position is less concerned with discrete achievements and more with the overall quality of life. Paradoxically, the male subject stands in horror of being female (since in that position the meaningfulness of male success evaporates) and yet is vitally concerned to have a secure relationship with the female.

If we are to deal with worth thinking as a live moral scheme, we should watch out for moral distortions in worth thinking that would be attributable to the pressing of one class of humans for advantage over others. The categories, examples, principles, and conclusions that appear in a philosophy of worth should likewise be under suspicion. But suspicion should not preclude appreciation of contributions to our worth understanding made from limited perspectives. Think of the help some ancient Athenian gentlemen have given us with our political ideals—ideals of personal freedom and collegial action that ultimately lend themselves better to enriching many lives than to restricting them.

ை

Our worth domain studies of play, work, love, and action will follow a common plan.

Each domain is most naturally entered by determining first what is essential to its type of action, and making this determination in each case opens up a distinctive anthropological and cosmological perspective. For the general theme of a species of worthy action is the active relationship of a certain kind of being with a certain world-formation.

The second major phase of each domain study consists of tracing out the structure of a domain's distinctive system of practical intelligibility—how that mode of action makes itself appreciable—by discovering the order implied by its most frequently used evaluative concepts.

In a third phase, we shall scout the frontiers of each domain to consider the difficulties that are inherent in attempts to apply the ideals of a mode of action beyond the frame of reference in which they normally make sense; we shall also consider how to make sense of amazing proposals of transworth that are flung, as it were, across these frontiers, using clues from worth thinking as we are able.

Chapter 2

༺ঔৎ༻

PLAY

2.1 The appeals of possibility

Much activity that we categorize as play seems so spontaneous that it comes into the regime of worth crediting not at all, or only ambiguously ("Just do it"). And yet certain rewards of play are so sweetly desirable and humanly fulfilling that thinkers have found in it a paradigm of human worth or even of transworthy life surpassing the usual terms of worth accounting. "Human beings are contrived as playthings of God, and the best part of them is really just that; and thus I say that every man and woman ought to pass through life in accordance with this character, playing at the noblest of pastimes" (Plato).[1] "Human beings only play when in the full meaning of the word they are human, and *they are only completely human when they play*" (Schiller).[2] "Civilization arises and unfolds in and as play" (Huizinga).[3] "You can have peace without the world, if you opt for death, or the world without peace if you decide for doing and having and achieving. Only in play can you have both. . . . Play, then, is the answer to the puzzle of our existence" (George Sheehan).[4] Really?

To associate play purely with animal spontaneity and pleasure and to leave it on that account out of moral reckoning would be to miss the depth of play's anthropological import and the detail of its own logic of worth. It is another question, however, whether an embrace of play as "the answer to the puzzle of our existence" is justified.

༺ঔৎ༻

What is play? Rival definitions reflect different practical interests and programs. Positive approaches define playing by its intrinsically satisfying form

25

(beautiful, perfect) or object (possibility) or attitude (openness) or affect
(fun).[5] Play can also be defined negatively as whatever doesn't help in doing
what is considered necessary to be done.[6] Positive and negative perspectives
agree on the gratuitousness in play, but one side sees the motivational sufficiency of play's beauty or fun as its fundamental principle, leaving open
the question whether it has effects that are valued from a nonplayful perspective, while the other sees its instrumental nonefficiency as the key, leaving open the question whether or to what extent play activities are attractive. More ambitious approaches want not merely to assert that play has
important attributes for human purposes but to define it as a principle, or
the principle, of the realization of the world or humanity, so that our ordinary feelings and judgments about play have to be worked into a central
position in our total understanding of life. (We will consider two such
approaches taken by Schiller and Nietzsche, respectively.)

The oldest linguistic evidence bearing on the meaning of play is discon-
certing: Indo-European *plegan*, meaning to exercise, to put oneself out, is the
root of the German word for duty, *Pflicht*, as well as "play"! (I will concentrate on English; for a report on other languages, see the second chapter of
Huizinga's *Homo Ludens*.) Diverse uses of the English word "play" show
movement between a very general sense, almost the same as activity as such,
and more specific senses in which various features are highlighted:

1. The swordplay was fast and furious.
2. The compass needle should have free play.
3. Don't be offended; I was only playing with you.
4. She brought her best arguments into play.
5. The lead guitarist played brilliantly.

(1) and (2) are an interesting pair, because they round out the physical
or metaphysical picture for us: the swordplay is an especially energetic
activity, force expanding impetuously to fill available space, while the compass needle's play is sheer freedom of movement, space in which activity
might happen. We arrive at the composite portrait of a certain happy relationship between agent and field of possibility. The two meanings interpen-
etrate: to speak of swordplay rather than of sword-work (as you might if it
were a long or bloody battle) is to suggest a certain delightfulness and a
gamelike uncertainty of outcome, while to say that the compass needle
should have play is to say that the needle must be able to point this way and
that, not merely that space exists.

The retreating force of (3) and the attacking force of (4) make them an
interesting pair as well. Whether an activity is getting the field of possibility

it requires, how its consequences impinge on us, and whether it is welcome are all issues that these distinct uses of "play" adjudicate rather sensitively.

The "brilliant playing" of a guitarist (5) seems like a fully authentic specimen of playing as such (in the way that "works great" is equivalent to "really works"). This was what was supposed to happen in playing all along. "Oh, he could *play*," we say about a guitar legend. We are talking about what a fully realized agent he is and, at the same time, how we are swept off our feet in listening to him. Note the finality in "He could *play*": there is nothing to add about his ability or our satisfaction in it.

The guitarist's playing is more strictly bound by standards than the free play of children, and yet we would miss something important if we spoke only of his proficiency in handling the guitar well, construing his music as work and his instrument as a machine. We would miss the wonderful bursting forth of music from his soul (and ours), an instant self-realization and satisfaction. We can, however, import all this meaning into work if we choose a play characterization for it: "The ditchdigger played his shovel like a master." (Compare: "He's just playing around with that shovel.")

The best general inference from usage seems to be that play is that kind of activity that occurs just because it is possible; it is attractive enough and rewarding enough not to depend on compulsion, even if the possibility to which a player responds has need and tension within it.[7] To have play is to have possibility. To be played out is to lose possibility. Play is thus an apt metaphor or model for any aspect of life considered as intrinsically meaningful or as beyond motivational doubt (fun, delightful, absorbing). Since play is a kind of elopement with possibility, an already-having-chosen or an already-having-arrived of appealing possibility, a player cannot meaningfully ask about it, in the way one can otherwise ask about any actual state of affairs, whether an alternative would ideally be better.

Now let us see to what extent this idea is confirmed by observable play activities. Roger Caillois's scheme gives a useful overview of these.[8] Caillois classifies play activities according to (1) two primary principles, *paidia* or childlike exuberance and *ludus* or the interest in gratuitous difficulty and form, and (2) the four primary domains of competition, chance, mimicry, and vertigo, in which *paidia* and *ludus* strike various balances—as, for instance, competitive games range from the wild exuberance of informal racing to the elaborate constraints of organized chess, and the pursuit of vertigo comes not only in the raw form of children whirling to make themselves dizzy but also with the technical refinement and deliberateness of mountain climbing.[9] Caillois traces a cultural development from tribal societies' "Dionysian" absorption in mimicry and vertigo to the predominance of rationalized competition and chance in civilized societies.[10]

The *paidia* and *ludus* principles represent seemingly opposite drives, one to discharge energy, the other to create and adhere to fixed form; and this schematic opposition fits the appearance that activities labeled "play" can be drastically dissimilar both physically and emotionally. One quality that does unify these opposites, however, is play's gratuitousness. The form of a complicated game, perhaps an intent elaboration of human culture, is sought sheerly for the form's sake; the energy in whirling or noise-making, a frivolous diversion, is released sheerly to discharge energy. The social purposefulness of rationalized play doesn't necessarily destroy its character of play. If a society's playing achieves certain economic or political or spiritual goals, working for that society's advantage, it works *because* of its character of play—that is, the society must benefit from the circumstance that these particular activities and social relations are chosen and enjoyed in the aspect of appealing possibility.

The distinctive happiness of play is honored by setting aside special places and occasions for it. By the same principle, the delight taken in play is internally separated by the subject from other kinds of satisfaction, and it is senseless or insulting in a peculiar way to ask why the subject seeks or prefers that experience. Play happiness is distinguished from ordinary sensory satisfactions, in part, by the way in which it is felt to involve the whole subject. When I register sensory pleasure, it is just as natural to say that the body part affected feels good as to say that *I* feel good. A good dinner makes my belly feel good. But I would never say that playing ball makes my arms feel good—not while commenting directly on the experience of play. I feel myself wholly mobilized in play, gotten together; it was an activity I *could* give myself to entirely.

Another ground of play-delight's separateness is its immediacy. In contrast to other ways in which I might come to feel a global sense of happiness, as for instance in passing a major test or being told that I am loved, the play experience does not stretch roots into past and future. We do often make play historical and consequential, to be sure: we keep records and give awards in sports, for example, and our immediate perception of most sports is permeated by awareness of these dimensions (see section 2.4). Play as such, however, is right right now. We relish that simplicity of happiness. At a given moment, I can meet anyone—a foreigner, a child, a romping dog, even (most amazingly) a patriarch or matriarch—on play terms.

Can the animal simplicity of play happiness be reconciled with the Schillerian ideal of a grand human fulfillment in play? This depends on what Schiller actually meant by identifying full humanity with play. Play is introduced in the *Letters on the Aesthetic Education of Humanity* as the healing of division between the sensuous and rational sides of our nature. As sensuous beings, we are essentially finite, particular, and receptive, subject to the determinations of the temporal, material world; as rational beings, seeking and grasping universal form through our own active intellectual determination, we are infinitely "enlarged," eternal, and free.[11] To highlight the opposition between determining and being determined is the German idealist way of expressing the age-old intimation that humans are akin to both beasts and gods. We are aware that we cannot take for granted being whole and at peace with ourselves and our worldly environment. But:

> [If humans] were to be conscious of their [rational] freedom and at the same time sensible of their [sensuous] existence, were to feel themselves matter and at the same time come to know themselves as mind, then they would in such cases, and only in such cases, have a complete intuition of their human nature, and the object which afforded them this intuition would become for them a symbol of their *accomplished destiny* and thus . . . serve them as a manifestation of the Infinite.[12]

For Schiller, the essential quality of any such symbol of fully realized human potential is beauty; the appreciative response to beauty he calls aesthetic freedom; and the exercise of this freedom he calls play.

Freedom is one practical meaning of what I called "simplicity," an entirely self-contained, unfragmented, and unhindered subjective state. The sporting dog and the sporting human—or the aesthetic spectacle of an artist's "sporting" materialization-of-spirit-and-spiritualization-of-matter, appreciated in a companion sporting of the audience's imagination—are equally specimens of free simplicity. But the crucial point in Schiller's perspective is that the human specification of simplicity is uniquely ambitious, complex, and universally inclusive. The human "play-drive" moves us not merely to kick up our heels, expressing vital spontaneity, but, beyond that, to design the decathlon and the intricate computer game, to savor every possible symbol of joy, and, beyond that, to take an intelligent position with respect to everything we know and worry about in our lives, even by composing a *Remembrance of Things Past*.

It may be that play always tends toward greater formal complexity and adequacy of life-representation if circumstances allow. I can imagine a dog playing increasingly complex stick-games with its master and progressively adjusting its game behavior to express awareness of how life is really going for itself and its partner—for instance, being slower at times to return the stick so as to chide the human for inattention. But even if the dog can express a grudge in such a way as to *enforce* it, I cannot imagine that the dog could ever mean to *represent* it, for the sake of representing it justly, as part of a just representation of the whole of life. The dog's romance with possibility is more limited than ours inasmuch as its lesser abstractive ability does not allow it to be in relation, as we can be, with *possibility as such and as a whole.* The dog is neither a self-realizer (treating "self" as the object of free reflection and imagining) nor a world-realizer, and we, potentially, are both. The dog-human difference is manifested in the fact that our spectrum of play runs from gambols and games up through high art, from physical movement up through complex mediations of the import of material existence. Heeding the siren song of possibility, we ferret out, in our personal and cultural evolution, ever more delightful possibilities of our own existence.

The spectrum of play is in fact a scale. The height of human fulfillment, in Schiller's account, implies not only a general human excellence in play but a way of ranking different human play activities. One can say that the worth of a play activity matches the degree to which it actually accomplishes an embrace of the full possibility of the playing individual's selfhood and world, or would tend to do this or (we judge) in principle should do this for any individual. How shall we measure? Schiller warns against judging play by its fruits in the ordinary sense. If we redeemed play activity with knowledge or moral scruple or sensuous gratification, we would be plunging into one or more of the separate departments of our life instead of harmonizing the whole by taking up a relation with our whole possibility. "In the aesthetic state . . . one's personal worth . . . remains completely indeterminate; and nothing more is achieved by it than [that] the freedom to be what one ought to be is completely restored. But precisely thereby something Infinite is achieved . . . the gift of humanity itself."[13]

Schiller seems to imply that play, infinitely worthy, can never be judged worthwhile. Yet we do make such judgments. One might think first of the familiar claim that engaging in sports is worthwhile because of the lessons it teaches about fairness, how to handle winning and losing, and (in team sports) how properly to identify with and be responsible to collaborators. And this might be fleshed out further to commend a particular sport for the development of dispositions and abilities that are advantageous for a particular social order, whether as reinforcing or as complementary—as baseball has been seen to serve industrial capitalism both as a clinic of entrepreneurial virtue and as a healing pastoral retreat.[14] On the other hand, dangerously popular games ("crazes") might be condemned for lack of social relevance.

The idealist definition of play seems to sail high above such considerations. Schiller has declared that playing is lost, or compromised at least, when it consorts with moral or economic projects. We might even mean to make this point when we say, "It's not whether you win or lose, it's how you play." But something is odd, even on Schiller's terms, about denying that play bears any particular fruit. The glory of play is supposed to be that it reconciles all sides of our nature, including our material nature; but our material nature is constituted by the whole set of life's actualities, including the economic and moral system we participate in. If our play activities bore no relation to economic and moral projects, if in play we really did sail away from our world and our own initiatives, the promised reconciliation would be incomplete. Understood thus, play activities *must* relate us to our worldly projects in a representationally detailed way, for the sake of adequate awareness, and in some sort of constructive way, for the sake of honoring our intentions in those realms.[15]

In fact, play forms always do combine abstractness and nonabstractness in their relation to actual life, whether in games or in the arts. Chess, for example, is on the one hand relatively nonabstract, in that its pieces represent such specific human figures as mounted knights; on the other hand, the powers of chess knights are highly abstract in relation to those of actual knights or knightlike people, as are the situations they get into. Tic-tac-toe is much more abstract than chess, but if its connections and blockages and choice-making were utterly unrelated to possibilities of maneuvering that engage us in the actual world, it is hard to see how we could understand it at all, let alone take an interest in it. Perhaps its most important feature is the sheer finitude of it, the fact that you can only go *here* or *there* and that you end up in a fix where nothing more can be done. This most elementary finitude entails that succeeding and failing are crucial to play, for playing virtually always involves pursuing some desired state of affairs that might fail to obtain. The subordination of the agent's initiative to the initiative taken by the game itself (as Gadamer puts it) can hardly cancel the agent out; the playful agent still makes decisions and takes actions that go well or badly.[16]

The nonabstract aspect of play is an important point to remember in any discussion of abstraction in art. Consider, for instance, the supposed abstractness of music. Many people feel that musical experience lifts them out of the actual world, or any world; some would say that music as pure sounding form offers the supreme aesthetic exaltation, while others would say that all art, insofar as it is true art, has the purity most commonly recognized in music. But music cannot be more abstract than tic-tac-toe. The successions and simultaneities of music take similarly lifelike positions. Music is, to be sure, interestingly different from prose or representational painting in that its relations to actual life are established in the relative darkness of discursively indeterminate forms of feeling; but even realistic prose and painting succeed, when they do, by establishing a somewhat mysterious relation between defined life and transcendent possibility.

If we take seriously the world-representing function of play at the same time that we admit Schiller's claim of play's transcendent worth (or transcendence of worth), we will want to say that play both is and is not subject to scalar evaluation—is not, insofar as we are leaving the world, and is, insofar as we are coming back to it. A question like "Is chess more worthwhile than tic-tac-toe?" will be answerable in one way and not in another. We can say that chess is more worthwhile on the grounds that it is more objectively complex, more intellectually demanding, more of a test of character, and thus a means of fuller human self- and world-realization. But play is play. One person's enjoyment of tic-tac-toe betokens the infinity of ideal human nature just as much as another's enjoyment of chess. The aesthetic satisfaction of "Yankee Doodle Dandy," to one who experiences it, means this as much as that afforded by Mozart's *Don Giovanni*. One thinks of *Don Giovanni* as a richer world, going partly by the test that it will nourish books' worth of interesting criticism, but "Yankee Doodle Dandy" is infinitely deep, too, even if we can't articulate so much about it. The opera and the song compare like the infinite sets 1, 2, 3 . . . and 1,000, 2,000, 3,000 . . . Both are infinite because both can be used by human subjects as filters through which to feel all possibility and all actuality.

This play conception is borne out by *violence* as an absorption in possibility. Violently playing subjects "leave the world" and "betoken the ideal infinity of human nature" just as chess- or violin-playing subjects do, except that they leave messes and deprivations. The infinity of violence is -1, -2, -3 . . . as playful torturers, for example, inflict ever-new losses on their victims. The absolute sense-captivating thrill of violence in any form (in which the firecracker is equivalent to the hydrogen bomb) transcends scalar evaluation. In the lure and delight of violence lies a power to suspend ordinary evaluating altogether.[17]

One can reasonably say that violence distorts play. The ideal self of violence is powerful in a fantastic, world-disconnected, and thus ultimately powerless way, and communicative in a socially disconnecting and thus ultimately isolating way. But we must remember that violence *is indeed play* if we are not to underestimate its worth appeal. And as violence does factually belong to the world that play represents, it also ought to find some correlate in nonpathological, more adequate, and fulfilling play representations; thus, if we find ourselves worrying about an apparently violent aspect of a play form like football or hockey, or the violent content in popular film and book narratives, we should be prepared to discriminate between violence getting the better of play and play getting the better of violence. (The distinct question of the worth of fighting arises in a quite different context [see section 4.3].)

∽

Now I propose to interrogate more specific, determinate notions of play worth, following an arc of articulation that runs through play's feeling, accomplishing, and knowing dimensions.

2.2 Play as felt: fun, gladness, and joy

Play worth begins to become articulate in the dimension of feeling. We measure play feeling by asking, for instance, "Was it much fun?" Teenagers at an amusement park can very precisely compare their thrill-ride reactions, allotting tickets and time accordingly. More often, we incline toward play activities with vague hopes and without much apparent chance of meaningful comparison. Should the family devote a whole Saturday to a canoeing expedition? Should I spend another dollar on an arcade game? Decisions are vindicated by a purely subjective gratification check: "I find it relaxing." "It was very exciting." On the face of it, nothing in personal identity depends on whether or how much we are gratified in this way.

Our standards of play gratification can be placed in an order. At the lowest level of intrinsic interest is the merely relaxing (perhaps "agreeable" or "pleasant"). But the relaxing has only a tenuous connection with play, because it corresponds to a need for relief. The first clear play pleasure is *fun*, which can have any degree of intensity but is always at the same time "light" ("delightful") insofar as it lacks worldly consequence or implications for selfhood. Fun, like pain, passes right through the subject. (Making fun a content of a relationship, as in an appreciative "We had fun," can transfigure it—capturing its inherently transient quality in the ongoing relationship, as a sunbeam is captured in a painting.) More considerable than fun is *gladness*, involving a kind of effulgence of the subject, a growth in being, not a transient ripple; one says "It was fun" and "It was fun while it lasted," but one has to say "*I* am glad" and only strangely would say "I was glad while it lasted." Beyond gladness, finally, is *joy*, in which the subject's gain of being is rooted in a larger reality. One isn't merely glad to be playing baseball in the major leagues, for example; one says "It's a thrill," referring not to titillation but to joy. A telltale declaration of joy is "This is what it's all about," indicating a finding of both self and world. The rejoicing subject is fittingly, perhaps even necessarily, collective, since the question of a human subject's larger reality is so commandingly a question of fellowship; thus, a deep reason for team sports is to promote play pleasure with this greatest amplitude.

Schiller's grand play theory throws light on how the play pleasures belong together. It marks the threshold of play significance, separating play from complacent or therapeutic pursuits that fail to lift us toward total freedom. And it helps us to understand how true play gratification can take relaxing, exciting, easy, and difficult forms. What kind of pleasure is common to unwinding with a game of solitaire, feeling your stomach drop out of your body during a thrill-ride, and cringing as Oedipus puts out his eyes? Schiller implies that each of these experiences puts us in touch with eternal happiness by symbolizing the end of competition between sense and reason. All play does this. There is a specific effortlessness, a being carried along, in all three examples—both in the lack of a need to strive (which does not preclude zestful trying) and in the irruption of contingencies to deal with (which distinguishes the play-calm of solitaire from the simple calm of walking on a treadmill). There is a forcing together of sense experience and abstract awareness. (Thrills and shocks have a special interest in that they almost overwhelm rational or moral consciousness; a too-violent roller-coaster and a too-shocking horror tale are simply nauseating, and no longer rewarding as play.) We are given an extraordinary license to court, or actually to experience, unfettered possibility: within safe boundaries, we "go all out" in feeling in a certain direction, in reveling.

The Schillerian idea that play is our *education* implies a standard by which to assess play-satisfactions. Even if we take play to be in every case an experience of perfect freedom in principle, the real world is always somewhere on play's horizon, which means that players must discern and adjust to concrete practical opportunities of unequal worth. Presumably Schiller pays more attention to beauty than to casual fun because he believes that "high" aesthetic experience is most effective in developing and harmonizing human powers. The experience of beauty ought to be the most authentically attractive, the best at getting and holding the attention of sensuous humanity in a profoundly encouraging way. To illustrate this idea with reference to a classic aesthetic formula, the formal *unity in variety* that a subject beholds in a beautiful work of art awakens the subject's power of universalizing reason and harmonizes that reason with the perception of material surfaces. In taking rational pleasure in the experience, one is strengthened as a rational subject. A parallel example from the physically active side of life would be the spiritual satisfaction of controlling one's body in highly formalized and disciplined kinds of play (here ballet and martial arts would rank high).

We can also derive a standard of play quality from the order of the play pleasure concepts. In any play, the subject reaches for the best possible existence and feels its worth in play pleasure. There is no sense of hollowness, no sense of relative inferiority or disadvantage. But as the life of players stretches out and becomes complicated in thought and time, players push with playful seriousness beyond fun to gladness (a happy, deep vibrating of self) and beyond gladness to joy (a happy resonating of self with the global situation). The subjective fullness of joy at the top of play's feeling scale corresponds to the objective fullness of beauty.

But play's attractions and gratifications are interestingly mixed more often than they are ideally pure. This is predictable, partly because of play's nonabstractness: if players really are coming home to the real world as well as leaving it, play should combine transcendent exaltation with realistic sensory and conative frustrations. Another, more troubling reason to expect a mixed play experience is that the play self, bumptious as it is, is no more guaranteed to be perfectly sincere and pure than any other form of the human self. Who knows what lurks in the player's heart? The idealist Dr. Jekyll's aim is to commune nobly with ideal human freedom, while dark Mr. Hyde merely wants to express resentment or escape responsibility. Practical evaluation of play will be concerned with sifting mixtures of motivation and distinguishing affirmable from regrettable kinds of mixture.[18]

Suppose that one day our softball player's father notices that she is *serious* about softball. He sees that she is not playing softball merely to kill time or as a means to some questionable end. There is an impressive amount of intrinsic joy in the activity. He judges that he ought to encourage her. (Naturally he still has to limit her, reminding her of other matters that need her attention also; we might say he is holding her down to earthly life.) But suppose that a later day comes when he starts to wonder if she is *too* serious. Has the air gone out of her play-spirit? Has she taken to treading too heavily on earth, intending only to gain prestige or glory in domination of her opponents, or perhaps avoiding nonsoftball concerns? In this instance it is possible for the father, going strictly by his sense of the quality of his daughter's play-gratification, to make a very consequential decision about how to try to influence her. Certainly she could make the decision herself; but she could decide badly, just as her father could decide well. (We can imagine similar decisions based on the apparent quality of the pleasure she takes in the movies she goes to, the music she listens to, and even the people she calls friends.)

"Have fun doing it" is a piece of advice that is increasingly acceptable outside of recognized play settings. A manager might induce workers to check their degree of enjoyment as a way of assuring that they intend and are achieving the best possible state of affairs. Here is a fascinating play of meanings of "best": Is play being subordinated to work, or work to play? Can "best possible" be applied simultaneously to useful results and to immediate human self-realization? What about the presumption in one person's issuing any sort of directions to another to be gratified? Does my boss have the right to ask me, ever so lightly, whether I am having fun?

2.3 Play as accomplished: games, prizes, tricksters, and gamblers

What, other than an emotional state, can be the referent of a claim of play worth? An *event* of playing, one wants to say. But how exactly is a play event fit to bear worth?

It seems that play is oriented to a distinctive kind of practical challenge. Possibilities whip us like a wind, "exciting" us, we say, if we feel our own powers surging forward to meet and exploit them. (If I have become completely familiar and comfortable with an activity—say, a puzzle game that I now have under perfect control—can I be said to play it?) The challenging play question, "Will I, or will we, pull it off?" becomes one of winning and losing as we shape play activity into units, "games." In a game, the play challenge is explicit and approaches to meeting it are explainable. Hence games have a central position in the play realm.

Winning and losing implies that something is to be gained or lost. "'There is something at stake'—the essence of play is contained in that phrase" (Huizinga).[19] Yet the identification of what is at stake in games is easily confused, for although games are normally conducted in their own charmed circle set apart from the rest of the practical world, they often have major worldly consequences—acceptance or disgrace, enrichment or poverty, survival or death. We want nevertheless to say that the worldly consequences fail to determine the specifically playful aspect of winning and losing. By insisting that play actions can make all the difference in the play world without making a difference in the real world, we mark an all-important distance between possibility and actuality. Without this distance, there would be no room for play to rise to better, ideal life, nothing to hope for from play. Nor would there be any room to maneuver in discussing and reflecting on actual life by the powerful, potentially all-inclusive metaphor of play.[20]

That which is at stake in a game, that which is added to the victor, is the prize. (We can always momentarily read a prize as *the* prize, nothing less than personal and social salvation.) Tangible prizes stand on the border between the play-world and the real world, lending silver trophies and money the significance of play success and play success the significance of precious objects and buying power. When tangible prizes are lacking, there is still the congratulation of victory; at a minimum, a game winner acquires a proud self-characterization that, like externally bestowed honors, mediates between the ephemeral play event and the ongoing world in which play is set. In pride, one considers oneself the owner of a desirable attribute. Beyond the fact that one did something, one *is* that doer. If the accomplishment belongs to a team, then the co-doer is proud of having measured up fully to a promise of collaborative help (a most virtuous contentment).

Thinking only of nonteam games, we can perhaps imagine a player, especially a consummately good player, utterly unself-conscious in playing, who sincerely says, "I play just to play, not for any prize." Such a player is in no doubt about doer-identity, sees no peak of possibility that has not already been scaled. A very good player could say this out of the experience of full self-realization; an indifferent player could say it out of lack of ambition. But what human being *is* fully realized? How can a true player set a limit to ambition? How can nothing be "at stake" in play, contrary to Huizinga's dictum?

We want to *show* that something is at stake in play. Material prizes are fitting. Nevertheless, if one becomes rich as a result of play, or walks away from a lethal contest with one's life, the worldly good gained in the prize counts as something one wanted *as a player*, not merely as a thing one would have wanted in a different spirit. Since what was at stake for the player was the ideally best life, or contact with the Schillerian infinity of human destiny, no finite economic value, not even survival, can be the prize's essential point. The worldly goods serve to symbolize the play success. A long, wealthy, and privileged life is, after all, the best symbol the world can provide for the attainment of ideal humanity. Are superstar athletes paid and celebrated too much? We can say from a play-appreciative point of view that the world doesn't hold *enough* to reward adequately anyone who excels in play, or rather that our only adequate gesture is to reward winners with the *most* goods that our economy can make available.

No price for play is too high, from the play-appreciative point of view, unless it is so high that it squelches play itself. Gladiatorial games can't be allowed to kill off all the gladiators. Basketball stars can't be paid so much that no one can afford to watch them play. Football games can't become so important to a community that players for the team representing the community are made miserable by social pressure. The demands of competition mustn't force athletes to disfigure themselves. (Standards change. It used to be considered unsportsmanlike to train for an event, and as late as the early 1970s a college football linebacker could refuse to lift weights because "When I go out on the field, I want it to be the real me, not some artificial monster built up by weights.")[21] We want to see what extraordinary things humans can do, by any and all means, and yet, overridingly, we want to be able imaginatively to weave what is done into the fabric of our existence. A sports accomplishment cannot be so wicked or freakish as to prevent this. But there are many examples of the play spirit pushing at these limits.

The glory or evident worthiness of winning is, at a first level, the superiority of the winner shown in besting the play challenge. This basic winning-glory shines brighter in proportion to the magnitude of the challenge, and we grade its luster. A second level of glory is constituted by the winners' own appreciation of it in the context of their whole lives, feeling it proudly. This we measure by finding out how fulfilled they seem to be; and much depends on a winner's ability to form a coherent understanding of a whole life in which play success is only one ingredient (hence our interest in how he or she "handles winning"). A third level of glory is added when winners are appreciated by their fellows and granted a reward of social eminence; their play success offers a worthwhileness-for-the-beholder that the players and audience can enjoy collectively. (This play glory tends to blend with, or be confused with, the glory of the worthy *deed* [see section 4.4].) We can ask at this level whether the reward we give winning is rightly measured in purely social terms: Is the magnitude of the attention-prize proportional to the extent to which we (or ideal observers) are able to read human potentialities and hopes into the event?

We are avid for winning to occur in some form, and the more winning the better, for it assures us of the human capacity to realize the best possible life. But in celebrating winners we always show also that losers have fallen short. Is losing in some sense worth doing? So long as a game is in progress, the prospective worth of winning throws a justifying light on all players who hope to win and who still have a chance. Players who eventually lose have a chance at winning during much of their playing. This chance defines the play meaning of their "participation" in the game. In this sense a losing effort can be worthwhile, but only insofar as it is not yet qualified as losing. What then is the meaning of losing as such, a meaning that applies equally to all players up to the end of their effort, while all have a chance of losing?

The consoling thought after the game that "Someone had to lose" vindicates losing in the perspective of those who instituted games as occasions of victory—a perspective that, ideally, all participants share. To accept the role of possible loser is to uphold this victory-enabling order and thereby to participate in the collective subject of game playing that always relishes the winning. But it is also to agree to face failure itself and the nothingness that failure represents, not only individually but in the collective subject. As before, the logic that shares out the meaning of winning also shares out the meaning of losing.

The play negativity of losing represents a serious negativity of life. Losing is worth doing as a way of standing up to death. Not to have lost is not to have learned how to live as a mortal.[22] But to lose too much while winning too little, or not at all, is a path of despair. Sane people withdraw from forms of play in which the balance swings, for them, too much to the negative.

The meaning of losing depends also on the conditions under which one is liable to lose. To this point I've had in view fair losing, losing caused by insufficient talent or effort on a level, bounded playing field with clear causality; but winning and losing aren't always fair, according to ordinary expectations, and winnings aren't always unambiguously affirmable. Trickster-heroes, for example, are poor winners by conventional standards, and peculiarly dangerous, in principle, to everyone. Yet by expanding the realm of human possibility beyond convention, they gain, in a way, the best victories of all. They are the heroic embodiments, not exactly of leaving the world toward the ideal, but of the growth of the actual world. The world to which we return from hearing of a trickster's exploits is a practically richer world now that new clues have been given to possible action in it. Tricksters reward faith in the inexhaustibleness of human resources. (At a minimum, trickster victory is comic: we discover in it the strange acceptableness of an incongruity. The basic everyday trick is the joke.) To be the one who loses to the marvelous trickster, however, is to be a chump, a dismissible agent, one unable even to recognize the nature of the game being played.

(Are cheaters failed tricksters? We can attribute two kinds of failure to mere cheaters: one outward, consisting simply of not winning in any sense, and one inward, lying in a cheaters' confused affirmation of the violated game rather than of a higher trickster-game as the frame of reference for seeking victory.)

Trickster games are apt symbols for our struggle with forms of life or character that really are inadequate. But we cannot accept that the casualty of trickery will be a person. Putting the matter in this light, it becomes possible to say that losing to a trickster is worthwhile when it serves as the occasion of overcoming a feeling, belief, or disposition that the loser embodied in the encounter, lacking which the loser is actually better off. (Which feelings, beliefs, and dispositions do and do not play a role in our ideal lives? For instance, is it better for me to lose my virginity to the seducer, or to keep it? Is my virginity only worth retaining if it is connected with moral and intellectual strengths sufficient to see through the seducer's trickery?)

In games of chance, players ritually submit to Trickster Fate, or Dame Fortune, whose miraculous superiority to all known laws they participate in, whether in winning (showing possession by a greater power, thus conferring prestige and emboldening ridicule of regular worth conventions) or in losing. In the extreme case of playing in a lottery, we let fortune make fools of us all—for we know, reasonably, that we will lose—although we feel at the same time in a peculiarly strong way that we are in the game with a chance of winning. Even if your state lottery ticket gives you a smaller chance of winning the ten-million-dollar prize than of being hit by lightning, you can still record your satisfaction at being part of the game by feeling afterward that you lost. It would take great skill to be the loser, in a meaningful sense, of so big a prize in ordinary sport. In golf, you would have to get to the last stage of a tournament at least tied for the lead. But in a lottery you are wholly in contention until the moment the winner is revealed.

As in all other games, the collective subject of chance-play can be sure that it will experience winning. The reward each of us gets from participating in this larger subjection to chance is, again, assurance of the durability of our social fabric, but now with reference to the perturbations of chance rather than to an order of merit. Since any society is in fact buffeted by uncontrollable chance, one could plausibly assert that a viable society must find a stance and practice a style for undergoing it; and one could draw the corollary that the balance between principles supported by a society's games ought to accord, so much as practical exigencies allow, with the balance of chance and merit effects that are felt in the society's life apart from its games. (Note that a game-crazed society could create the illusion that life really is a lottery more than anything else, while an excessively sober society, supported by belief in cosmic providence, could maintain the contrary illusion.) Admittedly, we do not ask this critical question while we are caught up in a particular play illusion. But the question is not foreign to the play spirit, either. As we create and refine our games, feeling our way through greater and lesser play satisfactions, our sense of chance's share is always important.

It might be objected that playing games of chance is not properly a doing at all, but merely a submitting; that winners in such play therefore deserve no credit of any sort; and that, in the absence of any glory in winning, the game, which could only be redeemed by a winning, is meaningless. Let us ask then about the chance-player in whom we see a possibility of impressive accomplishment: the gambler.

Perhaps the successful gambler is a trickster at bottom; in that case, wit and skill supersede fortune in determining success. We could say, though, that a trickster-gambler's agency fills the role of fortune, or becomes indistinguishable from fortune, for those who are defeated. Looked at in this way, the gambler is a cheater, systematically taking advantage of rules observed by suckers. (A gambler who breaks no formal game rules is still a cheater in the perspective of the industrious good citizen, insofar as gambling success breaks the rule that life's rewards should come in proportion to productive, socially responsible effort.)

But suppose that the gambler need not be a cheater. Posit a virtuous gambler. What satisfactions will we find in and around the victories of a gambler who plays fair, only on Saturday nights, in respectable company, and gives generously from his or her winnings to good causes?

The virtuous gambler is likely to say that gambling is worthwhile primarily for its fun, and that victories are worthwhile only as required to sustain the fun. But any sort of player might say the same. Do gambling victories have a unique way of spicing the generic play fun of facing uncertain developments with your own powers mobilized to meet them as best you can? Is there any difference between the way a poker player contemplates the other players' hidden hands and the way a batter in baseball looks forward to the next pitch? Between a given poker player and a given batter, at a given moment, there might be no psychological difference at all. But if we recur to the idea that play realizes an ideal infinity in human nature, we can articulate a great structural division of meanings that might apply to the events. The difference is reflected in the accepted definitions of baseball as a game of skill (notwithstanding the importance of chance in it for every player's experience of every play) and poker as a game of chance (with a large place for skill). Poker players are understood to confide themselves to chance in a more radical way than baseball players do. (Part of the intentional form here is intoxication [see section 6.4]; another part is the celebrated virtue of nerve.) Considering poker a legitimate game implicitly grants a greater role to chance in ideal human realization. The gambler in effect says, "It's not up to me to achieve or to deserve the breakthrough to infinity in winning. I can accept and live with this lack of control. By playing, I symbolically establish the possibility of my survival and self-realization in a chancy order, and by winning I symbolically lunge forward toward salvation on those terms." Insofar as life is chancy, the gambler is right, and gambling nerve deserves a high moral rating. Gambling is most at home, most logical, as it were, among those who really are most at the mercy of chance—soldiers, sailors, the down-and-out—and those dissolute aristocrats who are correcting for their excessive economic security by tilting to the opposite condition of life.

Insofar as gambling is part of any sort of playing (as, for instance, a baseball batter gears up for an early swing, betting on a fastball), all players can be right, and good, in the way that the gambler can be right, and good. But even though gambling is part of a sport, the dominant meaning of sport, treated as a game of skill, is quite different: the player accepts objective order and (with fingers crossed) banks on control, and players and audience are in suspense about how, not whether, order and control will be manifested.

Imagine a climactic moment in a novel when one major character says tellingly to another, "You've never been willing to gamble." The real issue could be a refusal (domineering? timid?) to submit to life's indeterminacy. But the actual force of this sort of observation, and the worth of any given form of gambling, depends on how one's confiding oneself to chance matches the real or realizable contours of determinacy and indeterminacy in life. On the one hand, no sane person gambles with the lives of children by not having them wear seat belts in a car. On the other hand, no sane person expects order and control in the stock market, where (like it or not) everyone's wealth is directly or indirectly at stake. How do things really happen?

2.4 Play as known: arts and sports

What is directly intended in play action is winning, which is immediately congratulated by the prize. But agents and spectators alike usually see the winning and the prize against broader play horizons. How is it that larger truths of play become established and known over the course of winnings and losings? What does *all* this playing accomplish? We can always ask what we have learned about ourselves, our society, and our physical universe through playing—for example, whether my preference for team sports represents a healthy interest in cultivating play-relations with teammates or an unhealthy aversion to choosing goals and styles for myself; whether a particular society's zeal for competitive sports betrays the pathology of its alienating economic system; what playful humans *can* do in water, or with a ball, or with words.[23] But I would like to ask about a more play-centered sort of measurement. What has play wrought that can be a continuing object of reference and interpretation in that play-character, as part of a play world rather than as part of general history?

If play consisted only of having fun, or being glad or joyful, we would be bound to say that it produces nothing at all. The practical achievements of play, if any existed, would be irrelevant to the intrinsically worthwhile subjective condition of playing. Games are won, to be sure, but within the perspective of play-exuberance it doesn't matter *afterward* which contestant won or which sort of prize was awarded. So we might turn the question at a different angle and ask, Where, if anywhere, do we encounter a defining and an ongoing interpretation of play achievements? Who, if anyone, is in a position to say, or about whom can it be said, that play has wrought something?

Knowledge of play-accomplishment is developed in the frames of art and sport, two explosively growing cultural sectors in an affluent society.

The art world is built up as a metaphysical confirmation of play. The joke and the snowman, for example, are fine outbursts of play—fun (funny) and ephemeral. But if we take them to be *really* fun, the intensity of the play-experience asks for an extension in time and memory. The joke turns into an epigram, a poem, a story; the snowman becomes a "work" protected from the sun, or forms the basis for a picture or statue. Specific play-delights can now be visited and shared at will. If these play memorials are *really* delightful, further elucidation is demanded, and art criticism arises to help us consort with the works' full abundance. Art is a realizing of play that does not destroy its play character. An artist indeed "works" (as the athlete, in the parallel case, "gets a job done"). But in spite of the fact that the artist whose work is most often the most worthwhile, namely, the specializing professional artist, *needs* to work to live—and in spite of the fact that human life *needs* art to define and maintain itself symbolically (so that we can speak quite properly of various kinds of cultural work that art does)—*what it is that is wanted and needed* in this case is *gratuitous delight*, which we enjoy as free beings.

Something else in play is uniquely realized and rendered knowable through the adventures of sports contestants. The great clue here is that sports generates sports pages and sports shows. Play becomes sport in order to produce knowable and interestingly discussible material—material that is not merely gossip about players or speculation about the background significance of their playing but that belongs essentially to play, so that knowing and discussing these matters is integral to the players' play and also becomes the basis on which spectators enter into the same play-world. To put it a little differently, we could say that sports are the leading edges of the *articulation* of play, making play worth more *perceptible* (in the sheer display of actions and of a range of actions), *comprehensible* (in the way that sports' rules and playing conditions enable analysis and evaluation of what is done), and thus *attainable*.

Baseball commissioner Bart Giamatti had a keen sense for this: "I'm standing in the lobby of the Marriott in St. Louis in October of '87 and I see this crowd, so happy with itself, all talking baseball, and I want to be in this game, so I spend two hours moving about, listening to them talk the game and hearing them getting it right, working at the fine points the way players in the big leagues do, and it comes to me slowly, around noon, that this, *this*, is what Aristotle must have meant [in the *Poetics*] by the imitation of an action."[24] Critics of sport who contend that modern sports fans are alienated from physical and social action miss the flourishing that Giamatti here records.[25]

The arts, like sports, are dedicated to the articulation of play experience. What then is the difference of worth principle between arts and sports, if our conception of play is broad enough to include both? The difference doesn't lie in the gap between spectator and performer or in the possibilities of being knowledgeable and discerning. In either frame, spectators can be expert or naive, fully competent peers or gauche fans. Great performances are as memorable as great games. Still, we don't compare great artistic performances as we do games and seasons in sports. A Horowitz performance of Chopin was great; so was a Rubinstein performance. The two performances had different qualities, which can be indicated and savored. But it would be extremely difficult, if not nonsensical, to argue in any reasonable fashion which was greater. In sports, however, just such arguments are encouraged by the structure of the activity and the record-keeping that goes with it. Admittedly there is a sense also in which one cannot argue whether Mays or Mantle was the greater baseball player—the sense in which their baseball activities are stunning performances, like those of Horowitz and Rubinstein. And there is a sense in which Horowitz and Rubinstein can be measured just as baseball players are, looking at the size of their repertoires, their technical strengths and weaknesses, and the fruitfulness of their collaborations with other artists. Why, then, is it so much more *pertinent* to stack up the numbers posted by Mays and Mantle for statistical comparison? Why does this sort of view take us so much deeper into the baseball world than an analogous comparison of pianists would take us into the music world?

Excellence in baseball is made up of victory-bits of all sorts: successful hitting of pitches, successful catching of balls, successful runs to home plate, game victories. These are countable, and one player's totals are commensurable with another's. Should we say that sports are set up in this way fundamentally for the sake of maximizing the number of winnings (a major league baseball season contains the greater part of a million detectable winnings) or rather for the sake of drama and narrative appeal?[26] There is no gap between these aims, actually. Sport is eminently recountable precisely because we can display the winnings it contains at any level of magnification. It would almost surely be absurd to include the report "Then Horowitz touched the F# gently" in a description of a concert, while it is not at all strange to say "Then Mantle let a high fastball go by," and many other things like it, in telling about a baseball game. A baseball result is compounded of almost innumerable component contests and winnings, each an occasion of suspense, each trailing infinite implications for character and situation.

This point might serve as a backdoor entry to interpreting the more obvious difference between the structures of sport and art, namely that every game in a sport offers the same structural opportunity for individuals to win and lose in precisely defined ways—the primary meaning of the game-event to be determined by how that open structure is filled in—whereas the primary meaning of the work of art is the unique structure of the work itself as a whole, which constitutes a freshly discovered and essentially unrepeatable "game." We can of course appreciate baseball itself as a work of art, and baseball teams as performers of the work, and this is not an insignificant part of the fullest enjoyment of the sport. And we can read the reviews of a musical performance with the same score-keeping interest that attends baseball game reports, which is not a negligible dimension in music criticism. But baseball and music are oppositely polarized. What is in the background for one is in the foreground for the other.

Art is not as articulable as sport quantitatively; but art becomes highly knowable and discussible through the qualitative articulation of aesthetic criticism, building on the articulative achievement of artists. The successful artwork works in ways on which critics can expatiate. But the teleology of sport works is obvious and precise, in comparison with the teasing teleology-without-a-definable-purpose of artworks, because sports are set up for the sake of this precision.[27]

Another feature of art and sport that serves the end of making play achievement knowable is that artists and athletes acquire a special kind of identity, a personal play reality lifted above play events, by having *careers*. I suppose the notion of "career" has an ineradicable work meaning, notwithstanding that I mean to apply it very broadly, as much to a year on a high school basketball team as to the principal livelihood of a whole adult life (see section 3.5). Still, one can commit oneself and construct an identity over time purely as a player, provided that play-achievements can be made knowable in the right way. In fact, there is more room for personal individuality at the level of the career than at the level of the single act or game. Even to be able to say, "Oh yes, I had a basketball career—I was a benchwarmer my junior year in high school!" is to have a distinct player's identity and with it an enrichment of one's whole personal identity. This is to be something to talk about in the play world.

Because sports occasions are well-organized and their results are precisely measured, sporting effort is subject to a discipline that seems at odds with play spirit. An exuberant, talented amateur could romp onto a sporting field and achieve something of note at a given moment, surprising everyone, possibly even setting a record, all in a carefree way; but no such undisciplined person could make an ongoing contribution to a team's success or to a sport. Paul Weiss is exaggerating but not fabricating when he writes: "Though the athlete is rarely playful, he often has his moments of innocent exuberance and pleasure; [yet] his primary tonality is satisfaction for having done what he ought, and not, as a child, for having done what he wanted to do."[28] In offering the opportunity to have a career, sport demands training and dutifulness. (Cal Ripken's dutifulness expressed through a sixteen-season streak of consecutive games played proved in 1995 to be one of the most popularly impressive accomplishments in baseball history.)[29]

Athletes are always asked how winning and losing feel and what they think about it. The reports they give us, stepping back out of their artificially limited game identities, anchor the idealism of play in real life, rounding out the return stage of the circuit of play meaning. But why do interviews with sportspeople so obsessively turn on comparisons and constructions within the play-world? "How does this victory [or disappointment] compare with last year's?" "Which record means more to you?" "Which team would you rather face?" We like to say that play is properly carefree, but no one constructing a sport identity is carefree; the challenge aspect of play, in this context, is too much in the foreground and too complex for that. You might relish the pure play spirit in an outfielder who says, "I didn't think about the errors I made in the first inning; I'm just out there to play hard and have fun." But if you ask him to comment on his making twice as many errors this season as last, or getting half as many hits, he will treat these as serious issues; if he doesn't, he is shamefully self-negligent in sport terms. The issue doesn't arise only for professional athletes, whose employers hire and fire on the basis of what they "produce" (in what critics of modern sport see as the capitalist deformation of play).[30] It arises for all who cultivate their play powers over time to arrive at a satisfactory condition and identity. Regarded in this light, the decisions of professional sports management simply ratify or symbolize values that exist quite apart from money.

Not rarely, an entire career comes to be defined by its most memorable moment. Any football fan who thinks of Franco Harris, for instance, thinks of one miraculous catch he made to win a playoff game for the Pittsburgh Steelers in 1972. Such a moment represents a pinnacle of peak value, immediately firing the imagination as strongly as football can fire it. I suppose that if the young Harris were choosing which identity to wish for, he would take "all-time leading rusher" over "maker of The Catch." There is a sense in which he is robbed of his playing career, or 99.99 percent of it, by his one shining moment. But there is another, at least equally pertinent sense in which making The Catch makes Harris more knowable to us, more usable in our discussions and in framing our own scales of satisfaction. (It might even have been *worse* for him, more alienating, to set a quantified record. Jim Brown said, "I hold more than a dozen records and as a result have been turned into a statistic.")[31]

What, then, is the relation of this play self—for instance, an athlete as the maker of a memorable play—and the human being who (presumably) intends to live well?[32] In what way are they the same person? They seem a little like siblings, in that there is room for one to glory innocently in the other. Greg Norman said, upon winning the 1993 British Open, "I'm not one to boast, but I'm in awe of the way I played today."[33] (A pianist might say the same after a triumphant performance.) His play self is at a distance from him such that he can contemplate it just as you or I do, except that he is allowed extra delight on account of also being that self. (Many athletes fall into the habit of referring to themselves by name, in their play identities; John Jones says, "I still think John Jones can play.") Is the play self to the main self as a limb is to a living body? One acts and accomplishes through it, one feels or appears impaired if deprived of it (hence the dread of retirement from a sport).

It would be nearer the mark, I suggest, to construe the play self as the whole person implemented under a particular set of conditions, tested in one kind of laboratory. Play as such would not be delightful if the whole person were not committed to it; therein lies its seriousness. But the knowable identity of the play self features only a very limited set of abstract accomplishments, like a certain number of hits, together with some measure of generic sportsmanship and some trace of a style. Perhaps we should say, then, that the play self *challenges us to read it as a representation of the main self*, as a ritual mask is to be read as a representation of a god. The player has obscured much of his or her full dimensionality by entering a framework in which pleasingly definite successes can be obtained. It is up to the player and to us to *make* play happiness a real person's happiness, to engineer the necessary resemblances, to avow the identification. This account suggests that there will be differences between appropriations of play that are more and less mature, more and less aware of play's apartness-in-context, more and less tactful about carryovers of personal identity elements.

The concept of play identities might help us to understand the curious act of rooting, which forms so large a part of sports experience. Why would it be worthwhile to root? What argument could a rooter use to try to change the attitude of a nonrooting spectator? Isn't the more authentically playful response to sport simply to await developments, ready to appreciate victory no matter who wins? Does the rooter's passionate partisanship spoil the innocence of play?

The most obvious rationale for rooting, and I think a solid one, is that it involves the spectator in the struggle-character of the contest. Without this virtual trying, the spectator would not follow the contour of the players' practical display. But it is also important to recognize that each player tries to best others by *being* the best (having recreated and perfected him- or herself in the play field). Without rooting, the spectator would not intend the essential thing the players intend and would miss out on their newly created selfhood. Thus the nonrooting spectator is defective in play terms.

Rooters make the fortunes of players and teams their own. This identification is to be marked as a second reason for rooting: if spectators did not care about the play identities of the players, they would not take their own risks in this dimension. It is possible, of course, to root shallowly for a given team on a given occasion and care no further about them in future. But deep rooters care over time, as though their favorite players were family members—they let part of their own identity be contingent on the formation of someone else's. Rooters can feel shame in the midst of victory and pride in the midst of defeat, depending on how their players perform.

We ought not to adduce this as the primary reason for rooting, I think, but surely a most significant byproduct of rooting, and perhaps a psychologically and sociologically demonstrable motivation for it, is the sharing of acquired play-identity with fellow rooters for the same cause. Like patriotism, sports rooting realizes ideal community, citizenship in an ideal city. (And is the whole phenomenon of patriotism better captured by any other single category than rooting? Is a national promise of liberty, in particular, better aligned with any other aspect of human experience than play freedom?) One could argue that precisely this ideal city is the final goal for the sake of which sports make play more knowable. This play knowledge forms the benches of the parliament-house in which we sit in energetic concord and offers notes for the melodies and harmonies of the music of the public sphere. In a purer play perspective, however, which looks at things the other way around, the final cause of rooting will be seen not in a larger politics but in the fact that play itself is formally advanced and enriched by human sociableness.

Much as patriotism can function as the last refuge of a scoundrel, so the cultivation of play identity in rooting can function as a mere vacation from the task of sustaining the selfhood for which one is more properly and urgently responsible—a harmless, shallow diversion at best, a grotesque escapism at worst. If everything depends on the Braves winning the pennant this year, then nothing depends on my own living well in my own community and career. A reflective worth judgment mediates between these perspectives. Rooting is worthwhile so long as it develops play identity, part of the largest possible human identity, without suppressing other important aspects of personal identity.

୭୨

An unsympathetic critic of sports or the arts may accept the logic that deduces sports and arts from the goal of making play-experience more knowable but object to play taking over so much of human knowing. Aren't there better uses for the mind? Grant that the refreshment of sport and aesthetic experience is important for many; let them have their games and shows; but wouldn't the newspaper pages now devoted to sports and art reviews be better allocated to business news, political news, scientific news?

Another objection arises in a quite different spirit, out of a certain love of play, yet strikes to the same root: Do sport and art make play pseudoscientific, pseudopolitical, pseudobusinesslike? Shouldn't play transcend worldly care? Granted, meaningful play must somehow represent and return to the actual world, but aren't our sports and arts too heavily earthbound?

The underlying question either way is whether play can be fully human. Schiller's proposition is that *we only play when we are fully human, and we are only fully human when we play.* The critic of play would like to ignore the first part of this claim and water down the second part to the easily accepted notion that playing is *part* of the whole recipe for human happiness. (Schiller means, to the contrary, that we are only fully happy *in*, not merely *with*, playing.) The second objector, who thinks play is sublime, favors the stronger sense of the second part of Schiller's claim but is just as ready to drop the first part; this objector is ready to leave part of actual humanity behind in reaching for ideally full humanity. I want to uphold Schiller's ideal against both objections, not to rule out other ways of construing authentic humanity but to let his play thesis be one of the prime contenders for that truth. I construe sports and arts as attempted proofs of the thesis.

Various grounds undoubtedly exist for saying that our sports or arts don't succeed on these terms, but we should keep the weaknesses of actual sports and arts in fulfilling the Schillerian ideal distinct from the absence in them of meanings they can never have. All play is absurd in a way. An elaborately orchestrated football contest is just as silly as a kid doing cannonballs into a pool. Everything we do to make play more knowable heightens this absurdity by investing such a great proportion of our resources in it. To laboriously learn baseball batting or oil painting—two of the most difficult activities ever attempted by humans—is, in an odd way, extra fun, like doing a long, bruising sequence of cannonballs. The gratuitousness of the sports and arts pages is more delightful the longer and more colorful they are. And this elaboration of play-silliness is in itself ennobling in that it puts playful sincerity, purity, and ardor into all our intellectual and moral operations. But such a benefit presupposes that play subjects have been fleshed out to fully human dimensions. Play subjects must have personal play identities (including play careers), must be able to make play promises and keep play covenants, and must be able to exhibit all human excellences, including a full range of virtues of character, skill, creativity, style, and grace, both as protagonists and as role-playing complements to others.

Wonderful literatures of sport and art seem to show that our conditions are richly met. The testimony of partisans on this issue is, of course, suspect. They want vindication, after all. Since they pack into sport and art every extra meaning it could conceivably have, naturally the features we have called for may be found in their interpretations. They want their favorite activities to justify themselves in the highest way possible, which is by fulfilling the Schillerian ideal. If we do not see what they see, they may be bold enough to tell us that we fail *their* test: "I have never met a person who disliked sports, or who absented himself or herself entirely from them, who did not at the same time seem to me deficient in humanity" (Michael Novak).[34]

2.5 How much should we play?

We have been discussing criteria by which individuals and groups can assess the comparative worth of play activities: Is it maximally fun? Is it maximally challenging (in a rewarding way)? Does it represent actual life interestingly while reaching out at the same time in a robust way toward ideal possibility, answering in the most satisfying way vital questions of human possibility? (Can physical power be imbued with intelligence? Can persons compete against each other and remain friends?) But a distinct evaluative question remains so far untouched: How much playing is not enough, or too much? The total amount of time and effort we give to playing is determined by our choice, to some extent, and this choice can importantly affect the felt tone and meaning of a day, a week, a year, or a life. Our sense of the possible worth of the play-maximizing ("playboy") or play-minimizing ("puritanical") approaches to life reflects an overall adjudication of this issue.

The hallmark of insufficient play, in Schillerian perspective, is spiritual cramp. Nonplayful life does not offer the singing, soaring, going-all-out kind of satisfaction that points feeling and imagination toward uncompassed horizons. Without a doubt, we often suffer from play deficit. But could there be an opposite problem?

To test for possible pitfalls in excessive play, let us imagine Planet Play, a technically and culturally remarkably world where the nonplayful aspects of life have almost been eliminated. I postulate a whole planet of play to set aside all the competing demands that might make us reproach play devotees in our world. Let Planet Play be a point of reference for any real human life to the degree that the question arises apart from any such reproaches (about work that should be done, and so forth) whether playing should be dominant, in fact or in intention, as much as it is. You may wonder if you are headed toward Planet Play if you spend several nights in a row at parties, or if you are planning an early retirement. Now, on Planet Play, no one form of play prevails; the people enjoy an infinite variety of games, shows, and gambols. Do they have a worth problem? We haven't yet articulated worth claims made by work and other modes of activity, so we are not in a position to fault Planet Play for lacking these other meanings. Can there be any hint *within* play's delight that play is overdone?

We earthlings feel a deficit of seriousness in this alternate world. But *they* experience a full measure of play-seriousness, of mattering and "making a difference," in the forms of play they take less lightly, to which they give their greatest passion and dedication. There is plenty of intentional contrast between their major sports and their incidental foolery, enough to prevent boredom. For us, their most serious seriousness is still light—but for them that lightness is what makes life consistently delightful and choice-worthy. That constitutes their victory in the game of securing the best life.

On which of the play principles that we have discovered might we base a criticism of Planet Play?

Play Principle #1: The energy of play-liberation is a function of the constraints from which we are liberated. The heaviest constraints would be those from which no human being *can* be liberated. The residents of Planet Play are, like us, liable to suffer and bound to die, and they are also responsible to and for each other, just as we are. Since these attributes are expressed in play, it might be thought that whatever else characterizes their life, they must share with us the heaviest constraints of all. But it is not certain that the meanings of physical vulnerability, mortality, and moral responsibility have the same inflection when they are represented in play that they have when represented in other kinds of activity. Nor is it certain that the heavy constraints that are expressible in play include all the constitutive constraints of human life. We won't know what other constraint-meanings exist, filling out the full human potential for intentional gravity, until we identify other major modes of practical worth.

Play Principle #2: Play is representational—a portrait of, and thesis about, actual life—so *that its meaning is a function of the meanings of life as a whole.* The meaning of play is impoverished, therefore, if it can't draw on nonplay meanings. For instance, a "battle" between volleyball front lines in one of our gyms draws some of its meaning from unplayful exercises on our real battlefields. For the people on Planet Play, however, the *whole* meaning of "battle" is found in its play-meaning, and from their perspective it is only a sordid addition of hatred and hurt that makes the battles of our world different. Whether the nonplay-based meanings that are missing on Planet Play are constitutive features of human life, or simply removable imperfections, again cannot be decided until we explore other modes of practical worth.

Play Principle #3: The greater the difficulty of a play activity, the less purely playful it can be. For instance, the sport of baseball requires hard practice and patient organizing. A play-life that comprehends all meaningful practical possibilities is bound to be contaminated by work and other nonplay activities, so that the contrast between play and nonplay as we draw it on Earth will have to reappear somehow on Planet Play, too. Thus, the two planets are not so different after all. Planet Play's folk might agree that play draws on nonplay and argue that the unavoidable "impurities" in their play create a more interesting total effect; yet they could still maintain that play puts the ultimate spin on all their practice. All modes of practical worth are effectively represented in their master playing, all becoming fun. But whether we feel in their practice a loss of other worth meanings depends on how we come to appreciate other practical modes. If our total view of human worth calls for serious self-centerings on occasion in modes other than play, we could not be deeply satisfied merely by qualifications of play by nonplay values.

2.6 Being as play

> In this world only play, play as artists and children engage in it, exhibits coming to be and passing away, structuring and destroying, without any moral additive, in forever equal innocence. And as children and artists play, so plays the everliving fire.
>   —Nietzsche (commenting on Heraclitus)[35]

Play can be made the master interpretation not only of humanity, as in Schiller, but even of Being, as in Nietzsche. A highly abstract but still very powerful reason for making this move is the evident impossibility of closing any quest for understanding by showing a determinate structure or reason. The point of being alive is to meet the challenges of embodied reason successfully, perhaps, but what then is the point of the whole scenario of birth and death? It just exists. Perhaps the world exists because God made it, as theists say, but why does God act? God just does. Both in the dialectical elaboration of theory, which always drives us to think of opposites and ask for more encompassing structures, and in the lived experience of practical motivation, where we are always liable to be touched by a deeper "Why?" or "So what?," we encounter an elusiveness that we can call play despairingly (taking it as frivolous) or joyfully (taking it as a lively whole).

Huizinga argued phenomenologically that play possesses a supreme kind of practical meaning: "The significance of 'play'. . . is by no means defined or exhausted by calling it 'not-earnest,' or 'not serious.' . . . The play-concept as such is of a higher order than is seriousness. For seriousness seeks to exclude play, whereas play can very well include seriousness. . . . You can deny seriousness, but not play."[36] Play resembles Being in that it cannot be denied.

If Being is play in such a way that we are exclusively or most fundamentally played by Being, then we might infer that the worth of our existence as a whole and essential tenor of every species of worth is play worth. But the notion of Being as a player—"as children play, so plays the everliving fire"—is incoherent. Being faces nothing, opposes no one; rather, Being sets up and encompasses facing and opposing. If our play is conceived as part of Being's play, then, it is not as though we are players on a team of which Being is the manager, our play purposes subordinate to Being's. The innocence of playing Being is not the temporary unreproachableness of human play, a delightful kind of agent virtue; rather, it supersedes the category of agency and the question of virtue. What we do conjure up in the figure of Being as a game player is our own felt opposition to the Whole of which we are willful parts. We say that Being plays us when we are actually thinking of ourselves playing a game with Being. We are impressed by the reflection of our own play worth back to us from an ontologically ultimate referent, seemingly magnified.

It will be pointed out that game playing is too restrictive a conception of playing in this context. "Being plays" could be taken to mean that Being's display is like the play of light and dark in a flickering fire, or that Being consists of a dance of Chance with Necessity. But someone has to play *with* such play, or take it over, to make it practically meaningful in play terms. Mustn't the contact with possibility *matter* to someone if any attainment of worth, or any sort of halo of worth whatever, is to be associated with it? I think we have arrived at a good place to mark a boundary between play and transplay. Play's promise of carefree spontaneity gets perfected in the transplay of a Being beyond beings—that is the quality that makes Being transplay and not trans-something else—but only by dropping the relations with care that make play worthy in our world. For worth thinking, then, the play of Being (if we think of Being that way) *subserves* the worth of our playing (such as it is), and although we may be playthings of gods or a God, deriving the meaning of our activities from a superior meaning of divine activity, our belonging to Being's play does not make us playthings of Being. (We can't pretend, of course, that we decide what to do with Being or handle it, since our doing is always an operation within rather than upon Being.)

The point of conceiving Being as play, or more properly transplay, is to place it beyond all theoretical and practical enframement. Being does not have ground or aim or worth. To identify with Being's transplay is to remove oneself from the ordinary division of worth domains. It is not to conquer all fields of worth on the terms of play. A real player can always *do* something other than play. Thus, the distinction between work and play (or some similar practical distinction) will survive and confound any utopian prescriptions for turning life into play, so long as these appeal in any way to the ordinary worth of play. It must be meaningful to draw such a distinction, because play freedom involves players' *turning* from the limits of actuality toward ideal possibilities. Players shut off their engagements with various things in order to be engaged differently and live more purely. That is not to say that they are wholly unaware of that from which they are disengaged. To the contrary, I have argued that play must always represent actual life in some way, and is more rewarding to the degree that this representation is comprehensive and rightly proportioned. One could push this point to the extreme and say that players are therefore not ultimately free from anything in the world. Yet a successful player must be free at least from the forces and even from the justification questions that interfere with playing. Playing is lively and organism-like (unlike Being), because it maintains itself over against other practical realities. It has wholeness and completeness, and therefore we know that (unlike Being) it excludes something.

૭૭

In this chapter we have come upon various reasons to think that play is a humanly adequate strategy and arena of practical self-realization. It provides peace together with the world, in Sheehan's conception—a psychologically sufficient happiness and an unlimited field for the admirable expression of our skills, strengths, and interpersonal concerns. Play principles generate a structure in which judgments of worthiness and relative worthwhileness can be made with a good degree of intellectual interest and intersubjective concurrence. We have also seen, however, that the meanings of play are conditional on the meanings of other modes of action that are excluded from play for the sake of play-freedom and that get represented within play for the sake of play's interesting content. We have reason to hold back, therefore, from fully accepting the play anthropology of Schiller or Huizinga and the utopian ethos they imply, although their grand play claims are useful guides in appreciating play worth. We also have reason not to grant an unlimited worth appeal to a play ontology. We will continue with the presumption that it takes more than one worth form—indeed, it takes a rich ensemble of worth forms—to make an affirmable human life.

Chapter 3

꩜

WORK

3.1 The claims of necessity

"The one sole truth lies in Work; the world will some day become such as Work will make it."[1] This pronouncement by a Zola character isn't strange at all in its Victorian context, a period in which the "gospel of work" had become a commonplace—in glaring contradiction to the classical ideal of a "liberally" cultivated life in which the burden of work is minimized. In our own time one can still be caught by the specific fervor and endless practical vistas of this proposal. But we can't miss its sinister overtones as well. *What* is the great work? *Whose* is it? What does work displace, distort, suppress—whether as a practical worldly program or as an exalted ultimate ideal?

꩜

Does work have any one essential feature? It needn't be useful or productive: one can work hard at paper-shuffling. It needn't be unpleasant: workers who enjoy their work are by no means freaks. It needn't be unchosen: a worker who freely decides on a course of work is admirable, enviable. It needn't be paid: one can work for oneself, or pro bono. And although work is the most reliable source of acknowledged worth in most cultures, it isn't even necessarily *worthwhile*, for the most prestige-laden professionals have room to wonder whether their lives are misspent.

Tom Sawyer's definition may still be best: "[W]ork consists of whatever a body is obliged to do."[2] Work is necessarily a relationship with necessity itself. Whatever possibilities attend it, we are aware in it of fronting necessity—as we could say earlier that whatever necessities attend

57

play, we are primarily aware in playing of our happy relation to possibility. (We *need* to play, but we do not play *to meet a need*.) Underlying our many curiosities about forms of work, therefore, is a generic work question about what in our world or our existence we are really unable to withdraw from and what our fundamental stance is with respect to necessity.

The distinction between necessity and possibility shouldn't be confused with the distinction between the "extrinsic" significance of an action as a mere means to something else and the "intrinsic" meaningfulness of an action as an end in itself.[3] A leisure-minded person will perform a work activity as a means to an end lying beyond it; but someone else, worried by a bit of undone work, will turn with some relief from a game back to work. Work, *as* work, can perfectly well be an end in itself. To deny that we have an intrinsically meaningful relation to necessity is to deny (wishfully) that necessity is an aspect of our at-homeness in the world.

I warn also against thinking of necessity so hazily and reverently that any really good or consequential way of being active is deemed "good work." To take this view is to be swept away by the still-powerful cultural current that privileges work worth above all other forms—and to return, in effect, to a preprismatic conception of action in the loss of meaningful worth distinctions.

The proper aim of thinking in the category of work is to bare the sharp edge of necessity as such. That is why it becomes *harder* to speak of work or to make a work-related evaluation that seems normal in cases of non-productivity, pleasantness, voluntariness, or material or spiritual nonremuneration. Lacking "something to show for it," what makes an activity other than gratuitous? If an activity is pleasant or voluntarily chosen, how do we know that it isn't a work imposter—an activity that perhaps looks like work when viewed objectively but isn't done for the work reason that "a body is obliged"? And how can an activity not be recognized by pay or prestige if it does answer to a generally recognized necessity? We can always pertinently ask about an activity alleged to be work whether it is productive, repellent in some way, obligatory, compensated, and honored.

☙

In one German household in some earlier century, a visitor learned that the ashes of a dead grandfather were to be found in an hourglass on the mantel because, living or not, "Everyone in our family must work."[4] Horrible people, not letting their grandfather rest in peace! Yet there is something delicious in the thought of prolonging one's own usefulness forever in an hourglass. (And what if your ashes had a special fine quality needed for the most reliable time-telling?)

We are ambivalent about work. We think of work as the royal road to salvation, and we think at the same time that ladies and gentlemen (or lottery winners) don't dirty their hands. Work is stability, security; work is the antithesis of peace. Work is certain accomplishment and proof of mastery; work is loss of one's substance and entrapment in servility. Work is social ingratiation; work is social onus. Work forges the true self; work interferes with true self-cultivation. How is it that our answering to necessity can be either painful and destructive or sweet and nourishing? Does it simply depend on which necessity we are willing to be related to?

Work might be despised because it seems to pertain to our corruptible part, our "biological requirements." It reminds us of a kinship with other beings that we cannot proudly acknowledge, a natural order with which we cannot gladly cast our lot. The bird has to find a bug, the beaver has to build its pond, and we have to do our jobs as well. It might be objected, against this dreary view of animal work, that we humans go about work in a unique and estimable way. Marx, for one, wanted to conceive "production" as the most comprehensive and essential attribute of humanity, and to support this idea he had to attack our apparent similarities to the "productive" nonhumans:

> Of course, animals also produce. They construct nests, dwellings, as in the case of bees, beavers, ants, etc. But they only produce what is strictly necessary for themselves or their young. They produce only in a single direction, while man produces universally. They produce only under the compulsion of direct physical needs, while man produces when he is free from physical need and only truly produces in freedom from such need. . . . The products of animal production belong directly to their physical bodies, while man is free in face of his product. Animals construct only in accordance with the standards and needs of the species to which they belong, while man knows how to produce in accordance with the standards of every species and knows how to apply the appropriate standard to the object. Thus man constructs also in accordance with the laws of beauty.[5]

Marx's argument doesn't show that production is uniquely human; it shows that there is a distinctively human way of producing, just as there might be distinctively human ways of doing many other things. But whatever the cause of our peculiar productivity—whether it be reason or the opposable thumb—Marx witnesses in this passage to the association of *excess* production with practical *freedom*. We may not have made a conscious, free choice to produce a certain new array of tools, but in doing this we bestowed freedom on ourselves in two ways: we now have more choices to make about *which* tools to use, and we also can choose *whether* to use such tools, since they are not simply a survival requirement.

Humans establish the human place in the world by treating their proliferating nonnecessities as really necessary. An outside observer might suppose that humans could just as well eat and reproduce without building, say, totem poles or menstruation huts, but the humans themselves *don't admit* that. So it is with all customs and standards. Now, insofar as we are unconscious of the difference between vital and added necessities, we are on a par with beavers building their ponds. What makes for a uniquely human work consciousness is *a paradoxical awareness of the nonnecessity of what we understand to be necessary*—a sense of maintaining standards, of choosing and creating ourselves, and not as artists or adventurers but in the very posture of addressing necessity.

Many of the added necessities in human life we inflict on each other. If we were not in competition at various levels, our economies and polities would not develop as they do. The fear of adverse consequences of interhuman competition is a more consistent and profound motivation than the desire for luxurious pleasure, and what we believe about our security requirements is, for the most part, well founded. So our awareness of the nonnecessity of working is by no means pervasive or dominant; it is only one thread woven in with others in the fabric of our work experience.

The human working posture should not be defined exclusively by the sense of nonnecessity that divides us from most nonhuman animals, or by necessity as rationally conceived, or by necessity as instinctively submitted to. It involves a combination and mixture of these elements. Nor should we define ourselves supremely by work (*animal laborans, homo faber*), or, at the other extreme, believe that work is an activity in which we engage only contingently—as though the whole human experience of having to get so many things done represents a run of bad luck. Here, too, the truth is to be sought in a combination and mixture of the senses in which human authenticity is separable and inseparable from work. We register all this in our ambivalent valuations of work.

Can we be reconciled to the world in all our necessary ties to it? Supposing we can cope, can we, in our coping, be at home? Posed in a global way, as concerning all of us together, this work question has a moral point but lacks political relevance. We can contemplate our collective work enterprise gladly or regretfully, proudly or ashamedly, perceiving our "human condition" as rich or poor in work worth, without focusing on practical questions having to do with who is able to realize which sort of work worth. There is a sense, admittedly, in which what matters most is what is done, not which of us does what—so long as the meaning of what is done is accessible in principle to all of us through shared representations. An aristocrat can say, complacently, "It takes all kinds to make a work world," and not worry about the proportions. But if each of us aspires, on behalf of ourselves and our associates, to maximal work worth, then the distribution of work worth becomes an important issue. For the identity of each of us is determined by what we and our intimate associates actually do and can't or don't do, just as our humanity is defined by what humans collectively can and can't do. I will bring up later the general politico-economic question of worth allocation (chapter 7); here, as part of discerning how work relates us to necessity, I want to ask how necessity imposes itself on the distribution of work worth.

By vastly increasing our forces of production, the Industrial Revolution transformed economic ethics. Today one can plausibly recommend a massive redistribution of work opportunities in the technically advanced societies—for example, a twenty-hour work week as a cure for the unemployment rate associated with current job standards, or the automation of all unrewarding labor.[6] These are politically meaningful proposals inasmuch as public policies could actually be adopted to implement them. Yet the autonomous force of our economic system places a question mark against any intended reform. The forms of work that are available to us are dictated in part by market competition. We know that politically negotiated constraints can be placed on the system when its costs become too frightful—if, say, everyone can see that it is killing or stunting humans, or poisoning the natural environment; but if well-meant constraints interfere too much with the capacity of productive organizations to take advantage of market opportunities, they subvert themselves (as happened in many twentieth-century socialist states). Obviously, the autonomy of economic process can be exaggerated. Employers of the nineteenth century claimed they were bound by "iron laws" to work the life out of little children. But it is also possible to exaggerate the amount of discretion we have in dealing with economic issues. Thus, a recurring prior question to be faced is: To what extent is the distribution of work worth a genuinely ethical or political issue and to what extent is it a scientific or technical one?

For illustration, I will offer assessments of practical necessity in two contemporary work areas: domestic work and waste removal.

(1) "Everyone ought to clean their own bathtub."[7] This maxim seems to make a legitimate appeal to discretion for the enforcement of a worth judgment in the realm of economic behavior. Most people would find it ridiculous or degrading to ask others to take care of their most intimately personal cleaning tasks, so long as they are able to perform them themselves; we might well extend the circle of tasks we already feel that way about to include most of what is called housework. (Norms can shift the

other way when servants are cheaply available and cultural barriers are removed; Europeans in Third World colonies often used "native" servants in ways that would be thought degrading in their home countries, for instance.) But if everyone in the United States did their own housework, there would be massive disemployment of domestic workers. What would *they* do? If the erstwhile domestic workers were immediately able to enter other morally acceptable lines of work in which there were insufficient openings, the society would be obliged to redistribute work opportunities; if they were not (yet) able to enter other lines of work, they would have to be given access to the necessary preparation. Either way, a major social challenge would be posed, and perhaps a major social change initiated, just by the collective making of a simple practical decision that is evidently within our discretion.

It will be objected that forces of economic competition insure the existence of a domestic worker class regardless of our feelings about housework. The fact is that a large number of workers who are relatively high-paid can get a significant advantage by freeing time from housework for the sake of their paid work. Not only does it cost them less to pay someone to do housework than it would cost them to do it themselves, but the time advantage they gain is a sine qua non of career advancement. As long as the lower-pay labor pool exists from which these higher-paid workers can draw—and there will always be a pay differential on which higher-paid workers can capitalize—domestic work as we know it will continue.

I am not very impressed by this argument. It assumes that the job market will continue to deny more attractive opportunities to the people who now do domestic work—or, to state the truth harshly, it assumes that current patterns of sex, race, and class discrimination will continue to constrain these people. But we ought to aim to eliminate these patterns. Furthermore, the argument is complacent about the current portfolio of nonwork activities that career competition tolerates very well. Not so many high-paid workers, after all, give all their waking time to work. Various recreations are considered necessary and suitable even for the "hungriest" professionals. And time is allowed to be spent with family, since we agree increasingly that dedication to work is grotesque when it gets in the way of parenting. I cannot see, then, why we might not become further enlightened to the point that "domestic service" comes to seem grotesque to us.

(2) On another front, it might seem that we could resolve on similar grounds that no human being should be so degraded as to have to specialize in waste removal. But here is a task that outranks others in exigency and that could not be done by everyone for themselves without cataclysmic inefficiency. If waste removal were not allowed to be a full-time job, we could not have cities. Even if we drafted young persons to do this sort of work,

as a benign equivalent of military service, we would still need career soldiers of garbage to direct them. One day, even that necessity might be mitigated; but for the near term we realize that we cannot do without cities, machines cannot do all of the waste removal work, and it is pointless, therefore, to attack waste removal jobs in principle. The crucial point is that the acknowledged necessity of these jobs not only places them outside ethical haggling, *it dignifies them*. They claim more respect than does domestic work. This is a case of moral evaluation adapting to technical requirements—not in shabby compromise, but in intelligent recognition of where the necessity line runs through one sector of our affairs.

∾

Our task now is to make soundings in human work experience to see better under what conditions we can affirm work. Adapting an approach pioneered by Hannah Arendt in *The Human Condition*, I will use the categories of labor and "work proper" along with a set of specific worker achievement conceptions to develop a more detailed portrayal of our practical relations to necessity (this structure paralleling that of our relations to possibility in play).[8] Arendt's immensely suggestive phenomenological distinctions between labor, work proper, and action (the latter a focus of chapter 5) make possible a much more intelligent discussion of anthropology and politics than the simplifications of modern "labor" theory (Locke, Marx) have admitted. There is a lot more of this sort of work to be done.

3.2 Feeling work: labor

On Arendt's showing, the hallmarks of "labor" as a distinct work type are that it is bodily, effortful, unintellectual (probably repetitive), and unpleasant.[9] While labor unquestionably needs to be done, there is nothing, or very little, to show for it, except that some necessary process in life has been sustained. The identity of laborers is submerged. They cannot point to any lasting product of their own in which they might take pride. (This anonymity in labor is the deepest reason why, if any sort of "labor-saving scheme" is proposed, no one can intelligibly ask, "Why save labor?" Concern about the evils of idleness has to be pursued differently than by sticking up for labor as such.)

We often call the struggle aspect of work "labor." At a given moment, we can labor at anything, and yet even in the midst of the most strenuous and apparently pointless exertion we can address a work challenge in such a way that we rise above laboring. That happens when we see a way to win in a work situation. Laboring is not to win but to prevent defeat. (An activity or occupation in which this characteristic is generally dominant thus acquires the title of labor. But we mustn't assume that a person called a laborer or performing an action considered labor is necessarily laboring.) As we generally prefer to win, we have a strong tendency really to change labor to something more rewarding—but also to misconstrue labor. John Henry, the labor hero, *can't* win against the rock and the steam drill ultimately, but we entertain the fantasy that he can.

An organism can be said to owe its most fundamental unity to its need to find sustenance outside itself.[10] Unity is the reverse side of alienation: because the living being does not have what it needs, because it does not contain the ingredients of its own future reality, it does possess now the functional unity of its self-maintaining activity. In labor, we find ourselves on the alienation side of this coin. We are close to being pulled apart by unfriendly forces. We even risk helping our own disintegration along instead of alleviating it when our minds range far away in time and space, trying to escape the painful present. Laboring exhibits the organic unity of our life as a harsh unity of vulnerability and a compromised unity of forced partnership with our surroundings. That is why the nicest labor prospect is one of smooth rhythm, an activity eminently maintainable, like the mowing of Tolstoy's peasant in *Anna Karenina*:

> The old man, holding himself erect, walked in front, moving with wide, even strides, his feet turned out and with precise, regular motion, which apparently cost him no more effort than swinging his arms in walking, as though in play. . . . It was as though it were not he but the scythe itself that went swishing through the juicy grass. . . .
>
> In the wood they continually came upon birch mushrooms, which had swelled in the succulent grass and which were cut down by the scythes. But whenever the old man came upon a mushroom, he bent down, picked it up, and put it inside his jacket. "Another present for my old woman," he kept saying.
>
> Easy as it was to cut the wet, soft grass, it was hard work going up and down the steep slopes of the ravine. But the old man was not in the least troubled by it. Swinging his scythe just as usual, he climbed slowly up the steep slope, taking short, firm steps with his feet shod in large bast shoes, and though his whole body and his loosely hanging trousers below his long shirt shook, he did not miss a single blade of grass or a single mushroom, and went on cracking jokes with the peasants and Levin.[11]

Here laboring holds survival issues at bay so firmly and calmly that the agent's consciousness is free for collecting presents and joking. But the shaking of the mower's body reminds us that he is really laboring. He is not free to daydream.[12]

John Henry and the mower represent the form of labor, male-associated in Western culture, that takes one away from home. Does labor look different in the domestic sphere? That sweet and tranquil refuge is really the front line of the struggle not to be overwhelmed by unfriendly nature. Here damage and loss can be held at bay only by the exertions of "homemakers." The ridiculous alarms sounded by advertisements for home cleaning products always resonate with our deep knowledge that, in principle, every home is sliding into ruin.

An impressive domestic counterpart to John Henry has been drawn by Gabriel García Márquez in *One Hundred Years of Solitude*. When the swamp-city Macondo is afflicted by a four-year rain, the ancient, blind mistress of the Buendía household, Úrsula, is galvanized by the challenge:

> She did not need to see to realize that the flower beds, cultivated with such care since the first rebuilding, had been destroyed by the rain . . . and that the walls and the cement of the floors were cracked, the furniture mushy and discolored, the doors off their hinges, and the family menaced by a spirit of resignation and despair that was inconceivable in her time. Feeling her way along through the empty bedrooms she perceived the continuous rumble of the termites as they carved the wood, the snipping of the moths in the clothes closets, and the devastating noise of the enormous red ants that had prospered during the deluge and were undermining the foundations of the house. One day she opened the trunk with the saints and had to ask Santa Sofía de la Piedad to get off her body the cockroaches that jumped out and that had already turned the clothing to dust. "A person can't live in neglect like this," she said. "If we go on like this we'll be devoured by animals." From then on she did not have a moment of repose.[13]

If we live in neglect, we will be devoured. And there is never a last battle in the war of survival. The feeling of home peace is leavened with fear of home loss. The most solid ground for confidence in the preservation of our homes must lie in an experience of stability *in*, not away from, home laboring. Although it is not pleasant to be tied down on a bed of nails, that stability realizes our humanity in its relation to necessity. We feel an earnest solidarity with "home" and "homemakers" not disregarding but taking account of this struggle. Home is where the heat is. A totally leisured home life would not be home life at all but a hotel stay.

The problem of maintaining a home is all the greater for beings whose intellectual freedom to question, evaluate, and imagine alternatives to what they experience is liable to alienate them from their own bodily circumstances. We can fracture ourselves very unhappily by disowning aspects of our life that cannot, after all, be escaped, and practices that enable us to enjoy goods to which we cannot sanely be indifferent. Labor can reasonably be touted as a cure for solipsism, because it imposes on us the sanity of organic unity and, directly or indirectly, the higher sanities of labor-based human relationships. Labor to maintain a home has this virtue to the supreme degree, since its point is the safe embedding of a person in the world, and its logic applies to everyone. (The labor factor is a significant part of the worth of having "a real home," that is, a real maintenance challenge.)

But labor is radically threatening, too, and so there is much sense also in touting contemplation as a cure for labor. Contemplation promotes an intentional unity that labor disrupts, a sharpness that labor dulls, a flexibility that labor rigidifies. For contemplation, satisfaction and finality are meaningful goals, whereas for labor there is only the fatality of a struggle never won. Labor's discipline of holding course under pressure, though fundamental for all practical enterprise, is not the same thing as concentration. It can become stupidity. The advanced concentration of contemplation holds eternal life, a gathering together of time, while in the forcibly dispersed time of labor there is only the deferring of death.

Labor can be either the most moribund or the most vital of activities precisely because it is participation in a process that always ends in death. Nothing besides execution is as intimidating as the living death of chain-gang labor; but nothing, on the other hand, is more encouraging than the indomitable efforts of Úrsula, which admit our competitive equality with our fellow animals only in order to win a distance from their fatal game. Arendt suggested that because labor is so closely bound up with consumption and thus with vital gratifications, it contains "the blessing of life as a whole," the benefits of nature's fertility, and an "elemental happiness."[14] It is true that gratifications belong together with laboring exertions in a rhythm or great system. But such enjoyment is not taken *in* labor. We can, as it were, hold labor in our left eye and "elemental happiness" in our right for a stereoscopic appreciation. That will give us a fuller view of the happy home and the happy society. But we shouldn't erect a false paradigm of "happy labor" or "the happy laborer." What makes laborers happy is finding a rhythm or producing an abundance that gives them a respite from struggle.

Another strong, dangerous reason to believe in laboring happiness is the fellowship made possible when individual projects are submerged in the general effort of maintaining life as such. Christianity and democracy, two great cultural programs that call for maximized sharing among their constituents, have countered the distinctness claims of more articulate forms of work with the notion of a common human "dignity of labor" and thereby have mitigated class division. But each tends to go too far, Christianity by losing sight of the material effects and spiritual rewards of labor-transcending kinds of work and democracy by dissolving important differences of value-kind into a utilitarian sea of "experience" and "satisfaction." Each program undermines itself by destroying what there is to share in the way of work worth. Each must bear some responsibility for the ethical nightmare of Taylorism in which all worker autonomy is erased.[15]

The interpretation of labor as a common lot of humans must depend on what the interpreter believes about life, death, and human destiny. For theists, labor will count as submission to a divine ordinance of creation (the commonly measured participation in existence of all material beings) or salvation (a punishment to restore relationship with God). "Physical labor willingly consented to is, after death willingly consented to, the most perfect form of obedience" (Simone Weil).[16] But this means also that the lived cogency of theism depends on the possibility of finding a relationship to God in or through labor. A world in which labor is distorted is, in that respect, an antitheistic world (even if it breeds "opiates of the people").[17]

Labor can, for the religious, take on infinite significance, yet we have to be careful while interpreting it to respect its own inarticulateness. Labor is the oppressed and feeling side of work; it becomes an appreciable deed or career only when some other work-character supervenes on it. A theorist like Weil who is primarily interested in the unity of the work world, with a special sensitivity to its labor aspects, can help us to appreciate the pervasive relevance of labor but also can confound the meanings of labor with the more definite and positive meanings of work. An approach like Arendt's that dramatizes distinctions between work categories can help us to avoid that pitfall but, on the other hand, can misleadingly sequester labor's meanings.

A common way of mistaking the meaning of labor is not explicitly theoretical at all, but breathlessly practical. It is the use of the inarticulate and ephemeral means of labor to express love. Labor can seem to be the perfect expression of love because of its humility. If I "slave" for you, we are both to know that I have really given myself over to you. But there is a double catch here. If I do succeed in submerging myself in labor, I dedicate myself to the production of ephemeral, nonnoteworthy effects, and you receive no message. (Perhaps I made the house sparkling clean for you today, but tomorrow it's dirty again. Perhaps I've made the house clean for you for twenty years, and when I walk out, it gets dirty and you *realize* what I've done for you—but then it's too late, love is gone, and the message has been lost in another way.) Or a message does reach you, but without a sender. (A maid could have cleaned the house for twenty years just as well as I did, so how can that be a manifestation of *me* to you?)

Because the intensification of a love relationship requires the intensification of the personalities involved, lovers want a combination of submission and glory. Any labor involved should be Herculean. (I must find and realize myself in maintaining a *uniquely* wonderful household for you.) Now the meaning of labor must be overlaid by meanings of work, creativity, adventure, and service. Still, the labor meaning must remain in this mix, so that service and devotion are appreciable. When such expressions of love succeed, they hold a teasing, pleasingly contradictory mixture. When they fail, it is by resolving the contradiction in one way or other, more often on the side of futile servitude, where the ability of the beloved to appreciate what is done wanes just as fast as the felt intensity of what the beloved *ought* to appreciate grows. Lovers fail to understand the workings of this syndrome precisely to the degree that they sincerely submerge themselves in labor, wallowing on the purely passionate, disaster-prone side of love.

If a lover's labor relieves the beloved of labor, enabling the beloved better to flourish, then the worth enjoyed by the beloved registers in the lover's own life in the other- or relationship-centered mode of love. Thus, it is worthwhile, in both labor and love terms, for me to wash the supper dishes on my wife's turn so that she can get to an art lecture downtown. (Yet some people cannot be rescued from labor. Spared one chore, they will only submerge themselves in others; they are not ready to pursue worth more ambitiously.)

☙

Because labor is inarticulate, it carries the form of work worth that we are least able to discuss. It is more like the lower border of the work realm than a region in it—all while and no worth. The press of necessity on laborers, their absence of discretion, makes it laughably beside the point to ask whether their kind or quantity of labor is optimally worthwhile, *for them*. The question we can ask on their behalf is whether a true or illusory labor situation exists: whether, for instance, a homemaker who mops the kitchen floor every day might be going beyond the minimum effort necessary to stave off the decay of human life, or whether the Europeans' sweet tooth warranted the enslavement and grinding down of Africans on sugar plantations. Since labor, supposedly answering the call of necessity, is grotesque when it is unnecessary, we have grounds for demanding change in such cases.

But there is a quite different "economic" way of asking about the worth of labor. Labor can produce wealth. The sugar laborers produced profits for the planters; overzealous floor moppers enrich the employees and stockholders of polish companies. Does labor's worth change when our attention shifts from the immediate struggle for survival to the producing of "wealth"? This depends on the practical significance of the wealth involved. If a quantum of wealth is a survival necessity, under a given set of economic conditions, then activity undertaken for the purpose of producing it is labor. If, however, "wealth" or any other effect of labor is necessary *for improving one's lot in life*—so that a project of changing one's world is in hand—then activity for the sake of this electively necessary wealth moves into the category of work proper, even though it may look in its immediate description like labor. An ethically defining difference between the lowest social class and all others is that the lowest-placed people cannot make this move.

3.3 Work as accomplishment

In the preceding discussion, we had to keep labor pushed down so that it wouldn't stand up and turn itself into work. But one of the strongest currents in practice is precisely to transform labor into work proper, the latter being a more impressive demonstration of human power and understanding and the true object of most of the encouraging things that are said about work in general. That "life grants nothing to mortals without hard work" (Horace) is true in the sphere of labor as a fate, but in the sphere of work takes on quite a different meaning as a frontier on which effort will reveal new and admirable acquirements. I have to clean my house—but I can try different techniques and tools. I have to put in time at the automobile plant—but the assembly line can be set up in such a way that my team follows a car down the line and takes responsibility for the ultimate product, and my colleagues and I can attend board meetings at which the relations between the firm and the larger society are reviewed. I have to put in time—but I can systematically put in overtime in order to retire sooner. These added possibilities show the important role of freedom in the realm of necessity. It isn't that we are free from the task at hand, but we lengthen our tether to it, and we define by our own conceptions what will take place within the tether's constraint. When we do this with an eye on freedom for its own sake, we play (can I beat my best laundry time this week?); when we do this with an eye primarily on the satisfactory accomplishment of what needs to be done, our freedom serving necessity, we work.

We can want to get work done, for the sake not of getting it over with but of pulling it off. Indeed, work can be infinitely seductive, even without taking on attractive nonwork meanings. The worker stays up late to finish a piece, or can't be pried out of the workroom for months. A team of workers are caught up in the thrill of their heightened efficacy together, enthusiastic about the big achievements that come within their collective reach.[18] In a stirring scene written by Solzhenitsyn, a gang of prisoners go all out one evening to finish building meaningless walls in frozen Siberia: "Why do these bastards make the work day so short?" cries one, only half joking.[19]

The key to the transition from labor to work is the accomplishing of things. (Arendt's attention was fixed especially on the significance of the making of *material* things in work, which led to two biases that I wish to correct: too little appreciation of the immaterial "things" that are accomplished in work, and a somewhat misleading blending in principle of work worth and creation worth.)[20] To think about work, we may and must attend to the particular well-differentiated things (of whatever sort) that workers get done. Thus, if we review the process by which cotton is formed into textiles and notice the part taken by the cotton pickers, our interest in the specific accomplishment of cotton picking leads us to construe the pickers' activity as work and as a distinct occupation. In work proper we first encounter the "job," the objective work quantum.[21] The cotton pickers get a job done. If they are treated as workers, they are paid for getting that job done. They have entered a social process of exchange more concretized and negotiable than the basic social complementarity of labor as such.

Work means gain.[22] Only in the realm of work proper is real payment possible, and pay is proper to work. Work *as work* is never lowered by being paid. The difference between "instrumental" and "intrinsic" satisfaction, between working "to get something" and working "for the sake of the work," generally counts for much more in theory (where nonwork worth standards of creativity, love, etc. can exert their influence more powerfully) than in work practice. Earning pay, workers worthily embody the getting-ahead that work is supposed to represent for everyone; their activity is worthwhile according to the market price of their accomplishments. Unlike workers, laborers are compensated directly for the whole undistinguished business of living the toilsome life: the labor administration allows them resources they need for survival and comfort so long as they labor, and perhaps in retirement as well. Whoever receives "minimum wage," the wage that is set solely for maintaining life at a tolerable standard, is, in that respect, a laborer rather than a worker. Whoever receives more than a minimal wage has by that fact gained the prestige of work proper.

Working well means getting ahead in the double sense of adding lasting new objects or arrangements to the world and acquiring personal capital.[23] Praises of work are sung loudly whenever people see a chance to get ahead materially; a great thrill about material "progress" has animated the age of capitalism, with progress indeed so wide-open in our era that it has encouraged a confusing transposition of work meanings into adventure meanings. Work's meaningfulness is threatened if it can't prove itself on either the productivity front or the pay front. Not the least of Michelangelo's agonies in carrying out the Sistine ceiling commission—one of the most worthwhile jobs ever, if we measure by the product—was caused by the pope's slowness to pay him.[24] It is all very well to say that Michelangelo got ahead in the world marvelously just by painting the ceiling, and that a great artist should show a sovereign contempt for finances. But insofar as the artist is a worker, insofar as the artist *is making a living* (and no small part of any professional's claim to respect attaches to making a living in the practice of her or his profession), not getting paid means failure and dishonor. If we say, as we certainly want sometimes to say, that it is more important to produce than to be paid, we are either superimposing another scheme of valuation on that of work or moving outside of work's worth domain entirely. In the case of someone whom we postulate to be a great artist, our interest in the free and innovative exploitation of possibility is so strong that we would prefer not to think of the artist as a worker, a respondent to external necessity, at all. The productivity in question belongs to play and creation. Nevertheless, Michelangelo was a worker, and I say he should have been paid in a timely manner.

While the paradigm case of work proper is paid productivity, we find analogies and imitations of this structure in all forms of activity. "Nice piece of work," says a teammate after a batter waits for the right pitch and pokes a double down the line. In baseball, a hit is a "product," and victories or other prizes are "payment." The play "work" of an amateur softball game collapses into play "labor" when such "products" and "payments" are not attained: then we are just sweaty and tired with nothing to show for two hours of effort. Here the work meaning of the difference between work proper and labor mixes with the play meaning of the difference between victory and defeat.

We are little disposed to question the worth of work proper, because it is set up precisely to be the most favorable field of worthwhileness. Work proper is a broad and mostly straight highway toward self-empowerment and self-knowledge. The identity of the good worker has both material and social solidity to the greatest possible degree. The "bums" who cannot stay on this road are objects of contempt and pity. (Yet there are voluntary vagrants, "hobos" and "hippies," who choose not to cash in on the worth-lucrativeness of work and who prove thereby that work's worth can be questioned after all.)

Work is a blue-chip worth form, yet the heroes of work tend to be notable for accomplishing through work something more than work. For example, Florence Nightingale performed an amazing work feat in organizing health services for soldiers in the chaos of the Crimean War, but she is appreciated more as a philanthropic "angel of mercy" than as a worker. James Watt was a most industrious worker and had a tremendous impact on work life through his refinement of the steam engine, but his most celebrated achievement, his "invention," is commonly lifted up and placed on the plane of creativity, together with the most memorable achievements of scientists and artists, rather than on the plane of work. How do we imagine the worthiest work as such, with less distinction available perhaps than in public service or inventing, but certainly more than in labor?

In principle, there ought to be an impressively effective hero for every serious occupation. To represent many possibilities, I nominate a man who is so thoroughly caught up in a work process that he is visible in no other way. He is a steamship's chief engineer whom we are used to calling "Scotty," grimy below decks, tending a cranky engine with an almost magical touch. We attribute the ship's motion more to him, to his competence and will, than to anything inorganic. We communicate with him by a speaking tube, straining to hear what he shouts over the roar of his boilers. Anything that is logically possible for the ship is within Scotty's power: he can coax thirty knots out of her if we absolutely have to go that fast. Were the ship wrecked on a desert isle, he could set up a smithy for rebuilding. No matter what he does—and this is very attractive in him, but also frightening—he is intent on his work and he is as "objective," fair, and responsive as a human being can be. His attitude is the more noble in that it is not impersonal or self-forgetful, since he is living passionately through his work. The life of his engine is *his* life, an amazing synthesis of steam and pistons and Scottish character traits.

Critics of industrialization have seen an unwholesome contrast between working with machines and a more direct working relationship with "nature." But we have always recognized that the vitality of *homo faber* grows through tool use. Large-scale mechanical processes, unlike ordinary tools, impose their rhythm and material requirements on humans, and experience shows they can catch us in horrible traps, as in the worst factories. They can intensify the unpleasantness of work and tighten its bondage. They can draw us deeper into fantasies and practices of a necrophilic sort of mastery of life. But we repeatedly rise to the challenge of putting machines in place as tools. Could humanity choose at any point to avoid the issue? Scotty seems the perfect work hero partly because his ship symbolizes the whole artificial world in our life-and-death dependence on it (Nature foaming outside the hull). The building, operating, and fixing of this contraption is *homo faber*'s responsibility. And the good mechanic—specifically, the one who can make repairs, going by the book or improvising as required, enabling us to do what we had intended to—is the unsurpassably important work team member.

But the Scotty example takes us far away from home—out on the high seas, where we are manifestly dependent on a moving substitute for home. Could we not equally well hold up a proper homemaker—say, Úrsula Buendía herself, wonderfully accomplished (we are told) in home construction, interior redesign, and even in making candy items for sale—as a model of work? For the important labor aspect of homemaking should not obscure its work aspect. An even richer example is the real Hildegard of Bingen, the medieval abbess, who not only accomplished marvels of administrative work in a monastic superhome but had to cope with bad health, hindering church rules, and hostile superiors. She attained success for her abbey by working with and around most of the major challenges a worker can face. She represents the great worker generalist, whereas Scotty is the specialist; Scotty would not know how to talk to a bishop or a mayor or a milkmaid, but Hildegard would know how to find someone to fix a machine if she couldn't do it herself. As in Scotty's case, though not as extremely (for she maintains a private creative and spiritual life), Hildegard becomes her vessel, that is, her abbey, and her abbey becomes hers.

Both examples show that work is attractive because of the magnification of the worker in the work—it is a way for the worker to grow—and because of the intimate bonding of the worker with artificial elements that makes the artificial world not dead and alien, but human past all doubt.[25]

3.4 The verbs of work

Which forms of work are most worthwhile? Even before we form larger or more analytical ideas about the structure of work life (see section 3.5), we can ask what kinds of work we'd ideally be attracted to or want to get involved in. Some general practical rules are obviously applicable: for example, to seek the optimum balance of breadth and depth, of flexibility and specialized excellence, of self-regard and other-regard, of self-sufficiency and interdependency, of joy and challenge, of freedom from oppression and safety from corruption. Many work options can be ranked or ruled out by matching such principles to particular circumstances. But for a more helpful answer, we need indications of the character of different kinds of work, concrete forms gathered from experience that we can imagine ourselves in.

"I don't like work—no man does—but I like what is in the work—the chance to find yourself," said Marlow.[26] There is a presumption that by working one can become a more desirable version of oneself, expanded or proven. There is also an immediate practical curiosity about what one can do in the modality of work, a curiosity that would express itself in any age or culture, though of course not always with the same encouragements. A way to get an overview of the possible opportunities and dangers of work doing is to scrutinize some leading verbs of work proper with respect to their possible inclusion in one's life. I will set out six of these—making, tending, operating, finding, serving, and managing—in a sort of zodiac and comment afterwards on why this particular array should emerge.

Making

The maker impresses us in the way that a mountain takes over lines of view in a landscape. "That's one of *her* dresses," we say of a good dressmaker's work.[27] Our ability to do things well is contingent on the good maker's work; the maker's prime affiliation is with opportunity, and that is why it would be a mistake to look for the amplitude of the maker's work-self only in mastery of materials or in the shape or intricacy or durability of the thing made. A good boat-maker opens up a world of good boating. There is usually room to excel, to distinguish oneself, to become famous in the relevant circles, in making. But there is an implicit restriction: the good boat-maker *as such* stays on land, mountainlike, as the fixed point from which mobilities fan out. Excelling in making normally precludes excelling in use. And yet the maker must be a profound student of use and so must master the concept, the unity, of use. (The best users have a reciprocal insight into making.)

Tending

The tender is less authorial and bold but more continuously necessary, protecting and rescuing opportunity. The tender falls more in the shadow of what we have already determined we want to do. If boats are made to go boating in, it follows that we need people capable of fixing the boats; if farms are to be productive, someone has to take care of the crops and animals. Is the tender more a lackey, then—a more intrinsically subordinate sort of worker? There are, as we've recalled, specially valuable wizards of maintenance, like Scotty, but inasmuch as tenders are busy restoring other people's creations and uses rather than injecting novelty into the world, they tend to be less eminent. Moreover, our desire to possess and use the best things is more conscious and competitive than our desire for the best security of repair, so there is little upper range in the tending market. Since the practical issue in repair is so largely basic competence rather than distinctive excellence—since excellence in repair *is* competence—a tender is more likely than a maker to be submerged in the generic identity of the work-type, though without becoming as interchangeable as laborers are. That generic identity is a kind of strength and claim on gratitude that the tender is privileged to wield. Getting the attention of a competent mechanic when your car is broken down is as sweet as getting a date with someone you've long admired.

If the point of work proper, in contrast to labor, is to get ahead, to enrich and not merely maintain the human world, then it might seem, ironically, that those who merely tend things are not actually working at all, however much skill they possess. But the tender is the proximal key to our getting ahead in the use of things, a partner and not a background precondition.

Operating

In *homo faber*'s world of made things, the operator or skilled thing-user is as essential as the maker and the tender. Operating can be the most extroverted way of working, an attention-getting performance like that of an artist or athlete. (Is there, after all, a distinction here? Is, for instance, a symphony violinist—who undoubtedly "goes to work" each performance evening—an operator?) In return for accepting the restricted identity of a something-jockey, the operator is allowed to present a personal style to the world. No other sort of work involves such an intense amplification of human powers and qualities through thing-powers and qualities. If we appreciate operators for mastery, the greatest are the ones charged with the biggest machine (swinging a giant crane) or the most difficult trajectory (landing a lunar module); if we appreciate them as ones *entrusted* with effects as well as things, the supreme operators are the ones like heart and brain surgeons, pilots, and bus drivers, in whose hands lie our most precious resources. What ambition could be more worthy than to become worthy to be entrusted with what is most precious? And in the most difficult sector of work? Hence "brain surgeon" becomes a proverbial high-status reference.

Finding

The finder is a distinct type that I might not have found if I had not needed a category for my own researching. This is a sign of the greatly reduced prominence of hunting and gathering in many people's lives due to agriculture. For most people and most kinds of food, food sources no longer have to be found (although it is still true for many kinds of fish that eating is enabled by finding). As our planet gets more thoroughly settled and exploited, relatively fewer people work at finding mineral and energy resources. The finding needs of our time more often concern abstract information than material things.

Finding differs from direct service (conveying needed resources) to the degree that it brings about a new arrangement and new availability of things at the worker's discretion. The discretion of finders is so great, in fact, that if they are not job-holders it may be hard to tell them apart from hobbyists. What is the difference between Darwin collecting biological facts as a minimally paid naturalist on the *Beagle*, Darwin collecting the same sort of facts as a self-supported private scientist, and some other gentleman collecting butterflies? (Does it make a difference if the gentleman is "working on a book"?)

The finder's distinctive objective is useful awareness. Heroes of finding lurk in libraries (in offices as well as within the volumes), are proclaimed on plaques beside exhibit cases in natural history museums, and are gratefully acknowledged in memoirs of childhood learning experiences. The finder's work is not often *urgently* necessary in civilized society, on the scale of a day or a week, but that is just what we relish and aspire to in finding, namely, the prospect of unexpectedly advancing the human world. Insofar as the finder subordinates his or her own creativity to the preexisting integrity of the things to be found, there is a noble humility in this form of work as well. It is different from the people-oriented humility of service proper; indeed, the finder is freest to turn entirely away from fellow human beings and runs the greatest risk of becoming inhuman.

Assisting

Assisting includes the many forms of "going between" or representing—for example, selling, litigating, and the work of government officials. The assister is the means of someone else's coming into possession of something. All work is assistance in a sense, of course, but the assister is the one worker who cannot work for her- or himself and whose skill pertains primarily to active relationship with clients and only secondarily to relationship with things. A car salesperson, for example, doesn't need to know as much about cars as a mechanic; he or she needs to know only enough to mediate effectively between the interests of the buyer and the vendor. A diplomat must know enough economics to converse productively with a foreign leader, but not as much as an economist. Here lies the ambiguity of assisting's worth: in its noble form, assisting subordinates technical matters to the properly higher concern for human fulfillment, but in its base form, assisting has no firm anchorage in work-world mastery and merely manipulates its clients without getting them ahead. When corrupt assisting is common, honorable assisting becomes noteworthy.

Managing

The manager is the watcher and planner of the work ensemble. All work must be managed if it is to get us ahead the most. Historically, the preeminent manager was the ruler of a family, community, or state—management being only one of a ruler's tasks—but now a class of professional managers answers to new demands for concentrated attention in an increasingly complex work world. In practice, management specialists perform a synthesis of making (plans and reports), tending (operational structures), operating (as "executives"), finding (to the extent that they are unavoidably involved in "research and development"), and assisting (as mediating between other employees and other managers, customers, stockholders, and regulators); the complexity of this synthesis is a noteworthy challenge, and grounds for honor. But it falls to the manager to do another distinctive and indispensable kind of work, the same work that Aristotle assigned to practical intelligence in his ethics: to discern the connections between means and ends in such a way as to sustain awareness of valid ends.[28] Among workers, the manager is expected to have the most disciplined, sensitive, or in any case reliable apprehension of what is most worth doing. Like all who work, the manager answers to necessity and so in one sense cannot determine what is to be done. But to the extent that there is room for interpreting a work activity's larger scheme of necessity, the manager is chief interpreter and negotiator. Managing thus presses on a boundary with leading in the political sense (see section 4.5) and makes us look for agents fit for eminence; at the same time, managing is evidently something that no worker can afford not to do well. Working without managing is like shooting arrows without seeing any main target. Working with good managing, we can lose technical battles and still have a chance of winning the work war.

꩜

The principal verbs of work coincide here and there with actual occupation-classes but are best conceived as dimensions of possible experience, duty, and reward that open up before each of us, whatever work we are doing.

How vivid and accessible they are depends on the individual worker and the particular work. But there will be a correlation, by my hypothesis, between vividly perceiving work worth and a display of one or more of these main kinds of work. The principal work actions are centers of worth resonance whenever we take stock of what we are really glad is getting done in relation to human necessities.

I don't claim that these six work action types are the corners of an eternal hexagon of work, but I think we can reasonably infer them by considering various combinations of values on basic axes of practical attention, such as from things (finding highest) to persons (assisting), from possibility (managing) to actuality (operating), and from preservation (tending) to transformation (making). A complementary explanation of the types is that they emerge near the boundaries between work proper and the other great practical spheres of labor (tending), creation (making), play and action (operating), owning and experiencing (finding), leading (managing), and helping (assisting). These proximities map out the relationship of necessity to opportunity. Each verb of work reaches out toward freedom's transcendence of necessity or else reaches in to necessity with freedom to humanize it.

ଊଓ

We have recognized that working entails earning, but we have not seen yet *how* material and spiritual rewards attach to work activity (and why in differing amounts). The next step is to push our inquiry out to the most comprehensive bounds of work's meaning by asking how work comes to be figured as an array of items to be known, discussed, and evaluated. What are "job," "occupation," "profession," "career," and "vocation" that worth may attach to them and be measured?

3.5 Knowing work

In asking how in the sphere of work we observe a general human drive to make life more articulately knowable, I follow the notion that a trend of dominant interest in cultural evolution is the differentiation of what is first compact.[29] Practically, this generally means a division of functions for greater effectiveness and wider scope (risking the alienations cataloged by Marx); theoretically, it means a multiplication of reference points yielding initially poorer but indefinitely enrichable unities of experience (risking murder by dissection). Thus, humanity can grow while remaining human. The elaboration of work forms makes a fine illustration of this principle.

Clayre rejects the notion that noncivilized folk have an unalienated work life.[30] Nevertheless, evidence he has collected from poems and songs, many recorded at the point of first contact with Stone Age peoples, suggests a more vivid involvement of hunter-gatherers in their necessary activities, a livelier work present, than is usual for workers in civilized societies. Gabon pygmies, for example, seem very immediately results-oriented in one of their elephant-hunting songs: "Hunter, lift up your heart, leap, and walk. Meat is in front of you, the huge piece of meat . . . the meat which will roast on the hearth."[31] Thus their work *doing* is displayed. They are not highlighting here the craft attainment or occupational identity or status or social gain of the hunter. After the feast, though, I think we can be fairly sure that pygmies discuss how the hunters who did most to bring in the meat have earned the gratitude of the community, have exhibited memorable skill, have added a chapter to a history of feats, and so forth. Work assumes these knowable aspects for them and is interesting to them just as it is to the civilized. Because of the functional compactness of their life, they do not have a large conventional vocabulary for this discussion—not the thousand-and-one "occupations" and gradations of material success (and breeding grounds for malice and vanity) that civilizations have elaborated. But if they do not use civilized distinctions, it may not be inferred that they lack interest in distinctions. If circumstances favor the development of this interest, they will catch up with everyone else in the elaboration of things to know about work. For knowing more and more about work is a way of producing work worth, fulfilling the basic work intention of getting ahead and building up the world.

Product, job, occupation

The first unit of knowable work worth is the *product*—the meat or the berry, the basket, the arrowhead—and products can already be relished, counted, weighed, and compared; given products, a work economy exists. Workers have no portfolio, no proof they have answered to the challenge of necessity, if no products are discernible. The product is a touchstone for understanding both the human need work addresses and the concrete way in which it advances us in dealing with that need. The most highly trained, skilled, and paid workers are still working trivially, except in the respect of making a living, if their products are inconsequential. This is a demoralizing or confusing factor in many work lives in late capitalism. For example, the "creative director" of an advertising firm laments that, in his business, "They're aware that they're talking about little bears capering around a cereal box and they're arguing which way the bears should go. It's a silly thing for adults to be doing."[32]

The *job*, the next larger unit of work, has a double sense: the whole of a sort of thing that needs to be done and the whole of a person's working action or activity. To call an action or activity a "job" is to write a check of worth against a conception of what is truly necessary and obliging. To have a job, a *real* job, is to have the social solidity and weight that come with membership in the team that is coping with what needs to be done. It is also to represent a knowable and reliable bundle of work powers, these being capable of analysis and negotiation to determine a worker's market value.

But jobs are worth checks, not worth money in themselves; they can bounce. The worthwhileness of doing a job, as such, is contingent. Doing a job could mean saving lives with a rescue team, but it could also mean listening to purposeless complaints from neurotic customers while your boss takes long vacations; it could mean building some of the world's finest furniture, or it could mean selling shoddy gimcracks by telephone. The search for a good way of spending work time moves on from the job, therefore, to the *occupation*, which we take to be an ongoing work, possibly taking a whole working lifetime. An occupation might be shady, of course, yet "occupation" inspires more confidence than "job" because of the unlikelihood that an individual could tolerate worthless activity on a long-continuing basis or that society could afford a large investment of its members' work time in an activity that isn't really useful. "Job" leaves any amount of time over for doing whatever else, but "occupation" recognizes that work *takes up* a life and thus defines it. The choice of occupation is scarier than the choice of a job: it is the threshold of adult participation in the work world, a more settled, reliable, powerful mode of working.

Marx saw a decline in the significance of occupations due to the job mobility of more and more workers in modern times. Commenting on Adam Smith's theoretical breakthrough in deriving all value from "labor as such," he noted:

> This abstraction of labor as such is not merely the mental product of a concrete totality of labors. Indifference towards specific labors corresponds to a form of society in which individuals can with ease transfer from one labor to another, and where the specific kind is a matter of chance for them, hence of indifference. Not only the category, labor, but labor in reality has here become the means of creating wealth in general, and has ceased to be organically linked with particular individuals in any specific form.[33]

Increasing use of machines and improved education, transportation, and mass communication are some leading positive reasons why the work economy can become flexible and dynamic in this way. The dark side of the trend is its destruction of the worker's proprietorship of competence. As workers become more interchangeable, they are increasingly nomadic and lose their leverage to command higher pay. Still, as we have seen in the prosperous United States, if there is a lot of wealth to go around, the predominant experience will be more of opportunity than of expropriation.

Another assault on occupations comes with what Toffler called "the prosumer revolution." On our newest technological plateau, even as fewer of us than ever produce the means of our own subsistence, we often perform work tasks for ourselves instead of relying directly on the competence of others.[34] We pump our own gas, fix our own houses, operate our own computers, and doctor ourselves. More often now it is cheaper to replace things than to get them fixed, or to buy tools to do necessary work oneself than to hire the people who specialize in using them.

A consequence of these trends that is congenial to democracy is that working experiences are more broadly shared. Three centuries ago, Russia's Tsar Peter was famous for plunging into the working life for several years (how could it be less?) as a carpenter in a shipyard; today, an American gubernatorial candidate can build a successful campaign around experiencing a different job every day for hundreds of days.[35] Remarkably, this stunt isn't widely perceived as an insult to the occupations. It is actually the democratic way of taking the occupations seriously. Christianity, too, wanting to free us from the forms of the world that pass away (whether for the sake of a transformation of the world or to facilitate departure from it), has reason to rejoice in the erosion of occupational division; a Christian theologian asserts that "life in the Spirit" is less well served by the traditional concept of *vocatio*, which holds that a duty to God binds one to a particular work station one finds oneself in, than by the concept of *charisma*, which allows for diverse empowerments from God throughout life (Miroslav Volf).[36]

What are the best relevant reasons to give a major part of one's life to an occupation, if much of the old wisdom in learning a trade is undercut in the newer economy? Let us gauge the attractiveness of the craft ideal. We surely admire a man who can build a sturdy boat that will be just right for the uses of a particular customer; it requires choosing the right woods from the right trees at the right times and shaping and assembling them by rules of thumb that reflect both the tradition of generations and long, hard-won personal experience.[37] This is one kind of human plenitude—a compelling answer to the riddle, "How can mastery and serviceableness, personal expression and generic relevance, be maximized at the same time?" It is all the more beautiful because we perceive it to be dying out. We even recognize that factory-made boats can be not only cheaper but *better*, judged by utility, than this man's works—a circumstance we resent (just as we did not want the steam drill to beat John Henry).

There is no question that this boatbuilder is wanted in the community. Whether or not one directly benefits from his work, one basks in his presence. But why would you want to *be* in his position? Isn't it more advantageous to let someone else be the excellent boatbuilder while you, as a generalist, remain free from immersion in a craft? How do you assess the tradeoff between the solidity of the boatbuilder's work identity and the flexible availability of the generalist? Do you notice how the craftsman seems to get the better of this alternative as he gets old, as actuality becomes increasingly more relevant than possibility in assessing a human life? What does the generalist become, over the years? Someone capable of telling stories about diverse work situations? But does that amount to "work experience" in the full sense, experience possessed by a worker as a worker? (A hobo has a lot of stories, too.) Does the generalist's experience fund, ever more powerfully, the effective doing of work and a mutually enhancing interpenetration of worker and world?

I am raising a question about the generalist, but my aim is not to condemn a looser relationship to occupations. I do think it is possible to fulfill oneself and become impressive as a worker in a series of occupations. This work diversity could be the trace left by an exemplary willingness to respond to needs as they present themselves. But it seems that master craftspeople are enabled by their occupational immersion to more directly and unambiguously represent the worth of work experience accumulated in a lifetime. I use the boatbuilder, therefore, as a symbol for a potentiality in any working life. But one should take seriously the boatbuilder's practical advantages (and risks, too) in realizing this potentiality.

A more communally oriented reason to esteem occupations is that they structure our social interdependency in a practically useful and morally affirmable way. This is the point of Durkheim's praise of division of labor:

> Everything which forces man to take account of other men is moral. . . . This is what gives moral value to the division of labor. Through it, the individual becomes cognizant of his dependence upon society. . . . In higher societies, our duty is not to spread our activity over a large surface, but to concentrate and specialize it. We must contract our horizon, choose a definite task and immerse ourselves in it completely, instead of trying to make ourselves a sort of creative masterpiece, quite complete, which contains its worth in itself and not in the services that it renders.[38]

Durkheim argues that personal development and occupational specialization go hand in hand because a person is truly autonomous "only in so far as there is something in him which is his alone and which individualizes him, as he is something more than a simple incarnation of the generic type of his race and his group."[39] This makes it clear that he is not thinking of the anonymous work at Adam Smith's pin factory. Neither, however, could he approve Marx and Engels's utopian ideal of "hunting in the morning, fishing in the afternoon, rearing cattle in the evening, and criticizing after dinner, just as I have a mind, without ever becoming hunter, fisherman, shepherd, or critic," which expresses either a retrogade nostalgia for a form of society in which personality was less developed or an irresponsible disregard for the social conditions under which one can meaningfully engage in those specific activities.[40]

Boats aren't built by specialized boatbuilders in utopia, and they aren't built at all in an otherworldly heaven. But good boatbuilders have manifestly become cosmogonic agents. They have made themselves *of* a tangible world-system; they have become a sort of species like a seal or a crab, with both the limitation and the ecological security that that comparison implies. Whether it makes sense to go their route depends on whether one can confide oneself to the actual world to that extent. For one whose goal lies outside the world, this worldly formation may seem a deformity.

However society in fact develops, and whether or not there is a supramundane reality to reckon with, each of us faces now, in some form, the question of how to relate a maximized worker worth to a maximized worth of life overall. It is at this outer boundary of the work sphere that the concepts of profession, vocation, and career have work to do.

Profession, vocation, career

Are all occupations of equal worth? They aren't equally honored by deference or pay. So-called occupational prestige, the conventional social valuation of work, seems to be determined by perceived difficulty of attainment and degree of social investment (long years of schooling, expensive facilities, etc.) as well as utility. Those who are supposed to have worked hard to prepare to do their proper work, like professors, enjoy higher prestige than those who work hardest in doing their work, like farmers. If professors do work hard, so much the better, although the evidence of their hard work may contribute less to their prestige than the exceptional leisure components, like sabbaticals, that form part of their popular image. (This supports the notion that the best work is that which brings the greatest freedom to necessity.)

Sociologist Edward Shils suggested that "the most esteemed occupations . . . are those which in their internal structure and in their functions are closest to the *centers* . . . roles [enabling people] to control society or to penetrate into the ultimate laws and forces which are thought to control the world and human life."[41] This theory hints at a seepage of nonwork value into the esteeming of occupations; I suppose that political leaders rate higher because they lead (see section 4.5). Indeed, we might question whether "occupational prestige" is properly a work variable at all, since all true work is necessary, and the slighting of a supposedly lowly occupation diverts our attention from this vital point. But if we assess work with regard for the richness of the knowable fulfillment of the worker in the work, rather than with regard to objective necessity as such, we will be able to recognize distinctions and make rankings at least roughly coordinate with the rankings on a sociological chart of occupational prestige.[42]

A chief clue to our intentions in drawing occupational worth distinctions is the concept of *profession*, which marks out the high-prestige class of occupations. The hallmarks of professionals are thought to be that (1) their work mandate takes in an infinite diversity of unique "cases" rather than routine situations, involving human needs with much individual inflection, and (2) for this reason, they must be given the largest possible license in determining what the needs are and how to deal with them, with extensive preparation of their judgment capacity so that they earn and continue to justify the exceptional trust bestowed on them. These latter points imply that, ideally, professionals are accountable in fully specifiable terms only to themselves and other initiates in their profession—as they alone really know what adequacy and excellence mean in their work areas—even though their general and ultimate responsibility is to the larger community.[43]

A profession shows itself to be a more knowable form of work in its ability to define itself, promote itself, teach itself, and police itself. This autonomy tends to disrupt the ordinary relationship between work and pay: a lawyer is not regarded as doing more or better work, or as subject to a greater obligation, when billing a corporation at five hundred dollars an hour than when defending an indigent pro bono. We say that some athletes are "professional" mainly to indicate that they do get paid; to them, however, being "professional" means defining and enforcing the highest possible standards of performance for themselves, not directly for the sake of earning more but to promote the quality of their sector of the work scene, acknowledging that the greatest responsibility for the quality belongs to them. Knowing that they define the very standards of their activity adds to our fascination in watching them. Conversely, the more strictly work and pay are proportioned to each other, or the more knowable work is by pay, the less personal excellence matters in knowing it. Yet pay and work are integrally related, so the looseness of the professional's relation to pay is an indication that some sort of nonwork worth helium is pushing professionals upward at the top limit of the work sphere.

One work-transcending element on this scene is personal relationship appreciated as an end in itself. In professional work, the work sphere overlaps with the superordinate sphere of personal ties. The family lawyer, the family doctor, and even (in a strange way, predicated on bridgeable distance) the family baseball favorite have standing as major family allies. To comport oneself well in human relationship is a worthy ambition and so an ideal draw to professional work. Perhaps the most important reason that clients trust professionals is that they credit them for wanting to be in relationship (and holding up a difficult end of it, at that).

It might seem that a professional can be an out-and-out misanthrope and still achieve a sort of transcendent work worth in exercising a professional's control over the definition of necessity itself. A boatbuilder is down on the shore, where the people (as customers) are boating, but there is a sense in which people (as clients) have to go up to the mountaintop to engage the lawyer, because the law is a special realm administered by lawyers. To be sure, legal needs in contemporary society can seem just as ordinary and inescapable as transportation needs. Yet we know we *could* live without courts, hospitals, or schools. We imagine ourselves slogging along, economically active and viable but afflicted by disputes and sickness and ignorance, in a life not *graced* by the professions and the higher needs for legal counsel, medical attention, and education that they address. Thus, professionals are leaders in forming our idea of a more desirable, more proper shape of human existence. How, then, could a professional be allergic to personal relationships? For the negotiation of our idea of human existence is one of the leading functions of relationship. Professionals who do not invest themselves in personal relationships are likewise strangers to this exalted humanity-defining function of professions. They become technicians.

Professionals are typically careful to sharpen the visibly distinctive profile of their activity. Doctors do not take temperatures; lawyers do not type legal documents. There is a comic side to this, an implication of vanity, and a dark side in the insistence on privilege and domination. Is there a real risk, though, that professionalism would be lost or degraded through submergence in more routinizable activities? Isn't it true that typing is not the best use of a lawyer's time? Or is there a worse danger that a too-specialized professional will lose touch with the vital dynamics of the work?

The polarization of the nonroutine and the routine, the more commanding and the more menial, in the division of work between professionals and their assistants furnishes a helpfully clear illustration of the general principle of interdependency in work. If popular narratives are any indication, we take much more satisfaction in seeing professionals (or workers with more initiative and discretion) teamed up with nonprofessionals (or less-free workers) than we do in seeing a pure exhibition of professional activity. A lawyer story is better if the lawyer's secretary takes care of a crucial witness; a detective story is better if the detective gets help from a friend who works in the police records department; a baseball story is better if a batboy finds the great hitter's bat for him.

Notwithstanding the beauty of interdependency in work, is the best work identity that of the professional? Is it possible to professionalize any line of work? Is that always desirable? One of the lowest-prestige occupations is waiter, and yet an excellent waiter can espouse "professionalism":

> I have to go between those tables, between those chairs. . . . Maybe that's the reason I always stayed slim. It is a certain way I can go through a chair no one else can do. I do it with an air. If I drop a fork, there is a certain way I pick it up. . . . I tell everyone I'm a waitress and I'm proud. If a nurse gives service, I say, "You're a professional." Whatever you do, be professional. (Dolores Dante)[44]

This is stirring. But Ms. Dante is probably using the term "professional" in a looser sense, meaning "dedicated to excellence." Or do waiters, like lawyers and doctors, minister to a relatively exalted and gratuitous need, helping in that way to draw the profile of human nature and thus satisfying the stricter criterion of professionalism? My own experience does not equip me very well to make this judgment, but I would say that excellent table service could have a constructive influence on my envisioning of human life. Some have admired it greatly. It is hard to say it is less technically impressive than excellent legal or medical service. The standards are subtle and elastic, and their portent is illimitable. But table service has lesser material consequences than lawyering and doctoring, for most people, and it would be ridiculous, probably, to cite an instance of table service as a turning point in one's life—which helps to explain why waiters are paid and honored less. The most ambitious and accomplished waiter, then, has to be content with a smaller portion of work reward, and a worth compensation for that limit must be sought outside work. This is a reason for waiters *not* to think of themselves as professionals, and, accordingly, not to accept the stipulation that *so much* of life's worth comes to them through work. Waiters should take advantage of their freedom from the problem endemic among professionals of being so much claimed by work worth conditions as to have to make life-deforming sacrifices of nonwork forms of worth.

The general sanity demands that many occupations be less obsessive and sensitive than professions. But the high prestige and intrinsic personal rewards of professional work are not the only solution to the problem of finding a fully affirmable kind of work and work identity, even if they provide impressive resources for a solution. The concept of *vocation* lines up squarely with the broad problem. One has a vocation if one can unreservedly identify with one's work, whatever it consists of. One is called *away* from alternative pursuits—that was an important aspect of the original monkish vocation, the rejection of "the world"—and *to* one's specific work, which one inhabits not as a passerby but as one who belongs to it. Those who take the whole initiative in choosing what to do are, in principle, passersby, since their activity will change whenever their feeling or judgment changes. The instability of the vocation-seeker is different. However chancy and muddled be the process of discerning vocation's call, the intended end in the worker's *answering* to the work is an arrival home.

The idea of answering to one's work is not the same as answering to persons through work—meeting a family's need for income by holding a paid job, for example. That is another dimension of work fulfillment. Vocation is a fulfilled relationship of the worker to the work itself as well as to those who benefit from the work; besides addressing a human need, it involves a material bond with the work, as the good smith, seeing a hammer, is drawn to swing it, or the good teacher, seeing a roomful of people, is drawn to stage a discussion with them. A worker without vocation gets no inner prompting to come back to work.

The strongest possible conception of vocation is represented by a belief that a task is given uniquely to me by a divine power or plan. Even without believing in divine assignments, I can have a sense that my own abilities answer so well or so unavoidably to a particular work challenge that it has my name on it—or, in a less personally inflated way, I can feel that the sort of worker I am belongs to the sort of work a given task is. Having become part of self-knowledge, the work and its worth terms are inescapable. It might be objected that I can't meaningfully imagine, let alone pursue, this question of personal fit unless I partake of a social elite's privilege of making the freest of bargains with necessity. But the best examples of vocation do not reliably come from a most-privileged class. Perhaps the more important point, though, is not that we can imagine virtually anyone finding a vocation, but rather that it would be unrealistic and unfair to expect all theoretically free workers to seek worth success in vocation. Work worth isn't the only worth. What is morally worth doing in all work assessment is to try to discern a gradient of worse-to-better fit and shallower-to-deeper attunement in whatever range of work opportunities any individual faces.

An occupation that cannot be a place of belonging for a significant part of a worker's life, that does not allow a sustained, full answering to the work, cannot be an object of vocational choice and so ought not be tolerated in our work world. Many occupations cannot with a straight face be called places of belonging. I am not thinking of the honorable occupation of waste disposal (although one had better not affirm that certain human beings belong together with waste without linking their occupation strongly to the universal human belonging to waste that they are specially helpful in dealing with). I am thinking of the sort of sales or managerial work that depends on avoiding truth, of the sort of manufacturing or service work that forbids thought, or of any work outside comedy that makes a ridiculous spectacle of the worker (like posing naked). My objection is not on the more familiar ethical grounds that pertain to particular actions but for the domain-specific reason that a work life trapped in such occupations is not worth living.

What about a person whose work is objectively worthless—say, a telemarketer of bogus products—but who enjoys doing it? By hypothesis, this ace telemarketer is genuinely fascinated by the ins and outs of her work and often feels surges of satisfaction in exploiting her great aptitude for it. She is eager to start work every day. If the social utilitiy of her work is challenged ("It's just a game for you!" or "You're a sort of pirate!"), she answers that she brings interest, sheer entertainment at a minimum, to the lives of the people she calls. She really believes this. Can we deny that she has found a vocation? No and yes. Although she is called to her work, she ought not to be. No one should be so lacking in sense or so malicious as to let themselves belong to a deceptive or destructive activity. If we find a moral defect in a person's belonging to a work, we cannot label the work "vocation." Having a vocation is stipulated to be an adequate solution to the work worth challenge.

A far more honorable test case is found in the worker who resourcefully, tenaciously, and ambitiously holds a series of jobs to support her family. If she is a committed and embattled parent, a single mother, we can more easily imagine that she sees her work as the meeting of her family's needs, an extension of homemaking, rather than as something unrelated that she undertakes in order to produce income to support her family. She feels an aptitude for this struggle and a worker's pride in succeeding in it. If she happens to do very well in waiting tables or typing or babysitting, she is satisfied not as a waiter or typist or babysitter but as a good provider.[45] Is this not an experience of vocation? Yes and no. We appreciate what is present but we see the gap between her actual work activities and the description under which they would be satisfying.

In no system will all workers find vocations. But a morally important social problem exists when a given work economy condemns whole classes of workers to occupations that cannot be made vocations, or can only be made vocations by exceptionally serene or inventive or odd-minded individuals. Mass-production industrialism did this by turning millions into factory automata, and late capitalism does it by involving millions of people in the making and selling of gratuitous goods and services. We cannot realistically hope ever to be free of this kind of social problem, which is, after all, just an exaggeration of that overproduction that gives us our relatively free work stance in the world. We must dignify the forms of work that prevail as best conscience will allow; but we should not be complacent about the problem.

The concept of vocation operates on the interior of work, where the criteria of fitness and the pertinent adjustments of attitude are elastic, overloaded with meaning, and very likely hard to define with precision. Work turns into vocation in the heart of the worker. For the more specifiable exterior of work, we use the more technical concept of *career*. To have a career is to have, as an achievement or as a prospect, an entire work life the success of which is publicly measurable.

If the basic aim of work is to get ahead, then "career" is a more central work concept than "vocation." One's career is one's progression and self-construction *by* work; one's vocation is one's self-harmonizing *with* or attunement *to* work. There is, of course, a standing question about what really constitutes success. From the perspective of concern for vocation, which is supposed to rectify work now-and-forever, "careerism" is a foolish attempt to get somewhere without ever being somewhere; from the career perspective, meanwhile, "vocation" can seem but a pleasant fiction. Within the work sphere, the career principle rules this discussion. In work terms, the success of getting somewhere is superior to the success of being somewhere. If we feel a distortion in this perspective, we are reminded in another way that work meanings ought not to be the only ones in our portfolio.

Careers are the work *of* work, the building up of what by our discretion we deem necessary in our work selves. The importance of this dimension of work is generally sensed. Employers in all sorts of business hold out prospects of advancement to their workers; they hope to motivate harder work and happier attitudes, and they may conscientiously want fairness of opportunity. In a typical work organization, however, the greater number of employees can advance in little besides seniority, and younger job holders often feel constrained to say about their work satisfaction, "It's not a career." Where, then, will their careers be found?

Many workers will have to settle for money alone. Seniority means more pay. Now, pay is so far from being a negligible work value that a career without any increase in pay would be a cruel joke. To earn more is a central kind of work success. Yet there are different meanings that higher pay might assume. Is it a compensation for investing a lot of one's time in a line of work—the balloon part of an overall payment? Or is it the rightly measured reward for more skilled, more productive, more leaderly work? Workers who believe themselves to be getting higher pay due to pure seniority as such cannot be as happy as workers who believe that they have advanced in work value. They may justifiably feel that they have earned their raises by plugging away, that they have a "career value" just in the accumulation of work actions on the same plane of quality. But "career value" in this sense is relatively insubstantial. "What have you done lately?" and "What can you do for us now?" always displace "What is the sum of your accomplishments?" in present interest, and even retrospective assessment is often more interested in the qualitatively highest point of attainment than in sheer quantity. This is why almost everyone would avoid or leave a qualitatively dead-end job, given a good alternative, even if a rich pot of gold were placed at the end of its thirty- or forty-year rainbow. A person who would be happy working solely for a big ultimate payoff would be a person for whom work's instrumentalism is not what it is for the careerist, who aims to get ahead in it, but rather what it is for hobos or slackers, who want to escape the worker's relationship with necessity. Such a person could exemplify only inferior worker virtues at best. Not wanting to be that person, workers who are really advancing only in seniority cannot be satisfied with their work life stories.

My thesis here is that careerism is fully proper within the work sphere, and that every worker should seek forms of work in which interesting and impressive developments of the work self can be attained over time. By what logic would "careerism" be a term of reproach, then? We fear careerist pathologies of deception and exaggeration: deception, when manipulation of appearances (perhaps to the disadvantage of other workers) substitutes for real growth of the work self, and exaggeration, when the story of the work self becomes not merely one component of or one parable for the progress of the whole self, but its whole identity. An adequate career plan is not an adequate life plan.

An adequate plan for one's personal career may not even be an adequate work plan. The third great pathology of careerism is excessive self-centeredness. Work life is collaborative; workers have to get ahead together, since their project is the construction of a human world that has to be jointly habitable, and so workers properly identify with the careers of teams and organizations. (The merely senior workers of the preceding discussion, unable to take pride in development of their personal powers, may rightly find satisfaction in the development of their companies or their societies, in "having been a part of something.") We condemn too exclusive a focus on individual development, because we judge that the necessity to which human work responds is a shared one, a qualification of our species-life.

When the quest to get ahead turns us against each other, we lapse from the distinctively human relationship with necessity into mere scrabbling. (We can ambivalently admire the robber baron or the hotshot investor only on the understanding that our social work-fabric can survive and even profit from intense expressions of individual enterprise. We feel we can't completely discourage their sort without also discouraging our real heroes.)

Work and democracy

What is the best way for an individual worker to participate in the career development of a business organization (or trade, or profession, or society)? The irresistible principle of democracy has been applied to the work realm in an unprecedentedly sweeping way in recent times. Popular self-determination in the work realm would mean equal sharing of responsibilities and privileges, especially of operational and strategic decision-making, among all workers, entailing a more fully shared awareness of all of a work enterprise's meanings. It has not been clear, however, whether so-called economic democracy is really a political principle imposed on work, forcing a sort of compromise—as even some of its proponents think—or a properly economic development.[46] How could productivity be enhanced by giving up the advantages of the division of labor, including the divisions between entrepreneurial initiative, management, and production proper? How could work virtue or career success be promoted by giving up specialization?

The currently prevalent answer to these questions is that although we must work, we who work are also (more importantly) human beings, and our humanity must be respected and if possible enhanced in our work arrangements. The workplace should be free of avoidable injury and disease risks, workers who are going to be laid off should be given decent advance notice, and so on. It is very evident, however, that some evils of the workplace, like Taylorism, are distortions of work itself and not merely of human beings while they happen to be in a work zone. So I ask: Is an undemocratic workplace not a distortion of work also? Isn't the problem with Taylorism precisely its undemocratic extreme, its total separation of those who decide from those who must exert themselves?

I want to keep clear the difference between saying (a) that an undemocratic workplace prevents people from working well, and (b) that it keeps people from sharing in the determination of their destiny, on which work happens to have an impact. In the work worth context of evaluation, everything depends on whether we identify with the aspirations of workers to get ahead by working. And this context is inescapable, for ironically, even when we distance ourselves from work by asking how we can minimize its negative effects on us, treating it as an alien threat, we are caught up in "working for a better world." People who want to impose sharply distinguished political requirements on the work sphere have to show us that we can get farther in *work*, and not merely in debating privileges, by following their advice. If we admit that we all have a stake in working and that in that capacity we all want to get ahead as a team—and some rough realization of this principle is a lesson perennially thrust at us by actual work experience—then our conceptions of work and democracy can hardly be kept separate.[47]

Must a consistent democrat condemn the interdependency of specialized workers that evolves for the sake of the greatest work effectiveness? Democratic politics itself involves divisions of responsibility. The electorate has oversight and adequate voting opportunities to make the oversight meaningful, but it cannot exercise every governing function as a committee of the whole. Do we concede this only to compromise between our purely political motivations and the *need* for a *working* system of government? This is part of the story, no doubt; but the sphere of deliberation and leadership is always already segmented into issue areas, and specialization is required simply to address issues competently. There is a logical reason that no one could campaign simultaneously for mayor, governor, and senator, and that is that no one could form a coherent discourse on all the issues associated with those offices.

One might admit that functional division is a feature of democratic politics, yet insist that inequalities of participation are greatly mitigated in this system by the fact that its main object is to allow people to speak and to give them satisfaction, rather than to produce things in the manner of work. The ordinary business seems less like a democratic government and more like an organization of the opposite kind, like the army (or its play analogue, a sports team), where life-and-death (win-or-lose) necessity, and above all a premium on timely and precisely coordinated action, require hierarchy and discipline. Could Henry Ford have made a commercial success if he had involved all his employees in regular deliberations on company policy? One supposes that competitors would have left him in the dust. Ford's autocratic approach *worked*—in certain important ways, under a given set of conditions.

But the great entrepreneur Ford paid homage in a different way to the principle that workers have to progress together. Realizing that the health of his industry depended on expanding the number of people able to buy cars, he paid his workers more than the industry standard in order to make them better consumers. More wealth led to more power on labor's part to resist management, which ultimately led to more worker participation in high-level decision-making. And this was an economic development, not merely an external imposition on business of "democratic values."

I don't see support in this example for a "trickle down" theory that justifies economic policies benefiting rich employers primarily and their employees secondarily. My point is that in most sets of circumstances there will be some way to obtain a real, beneficial yield from the principle that all workers' prospects for success are interconnected. Antagonistic principles will always be operative as well, and will often have the upper hand. For example, high industrialism was very inhospitable to economic democracy, as the commodities that dominated the market and the conditions for producing them fostered huge organizations with rigid procedures. Now, however, in many areas of business the most effective organization size is much smaller, and procedures may or must be more flexible. Under these conditions, a growth in work democracy is unavoidable.

Workers, managers, and owners all have a greater stake in competitive advantage and producing wealth than in any purely aesthetic or political refinement of the work experience, provided their dignity survives the work. This implies that radical reform of work will come not out of any desires regarding *how* work should be done but as a consequence of a change in what we want the *result* of work to be—what, in a broad sense, we want to produce. High industrialist culture's ruling desire was to produce huge quantities of goods, which entailed putting millions of workers in the modern type of factory. If the ruling desire had instead been for finely made things to be enjoyed by a stable population, Western societies would not have gone down this path. What now do we think we need to produce?

3.6 "Dhamma work": the transworthy reconstruction of work

The concepts of profession, vocation, and career permit us to examine the worth of work from various larger perspectives that we are somewhat free to use or not, depending on how we think we can maximize the meaning of our work or deal with work in such a way as to maximize the meaning of life. The more work extricates itself from the immediate material bondage of labor and develops itself, the more room it gives us to wonder what our true necessities are. Our place in reality becomes less resolved, more an open question. We are called increasingly by the work of thinking about our life, developing or rescuing its knowableness. Thus work leads of itself toward philosophy and religion.

The religious strategy for tackling the most open form of the question of human beings' proper aim is to affirm that a resolution of the question does exist, though not within our ordinary horizons. Religiousness involves a strong inflection of our notions of necessity and work. (1) There will be something we have to do to *really* live. (2) The character of this activity will be noticeably different from ordinary secular work, just as real life differs from the ordinary experience of life. (3) We will be able, nevertheless, to recognize the truly needful activity as work, and there will be some continuity between it and what ordinarily counts as work, just as real life cannot be wholly alien to the life we are now embroiled in.

Buddhism offers an explicit preparatory counsel regarding work. One point of the Eightfold Path is "right livelihood," which means avoiding occupations in which immoral actions or excessive moral peril are inherent. Most forms of work can, in fact, systematically hinder enlightenment, but Buddhists aim to neutralize the bad aspects of jobs and occupations by working within them in an enlightenment-tending way. Then, beyond such worldly coping, there is a proper Buddhist work of attaining what is truly needful. Buddhadāsa calls it "Dhamma work," that is, "Truth work," but emphasizes that he can only say this in "Dhamma language":

> Everyday language is based on sensory things and experiences accessible to the ordinary man. . . . By contrast, Dhamma language has to do with the consciousness, with the intangible, nonphysical world. In order to be able to speak and understand this Dhamma language it is necessary to have gained insight into the consciousness. . . .
>
> We have to work in order to eat, to fill the belly, and also to get the things we desire. This unavoidable chore of earning a living is what is meant by the term "work" taken as everyday language. Taken as Dhamma language, work refers to mind-training, that is, the practice of Dhamma. In its most profound sense, work is the acting out of Truth.[48]

Looking for the locus of mind-training, we might think first of a specialized and seemingly "unworldly" activity like meditation. Perhaps "work" is only a jumping-off metaphor in this context. Yet Truth is *the* truth, the truth of everything and a truth in everything, according to Buddhadāsa. "Though our work may be of a worldly nature, if we do it in the right way, ultimately that work will instruct us beyond the activity itself. It will bring us to an understanding of the true nature of the inner life; it will enable us to recognize impermanence, suffering, and nonselfhood."[49] The claim is that we can make a double living, meeting economic needs predicated on the demands of desire and the durability of things at the same time that we meet our religious need of realizing that desire is doomed and nothing endures. Work thus becomes a supremely tense metaphor in action, thriving (in principle) by contradicting itself. But the fully successful practice of work is, of course, the opposite of tense and contradictory; it has the character of going with the flow. It retains its work character in that it aims to "get somewhere," and does get somewhere, but its destination is the time- and space-transcending enlightened mind rather than a visibly improved future world. The "self" that arrives in it is not the self that set out in it.

Christian discourse on work typically seeks the same doubleness of worldly and spiritual meaning. "To pray is to work, to work is to pray" was an early motto for Christian monks. Luther brought spiritual and economic "vocations" into close proximity for all Christians in principle.[50] At the core of John Paul II's encyclical *On Human Work* is the idea that divine and human productions coincide in a way, as the human being "shares by his work in the activity of the creator."[51] The human, worldly side of this theistic work meaning is very strong, for God condescended to create and work in our world, our history: "[W]ithin the limits of his own capabilities, man in a sense continues to develop that [divine] activity, and perfects it as he advances further and further in the discovery of the resources and values contained in the whole of creation."[52] So part, at least, of Christian truth work can consist of getting ahead in worldly wealth, this not merely as a sign of stewardly virtue *before* God but also as the practical goal of a true workers' collaboration *with* God.

It seems, however, that collaborating with God cannot be manageable in the way that an all-human collaboration is. Christianity symbolizes as "resurrection" and "last judgment" the inability of humans to know or control God's relation to worldly works; these ideas challenge Christians to question what in human experience *really* is sponsored by God. According to Volf, Christian work cannot amount only to sharing in the creation of the world, in the sense of perfecting or richly developing the world's given possibilities; it must envision the *new* creation, the eschatological transformation of the world, not *elsewhere* than in this world but *otherwise* than the world now is.[53] "Life in the spirit," including specific gifts from God that empower work activity, is marked by both a yearning for the new-that-is-not-yet (depending entirely on God's action) and a realization in Christian living of the first fruits of the new. That is a Christian contradiction paralleling the Buddhist contradiction in locating Dhamma work in ordinary work.[54]

The new creation in the Christian view is a "raising imperishable" of human and all beings (1 Corinthians 15.52). What could be the place of work, specifically, in a raising imperishable of humans and their world? Volf argues that even though the direct results of work typically pass away, their cumulative effect does not; the world does get somewhere. Most importantly, *we* get somewhere with each other, for personhood itself is partly a product of work. What in our personhood belongs to a new creation? A central Christian claim on this matter is Paul's assertion that love will remain while knowledge passes away (1 Corinthians 13). Yet personal love presupposes a diversity of faces, powers, and histories, a loving Hildegard (the one who ran the abbey) interacting with a quite different loving Scotty (the one who ran the ship's engine). One cannot be certain now what in knowledge will pass away and what will ultimately make persons knowable, but one sees that love's knowing depends on work. That is a Christian concession of infinite importance to work.

∽

The perspectives of Buddhism and Christianity imply a vexing but fitting question at the end of this part of the investigation. While we know that various things do need to be done and that the worth of work in general is unimpeachable, can we know that any specific form of work is worthwhile? And does it undermine the whole worth system of work—which we might justifiably have taken to be the firmest of our worldly worth systems—if we cannot be confident that any work activity is actually taking us in the right direction? Although they are relatively worldly insofar as they affirm the goodness of material "creation," Christians should be more afflicted by skepticism than Buddhists are in this connection, for Buddhists can in principle taste enlightenment in whatever they are doing, while Christians must wait to see what survives the fire. And Buddhists have less reason to build up a personal identification with a type of work, in any case, since personal distinctness is no prominent part of their vision of salvation.

One advantage of any relatively worldly affirmation of work, balancing the danger of eventual disappointment in it, is that because the *results* of work count, one can find out *later* that one's work was worthwhile. Work worth plays out over time. It would be an absurdity, or at best a weird limit-case, if I claimed to realize now that I had had fun playing a game a year ago; but the subsequent "paying off" of work, even many years down the line, is a regular enough human experience that we advise, reassure, and warn each other constantly about how and when work will turn out to have been worthwhile.

3.7 Would God work?

Could God, an omnipotent world-maker, properly be the subject of any of the verbs of work? This question raised by theism can help us to assess the prospect of a transwork that would be in some way a human possibility.

John Paul II founds the dignity of work on humanity's resemblance to a working God. His argument is founded in the representations of the book of Genesis:

When man, who had been created "in the image of God . . . male and female" (Genesis 1.27), hears the words: "Be fruitful and multiply, and fill the earth and subdue it" (1.28), even though these words do not refer directly and explicitly to work, beyond any doubt they indirectly indicate it as an activity for man to carry out in the world. Indeed, they show its very deepest essence. Man is the image of God partly through the mandate received from his creator to subdue, to dominate, the earth. In carrying out this mandate, man, every human being, reflects the very action of the creator of the universe.[55]

One problem with this interpretation is the possibility it assumes of determining the specific content of the "image of God." The Hebrew Bible combines anthropomorphic boldness with idolophobic circumspection, so that we find, on the one hand, pictures of God walking in the garden of Eden in the cool of the evening, and haggling with Abraham and Moses, but on the other hand, the pronouncement that no one can see God and live. God is said to work for six days and rest on the seventh, but God also says, "As the heavens are higher than the earth, so are my ways higher than your ways" (Isaiah 55.9). To link humanity with God by an "image" (Genesis 1.27) is to assert with great temerity a parent-child connection between God and ourselves (Adam goes on to have a son in *his* image [Genesis 5.3]). It is also to open the door to our projecting upon God any human quality we specially fancy—philosophers tend to jump to the conclusion that the image of God is rationality—unless we are circumspect. But if we are too rigidly circumspect, insisting on an abstract divine transcendence, we fail to leave open the door of divine proximity to, concern for, and solidarity with the world.

If we do think that there can be some describable isomorphism between divine and human life, what would justify including work in the shared form? The pope notes that Genesis mentions the human mission of subduing the earth right after the creation of humans in the divine image, as though the purpose of the image is to equip us for the mission. Certainly the giving of the mission speaks to the question, What is the right activity of these new human creatures? Of equal prominence in the mission, however, is "being fruitful" (reproductively active), and even closer to the mention of the image is sex difference. The pope does not attribute either sex difference or sexlike generation to God. Why then worklike action?

The action of "creating" is essential to a monotheist conception of God. How does God's speaking-creating of the structurally greatest elements of the world in Genesis compare with the scenario of humans "subduing" and "having dominion" over the earth, or tilling and keeping the Garden of Eden (2.15)? There seems to be a great difference between God as an unconstrained metaphysical power and the human earth-creature fashioned from ingredients of the material world and animated contingently by the breath of life (2.7). Do humans do what God would do if God lived in a fleshly form? That notion seems absurd; but if humans always do something categorically different than what God does, then God's activity is irrelevant as a model for human practice. Supposing, then, that some human activity can significantly resemble the activity that is designated "creation" in God's unique case, it must be a "getting ahead" of the world's most basic limits (similar to God's getting ahead of primal chaos), that is, a transworking—perhaps the "building" that the New Testament writer Paul indicated in the phrase "Love builds up" (1 Corinthians 8.1).[56]

The pope embraces the anthropomorphic imagery of Genesis 1 so wholeheartedly as to affirm that "it teaches that man ought to imitate God both in working and also in resting, since God himself [that is, in revealing his Word] wished to present his own creative activity under the form of work and rest."[57] It is hard to dispute that the Genesis text means to sanctify work and rest by using them as structures in the creation story. But equivocation must result from using the word "work" both for God's activity and for the human activities with which we are primarily concerned under the usual rubrics of work. The monotheistic Creator's activity could not answer to necessities as do human work activities. Theologians reason that God creates the world out of superabundant goodness, not to satisfy a hunger. There is thus nothing laborlike about God's activity. But might God's activity be the perfect form of work proper, a pure "getting ahead" with any materials wanted, restricted by nothing? Wouldn't an all-powerful version of human work make *a new world*, just as God did? But work would then entirely lose its character of coping and turn into something evidently more godlike, something for which a distinct term, like the theological "creation," would be required. On the other hand, couldn't God *assume* the necessity of looking after the created world, using divine discretion, just as humans give much of their work attention to goals that are only electively necessary? Perhaps. But it seems that God's self-binding to necessity could not have that harsh firmness by which we distinguish, in the human case, between work proper and pursuing a hobby.

Another possibility to consider is that God "works" in the broader sense we use in sayings like "The work of a madman" or "Know them by their works," a sense used also when we say that wind works on sand dunes or a sculptor works in marble or one person's happy or miserable demeanor works on the attitudes of others. (This I take to be the sense of ἔργον, the

Greek word behind most of the appearances of "work" in English transla-
tions of the New Testament.) God's working would then be God's being
active in a way that changes things that are related to God; in these changes
would lie a revelation of what one is here dealing with. In addition to the
unique, all-originating action of "creation" (which makes all things "works
of God") there would be a further divine working of and in the created
world. It could be conceived as an intentional making, like a potter fash-
ioning a pot, or as an impersonal process, like rainfall. The only necessary
meaning is that God is active and effective. But this attribute, which God
would indeed share with finite agents, does not pick out the human activities we designate as "work" from others.

I suggest that theism especially stands to benefit from a strong reservation about the relationship of human to divine working. For the interest
of an assertion like Jesus' "We must work the works of him who sent me,
while it is day: night comes, when no one can work" (John 9.4) lies in the
intersection between divine and human modalities of action, not in a given
commonality between them.[58] The speaker, writer, and primary audience of
this saying do not suppose that the sun ever goes down on God. The whole
structure of work meaning that goes with mortal limits is not applicable to
God. Yet God's way of being active and effective comes into the mortal
frame of reference (as "the work of sanctification," for example). It can be
a blessing or a salvation, because it is other.

A nontheist could draw a formally similar conclusion: for example, a
Buddhist-influenced program called Constructive Living features the
slogan, "There is Reality's work that only you can do."[59] One can imagine
a Heideggerian account of the enabling by Being of the basic structures of
occurrence—"practical necessity," as we call them—in which human work
is enacted.[60] The transwork of Being could not be distinguished in itself
from the transplay of Being (see section 2.6) in the same clear categorical
way that human work is distinguished from play. *As workers*, and with as
much worth force as work can supply, we would have a reason to speak of
"Being's work" and to construe this as a horizon of meaning that must be
addressed in authentic human existence. As ontologists, on the other hand,
we would scruple to speak of Being's transwork. The point of doing this
would be to allow for an ultimate nondifferentiation of transwork and
transplay and thereby to open ourselves to profound reinterpretations of
our worldly activities, glimpsing play in work and work in play.

৩৩

The practical categories of work and play can encompass all of our actions,
if we hold a focus strictly on the disjunction between necessity and

possibility as basic facts and motivations. Perhaps the most basic representation of our active lives that is practically relevant is the model of an alternative (present at every moment) and an alternation (through time) between actions that respond to acknowledged necessity and actions that leap toward appealing possibility. The person or team that does these things well is, to that extent, a worthy *worldly* agent in the relatively simple, relatively objective sense of "world" that centers on tangible practical constraints and openings.

Because we are spiritual beings, however—because the worth of our lives is contingent on our comportment in relationship with each other, not merely instrumentally as teammates but intrinsically as sharers of self-definition, very much in a world of *our own*—we are also concerned with necessity and possibility at a different level and in a different relation. Different major types of worth are most pertinent to those actions of ours that are primarily motivated by the acknowledged necessity (not as objective as that of work) and embraced possibility (not as optional as that of play) of affirming and amplifying our fellowship with each other. The way we talk about worthy and worthwhile actions reflects this, as will be seen in the following chapters on action proper and love.

Chapter 4

◌◌

ACTION PROPER

4.1 The conditions of honor

At the same time that the "action theory" of the late 1950s was trying anew to make sense of voluntary agency in general, Hannah Arendt accomplished in *The Human Condition* one of the great feats of intellectual re-creation by bringing back into focus the classical Greek conception of a particular domain of action worthy to be called action proper.[1]

The crux of Arendt's case is a correlation between personal identity and the public sphere. Action proper consists of those acts which disclose *who* an agent is, in his or her personal distinctiveness, necessarily *to* an audience of other persons in whose eyes identity is realized and through whose acknowledgment worth is constituted.[2] This disclosure fulfills and extends the event of each person's entry into human life as a new constituent. Every existing person is, in principle, one of the dramatis personae of the story that, in principle, controls our understanding of what is going on in the world. Many of our actions do not illuminate who we are in a way that develops the great story. We may play games and get jobs done without thus far disclosing ourselves in personal distinctiveness. Yet we *may* so disclose ourselves in anything we do: it has already become evident that the worthiest identity in any practical field is constituted in just this way, when an agent appears most clearly as *the one who* plays in a certain way, works in a certain way, and so forth. Thus we have not assumed that certain pursuits are inherently separate from action in the eminent sense. But we cannot fail to notice that certain forms of activity are more difficult to shine forth in than others—as labor, for instance, tends more to obscure the person than work proper—and this is one of the weightiest considerations in evaluating any organization of practical life.

Certain worthy acts, including some that might be regarded as supremely worthy, seem to belong in a distinct category of action proper, because their goodness doesn't affiliate with any other category we recognize. No other category is defined at its root by the quest for distinctiveness; no other category looks to incommensurable excellence as its prime evaluative criterion. "Action can only be judged by the criterion of greatness because it is in its nature to break through the commonly accepted and reach into the extraordinary" (Arendt).[3] Action is uniquely *daring* in that it elevates the ordinary quest for justified interpersonal relationship to the level of a maximally active justifying, a renegotiation of the terms of justification. The extraordinarily bold move and vivid presence of the successful actor influences the meaning of "good" and "evil" and so helps to fill in the worth horizon for every form of practice. There is great risk in attempting this, and yet a great, often decisive, practical advantage for so bold an agent is that his or her action becomes in itself a magnetically strong ally, a *cause* to which any number of fellow agents can loyally subscribe.

A good classical example of action's pursuit of greatness is Alcibiades' argument for the Athenian expedition against Syracuse. Was the expedition supposed to be fun? Would it count as a winning move in the contest with the Spartans? Was it necessary for military or economic security? Would it yield wealth? Did it promise to be a "great experience"? All of these recommendations could be argued for; some were; at least one of them, I suppose, had to be; but none was primary. The dominant appeal was Alcibiades' bid to be brilliantly outstanding on his own behalf and as a type for Athens. Success would indeed mean enjoyment, security, and prosperity for Athens, but it was an overwhelmingly interesting prospect in itself as a glowing next chapter in a life story, a chapter of honor.

> There was a time when the Hellenes imagined that our city had been ruined by the war, but they came to consider it even greater than it really is, because of the splendid show I made as its representative at the Olympic games, where I entered seven chariots for the chariot race (more than any private individual has entered before) and took the first, second, and fourth places. . . . It is customary for such things to bring honor . . .

As Alcibiades transposes the logic of distinction back and forth between person and state, individual style and communal spirit, he forces on our attention the hubristic danger in an uncontrolled pursuit of action greatness:

We have reached a stage where we are forced to plan new con-
quests and forced to hold on to what we have got, because there
is a danger that we ourselves may fall under the power of others
unless others are in our power. And you cannot look upon this
idea of a quiet life in quite the same way as others do—not, that
is, unless you are going to change your whole way of living and
make it like theirs is.[4]

Acts of "senseless" violence or excessive display can make powerful sense
in this way.

At the opposite extreme of action from the swashbuckling hero we can
find a certain kind of martyr, implosive rather than explosive, communally
oriented rather than individualistic, like Simone Weil starving herself in
London in solidarity with the suffering French during World War II.[5] Weil's
action had no ordinary utilitarian purpose. It added to the world nothing
except the awareness that an individual did a distinctive thing in commitment to a meaning. It was not meant to make Weil shine more brightly like
an individual star in the sky; it was meant to bring a transpersonal reality
to a shining focus:

Today it is not nearly enough merely to be a saint, but we must
have the saintliness demanded by the present moment. . . . A new
type of sanctity is indeed a fresh spring, an invention. If all is kept
in proportion and if the order of each thing is preserved, it is
almost equivalent to a new revelation of the universe and of
human destiny. It is the exposure of a large portion of truth and
beauty hitherto concealed under a thick layer of dust. More genius
is needed than was needed by Archimedes to invent mechanics and
physics.[6]

By active greatness, an agent propels himself or herself forward, on his
or her own terms, into a communally expanded identity. Greatness in this
sense is the maximum of action proper. Approaching this maximum, however, where the "great" agent would so much dictate the meaning of events,
action threatens to defeat its own quest for justification. To be successful,
to animate a valid answer to the question of life in relationship, action
requires a hearing from the audience to whom the actor appears. Action is
interaction. But an Alcibiades runs roughshod over his audience, and a Weil
hides from hers. They show how the ideal of greatness can distort practice.

Another difficulty with greatness is that the maximum of agent
distinction must be in short supply relative to the total demand for estab-

lishing personal identity. "We admire geniuses, we love them, but they discourage us. They are great concentrations of intellect and emotion, we feel that they have soaked up all the available power, monopolizing it and leaving none for us. We feel that if we cannot be as they, we can be nothing" (Trilling).[7] There is a necessary minimum of action proper for all agents, a condition for being active at all as one of life's dramatis personae, usually articulated in terms of "honor," "self-respect," and being serious and being taken seriously.

Seriousness means singleness: being fully present, meaning one thing and in no way its contrary, doing something and in no way backing off. This all sounds simplistic, perhaps, and tedious, unless we are not willing to lose what lack of seriousness might cause us to lose. Then it matters. We want serious absorption in play to maintain the alert focus on possibility that goofing around would dissolve. We want serious application to work so that what needs to be done will more surely get done. Action proper *must* be serious, because if one cannot communicate and justify one's uniqueness, one loses one's "who"-portion of humanity.

To try to engage in action proper and to fail is ridiculous. It is the main ridiculous thing. The laugh of ridicule witnesses in its malicious way to the grand claim each participant in the personal world makes, as if to say: "So *that* is what he comes to! How then could he presume to be one of the makers of our story?" But action and honor are fragile for everyone. Whether and how I shine forth depends on much outside my will. If I do produce words and deeds, their meaning is ephemeral and mutable. The Greeks addressed this problem, Arendt says, by creating the polis "to enable men to do permanently, albeit under certain restrictions, what otherwise had been possible only as an extraordinary and infrequent enterprise for which they had to leave their households. . . . It is as though the men who returned from the Trojan War had wished to make permanent the space of action which had arisen from their deeds and sufferings."[8]

4.2 Self-display and the potentiality of collective power

Before our self-announcing words and deeds further develop our public story, something else is already going on. Promenading in the town square, on a boulevard, on the beach; congregating in a restaurant, store, office, or classroom; "rallying"; "partying"; causing disturbances, perhaps—and *preparation*: acquiring and practicing with clothes and jewelry, putting on makeup and scent, fixing hair—we devote more time and interest to the sheer displaying of ourselves to each other than most of us can honestly admit. I am not sure that philosophy's famous critique of appearances does more to resist than to confirm this principle. Every great thinker has a cult of personality. Writing and speaking have all along been self-displays, means of imposing a subject in a personally advantageous way on his or her fellows.

One would be led to believe by women's magazines that many millions of woman-hours are devoted annually to the improvement of personal appearance. I won't offer a guess on how the number of similarly spent man-hours would compare. I want to ask what drives all this effort, given that it is not pleasant or productive in any obvious way. It is as though there is a competition in daily life to present the most impressive appearance. What then would be the reward for impressive appearance?

It is impossible to explain the male and female body types, and probably also some male- and female-associated psychic structures, without considering the consequences of self-display in Darwinian evolution. In evolutionary perspective, no purpose could be more important than mating in forming the means by which we signal each other, no purpose could be evoked by another purpose (like governing or marketing) to greater advantage, and no purpose would be likelier to occupy our intelligence.[9] High-minded protests to the contrary, we in fact throw ourselves into judging human books by their covers. Looking good in any sex-related way is a promise of being good in practical matters bearing on reproductive success—for example, in the fighting aptitude of broad shoulders or the nursing capacity of breasts—and there is little in human life that isn't relevant to reproductive success. But whether or not a strategy of self-display has an evolutionary or reproductive rationale, it is clear that some form of cooperation is the reward that makes it worthwhile.

The attractive agent, under most aspects of practical association, must also be *the one who* possesses generically desirable attributes in a distinctive way. Projecting individuality is as much a mandate of self-display as are the chief manly, womanly, or sex-neutral human powers. Impressive active excellence in this dimension seems to form the largest part of the value of what "entertainers," as such, do, and of the personal worthiness, endlessly scrutinized in the mass media, of being an entertainment celebrity.

We can look at the competition to look impressive in either a positive or negative light. Positively, it's as intrinsically healthy and rewarding as the competition to write great novels or excel in any other way—an engine of beauty and a spice of life. Negatively, it's a rat race, a drain on energies that could be better spent. When we are not zealous to look great, we find blessed relief in a stabilizing of the competition, a stipulation of "enough" so that each of us has a secure place at a given level of effort with nothing to gain by investing more. The "enough" point may be renegotiated, but renegotiation may not be easy. Many women I know are still bound by a traditional classist and sexist presumption that a respectable woman disposes of the time and resources needed to refine her appearance extensively; her failure to use time and resources in this manner creates (it is thought) a dishonorable effect. Meanwhile, many of the same women enter public settings governed by the idea that one should be intent on excelling in a more impersonal way, seeking profit only for one's constituency—that is, wearing a plain business suit—apparently serious about the greater task (and yet not neglecting oneself!).

To be out in public and to look one's best are to reach for a portion of collective reality, a share in an economy of attention—ultimately, a reputation. In any community, the issues of seeing and being seen are felt with moral seriousness. Not to make a good appearance is to suffer what seems a fundamental harm. We are fascinated by tales of people we know being seen in embarrassing situations. If I am *not* in your community, it hardly matters to me if you knock my hat off with a snowball or get your own hat knocked off (I have exchanged snowballs on this understanding); but if you and I are tugging on each other's appearance within one economy of attention, a snowball could trigger a war. In such cases the issues of personal impression and personal honor are joined. Personal vividness is a precondition of action insofar as one needs to evoke the initiatives of others (a leader must *win* followers); personal honor is necessary insofar as one's own initiatives must be allowed (a merchant must *earn* the trust of customers).

One cannot succeed in holding a portion of collective reality without exhibiting a style. Often people can achieve style together by following fashion. The best thing to say for fashion is that in principle it allows everyone to excel; it combines the delights of individuality and novelty with the peace of sharing. Unhappily, fashion is conformist and invidious in practice, marking off those who follow it better from those who follow it worse. But it need not be a tool of discrimination. Whole communities can be avid for the latest tunes or dances or clothes designs just for the sake of freshening the collective appearance they make on festive occasions.

We love pageantry, and the possibility that everyone can be a peacock. Parades are humanistically worthwhile because they affirm all of their participants, often by implication the whole of a society, in this way; the experience of equal access to beauty means far more than any one person's achievement of it. But we indulge the sentiment for showing off only at designated times. In other dramatizations of the issue of appearance, we usually cast the insecure and evil personages as the bigger, more beautiful, more glittering ones. This is due, I suggest, to two layers of dramatic perspective, two kinds of foreseen reversal: we see the superficially impressive persons as the ones who are doing well *now* but, when true worth comes to be discovered, will be much reduced; or we see them as the ones who "have their reward in this world," while others win our favorable attention in a superior world of true worth. A Cinderella story captures both our aversion to obscurity and our distrust of eminence.

෨෧

The public "space of appearance," on the conception recommended by Arendt, is sustained by "power," an infinite potential of what might be done by agents together.[10] Students of history, politics, and social psychology are well acquainted with the enormous effects of collective enthusiasms and concerted action, of course, but the matrix of these phenomena, the concrete possibility of concert, is greater still in its indefiniteness. Because the plurality of agents is intrinsic to collective power, it cannot be identified with either motive force or results as such. Power in this sense can preserve a state of affairs, but without insuring anything's endurance; can bring our affairs into a new order, but by no specific pattern necessarily; can open future prospects, but with no predictable result. To display oneself is to participate in this communal potential, to underwrite and entrust oneself to it, and not merely to stake an individual claim to some share of attention. Voluntary slobs and recluses are thus, in one crucial sense, treacherous (although they may enhance the community's power if they are pointed out as its foils). Every tactic of self-display, even the most patently sexual overture, signifies on the communal level a certain contribution to our awesome collective power. When we reflect on courtship behavior, we think as much of gods as of animals.

The aspect of action proper in any doing is rooted in power in this sense. Action is ephemeral and unpredictable because power comes under anyone's command only momentarily and with luck. Action is especially sensitive to personal identity, not in the more precisely credited way of play and work but in the volatile and dialectical manner in which power is realized. (Think of how a celebrity or political leader's stock can rise and fall dramatically.) A successful, telling, historic action embodies in perceptible and discussible form the otherwise inchoate, awesome potentiality of the power-field in which our lives are lived. Actions in this category reveal power while minimizing the distractions of charming possibility or practical necessity. The mightiest acts of collective action—the pyramids, the mass demonstrations, the battles—ring in our ears for generations with their staggering gratuitousness.

4.3 Helping and fighting

We cross the threshold from the potential of collective "power" to actual action proper in the simplest and humblest expressions of cooperativeness.

To be sure, most cooperative behavior is automatic and instrumental, as, for instance, motorists stay in their lanes and take turns at crossings in order to travel most efficiently. But to intend cooperation for its own sake as well as for an ulterior end is to be, worthily, *one who helps.*

The occasion of help is always an appearance of need or advantage, but its true telos is different. If you see my wife jump up to help me in with some groceries, you will naturally relate her act to the two presumptions that groceries need to be gotten into the house quickly and that spouses habitually cooperate to keep their relationship on an even keel. As these doors of presumption slam together, you might miss the glimmer between them of pure helpfulness, the reward of actualizing collective power for its own sake—which has already contributed much to the ideal meaning of spousehood. When you hear of a great exploit of helpfulness, like Florence Nightingale's contribution during the Crimean War, you may be so much affected by the compassion or impressed by the professionalism in it that you miss the marvelously gratuitous character of help, the maximizing of collective power purely for the sake of that power (with its associated personal identities) existing and being recognized.

Humans are much more reliably helpful than they are compassionate or conscientious. We could not be consciously social beings, allowing our identities to be shaped by cooperation, without a disposition to help. It is stretching the point to say that there must be honor or charity among thieves, but certainly there will be helpfulness among thieves, and not because of the special requirements of their work.

Help is never pure work or play. The social joy of cooperation is not promoted when an act is ruled by the sense of a *thing* to be done; help is inspired by the sense of *someone*, the helper and the helped. Work and play become more eminently personal in the measure that they call for and embody help. But this personal quality is of a specific kind. The helper is the servant of the helped. The worthy or worthwhile result that the helper tries to bring about belongs to the helped. Thus there is an element of obedience and heteronomy in help. The worth realized in helping might be called "heteroworth," either from the point of view of the helper, whose good is subordinated to the good of the helped, or of the helped, whose active efficacy is posited as insufficient and so in a sense is eclipsed by the action of the helper. If the helper reaches for too large or too central a share of ownership of the good of the helped, perhaps by taking too much credit afterward for helping—or if the helped makes either too much or too little of his or her own activity—the worth form of help will be undone. The balance here is so delicate that it must be heavily protected by formulas and rituals and institutionalized tacit understandings. In the serious joke of saying "Thanks a million," the helped acknowledges the helper with everything that can be called up in a moment, that is, just in words, looking ahead to free and clear possession of the benefit; the gratuitousness of the help-relation is confirmed by the passing away of its moment.

The greatest helper identity is that of the amazing *savior* whose own chief good is incomprehensibly hostage to the chief good of many and whose superior strength is entirely at the service of the weaker. ("You're a godsend.") The savior's pathological opposite is the *lackey*, an auxiliary without discernment or true strength, really most at home assisting in unworthy pursuits. In stark contrast to the lackey, the savior defines the good for which she or he acts. We cannot say that a Christ or Buddha "gave himself unconditionally" for the good of others without being mindful also that these saviors aimed to revolutionize their beneficiaries' lives.

Help becomes a preworthy category when approached from higher planes. Moral conduct and love, for example, each require something more than helpfulness. But help is also a test of worth, for an effectively unhelpful style of morality or love would forfeit its claim to appreciation; and help can be a redeemer of worth, for challenges to apparently self-serving acts can be met by a showing of helpfulness ("Yes, the concert tickets are expensive, but it's to support Willy's choice of pieces"). Of course, there is plenty of room for falseness in help, as well. A pretended helper can stay free of help's perplexing interaction of agencies by operating philanthropy like a business, scoring gains and losses on paper, or by abusing Thoreau's idea that the greatest help one can give others is simply to exude one's own quality.[11]

⟨⟩

If this life be not a real fight, in which something is eternally gained for the universe by success, it is no better than a game of private theatricals from which one may withdraw at will. But it *feels* like a real fight.

—William James[12]

Must life be a fight if one is to feel fully invested in it and bound not to withdraw? There is a circularity in James's conception. He seeks grounds for answering the question "Is life worth living?" in the affirmative. But it seems that one would only throw oneself seriously into the life-fight if one had judged the fight worthwhile. Perhaps he means that the judgment of life's worth arises from the immediate experience of being caught up in fighting. (On James's theory of emotion, the bodily event is the basis of the feeling—anger comes from bristling, fear from flinching, and so forth).[13] Is the point, then, that when I *am* in a fight, my adrenaline rush keeps me agitated and focused? Does my body sense that relaxing could mean getting hurt, and does my unbidden, continuously strong aversion to pain and loss keep me eager to act? Do I then project these near prospects upon the universe in my benchmark experience of the worth of living? This view seems too restricted. The persuasive strength it gets from a bodily state will disappear when I happen to be relaxed. To give the principle of fighting spirit a cognitively and morally inescapable form, it has to be generalized in such a way that bodily fighting will be seen as one of its occasions, not its ground.

If instead we understand fighting as a structure of cooperation and look for its motivational thrust and meaning in the interagentic exploitation of collective power, we can readily appreciate the crucial position that the body holds in it. To do this, we will have to think of "fighting" even more literally than James did—not just as any sort of struggle, nor even as "competition," but as a direct, active opposition of agents.

One might object that fighting is essentially antisocial insofar as it is dedicated to harm—harmfulness being an obvious criterion by which to separate real fighting from its ritualized alternative, competition. But fighting and harming cannot be equated. Harm occurs under all sorts of conditions, with or without intention, whereas fighting implies a personal fighter-foe pair just as rigorously as help implies helper and helped. The ultimate Adversary is symmetrical with the ultimate Savior. Fighting implies strength against strength, but not necessarily with a harmful result. In war, the enemy can be defeated by temporary capture or disorganization rather than destruction.[14] A pitcher-batter battle is normally decided by a hit or an out, not by a beaning. It is essential to fighting, but not to violence, that the strength of one's foe forces self-exertion: as a key to the rewards that depend on increased exertion, the foe is posited as present, not as canceled. (The ever-renewed battles of Valhalla are the true extension of the fighting spirit after the fight, not the abuse of the foe's body, which has to do with expunging fears and resentments.) More importantly, the foe's insight into worth becomes a foil and a test, and the fight becomes a clarification of worth. By virtue of which attributes does a combatant most fittingly or effectively triumph? What does an agent's individual synthesis of attributes amount to when put to the sharpest practical test?

Fighting is not identical to harming, but we cannot pretend that the two are unrelated. The overcoming of the foe is the destruction of a project, and projects are always prosecuted by embodied agents. We readily recognize the pitcher's competition with the batter as a fight, because the players' physical efficacies are at stake. A pitcher who gives up a hit is that much weaker as a baseball force. A contest between two boardroom factions for corporate control is a "fight" if it strengthens the winner and weakens the loser in materially meaningful ways. An "argument" between parents is really a fight—as the children sense or fear—if they try in some significant way to undermine each other. Since strength and weakness are vitally at issue, fighters cannot neglect opportunities to weaken their foes. A pitcher may threaten a batter's very life by throwing high and inside (near the head) and may even be culpable in baseball terms for failing to use this means to reduce the batter's chances of success. Yet fighting does not of itself entail an interest in *unmaking* the foe. The fighter and the torturer are not close kin.

The harm-bound character of fighting registers also in the fighter excellence of disregarding one's wounds. But here fighting gives a different turn to the issue of harm. Experience and discipline in fighting are desirable assets in coping with wounds and threats, whatever their nature, so long as one is pursuing ends of greater importance than one's own bodily well-being. Part of the discipline may be a deceptively jolly, blackly humorous language of combat that makes light of personal harm or treats it as a purely technical problem. This is intolerable to the compassionate helper, who negates harm from the position opposite that of the hardy fighter. The helper moves from the fullest conscious acknowledgment of hurt, which makes for full seriousness about preventing it or healing it, to its negation (which carries the most conviction on the premise that hurts are avoidable); the fighter moves from denying the hurt, in order to stay serious about fighting, to renewed affirmation, in fighting, of hurt's positive relevance to overcoming the foe (and thus of the general proposition that harming can't be eliminated from life or from responsible agency). Embodiment can be shown to give the lie to both positions. On the one hand, the helper's cause is lost, in an important sense, because every embodied agent is in fact irremediably exposed to strife, injury, and death. The fighter is strong in this knowledge; fighting can represent worthy candor on this point. On the other hand, the fighter's prescribed indifference to harm won't be sustaining, because no success is meaningful unless it somehow promotes someone's bodily well-being; and fighting and bodily well-being are inversely related in general. The tragic primal scene for the fighter is the return after battle to the burnt house and slaughtered family.

An unbearably powerful symbolic resolution of these difficulties in the meaning of helping and fighting—and thus also one of our standard worth jokes—is the Knight in Shining Armor, perfect both in helpfulness and in fighting strength. The knight of help and combat is doubly shadowed by death, poignantly doomed to run up against that final nonnegotiable limit to the power of human agency about which we say, with the same purport, "Can't be helped" or "Can't fight it."

A major worth irony in helping and fighting is that either activity can easily *reduce* the personal distinctiveness of agents. Our sex specializations promote and symbolize this effect (giving us one more reason to resent sex). The helper approaches submergence in the life of the helped, assuming the status of a faceless, nurturing breast, while the fighter in pushing off from the foe risks standing out too far, approaching the impersonality of "the strong arm," more a natural force like a thunderbolt than a possible colleague.

Sex is also implicated in the unfolding of the two worth profiles on different timetables. Early in an agent's life, the female-affiliated "helper" identity is one of the best that can be imputed to her or him, the male-affiliated "fighter" one of the worst; but later, and most of all at the end of life, "fighter" becomes high praise and "helper" sounds faint. In the schoolroom context, where vitality abounds and the great task is to teach the arts of peace, a helper shows the way and a fighter is merely a troublemaker; but looking back over life, thinking of our attrition and our irreversible decline, surer now of the social channeling of action and taking institutionalized helps for granted, we see in fighting a prime token of precious strength. When death is close, forcing us to recognize an ultimate futility in helping, the good fighter's disdain for death seems most apposite.

What did I miss if I didn't help or fight? What is lacking in a life without helping and fighting? Not necessarily any results, for helping and fighting are not prima facie successful or worthwhile. But since they are prima facie worthy, a question arises about character: *What* was I, what did I lack within, that I did not stir myself to live well in either of these ways? If I didn't have decent helping and fighting opportunities, and so haven't directly proven a disposition not to help or fight, then *where* was I, that I found no helping or fighting to be done? For we suppose that in the course of life any worthy agent will sometimes be in the thick of action and that the beneficial marshaling of collective power will depend on her or his performance. At stake in this is not only a practical need that may go unmet but a dignity, a share of power, which an agent ought not to be deprived of, or which an agent ought not to disrespect by declining.

4.4 Deeds, fame, and glory

Helping and fighting are prima facie worthy activities. The *deed* is a prima facie worthy action. There is no verb "deeding," although we have the expression "a man [*sic*] of action" for one who is ready and able to perform deeds or who has a career of performing them. The deed is a unit of practice, an aim and an evidence of success; it is also a unit of history, a point where we can see a noteworthy difference being made in the interactive situation.

The deed is the precondition of *glory*, a specifically historic communal maximizing of individual agent worth. Because the purpose of fame is to transmute the ephemeral and elective into the enduring and inescapable—glorying in sheer memorableness after an action and its direct material effects have disappeared—we fall easily under the illusion that public attention in itself, *mere* fame, mere talk, constitutes glory. Our very attending to someone, or being attended to, is meaningful to us, so we are happy that in a democratic mass-media culture everyone can take a fifteen-minute turn at fame. But this egalitarian fame, or that of the myriad celebrities who represent the popularity principle, is distinct from glory, since the condition of memorableness is not met. Glory is not fashion, the formula for a moment; it is antithetical to it. Depending on one's purposes, popularity can be worthwhile, but it has only the slenderest hypothetical claim to implement worthiness.

A well-drawn distinction between fame and glory will make clear that fame (as usually conceived) cannot confer a personal sort of immortality. Typically a person is famous *for something*; our attention is directed to the famous individual only because we are interested in the event that she or he is associated with. For instance, Einstein is famous for formulating relativity theories, and in the minds of most people who have heard of him, "Einstein" means only "the discoverer of relativity." Some people now living do remember interactions with Einstein and his look and style, but as time goes by, the meaning of his name becomes less and less personal.[15] For glory, in contrast, the concrete individuality of the agent is central. Glory's logical home base is not the eye-catching phenomenon but the ensemble of agents; already knowing Cynthia, or at least knowing of her existence, you are impressed by the fact that she turns out to be the one who performs a memorable feat (she fought the power company in court, and won). She becomes immortal because when later generations hear of what she did they are moved to regard *her* as an active member of the ideal ensemble of agents. Remembering her in this light evokes her presence; it is not a matter simply of honoring the accomplishment, in the way in which we honor the "discoverer of relativity," or the discoverers of seed-planting or tool-chipping, whoever they may have been. A nondistinctive feat like "winning a tough battle" can earn glory because we are related (in fact or in imagination) to the doer. Individuality *in* the deed, "brilliance," forces on our notice the individuality of the agent, causing a sudden and vivid acquaintance, but brilliance is not a condition of glory: there is no contradiction in Pericles' proclaiming the whole earth the memorial of the glory of fallen Athenian soldiers while not mentioning any of their names or describing any individual action.[16]

If a pertinent description of a glorious deed contains no personally individuating content—if either Claudia or Cynthia could equally well have performed a given nonbrilliant glorious deed—then it might be objected that glory as such has even less to do with personal immortality than fame does. Doing a nonbrilliant glorious thing seems more like being rich, that is, like coming into connection with something of value, than it is like being creative, developing and imposing oneself. It calls only on generic virtues like strength and courage. But, I reply, we are not to think of glory-immortality as "personal" in the sense that the glorious doer makes a distinctive mark. Claudia or Cynthia, either one, acquires worth by associating herself with a permanently meaningful constituent of a greater human story, but the association is engineered by virtue; it is not a matter of good or bad fortune alone, and this means that the agent is not separable from the worth as the rich person is separable from riches. The worth is enjoyed as the individual joins the humanly generic. Since our attention in appreciating this kind of worth runs *from* the individual *to* the generic, we are not unduly frustrated in our ignorance of the personal distinctions of the fallen Athenians. It is enough to know that they were individuals and that someone did know them in their individuality. Precisely because glory accommodates ignorance of personal identity in its affirmation of individuals, it offers an unlimited worth reservoir.

Popularity-fame, though superficially democratic, is really discriminatory against merit, for it creates shares out of a finite pool. The public can only attend to a certain number of agents—a large number, perhaps, but never more than a tiny fraction of the living and the dead. Glory, however, does not involve actual basking in public regard. It involves a claim on regard. We allow that agents who qualify for our ideal ensemble, whoever they may be, in principle can make an invaluable contribution to our life. Any one of the now-unknown soldiers whom Pericles praised is, we suppose, worth having on our side, and we can imagine concrete circumstances in which we would want their partnership. That the soldiers hold that place without our knowing who, otherwise, they are impairs their fame but not their glory.

Although popularity does not create merit, there is nevertheless a power in popularity that is itself valuable and a key to action worth. Shakespeare's fame has meant the creation of a huge complex of thought and sentiment developing Shakespearean concerns. If Shakespeare weren't popular, a great cultural potential would be wasted. And we should not pretend that the nameless fallen Athenians are as well off in worth terms as the Horatii whose personal story we have heard. We insist that the Athenians are fully worthy in our definition of glory, but still we reach out toward them, somewhat frustrated, trying to fulfill the interagentic relation to which they confided themselves as they pursued deed worth.

Aristotle points to the disadvantage of fame's scandalous contingency in a famous passage: "But honor after all seems too superficial to be the Good for which we are seeking; since it appears to depend on those who confer it more than on him upon whom it is conferred, whereas we instinctively feel that the Good must be something proper to its possessor and not [easily] to be taken away from him."[17] Self-sufficiency is one of Aristotle's chief criteria for true well-being. But those who consciously attempt worthy deeds reject the ideal of perfect self-sufficiency, for they desire to become attached to a good of which they are not the sole proprietors.

4.5 Collective action; leading and following

Helping and fighting imply a "we," for they are structures of cooperation, but we have discussed them on the model of the single agent, a dramatic protagonist. How do worth opportunies change when the agent of action proper is "we"?

A collective subject can act as a quasi "I": for instance, we, the citizens of Rosehill, can help the flood-struck citizens of Greenville, or we, the Chicago Bears, can battle the Detroit Lions. In these cases we take the usual readings of virtue and efficacy in evaluating agency, but we also ask: To what extent did the teammates help each other and thus help the cause? To what extent did they hurt the cause by fighting among themselves? The ideal preference for help is strong. One kind of worth-supremacy of helping is entailed by the practical superiority of the group to the individual, both in authority and in ability to produce results. Thus the happiness of helping in a greater cause is of an exalted kind, and collective responsibility in disgrace, like war guilt, is peculiarly poisonous.

Another kind of collective agency, more difficult to understand and evaluate because it is more diffuse, is the "we" of a community insofar as it tends purely to "us," to "our affairs," and does not oppose anyone else. This kind of "we" supervenes on individuals in clan and town life, on clans and towns in national life, and finally (in unique freedom from the quasi "I"-hood of inter-"we" action) on nations in universal life. It is the agent of cultural endeavor, political process, and morality, the "we" whose story is, on a given historical horizon, the main story. It displays itself, from one member to another, in courtesy and other forms of collective style. Within this self-directing "we" there is not so one-sided a presumption for helping over fighting; fighting again becomes relevant and necessary in various ways, as the identity and direction of the community are continually liable to be contested both by those who mean well and by those who do not.

A self-directing "we" with too little fighting lacks vitality. It a requirement of the democratic "we," however, that contest be sublated in the final
vote into consensus: the voter acts at once as a member of a party's fighting
"we" and as a member of the deliberating, inclusive "we," helpfulness in the
latter role redeeming belligerence in the former. No one can fail to notice that
voting in a mass democracy is peculiarly unworthwhile, inasmuch as a single
vote scarcely ever affects an election's outcome. Yet voting is peculiarly
worthy, because it harmoniously realizes these two main modes of membership in a vastly comprehensive collective. The share of personal reality one
achieves by voting is tiny in immediate practical terms *because* it is enormous
in terms of socially expanded identity. The more powerful your single vote,
the less true it is that you are participating in democratic process.

Voting is a paradigmatic act of collective action, important not so
much for bringing about any particular result—for the voter and the whole
vote often "accomplish nothing," at least nothing new—as for sustaining
the power of the collective. The power implicit in the togetherness of persons evaporates if persons fail to gather. Thus we feel that it is more fundamentally important that a vote or a class reunion or a birthday party
simply take place with "good participation," assuring the continuance of a
certain social potentiality, than that it be productive or enjoyable. If we can
find evidence that the gathering was worthwhile, a "good one," so much
the better; that refreshes our appreciation for what we have to gain or lose.
A good vote is "decisive." It firms the collective will. Since the quality of
collective will is the most important thing at stake, a vote gains decisiveness
more by involving more members than by enlarging a margin of victory; an
American presidential election decided 50.2% to 49.8% with 80% of all
voters participating would be far more decisive (in the most important
sense) than a 55% to 45% win with only 40% participation.

The "popular uprising" has often been taken as a thrilling paradigm of
collective action. It is thought that "the people" can act in concert on the
basis of their shared awareness of a shared practical reality—for example,
the reality that all Russians, urban workers and bourgeois as well as sailors
in the navy, are oppressed by tsarist rule. (I am thinking of Eisenstein's
sharply synthesized presentation of "the people's" action in *The Battleship
Potemkin* as a token of the Russian Revolution's commitment to this paradigm.) On the other hand, political thinkers have usually been skeptical of
the political value of popular action, viewing the power of "the mob" as an
erratic, quasi-natural factor similar to stormy weather. Now, to act as a
member of a "mob" is not a worthy choice; mob reality, however exciting,
is contemptibly subpersonal. What then is the difference in principle
between democracy's enhancement of personal worth and the mob's
diminution of it?

It is dangerous to ask either for wholeheartedness in the individual agent or for effective coordination of the group as hallmarks of collective action. At the back of either appeal might be the fascist ideal or fantasy of the many as *purely* one. In a communist perspective, it is a great breakthrough, an overcoming of alienated consciousness, when an individual realizes the identity and mission of the working class, not merely in theory but in practice. An Odessa citizen's practical self-subordination in helping the *Potemkin* sailors involves a redeeming retrieval of her or his truer self in solidarity with the working class. But the submergence of the individual in the class story, the shoving aside of the practical question of how helping the rebel sailors at this juncture will relate to carrying on one's own distinct life in future, is a fearful alienation in turn. Realizing the collective as *purely* one, its divisions of consciousness and potential for discord negated, banishes the very form of collective power that is of positive worth interest. No one disputes that a mob wields awesome material power; no one disputes that individuals are capable of fanatical devotion to a group effort, or that fanaticism is exhilarating. But we use the categories of mob action and fanaticism to mark failures in worth.

The contrasting liberal paradigm of the American Revolution does feature popular uprisings, notably the Boston Tea Party, but its centerpiece is something quite different, in comparison with which the Tea Party seems silly. It is a written statement of collective intention *signed* by leaders of the rebellion. They inscribe their individual identities in the collective manifesto in this posture: "And for the support of this Declaration [of Independence], with a firm reliance on the protection of divine Providence, we mutually pledge to each other our Lives, our Fortunes and our sacred Honor." One might justifiably object to the imperfections of leadership that flaw this collective action. The signers don't mean to represent Americans as inclusively as we would now require. One could say also that the worth language of the Declaration partly sanctifies, partly dissimulates the social dominance of the signers' class—and not just contingently, as an available manner of speaking that happens to be useful for this end, but as the essential expression of that class's interest, which depends on a hierarchy of worth and a prerogative of defining worth. Nevertheless, this worth talk creates a logical space for collective action distinct from mob action and fanaticism. To "pledge" with "honor" is to effect a subordination of individuals to a collective that does not cancel individual selfhood.

༄

Human social life, as such, is not collective action. Even if the forms of cooperation that now prevail were once consciously devised by some agents and agreed to by others as a means of maximizing power, the essence of the "social" is to be *in place*, that is, to be the supporting platform, not the object, of initiative. Institutionalized pledging and voting in a democracy set up, therefore, an ambiguously half-social, half-political current in citizens' lives: political obligation both is and isn't to be taken for granted. Accordingly, the initiatives of elected officials both are and aren't examples of *leadership* as a species of action.

To lead is to initiate cooperation for a common good, but more gratuitously than as a job—that is, not as "administration." Following, as the correlate of leading, sustains that cooperation, but not as "staff." Notwithstanding the distinction between work and action proper, good administrators tend to be good leaders, and good staff tend to be good followers—which indicates that the normal conditions of cooperation are not entirely technical.

Robert Neville offers an interesting argument concerning leadership that backs up to our subject.[18] Reformulating for democracy the principle of public responsibility that he finds in Plato's *Republic*, Neville sees leadership's ruling aim as conservation of value. The prime leadership occasion in a society like ours is when *things going wrong*. When things are going tolerably well, our roles are differentiated so that each of us is free to pursue happiness and virtue in a highly individualized way, and our public responsibilities are mostly deactivated. "But where the society's structures fail. . . . When a society's legitimate political processes lead to a deeply immoral war, to the oppression of certain groups, or to the denigration of learning and the arts, or to any other serious failure of the values that require public conserving, it is everyone's responsibility to do something about it."[19] A new problem arises with the reactivation of everyone's public responsibilities: How, with the social structure broken down, are we to be organized to fulfill them? "Leadership is required . . . to create the organizational structures that make the public effective. Leadership thus is the initiation of cooperation."[20] Leaders and followers must spontaneously find the form of cooperation, leaders inventing and persisting, followers recognizing and upholding.

Neville's account highlights the relation of leading and following to freedom. But he takes back what he gives. Since the opening to freedom in this case is caused by a breakdown of social machinery, the freedom of leading and following is subordinated to necessity, and the two forms of action become forms of work instead. Unlike the enterprise that *first* created a social structure, when it was a desirable option rather than a necessity— when someone said "We can do better"—the point of leading and following now is to protect or retrieve something, the loss of which is unacceptable. So long as one thinks of leading and following on this paradigm, one assumes that everything worth doing *has been done*, or that we can get to the point in any practical sphere where this is true; and that is to assume, in turn, that the goal and success of acting is to "set things up in the right way."

It is true that within the realm of work we specially value the organizational faculties of leading and following, especially in the heroic situation of having to avert a disaster brought on by social failure. But if leading and following really belong to a category other than work, then we ought to be able to show them best as responding to their own distinctive occasion, not an occasion of work necessity. Supposing they belong with other structures of cooperation in the category of action proper, we should find in them a capitalizing on collective potentiality for its own sake.

Let us reset the stage. Now it is undisrupted. Social and technical routines are working. We are in an eighth-grade English classroom where all necessary books and supplies are on hand, desks are occupied by students who do not need academic remediation and are not causing discipline problems, and a qualified teacher is in charge. The thermostat works. The students know what is going to be on the next test—a comparison of epic heroes—and how they should prepare. The day's business is to discuss *Beowulf*, and it is clear how to do this: questions will be asked by the teacher and a couple of delegated students, everyone in the class will be invited to respond to the questions, and someone had better respond somehow to each one. We readily imagine the class time passing in routine fashion, decently but without impressive profit, everyone doing their jobs. But on this occasion the class goes better. Unexpectedly, one of the assigned "leaders" *actually leads* by proposing a link between Beowulf and Batman; and the leadership *succeeds*, as it turns out that most class members have seen the *Batman* movies and want to give the leader's suggestion serious attention, while a few are ready to articulate afresh their own perceptions of threats to society, monsters, and heroism. This class rises above routine not so much because it brings forth a remarkable new idea as because a dormant collective potentiality has awakened. A new idea was indeed a necessary condition—there had to be somewhere for the awakened group to go—but the going somewhere together, the improbable coincidence of thrust among minds that normally run in divergent directions, was in itself the chief reward.

Is there a difference between what the leaders and followers "got out of the class" that would make a worth difference between leading and following? One reason leaders are in the more ideally enviable position is that they do *not* get a greater measurable benefit out of the cooperation than the followers—they *nobly* exert themselves and take the risks of initiating without a greater payoff for themselves in view, since the collective good for which they act is in principle to be shared by all equally. Consequently there is a mandate in any collective to rotate leadership, circumstances permitting.

There should be fair distribution of the worth bonus of leading as well as of its burdens. If someone retains the leader role for everyone's good, material bonuses oughtn't to be piled on top of the worth bonus. (Alcibiades doesn't look at the matter in this way; the austere Pericles does.)

Leading and following jump out to claim our notice in the surprisingly good English class, but I do not mean to suggest that they are otherwise absent. Ordinary life must be redeemingly leavened with leading and following, for a collective endeavor that is utterly perfunctory, like the dreaded dead class, is in fact no more normal than the inspirational event. It seems more accurate to say that the courage of leadership and the loyalty of following are threads in the fabric of humanity which on the most memorable occasions shine forth more purely and are more appreciable by themselves.

In the most comprehensive scenarios of cooperation we are all followers; no one can presume to offer relevant leadership, because the decisive initiative has already been made otherwise (retaining, however, its character as an initiative, not to be confused with taken-for-granted social structures). For example, American citizens pledge to uphold a political project defined by a charter two centuries old. In effect, the charter is the primary leader. As moral agents, conducting ourselves and honoring and punishing others according to a definite set of scruples, we follow the ideal charter of the moral law or the order of values. Thus, personal moral worth does not derive directly and simply from a principle of moral obligation: rather, moral life is a collective endeavor within a larger field of collective potentiality, and moral virtue *both* owns the narrower meaning of fitness to fulfill the obligations of morality *and* implements the larger meaning of loyalty to collective good. That larger meaning grounds a strong standing presumption in favor of discussing moral issues with others. That is mainly why we do ethics.

4.6 Crime; war

Let us call "crime" any act regarded by the agent as beneficial that involves a conscious negation of the well-being of others as defined and protected by social covenant. Let us set aside for a moment the more familiar explanations of crime as the product of passion (overcoming reason) or selfish calculation (overcoming altruism) or mental or emotional incapacity (thwarting social control). We are in position now to bring out another explanation that could, depending on the case, be as relevant as any other. Crime can be a way of attaining worth. But this explanation will be hard to sustain, since noncriminals and criminals agree that crime negates the standards of worthiness.

At the threshold of crime, but also of many noncriminal acts, is a conscious resistance to social control. Whichever system I am up against—parental policy, school policy, store policy, the soft drink machine—it is always a human thing, not intrinsically holy and sovereign; why should it hold sway over me? Or, to put the question more objectively: Why should the system be exempt from challenge? To submit to it is perhaps to collude in mediocrity or injustice. Worth is endangered. If we act against the system, it will be completely clear that we *are* acting; for all true initiative, whether at the level of intent or at the level of material repercussions, involves some boat-rocking.

Acting against the system is mischief. It carries the positive value of strengthening the independence of the mischief-maker; it does not carry the negative value of personal harm or betrayal, because the system is seen as an external device of society rather than a token or incarnation of social fellowship.

When mischief-makers grow up, understand issues of cooperation better, and become more established in the social world (especially as workers and owners), their disposition to challenge the system might yet flourish in the practice of art, or law, or politics. They might form the backbone of a profoundly constructive campaign for social change. Their ability to see beyond the questionable present social reality is now complemented by an ability to focus on an ideal that better satisfies the benign intentions of their society.

In crime, the gesture toward the present imperfection of society is finished in the other way. Criminals see, beyond the system, nothing—neither an ideal of better social arrangements, nor an intrinsically important reality of living agents for whom the system is an instrument. But *that does not matter*. An absence of concern matches the absence of meaning. If criminals philosophize like existentialists about the ultimate void of meaning, implying their concern for it, that is only a sort of leisure pursuit for them, or a smoke screen. And since crime has no ulterior goal for social fellowship, the opposition between the agent and society becomes absolute. The meaning of the successes and gratifications of the "I" is now controlled by the *versus* of the "I-versus-them" relationship. Too weak to escape this *versus* or too strong to settle for anything less, depending on how one looks at it, the criminal triumphs not by gaining pleasure and material efficacy as ends in themselves but by besting society and thus pinching the fuse of the otherwise explosive question of practical rightness. Yet there is no real contest between the criminal and society. Either fighting or sport proper would involve a stronger affirmation of the opponent than crime allows. Instead, the gains and losses of crime are scored in the manner of a solitaire game. (A sort of sport or fight between cops and robbers may supervene on this structure; alternatively, a criminal may take the perfectly criminal attitude just toward the police or some other designated segment of society.)

Criminals have chosen, like Milton's Satan, to reign in hell rather than serve in heaven, but they would not *say* that—they would not be caught in the contradiction of desperately, pseudoheroically asserting their independence from the conditions of meaningful life—because they do not acknowledge heaven at all. They are "hard," "cynical." The paradigmatic crime is the one of maximum callousness: murder. Jack Abbott, writing from a maximum security prison (where "society" presents its most disingratiating face), sees the soul of crime in the need of inmates to be prepared to murder:

> Have you ever seen a man *despair* because he cannot bring himself to murder? I am not talking about murder in the heat of combat—that very seldom occurs in prison—I am speaking of cold-blooded premeditated murder. The only prisoners I have ever seen who do not suffer from that despair of being incapable of murder are those who *are* capable of it (not a few).
>
> Most of them find—somewhere down the line—that they *are* capable of it. To discover that there was no basis for your anxieties about murder is a feeling similar to that of a young man who has doubts about being capable of consummating his first sexual encounter with a woman—and when the time comes, if he did not perform magnificently, at least he got the job done. You feel stronger.
>
> If you can kill like that, you can do anything. All of the elements of every crime come into play. There is the deception; the ability to hold a secret; the calculation; the nerve. . . .[21]

Criminal agency can exhibit every strength noncriminal agency can, but without including social interest in its equation, and thus, for lack of restraint, can excel all the more. The criminal reaches for a purer worth, or rather, a purer alternative to worth (it isn't what noncriminals mean by worth), predicated on honest recognition that one is on one's own. The essential point of crime is not what it pays—as though the worth question were canceled in favor of calculations of worthwhileness—but *that* it pays as the reward strictly of the exercise of power of a desocialized self.

For some reason, a criminal has not been offered by society a sufficient inducement to be prosocial, and other-regard has insubstantial appeal. One can object that this way of stating the problem already assumes, like a criminal, the absence of valid social authority. Rightly seen, society presides over its members spiritually; it doesn't offer a deal or an appeal as a merchant would. Blame Cain! He shouldn't have been weighing his prospects so selfishly.[22] But the creative and productive mischief-makers, the redeemingly uncomplacent members of society, will blame familial, economic, political, and penal structures for unnecessarily squeezing people into the Cain position. They are bound to try to prove their nihilistic cousins wrong. They will want to help them or fight them (punishment can bear both meanings) for the sake of drawing them into cooperation.

⟳

Is war a form of criminal activity, as its critics like to assert? The question can be approached psychologically, for example by looking for similar evidences of paranoia or sadism in the spheres of crime and war.[23] As a question of political science, the crimelike incivility of war—"an act of violence the aim of which is to force the adversary to carry out our will," in the words of Clausewitz—will be balanced against the prospects of restricting the occasions and methods of war in civilized fashion, according to the interests of an international community.[24] I'll ask now about similarities and balances of worth.

The martial virtues form a provocative ensemble of seemingly criminal and anticriminal elements. Important, on the one hand, are fierceness, cunning, and ruthlessness in relation to the enemy, but so too are loyalty and self-abnegation. With an army of proud, fierce, but totally selfish soldiers, you might as well have a gang of robbers; but an army of loyal but unrestrictedly compassionate soldiers might as well be an order of monks. Critics may argue that war draws vast numbers of morally normal people into criminal behavior with a misleading promise and seasoning of virtue and a larger loyalty. War's defenders can say that our best or potentially best aggressive qualities, qualities that go sour in crime, are ennobled in war thanks to the indispensable presence in it of the prosocial virtues. It may even be claimed that *only* war mobilizes *all* virtues.[25]

War is a great theater of virtue mainly because it is evil. A theodicy can use the point that our most precious virtues are occasioned by evil to justify evil's presence within a divine providence. But even this argument does not declare evil good or justify the doing of evil. War is an evil we do. Once war is set going, all sorts of hardy, courageous, self-sacrificing, and even compassionate responses can be made to it. These are worthy ways of coping with the moral emergency of war. The worth of sponsoring it is something else. What can be said in favor of going to war?

Michael Gelven argues that the meaning of human existence is fundamentally conditioned by our finding ourselves always in the actual or potential presence of other members of a "we," with whom we share a sense of our "own" meaning, and also of those who are different, either a threatening "they" or an affirmed "ye." The "we-they" and "we-ye" possibilities, war and peace, imply each other, and neither can be eliminated. By denying that a we-identity could be worth fighting for, "a pacifist denies the very existential foundation of true, or authentic peace: the worth and meaning of a we."[26] Moral considerations could never properly lead us to forfeit our existential worth, because morality is built on this existential foundation.[27] This is why it is *intelligible* that a Polish partisan persists in acts of sabotage against the Nazis even though the loss of fellow Poles in reprisals is materially far greater than the damage inflicted on the Nazi cause: *before* moral and prudential considerations are weighed, "being Polish matters."[28] War reveals this truth "more brilliantly than any other mode of existence."[29]

This line of thinking, which well represents a worth-depth in war thinking, seems at least semicriminal. Significantly, Gelven allows for an unjustifiable attachment to "country" as the highest collective in the order of belonging, superior even to religion. He reasons that "my country is the land of my fathers, the place and hence the origin of my familial existence, of the looks I inherit, the accent in my voice, the lap from which I drink the milk of culture."[30] But this is all true of the planet, too—unless there is some reason to dwell on my *different* accent (yet not so much as to be sub-patriotically loyal to my clan or town?), some reason to *insist* on defining "we" so as to exclude a "they." For Gelven, there is such a reason; a priori, it is the structure of we-they opposition, and a posteriori, it is the actual threatening of one collective by another. But we-they opposition is a possibility, not an inevitability. We obviously have discretion in judging who is "different from us," and we can act to change the grounds on which we make it—indeed, that is how patriotism gradually forms out of regionalism, and (I would say) universalism out of patriotism. Why must there still be an opposing "they"/"ye" at the highest rank in the order of belonging? What indeed could civilize intergroup relations if not the principle that an all-inclusive identity outranks only partially inclusive ones in determining worth? (This is both an old "imperial" political ideal and, as Weber noted, an emphasis in salvation religions.)[31] Gelven's anti-universalist argument endorses, if not the hard, self-serving aloneness of the paradigm criminal, then the hard solidarity of the group that is ready under certain circumstances to act like a criminal, to set itself (no doubt in self-defense) "against the world." Thus Gelven helps us to see war behavior on its descending curve toward selfishness and callousness instead of on its more popular ascending curve toward noble sacrifice and historic glory.

War differs from gang violence—or gang violence resembles criminal activity less, and war more—in its largeness of scale. It is a maximum of collective action, the greatest of all such actions, except for voting, that can be focused and carried out in a day. But once we appreciate war in this character, we must see that it is hopelessly flawed, for the redeeming bigness of the collectivity is always only half of what it might be, due to the structure of opposition. (This limitation is obscured to the degree that participants think of war in friendlier terms as a pure *fight*, for there is a collegiality in fighting.) Now, opposition is not permanently controlling of the participants in war as it is of the participants in crime, for war is often partly redeemed by the fact that it will foreseeably end and give way to some version of peace. Still, one cannot look at two great armies on a field without being haunted by the thought that a greater deed awaits their combined effort, if only they can learn how to define and pursue that deed. The alternative, as we have seen, is voting.

4.7 Divine-and-human action:
Greek, Hebrew, and Chinese conceptions

Collective action brings complexity to agent identity. If a Bears receiver catches a pass in the end zone, who scores a touchdown, he or the Bears? We keep records both ways. If a woman delivers a dinner cooked in Rosehill to a Greenville flood refugee, who helps, the individual or the town? Gratitude would extend to both. If one of the Bears, unbeknownst to the others, bribes the Lions quarterback to play poorly, are the Bears cheating or only he? The Bears gain the unfair advantage. If one Rosehill caterer takes unfair advantage of Greenville's troubles to enrich herself, is Rosehill a corrupt town? Yes, though it is hard to say so.

"I did it!" is a mountain peak—a vantage point. "We did it!" is partly a still more eminent peak, more like *the* vantage point, and partly the occupation of many peaks at once, securing a world. The relations among these meanings make the complexity of collective agent identity interesting even in the easy cases just cited. But there is a deeper question about the sources and interconnections of agency. The question is forced on us when we find ourselves caught up in a forming of purpose and efficacy that we cannot see and define—not immediately, or clearly, or wholly—and yet, sensing a combination of streams or layers of agency, we are eager to appreciate the dilation of practical worth that comes with it. We may be trying to reach a practical accommodation, in theory, with the First Cause or Causes. We may be feeling our way toward transworthy action.

Let us sample different approaches to the transworthy enlargement of action in a range of classic traditions, beginning with Greek epic.

For Homer's audience, the Trojan expedition is the greatest of collective endeavors, drawing together a superteam out of the many Greek societies.

Its purpose and prosecution *could* be interpreted in entirely human, Greek-and-Trojan terms. It could be deemed a worthy effort. But the grandeur and fatefulness of it seem to go beyond the level even of actions normally called worthy. Accordingly, the war as a whole is represented as in the hands of the gods, and the most fateful single actions within it are never in the hands of human agents alone. It could be argued that empirical honesty demands this representation, for a finite agent's power is never absolutely sufficient to compel a desired result—a truth we are reminded of when the best Greek archer, taking a perfectly clear shot at Hector, misses (Apollo deflects his arrow).[32] So much less can a finite agent assure the ultimate outcome of an undertaking that is more complex than an arrow shot. But it is also true that human hope and fear reach out toward success-meanings that exceed even the greatest possible collective human competence and, for that very reason, are capable of sustaining and redeeming collective human endeavor. This seems to be the main point made by the divine orchestration of the superficially messy and absurd war. A reader who wants to root for Achilles or the Greeks in this story will be frustrated by all the interruptions of their control of events—do *they* really *do* anything?—and by the excessive scale of the whole action. But a reader who understands that human agency is indeed overmatched in these ways but who nevertheless perceives the Trojan War as one of the greatest possible actions will be interested in a deepened interpretation of who is acting and what is done. Thus, Teucron could not have killed Hector (*is* prevented by the god Apollo), because we know that the problematic glory of Achilles depends on his killing Hector later, and Paris could not have been killed in his duel with Menelaus (*is* saved by the goddess Aphrodite), because we know that he ultimately brought death to Achilles (by an Apollo-guided arrow), and so forth.[33]

A similar interpretation is at work in the Hebrew Bible's account of the Israelites' escape from Egypt. As with "Hellas," a greater "Israel" identity is at stake, caught in a humanly uncontrollable world-process, and the resolution of this frightful, hopeful prospect is found in a combination of human and divine agency. A great difference between the *Iliad* and Exodus, however, is that under the somewhat shaky and flexible reign of Zeus, Homer shows portions of fate allotted to jostling plural gods, while the message of Exodus is the perfect singleness of divine purpose and power in Yahweh. The Greek theology, "empirical," more in line with disorderly experience, reflects how things go; the Israelite theology, "moral," expresses a will to prescribe how things must go. Thus, the *Iliad* glories in the balance between heroes on each side, the tides of battle, the pushes and pulls of gods, its action seesawing along, while Exodus maximizes the power differences among its three principal agents—wretched, enslaved Israel, capable of so little; Pharaoh, greatest of earthly powers; and the unique Yahweh, who ultradecisively squashes Pharaoh-the-highest on behalf of Israel-the-lowest.

The Hebraic perspective on action is distinguished by conscious attention to the implications of a divine agency that not only affects human affairs with supreme power—that is the interpretive key to the larger contingencies and results of history used by the dominant biblical writers and editors—but also, at the same time, relates to human agency with infinite intimacy. One sees right through the charming anthropomorphisms of Homeric theology, which are evidently only signs for superhuman, largely inscrutable movements. But there is a daring humanistic presumption in Exodus adequately to disclose God's will, and thus the meaning of everything, in intelligible and justifiable terms. There is a striking symmetry between the mind of Moses and the mind of Yahweh, for instance: they argue over what to do next like an old married couple.[34] (Achilles can beg his divine mother Thetis to intercede for him, but he cannot go straight to a policy conference with Zeus.)[35] Hebraic theology will speak of God's inscrutable transcendence only as a hedge against crass distortion; the starting point will always be, not the mystery of the world-process, but the righteous will of the known world-ruler. If one were to "see through" the humanly intelligible plans Yahweh formulates for Israel, discounting them as anthropomorphisms, one would fail to take Israel's charter, the commandments, seriously enough.

The Israelite and Greek epics differ also in how they set up the relationship between the human individual and the human collective in the pursuit of worth. Homer is very interested in the dramatic tension between Achilles' individual honor and the fortunes of the Greek team. No Israelite hero can have so personal a purpose; no counterpart to "the wrath of Achilles" could be a main biblical theme. On the other hand, Homer has no room for a Moses or a David. There are human proxies and protégés of the gods in the Greek story, but never an individual whose acts amount to the decisive worldly point of entry of the divine will. That would destabilize the Homeric apportioning of destiny, *moira*, on both the human and divine levels. The decisive *moira* and drama for Israel are found in the balance between divine and human agency rather than among elements within either.[36] The divine sponsorship that holds uniquely for Moses (and then for subsequent prophets and sages) and for David (and subsequent kings) holds through their leadership for the Israelite collective, God's chosen national agent; and it holds also through the example Moses and David set for each individual member of Israel. Thus, the nation and the individual are coeval and, in a sense, interchangeable points of contact between divine and human agency. When we listen to the songs of the Suffering Servant—"This is My servant, whom I uphold, My chosen one, in whom I delight"—we don't know definitely whether an individual messiah is meant, or Israel as a whole, or any individual who identifies with Israel's mission.[37] All of these meanings are potentially in force; the question they collectively raise is, How do they apply to us, and to me, now? And how do they pose not only constraint, a demand for compliance, but opportunity, a path to the best kind of personal distinction? Divine sonship and messianism become Jewish categories for corporate and individual moral endeavor, neither to the exclusion of the other and neither to be eclipsed by unilateral divine action.

The Hebrew Bible places the epic of Israel within a larger epic of humanity that is also governed by a vision of the most worthy action. From the beginning, the grandeur of divine-human cooperation is represented in Adam and Noah, the fathers of all humanity, "walking with God."[38] (If we were tempted to equate walking with God with adherence to a certain moral line, we would be checked here by the absence of any defined line. We don't know what exactly would constitute "missing the mark." Given the normative possibility of cooperating with God, however, any departure from walking in God's way is implied from the beginning to be a distinctively dreadful action or action impairment—"sin.") Humanity having been corrupted by Noah's time, Noah's construction of an ark under God's direction turns out to be the only action in his generation that is not in vain.[39] When the tower builders of Shinar bid for greatness without God's cooperation, God throws them into confusion.[40]

Early in Israel's story God indicates that Abraham and his descendants are to "walk in My ways."[41] After humanity has splintered into opposed national communities, Israel is refounded as the nation with whom God walks. "I will be ever present in your midst. . . . O Israel, what does the Lord your God demand of you? . . . To walk only in His paths."[42] From this viewpoint, cooperation with God must be conceived on a group basis, inasmuch as its primary goal is a distinctively high standard of justice. The justice outlined in the Mosaic covenant is to be Israel's glorious deed. Then, after the Israelite states are destroyed, the Jewish community serves as a cultural matrix for the pursuit of Israel's action. The continuing existence of the Jewish people as a "light of nations" will prove that practical partnership with God is an eternal condition of human life's superior meaning.[43]

One contemporary Jewish thinker, Michael Wyschogrod, can make only the most negative sort of case for the corporate election of Israel:

> Simone Weil is far from wrong in speaking of society and the nation as the "great beast" to which men sacrifice their individuality, so that they never dream it possible to become a "single one" before God. No one who has read the prophets of Israel can be unaware of the extent to which Israel's faith fears the arrogance of

the collective. But the question is, What to do? Shall the domain of the state be written off as the domain of the Devil, beyond the hope of sanctification, or shall it be seen as the most difficult challenge of all, which must be won for the holy precisely because of its remoteness from it?[44]

Such a way of putting things shows how far the modern nation, or "society," diverges from the action-fostering polis.[45] But the traditional meaning of corporate Israel is closer to the polis, even if its ideals are obviously not identical to the Greek ideals. Israel is not merely a set of material conditions for the worldly life of its members. It is a theater and an ensemble of dramatis personae for whom a national story ("We were slaves of Pharaoh in Egypt," etc.) and 613 commandments make up a script outline.[46]

In the Exile and the Diaspora, a sense of being on one's own, a sort of normatively solitary partnership with God, developed among Jews alongside their continually renewed assertion of corporate identity. Persecution and responsibility alike come home to the individual and reach their peak in her or him—as most of the prophets warn by their example, if not by what they say. These are the sternest tests of agency. "My God, my God, why have You abandoned me?"[47] Correlated with the ontological uniqueness of God is the uniqueness of the "suffering service" of the moral subject allied with God.[48]

This practical conception continues to be an important part of the appeal that Judaism can make. Abraham Heschel, for example, related the Jewish conception of action to a mystery in selfhood that might strike anyone, a realization that the self is not its own ultimate ground of meaning but rather is an object for a transcendent Other subject.[49] This leads to a practical doctrine:

> There is *an ecstasy of deeds*, luminous moments in which we are raised by overpowering deeds above our own will. . . . To him who strives with heart and soul to give himself to God and who succeeds as far as is *within his power*, the gates of greatness break open and he is able to attain that which is *beyond his power*.[50]

The commandments (mitzvoth) of Israel are the program for such deeds:

> The purpose of performing a mitsvah is in the meaning, in the light which emanates from it. The act is performed by man, but the light emanates from God. Every mitsvah adds holiness to Israel. . . . "If a man sanctifies himself a little, he becomes greatly sanctified. If he sanctify himself below, he becomes sanctified from

above" [*Yoma* 39a]. Holiness is not exclusively the product of the soul but the outcome of moments in which God and soul meet in the light of a good deed.[51]

In this passage Heschel invokes a corporate dimension of holy action together with the individual dimension that is his main theme.

Within the biblical history of holy action, the psalmists explored the prospects of cooperating with a preeminent Helper-Fighter, keeping an eye on the extraordinary power and justification this association holds—or should hold ("But I wait for You, O Lord").[52] They relish the extraordinary situation in which the supreme power of the universe acts with certain creatures and against others: "Were it not for the Lord, who was on our side when men assailed us, they would have swallowed us alive. . . . Our help is the name of the Lord, maker of heaven and earth."[53] Even though the foundation of worthy purpose and power is strictly divine, God is bound by covenant to serve Israel: "Destroy all my mortal enemies, for I am Your servant."[54] God is "my portion in the land of the living": the projects of installation *of* the world and of humans *in* the world are yoked together in such a way that within the divinely governed natural and historical order there is a certain human autonomy ("The heavens belong to the Lord, but the earth He gave over to man") and a particular reward in conducting oneself in the *name* of the Lord.[55] God is the redeemer, the guarantor of ideal worth, and Israel, "an alien" in the world (but ideally representative of all humanity), is the implementing vehicle through which God's plan is seen to be practically worthwhile.[56]

Hebraic tradition is an advantageous point of reference in an investigation of action proper, because it draws so boldly the interpersonal conditions under which the meaningfulness of action is greatest. Whereas the dominant tendency in Christian and Muslim theology has been to conceive divine action as a universal foundation on which creaturely action supervenes (as "secondary causation," in some accounts), Judaism has kept the premise of divine-human cooperation more central and vivid—possibly as a survival of clannish or nationalistic perspective but certainly as a strong worth strategy.[57] Jewish life shoulders its distinctive burden of 613 endlessly interpretible commandments so that it can rise to become, as a whole, an action of God, a definite community, and a definite individual together. Is there any fuel for action that isn't burning yet?

∽

An instructively comparable ethos of human-and-divine action may be found in Confucianism and neo-Confucianism. I will briefly sketch the apparent worth evolution in this case. The ancient Chinese counterpart to the Greek and Hebrew national epics is the story (set at roughly the same time, toward the end of the second millennium B.C.E.) of the great event in which the Zhou overthrew the Shang by divine permission, the corrupt Shang having forfeited the Mandate of Heaven.[58] The Chinese ruler was conceived as a son of Heaven, ruling ultimately by the entitlement of right-eousness; and righteousness was measured by the harmony of the whole people. But the Zhou order was falling apart by Kongzi's (Confucius's) time (as was Israel, also, in the time of the great writing prophets), so it came to seem necessary to place the morally serious person as such, any such person, in direct relation with Heaven, according to the example set by Kongzi himself (just as the prophets' faithfulness to God became a model for all Jews). The Confucian who is sincerely devoted to familial and social duties and ardently studious of proper behavior, *li*—which by this time has become a practice with human referents instead of supernatural ones—real-izes in his or her actions a traditional right relationship of the community to Heaven (much as a Jew's observance of mitzvoth realizes the Torah-way of Israel).[59] The community is vividly present and freshly articulated when-ever such an individual acts with ritual correctness; and because ruler and subject alike are primarily concerned with the harmonious operation of the social system rather than with individualized exploits, such action is a pos-sibility for anyone. It is typically celebrated in *unusual* deeds performed for the sake of good *order*:

> [Mengzi:] "Duke Ching of Ch'i went hunting and summoned his gamekeeper with a pennon. The gamekeeper did not come, and the Duke was going to have him put to death. . . . What did Confucius find praiseworthy in the gamekeeper? His refusal to answer to a form of summons to which he was not entitled."
>
> "May I ask with what should a gamekeeper be summoned?"
>
> "With a leather cap. A Commoner should be summoned with a bent flag, a Gentleman with a flag with bells and a Counsellor with a pennon. When the gamekeeper was summoned with what was appropriate only to a Counsellor, he would rather die than answer the summons. . . . Rightness is the road and the rites are the door."[60]

Because exemplary individuals are strongly mindful of the expansion of their agency into the communal dimension, they disdain the more common, selfish kinds of striving, accomplishment, and pride. The incon-gruity between their modesty on the lower worth plane and their ambitions and rivalries on a higher plane is savored by Kongzi, who could say,

"Gentlemen never compete," but also said, "In a hamlet of ten houses you may be sure of finding someone quite as loyal and true to his word as I. But I doubt if you would find anyone with such a love of learning."[61] An individual's involvement in this higher worth or transworth is superficially measured in familiar worth terms—"A gentlemen is ashamed to die without having accomplished something"—yet is so little like ordinary worth that it is liable to be marked by ignomity rather than glory (as in the biblical portrait of the Suffering Servant).[62] "The Master said, A Knight whose heart is set upon the Way, but is ashamed of wearing shabby clothes and eating coarse food, is not worth calling into counsel."[63] And he lamented, "I have never yet had a chance to show what I could do."[64] The adversity Kongzi faces is contingent, admittedly. If the world were harmonious rather than competitive, then it would be "a disgrace" for the exemplary individual to be "needy and obscure."[65] But then again, if competition disappeared, ordinary meanings of honor would disappear with it.

The action of the exemplary individual is "heavenly" in a stronger sense than in merely relating the individual or the community appropriately to Heaven. It is part of Heaven's own action—which is to say, finally, that it is an act in solidarity with the whole world, for Heaven is understood by the classic Chinese thinkers not as a transcendent person or separate place but as an enabling structure immanent in all real things. Fundamentally, Heaven's power prevails in spite of chaos and evil, and the sage prevails with it. "The Master said, Heaven begat the power that is in me. What have I to fear from such a one as Huan T'ui?"[66] It is true that Kongzi and his disciples have just been harassed into leaving Sung when he says this, but their seemingly unfortunate departure is actually part of a larger transworthy pattern: abandoning an unrighteous ruler is the sage's trademark action.[67] The sage's disdain is, at times, the highest instruction.[68] Greatness prevails by separating from the small. And Kongzi need not long for any sort of otherworldly redemption, for the validation of what he stands for is immediately (if not always happily) perceived.[69]

On basing the greatest action in Heaven there is fundamental agreement between Confucians and Daoists, although the latter criticize the Confucian fixation on merely "human" standards:

> "The Heavenly is on the inside, the human is on the outside. . . . Understand the actions of Heaven and Man, base yourself upon Heaven. . . ."
>
> "What do you mean by the Heavenly and the human?"
>
> "Horses and oxen have four feet—that is what I mean by the Heavenly. Putting a halter on the horse's head, piercing the ox's nose—this is what I mean by the human." (Zhuangzi).[70]

Confucians, too, can say, "What man exalts is not truly exalted."[71] They think their model of action is greater than Daoism's, however, because it brings together the Heavenly and the social. The Daoists seem to them to lack a strong program for interhuman cooperation. But the Confucians' insistence on binding the Heavenly so tightly to the social becomes their vulnerable point in the worth debate. Zhuangzi uses the character of Kongzi to ridicule the plans of a dedicated Confucian:

> Yen Hui said . . . "Suppose I am inwardly direct, outwardly compliant, and do my work through the examples of antiquity? By being inwardly direct, I can be the companion of Heaven. Being a companion of Heaven, I know that the Son of Heaven and I are equally the sons of Heaven. . . . By being outwardly compliant, I can be a companion of men. Lifting up the tablet, kneeling, bowing, crouching down—this is the etiquette of a minister. . . . By doing my work through the examples of antiquity, I can be the companion of ancient times. . . . If I go about it in this way, will it do?"
>
> Confucius said, "Goodness, how could *that* do? You have too many policies and plans and you haven't seen what is needed. . . . You are still making the mind your teacher!"[72]

Whereas the Daoists can reflect freely (and mischievously) on the extraordinary character of the divine, the ultimate Way, so as to portray more impressively the strange transworth of the Daoist sage whose wandering is in that Way, the Confucians seem to appeal only to a domesticated Heaven in which the discriminations of social etiquette, the exigencies of politics, and the ordinary mind in general are reduplicated. Heaven becomes an insignificant worth partner. (Is Israel's god Yahweh too fiercely independent to dissolve in this way as a constituent of the greatest action? Or is Yahweh too human after all, too much a magnified Israelite king, to withstand a Daoist-style worth critique?)

Greatly influenced by the long conversation with Daoism, Neo-Confucianism became explicit and ardent in its practical inclusiveness; we read, for instance, in Wang Yangming's *Inquiry in the Great Learning* (1527) that the exemplary individual forms "one body" with all beings:

> The great man regards Heaven and earth and the myriad things as one body. He regards the world as one family and the country as one person. As to those who make a cleavage between objects and distinguish between the self and others, they are small men. That the great man can regard Heaven, earth, and the myriad things as one body is not because he deliberately wants to do so, but

because it is natural with the humane nature of his mind that he should form a unity with Heaven, earth, and the myriad things. . . . Such a mind is rooted in his Heaven-endowed nature, and is naturally intelligent, clear, and not obscured.[73]

The mind that does not "distinguish between the self and others" can only sponsor actions for the interest of all things. It becomes outstanding by instanding. Thereby it distinguishes itself from the mind of the "small man" who pursues self-centered worth. Pursuing the same point, the contemporary neo-Confucian Tu Weiming makes an appeal more to deliberate initiative and less to sensibility:

To fully express our humanity, we must engage in a dialogue with Heaven because human nature, as conferred by Heaven, realizes itself not by departing from its source but by returning to it. Humanity, so conceived, is the public property of the cosmos, not the private possession of the anthropological world, and is as much the defining characteristic of our being as the self-conscious manifestation of Heaven. Humanity is Heaven's form of self-disclosure, self-expression, and self-realization. If we fail to live up to our humanity, we fail cosmologically in our mission as co-creator of Heaven and Earth.[74]

Compared with the Jewish action maximum, the Confucian paradigm involves a less sharply drawn community and divinity, and it promotes calm reasonableness and discipline far more than anything like messianic passion (although one might hear that note in Tu Weiming). A Confucian will not look for a climactic encounter with the divine and is less disposed to bet everything, so to speak, on a single decisive "holy deed." The heroes of this tradition are memorable more for their attitudes and wise sayings about the conduct of life in general than for astounding actions like Hosea's marriage to a prostitute or Jeremiah's bearing of a yoke.[75] Discernibly, however, the Confucian action ideal has been built up out of the same basic ingredients, to the same worth-impressive effect; and this effect indeed accrues to the individual, who can become awesome: as Kongzi says, "The exemplary person has three things he holds in awe: The will of Heaven, the great man, and the words of the sage."[76]

〇〇

The biblical psalmists point on a number of occasions to our next transition between worth domains. Although they like to talk of God's fighting on behalf of Israel and guiding it, their attention is led to another dimension of action, or to a worth form beyond action, for several reasons. There is the inadequacy of any worldly description of divine efficacy; there is the overwhelming asymmetry between divine and human power, and the already-complete attainment and givenness of God's glorious distinctness; and there remains the need, notwithstanding, for a supremely strong reason with which to appeal to God and a larger background question of practical orientation. The touchstone for which the psalmists reach, beyond "deeds" for their own sake, is *chesed*, faithful love.[77] (Compare the Confucianist *ai ren* and Wang Yangming's stress on love as the means of forming universal unity.)[78] "I call on You; You will answer me, God; turn Your ear to me, hear what I say. Display your *chesed* in wondrous deeds, You who deliver with your right hand those who seek refuge from assailants."[79] "O Lord, be mindful of Your compassion and Your *chesed*; they are old as time."[80] "Truly Your *chesed* is better than life; my lips declare Your praise."[81]

Love would appear to be a mighty, or transmighty, worth reservoir.

Chapter 5

❦

LOVE

5.1 Loving as doing

Poets describe love as a game. There is winning and losing in love, and stylized conduct; but if love were a game, its victories and losses would be less fateful. One who walks away from love as from play has not loved.

Moralists say we ought to work at love. There are needs for it and careers in it. But work could not be so sweet, so purely intrinsic a good. If love were work, we would need rest from it, but love is an ultimate invigoration.

We have come closest to love, categorically, in studying action proper. Action proper produces meaning directly from the togetherness of subjects, as a radiance of their cooperation, and love, if successful, is undoubtedly a powerful togetherness and consciously enjoys itself in this aspect. Lovers can speak of their love in the way that soldiers speak of a great campaign. Significantly, however, lovers try to rally each other to their love as a worthy cause only when the primary concern of love, the devotion of each lover to the other, is in doubt.

Is love a worth realm at all?

When love *happens*—the event, the "crystallization," the ravishing—the worth chase seems to be finished. Worth's definition is now stamped on the lover's soul with the face of the beloved, quenching all doubt and idle curiosity; the "world," as a system of shares, is dissolved in concern for the beloved and reconstituted as an overflow of appreciation from the beloved, stripped of the power to make demands or offer rewards of other sorts; the lover is "surrendered" to the unsurpassable good of the beloved and so liberated from all previous accretions of character, all previous formations and frustrations of project.[1] This describes the experience of love. Normatively,

137

too, love ends the worth chase insofar as it represents the maximum in value-realizing, the most powerful and benign strategy conceivable for growth and appreciation. From neither of these angles, however, can we tell much about love as an *action*, that is, as an object of meaningful practical choice. One might try to maneuver oneself into the path of the experience of love—lie down on the train tracks, as it were. And one can hardly refuse to endorse the value-maximizing enterprise as such. But what does it mean to go about loving in one particular way rather than another?

"I played softball" or "I did my homework" or "I bought a bicycle" are prima facie good answers to the question, "What did you do this afternoon?" Can one also answer, "I loved Henry"? The love report seems even more powerfully self-validating than the others—and yet it bears a strange relationship to "this afternoon" (it would fit better with "that period in my life") and is more inherently abstract, less informative, than the other answers (unless we take it in one special sense). The practical force of the statement tells us that agent worth is at stake, yet the notion of lover worth takes a strange turn. We can naturally ask whether a player or worker or owner performed well enough to earn credit, but one can only be a "good lover" in one restricted sense. It seems that we are called on to widen the timescale. We think of those who "love well" as long faithful.

Perhaps love worth is anomalous because of a special characteristic in loving action. If the love character of an action is constituted by something other than a character assumed in any other worth domain, then the key to this character must lie in the relation between lover and beloved. The distinctive love action must occur vis-à-vis the beloved. What does a lover necessarily do, just in loving, in relation to the beloved? What have frustrated lovers not done yet that they want most of all to do? The prime practical necessity for the lover is to *approach* the beloved. This is the precondition of other valuable things happening, of course, but in the first place it is, in itself, the uniquely worthwhile lover's act. Even when lovers have come together, their love will remain vital only if their togetherness is not a static fact, like a tied knot, but an unceasing and unstoppable approaching. (Can one sustain or jump-start this act by "working on a relationship"?) Love will tend to be indefinite and publicly uninteresting in practical content because the movement as such, which takes place *through* manifest activities (loving *by means of* playing together, working together, and so forth) or even *apart from* any manifest activity (loving "in spirit"), is its essence. Yet if it is to be expressed as a life policy, as in friendship or marriage, love needs a vision of how lovers' approaching each other and their cocentering of the world are to be sustained in manifestly worthwhile activities.

Love must be moving. If I say, "Love moves me," *I* must nevertheless be moving in it, that is, my power of initiating action is moved. Moving, I can never satisfactorily point to an accomplishment or even a state of my self in love and declare it worthy. Not that I am humble; rather, I am ambitious. The lover resembles in this respect that most playful player who cares more about the game coming up than the game just concluded, or the workaholic, or the political glory hound. We say in such cases that agents *love* what they do. To venture to do anything is to rouse oneself and move into a field of uncertainty, intending to master it, trying to do so. Yet we flinch from the notion of trying to love as from a sour chord; love is so much a moving that it seems to us more proper to speak of love trying us, and we often experience it or interpret it as a "passion" because of this excess over ordinary voluntary control. I am overmatched, in a sense, by the imperative attraction of the beloved and by the psychic energy configuration of love within me. But *I* run with the latter to meet the former, insofar as I love. I borrow these grandeurs as a surfer borrows the height and force of a wave.

Self-abnegation is characteristic of love, because it makes the lover's movement directly apparent and also dramatizes the stakes of the relationship, the difference between what is possible apart from the love and what is possible through it. The extreme sacrifice of suffering or death brings out the tragic aspect of all loving self-abnegation: what is lost for the sake of love might finally be lost *to* love as well. Jealous lovers react angrily to this prospect, positing their own love happiness as necessary.

A worth domain always makes a strong prima facie claim to be included in a good life. Love may make the greatest of all such claims, for we think of a life without love as gapingly incomplete. But someone whose love is now over with is not like someone who has done a job or performed a great deed. The memory of past love is melancholy. One is glad to know the point of love, but that point always is just to love. Analogously, the memory of past creativity is cold comfort if one is unable to create anew. But love's argument is even more dynamic than that of creation. The main premise of love is not "This good new thing *can* be realized and you *may* be the one to realize it"; it is "You *must* be nearer this Other, in intention as well as in real engagement, because *all* goodness in your life belongs in a network of connections with this Other." Love worth is so profoundly urgent, such a direct and exorbitant pull on concern, that it is of all worth portfolio items the least collectable.

5.2 "True" and "higher" loves

Discriminations of "higher" and "lower" are common in love discourse, but in two different main senses. We may *rank* forms and occasions of love according to different degrees of goodness, regarding all as healthy and equally essential to the good life ("the highest does not stand without the lowest");[2] but whether or not we have ranks of love in mind, we are often willing to *rate* manifestations of love as more worthy or less worthy according to our normative expectations for the form or occasion concerned. In rating love, "lower" means bad or false and "higher" means good or true. Our generic criteria for "height" in love can all be interpreted as manifestations of purity in the three elements of love's triad; the lover, the relationship, and the beloved. We look for a purity or coherence of energy in the subject, an *intensity* of devotion, in the lover's loving; we look for a purity in the lover-beloved relation itself as it is sustained by understanding and practice, a *clarity*; and we look for a purity in love's effects on the beloved, or *benignity*. Thus we look down on a "lower" form of sexual love, "lust," because it involves less than the whole subjective energy of the lover, it fosters confusion about who the lover and beloved are and how they should deal with each other, and it only inadequately benefits or threatens harm to the beloved. Someone may want to extend the benignity criterion to all who stand to be affected by the relationship; for example, a girl's parents may insist that a suitor's love is impure if he is not devoted to their happiness as well as hers. But that is nonsense. The condition of the lover's subjective intensity is its focus on the beloved, which lifts the beloved up from the level of everything else that exists.

Plato's love doctrine is a little like the argument of the family that wants a suitor to be devoted to the larger unit. The larger unit in this case is Beauty itself.[3] For Platonism, the real lovableness of a beautiful individual is based on the generic *pure* Beauty instanced in him or her. A lover devoted to an individual as individual is like a miner making off with a hunk of ore and abandoning the mother lode of gold. The Platonic purity argument goes wrong in an interesting way, I think. Aiming to secure a purity of intention in the rational, Form-responsive consciousness of the lover, it sacrifices the carnal sincerity in which the loving individual is realized as something of his or her own, not to be assimilated to Reason itself. (Plato *acknowledges* that the lover's soul-life includes carnal desire, but he wants this "dark steed" to be rigorously disciplined and mortified.) Placing all its hope for clarity in the relation between Reason and Form, eternal with eternal, Platonism makes unintelligible the individuality of lover and beloved alike and throws a dark cloud over the physical world they inhabit, which it can explain only in terms of deficiency. Because it insists on true benefit in the form of imperishable Beauty, it cannot comprehend either anxiety for the beloved or grief over the beloved's loss—two essential strands of love's benevolence in our world.[4] Concerned to include everything worth loving, Platonism turns away from the depth of meaning in love's dramatic, fascinating approach to the particular beloved.[5] Instead of rising to the challenge of embracing the largest structures or the whole of being as lovable, in the manner of religion, it nags at existing experiences of love with extraneous ideal considerations, in the manner of philosophy.

Let us now consider possible rankings of loves. Do ranks of love correspond to differences in the possible intensity, clarity, and benignity of love actions? I will retrace the exemplary itinerary of C. S. Lewis's *The Four Loves*.

Affection

Affection is warm attraction to someone or something that has become familiar. Its hallmark and proper flourishing is comfortableness. I agree with Lewis that affection is to be admired both in its own right and as a supporting ingredient in other forms; it's at best a borderline case of love-as-doing, however, because there is so little movement in it. Even where there is strong physical drive—one of Lewis's examples is the coming together of hungry infant and aching mother's breast—we find that the tenor of the relationship is more one of a taking of each other for granted than of an intent approaching of the beloved.[6] The satisfactions of affectionate relationship are under one's belt, like a square meal, rather than out in front of one as a beautiful prospect. Affection's benefits lie mostly outside the realm of agent worth. For example, it is important to me, but no credit to me, that by virtue of a long rubbing of shoulders with a man I would never choose as a friend I have become affectionately appreciative of his good qualities.[7]

Affection is the lowest form of love, because the rule of comfort limits its intensity, clarity, and benignity. If I were to be extremely aroused in my affection for a teapot I've long used—if I were to realize an exceptional clarity in my relationship with it—if I were to take its well-being with utter seriousness . . . that would be unusual. Say the teapot is a fascinating, precious remnant of Chinese civilization. But does my love in this case show that affection can be as "high" a love as any other? No, because we have strained the paradigm of affection and evoked another without quite attaining it. The teapot must be made romantically mysterious, the relationship with it less comfortable. I have to begin to imagine Chinese people to make good on the crucial feature a teapot lacks: subjectivity. If I am to move wholly toward the beloved, the beloved must call to me with all the energy and interest of a new, other, world-centering enterprise. Just as the ontic simplicity of nonpersonal things makes them fine candidates for affection, it also sets up a reproach between persons: "You love me like you would a teapot."

Does affection represent a success in worth terms, a strong establishing of an agent in a world, or only a soothing suspension of the basic worth questions? At its best, affection delivers the best of both alternatives. In the bosom of affectionate family life, for instance, individual family members can, at their discretion, either find reason to feel secure or enjoy a holiday from concern. But affection cannot be pushed too far in either direction. It balances on a blunt edge, but an edge all the same. To take the object of affection too much for granted, too much as background, is to forfeit the joy and justification of love; to become too lovingly aroused toward the object, on the other hand, is to roll off the comfortable sofa of affection and into a more dynamic and uncertain relationship.

Friendship

Now we enter the field of necessarily personal forms of love, where ranking becomes more difficult and controversial. We can go straight to impressive testimonies to the supreme worth of each form, like Cicero's for friendship:

> What is sweeter than to have someone with whom you dare to say everything as if with yourself? What would be the great fruit in prosperous affairs unless you had someone who himself would rejoice in them as much as you? . . . How much power there is in friendship [due to the good will in it]: for what family is so stable, what city so unshakable, that it may not be completely overturned by hatreds and divisions?[8]

Friendship wants to pass all the love tests with flying colors. For subjective intensity, it offers something stronger than warm inclination: the famous friend Laelius says, "I loved [Scipio] because of a certain amazement at his virtue."[9] But however admirable one's friend is, appreciating a friend is always tied to a sense of affinity, a heightened clarity about oneself and the other at the same time, since friends have interests in common. Lewis says, "[T]he typical expression of opening Friendship would be, 'What, you too? I thought I was the only one.'"[10] Finally, friendship is superlatively benign for the friends themselves. Friends help each other personally (with chores, for example, or debts) as a matter of course for the sake of helping each other as bearers of larger interests. Friendship's main theme is to be confirmed and advanced in the largest version of oneself. (Tristan and Iseult had things precisely their way, as romantic lovers, when they were alone in the forest, but as friends they could not bear to deprive each other of social excellence, and so they came back into society.)[11] Friendship is uniquely expansive in this sense. It seems right to meet one's friends in public places, and it isn't directly necessary to bring them home. Clinging enters friendship only with an admixture of another type of love.

A critic of friendship's claims to maximal love value can point to various limitations in it. First, there is a certain affection-like placidity in friendship that makes us think of it as less than the most intense love, and this is essential: friends are "easy" with one another so that they can jointly be fervent about their objects of shared interest. It might be said in praise of friendship that the total appreciative involvement of the friend is as great as in any other form of love, but it is so well distributed among individuality and virtue and objective interests that friends are not cramped in any important dimension of their being. Second, it might be argued that friendship produces less than the greatest possible clarity about self and other because of the necessary similarity of friends, a quite deceptive affinity (if friendship is judged as a reckoning with humanity), at once magical ("What? You too?") and natural, unforced, utterly reliable. To share with one's friends an expanded enthusiasm and vision along a particular line, like politics or stamp collecting, is not really to grow. It might only aggravate a self-caricature. The housekeeping details of life that do not belong to the regular fabric of friendly association might be a key to maturity, after all. Thus it might be concluded that friendship is far from guaranteed to affect its object in the most benign way. Further, friendship puts people at greater risk of getting into trouble with the larger community, for friends form a secession party more likely to form socially hostile opinions or to perform subversive deeds. Hence Cicero is anxious to legislate to friendship: "Good people . . . should not think that they are so bound by friendship that they cannot part company with friends plotting against the state."[12] Many spouses will attest that friendship can be a powerful enemy of stable home life. But friendship will reply to these charges that the good of friendship is not overly narrow; critics have overlooked the complementariness of friends' virtues, which in the best circle of friends actually widens one's appreciation of humanity just as far as it can be widened with full and lucid enthusiasm. In any case, the narrowness and secessionism of friendship are all part of its precious focus on the human good, which can lead to the rescue of societies from bad government and of individuals from bad home life. Friendship is idealistic in a publicly responsible way without sacrificing realistic concern for individuals. This makes it a surpassingly pure vehicle of agent worth. Besides all the incidental advantages and pleasures of friendship, friends radiate with the goodness of the good to which their shared interest is directed. My philosopher friends are as noble as philosophy itself, and I, with them, embody something of that too. If a shared interest happens to be ignoble, then friendship love, so far as it can exert leverage in the situation, will militate in favor of a more admirable theme.

Romance (Eros)

The love that "unnerves the limbs and overcomes the mind" has won wider respect than friendship.[13] But it also evokes fear and loathing. It is too powerful and unaccountable. It is too thick with treacherous carnal reality, on the one hand, and too flighty and illusion-prone on the other. The lover goes overboard in this kind of love. It produces idolatry while it lasts and excessively bitter disappointment when it ends.

The preeminence of romantic love (as we now call it) lies in its subjective intensity. Since nothing can be held back out of it, it is an absolutely sincere devotion. The romantic lover is more easily recognized in an emptied, castaway guise, haunting the forest like Tristan or raving in the desert like Majnūn, than in prosperity or a responsible position. In romantic consummation, the dark steed of lust runs hard, reined but not hampered; the fair steed of honor proudly holds up its head, feeling an expansive confirmation not unlike that of friendship; and reason rejoices in a fulfillment of *all* ideals in the intensest and most pregnant beauty of the beloved, a setting right of everything in the world, *now*, far more powerful than the more selectively focused, calm, "in principle" shared interest of friendship. No wonder illusion has a field day, as consciousness works overtime to keep pace with enthusiasm! But to sneer at this hustling of consciousness is to underrate the enthusiasm it serves. The lover, at the moment before the huge idealism of love "crystallizes" onto the beloved, is in a state of energetic readiness to embrace the whole world in the most intensely affirmative way.[14] The beloved provides the almighty clue and effective vehicle for the coherent discharge of this energy. What makes the clue so powerful is that it calls on the lover in all his or her carnal individuality; what makes the vehicle effective is that the beloved likewise possesses a definite carnal presence commensurate with and able to be joined to the lover's own.

Of course, the exhaustive demand romance makes at the moment may feel and talk like Forever, but it is no such thing. It is all intensity and no extension—nothing, at least, after the fire burns out. The idea that there could be endless fuel for a fire so hot is marvelous, however; believing this, lovers have faith in Love and reality at the same time. A divine superbeing or ground of being is an especially appealing beloved, if one's imagination can cope with the indefiniteness of the referent, because it promises a fuel supply for love even if the whole world should be exhausted. But any romantic love is already on this footing, with emotional if not metaphysical propriety; the god is within, in the enthusiasm.

In this intensity lies love's clarity. Romantic love is overpoweringly revealing and true, in spite of all illusions, because it brings into luminosity feelings and beliefs and attributes of the first importance that otherwise stay deep in the dark. Friendship is pure only in its own safe zone, holding uncongenial matters at bay, but romance achieves purity in a sort of ravening candor. The high-temperature oneness of romantic relationship, more than a pooling of experience, more than an "opening up" of friends, is a collision between the lovers, a crash test, shaking everything about them out and forcing it all back together. A loss of balance here produces cruelty instead of clarity.

Terrible wrongs are done in the name of romantic love. Should the very form be blamed? Lewis thinks that romantic lovers characteristically take up a conscious and dangerous allegiance to a law of love superseding all others.[15] But a lover who would plead justification by love's law ("Yes, I abandoned my family, but it was for Love") seems to presume on love worth in an inauthentic way. What is of itself a dynamic principle of meeting between two lovers is treated as a claim for a stable apportioning, a right. If it is good to grant lovers some *license*, the justification would not be a "law" of love in that sense.[16] Yet romantic love isn't simply a thing to excuse, a temporary incapacitation like illness or rage, either. We do figure it this way retrospectively, after the fire has burned out, but we are not doing justice then to its seriousness and lucidity. The passing of illness or rage makes one well, but the passing of love makes one a melancholy loser.

Romantic love is indeed dangerous and bears close watching on the benignity front, but it isn't necessary that romantic lovers should flee the world or hurt anyone else. Romantic lovers and their audience do dream of their fitting into the world, and it does sometimes happen. We think it happens in the best marriages. I surmise that this is the ground of the license granted to romance—more a hope, or the honoring of a hope, than an excuse.

Charity

A love that is by definition unconditionally benevolent seems likely to appear at the top of any scale of love worth and so must throw a worth scare into all the "lesser loves." This love would be free of the inertia of affection, the partiality of friendship, and the tempestuousness and ephemerality of romance. One who loved with this love would be capable of the most difficult acts, like ministering intimately to a loathsome beloved or submitting to torture, mutilation, or death on behalf of the beloved. The "lesser loves" can only protest: Could there really be such a lover?

The more we emphasize the difference between charity and other loves, the more doubtful we make the possibility of a charitable lover. If charity is indifferent to comfort ("bears all things"), utterly consistent ("endures all things"), independent of personal traits ("believes all things"), how can it be regarded as a personal act at all?[17] In the absence of regard for either the distinctive sensibility of the lover or the individually defining traits of the beloved, a transaction between persons becomes difficult to recognize as part of a relationship, though it be as benign as air and sunlight. In fact, the theological impetus to conceive God as suprapersonal is closely bound to the ideal of unlimited benignity. God's "love," as general as sunlight, is therefore little like the love of any finite being. And the perfect form of love for a human being (according to Lewis's kind of religious love idealism) could *only* be love *of this suprapersonal Being*, a love so different from love in the world as to be inconceivable, but fated nevertheless to haunt all our love experience as an empty ideal.[18]

If we ask for continuity between charity and other loves, however, another picture emerges. Love's motto becomes "Hopes all things."[19] I hope that as one affectionately bound to my familiars I can broaden my comfort circle to include whoever here and now can get the most benefit from me. I hope for an expansion of the jolly friendship circle in which I share my liveliest interests. I hope that the intense energy and lucidity of the romantic focus need not be bottled up in romance but can be approached in my other relationships. As a vessel of love-hopes, charity would be an anthology of the loves, perfected by addition instead of subtraction. A religious love-heaven would reconcile all worthy affections, friendships, and romantic attachments under the umbrella (not the jealous dominance) of unconditional affirmation.

But charity looks in certain ways more like one of the loves than the sum of the loves. It is the opposite of romance in that its force arises in the benignity part of love's formula, and its blind spot lies in its subjective quality, inasmuch as its left hand is not to know what its right hand is doing.[20] Clearly the sick need visiting, but we have to be spurred to realize, in some bewilderment, a movement toward them. The romantic lover, in contrast, is sure of caring passionately about the beloved but relatively blind to the helpful or hurtful consequences of the relationship. It is a rare perfection of benevolence, a quality exhibited by saints, to care passionately, just as clear-eyed benignity is a rare perfection of romance. Similarly, charity's lack of discrimination with regard to worldly aims is at the opposite end of a spectrum of interest from the focused enthusiasms of friendship. Charity cares for happiness without knowing what the theme of happiness would be. Like romance, charity without friendship collapses in ennui—supposing that it does intend to sustain a relationship and isn't merely a utilitarian intervention. Finally, the comfort of affection may give a needed basic reassurance that charity or any love can sustain a real relationship, while charity can give affection an active inspiration and worthy goal without subjecting it to the personally fastidious restrictions of romance and friendship.

We should distinguish, then, between a Best Love that is superior to all other versions of love because it contains all their excellences and overcomes their limits, and charity as one of love's types complementary to others. The Best Love is an ideal; it isn't found in our experience, though we can strain toward it. Charity might be thought to have a specially close relation to the Best Love in its "unnaturalness." It might be claimed that the other loves are quite likely to occur in a human life whether they are deliberately pursued or not, while charity depends on an extraordinary inspiration and focus. But this view depends on the doubtful assumption that unselfishness is unnatural. In fact, while we do marvel at unselfishness, we also bank on it under the rubric of "decency."[21] We expect that people will often, even routinely, respond to prospects of goodness merely for goodness' sake rather than for self-gratification. If we are a little bewildered at our motives and acts being taken out of our own grasping hands, as it were, we are still not unfamiliar with the occurrence. But we must admit withal that we are somewhat bewildered by *all* the loves. Love is moving.

∾

I conclude from these observations that the notion of ranks of love can be seriously misleading. The "lowest" love, affection, is the least dispensable. The "highest" love is an ideal combination of the strengths of the real loves. When we do evaluate the quality of the real loves, we find that they complement and correct each other.

A question remains as to whether what we are evaluating in love is in any sense worth. The lover's approaching the beloved might best be understood as involving a departure from worth. Love seems to suggest that worth assessment of the lover's self is idolatrous—that the real question is about You. The portion of reality that the loving self secures is all in You, not as a possession but as a stake. Not that You *rules* I, in brutal heteronomy; but the flourishing of You in relationship with I—You first, me second—is love's answer to the deeply open question that worth generally addresses. The love self is worthy *as* the self of love of the Other, and from love's perspective is *nothing* otherwise. Normally worth is an expansive condition for the self, an ideal meeting with others by which the self is aerated, but not so one-sided a relation as this.

Although there is a certain strain in congratulating a lover on worth and treating love as a variable amount of credit in an agent's worth portfolio, we are familiar with the thought that lovers do try to be *worthy of* each other and, in general, not to be unworthy in love terms. To hear the call of love and not answer properly is to fall out of love's movement and lie still, in the dust, left behind, perhaps even causing the same mishap to befall another. Bearing this in mind, we can seek to identify the worthiest love actions.

5.3 The worth of sex

When I say "I loved Henry," what am I *referring* to? I may of course be referring to a host of things, picturesque or prosaic: riding bicycles with Henry on a rainy afternoon, taking him to the emergency room when he sliced open his thumb, combing junk stores in search of a certain gift for him. But if I mean to say this with a definite, complete, and generally understandable practical reference, as in, "That afternoon, I loved Henry," then I am probably talking about a physical encounter in which the moving energy of love eruptingly declared itself. In sex, preeminently, love comes to a point.

Many kinds of commonly observed sex, from the brutal extreme of rape to intercourse between affectionate but romantically uncommitted friends, are disturbing from the point of view that would reserve sex for an expression of full interpersonal devotion. (Attributing unworthiness to what is seen as a sexual "perversion" draws on this ideal also.) It seems that much sex occurs thanks to an intersection of two quite different evaluations of sex that happen to share a tactical principle: on one side, the view that having sex is the most satisfying *thing* that could be done *at a given time* (hence, say, *tonight*); on the other side, the view that having sex is the most inspiring *thing* to do *now* (hence *tonight*) to realize romantic love. The nonromantic and romantic worth visions diverge widely, yet we can see in either case how a compellingly energetic and definite candidate for "worthwhile act," namely, "sex now," exerts a great influence on thinking about worthy agency. It is well known that the gap between the nonromantic and romantic motivations for sex breeds misunderstanding and unhappiness, and yet, strangely enough, their combination does draw people into sex very often. Even after making due allowance for human powers of deception, we might wonder whether there is a more substantial convergence beneath what looks like a gap.

Let us begin with the pursuit of sex for its own sake. I propose to simplify the question by appraising "sex without love" only in the sense of sex in freedom from the total commitment of romantic lovers; our portrait of the four loves implies that only romantic lovers have a strong motive to regard sex as essential to their love and to reserve sex for their love. If sex has worth possibilities when it is detached from the normative demands of romantic love, it will of course be all the more available to serve the other forms of love—for instance, as a pastime of friends.

How, then, might we define and explain the worth of sex as such without any reference to love?[22] We can say: (1) Sex is great *fun*, and the fun is enhanced, as in the best sorts of "good time" generally, by a specially intense conviviality: one is not merely doing it with a friend, one is doing it to, and having it done to one by, a friend. (Even if the friendliness involved is superficial and opportunistic compared with the friendship love we were discussing earlier, the sharing and intimacy of the event are real and estimable.) (2) But we might emphasize the strangeness of the partner and say that sex is a great *adventure*. One doesn't know in advance what shapes it will take, what experiential qualities it will deliver. (In cruising, one doesn't even know who the partner will be.) Thus sex is extremely interesting and promises to confer an expansive sort of self-worth with success. (3) Sex is a notable *victory*. We understand the difficulties of "scoring," the need for skill as well as luck to succeed in the pursuit of sex. (Sex as a "score" within a firmly fixed conventional "game" framework is not the same as sex as an adventurous "exploit," although these characterizations can run together in sex bragging.) Or, better yet, sex is a win-win game between the partners, perhaps appreciable in the category of action proper as an intrinsically worthwhile collaboration (a meaning that is missed by the complaint that loveless sex amounts to "mutual masturbation"). Or sex is the successful culmination of self-display. (4) Sex is a crucial *proof* of capability. A person able to meet his or her own bodily and emotional needs, and at the same time to engage and satisfy a sexual partner, inhabits his or her body in a stronger, more self-assured, more respect-worthy way. A hostile critic will characterize the sex act as the dark steed of lust running away with a person, but the sexual agent may feel reconciled with that element and confirmed in mastery over it in having had a good ride on it. Sex without love proves specifically that the sexual agent is independent even in this ultimately exposed use of his or her body, and is not constrained to "melt into" a sex partner or to become an emotional hostage.[23]

So it appears that sex can get substantial worth recommendations without any mention of love. But it isn't fully evident that love has really been kept out of the picture. (1) Why would sex be the highlight of the most enjoyable evening possible in spite of its danger and messiness compared with other recreations? Perhaps the intense friendliness of the encounter is the best explanation—but what makes this unusual form of friendly expression emotionally possible? (2) Why, on the other hand, would so cloistered and relatively tame an activity as sex count as a great adventure? There must be a bigger tiger in sex's jungle than venereal disease or abuse by one's partner, since sexual adventurers often feel quite safe from these threats. What is it? (3) Why does "scoring" seem so uniquely important *to the agent*? (*Talk* about sexual scoring may put it on a level with scoring in basketball; but that conventional coolness does not, I think, match the agent's feeling.) Or why are the participants *so much* pleased by success in their encounter? Is it only because (4) sexual success proves the capability that was most in doubt? But why then the special concern for this capability? Does sexual capacity represent life-giving power, symmetrical perhaps with the death-dealing power that is proved in hunting or military combat? Why, if life-giving power is the issue, are sex pursuers usually either heedless of conception or careful to prevent it?

We will have to mention love, after all, if we hope to account for the magnitude of sex's meaning even to pursuers of sex without love. If love doesn't appear here in the form of conscious devotion to the sex partner, still it can lurk beneath the surface as a differently focused desire or an unresolved issue of desire in the sexual agent's life. Sexual motivation is so unclearly strong, so *moving*, that we must take its conscious part for the tip of an iceberg.

On a broadly plausible Freudian view, sex as such is profoundly meaningful to us because it speaks to the infant's condition of unhappy, anxious separation from the maternal source of life and nourishment. The emotional reality of infancy is not simply left behind in growing up, but remains foundational; and sexual connection is all the sweeter because it fulfills our primal desire in disguise, refining away the panic of the infant and the awesome tyranny of the mother, beautifully refiguring the beloved so as to represent (most often) both nurture and youth at once. Thus sex is a *great* time, a *great* adventure, *the* success, and *the* proof, because it moves us with the urgent movement of the supremely needy infant. And an infant's passion, though not the highest love, is undoubtedly love.

In remarks entitled "Love, the Answer to the Problem of Human Existence," Erich Fromm speaks of an ontologically fundamental problem of separateness common to all conscious beings and thus sidesteps the Freudian task of elucidating emotional issues with reference to a life story.[24] One might prefer this more adult-centered view. The two diagnoses are complementary, however. The anxious infant is on the front line of our ontological predicament and feels our foundational feelings about the possibilities of profound loss and bliss in that situation. We can say, then, that sex is a specially attractive objective because it obscurely *seems* to be, or so movingly resembles, "the answer to the problem of human existence." On either account, sex is a stalking horse for love. Sex without love is a false objective.

Now let us take up the romantic view of sex as a breakthrough to love. This case, which we may call the case of the romantic opportunist, presents a mirror image of the other. The sex pursuer's surface goal is a good time, with a somewhat repressed deeper goal of overcoming separateness from nourishing human warmth; the romantic opportunist, meanwhile, adopts that warm union as an explicit goal but has made a deeper, probably less conscious decision to locate and possess that union as a worthwhile item in his or her portfolio of experiences. Otherwise there would not be such anxiety about "missing a chance"—construing love as a special opportunity like meeting a celebrity or attending a fabulous concert. In the romantic opportunist's perspective, sex with love provides the best of everything: an unlimited reciprocal affirmation of persons (as in marriage) combined with the accessibility and excitement of *this* place to be dwelt in *now* as a world unto itself. There is adventure without distracting danger, victory in a unique, ineffable private "game" rather than in a conventionally discussible "sport," and proof of soul power as well as body power.

The sex pursuer is much more interested in the experience than in who the experience is with. On that view, the individual identity of the partner is replaced, in effect, with a perennially relevant but generic, vague, hidden beloved. The romantic opportunist, on the other hand, confirms the individuality of the beloved in the present moment but remains relatively blind to the beloved's past or future. Each of these approaches looks defective from the standpoint of a love idealism that ties the self-realization of a lover to the maximal movement toward a beloved, that is, to a maximal commitment.

Even granting a commitment principle, it can still be asked why lovers should care what happens outside of love. Why should they, or anyone, "hold out" for sex only with love? How would a general sexual ethic be implied by an act that concentrates entirely on a particular beloved? Lovers' answers to this question will of course differ in meaning (if not necessarily in prescribed conduct) from purely hedonistic answers, since their axiom is movement to the beloved rather than self-gratification; nevertheless, lovers' answers can vary widely, depending on how they are disposed to make ethical generalizations of any sort. Some will simply not care, even in their own case. A person may have dozens of casual sexual encounters before and after a love relationship, but within that relationship, just while it lasts, tie sex fiercely to love. Love makes for different rules. But another person may be so strongly interested in the prospect of "true love" as to want to watch for it for years before it arrives and honor its memory forever after it ends. This person need not judge that nonloving sex is wrong—only that "This isn't it." Sex is worth not doing in one situation because of the way in which it is worth doing in another.

Another person might weave an idealism of love together with other ideals of human dignity, fidelity, proper care for children, and so forth, into a code of conduct requiring that sex connect with love. The main practical site of this more ambitious worth pursuit is marriage.

5.4 Marriage and divorce; eloping

Romance leads to marriage when the unlimited enthusiasm of the romantic lover for the beloved wants to fill time and public space from the brimming Now. Without that overflow, love is less sure of its excess. ("Will you still love me tomorrow?" is a question about what is felt today.) But romance is averse to making any sort of compromise with public life. To what extent does this tension turn on worth issues?

Marriage ideally brings romance, moral aspiration, and the public interest into one colossal worth package that is bound to be central in the social imagination, whether or not it works out most happily for the individuals who try to take it up. The key to it, practically, is to make and keep a vow. One would think that romantic lovers would shy away from any semblance of a contract, and guard their spontaneity; in fact, lovers do hold the "piece of paper" (the marriage certificate) in contempt, and apostles of love argue that marriage ought not to be considered valid where love exists no longer. But romantic lovers are not alarmed at all by the vows that gush forth from their hearts, since they have no wish to imagine a future emotionally different from the present. Marriage can seem to them an enhancement of their portions in each other, not because it reconciles them with the world but because it brings to the here-and-now altar of their love every remaining thing about themselves, all their entailments. The moral good of keeping their promise to each other is figured as a romantic good of extra giving.

This romantic rationale for marriage is not actually marriage's own charter. It is marriage's attractive aspect when proposed to premarital romantics. In marrying, there is a turning of love's tide from the privately centered to the publicly extended. But this extension of love into the public world is indeed a modulation of love, and not a compromise or combination of love with other ideals. The immediate giving of romantic love becomes *committed* love; flushing intensity turns into a *constructiveness* of love; the zest for overcoming obstacles that in romance so characteristically means getting away from one's chores becomes *practical*, fully engaged with all the challenges of daily living; and the lovers' giving of themselves from the world to each other becomes the lovers' giving of themselves as a pair back to the world, with a feedback effect of strengthened confidence in their relationship and a steadier enjoyment of it. Although we must admit that marital love is amply exhibited in nonmonogamous formats, in its monogamous form marriage keeps continuity with romance and adds magnitude to romantic love, conserving romantic inspiration within itself, and thus attaining greater love worth.

Does the nature of marital love worth entail that divorce is an unworthy action?

As I examine what seems the most powerful modern case for fully binding marriage, that of Denis de Rougemont, I am uncertain at times whether he means to *characterize* love in its marital form or to *qualify* love by other "ethical" or "existential" conditions:

> Fidelity is . . . a construction. An "absurdity" quite as much as passion, it is to be distinguished from passion by its persistent refusal to submit to its own dream, by its persistent need of acting in behalf of the beloved, by its being persistently in contact with a reality which it seeks to control . . . fidelity thus understood sets up the person. For the person is manifested like something made, in the widest sense of making. It is built up as a thing is made, thanks to a making, and in the same conditions as we make things, its first condition being a fidelity to something that before was not, but now is in process of being created. Person, made thing, fidelity—the three terms are neither separable nor separately intelligible. All three presuppose that a stand has been taken, and that we have adopted what is fundamentally the attitude of creators. Hence in the humblest lives the plighting of a troth introduces the opportunity of making and of rising to the plane of the person.[25]

Rougemont's intent may be the same as mine, namely, to establish a distinct species of marital love and love worth. We both point to constructiveness. But there is a difference between a constructive activity *of love*, expressing love and succeeding on behalf of love—which is always primarily on behalf of the beloved and the relationship and only secondarily for the lover as a creature of the relationship—and a construction of *personhood* with the primary intention of "making" something. The former constructivism wants *love* not to be a sand castle washed away by time; the latter wants enduring significance for *a person's life* as a matter of adequate identity.

Rougemont wants to show that divorce is ruled out by an adequate conception of marriage. To bring forward the principle of marital fidelity in its strongest form, he combines his sense of marital love with his person-building philosophy—a judicious mixture, in its own right, of existentialist voluntarism (authentic subjectivity realized "by virtue of the absurd") and the classic objective conception of happiness ("Call no man happy until he is dead"). This makes a strong position, I think, but I question whether his conclusions, which evidently depend on appeals to creation and action worth, tally with considerations strictly of love worth.

There are four important distinct perspectives in which divorce might be considered. One is merely loveless: to people who happen to be married to each other but have no love, divorce is an eminently live option and probably an attractive one. A second is purely romantic: divorce is an *imperative* option for romantic lovers who no longer love each other, for they are bound to make themselves available to different people, whether present or future, actual or possible. A third represents properly marital love: divorce signifies a disastrous failure, to be dreaded and shunned as unworthy of spouse-lovers—and yet divorce may acknowledge a love failure that has already occurred. A fourth, maintained by Rougemont, insists on honor: the decision for marital fidelity having been made, divorce is ruled out unconditionally, as it would mean the wreck of a personal career.

Might the fourth response be as loveless as the first? A marriage gone sour can be suffocating. Holding a spouse in a bad marriage can express vindictive hate rather than love. (We can surely agree that a commitment in hate is worse, from any love-related point of view, than an absence of commitment.) Suppose a couple reaches their golden wedding anniversary in a state of long-confirmed mutual distaste. But these spouses are not snarling rats in a cage; they are proud of their marriage's durability. From the fourth perspective, they are to be applauded for standing by their vows. Only in the third perspective is there regret that they failed to hold their marriage together as a *love* accomplishment. They have shown a triumphant will to control their practical reality, perhaps, but (it can be objected) they have not persisted in genuinely acting for each other. The old marrieds may make the tough reply that they have acted for each other in the sense and with regard to the issue that counts. They claim they understood that in entering the practical partnership of marriage they were leaving romantic fancy behind. But, I ask, can marital fidelity have so little to do with tenderness and joy? This is a serious difficulty, and the fourth perspective apparently doesn't feel it.

I can see three strong moves to address the difficulty. One splices together love and the ethics of fidelity; the two others involve modifications of our idea of love.

(1) Marital lovers, like charitable lovers, flex strong muscles of voluntary engagement in love, rejoicing that there can be so much self-determined, well-thought-out movement auxiliary to the basic impulsion; still, love cannot be guaranteed or commanded. The marriage vow, then, if uttered without any implicit reservation, must invoke a moral consideration outside love. Marital lovers do extend themselves into time and public space far more confidently and effectually than romantic lovers, and they do trust their love to sustain them in this, but they still cannot claim to have the love completely under their control. An honorable person can stand by a promise, however, and proves worthy in doing so even if the path of honor leads into a desert. If, as seems evident, there are strong personal and social reasons to uphold the institution of marriage, the alliance of marital love with the ethics of fidelity is most precious. It is a natural alliance, for the ethics of fidelity does hold an appeal for marital lovers.

The partnership of love and honor might seem less than ideal if we want to understand marriage as a "blessed" condition of greater worth than other covenantal partnerships. We have uniquely high hopes in celebrating marriage, and the vow of spouses to be lovers of each other, not merely partners, is related to the expectation of a maximum of happiness. An emotionally dim golden anniversary might represent one sort of success, but (on this view) it must also represent a failure.

If we want to conceive an ideal sufficiency of love to marriage, we must see whether our understanding of love can be expanded to include the requisite principle of constancy.

(2) Our golden-anniversary spouses might appeal to a Kantian notion of practical love to claim that they do not, after all, lack love. "Love out of inclination cannot be commanded," and so cannot have been the real object of the marriage vow; the vow must rather have aimed at a policy of beneficence—as they have indeed doggedly carried out toward each other in their partnership.[26] *Ethical* love is the higher love, in any case. (3) Alternatively, the spouses might take a theistic line suggested by Rougemont and associate their "constructive" activity of staying together, despite the failure of mutual attraction, with the indefatigable divine love. Divine love can create the very goodness of its beloved even if the beloved is a vile enemy of goodness itself.

If we can adjudicate these two somewhat counterintuitive claims on love, we will thereby determine something crucial about ethics, on the one hand, and theology, on the other. *Can* we think about love in tough Kantian fashion? That would put it in our power to eliminate love tragedies, perhaps the main threat to the coherence and cogency of moral living. If, on the other hand, we admit that we are unable to save ourselves from such tragedies, *can* we regard as a real prospect what might better be dismissed as a fantasy of almighty love from beyond the world?

Whatever we think about love must proceed from a distinction between loving and nonloving motivations. I've suggested that the important difference love makes to motivation is movement. Love is an impulsion. Without the gracious revelation of the greater good of the beloved, greater than the lover could have fashioned or forecast, there would be no love worth in submitting to the beloved's claim. If we stay within these bounds in conceiving love, we must admit a contingency in it. Those who want to support Kantian answer (2) might argue that respect for one's covenant partner is relevantly similar to impulsional love insofar as it involves a rational "inspiration" and "enthusiasm." For Kantians, there is indeed a contingency at the threshold of moral conduct: Will agents realize their own true identity as agents of reason? When they come to themselves, see their best light, and act on it, they are (like lovers) exceptionally empowered—for reason stands where flesh falls—and they attain a happiness that is unconditional and therefore superior (though not necessarily complete). There is a sort of romance of reason—quite giddy, really, when it leads one into strange acts like telling the truth to a murderer or staying married to someone you dislike. Ironically, though, marital love meant to be less giddy than that. It meant to solidify the ordinary terms of happiness rather than unsettle them.

Kant himself admits the incompleteness, for finite agents, of a purely rational gratification; in fact, the distressing gap between the purely rational "supreme good" of fulfilling duty, which is in the agent's power, and the "complete good" of a gratification both rational and sensuous, which isn't, must provoke faith that virtue will be divinely rewarded more fully than it can reward itself. So we see lurking within the tough Kantian view of "practical love" an ongoing negotiation with the hope of happiness, necessarily including (we should add) love happiness.[27] The unpleasant old Kantian spouses should perhaps be warned not to put off their hopes of happiness to some future world in which they are freed from each other. That vision might reflect a disastrous misunderstanding of how eternity and God are met. Besides, their daily unhappiness is a live moral concern insofar as it weakens their ability to act beneficently toward each other.[28] Therefore they ought to hope for a miraculous grant of divine happiness *now*, *here*, overriding their old inclinations.

Somewhat surprisingly, then, the "practical love" view leads to a position very like the "divine love" appeal of answer (3). We hear answer (3) in a popular thesis of theistic wedding sermons: while human love can never be assured, God's can, and faith in God involves confidence that divinely inspired charity will make good on any failures of marital love. We ought to take seriously at this point the possibility that the marriage-guaranteeing divine love beyond human love is *translove*, a power or pattern in events resembling our paradigmatic loves yet differing from them so much as to elude human attribution. Is divine love an impersonal and universal supportiveness that, like gravity, is totally reliable once adequately understood? Or is it preferential and passionate, like a personal act, present only by free grace? Monotheist theology shuttles between these two characterizations, wanting the Good to be both ideally perfect and personally relevant. On the ideal side, as a universal principle, divine love is not anyone's moving or anyone's portion, and so is beyond all worth reckoning. Implemented in personal lives, however, it becomes dramatic, as in the love-worthy figure of the martyr.

One can make a parallel case for a more fundamental eros than the attraction of interhuman erotic love—a responsiveness to all existing things insofar as they are vital and beautiful.[29] This transworthy eros-sensitivity would be as ontologically inescapable as perfect charity-spontaneity. It, too, would be realized in human hearts only with twists of preference and lurches of passion. If charity is like basic physics, binding things together in relative indifference to their individual forms, then eros is like basic chemistry, its elements the noticeable identities of things and their relations. The sexual "erotic" is only one set of particularly intense moves within a general search for ways in which beings can be energetically, self-actualizingly together. Our erotic affirmation that every being has its beauty is as strong in principle, and as limited in practice, as our charitable affirmation of our own agentic flourishing in benevolence. (Eros on this definition is quite different from the world-denying, death-seeking, infinite longing that Rougemont finds in Tristan and associates with Gnosticism.)[30]

In marriage, it is charity, human if not divine, that provides the ideal anchor, not eros. "Love is not love which alters when it alteration finds" is the formula for marriage. Eros's potential consistency is opposite to charity's: the perfect erotic lover finds anything lovable, no matter how altered, *uniquely*, and so loves always differently, while the love of the perfect charity-lover is always the same, since it flows from the lover's own definite love personality. Eros has probably played a great part in captivating the marital lover, and can continue to sweeten and sharpen the love, but charity is in the driver's seat once the lover has determined to uphold relation with the lovable other. The marriage vow expresses this balance of the loves and provides the bridge between marital love and ideal faithfulness. At the same time, it tilts interpretation of divine translove toward a universal, reliable supportiveness.

☙

If tying love to honor is the essential accomplishment of getting married, there might seem to be no substantial objection to eloping. Running off to get married used to be a fine romantic gesture and a social scandal for the same reason: eloping vetoes everyone else's veto on a marriage. From a romance-affirming point of view, eloping is the sufficiently romantic way to enter marriage; for marital love's purposes, eloping is too romantically private and flighty, eligible only as a last resort. Marital love's judgment that eloping is unworthy is, in the marital realm, more substantial than romance's approval.

Eloping as a dramatic act of running off has become rare in contemporary Western societies, because it has become extremely common in another, more ambiguous form. Many couples now enter what they conceive as committed relationships without submitting themselves to social endorsement by formally marrying. They are allowed to do this by the absence of effective social restraints on cohabitation. And yet there is a sense in which a cohabiting couple is stipulatively married, like the couple that has run off in the old-fashioned way, while the world waits in suspense to see whether they will assume a respectable place in the social order. If they self-consciously present themselves to society as "partners," they evidently set up as an example of marital love while at the same time making, indeed more perfectly making and indefinitely extending, the elopers' gesture of rejecting external constraints. Sometimes the mood of this relationship is intensely marital and not at all romantic: the couple is paradoxically determined to create a public reality on privately improvised terms. But even when the lovers' mood is predominantly romantic, just in cohabiting they subject themselves to certain conventional notions of lasting relationship, including generally accepted moral norms of good or fair treatment. Their relationship to honor is not focused on a point in the manner of the old-fashioned elopers who have to find a justice of the peace before dawn. They have more negotiating latitude. But they are on a tether.

In a debate with defenders of conventional marriage, today's elopers might bring up reports of outrageous enforcement of marriage customs. In 1995, for example, a man in southern Egypt started a fatal gun-battle because his sister held her husband's hand at her own wedding ceremony, contrary to a tradition he cherished.[31] An extreme case like this makes clear, they might argue, that control of the public shape of relationship cannot be trusted to tradition. Once the authority of tradition is limited, responsibility for determining the form of a relationship necessarily belongs to the persons entering the relationship. Therefore, *not* to elope in some fashion would be maritally unworthy. (This claim is honored today even in conventional weddings by including personalizing touches in the ceremony.)

But we could argue the other way from scenarios at the opposite extreme. Think of an eighteen-year-old woman cohabiting with a man irregularly (but in conformity with her own ideals of relationship) in her bedroom in her family home and producing a series of babies that her parents are obliged to care for. Evidently the shape of a relationship cannot be entirely within the prerogative of individuals entering it. It might be replied that this argument misconstrues a general moral issue of consideration for other persons as a mandate for marriage customs. But it could likewise be replied against the earlier argument that the extreme enforcement of marital honor standards by the Egyptian man reflects a failure of moral consideration rather than a defect in custom. Taken together, the two examples show that marital love, by virtue of its public orientation, must undertake a negotiation between moral responsibility (in which conscience is sovereign) and social observance. Eloping remains unworthy, for marital love, if by eloping we mean an overbalancing toward the private in this negotiation.

5.5 Parenting

Begetting a human being starts an endless chain of immeasurably important consequences. Whoever has become a mother or father has by that fact won a significant share in the collective human reality. The awesome unworthiness of a negligent parent is the inverse of begetting's great worth; it is an intensely regrettable spoilage, as though Leonardo were to paint a masterpiece and then leave it out in the rain. Begetting does not require talent like Leonardo's, to be sure; it is part of our inherited design that befalls us, like breathing and eating, more than it is any sort of invention. (Religiously interpreted, as a participation in a divine power or scheme, begetting is transworthy.) But begetting *is* subject to choice. Even though the worth of begetting could be deemed merely potential, considering that it can be negated by withholding child care, we could put the point the other way around and say that child-raisers must be devoutly grateful to begetting for giving them their chance. Irresponsible pregnancies cannot be explained solely by thoughtlessness; the worth stature of the begetter is a great lure, particularly for women, whose actions of gestation and delivery are so impressive. Yet it must also be said that on mature consideration the good parent is far more impressive than the begetter as such.

The worthiest parenting action, partly because it is most difficult and partly because its effects are felt to be most precious, is conducting a relationship beneficently with new persons in order that they, in their unprecedented individual characters, and the world, a massively solid yet trembling edifice, can fit harmoniously together. This activity has a work aspect, for it is a necessary chore; it often has an obvious play aspect; and it has an aspect of action proper in that it exploits a collective potential just for the sake of doing so. But no one doubts that parenting is most profoundly marked as a form of love. Once the parent's good is captured by the child's, the worth of parenting accrues to the parent primarily in the rapt position of the lover, not in the independence of the worker or player or in the balanced interdependence of cooperators. At the same time, the disciplines of work, play, and cooperation are demanded of the parental lover.

The begetter, as such, has at most an imaginary relationship with the child to come. This is a tenuous expression of love, hard to separate in essence from a general adventurousness or inclination to make things. But parental love, much firmer in itself, also takes over a major part of begetting's worth. Begetting in barest form is a powerful relationship with the world, renewing it and determining its future composition; and since a beloved child *is* part of the future existence and identity of the world, is "youth" in a general as well as in an individually specific sense, parental love is a way of loving the world at the same time that its object is a person. Adoptive parents realize this no less fully than parents who happened to beget their children; it makes no difference that the physical production of the children was not their accomplishment. Educators, too, are love-worthy in this way. (Although educators at advanced levels seem to work in the opposite direction from child-raisers, introducing a world to persons more than persons to a world, they are still drawn to the good that comes about through the constitution of a new world by these persons.)

To miss being a parent is to miss the most deeply optimistic relationship with the world. From the point of view of parental love, it is to miss the real world. Not many do miss parenting entirely, in the broad sense of "parenting" that includes what relatives, friends, educators, and responsible citizens do for the sake of installing new persons in the world. But some people steer away from it—even educators, and even parents. Why? Are they incapable of appreciating, or insufficiently charmed by, the emerging good of the world-as-young? That would show a constriction of eros. Or are they afraid of the openness of the situation when dealing with the young, the necessary shortage of valid solutions to the questions and conflicts that will arise? Do they simply not see how they would conduct themselves? That would show a limitation in charity.

The normative balance between eros and charity in marital love prefigures a similar requirement in parental love. As a human love, parenting cannot thrive without the nourishment of youthful cuteness. But the parental relationship makes sterner, more far-reaching demands. The parental lover *means* to care for the child, even when the child is repulsive. Sometimes in explicit vows, parents link their parental love to larger humane considerations and to the ethics of fidelity, just as bride and groom make their marital love a point of honor. Thus parenting can be defined normatively as "life-long covenantal advocacy" (Hartwig).[32]

Although some worthy parents are single and some worthy spouses are childless, marital love and parental love are schools for each other. Each is expansive; each succeeds and gains confidence in making all sorts of accommodations. Each beckons to the other for the sake of a peculiarly powerful reverberation that can occur in their conjunction: in two or more parents loving their child together there is a collective realization for which "cooperation" and "teamwork" are not quite adequate categories. There is now a plural loving subject enfolding the singular lovers. The joint approaching of the child in parental love intensifies and confirms the mutual approaching of the marital lovers. Now there is a more personally binding expansion of marital love than was ever involved in the project of dealing with the public world as such, and a more passionate deepening of parental love than the cuteness of children could sustain by itself.

5.6 Love's limit-objects

Because love is a passion for communion, it does not want to accept limits. I'll consider here three extreme possibilities of love corresponding to three kinds of objects that seem initially to be beyond love's reach.

The dead

According to Kierkegaard, the "work of love" in remembering the dead is the purest proof of love: "When one wants to make sure that love is completely unselfish, one can of course remove every possibility of repayment. But this is exactly what is removed in the relationship to one who is dead."[33] Often there is no call to prove unselfishness in love; love can be celebrated as a great benefit to the self. But we understand that love's benefits come through motion toward the other, looking toward the other *more* than back on oneself. Love involves freedom from oneself as hitherto known and as presently graspable. One is caught by the other, receives one's love-self back from the other, and is then able to go on more happily. Loving someone dead is the most perfectly free movement outward from self, receiving a love-self back only as a question. To be sure that we are not thinking of some comfortable arrangement of memories, or of a pain-relieving or exhilarating fantasy, we must look for this love only in *grieving*, a frustrated moving toward a beloved whose absence is felt.

There is already a popular psychological discussion of the conditions and amounts of worthwhile grieving. Our question here is: What *love* sense can it make to approach the nonexistent *as* nonexistent? If I affirm the continued existence of my dead beloved as a past or future reality, I nurse our relationship through a period in which we are challenged by separation. Or I intend the holding of our time-dispersed realities together in eternity. *Remembering* the beloved would seem to be precisely the work of sustaining relationship, a work of presencing, while grieving, in contrast, means reaching vainly for one who isn't there and incurring bruises from impossibility. Remembering can be practical as grieving is not. If I carry out the provisions of a dead person's will, or build a monument, I at least benefit him or her as an agent in our larger history. Would it be unworthy, then, for grieving not to give way to remembering?

The wholehearted griever feels that remembering as "presencing" is really disloyal to the dead beloved. The rememberer's will establishes itself in its own power and becomes all, whereas grief is only ashes. In fact, the griever ought to be disturbed by Kierkegaard's suggestion that love for the dead is the most perfectly faithful, hence godlike love, since that makes grief into a sort of spiritual athleticism.[34] The griever is not trying for happiness, but trying to be honest about unhappiness.

The griever does have one sort of satisfaction. Grief proves that the dead one is not unlovable in being dead. Death can deprive love of happiness but not its dynamism. Death does not shrink love's domain. Love must be a very large domain, then (albeit dark), and those who attain portions in it must be (though painfully) great.

The enemy

How can one lovingly approach another being who is engaged in the antithetical movement of spoiling relationship? Christianity and Buddhism both make a major theme of enemy-love, which for their purposes is a proof of purification from worldliness. Christians hope for human participation in the uniquely unconditional love that the world's Creator can show creatures; Buddhists work for a dissolution of selfhood, the root cause of suffering, through unconditional compassion.[35] But these are transworth claims. How could evil be embraced worthily by love?

Aquinas suggests a couple of oblique approaches to the enemy. Loving one's value-contrary, evil or the enemy as such, is admittedly impossible; and one ought not to trivialize the enemy by focusing on some more congenial attribute that is artificially abstracted from a hostile gestalt. But one can love the enemy under a different description. One can love humanity generically and the enemy as a human being. (A closely related though distinct possibility is to *sympathize* with the enemy as a fellow tenant of the human *condition*.) Or one can love an individual as loved by someone else, for the other lover's sake. "For since man loves his neighbor, out of charity, for God's sake, the more he loves God, the more does he put enmities aside and show love towards his neighbor: thus if we loved a certain man very much, we would love his children though they were unfriendly towards us."[36] But love on either of these plans reaches through the individual to a different object: the beloved genus or the other beloved individual whose "sake" is the lover's true concern. The enemy may get benign consideration on this approach, but the core of the love challenge has not yet been addressed.

Another model is suggested by ordinary forgiveness, a noble manifestation of ordinary decency. The forgiven person is reckoned with as evil in one way—there *is* something that needs to be forgiven—but finally posited as lovable. The goal of forgiveness is an affirmative relationship and happiness. Often difficult, forgiveness is also often a practical necessity: aggrieved parties can see that everyone's interests are best served by setting offenses aside and making new, hopeful starts in personal relationships. In that sense, forgiveness belongs to the fabric of ordinary life, although it is perhaps most often a blind or spasmodic act, a shrugging off, rather than a genuinely loving approach to the offender. It is a sort of cleansing act that makes the interpersonal atmosphere immediately fresher.

True enmity, however, rejects forgiveness. Thus, love of the enemy must be more extraordinary than love of the momentarily misguided.

We might seem to have come close to the possibility of enemy-love when we appreciated fighting as a kind of action (see section 4.3). But the rewards of fighting lie in the fighting, that is, in attacking and thereby testing one's own and the other's good. Enemy love means approaching, as a good to promote and bind yourself to, an agent who disallows your deepest basis. One can intend to oppose the project and love the person, but the road to the other person is barred, for the moment, by the inimical project. How can one approach and bind oneself to one's own undoing? The good that I have tried to build into my identity, if I am loyal to it, forbids me to set enmity aside unilaterally. (I may humbly disregard what is *merely* my own—but more than that is at stake.) A would-be enemy has no power, of course, over an almighty Creator or Enlightened Mind or ontologically necessary communion of all beings, but within the world, where the portions of existence and goodness are contested, an enemy can be frightfully dangerous to love's designs.[37]

One can place the problem of the enemy within the presumptions of ordinary forgiveness, holding out for an ultimate turnaround in the relationship. A Christian's martyrdom, for instance, may be the very thing that changes the attitude of persecutors and makes heavenly communion with them possible. How, though, can a Christian aspire to be part of the implementing of unconditional love in the strictly worldly relationship of enmity? The most extraordinary practical possibility of all would be that of *dealing with* the enemy, *as an enemy*, *lovingly*. Augustine needed to establish this possibility, because he thought that Christians are obliged to take part in the maintenance of the world, even by using lethal force on behalf of the state. He conceives the Christian police officer or soldier as dealing with enemies of justice (1) in sincere, intense devotion, (2) in pursuit of a clear understanding of persons and relationships, and (3) benignly.[38] Let us assess these aspects of enemy-love in turn, bearing in mind that it contains now the shocking possibility of *loving killing* of enemies.

(1) The sincerity of enemy-lovers appears in their regretful demeanor and their scrupling to commit no more harm than is necessary. We see that love is relevant to the relationship of enmity, because there is a distinctively loving way of conducting oneself in it. The enemy-lover realizes subjectively, passionately, what has always been a prudential consideration in war: the best belligerence is that which least compromises the peaceful coexistence that must follow. Now, one may doubt whether it is realistic, or even desirable, to expect warriors to conduct themselves sorrowfully. A consistently sorrowful soldier would have lessened chances of success in a just cause. But a gleeful killer isn't wanted either. In popular narratives, combatants of good moral character always fight with noticeable regret and restraint, enthusiasm for violence being reserved for the villains. To the extent that the restraint of the good uniquely handicaps them in fighting, a higher-level drama of opposition between good and evil is brought out. A complete "fight fire with fire" approach would suppress that drama. So a *decency* at least, a minimal love, is already manifest in the scenarios of just use of force that we ordinarily imagine. A more devoted enemy-love turns this ordinary glimmering into a bright light, intensifying the dramatic opposition to evil.

An advocate of nonviolence may claim that love of enemies prohibits harm entirely on this ground of subjective purity. Popular narratives do not take the logic of restraint far enough; a purely loving agent must always participate in enmity by suffering harm rather than inflicting it. The ancient ahimsa (no-harm) ideal nurtured by Hindus, Jains, and Buddhists supposes that the supreme task of every soul is to free itself from entanglement in worldly actions, of which violent actions are the most oppressively binding. Gandhi brought ahimsa into the political mainstream, arguing that nonviolent action alone can neutralize the poisons of injustice.[39] But while there is clearly much to say for ahimsa as a strategy for departing from the world, or as an approach to personal tranquility, it is less clear that a nonviolent agent can, in that character, take adequate responsibility for the course of life in the world. Arjuna, after all, had to fight, even if Gandhi would have steered him differently.[40] The crucial issue becomes one of interpreting the true dimensions and consequences of conflict, and so our attention is directed to the love criterion of clarity.

(2) The strongest argument for Augustinian enemy-love could be that it promotes clearer recognition of the moral reality of conflict. Unjust aggressors are met in the evil character they have adopted, their unacceptable threats to the innocent are acknowledged with appropriate intolerance, and the loving officer of justice becomes the means by which an obligatory intolerance of evil is realized within the fabric of worldly life (rather than haunting the world from outside it). The enemy-lover neither surrenders the world spiritually nor surrenders to the world. Like a parent who sometimes punishes a child because love itself requires not letting the child fall into the illusion that evil is good, the enemy-lover teaches the terms of true worth to offenders by resisting their evil.

Gandhi's nonviolent pedagogy has the very same intentions, however. The suffering of harm by nonviolent resisters clarifies injustice for the offenders by evoking their shame; at the same time, the resisters clarify through their loyalty to coexistence with the offenders the prospect of a *personally real* peace that can replace the conflict. Because it is confrontational and politically purposive, Gandhian nonviolence is responsible to the world just as Augustinian enemy-love means to be. It has the love advantage that it avoids the terrible passions and estrangements of violence that make Augustinian enemy-love such a tenuous possibility psychologically. It has the disadvantage that it has only been shown to serve love's purposes under special conditions—with a certain type of issue, a certain caliber of opponent, and a certain discipline and teamwork of lovers—outside of which it may do more harm than good.[41] But in any conflict situation a worthy lover will want to ask, Can we devise a way of confronting evil and working for the true well-being of all without harming the other? The "nonattachment" of love can prove itself in the lover's sacrifice not only of bodily well-being but also of ordinary practical assurance. Love, moving, will run risks. Love will balance hope and perception, aiming for the middle ground between irresponsible fantasy and the practical status quo. Gandhi and others have proven that nonviolent action is not essentially fantastic and thus have made nonviolence a permanent and imperious item on the menu of enemy-love. Augustinians who decline to try the Gandhian method may have to admit that their main commitment is not to love.

(3) The question of benignity brings out most plainly the different metaphysical assumptions that divide Augustine and Gandhi's conceptions of enemy-love. Both hold that love means bringing a transworldly spiritual reality into the world. Both speak for religious traditions that tend to emphasize a discontinuity between ultimate spiritual reality and the world

we now live in. But the Christian twist on discontinuity is more dramatic, more imbued with adventure and fighting worth. For Christians, a great turnaround, repentance, is central in the paradigmatic spiritual life, and death is conceived as a wrench away from physical existence into a qualitatively different and final spiritual existence. Hinduism thinks of persons changing gradually, incrementally, rather than by sudden reversals (not that these are precluded); assumes an unending stream of lives rather than a single finite life per soul; and thinks of victory over the world as a state, a realized happiness, rather than an event like winning a contest. Thus, to the Christian Augustine, it seems less improbable that a violent confrontation could yield clarity and spiritually benign consequences. A violent *handling of* offenders, harming them in body, could be the most honest and effective means of *dealing with* them so as ultimately to benefit them and strengthen communion with them.[42]

It is not easy to make Augustinian enemy-love work even within the Christian imagination. The scenario must be something like this: Unrighteously aggressive soldiers or criminals are about to kill innocent people, and Augustinian defenders prevent these crimes by killing the aggressors. According to the intention of the loving killers, the would-be aggressors actually benefit in that they subsequently meet their Maker without that crime (and all evil that would follow from it) on their record. But the darkness of the crime was already in their hearts. Killing them trapped them in that darkness. Thus killing, which precludes repentance, seems the one measure Augustinians could *not* take. (If salvation is determined at one juncture on a yes-or-no basis, the danger of the deeper evil the aggressors might get into if they are not resisted is probably irrelevant; all that matters is whether their basic orientation, especially at the critical moment of death, is toward or away from God.) Or is the idea that the offenders will appear before their Maker at judgment time *chastened* by their earthly punishment and so more probably turned toward salvation? We can obtain this effect only if we import into eternity the pedagogical conditions under which parents and children interact in the temporal order. It is hard to see how this is possible.

Capital punishment affords the one scenario in which these Christian objections could be met. The condemned do have time in which to be chastened and to repent, and the enemy-lovers have time in which to try to make their relationship with the condemned more affirming—although the real payoff of these changes must lie elsewhere than in this world. The remaining difficulty is that execution does not always find its victim in a better frame of mind, and the killing is required to take place regardless; in this case its spiritual upshot turns out to be no different than in the more categorically objectionable cases of police and military violence. This possibility should give a Christian pause. To rest content with having given a condemned person a finite chance to repent may be honorable, but it is not loving. The enemy-lover ought to want to widen as far as possible the pedagogical opportunity to turn the offender toward God, which requires keeping the offender alive.

I believe that the benignity test touches the relatively strongest point of the Gandhian alternative, which rests on a bias toward tranquility and constructive action in the longest term. Conversely, Augustine's loving killing can excel in passion and decisiveness but can present only the shakiest assurance that the consequences for the beloved are the best. It needs the support of faith that God also acts for the best in and through these confrontations. (The biblical portrait of God acting providentially through numerous violent events in the history of Israel is foundational for Augustine's way of imagining enemy-love, even though it doesn't entail that violence is generally desirable or permissible for God's followers.)[43]

Self-love

Moving toward the greater good promised by the other, the lover cannot be self-centered. But since the greater good is one of communion, the loving self can never drop out of love's sight; a complete self-sacrifice in love is tragic. Lovers affirm themselves in loving and ideally benefit from love more than they could benefit from anything else. Still, love involves a concern primarily to benefit the other. The lover's self-recreation and self-benefit is a function of this concern. It is a question, then, whether the self can *worthily* be a focus of its own love.

Bernard of Clairvaux's scale of love is interesting in this connection, because its top, as well as its bottom, is a form of self-love.[44] Bernard thinks that as fallen, merely "natural" beings, we are caught up in movement toward goods prescribed to us by our appetites. In this first degree of love, we love ourselves for our own *sake*. Then love may be raised to the second degree by enlightened awareness: gratefully acknowledging their debts to God, believers love God for their own *good*. In the third degree of love, humans love God for God's *sake* as a result of tasting God's sweetness. In the fourth and highest degree, humans can love themselves for God's sake, tasting the sweetness of God's will being done in their obedience to God.

Only Bernard's third degree of love conforms to the model of love I have used in this study. That is where ecstatic love worth first appears. But it is also where a difficulty inherent in love, the unsecured status of the lover, is raised most sharply. A divine beloved, on the theistic conception, is beyond the world. The lover of a worldly being at least has that place to stand at which the beloved is beheld and served; the basic reciprocity of worldly coexistence keeps lover and beloved in some sort of balance. But the Ultimate Lovable of the theist is greater than any being with which one can be in such a definite position—so great that one must fear oneself incapable and unworthy of communion with so unequal a good. Suffering now seems worthwhile, not only as a disruption of the lover's present reality but also as a station distinct from, and somewhat safe from, annihilation. "Because it is Thou who has made me, let it not be Thy will to destroy me utterly. Scourge me so that I may be made better, not so that I cease to be; beat me so that I may be given a better shape, not so as to crush me to bits" (Augustine).[45] Love of God requires a most drastic mortification of the basic attachment to self that is love's point of departure, threatening at the extreme a loss of love itself in the disappearance of the lover. One can make the most of the difficulty by claiming that only God is able to love God, that the appreciative human love of God must be borrowed from God; but then God's self-enjoyment cancels the structure we were interested in, the moving of one being toward another. An alternative is to rescue the loving self as recreated by God, maintaining the plural structure of love. This is what happens in the "self-love" of Bernard's fourth degree of love, which is anything but selfishness and yet is the ultimate good news for self-concern, an unconditionally worthy happiness. It is good news for love, at the same time, since it means a freeing of love from the last impediments of unworthiness in the lover.

In the higher love of self, love clears its last hurdle. But this is not an ordinary worldly possibility:

> It is impossible to draw together all that is in you and turn toward the face of God as long as the care of the weak and miserable body demands one's attention. So it is in a spiritual and immortal body, a perfect body, beautiful and at peace and subject to the spirit in all things, that the soul hopes to attain the fourth degree of love, or rather, to be caught up to it; for it lies in God's power to give to whom he will. It is not to be obtained by human effort. That, I say, is when a man will easily reach the fourth degree: when no entanglements of the flesh hold him back and no troubles will disturb him, as he hurries with great speed and eagerness to the joy of the Lord.[46]

Every form of love, I submit, aspires to some version of this condition. Bernard's account is warranted as much by a general appreciation of love as by a special theistic metaphysics. The dramatic unworldliness of romantic love, the world-harmonizing of marital and parental love, the "make no fuss" ethos of friendship and charity, and even the humble comfort of affection are all overtures toward this ideal of untroubled freedom. In a happily approaching lover's "speed," proof of free availability for a superior good, lies worldly love's intimation of immortality.

⧬

A crucial feature common to worthy actions in all genres, including love, is that they are ways of claiming a share of time. That is how they can furnish the contents of a life portfolio, each sort of worth attaching to a shorter or longer *while*: I worked in the morning, played in the afternoon, went to a political meeting in the evening, and later went romancing. This *adds up*. But there are other worth-related acts that do not occupy a while and cannot acquire the vindication of adding up. They do take time, of course, but only incidentally; they are really more positions taken with respect to time—functioning either to hold life-time all together or to release it from our grasp—so that asking whether they are worthwhile seems at once relevant and odd. We can proceed through time very thoughtfully and busily without straying into these areas at all. They may not be missed if they are not mentioned. But they are possible, they have in fact taken on great practical importance in the mainstream of common life, and their effects in worth thinking should be examined.

Chapter 6

❦

ON THE BORDERS OF WORTH

6.1 Fulfilling a life plan

A planned life is a closed life, Colonel. It can be endured, but it cannot be lived.
—The Mandarin, in the film *Inn of the Sixth Happiness*

The ideal of living by a plan is highly suspect. How can one preclude checks and upsets that will change one's purposes? How can life's potentialities be crowded into one corral? Suppose a teenage boy announces a plan to earn degrees at top schools, teach at top schools, publish a number of well-reviewed and discussion-provoking books in different areas, and retire comfortably to the seashore. It is a lovely vision. But suppose he then carries out his plan exactly. We tip our hats to him, yet reluctantly; behind the praise we must give him for his discipline and ability, we pity his confinement. What he might have missed by carrying out his plan, what he *must* have missed, looms larger in our minds than what he achieved.

Had the young scholar been influenced by the preceding account of the worth manifold, he might have formed a scheme to optimize life worth—playing on Monday, working on Tuesday, and so forth. Scheduling worth in this way cannot be completely absurd, since most people do arrange their days, weeks, and years according to certain ideals of movement between practical domains. But we know that none of the worth species are guaranteed to come into our lives just when we summon them. Play worth presupposes the saucily raised eyebrow of possibility; one can run around on any designated playing field and never see this eyebrow. There is no work worth without the imposition of practical necessity; one can show up regularly for "work" and yet never manage to be part of doing something that really

171

needs to be done; on the other hand, one can be caught by an inordinately large work demand that never lets one go. Action assumes a concord of free agents. Love assumes an onset of movement. And so one could arrange one's life by a scheme, hoping to include every major color in the worth rainbow, and fail to realize any of them. Or one might be enslaved to work throughout one's waking hours and yet play, help, fight, lead, follow, and love richly in one's work. Thus no worth schedule formulated in advance can be followed with confidence. Achieved worth lights up in the retrospections of the fortunate. Worth results in life always say as much about the structure and vicissitudes of life as they say about any individual character.

Yet simply being "open to life" is not a tenable alternative to following a life plan. Royce's point (revived by Rawls) has considerable force:

> If a man could live with no plan at all, purposelessly and quite passively, he would in so far be an organism . . . but he would be no personality. Wherever there is personality, there are purposes worked out in life. If, as often happens, there are many purposes connected with the life of this human creature, many plans in this life, but no discoverable unity and coherence of these plans, then in so far there are many glimpses of selfhood, many fragmentary selves present in connection with the life of some human organism. But there is so far no one self. . . . You are one self just in so far as the life that goes on in connection with your organism has some one purpose running through it.[1]

The principle that a worthy human life is unified by a single purpose turns up on several different lines of reflection. One is moral: an agent is expected to carry out a consistent program of virtue and justice, or at least to be able at all times to be reminded of a higher-order desire to have the right desires.[2] A serious audience would be horrified to hear that a certain person "was moral, for a while." Another consideration is biographical: one wants to be able to determine the significance, for better or worse, of everything that unfolds in one's life, so as to be able to tell one's life story adequately, and this seems to require some imputable long-term purpose by which "better" and "worse" may be gauged. One may not care about collecting all the details of one's life into a unified account and yet still need to face up to a fundamental question like "Has it been worth it?" or "Did I do what I really wanted to?" Finally, the forward-looking counterpart to these retrospective assessments is practical rationality itself. How can I look ahead into the future *at all*, let alone toward a "life worth living," without making plans, and how can I plan seriously and effectively without a guiding purpose? What would happen to our society's provisions for higher education and "career development" without a universal presumption of large, life-guiding aims?

None of these conditions requires the exact carrying out of a plan. The moral point of view does impose certain constraints on our practice, but it leaves wide freedom in choosing our material ends. The retrospective search for meaning in life is all the happier if important ingredients are seen to have come as surprises—best of all, if the great theme of one's life bursts out as a climactic discovery. Practical rationality is perfectly capable of foreseeing unforeseeableness and providing for flexibility. So it is easy to see that optimal worth (like good music) must lie in some balance of control and contingency.

The same structure shows up in our appreciation of others. We *respect* people for sticking to a program, and may even love them in gratitude for the benefits we reap from their consistency, but we *delight* in people for their ungoverned qualities. They are interesting and charming insofar as anything can happen to them, and from them, in their encounters with the world. That suspense and carnivalesque potentiality is what draws us into their lives. Romantic love, an adventure in mutual re-creation of the self, presupposes this uncertainty.[3] So does any relationship that deserves to be called intimate. Thus, a person who lives too much by plan is lost to romance and friendship. One obvious reason why I could not have included love or friendship in my sketch of the young scholar's life plan is that he needs luck to find lovers and friends; but it is also true that one needs flexibility to *be in* and hold up one's end of such relationships. More precisely, one needs flexibility together with consistent identifiability. There must be suspense *and* clue, surprises *and* a thread to follow.

As the worth balance of our lives gets composed, partly in our control and partly not, we tumble more or less blindly into major worth additions, particularly in the first third of a normal life span. We choose circles of friends, school programs, and jobs without understanding our options at all adequately, simply because we find ourselves willy-nilly in worth realms where some choice or other must be made. In some cases, one has enough room to stay clear of an ordinarily large worth addition. Many of us can avoid marriage, for instance. Or one can move forward in something like blind faith—which is how many people marry, or how they have children. The conscientious or prudent move in this situation might seem to be to hold back, showing the proper caution of drivers at night who won't drive beyond where their headlights shine. But there is a sort of daylight on the highway of life, after all, in the grand spectacle of what folk do; and another conscientiousness, a loyalty to life's large patterns, can bind the agent to a more broadly valid optimizing of the worth chase than the agent could have devised on his or her own.

The same logic applies to limitation. If forces beyond my control block me from some forms of worth, I may draw from life's spectacle the reconciling insight that individuals must have different, complementary shares of worth. In this case, though, the logic is treacherous. It can rationalize cowardice and oppression. Only when we are assured that the strongest possible conception of agency is applied to every agent, and that the greatest effort has been expended by each agent and for each agent's worth sake, can we go along in good conscience with life's planning life for us in this regard.

The acid test for the possibility of realizing worth by agreeing to life's plan is death. Death of all things makes it clearest that "life," as an event or process of worth-determination, cannot be *our doing* even though we *are* carrying it out—or, put differently, that our doing takes place within a larger reality that it can interact with but not change, rather like a fetus in a womb. Death makes the point that we (as worldly agents) don't ever come out of this womb.

6.2 Dying

What shall we *not* talk about under the rubric of worthy or worthwhile dying? I propose not to consider (1) dying taken to be instrumental to further life, since it's then understood as not really dying, and (2) dying simply as release from intense and otherwise interminable suffering, since this is obviously good (and "worthwhile" in a weird yet plain negative sense). I would also set aside problems of the definition of death—whether as regards (3) rival criteria of physical death as an event or process, or (4) death's phenomenological mysteriousness—except to note that since death involves a change from a condition in which the subjective evaluation of personal well-being is necessarily supreme (insofar as no one can sustain against you a different estimate than your own of how well you are) to a condition in which objective evaluation is necessarily supreme (since you no longer have anything to feel or say freshly about the matter), it *must* be an "enigma" *to* the subject who will die, while at the same time it *must* be a central point of reference for public assessment of a life ("Call no man happy until he is dead").[4] I want to focus on the worth of choices concerning how to die.

As to whether we have reason to go gentle into that good night, agreeing to death as part of life's plan for us, there are powerful things to say for death's contribution to larger patterns of living that we appreciate. Death is an integral part of the sexual reproduction scheme. According to the sex strategy, a life-form increases its chances of continuation by a strategy of self-diversification. Rearranging its genetic materials through sex makes a species a series of adventurous *experiments*, its continuity arising in conservation of its successes. A peculiarly momentous *partnership* defines the life of sexual mates and of parents and children. Members of the species *cooperate* in quite detailed ways as units of the species experiment, whereas an immortal individual would have to be regarded more as an experiment unto itself and would never get close to the worth neighborhood of action proper. Furthermore, the members of each finite generation have a definite window of opportunity, a shot at success yielding *victory* or defeat; and this portioning of time and effort is structurally fundamental for our worth thinking. The famous tedium of immortality is a worth effect.[5]

To test this claim, imagine that breakthroughs in physics and medicine have made us securely immortal. Each of us still controls a portion of what happens, and each strives to make his or her own portion beautiful and interesting. Although we are not playing against limited time, we are still playing against uncertainties of creation. Thus we are like musicians evolving ever more complicated parts in a universal symphony. The music grows ever more beautiful, and we are never bored. (It may be claimed that we would have to change into different persons over and over again to stay subjectively commensurate with this growing beauty. I don't see the necessity of this; but suppose for the sake of argument that our personal growth does not rupture our identities.)[6] Now, within any given time segment, some contributions might be more impressive and some might be relatively lame. So there does seem to be motivation for a worth chase. We can see that some members of the orchestra would be zealous to do well. Some others, however, would surely be content to do less, knowing that there will never be a time at which it turns out that any individual is more or less worthy than any other. Indeed, the short-term worth difference of low achievers never carries over into a long-term worth identity, for *there is no long-term worth identity*, either in amount of achievement or in quality (since anyone might ultimately take a turn at any contribution). That is a deep difference between the immortals' sort of personhood and ours. Do they have a life less anxious and jealous than ours? If so, they attain it by giving up our presumption of equal human responsibility and the passion that makes us glad or disappointed in each other's performances.

Religious conceptions of personal immortality guard against this worth problem by finalizing worth at the threshold of eternal life. The ultimately relevant sort of equality may be assured by a fire burning off everything unworthy in each person and burnishing everything worthy. Worth rankings implied by differences in earthly performance may be confirmed in an eternal hierarchy (like the levels of hell and heaven in Dante's *Divine Comedy*). Thus endless life is made intelligible by an end of life. Even an earthly life of endless rebirth, as conceived in Indian traditions, must come to a decisive point in the winning of deliverance, although on these assumptions it is the spiritual death of the false self, rather than physical death, that plays the terminator role.

We do not have the choice whether to die, but we do make practical choices affecting our exposure to the risk of death and our approach to death. Under what conditions does dying hurt one's campaign for a worthy life? What sort of dying makes the fitting conclusion or greatest enhancement of a worthy life?

With dignity

No one would choose to die in a worth-reducing or worth-mocking manner, except out of spite, or (in the case of a philosopher) to make a point about death's essential indignity. We have now a fairly firm moral consensus, I believe, that to claim dying's share of living and ideal human agency, one does best to participate fully, if not overweeningly, in making all necessary decisions respecting the approach to death and its consequences. The paternalistic medical model for treatment of the dying, prevalent in Western societies till recently, denies the dying a chance to exhibit the most meaningful self-control, that of judging: the only question of agency regarded as open on this model is whether the patient can stay calm in a sickbed, and the only power acknowledged in dying is the logistical nuisance of it. But the ideal of keeping the dying as unaware of their predicament as possible now seems drastically wrong as a general rule.[7]

The most popular loci of good dying all touch issues of dignity.

Suddenly

"Sudden" death, now wished for by many, used to be generally feared.[8] (It is a question here of *very* sudden death; scarcely anyone, I suppose, regards protracted death as desirable.) I see two sets of reasons to want to hold the experience of death in one's subjective portfolio: (1) Those who see earthly life as the gateway and qualitative key to eternal life will want to meet death deliberately in order to put their intentions in the best final order. Their prime concern will be their spiritual momentum at the point of death. They may want to appreciate their lives as whole units, from this ultimate retrospective point of view, or they may care about earlier details of life just in the practical way that a housekeeper cares about sweeping out every corner. (2) Those who simply aim to maximize the value of earthly life may want a full chance to appreciate it retrospectively, perhaps as a social event (friends and family gathered round); or they may be concerned not to fail in an integral part of the project of knowing oneself and understanding the human condition.

But there might be something to say for sudden death. Suppose I had an Uncle Herbert who was quite unexpectedly killed on the sidewalk by a piano falling out of a fifth-story window. This is just the sort of death a sudden-death fearer is afraid of. Why, then, does so unfortunate an occurrence strike me as funny? The answer is not (as on some theories of comedy) that I glory in not being Uncle Herbert. I am in no way gloating. On the contrary, I am drawn to the idea of dying in this fashion myself so that I can be someone else's amazing Uncle Herbert. There is something acceptable, survivable, about his indecorous demise. Herbert himself held religious beliefs that would have motivated him to confront his death carefully. Why am I not anxious about the final state of his soul? I must be thinking of him as *realized* already, solid and acceptable in worth terms. (My thought experiment is spoiled if death catches Herbert too young, or when he is in the midst of writing what would have been his great novel, or just after he has first taken a bribe.) My background thought seems to be that we cannot control the manner of our ending, but our lives are not thereby ruined. Thus, I make Herbert bob up from under the piano, in a way. The abruptness of his death is desirable also in making the point about the survivable contingency of life in a pure way, without the distraction of suffering. The self-knower may demand a full experience of dying, but sudden death is the more philosophical death for the onlooker. So in inclining toward a piano death I am not only flinching from the unpleasantness of an extended dying, I am partly also taking the onlooker's view of myself, as is characteristic of worth thinking.

At home, at peace, surrounded by loved ones

Sudden death, as such, is not in any sense a worthy death, whether or not its context lends a worth message to it. It is no sort of achievement. But the death most often desired by sudden-death fearers, the death that sudden death spoils, seems equally passive as far as the one dying is concerned. That the one dying has peaceful leisure in which to gather thoughts and intentions, and that the relevant others are supportive, is surely a kind of good fortune. The gathering of people proves reassuringly that worth *was* realized in all those relationships. The worth *of the proof* comes into the category of worthwhile experience, as "education," if it has a significant effect on the character of the one dying or of the onlookers. Can the one dying get credit for bringing this scene about, though? It seems that we would not esteem a dying man if he had chosen to avoid all hazards, hanging around his house so that he would have the best chance of dying in this fashion. Nor would we disesteem him if he raised his chances of not dying at home above the average by, say, hiking through the national parks. Would we esteem him for choosing to leave the hospital so that he could die at home? Yes, if he had to pay some price of discomfort or had to accept an earlier death.

Traditional sex roles make it easier for us to imagine a woman whom we admire for staying home so consistently that she is virtually bound to die there. But that is because we impute to her a life's work in the home. She is actually dying in harness, which represents a very different sort of dying worth from the death of peace.

In harness

To die *engagé* is to insist infinitely, as best a mortal can, on the worth of the activity in which death finds one. This may be a way of stamping a desirable meaning on one's own career. So Pericles supposed for the Athenian casualties:

> The consummation which has overtaken these men shows us the meaning of manliness in its first revelation and in its final proof. Some of them, no doubt, had their faults; but what we ought to remember first is their gallant conduct against the enemy in defense of their native land. They have blotted out evil with good, and done more service to the commonwealth than they ever did harm in their private lives.[9]

If I die in the act of writing this book—best of all, if I struggle, gasp, and just manage to rap out its last words before falling from my chair—it will seem as though I committed myself to the book, or rather to the ideal of the examined life, entirely. There would be a kind of noble unselfishness in this sort of commitment even if the object of my final concern had been only to straighten a roll of toilet paper: something *is* worth doing, one *does* hear a call. But if, on the other hand, death's approach makes me drop what I'm doing, a suspicion might be raised that I have merely been *passing* the time, seeking pleasure and avoiding pain, all along.

As purification

Another intensely purposeful death is sought by one who means to disengage from the practical world rather than to give it emphasis. In one clear instance, a "dignified yogic death" involves formal withdrawal from all worldly responsibilities, a carefully controlled fasting program, and a calm and deliberate embrace of the moment of death.[10] But outside the category of suicide (which I have been deferring) the same effect could be obtained by an ascetic approach to any worldly activity. One's death could come as a by-product of one's self-denial. It is possible that Simone Weil fatally malnourished herself because of her sense of responsibility for the hunger of others in wartime France.[11] If this is so, then her dying was approvable in her view insofar as it followed from an ethically requisite purification. (It is difficult to appreciate in the *engagé* category, because her starving was not a "work" and did not accomplish anything in the world other than her death.) A logically similar example is the military or political leader who dies as a result of refusing to duck or to wear a bulletproof vest. This person's choice not to be intimidated by the possibility of death was foolish from a utilitarian point of view, but it is a worthy emblem of freedom. Dying implements the choice unluckily yet consistently.

Consequentially

According to Plutarch, the Spartan lawgiver Lycurgus had an unusual opportunity to accomplish something worthwhile by dying. He got his fellow citizens to agree to abide by his laws until he came back from consulting the Delphi oracle. Then he died on purpose in Delphi.[12]

Anyone who writes a will hopes to accomplish something by absence—hopes that the absolutely vulnerable will of the dead will be held inviolable by the living and thus constrain them. St. Francis in his will forbade the members of his order ever to change his rule in any way.[13] Rich people often leave bequests with strings attached. Although most of us lack the spiritual authority or the control of wealth to compel our fellow creatures to follow our explicit instructions after death, everyone who dies binds the living in some fashion in leaving the world, encouraging them in some ways and inhibiting them in others, with better consequences or worse.[14] One of the strongest arguments against suicide is its horrific effect on one's survivors; a good argument for it, on the other hand, is that it can set (on Stoic or Epicurean premises) an inspiring example.

To summarize, my best death is shaping up as follows: at a suitably advanced age, I expire in the bosom of my warmly united family a few hours after collapsing on the important job I am doing, where I have grown gaunt through altruistic self-neglect; afterward, my life insurance payoff puts my grandchildren through college. Conversely, I most want to avoid dying alone, fat, gorging on chocolates, and leaving massive debts.

By one's own hand

Since we are mortal, any talk of choosing death can refer only to a manner or a meaning of death, not to death's occurrence. That is the trump card of the thoughtful advocate of suicide. An autonomous agent cannot turn a blind eye to any part of life that opens itself to his or her determination. To die in control of his or her faculties, true to a vision of worthy life, may be in an agent's power. Self-killing might offer a uniquely impressive proof of his or her capacity to make principles prevail over the inclinations of the flesh.

But there are considerable risks of self-contradiction in the suicidal project. As Augustine pointed out, Cato had to commend his son to Caesar's mercy before he killed himself to defy Caesar's tyranny.[15] What Cato meant as a courageous gesture could be interpreted as cowardly refusal to deal with a difficult situation. He was also denied straightforward suicidal efficacy, as he had to reopen a wound that a doctor had bound up.[16] Zeno the Stoic, in order to preserve his dignity and "life according to nature," committed suicide on the ridiculous occasion of falling and breaking a toe. He construed his accident as a sign from God that his time had come. (For Chrysippus, God's call was an inflammation of the gums.) At least Zeno's legend spares him any uncertainty in doing himself in; we are told that he simply held his breath.[17] Seneca, however, the greatest apostle of suicide as a road to freedom, could not get blood to come fast enough from his veins, or poison to work, and finally had to have himself carried into a vapor bath to die of suffocation; meanwhile, his wife's cosuicide was prevented at Nero's command.[18] A man who cut his own throat in England in the 1860s was saved, convicted of the capital crime of attempting suicide, and accordingly hung, but the hanging was not fatal because it reopened his throat wound and enabled him to breathe.[19] These are some of the more striking reminders that a suicide needs luck, like anyone else, to die in a desirable way. Death is not, after all, entirely within the would-be suicide's power. But I dare not deny that suicides can control some aspect of dying for morally important reasons. That would be unfair to many who have courageously given up their lives to show intolerance of their own inadequacy (as in shame suicides) or of an evil situation.

The best-known proponents of suicide worth in Western literature are Cynics, Epicureans, and Stoics who deny an afterlife. Rather than being overawed by the thought that earthly life's filling of time provides the sole possibility of good, they aggressively master time, impressed by the discretion of the agent to determine the meaning of the spending of time moment by moment, as especially on Epicurean reasoning, or altogether, as most dramatically in Seneca's celebration of the freedom one has to dispose *of one's life.* In contrast, those who suppose like Plato and Augustine that the meaning of earthly life is determined by its relation to eternal life argue that human time is not fundamentally at the agent's own disposal. We are like soldiers or servants of our "good masters," the gods, and we are bound to our posts.[20] By marrying time to eternity, one trades the prerogative of suicide for the transcendent expansion of life's meaning in divine providence. A sharp edge of this expansion within earthly living is the necessity of coping with any and all difficulties life may present. Life is a task given by eternity. But since eternity means the all-togetherness of *all* time and all interrelationships, not merely the unity of an individual agent's life, the exact outlines of the task posed the individual by eternity can never be made out entirely within the individual's own practical horizon. Thus the Stoic scenario of single-handedly implementing divine providence by suicide never obtains. Zeno and Chrysippus thought to imitate Socrates by seeking death only on a divine command, and yet the remaining and crucial difference in Socrates' case is that he was killed by others, that is, he submitted to a larger mechanism of fate than his own practice.

We come close to a rapprochement between these two views if a genuinely voluntary suicide is understood to be the divinely mandated *standard* response to a kind of unchosen event. The leading meaning of the act is then loyalty rather than mastery. Self-immolating Hindu widows might explain their action in this way; so might the overabundant volunteers for suicide bombing missions in terrorist causes.

Epictetus was fond of the game analogy for life and death. "I think it fitting for me to join in the game while the game lasts."[21] (Contrast James's portrayal of life as a *fight* from which we may not withdraw, cited in section 4.3.) In a sport, actually, there are four different kinds of unit of achievement: the event (in baseball, for example, the at-bat), the game, the season, and the career. The relationships between these units are evocative or symbolic of different configurations of the question of suicide worth.

The elementary baseball sin is to refrain from trying to get a hit or make a play. One shouldn't take up a position on the playing field if one hasn't "come to play." (The listless sort of suicide: "I didn't choose to live and now don't want to—so let me out!" Antisuicide: "But you *are* living nonetheless. The game has started and we're all in it. No other *you* is available to step in for *you*.") But suppose a player has had three hits in three at-bats, including a grand slam, has made a splendid play in the field and no errors, and in his ripe feeling of personal satisfaction wants to take himself out of the game in the fifth inning. Clearly the meaning of his activity precludes this: he has a nice collection of event-performances, to be sure, yet he is a player *of a game* that is won by a team in nine or more innings. (Stoics would make the analogical point about playing one's role in life.

Notice that if the player *had* to leave the game at this point, say with a pulled hamstring, he could justifiably say he'd had a good day.) Suppose next that a player comes to the last game of the season with a .425 batting average, already having passed the number of at-bats needed to qualify for a record. If he sits on the bench he will become the best all-time hitter for a season. (Players *have* been benched in situations like this.) But the player's team is in a down-to-the-wire pennant race. They need his help to win their last game. Even though he risks losing a momentous personal record if he doesn't get any hits, he is clearly obliged to play. Again, he is a player *of a game* that has this structure, a season's "race"—as it is equally part of baseball's structure that members of a twenty-five-man team can fill in for each other, which under other circumstances would enable him to sit the last game out.

Suppose next that the season is over and the player decides to retire rather than see his career go into decline. Or he simply doesn't have the heart for the game any more, so that it would seem disgraceful to him to continue. Although the team's management and fans will be disappointed, the player is bound by no obligation to the sport to play further. (There would be inordinate disappointment if the player retired on the verge of setting a major career record, say, one short of 755 home runs—but the decision would still be at his entirely free discretion.) Career performance is not bound as season, game, and event performance are. The player has freedom at this point because he *is* out of the game. The game stopped and he continued; therefore, he may decline to continue with the game when it resumes. (Similarly a "liberated" soul decides from a vantage point outside the round of rebirth whether or not to reenter it, on Buddhist views.)

Because we have drawn the boundaries of the game within life, we know that life is other than, greater than, and in crucial respects unlike the game. The meanings of a game are laid down like straight tracks, whereas the meanings of life, in which interpersonal exposure is *wide open*, are subject to continual struggle and re-creation. If we want to interpret an act of suicide on the analogy of retirement from a sport, we must discern a game-like-ness in life and fill in the counterpart to the larger ungamelike thing, "life" as it reclaims a retiring athlete, in the frame of reference the suicide enters by departing out of life. For Epictetus, life is fittingly regarded as a game both because it has its internal constraints, while one is in it, and because rational self-mastery places one in a position of judgment overlooking all temporal events. The larger and relatively mysterious frame of reference for him is divine providence. One wonders, though, how gamelike the reason-loving moralist has made providence itself, how artificially legible he has made his rules of "nature," how committed he is to suppressing any real complexity (and new challenge for judgment) in life outside the game:

Whatsoever station and post you assign me, I will die ten thousand times, as Socrates says, or else abandon it. And where would you have me be? In Rome, or in Athens, or in Thebes, or in Gyara? Only remember me there. If you send me to a place where men have no means of living in accordance with nature, I shall depart this life, not in disobedience to you, but as though you were sounding the recall for me. I do not abandon you—far be that from me!—but I perceive that you have no need of me. Yet if there be vouchsafed a means of living in accordance with nature, I will seek no other place than that in which I am.[22]

6.3 Sleeping

Consciousness is a kind of mastery of the world by the self, but—as the affliction of insomnia proves—also the world's tyranny over the self. The conscious self needs a "dimension of retreat" to maintain its separateness, and it has this in its ability to sleep (as Levinas argued).[23] Going to sleep is like a little Stoic suicide, a proof of freedom. This would be true whether in oblivion or in a busy, psychically worthwhile "dream-work." But sleep's liberation is only temporary. Jonah, the prophetic antihero who could go to sleep in a ship's hold while God's storm howled around him, still had to wake up to face his mission.

It might be objected that while sleeping does prove the power of the self to be by itself for a while, sleep is more typically an interruption of the self's projects. After all, without the need to sleep, one could farm an extra tract of land or hold down an extra job or read or write an extra set of books. Sleep is a limit to getting ahead, and to vigilance. Thus the sanity of workaholics and moral rigorists depends on their seeing sleep as worthwhile, which means acceding to sleep as part of life's plan for them. (I must accede to *more* sleep than my philosophy strictly requires, eight hours a night.) It seems, however, that in these projects of the self that are thwarted by sleep, the self must already have been stampeded by external circumstances. Why would one need to accomplish *that* much, except to prevail in a competition that was imposed on one—a competition that would escalate endlessly were it not for universal limiting factors like sleep? So the gracious necessity of sleep does protect the self, perhaps in spite of itself. One can always dance all night if one really wants to, and sleep later.

Sleep protects the imposed-on self but is no friend to lovers, for whom an infinitely zealous movement toward the other is joy and fulfillment. From devotion's point of view, no single act could be more worthwhile than waking up and becoming a candidate for togetherness. But waking up is not an act. It is more like a birth. We contemplate the enabling miracle of waking up to love in the otherwise maddeningly passive figure of Sleeping Beauty.

From the thought that there could be no real wakefulness without a sleep, no real freshening of life without a hiatus, there comes a sort of argument for reincarnation:

> Rabbi Zusya's younger son said: "The zaddikim [holy men] who, in order to serve, keep going from sanctuary to sanctuary, and from world to world, must cast their life from them, time and again, so that they may receive a new spirit, that over and over a new revelation may float above them. This is the secret of sleep."[24]

6.4 Intoxication; the Bataillean act

The choice to get intoxicated seems like defiance of worth questions, and in a more profound way than choice of "pleasure" or "recreation" or "frivolity" pure and simple. How merrily today's party animals (not like the crew of Plato's *Symposium*) would slam the door in the face of earnest inquiry!—so long as they were acting as party animals. But any choice of action is an affirmation of worth. Conscious beings cannot escape our question, not even conscious beings aiming to reduce or lose their consciousness.

Defiance is here, all the same. Of what kind? Is there a deliberate cultivation of ugliness, as in the use of profanity in speech? People do sometimes seek intoxication in order to be emotionally assaultive. But if this were a predominant or typical reason to get intoxicated, the use of drugs would be in much greater social disfavor.

We might look for an affinity with the sweeter, more sociable kind of defiance found in comedy. Charlie Chaplin's *Modern Times* (1936) contains two hilarious intoxication scenes. In one, some accidentally imbibed "nose powder" makes him spin like a top; in another, rum puts him to sleep in a bin of ladies' clothing. These misadventures are of a piece with everything else that makes us laugh in the movie. Intoxicated figures are comic for the same basic reason that clumsy figures are: they represent exceptions to good order, survivable incongruities that relieve us from having to believe too deeply in our unreliable arrangements for security and salvation. Unlike bumblers, however, who inflict their purely individual shortcomings on the world in order to prove that you and I can survive *acting like ourselves*, the intoxicated are gripped by a transpersonal power, like leaves blown by a great wind; they show, if they are resilient enough to be comic, that we can survive acting *not* like ourselves, that we may confide ourselves in a profound way to what transcends us. (The root meaning of the German words for intoxication, *Rausch* and *Berauschung*, is the movement of a great force, as in the English cognate "rush.") One reason to party, then, is to gain this comic/cosmic reassurance, jumping deliberately into the wind that blew the tramp around. Whether the wind is something in ourselves is a teasingly interesting possibility.

It may be objected that the proper and distinctive meanings of intoxication are darker than this interpretation recognizes. Doesn't Chaplin have to neutralize intoxication after a fashion, render it unreal, in achieving his comic effect? What, then, must be added to this picture to make it truer?

Some of the usual descriptions of intoxication are shockingly negative. The intoxicated subject is wasted, plastered, smashed, stoned, or blotto. "To intoxicate" means to poison. A legal synonym for "intoxicated" is "impaired." Such terms suggest that getting intoxicated expresses despair about worthwhileness and an abdication of action. We know that a classic reason to use drugs is to wipe out awareness of an unpleasant reality or to escape having to do anything about reality. On the other hand, happy people seek intoxication too. Is it possible that the negative descriptions properly apply only to the dregs left by the activity of getting intoxicated and not to the chief attractions it holds for nondespairing people? That to say, "Let's get wasted" is jokingly to label the whole experience by the apparently senseless part of it—as campers might joke that it's time to collect their mosquito bites? Yes; except that camping would go off all the better if one never ran into mosquitoes, and campers would take the option of bite-free camping if they had it, whereas intoxication-seekers very often (if not always) want to be wasted in some way. The mosquito parallel extends only to nasty coming-down experiences, not to being wasted as such. This is what we have to account for.

Some very positive adjectives are also used for the intoxicated state, like "high," "lit," "lush," and (meant one way) "loaded." Is it the case that intoxication-seekers attain an extraordinary fullness of power or sensation when the intoxication experience goes right, and only become "wasted" when the experience is spoiled by overindulgence? Then the attraction would be spiced by risk; intoxication-seekers, like surfers or skiers, would gamble on getting it right, avoiding wiping out. But intoxication doesn't typically resemble sport this much. The risk isn't so much the substance of the experience; in this respect intoxication seems more similar to love, which is also excitingly risky but not normally undertaken for the *sake* of running risks. Is it, then, that the arc of the intoxication experience moves through a delightful part and on to a "wasted" bitter part? Then the pleasure of intoxication would be melancholy, shadowed by knowledge of the coming wastage. But this doesn't seem essential to intoxication either. It seems rather that the goodness of intoxication somehow is partly *made* by the elements that ask for negative description. We already saw that the negatively described elements are not like the mosquitoes that plague camping. Can we say that intoxicated subjects are high in a way that is low and low in a way that is high? Lush in a way that is wasted and wasted in a way that is lush? If there is a kind of wastage even in the optimal intoxication experience, what makes *this* worthy or worthwhile?

A clue to darker meanings is that we regard nighttime as the appropriate setting of intoxication. Which of night's meanings is most relevant in this connection? Nighttime is primarily sleep time, and sleep introduces a healthy discontinuity between our get-up-and-go periods of industrious self-definition. But other nocturnal activities have the same significance: in them we are released from what we have been doing in the day. The night redeems the day by offering us alternative experiences and perspectives, all of which (whatever their intrinsic interest) clear the counter so that we can start over again on the following day. And sometimes we have a peculiarly fascinating chance to go all the way over the night-bridge to the new day, staying up to see what dawn will show us to be, as in the all-night party that brings teenagers to the dawn of adulthood.

If intoxicated consciousness is to ordinary consciousness as night is to day—much darker and so more charged with unknown possibilities and with a specially intense interest attaching to the things that *can* be seen in it—then I might seek intoxication because I expect it to redeem my ordinary living by adding new perspectives to it and making space for new beginnings in it.

People invoke the sleepier meaning of darkness when they speak of using intoxicants for relaxation, as for instance to unwind at the end of a hard day at the office, but the meaning of getting intoxicated cannot be the same as the meaning of taking a nice warm bath, which for most of us would be much cheaper and safer.[25] The issue of new beginnings creates excitement. Intoxication is not just lying down, or catching a breath; it is something like knocking yourself down to study yourself in ruins, or burning some of yourself down to see what might appear in, or rise from, the ashes.[26] More fundamental than the overt behavioral destructiveness sometimes seen in intoxicated people is a destructive intention proper to all intoxication-seeking. Intoxication is a fire that throws heat and light in its "rush," its energy increase, but also intrigues us in clearing space for new possibilities we might like. It is a form of sacrifice or gambling, of throwing things away hoping to get better things back.

The new possibilities promised by intoxication are not actually delivered within it. If I do come to a new understanding under the influence of a drug, I am in that respect enlightened, not intoxicated. Whatever we think of the truth-value of drug-based enlightenment, the very appearance of enlightenment is qualitatively opposite to that tending toward stupefaction, that stopping down of consciousness, by which intoxication is defined. Intoxication in itself is the night before the dawn, not the dawn.

Why would it be important to live in a hampered way? Are there important issues that can be handled (I mean handled, not escaped) only by a stopped-down consciousness? Intoxication's answer could be that I need to be mentally hampered if I am sincerely to welcome unknowable new possibilities like "This person, whom I don't know, could be my friend," or "I can sing in public," or "Having just lost my job, I can still be happy." We can connect with such surprising possibilities because intoxication dims our powers or habits of discrimination. What is normally unacceptable becomes acceptable.

Nietzsche offers something like this answer in a section of *Thus Spake Zarathustra* called "The Drunken Song."[27] The song comes at the end of Zarathustra's long day, when he and his companions, having worked out new ways of affirming life, must reckon directly with death. Zarathustra asks, *What does the deep midnight declare?*, and answers, in the "drunken happiness of dying at midnight," that "the world is deep, *deeper than day had been aware*."[28] The brighter-and-deeper "midnight soul" takes account of a woe in the world that goes deeper than any daytime happiness, an ultimate woe called "God's woe":

> God's woe is deeper, you strange world! Reach for God's woe, not for me! What am I? a drunken sweet lyre—a midnight lyre, an ominous bell-frog that nobody understands but that *must* speak . . .
> Gone! Gone! O youth! O noon! O afternoon! Now evening has come and night and midnight—the dog howls, the wind: is not the wind a dog? It whines, it yelps, it howls. Alas! Alas! How the midnight sighs! How it laughs, how it rattles and wheezes!
> How she speaks soberly now, this drunken poetess! Perhaps she overdrank her drunkenness? She became overawake? She ruminates? Her woe she ruminates in a dream, the old deep midnight, and even more her joy. For joy, even if woe is deep, *joy is deeper yet than agony*.[29]

The equation that has to be solved is easily stated: affirmation must embrace and supersede the negative, love must be stronger than death, good must be brought out of evil. But how can human subjects realize such a solution? How is it humanly possible to *see* or *believe* that joy is deeper than woe—when it is *midnight*, that is, when we are facing up to a No so overwhelming that no ordinary valuation can stand before it? In sharp disagreement with Stoic and Buddhist strategies of detachment, Nietzsche suggests that only a hyperintoxicated state (an "overdrinking of drunken-ness") puts a human subject in touch with joy behind all agony.

"Pain too is a joy . . . night too is a sun," concludes Zarathustra, by which he means that the encounter with death and woe is an occasion of insight.[30] Has Zarathustra stepped *outside* drunkenness in wresting a phi-losophy of eternal joy from the challenge of midnight-death? But the sub-stance of the insight is an utterly undiscriminating love of pain and pleas-ure, life and death, all entangled with each other—an ecstatic Dionysian union with everything. Midnight's song has to be "drunken," because the circumstances of midnight cannot be affirmed except by a Dionysian lucid-ity of which drunken self-resignation forms part. Such rapture must be an event primarily of the heart—but not, be it noted, a muddling of the head, for the head is still required to know and to speak what the drunkenly changed heart grasps.

Nietzsche certainly did not think that literal overdrinking is the path to Dionysian insight. In his notebooks he expresses the same misgivings most people have about substance abuse: that it produces a false sense of a plen-itude of power, offers false escape from a feeling of emptiness in life, and manifests a will to self-destruction.[31] But in relying on intoxication as a metaphor for life-accepting consciousness, he showed how actual intoxica-tion can draw its meaning from this existentially crucial need for a trans-formable heart. (So can suffering).[32]

A person is the subject of transformation only in an equivocal way. Transformation separates the one who can say she or he has been trans-formed from the one who became transformed. But transformation cannot be equated either with creation or destruction. There must be some change-ableness of form, or else there would be no transformation, and there must also be some continuity of form, or else we could not identify the person who has been transformed. In intoxication, the equivocal status of a trans-formable subject becomes something we actually experience. Beyond our extraordinary drunken joys or angers we are aware while intoxicated of our own extraordinary changeableness.

My changeableness is a matter of more gravity than the sheer existence of multiple possibilities of selfhood within me. Intoxication might be inter-preted as the liberation of such possibilities from the censorship of the day-time ego.[33] This would involve a suspension of the teleology of self-forma-tion. But taking the issue of my changeableness seriously assumes and deeply reinforces that teleology. I am aiming toward what I will be "in the end."

The changeableness of my being is as uncanny as the darkness of mid-night. Intoxication's adventure is to reach that midnight place where the ordinary subject is absent—accepting pain, seeing unseeableness, and being someone else, swimming in a crashing sea out of sight of land. The adven-ture would fall flat without a corresponding truth of intoxication, and the truth is that to live fully I must accept pain, face unseeableness, and realize that I am potentially someone or something else. The truth is that life is wild in such ways. Any profound event of transformation, like falling in love or having an ecstatic encounter with Nature, is likely to be called "intoxicating" to point to this feature. If no one ever got intoxicated, would we have an adequate metaphor for the force of such experiences?

I cannot say that a person is missing part of the meaning of life simply because he or she is always sober. But an always-sober person *may* be missing part of the meaning of life that an intoxicated person is not missing, if the intoxicated person happens, by virtue of intoxication, to be dealing with a basic problem of human life that the sober person is not dealing with in any way. Does the sober one know as much about pain and loss? Has the sober one noticed how dark the night is? Has the sober one dared hope to fly, or felt how glorious a phoenix might fly from the ashes of the already-known? (People who sit in bars overdrinking are given credit by popular songs and stories for being in touch with life's greatest problems, even if not for dealing with these problems in the most effective way.)

Perhaps we discover a self-contradiction in this. Wouldn't anyone who wholeheartedly wanted to do something new or to solve life's problems see intoxication as hindrance, not help? Wouldn't such a person want to take concrete steps rather than wait in the dark for phoenix wings? Are the steps knowable, though? One person thinks so, another does not. The antithesis to the intoxication-seeker is the industrious person whose ambitions are already definite and apparently valid enough to sustain serious effort. Whereas intoxication-seekers are helping something good happen by getting themselves out of the way, the industrious know that they can secure good things by continuing with what they are already doing. As far as valuing is concerned, the industrious have taken complete control of their destinies. In contrast, those who are open to the coming of new things in their lives apart from their own actions—even if they happen to be well-occupied people with strong convictions—do not have the deep reason to fend off intoxication that the industrious have.

To the industrious, the prohibition of intoxicants makes sense, not only because many intoxicants are physically and morally dangerous (as anyone can see), but because in their eyes nothing really meaningful is added to anyone's life through intoxication. Is the self-assurance of the industrious itself a moral problem? (This question will come up again in thinking about worship.)

૭౨

People do often pursue intoxication collectively; let us see whether there is a worth reason why they should. Intoxicated conviviality might well be taken for a good cheer attending shared pleasure, a quantitative rather than qualitative addition to satisfaction. But if intoxication is other than or more than pleasure for the single subject, if it is a dabbling in profound transformation, then it must also have this or a related character as a collective action. Let us consider two main possible structures of joint transformation. One is mutual aid and encouragement. As scholars working on the same topic might help each other by exchanging references, so intoxicated subjects might support each other in deriving their personal rewards from the experience. The other possibility is of a *communion in transformation*. Lovers give themselves to their relationship in such a way that they are liable to be changed by each other and by the greater reality of the relationship. Scholars, too, as a matter of fact, do more than trade advantageous bits of information or technique; they affect each others' basic appreciation of the meaning of scholarly work and jointly advance and taste the rewards of a public understanding of their area. Convivial intoxication seems to be more of this communing type. Indeed, the most substantial reason why there should be drinking at a party seems to be that it helps or makes individuals give themselves up to a collective transformation process and thus to be more profoundly indebted to each other and to the society they form than they could otherwise be. (Is someone who *won't* dance in this way with others, who keeps her or his heart on a separate track, a dangerously antisocial individual?) Yet communal intoxication could be undertaken to create, or could unintentionally create, a heightened *uncertainty* about the mutual acceptableness of persons—a more dramatic and dangerous situation than everyday civility allows.

We have been standing outside intoxication, as it were, asking why a group of people would want to get in; but there are also reasons inside intoxication for pursuing it collectively. One is that we may be more likely to be changed if we surrender ourselves into the power (friendly or antagonistic) of other people's perspectives and transformations. It is also possible that a cohort of like-minded intoxication companions may keep everyone's transformations on a safe track—or even on so narrow a track that one really has to get away from them to seek the proper end of intoxication. But a nonsuicidal intoxication-seeker must strike a balance between the risk of conformism and the risk of departing too far from normal consciousness in a destructive way. Companions are insurance against some form of self-immolation coming as the unwelcome conclusion of intoxication. Beyond the obvious practical help in preventing destructive behavior ("Friends don't let friends drive drunk"), companions provide a kind of safety net within the intoxicated shift of consciousness. To be in their presence (even if they are besotted at a given moment) is to have some surety of the dawn beyond the night—to know, that is, that if you change drastically, future self leaving present self behind, someone else will catch you. At a minimum, if you *get away with* being intoxicated in company, you have reassurance that society will indulge you even under extreme provocation. (Theists might feel reassured of God's indulgence also—dramatically so, if in their intensified private reality of intoxication they jettison the whole question of social acceptance.)

೦ᥩ

If getting intoxicated can be worth doing, not simply in the way that trying one more flavor of food is worthwhile, but in the way that raising one's power of life is worthwhile, one might suppose that to eschew intoxication must be to miss part of life's meaning. But this conclusion is barred by the very logic that makes intoxication worthwhile. For intoxication is significant because it is *about* a fundamental human problem, namely, the problem of finding a way to affirm life wholeheartedly under all its conditions. That this problem exists apart from the work of intoxicants means that there can be other approaches to it than intoxication. We would also lose our grasp on intoxication if we defined it as the *only* subjective correlate to the objective life-problem. (Nietzsche runs this risk in Zarathustra's metaphorical "drunken song.") Heart and mind may be changed in infinitely many ways. Religious devotion is a comparably deep way of addressing the life-problem deliberately, insofar as it opens the heart to transformation, and is deeper still insofar as it enhances cognitive awareness. Of course, religious experiences may be called intoxicating just as intoxication experiences may be called religious, and both descriptions may be true, but the interest of crossing these categories would disappear if we did not understand their separateness.

There are probably numerous ways in which ordinary acts, without any resort to intoxicating substances, can bring on the nighttime of intoxication to some degree. Can so-called natural alternatives yield the meaningful rewards of intoxication—including its intrinsic riskiness—without its excessive hazards? Mightn't an individual achieve intoxication-transcendence by running or yoga, for instance? The "natural high" has a great advantage besides safety: its reward comes on top of the reward of something else worth doing, something pleasant or empowering in its own right, so that a double gain is produced.

For the most part, however, "natural highs" are not actually different ways of realizing a single intoxication-meaning; they realize different meanings. They are considered healthier not only for their greater safety (when they *are* safer) but for their sunnier purport, their power increase being shadowed perhaps by death but not by life's sadness. They may betoken avoidance of life's sadness. They are much likelier than intoxication to contribute definitely and harmoniously to a recountable life story.

∽

Could there be an objective correlate of intoxication, a practical intervention in reality drawing heightened worth from its correspondence to the peculiar state of the intoxicated subject's consciousness? Since Bataille made a noteworthy search for this, I propose to call the act that seeks a practical realization of intoxication a Bataillean act.[34] (I call it an act rather than an action, because whether it cuts any definite figure in the economy of practice is uncertain.) What in the intoxicated subject is an overloaded "lit" or "lush" state is, in the Bataillean act, gloriously energetic and interesting *excess*; but as on the negative side the intoxicated subject is "smashed" or "wasted," the upshot of the Bataillean act is gratuitous and irrecuperable *loss*. Excess and loss are here relative to reason, are *of* reason, and so they forbid explanation or justification—yet they are urgently important, they make their own wildly superior sense, they raise up a worth or transworth that *clearly enough* divides itself from regular worthwhileness. Which acts in our repertoire, if any, are properly Bataillean in whole or in part?

One thinks immediately of violence. But the Bataillean act could not reduce to the simple thrill of suddenly releasing the energy in things. Considered either as excess or as loss, the pseudoeternal implosion of violence defeats itself in its immediate termination, its self-totalizing. The Bataillean act must be an *ongoing* discomposition of the acceptable, a bizarrely disturbing presentation as in surrealist art, or obscenity, or the rawer sort of sacrifice. We do participate in vast subcultures of surrealism (attending to the "weird" however we can find it), obscenity, and sacrifice (which in major religions remains blood sacrifice, in principle if not in literal fact). How many acts of play and help and love have really been ventures of this other kind? In any case, the preference of most of us, most often, is only to dip our toes in the Bataillean possibility. Are we mediocre? Are we in bad faith? Or does the possibility of Bataillean acts exist only as a fringe of justifiable practice, meaningful only in its contrast with reason? I take Bataille's endless vacillation on the sense of senselessness to be a proof that this is the case. He writes: "How would it be possible to feel the attraction of the void if the appearance of the opposite wasn't also there?"[35]

The religious would prefer to say: "How could we know the limits of 'world' and 'worth' if the eternal weren't also asserted somehow?" The faith premise of transeconomic grace or transrational reason is similar to Bataille's desperate premise in its extremism, but opposite in its optimism.

It recognizes the Bataillean alternative as its demonic complement. Its own act could be worship.

6.5 Worship; the Sabbath; music

Nothing is done with a greater sense of rightness than worship. To ask whether or under what circumstances worship is worthwhile seems out of order. And yet decisions to stop or to start worshiping and to worship in one way rather than another, with a greater or lesser investment of resources, are in fact made. What can agents go on in making such decisions?

The question is most tractable if we construe worship as a form of work. Supposing that the gods have to be propitiated if we are to live well, worship becomes one of our chores. We shall rain-dance as often as is necessary to bring rain, sacrifice enough lambs to keep our flocks thriving, or say enough prayers to reach heaven. On this view, worship gets us measurably ahead.

But the work model of worship must be rejected, for it makes unjustifiable assumptions about natural causation and rests on a morally unacceptable view of relationship with the divine.

The difficulty with regard to causation might not arise on some religious views of ultimate reality, but it does attend traditional Western theism. Theists have powerful reasons of their own, quite apart from deference to modern science and technology, not to expect their God to pull strings on natural events in response to human acts. The transcendence of the world's creator—so majestically portrayed in Genesis 1, so excruciatingly tested in the book of Job, so consistently underlined in the Qur'an—means that God is at all times playing God's own game. The theist's prayer must always end, "Your will be done," which is to say that it must end more or less in the dark.

This point bears on the second problem as well. To worship in order to secure divine favor is to try to manipulate the gods as though they were morally inferior beings, avid for the entertainment of the rain dance, hungry for sacrificed flesh, or greedy for the praise that prayers give them. But to revere beings of that quality as gods would be an enormous mistake in valuing.

The purpose of worship cannot, therefore, be to alter the external course of events. Is its purpose to work on the inner reality of worshipers? If that is the aim, what inner effect would make worship worthwhile?

We could bring worship under the model of intrinsically rewarding and frankly gratuitous activities such as play or aesthetic enjoyment. The primary vindication of worship would come, then, in the feeling of delight attending it (though not to the exclusion of a secondary vindication in realizing greater harmony with the divine and greater worldly success as a result of this).[36] I doubt, though, that worship is always delightful, or only considered worthwhile when delightful. Even if worship were always delightful, the question would remain, What is worship's special reason for being?—assuming that it is a significantly different way of seeking delight, and not merely one of various ways in which good music or good architecture may be enjoyed.

The analogy between worship and play is worth considering because of some striking resemblances between the two. Both are set apart from ordinary practical reality. Both typically take place in a marked-off space, following their own sets of rules. Both employ distinctive gestures or actions, many of which are intrinsically satisfying to perform or to witness. Both take themselves to be improvements on ordinary existence, and both have a special seriousness that can be shot through with joy.

But the analogy breaks down when we look at the objects of seriousness in the two cases. Players are serious about doing well, being "good at it," and attending to the contingencies of play. They are not serious (insofar as they are really playing) about the relationship between their play and the rest of their lives. They lapse from playmindedness if they start to care even about the relationship between one play event and another, because they are supposed to live in the play moment. Worshipers, however, are more serious about the relationship between their worship and the rest of their lives than about anything else. If they worry about how well they are worshiping, their concern is for sincerity, purity, and ardor rather than skill or grace; no one can be "good at" worshiping. And play is profoundly optional—all work and no play makes Jack dull, but not dead or bad. If worship is impractically gratuitous in some way, it isn't in this way. Worshipers feel worship to be their highest duty. Players enjoy lightheartedness, undutifulness.

What can the high seriousness of worship consist of, if we refuse to interpret worship as superstitious work? We reasoned that the effect of worship must be inward. If worship is so uniquely important, must we believe that our basic well-being is at stake in it? "All secular endeavor and no worship makes Jill"—what?

Al-Ghazālī (among others) compared acts of worship to doses of medication.[38] What medication does for the sick body, worship does for the sick heart. A main premise for al-Ghazālī, however, is that spiritual health is necessary to be welcomed by God in Paradise: "None shall be saved except him who comes before his Lord with a pure heart" (Qur'an 26:89). So while spiritual health may involve immediate enjoyment comparable to that of physical health, its paramount virtue is that it orients a person toward God as God desires. The reward of worship, accordingly, lies in its good effect on a relationship, and in this respect it is more analogous to relationship-tending activities like making polite conversation and giving thank-you gifts than it is to play. Worshipers' extremely careful attention to an Other sharply contrasts with players' reveling in their own well-exercised powers.

If the point of worship is to build a good relationship with God or with any greater source of goodness on which ultimate happiness depends, then worship might land in the category of work, after all. Part of our ordinary motivation to maintain relationships is that we know that negligence in this realm invites practical disasters. But worship that is authentic, at least as judged by religiously serious and thoughtful people, cannot be merely instrumental, undertaken for some benefit to be gained down the line. Absorption in divine goodness is of its essence. We must be careful to avoid valuing mistakes with regard to the quality of a worshiper's spiritual life as much as with regard to the conception of God. Surely ultimate bliss is not to be attained by obsequiousness, fullness of soul by groveling, or fullness of relationship by cagey policy. A credible divine savior would be geared to empower us to be better people; a salvation that was worth having would involve our becoming better people.

But worshipers are not always detached enough from worship to evolve these arguments for it, arguments that are still instrumental in the sense that they assume that we get somewhere worth getting by engaging in worship. Worshipers in theistic traditions do not typically understand themselves to have chosen, as though from an unbiased starting point, the most promising salvation program. Nor do they think they are making a do-or-die bet about the right path to salvation, in the spirit of Pascal's wager argument.[38] Instead, they believe themselves to be *responding* to a God already manifested as great, and they already feel that the substance of salvation would be close and harmonious relationship with their God. They do not say, "Let us try worship and see where it gets us"; they say, "Let us worship, since we realize that we are in the presence of the Holy One"; or "Let us worship, since we realize that we are indebted for all good things, and for the prospects we have of the best things of all, to our Creator and Redeemer." This realizing is the core of the distinctively religious attitude called piety, whether piety's object is God, parents, country, human society, Nature, or an Enlightened Mind.

Like the playful attitude or the industrious attitude, piety projects its own (different) definitions of worth. It poses a set of problems to be solved: how we can show adequate gratitude to God, for example, or how we can tell which worldly causes to support for God's sake. Still, the pious attitude is unique in the way that it eclipses worth questions. Even more than in work, where we feel imposed on by things that have to get done, in worship we feel we have no choice about valuing the activity's underlying rationale. Workers and players alike can reevaluate their actions and decide to abandon them; they are free to become sick of their standard or style of living, and even of life itself. But worshipers are totally constrained by the revealed holiness to which they are responding. As valuers, they are swept off their feet. They cannot stop worshiping without (as it seems to them) falling into evil. That is why they are so serious about it—in principle, infinitely serious. (If workers are *that* serious about work, is it because they are worshiping in their work? If dancers are *that* taken with their dance, is it because they feel themselves claimed by a supreme goodness that transcends their dancing?)[39]

Since the pious do not really have room to ask whether worshiping is worth doing, they obtrude a sort of blank spot into our field of inquiry. But there is more for us to attend to than this blank spot. Even the pious have room to wonder what sort of worship makes sense, and to find reasons why some forms of worship are more worthy or worthwhile than others.

For one thing, it is possible that not all forms of worship are equally good spiritual medicine. Al-Ghazālī thought that acts of worship produce the greatest benefit when the directives of the prophets are followed (notably, in Islam's daily prayer regimen). This is confirmed in every believer's experience, he maintains, although to be set on the right path one needs the prophet's extraordinary transintellectual insight into the heart's needs.

Another issue that assumes importance in religious deliberation on worship is how well worshiping will serve to establish a paradigm of good order in a disorderly world. The pious may think of themselves as forming a counterculture, and their worship may model the world to come—as, for example, early Confucians practiced rituals to model a future restoration of good order in Chinese society, or Christians celebrating the Eucharist represent an eschatological reunion with their Savior.[40] Or they may think of themselves more as ministers to the world, increasing or preserving its harmony—as the Christian Communion service also embodies a spirit of fellowship that is meant to leaven secular dealings and thereby make a more loving world. Now, if we postulate that worship is the activity in which human perceptions of ultimate good order are acted on, we can, even from a nonpious starting point, speculate what ultimate good order would look like and what its practical requirements would be. For example, it could be argued that loving fellowship is the essence of social well-being and, from that premise, that supremely serious rituals of fellowship ought to be instituted to form and spread that spirit. Or it could be argued that clearly defined hierarchy and scrupulous respect for role limits are the key to our happiness, so that our great need is for rituals that focus on harmonizing diverse functions. As long as we are thinking in this fashion, however, we are *working* on our social problems, making worship worthwhile in work terms. If the pious make similar-looking arguments, they do so with quite a different thrust. They want to align their world with the Holy for the Holy's own sake. And yet they are working or creating *in their way*; beyond maintaining an attitude and a relationship with their God, they are actually (as they think) building a new world. They may be building new *selves*—in a project that goes much farther than "saving" persons, in the sense of overcoming sickness—to live in this world.

If we place worship in the key of ambitious faith instead of dutiful piety, our emphasis must fall less on the stimulation of the act of worship by the holy Other and more on the projection outward of the believer's sincere zeal as, in a sense, an end in itself.[41] The worship imperative and the choice of manner in worship would reflect more than anything else the subject's desire to concentrate, to integrate everything—perhaps to transmute, redeem, and exploit normally unworthy impulses in the fire of the completely intent act—and thereby to maximize his or her own being.[42] For this act to be describable as worship, however, it must retain its reference to the adorable Holy. (We will consider what happens in the absence of this reference in section 6.6.) The worshiper, like the lover, expects to be changed not only *for* but *by* the better.

᭳

From the worshiping point of view, what constitutes enough worship? The Jews have famously accepted great inconvenience and resentment in their relations with non-Jews, and have sometimes died, for the sake of reserving an entire day each week for worship.[43] Until recently, many communities in the United States were still sufficiently in line with the biblical Sabbath principle that they required places of business to close on Sundays. The blue laws have mostly been phased out now and there is little prospect of restoring them, since they run counter to the principle of religious pluralism. But congregations, families, and individuals still deliberate on how to observe a Sabbath. Let us try to find the determining assumptions of this form of worship calculation.

The chartering of a Sabbath in the Genesis 1 story of God creating for six days and resting on the seventh posits a regular, ongoing relationship between time in its dispersal and time in its fundamental unity. (This is a development of the idea "God is the world Creator.") The week, a repeating gathering of time, is preunderstood in the Genesis vision as the unity of unity and dispersal. Creation is finished on the seventh day, but time is not. Unlike the conversion moment, which achieves all at once a proper orientation of temporal life to eternity, the Sabbath moment is instituted for the proper regular conducting of temporal life. The difference is clearest in relation to the future: a convert peeks ahead in *hope* of confirmation in an overall relationship to eternity, and in *fear* of lapsing from it, while a Sabbath observer *knows* that the future belongs as much to eternity as the past does, and accordingly follows a routine for that relationship. The "holy present" of worship has taken responsibility for the future; Sabbath observers know the worth of their acts in this fuller way in relation to time. But the convert, the agent in the grip of faith or piety as such, is the one who knows what sabbath observance "is all about," namely, the fascinating or tremendous character of eternity as this might extend in time. For this reason, Sabbath calculations have to take into account what al-Ghazālī might call the "taster's" point of view and the "physician's" point of view together.

The Sabbath worship event must be concentrated enough to refer human worshipers lucidly to eternity as time's foundation, on the one hand, and extended enough to encompass the wider dimensions of the time of living, on the other. No precise objective formula for adequacy in worship could be given, of course, because a key to adequacy is the individual worshiper's intent and experience. Anything between the sincere prayer of an instant and dancing for hours on end may be in order, depending on how a worshiper is able to bring everything in himself or herself to the junction with eternity. Yet the common human shaping of time can be discussed in its relevance to worship. From a sabbatarian point of view, by hypothesis, the twenty-four-hour day is a necessary microcosmic unit, because it represents a complete living cycle. If a program of worship takes place through a day and a night, it can refer to all the directly, biorhythmically experienced dimensions of being alive. But daily devotions, which have their own place, could not suffice for a Sabbath, because they could not fully occupy a living cycle without totally displacing profane activities and thus suppressing the relation between holiness and the world. If a whole community meets in worship on a daily basis, *that* worship cannot be *about* anything like a full range of activities and interactions in the world. It is a practical fact that within a week, producers and consumers need to come to market and workers need to rest. And that minimum of time gone by must also be the maximum, not only to respond to the impatience of worshiping zeal, but also because waiting fifteen days or a month for a Sabbath would give profane existence too much room to establish itself in forgetful independence.

Many religious folk, Jews included, decide to observe a Sabbath equivalent just one day per year. It could be claimed that catching a whole year with one Sabbath is most worthwhile, that is, most religiously efficient. (The annual Yom Kippur visit is likely to be much more personally moving than the weekly synagogue visit.) On the other hand, it could be claimed that an annual Sabbath is less worship-worthy, because it lets so much detail in one's life slip out of one's share in eternity.

⁖

Is a life without worship a lesser life? All secular endeavor and no worship makes Jill—just secular. That could mean that Jill is more vulnerable to the disorders of this world. It is as though she is wandering in a swamp without a map or quinine. But apart from the trouble Jill might eventually fall into, what is qualitatively deficient about her life if she is only secular? From a worshiper's perspective, Jill appears to be not merely information-deprived but dazed in her consciousness, sleepwalking, as it were, in the absence of the rousing and guiding of valid rites of worship. Can she be aware of this? Many people do feel dim or vertiginous, and some explore religions hoping to find relief. For them, worship could be the spiritual medicine of which al-Ghazālī spoke. But what about a Jill who does not feel at all lost—a happily busy Jill with a firm grip on the value of what she is doing, who feels that she has no time to waste grasping for metaphysical wisps of "eternity"?

The person who is furthest from seeing the good of worship bears more than a passing resemblance to the person who is furthest from appreciating the meaning of being intoxicated. We find in both cases that the chance of ecstasy fails to engage the subject who is thoroughly self-possessed. Maybe the sober and secular approve of themselves too much, or are too sure of what they must do to stay on the right side of the universe. (Note that those who bend the elbow and those who bend the knee might also act with too much assurance, blocking the chances of transformation that intoxication and worship are meant to provide.) Undercutting some of the ordinary grounds of self-possession, intoxication and worship both take away discriminations of value: in intoxication, all things are felt to flow together into a lake of equal lovableness (or sad poignancy or disgustingness), while in worship all persons and things are seen to settle on the flanks of one holy mountain and shine by one light.

The metaphors of lake and mountain point to a great structural difference between the more typical intoxication and worship experiences. Worship is most aptly called an intoxication when its effect on the subject is of a melting or blinding kind. Intoxication needs clear thought and aim to resemble worship. We find, thus, two great opposite yet complementary procedures of transformation: (1) loss of form, as in the self-submergence of intoxication, and (2) gain of new form, as in a worshiper's concentration on the Holy in order to receive what can be received from it. That these opposites can be intimately allied is proved by the use of music to facilitate both submergence and concentration in settings of intoxication and worship alike.

The principle of concentration or sharp focus underlies two virtually universal features of worship that make it more difficult to appreciate from outside the worshiping stance. (1) Worship insists on ritual. Whereas intoxicated subjects may have trouble walking a straight line, worshipers are asked to make the unusual movements of a special choreography. This is as silly as Simon Says in the view of anyone who lacks the motivation for it. But it sharpens bodily movement in accordance with the sharp focus of the worshipers' intention, making them present as whole persons in that intention. (2) Worship raises a qualifications issue: it is not for just anyone to perform whenever she or he feels like it. New worshipers must qualify by undertaking study or other tasks, by confessing their condition and declaring their intentions, and by going through ceremonies of induction. Special measures like fasting may be required in advance of any act of worship. Worship must be performed at the right time. One reason for such requirements may be that they make for a pleasantly clubby atmosphere, but the deeper reason is that the focus that makes worship worthwhile could not be attained and held without commensurate preparation and discipline.

Worshipers' seriousness about preparation and discipline seems misplaced to the secular-minded, but it does have a basic plausibility, for secular thinking well understands the value of job training and concentration on a task. The intoxicated totally give up this seriousness, however, and so no incongruity could be greater than the one that assaults us when drunken carousers parody the Last Supper at the end of Luis Buñuel's film *Viridiana* (1961). The surface clash of carnality with spirituality, of the impure with the pure, has the underlying structure of opposition between the submerging and concentrating modes of transformation. What gives such a scene its amazing poignancy is our sense of the readiness for transformation that the opposite styles have in common. We cannot call this shared quality "seriousness" in the ordinary sense of that word, and yet it is hardly frivolousness. It is really the opposite of complacency—a willingness to hazard the self, to hope for what tomorrow's dawn light will reveal.

Intoxication and worship are also both alike and opposite in their departure from time. The most general worthwhileness requirement that one "have something to show" for an activity can be satisfied, if one becomes happier as a result of intoxication or worship, but the usual correlation of reward units with units of time "well spent" is missing. Time is not exactly at the disposal either of the intoxicated subject, who wallows in the starting over of time (from midnight), or of the worshiping subject, who in effect suspends time by aiming at an eternal rectification of life. The submergence of the intoxicated subject involves an abstention from entering into time in its ordinary practical meaning, according to which actions have cumulative and binding implications; the concentration of the worshipper insists on gathering the practical meanings that are ordinarily dispersed through time into one integrated supermeaning. These extremes of chaotic potentiality and imperishable actuality are, we could say, the mysterious south and north ends of the continent of doing.

☙

How might worship worth carry over into, or qualify, other activities? What are significant ways of filling in the blank: "For her, to _____ was to worship"? You could not say "shop for groceries" except with comic effect. You surely could not say "write a report": activities that one would want to call "technical" require too narrow a concentration to allow the transworldly horizon of worship to appear. At least it would be an extraordinary accomplishment for someone to address a routine "technical" task in such a way as to set it against the widest horizon. Perhaps we can more easily imagine a ship's engine mechanic working worshipfully—so vital the task, so awesome the environment. Or, at a different extreme, a worshipful cameo painter—so fine the work, so beautiful the object. But to place these activities in the category of worship is still rather provocative. It would raise fewer eyebrows to say "Hiking in the wilderness is worship for her," since wilderness provides not only a great widening of horizons and a real hazarding of self but also a sense of more direct contact with the root causes of the world. (Any required preparations and patterned actions in these ways of spending time will substantially increase the resemblance to the paradigm cases of worship, if they serve to increase concentration on something transcendently valuable.) But wilderness is, in itself, diverse and unfocused.

How natural, though, to say that playing or listening to Mozart (or whichever sort of music one is most profoundly moved by) is worship! Why?

Would we expect music to serve its participant as a specially powerful method of concentrating on new personal form? There is some reason to think that music works in the exactly opposite way—that the effect of sonic beauties pouring into the soul in abstraction from any practical frame of reference must be to melt the soul into irrational and undiscriminating feelings like those associated with intoxication. Indeed, musical experience is very commonly said to be intoxicating. The unexcelled feeling of virtual power and the bottomless emotion that music evokes are accompanied by no lucid aim, unless custom has forged a link (as between anthems and state occasions or hymns and church worship). Music appears to be just as lacking in semantics as a bottle of whiskey. Like whiskey, it gets its effect from opening the floodgates of feeling within the subject; it is not able to make an intelligible representation.

It would be foolish, however, to suppose that music is completely lacking in semantics. Music has analogues to phonemes (notes and chords), syntax (rules of composition), propositions (themes), and rhetorical forms (genres). One knows the *meaning* of the difference between minor key and major key in Western tonal music, or the difference between the blues scale and the conventional diatonic scale. One cannot capture such meanings in words, not because musical meaning doesn't exist but because it is of a distinctive kind. The whiskey parallel breaks down: if the difference of flavor between Scotch and bourbon is a difference of meaning, it is for most of us a far less articulate one.

Music figures to be a specially powerful means of opening subjects to the acquisition of new and specifically *holy* form, then, to the degree that musical forms tally with the humanly available forms of holiness. That organized worship often gives a privileged place to music indicates that musical forms must be good analogues, at least, for holy energies, sensitivities, and vistas. Part of music's religious effect lies in its power to abstract listeners from their everyday frame of reference, to lift them (by the rhythm of their breathing or their beating hearts) to a kind of out-of-this-world purified experience in which a felt relation to worldly experience is preserved. To this extent music has no message. But music also has a semantics of extraordinary personal import. Thus, on the one hand, the concentrating intentionality of worship can be served by music in an official sacred role, and, on the other hand, any music is liable to generate an identifiable and repeatable exaltation, a practical equivalent of worship.

Now we can afford to look at the other side of the coin. In order to be available to receive new form, it is necessary to let go of old form; and to help set aside those forms of profane existence that interfere with sanctification, worshipers not infrequently resort to intoxicants like wine and peyote. Except perhaps for peyote, which may have a certain power to impose form on thoughts, no change agent can compare with music in its power *both* to dissolve the forms of the old self (superseding the ordinary mind's lucidity with its own more darkly intimate kind of meaning) *and* to contribute positively to the new formation of the self. The best worth view of music, therefore—which is also emblematic of a complementarity between intoxication worth and worship worth—sees in it a balance of the two great principles of self-transformation.

6.6 Zazen

Zen-sitting is the way of perfect tranquility: inwardly not a
shadow of perception, outwardly not a shade of difference betwen
phenomena. Identified with yourself, you no longer think, nor do
you seek enlightenment of the mind or disburdenment of illusions.
You are a flying bird with no mind to twitter, a mountain unconscious of the others rising around it.

—Meiho[44]

Seen from outside, Zen-sitting or zazen seems to belong among religious
acts that attempt to relate worldly beings to a fundamental (and necessarily
transworthy) Good. But the Buddhist goal is to refrain from identifying
goodness with any sort of being. The essence of good is taken in this view
to be openness to all beings in their impermanence, as "grounded" in a
great emptiness and nonseparateness. Like worship, zazen detaches itself
from ordinary practices, but its lack of an objective referent makes it opposite to worship and a major practical category unto itself.

The pose of zazen is not so exceptional. Without a vis-à-vis, there can
be no dramatic prostration or offering. One sits down, and sits still. One is
"just sitting."[45] Zazen becomes exceptional in the carefulness and duration
of the act. The transworthy possibility is perfectly universal, neither here
nor there, attaching neither to the sitting being nor to any other, neither
formed nor limited by any sort of interest—for sitting "severs the root of
thinking," in Dōgen's phrase, and causes desire to depart.[46] Giving up
intending and trying, the tree that is the person leans far enough over to fall
into the impersonal structure of goodness.[47] Since everything is given up,
even the conceits of worship ("If you see the Buddha, kill him"), zazen
could be called the practice of perfected transworth or of trans-transworth.
The test of this perfection is in the destination. Just as sitters did not take
off to somewhere else, but only sat down, so they do not end anywhere else
than in the world, going on—now in radiant compassion. Satori, sudden
enlightenment, is indispensable but not the entire "work of emptiness."[48]

In spite of the basic difference in premises, deliberations on how to go
about Zen meditation are analogous to those for the worship activities that
are appropriate to theistic creation faith. The key, again, is to maintain relation between the holy and the world. This requirement can be stated either
positively, as the goal of the quest to realize complete freedom from crav-
ing, or negatively, as a caution or check (Suzuki comments that a monastic
leader's insistence upon manual work "saved Zen from falling into the pitfall of antinomianism or from becoming a hallucinatory mode of mind").[49]
Thus, there is a need to gauge how much and what quality of sitting are

best. But valid evaluation can only come from the enlightened mind, so the guidance of a master is needed, and the worldly uncertainties of placing oneself under another's personal authority are unavoidable. The celebrated joking and whacking of Zen masters is needed partly to "kill the Buddha" in practical terms, that is, to prevent the congealing of worth in a master-disciple relationship.

In enlightened practice there can be no clinging, not even to the worth-ideal of the enlightened master. Yet the sitter at least tacitly accepts and aims at this ideal in devotion to sitting. Enlightenment must occur in *this* mind, *mine*. But if zazen or any other inherently individual practice has too dominant a position in life, there is in fact a building up of prestige in one site, a discrimination interfering with normative Buddhist openness, from which bad personal and social consequences may follow. How can this difficulty be overcome?

There is a relevant suggestion in Rodger Kamenetz's report of a recent conversation of Jews with the Dalai Lama in Dharamsala.[50] On Kamenetz's account, the spiritual leader of Tibetan Buddhism, now the national leader of Tibetans in a crisis of exile, wanted to know the secret of Jewish survival. Part of Judaism's "secret," one Orthodox Jew replied, is that its approach to sanctifying life is family-centered.[51] The pursuit of holiness must be interpersonally involving and laced with reminders in every dimension of worldly life. An Orthodox rabbi in the group noted further: "The rabbis are not celibate, so that in their answers and teaching, they would speak with the credibility of sharing the problems of everyday people."[52] Family is anything but a central practical category in Buddhism. The breakup of the Tibetan social system that sustained Buddhist meditation for centuries now forces a question not only of expedience but of enlightenment principle: Can Buddhists avoid a destructive delusion in their meditation-centered practice if they do not positively revalue family life, national life, and history—main elements in the "wheel of rebirth"? Kamenetz is keen to press the question from the other side as well: Can the Jews save themselves from spiritual sterility without opening up paths for individuals to an enlightened mind? For Kamenetz, these are questions about Buddhist and Jewish renewal. For us, they suggest a dialectical handling of the ultimate question of transworth credibility. The most ambitiously demanding thing to say from our speculative position is that transworthy life *should* combine the voyage to the far shore (or beyond "shores") with unstinting love of the world. This is precisely what the best-known representations of the seated, blissful, compassionate Buddha are meant to convey. But one has to conceive the sitting as belonging in a continuum with going about and doing things.

6.7 Sacrifice as a crossroads of categories; queering

It is harder than one might have expected to interpret sacrifice as a distinct type of worthy action. Sacrifice is heavily overdetermined in worth. Seeing how this is so, one can better understand why such diverse rationales are given for sacrifice by writers on morality and religion.

Sacrifice can be figured as a sublimely gratuitous gesture of gratitude for existence, registering the worth of existence in the dearness of what is offered.[53] From the point of view of an ongoing religious practice, however, sacrifice is the most necessary of all forms of work. Sacrificing addresses both the uncertainty of food-finding and the threat of moral pollution; it sluices out the mucked canals of worldly existence with water from a divine sea.

> Through sacrifice, life is returned to its divine source, regenerating the power or life of that source; life is fed by life. Thus, the word of the Roman sacrificer to his god: "Be thou increased by this offering." It is, however, an increase of sacred power that is ultimately beneficial to the sacrificer. In a sense, sacrifice is the impetus and guarantee of the reciprocal flow of the divine life-force between its source and its manifestations (Robert Flaherty).[54]

The "increase of power" wrought by sacrifice may be understood to lie not so much in a flow of life-force as in a symbolically well-arranged rapprochement between the living and their ancestors, time and eternity.[55] In any case, as the only practically consequential way of *dealing* with transcendent being, sacrifice offers the only responsible basis of thought about transcendent being. Theology, if not idle, is the theory of sacrifice. And theology takes on a more personal meaning, with the increase of individualized consciousness in civilized societies, inasmuch as sacrifice is a strong and perhaps the only bearable interpretation we can give death—each individual's unavoidable rendezvous with worldly life's Other.

Self-sacrifice is the last chore. Realizing this, mustn't we regard it as the main chore, in a sense the first? The trend in all the great Axial Age religious traditions has been toward inwardization of sacrifice. True sacrifice is thought to lie in the believer's detachment from spiritual hindrances to goodness, such as greed and fear, rather than in a ritual offering of good things. This perspective can bring a worth revolution. With the focus on proper attitude comes a sometimes explicit refusal to conceive the human-divine relation within the framework of work worth, as in the *Mundaka Upanishad*:

Between the offerings of the two portions of clarified butter one should offer his principal oblations—an offering made *with faith* . . .

[But] unsteady, indeed, are these boats in the form of sacrifices. . . . The fools who delight in this sacrificial ritual as the highest spiritual good go again and again through the cycle of old age and death. . . . Abiding manifoldly in ignorance, they, all the same, like immature children think to themselves: "We have accomplished our aim." Since the performers of sacrificial ritual do not realize the truth because of passion, therefore, they, the wretched ones, sink down from heaven when the merit which qualified them for the higher world becomes exhausted.

Regarding sacrifice and merit as most important, the deluded ones do not know of any other higher spiritual good. . . . Having scrutinized the worlds won by sacrificial rites, a Brahman should arrive at nothing but disgust. The world that was not made is not won by what is done [i.e., by sacrifice]. For the sake of that knowledge he should go with sacrificial fuel in hand as a student, in all humility to a preceptor who is . . . firm in the realization of Brahman.[56]

Since a believer's whole life ought to be founded on this inward sacrifice of attachment to worldly goods (be they heavenly!), Krishna can teach Arjuna in the *Bhagavad-Gita* to perform *all* actions as sacrifice.[57] The writer of the New Testament Letter to the Hebrews gives similar advice, arguing that Jesus' great sacrifice secures for Christians the world-transcending attitude that was always the religious essential:

By faith Abel offered to God a more acceptable sacrifice than Cain's. . . . By faith Abraham, when put to the test, offered up Isaac. . . . Through [Jesus], then, let us continually offer a sacrifice of praise to God, that is, the fruit of lips that confess his name. Do not neglect to do good and to share what you have, for such sacrifices are pleasing to God.[58]

A sacrificial "work" now reappears as the expression of a worshiper's victory over self and adequate attunement to the divine. In this, it runs together with a lover's appreciation of sacrifice as a token of devotion. The point of it is taken to be that it reveals the movement of an agent from private good to a larger good in communion with an other.

But there is a practical purpose and necessity to the expression of faith or piety in acts of sacrifice that gives them another sort of work worth.

Believers who have attained inward liberation from the pressures of worldly existence still live in relation with the world. The quality of their lives can affect the world around them, and that effect might be what the world *needs* most profoundly and continuingly. So the world-renouncing sannyasin will use his strange credentials to teach; the God-worshiper fighting paganism will suffer and be martyred; the politically active satyagrahi will, on Gandhi's principles, seek suffering and accept death also.

The self-sacrifice of suffering and martyrdom can become a decisive leadership strategy, as we see in the ascetic heroics of sannyasin-gurus and Israelite prophets. In Jewish and Christian writings of Hellenistic and Roman times there is ample evidence that ascetics and martyrs were the most important ralliers of the faithful. Christians' ability to suffer and die purposefully was the main thing the wider public knew about them in the second and third centuries C.E. and was a key to the movement's growth.[59] Suffering and death make such an effective proclamation because they are understood to occur on the fault line between eternal and temporal life. The discomposing of the flesh *means* the ultimate untenability of temporal life on its own terms. Thus, one who embraces suffering and death is not only active at the point of leverage where the personally beneficial work of redemption happens but is also "out front" for the benefit of others in a community, helping and leading, clarifying practical prospects.

At this point, the path of interpretation divides. There is a "sober," thoroughly constructive view of useful and exemplary sacrifice.[60] On this view, sacrifice is both inevitable and desirable, because we cannot be indifferent to the competition between goods. If we are valuationally serious, we must prefer that our devoted intention, not random circumstance, determine which goods survive and flourish, and we must prefer the greater value to the less. Following this policy will require us to give up goods of our own, but only where we *see how* we can realize a greater good in that way. On the Bataillean "intoxicated" view, however, the point of sacrifice is its blindness. We understand (or *thought* we understood) that there is no understandable good outside the integrity of the flesh, but sacrifice achieves an affirmation of something else. Whereas we admire the strength of a war captive in holding out against torturers for the sake of an intelligible and relevant principle of honor, the grotesque tortures in martyrology impress us rather as symbols of a wild unknowableness of death, or of what is beyond death, and as manifestations of a delirious "strength" in which one can hurl oneself in that direction.

The sober and intoxicated views seem to defeat themselves, however, inasmuch as they sharpen the two horns of a sacrificial dilemma. Sacrifice is supposed to involve loss of a precious good. But (1) if one sacrifices to achieve a greater good, won't the gain cancel the loss? —if, that is, one sincerely identifies with the gain? On the other hand, (2) if one sacrifices *not* for the sake of a greater good but "deliriously," can a subject so free of the claims of goodness be said to lose anything? Sober sacrifice boils down to discipline—noble, but not spiritually extraordinary. Intoxicated sacrifice is so extraordinary that it is no longer noble at all. The greatest interest of the category of sacrifice seems, therefore, to lie at a point midway between discipline and delirium where it is possible to observe an active negotiation between worth and transworth. It is a peculiarly interesting negotiation, because various forms of worth and transworth are involved. There is tending to the world and aligning with eternity; there is taking a share of world history, and resigning from world history; there is divine action along with human acts of helping and fighting; and there is love of the dead along with love of the living. In sacrifice, both transworth and worth sprawl across categories. This immensely relevant yet elusive prospect, engaging but exceeding so many of the grasps of worth thinking, seems uniquely compelling.

ᏸᏇ

Jesus Acted Up
—Robert Goss (book title)[61]

There is a good reason to bring up queering here.

Not long ago a narrowly targeted, contemptuous term for homosexual acts, "queering" has lately been adopted by antiheterosexist movements and "queer theory" scholars to refer approvingly to a broad subversive engagement with epistemic and practical norms of all kinds. ("Acting up" sometimes means the same.) Thus the sexual "deviance" of people called "queers" becomes a metaphorical vehicle for anyone endorsing and participating in the most radical kinds of difference, especially by putting forward a problematic personal identity. To be "queer" is to be worthy—ironically worthy, in defiance of the conventional meaning of the term, but nonironically worthy, as an agent of freedom, creativity, pluralism, and sophisticated awareness—and "queering," whether in gender-bending performances or any sort of deviation-enacting criticism, can be highly worthwhile, inasmuch as the restraints it challenges are among the most stifling and dangerous to humane life.

I am queering queering, in a fashion, by including it in a traditionally meaningful worth category—and not just any traditional category, but the one that for many generations has been a linchpin in a deliberately maintained order of life, an order in which sexual "deviants" often become sacrificial victims of a sort. Yet the profile of queering is remarkably like that of sacrifice. Like sacrifice, queering is a type of action that is difficult to account for within any one or two other worth types: for example, it could be discussed as a specially self-reflexive, body-citing sort of play, or as "lifestyle"-creation, or as a kind of rebellious fighting, or as a socially constructive helping or leading, or as a pursuit of highly individualistic love worth, or as a sort of intoxication or antiworship. As with sacrifice, we are led to the conclusion that queering derives a special practical appeal from the rich array of meanings and possible emphases in it.

Substantially and more importantly, queering has in common with sacrifice a central interest in saving the energy and quality of life and a central commitment to doing some of the most difficult, most mysteriously efficacious work necessary to that end. "Be thou increased by this offering" is the implicit intent of a morally appreciable act of queering. It is true that the flamboyance of paradigmatic queer acts looks far different from the piety of the traditional Roman who said those words, but beneath the surface difference is a symmetry. Whereas traditional sacrificers act to serve their divine superior and only secondarily to benefit themselves (on a revised understanding of themselves), queering works the other way around: it puts itself forward as self-assertion, but ultimately it brings a blessing for the community (in a way that "straights" must change to appreciate).

Sacrificers, if sober at all, think they act in a system of life-energy or life-goods that circulate between divine and earthly spheres. Queering, too, contributes to a circulation of practical value, bringing marginalized possibilities into the established order—paradigmatically, in the outlawed bodies of the sexually "deviant"—and inverting the established order's own meanings. (ACT UP members have thrown condoms in a Catholic church and dumped AIDS victims' ashes on the White House lawn.)[62] The upshot is a salubriously giddy realization of shared, though widely denied, conditions of human life such as polymorphous sexuality and mortality.

Judith Butler argues that queering social norms is a performance that discloses the performativity of all norms and the dependence of all personal identities on social power dynamics. As regards gender and sexual orientation, it is not demonstrably true that "straight" people express an original heterosexualist nature; on the contrary, we know enough about the historical and psychological contingency of personal identity to know that "straight" people are inducted into the performance of gender identities in generally the same way that "deviants" are.[63] But the special vocation of queering is to show up, from the disfavored "queer" position, the necessary hypocrisy of socially enforced norms. "A performative 'works' to the extent that *it draws on and covers over* the constitutive conventions by which it is mobilized."[64] A subject of heterosexual identity, for example, is supposed to be originally and naturally thus; a subject, as such, is supposed to be the author of all of his or her thoughts and acts; a society is supposed to mirror perennial archetypes of order like family, church, and state. Thus, they stiffen themselves against questioning. But actually all of these vectors are made up as life goes along, sustained (as long as they are sustained) by our performative repetitions, according to the opportunities and compulsions of social-historical circumstance. Because queering is now done in vivid awareness of its own impropriety—as the term is twisted away from its older opprobrious use, or rather as some subjects *try* to use it differently— it is a gesture that may be peculiarly safe, at the moment, from reinstating in yet another guise the falsely naturalized authority of a fixed right way.

> If the term "queer" is to be a site of collective contestation, the point of departure for a set of historical reflections and futural imaginings, it will have to remain that which is, in the present, never fully owned, but always and only redeployed, twisted, queered from a prior usage and in the direction of urgent and expanding political purposes. This also means that it will doubt-less have to be yielded in favor of terms that do that political work more effectively.[65]

The general political purpose Butler has in view is of course the mini-mizing of harm and repression. But the usual premise of emancipatory pol-itics, which is the independent authenticity and worth eligibility of each individual subject, is undermined in Butler's queer theory. Queering can be a relatively effective way of altering the flow of social power possibilities precisely because it is not taken in by the illusion that the individual subject (as defined in socially dominant discourses) has ontological or political standing outside that flow. The worth of queering would act like a fer-menting agent on all other forms of worth, not destroying worth as such but changing our understanding of our relation to worth. Queer worth is not transworth in the sense that it is better than worth; it is—supposedly!— worth *otherwise*.

It seems, as with sacrifice, that the most meaningful queering will walk a line between a conservative, ultimately earthbound alternative and a rad-ical grab for transcendence that does no recognizable good. Butler has com-mented on how queering can defeat itself by reinscribing in its own practice the order it contests. Thus the Harlem drag balls portrayed in the docu-mentary film *Paris Is Burning*, adopted in some quarters as exemplars of gay resistance, have come in for criticism for their perpetuation of hetero-sexist and misogynist stereotypes.[66] Drag becomes unqueer in its stability. The effect it has when first performed or witnessed is quite different from the meaning it assumes over time in establishing its own customs and style.

The most surely queer act has the character of an interruption. Interruption is the queer adventure. And as with other adventures, there will often be nothing to show for it.

∽

On the borders of worth we find a wide array of impressive practical initiatives and a lack of any systematic evaluative order in which to place them. That is because the point of all these initiatives is to launch us beyond the frame of reference in which there could be such an order.

Now that we have marked the limits of *terra cognita* on our map of worth, we can turn at the end of our inquiry to try to see the worth system whole and to think freshly about how the system works and what it means.

Chapter 7

༺ঔৎ༻

THE STATE OF WORTH

7.1 What does worth thinking accomplish?

One way to begin to assess the effect of worth thinking as a whole is to pose an antinomy between positive and negative evaluations of the practical value of a system of worth concepts.

Thesis: Worth thinking builds the house of practical self-consciousness that we live in. We cannot identify ourselves as agents—to ourselves or to each other—or recognize issues or changes in the quality of our practice except by referring to relatively firm ideal standards of action. Such standards do exist, with demonstrable intellectual and spiritual force (if never beyond challenge); and we can show, by examination of what people are willing and unwilling to say, how worth thinking produces them.

Antithesis: Worth thinking builds sand castles of evaluative stipulation that last only until the next tide of circumstances rolls in to change our ideas. None of us necessarily lives within a structure of self-understanding produced by worth thinking or necessarily shares such a structure with anyone else. On the one hand, we are always free to devise new forms for practice; on the other, we are always liable to be caught up, knowingly or unknowingly, in structures of practice that we are not able to evaluate. Even within a given economy of worth thinking, the provisional force of a figure of worth can always be eliminated by some other showing of worth—perhaps as the result of unforeseen shifts in the material conditions of life, perhaps by the appearance of an imperative or seductive good that transcends the ploys of worth thinking.

Both thesis and antithesis seem to me strong. I propose to address the antinomy at its hinge: the idea of building. In building there is both accomplishment and activity, solidity and flux. (1) If we thought we were building

213

but now see that no edifice is firming up, we realize that we have only been messing about. Now, the equivalent of a firm edifice in practical conscious-ness is a standard with normative force. So a reason to reject the antithesis, which portrays us as messing about, is that the *sense* of our use of worth concepts—however mutable or perishable they in fact are—must be one of building. Otherwise, these concepts would not have even the prima facie constraining force that they evidently do have. (2) But if we are too much startled or cast down by the collapse of something we have built, we forget that its meaning, even as a finished thing, derived from our having been active in building it. The stones of a castle are stones that were piled high and that could have been left alone or piled differently. (They need upkeep, as well.) The force of a worth concept, likewise, has been lent by a com-munity of subjects; and these subjects are engaged all along, not only in finding agreement with each other, but in struggling alone and together with all of life's pressures and uncertainties—including unforeseeable impingements of transworth. A reason to reject the thesis, then, is that it mystifies the meaning of our worth concepts by treating them as independ-ent, making us hostage to our own creation. (3) If, however, we hold both aspects of "building" in view, we can affirm that we are really living within our worth standards while admitting also that their constitution is an end-less and possibly messy process. I do not think that this conclusion "over-comes" the antinomy of worth thinking. Any antinomy worth stating iden-tifies a lasting tension between solidly grounded rules. I would rather say that this interpretation of the antinomy gives us a plan for conversation between its terms.

There is another alternation of perspectives we ought to consider—not a debate, but a matter of thought's phasing. We have seen throughout this study that worth thinking just as characteristically *opens a question* as it achieves evaluative *determinacy* for the sake of decision-making and justi-fication. Worth thinking is as vitally interested in asking, for instance, what *can* be a good sexual expression as it is in producing usable standards in sexual ethics. This asking is not the prelude to a conceptually controlled formulation of an answer; it is a real wondering. My own motive in pursu-ing this inquiry has been as much to wonder and solicit new possibilities as to get clear on the current operation of practical standards. So worth think-ing both settles and unsettles. It pries us free when it is not anchoring us, or frees us in one way while anchoring us in another.

The question of questioning could be built into the metaphor of build-ing in this way: We don't merely live inside a building, guarded by its walls. We look through its windows and climb around on its exterior, getting views. We keep raising towers (and going through Tower of Babel crises). Under certain conditions, we jump. These possibilities are understood, whether or not they are desired, all through our activity of building. But just as every tower is set on foundations and every window is set in a wall, every question takes off from a set of somewhat determinate assumptions. I could not begin to evaluate specific forms of work, for instance, before I took bearings in what seemed like evident necessities for a livable human life in the world (section 3.1). This point could be made of all forms of thinking, of course, but "worth" has a bolder, more insistent question mark after it than do most other topics of discussion since it pertains so directly to freedom, understood more as an adventure than as a task, and to goodness, understood more as a mystery than as a problem. The point of worth talk is to *consider*. It is not a proper locution to say "That's unworthy" or "That's not worthwhile" with even so much as the shaky firmness of "He's not masculine" or "She's an unusual sort of Englishwoman."[1] To be firm, I say "That's not right" or "You're making a mistake." You *can* discuss judgments of the latter sort with me, to be sure, but they easily pass as final; whereas it is odd *not* to discuss worth judgments.

Worth discourse is most at home in the freely cooperative relationships of action proper, and also in the various love relationships insofar as they involve a moving of lovers toward each other and jointly toward their objects of common concern. The language of considering serves the act of positioning oneself in relation to a fellow subject. If I venture to suggest to a stranger who is a fisherman where it would be more worth his while to fish, I posit a helping relationship or friendship between us and open myself to an interesting reply. Members of a democratic society are all poised in principle to address each other in this fashion.

Now let us apply these qualifications to an explanation of how worth thinking, in either its answering or questioning phase, can be rational.

Rationality is partly a *technical* matter of stable intellectual order. Any kind of thinking needs tracks to run on. If our major ideas about the nature of worth (such as the worthiness-worthwhileness distinction) and about the domains and subdomains of worth hold their shape through a review of usage and a sustained questioning, then we become more confident that we can make ourselves understood with them and wield them to good purpose. We come to trust linkages of *argument* when we find one sort of consideration leading regularly and nonarbitrarily to another sort. We also gain confidence that our ideas are phenomenologically *objective*, that they do justice to the intentional and interintentional structures in life that they purport to represent. The preceding discussions give sufficient grounds, I submit, to conclude that worth thoughts do form a relatively stable and generally intelligible (albeit richly differentiated) system, reliable and useful in finding one's way in practical reflection; which is to say that worth thoughts are not so mutable in form and ad hoc in application that they can be studied only in the exhaustingly empirical way that biologists study genetic variation or linguists study dialects.

The rational *intersubjectivity* or reasonableness requirement goes further: we must be able actually to rectify our relationships with each other with the concepts, propositions, or arguments at issue. Individual freedom could be conceived in such a way as to preclude the intersubjectivity of worth thinking. But our worth chasing is so consistently interpersonal and even public in its orientation that it seems few of us would be willing to let the freedom principle force that conclusion. It is important not to confuse the reasonableness standard with a requirement for agreement. I might never see eye to eye with Henry Ford, but the question is whether we can *reach* each other with claims stated in worth language, that is, whether by virtue of using this language we form a team in moral concern. There are circumstances in which practical understandings diverge so widely that key evaluative terms become almost useless (I am thinking of what happens to the terms "freedom" and "dignity" in a debate between communists and liberals, or between opponents and supporters of legalized abortion). But situations are also common in which interlocutors have almost no practical tendency toward agreement and yet know quite consciously that the use of worth language institutes moral fellowship. Worth language can be the *unique* means of redeeming relationship in such cases. If a father and his softball-playing daughter cannot agree on the best use of her talents, it is crucial that they can at least be brought together by the articulable question of the best use of her talents. If they could not speak to this theme, their commitment to each other would be neutralized.

We can ask still more of rational thinking than minimal intellectual and fellowship-guiding adequacy. We can ask for heuristic shrewdness and luck, as proven by rewards beyond prediction. Is worth thinking the best game in its part of town, the game with the most action? The object is to evaluate practical choices, so far as they are left undetermined by the more direct exigencies of justice and pleasure. What other approach might be more fruitful? We could take a more freely aesthetic approach, looking for *richness* above all: the best actions would be the most mutually accommo- dating, contingently pleasing ones (like the exhibits of artists in a gallery). Or we could take a more rigorously moralistic approach, looking for strong intentional *convergence* above all: the best actions would then be the ones that foster common purpose (like the optimal play of members of a football team), and our key references would be to collective maneuvers and stan- dardized virtues. My explorations of the worth manifold and its frontiers persuade me that worth thinking achieves a fruitful mean between an aes- theticist alternative that loses touch with evaluative rationality, too much weakening our hold on time and fellowship, and a moralistic alternative that unduly limits our freedom and vision of possibilities. The actual prominence of worth thinking in our lives must be due in large part to the success of worth thinking in actually maximizing the benefits of richness and convergence and minimizing their drawbacks—for the minimal constraints of rationality often leave us free to discuss our choices of action in either of the other, more one-sided manners. Worth thinking's superiority in fruitfulness, a dynamic feature, is related to its stability, as well, for we are most likely to reach evaluative equilibrium in a middle position between one-sidedly satisfying, higher-risk alternatives.

A complementary point can be made by observing how worth thinking's psychosocial work of establishing individual and collective identity intersects with its ethical work of elucidating the choice-worthiness of action types. A major aim in assembling a worth portfolio is to appear in the world as a distinct being, individually real. An agent's exemplification of standard virtues does not satisfy this interest. On the other hand, a nonmoral, purely "interesting" showing of personal distinctiveness is merely a spectacle or a diversion. In a *worthy* showing, the wider acceptability of one's actions is just as important as one's personal distinctiveness.

Worth is a peculiarly powerful dimension of identity, because it makes claims on the agent's audience. Consider this example: A National Socialist party wins control of the German government in 1933, having promised to boost the economic progress of German-speaking people. They might or might not do a good job for what might or might not be a well-conceived cause; they might have a good claim to stay in power. Pointing to their distinctiveness in relation to other parties in Germany (both personally and tactically), they argue that they are the worthiest leaders and should be followed. Thus far we stay within the bounds of ordinary politics. But now the stakes are raised. The Nazis say they want to act as the vanguard in Germany's fulfillment of its historic mission to save Europe from racial debilitation. They are laying claim now to an extraordinary worthiness that entails enormous demands, first on Germany to embody it and then on other peoples to fall in with it. Obviously, they will need a strong conception of worth identity to license their invasions and persecutions. The role of worth talk in this evil is dismaying; one might conclude that a strong worth image is dangerous, because it is liable to be turned to tyrannical, incontinent uses. But we can look at this the other way round and observe that no people could have a strong worth identity, *both* distinctive *and* publicly considerable, without important repercussions in their relations with others. After all, peaceful Switzerland proves the same point. Its strong identity as a neutral haven causes people and resources to flow to it from all over the world. But Switzerland proves the point more impressively in that it maintains its worth identity without provoking the formation of more righteously powerful worth identities in opposition to it, as the Nazis did. I take this as another indication that worth thinking is the arena in which we seek the mean or the best accommodation between free individuality and constrained community.

7.2 Worth economics and politics

Individuals and groups find moral fulfillment in worth. Can we assume that the preconditions of attaining worth are universally abundant, so that worth seekers are never thwarted by lack of opportunity except as a consequence of their own choices? Of course not. But this means that a question of justice arises. What ought to be done to apportion and administer worth's preconditions fairly?

I do not know who would seriously demur from the proposition that a society is obliged to arrange the education of its youth in such a way as to maximize each individual's access to worth. Probably it is more controversial to assert that the true arena of human education is nothing smaller than life itself, from the cradle to the grave, from the private home to the public forum and back, and that the obligation to maximize access to worth therefore holds for all persons with respect to all others insofar as their actions affect the others' prospects of achievement. But I will take these principles for granted in order to call attention to two structural difficulties in implementing them.

One difficulty is that a political discourse on justice in relatively large and heterogeneous communities will tend to mask or divert attention from all but the most vaguely generic forms of worth ("the dignity of work"). As a result, members of the large community will often be devoted publicly to practical issues different from those they care most about in their own lives. The good general normative reason for acting in this way is that people ought to leave each other free to specify their own worth goals.[2] Moral subjects *do* act in this way because, in relations between members of a large community like the state, the imperative of respect takes precedence over the imperative of positive appreciation. Respect in this sense is the programmatically neutral affirmation one gives other persons on the premise that one does not know their projects and may not presume to help in the production of their distinctive identities. One merely tries not to get in their way. Within a more intimate community like the family, however, one had better not try to avoid affecting the others; one is obliged to support a daughter's softball ambition or a father's back-to-school plan. The allocation of worth opportunities through friendly or loving collaboration is a *more* meaningful politics, in relation to an agent's own moral identity, than the worth-neutral politics of "preference satisfaction" or "capabilities fulfillment," even if public decisions of vast consequence can only be made on a more neutral basis. Thus, we may easily fall prey to either of two opposite ills. We may lose moral sensitivity to personal worth issues because of the dominance of liberally neutral worth discourse in the state, so that we lose much of our purchase on collective worth at that level and forget or deny that personal worth is a political issue at all. Or we may carry the passion of personal worth issues into the discourse of the larger community without respect for the concrete diversity of personal realizations of worth, rendering that discourse repressively unjust and hollow in the fascist way.

The second difficulty is that an injustice can arise in the relationship between individual and collective worth prospects. Patriarchy makes an appropriate and still urgent case study. Patriarchy is, among other things, a certain worth bargain. Its premise is that a family can achieve the worthiest standing if its male head is more empowered than any of its other members to perform impressive, socially valued actions. It teaches that submitting to the patriarch's leadership, or at least consenting to identify with the worth outcomes he produces, is prerequisite to building up a meaningful collective family worth on which all family members' worth prospects are dependent. Monarchy is the same arrangement writ large: let the king pursue glory so that the nation can acquire it with him. Thus, the recent sudden shift toward equalization of worth opportunities for female individuals in Western societies has caused anxiety for the loss of collective worth. When a wife and mother achieves professional excellence, we see not simply an addition of individual worth but a threatened loss of family worth—on the assumption that a family is more than an aggregation of individuals instrumental to their several welfares, that it is instead a unified purpose and presence (as indicated by the shared patronymic name).

A collective worth deal may involve the larger unity of an ethnic group or class, without or without the support of patriarchalism. The power and potential awkwardness of such deals were exhibited with scorching clarity in the 1991 controversy surrounding a U.S. Supreme Court nominee, Clarence Thomas, and a woman accusing him of sexual harassment, Anita Hill, both of them African American. Many African Americans felt Hill "violated a deeply held black taboo which is that we shouldn't air our racial dirty linen in front of white folks."[3] According to Evelyn Hammonds, the rule of race loyalty constrains women more than men. "No mention was made of how Clarence Thomas had failed in his duty to the race, especially to Black women. This deeply held ethic that Black women have a duty to the race while Black men are allowed to have a duty only to themselves, can only be challenged by a black feminist analysis. . . ."[4] In the feminist counter-movement, however, many women felt it necessary to respect Anita Hill *more* than Thomas because the worth of all women rode on her shoulders.[5]

An African American woman might reason that the facts of social life in racist America are such that her best hope of improving the social allowance of agency to herself and those she most cares for is to share in a gain in the collective standing of African Americans, which actually depends (ca. 1991) more on the public dignity of a Clarence Thomas than on an Anita Hill. In a dangerously sexist climate millennia ago, as patriarchal civilization was assuming its historically familiar form, women might have begun to argue similarly for the worth priority of the patriarchal family head, clan head, or king. I think we have to admit, unhappily or not, that these calculations could be right: in a given situation, the price women would pay for not acceding to the patriarchal worth bias, specifically a price of worth, could be higher than the price they pay in subordination to men. But we must distinguish between two dimensions of decision-making and possible action: one in which accepting patriarchal bias or any analogous inequality might be justifiable, and one in which it cannot be. The former is economic, the latter political.

A worth *economy* is a structure of practical evaluation that obtains in fact. In a sexist society, for example, it is a fact that women tend to be prevented from attaining as much or as many forms of worth as are accessible to men. In a capitalist society, it is a fact that control of production—which is to say, control of a form of work worth and of access to most other forms—belongs to an elite class of large owners or managers acting for ownership blocs and with interests partly inimical to the interests of other classes. Insofar as we face such facts, the foremost practical question is how to administer whichever portion of the worth economy happens to be under our control or subject to our influence. A mother might believe with justification that she is administering the family worth economy most efficiently and fairly by sending her sons to school years longer than her daughters, or by giving special advantages to her oldest son.

A worth *polity*, on the other hand, is an ideal structure, the very definition of which is subject to negotiation. To be sure, agents always find themselves with certain axioms and institutions of collaboration in place. Otherwise they could not converse. But politically no constraint is beyond question *except that we have to deal with each other*. The point of political activity is to peer over the obstructions of the factual economy and reconsider what might be done—to give a collectively formulated ideality in our minds the preponderant weight, for a time, in its seesaw balance with the reality we inhabit. I speak from a political perspective when I protest the submergence of daughters in a family or of women in sports or the workplace.

Economics and politics mesh intricately in the everyday discourse of collective practice, but whenever we try to clarify a question that arises in this discourse we find that if we are not making a technical, prudential claim on the administration of our affairs in a granted state of affairs, we are making a teleological and justice-oriented claim on the apportionment of life chances.

Simone de Beauvoir argued in *The Second Sex* that women have unjustly been assigned and have *basely* accepted a lower position in the worth polity of patriarchy. The male prerogative of "transcending nature" allows men to earn a share in eternity that is denied women, who have only the insubstantial consolation of viewing male projects with irony. Beauvoir's central aim was to renegotiate the balance of worth opportunity.[6] One of her tasks was to bring to light a political deformation of *love worth* under patriarchy, which assigns women the specialized vocation of seeking love worth above all, *in relation to men*; cast as men's generic love object, predetermined auxiliaries to male-defined needs and desires, women may not be loved robustly by women either as female or as individuals.[7] An established love economy of romance, marriage, and parenting implements the patriarchal polity.

Taking up Beauvoir's advocacy of selfhood for women, our contemporary Luce Irigaray tries to forge a worthier female access to love worth and transworth at the same time, appealing to female identifications of the divine as an unprescribable becoming and multiplicity that infinitely supports female selves in relation.[8] Although Irigaray criticizes male-affiliated worth assumptions of autonomous selfhood, the thrust of this, as of any recognizably feminist argument (or any justice argument), is worth-political, since it is concerned with personal shares in what is done and what is to be done.

I do not mean to imply that worth and justice follow exactly the same logic. A justice argument is categorical and generic, inescapably applicable to all agents in a specified situation. A worth argument is more escapable and individualized (even if it is not contingent on sensuous inclination in the way that Kant thought all noncategorical imperatives must be).[9] The heart of worth thinking, nevertheless, is the primordial justice issue of shares. Justice arguments always take for granted some prior definition of shares achieved by worth thinking. If this were not true, it would be incomprehensible how anyone could ever have thought a sexist polity just.

7.3 Worth religion

A church of Worth does not exist, but we can ask whether a worth religion flourishes among us in fact. The phenomenon of national religion is suggestive in this connection. Students of religion in America have long called attention to "the American creed" or "American civil religion"—a fabric of manifestations of faith and piety referring to an object of profound collective concern, a national enterprise, found outside the channels of formally recognized religious communions.[10] Since the dominant religious traditions in America are transnational in principle, a distinct nation-referring form of religion must arise when the nation's affairs are taken with religious seriousness, as seems to occur in certain political speeches and holiday observances. One might think that the dominant religions leave no comparable room for religious attention to the worth affairs of individuals, since they are relentlessly concerned with the individual's quality of life. But the true object of their relentless concern is *transworth*: the Abrahamic faiths place their adherents in an infinitely unequal position before a divine sole proprietor of authentic goodness, while the most influential traditions of South and East Asia look to the dissolution of the ordinary subject of worth in the realization of Brahman or Emptiness. So an opening for worth religion does exist, and any religious movement could succeed by exploiting it.

One might wish to argue that worth is time- and world-bound in such a way that it cannot be the object of religiously unlimited concern either in fact or normatively. But the same point is urged against national religion, and is readily answered in both of its dimensions. As regards the question of fact, human beings have shown themselves capable of attaching infinite importance to anything, however "superstitious" or "idolatrous" their orientation might seem to their critics, and we have much evidence that people have at the very least tended to be religious about national affairs.[11] As for the normative question of whether national affairs make a fit object of religious concern, the evidence of the "best" expressions of national religion, as for example in Lincoln's Second Inaugural Address, is that it "is not the worship of the American nation but [a critical] understanding of the American experience in the light of ultimate and universal reality" (Robert Bellah).[12] The objection can now be reversed: How real could a relationship with ultimate reality be if it is *not* interpreted with reference to the most practically important configurations of worldly life? And how could the life-nurturing, justice-upholding, war-making nation not be in the foreground of this interpretation? A person of faith who is also a citizen must bring the nation into "the light of ultimate and universal reality" or else split heaven from earth, de-realizing both. The same line can be taken with worth generally, as I suggested in my initial analysis of the worth-transworth relation (section 1.5). Personal life in the world cannot be assessed adequately without reference to worth. The discourses of economics, politics, ethics, and theology track roles and relationships; only worth discourse tracks the accumulation of meaning in an individual's existence.

If the full realization of any claim of transworth involves worldly implementation, therefore, it must involve worth reckoning as well. One can see this to be true in fact: for example, the language of secular "self-help" writing, packed with assertions of what the reader deserves and is or should be worth, is regularly aerated by appeals to a transworth horizon of self-forgetfulness and grace, while religiously accredited "spirituality" literature makes all sorts of discriminations between more- and less-successful practitioners (picking out "masters," for example) and practices. One can see how to maintain this idea normatively as well: worth thinking "at its best" will subject itself critically to the actuality or possibility of transworth.

Socrates' *Apology* is one of the most impressive examples we possess of a wholly resolute yet wholly self-critical pursuit of worth. Both aspects are shown in his manner of meeting death.

> I shall not bring any of [my relatives] here and beg you to acquit me. And why shall I not do so? Not because I am stubborn, Athenians, or lack respect for you. Whether I fear death or not is another matter, but for the sake of my good name and yours and that of the whole state, I think it is not right for me to do any of these things in view of my age and my reputation, whether deserved or not; for at any rate the opinion prevails that Socrates is in some way superior to most men.[13]

Socrates makes his course of action intelligible by referring to the issues of honor and reputation. But he never lets his audience forget that his distinctive reputation has been constituted by a certain relationship with the unknown, uncontrollable divine. His account of himself begins with the story of the oracle that summoned him to his philosophical task and ends with the reflection that his personal *daimon* or "prophetic monitor" has often stopped him from an act but does not stop him now.[14] (Another hero of self-critical worth seeking, Kongzi, was wont to appeal in a functionally similar way to an endless learning process.)[15]

Inspired by the Socratic precedent, Stoicism became the great Greco-Roman worth religion, retaining the gesture toward the divine and continuing to find in the encounter with death, "God's summons," a decisive realization of a worth-transworth relationship. The religious danger of deciding for death (and thus for a certain shape of life) by one's own calculations, for self-interested purposes, was a sensitive point with which Stoic writers grappled (see section 6.2). The question I asked earlier about the Stoic suicides and suicide arguments—namely, whether they presumed to know more than is knowable about the conditions of meaningful life—foreshadowed a general question I can bring up now about the danger in yoking transworth and worth together in a worth religion. I take a cue from Herbert Richardson, a Christian theologian unconvinced by Bellah's defense of national religion "at its best." Richardson pursued his objection in these terms:

> The religion of Christianity seeks to be not merely an effective critic of civil religion, but also an alternative to it. But it can be this only by rejecting two claims: (1) the claim of every earthly Caesar and *civitas* to be ultimate and (2) the claim that *civil categories* are adequate for conceiving the relation of man to God. This is why Christianity rejects not merely the worship of an earthly king, but also the claim that God is *like a king*. Christianity affirms that what is higher than all earthly kings is not some heavenly king, but the suffering crucified Christ.[16]

The analogous objection to a worth religion would be that it imposes worth categories on the relation with transworth. True religion's transformative, salvific impact on our very imagining of the good is then forestalled. We dress glorious grace in the shabby clothes of merit. From the religious position of primary alliance with a concrete claim of transworth there is a need, therefore, to keep up an attack on worth religion. A virtue of recognizing religious seriousness in worth seeking, from this point of view, is that it energizes an important polemic, enabling rival constructions of worth and transworth to etch themselves more sharply.

7.4 The pursuit of practical lucidity

What makes reflection most worthwhile? Cultural history suggests that one of the most influential contributions a thinker can make to the common life is a morally and metaphysically strong model of "the good life." Platonism and existentialism, doctrinally opposite positions, have each been woven extensively into the fabric of common life, because each could be perceived and practiced by individuals as a personal *stance* and *method*. The Socratic essence-seeker and the Nietzschean self-inventor are icons of sterling agency. So also are Kongzi and Laozi. In comparison with other sorts of icon, the special strength of these is rooted in their lucidity with regard to the presuppositions of action. Each discloses important general characteristics of practical possibility. Each is enabled by a metaphysical analysis to put forward a virtually irrefutable principle of practical justification.

The study of worth thinking does not yield an icon of the good life like those of Platonism and existentialism. Lucidity about worth leaves too many choices free for any school of worthism to form. More awkwardly still, lucidity about the possible relations between worth and transworth causes hesitation in accepting any such thing as a worth configuration as fully valid. To turn these embarrassments into virtues, however, we may confirm as strategic clues the notions of (1) *domains* of worth—as a standing pluralist reminder that whichever worth claim one responds to, there are others, each with its own anthropological depth and luminosity; and (2) *levels* of reckoning practical goodness—the collective distinct from the individual, the transworldly distinct from the worldly—as a reminder that however one is interpreting worth identity, a structurally different way of doing so is available. Our differentiations of "domain" and "level" correspond to dangers of ethical confusion, of course, but also to a promise of ethical richness—a richness that must, in fact, be attainable if we are meaningfully to pursue a *moral happiness* more morally satisfactory than individual happiness, as such, can ever be (even in the character of "blessedness") and individually happier than morality, as such, can ever be.

Another great contribution of reflection to culture is critical and antimetaphysical. It is well exemplified by ancient skeptics and by modern Marxists and feminists. Rather than set up an icon of good life, critical thought sets up a question that cuts infinitely deep—about the foundations of judgment, about the effects of social arrangements on thought, about the preformations of our thought according to real or imagined human-kind differences. Worth lucidity supports these critical projects by bringing further into the light some of their most important targets. For instance, it is important accurately to measure the extent of workers' and women's worth deprivation and the depth of the bias of a capitalist and patriarchal worth system against them. Worth philosophy's own critical initiative, however, is simply the obverse of the positive goal I called "richness." It is a disruption of worth complacency in any one domain or level.

෮෨

Writing from a socially privileged position, I have made what I take to be the best use of my perspective. That is to begin laying out a banquet table of practical possibilities that in the best-arranged life would be accessible to all. To anyone in a dissimilar position some of my inclusions and exclusions will seem odd, my proportions wrong, my urgencies misplaced, in a somehow typical way that calls for correction (this as opposed to my temperamental peculiarities that one would either like or dislike). Although thinkers are obliged to reckon with pitfalls of bias as searchingly as their resources permit, they would be foolish to suppose that an account can jump out of its own shoes to expose its own most basic shortcomings.

The ultimate resource and corrective is the most inclusive conversation. But my last word for now is this: I do not regard the larger conversation as external to my account, as though I were saying my piece—in a complete and self-enclosed act (incorporating *captured* quotations of others)—and only then opening myself to replies. I am a creature of the conversation. You have been responsible for me all along.

Notes

Chapter One

1. Frank Reynolds argues for multiple senses of "cosmogony," including both fully cosmic formation and teleologically specific human formation, in "Multiple Cosmogonies and Ethics: The Case of Theravada Buddhism," in *Cosmogony and Ethical Order*, ed. Robin Lovin and Frank Reynolds (Albany: State University of New York Press, 1985).
2. See Charles Taylor's explanation of the parallel notion of "incomparable goods" (which we apprehend in "awe") in *Sources of the Self* (Cambridge, MA: Harvard University Press, 1989), pp. 19–20.
3. These moves are found for example in John Rawls's and David Hume's theories, respectively.
4. See the "Analytic of Pure Practical Reason," book 1 of *Critique of Practical Reason*. Kant usually wields the formal-material distinction on the assumption that the matter of willing is always empirically conditioned and a prospect of gratification, while the form of willing is (properly) a priori and dutiful. But this is not the distinction that divides the realms of worthiness and worthwhileness, even though it exerts a sort of magnetic polarizing force on it. The issue between worthiness and worthwhileness is one of determinacy. Kant considers the need for moral determinacy and what I have called implementation under the rubric of "the typic of pure practical judgment" (ibid., Ak. 67–71), but here too he is preoccupied with protecting the free rational/moral will from empirical conditioning and misses the whole problem of how we may allow particular actions and practical complexes to count, to some extent, as bearers of moral worth.

5. For a different but complementary development of these ideas, see Charles Taylor, "What is Human Agency?" in *Human Agency and Language* (Cambridge: Cambridge University Press, 1985).

6. An exemplary working out of this point in the realm of ethical theory, with utilitarian calculation implementing and being redeemed by Kantian first principles, is R. M. Hare's *Moral Thinking: Its Levels, Method and Point* (Oxford: Oxford University Press, 1981).

7. Thomas J. Oord gives a perspicuous moral definition of love with a virtue rather than worth center: "I define proper love as acting intentionally, in sympathetic response to others, to attain a high degree of well-being given [*all*] the degrees of ill and well-being possible for a particular act." "Love Archetypes and Moral Virtue," *Contemporary Philosophy* 22 (January 2000): 13–17.

8. Alan Gewirth's *Self-Fulfillment* (Princeton: Princeton University Press, 1998) is a detailed study of this conception. He is willing to bar certain avenues of self-fulfillment, like the suttee that an Indian widow might choose to perform, on the grounds that a particular conception of self-fulfillment can be inconsistent with general protections of individual autonomy (such as, in this case, opportunities for critical reflection on cultural norms) (203–4).

9. Other major worth types that impress me as important are creating, owning, and experiencing. I have discussed owning in this perspective in "The Worth of Owning," *Public Affairs Quarterly* 16 (April 2002): 155–72, and experiencing in "Great Experience," *Journal of Aesthetic Education* 29 (spring 1995): 17–31.

10. I develop and support this claim in *The Concept of the Spiritual* (Philadelphia: Temple University Press, 1988).

11. Aristotle, *Nicomachean Ethics* trans. Martin Ostwald (Indianapolis: Bobbs-Merrill, 1962), p. 292 (1178b9). The sense of this ambition depends on the piously humble recognition that humanity as such (the frame of reference of "politics," "practical wisdom," and thus "worth") "is not the best thing in the universe" (1141a22).

12. In *The Concept of the Spiritual*, chapter 2, I argue for the propriety of calling "spiritual" the addressing of always-open relationship issues and locate in this conception the tenable core of all actual references to "spirituality," etc. In this work I will sometimes use the term "spiritual" to evoke the vague popular understanding of a higher life, but only when I see that a more definite, usable meaning of the term in the given context could be established along the lines I've indicated.

13. So Kant describes the metaphysical overreaching of Platonism in *Critique of Pure Reason*, trans. Norman Kemp Smith (New York: St. Martin's, 1965), p. 47 (B 8–9).

14. Joel Kuppermann has made the point well in a closely related frame of reference: "If people feel constrained by their misunderstanding of the implications of liberalism to eschew judgments, even unvoiced judgments, of other people's values, they lose an important source of thinking about their own values . . . extreme reluctance to judge, from outside, the lives of others . . . lends itself to a sense of one's own life as having no relation to standards of excellence. From this it is a short step to a sense of one's own life as essentially meaningless." *Character* (Oxford: Oxford University Press, 1991), pp. 116–17.

15. Cf. Charles Taylor's account of the properly ad hominem, gain-promising character of practical teaching in "Explanation and Practical Reason," in *The Quality of Life*, ed. Martha Nussbaum and Amartya Sen (Oxford: Oxford University Press, 1993).

16. Alasdair MacIntyre, *After Virtue* (Notre Dame: University of Notre Dame Press, 1981).

17. I draw on a summary anthropological argument for this thesis by Sherry B. Ortner and Harriet Whitehead in the introduction to *Sexual Meanings: The Cultural Construction of Gender and Sexuality*, ed. Sherry B. Ortner and Harriet Whitehead (Cambridge: Cambridge University Press, 1981). The generalizations I make in this paragraph seem to me broadly accurate for a cultural legacy that we are still vitally concerned with, although few today would argue that they are normatively correct.

Chapter Two

1. Plato, *Laws* 803c, trans. R. G. Bury (Cambridge, MA: Harvard University Press, 1926), 2: 53–55.

2. J. C. Friedrich von Schiller, *On the Aesthetic Education of Humanity*, my translation, based on that of Elizabeth M. Wilkinson and L. A. Willoughby in *On the Aesthetic Education of Man in a Series of Letters* (Oxford: Oxford University Press, 1967), p. 107 (15.9).

3. Johan Huizinga, *Homo Ludens: A Study of the Play Element in Culture*, trans. unknown (Boston: Beacon, 1955), foreword (n.p.).

4. George Sheehan, *Running and Being* (New York: Simon & Schuster, 1978), pp. 71–72.

5. On play as experience of possibility, see Joseph L. Esposito, "Play and Possibility," in *Philosophic Inquiry in Sport*, ed. William J. Morgan and Klaus V. Meier (Champaign: Human Kinetics, 1988), pp. 175–81; on play as essentially fun, see Huizinga, *Homo Ludens*, pp. 2–3. José Ortega y Gasset argues that sportive activity, simply because it is a

delight, is "the foremost and creative, the most exalted, serious, and important part of life" in "The Sportive Origin of the State," in *History as a System*, trans. Helene Weyl (New York: Norton, 1961), p. 18. Drew Hyland dwells on "responsive openness" as the salient quality of the "play stance" in, among other writings, *Philosophy of Sport* (New York: Paragon House, 1990), pp. 125–29.

6. With his eye especially on the sort of case where someone wants to call someone else back to what needs to be done ("What are you playing at now? Get back to work!"), Bernard Suits defines playing as "making a temporary reallocation to autotelic activities of resources primarily committed to instrumental purposes." "Words on Play," in Morgan and Meier, *Philosophic Inquiry in Sport,* p. 22. This approach is of least interest to us, because it centers play where the justification for it is invisible, only to be inferred in a sour way. Nevertheless, any adequate definition of play must contain negative moments; for instance, Huizinga has "connected with no material interest" among his criteria (*Homo Ludens*, p. 13), and Caillois calls it "unproductive" (Roger Caillois, *Man, Play, and Games*, trans. Meyer Barash [Glencoe: Free Press, 1961], p. 10). Both writers make much of an element at once positive and negative, that of make-believe, representing both freedom *for* creation of a new reality and freedom *from* ordinary reality. See also Randolph Feezell, "Play and the Absurd," *Philosophy Today* 28 (winter 1984): 319–28.

7. R. Scott Kretchmar draws attention to the basic presupposition of need and the "base values" of tension and uncertainty in his category of "acquisitive play" (encompassing games, contests, and drama). "Qualitative Distinctions in Play," in *Die Aktualität der Sportphilosophie,* ed. Gunther Gebauer (Sankt Augustin: Academia, 1993), pp. 6–7.

8. Caillois, *Man, Play, and Games*.

9. See Caillois, ibid., pp. 14–26, 36.

10. Ibid., pp. 86–87. Caillois sees a rationalization of chance in hereditary social differences.

11. Schiller, *Aesthetic Education*, chaps. 11–14.

12. Ibid., p. 95 (14.2).

13. Ibid., pp. 145–47 (21.4–5).

14. See Leverett T. Smith, Jr., *The American Dream and the National Game* (Bowling Green, OH: Bowling Green University Popular Press, 1975).

15. This gives me a reason to agree with Kretchmar ("Qualitative Distinctions in Play," pp. 9–13) that narratively rich forms of play are more valuable than forms mainly dedicated to immediate aesthetic

reward. But I think his praise of narrative play crosses into the different worth domain of experiencing. Abstraction is as important as representation in play: the player, as such, never wants to acquire a humanly full personal identity. That would be too much ballast to carry in play.

16. The taking over of the players' initiative by the play is stressed by Hans-Georg Gadamer in *Truth and Method*, 2d ed. (New York: Seabury, 1975), pp. 91–96.

17. On this point I particularly recommend J. Glenn Gray's interpretation of "The Enduring Appeals of Battle," in *The Warriors* (New York: Harper & Row, 1970), pp. 29–69.

18. Exactly this project is taken up in earnest by Peter J. Arnold in "Sport as a Valued Human Practice: A Basis for the Consideration of Some Moral Issues in Sport," in Gebauer, *Die Aktualität der Sportphilosophie*.

19. Huizinga, *Homo Ludens*, p. 49.

20. A compelling model of this possibility is the Balinese cockfight as portrayed by Clifford Geertz in "Deep Play: Notes on the Balinese Cockfight," in *The Interpretation of Culture* (New York: Basic Books, 1973).

21. Hyland, *Philosophy of Sport*, p. 56.

22. Michael Novak develops this point eloquently in *The Joy of Sports* (Lanham: Hamilton, 1988), pp. 47–49. Edith Wyschogrod shows how in some sports a deliberate courting of death enhances the joy of merging one's effort with elemental natural forces in "Sport, Death, and the Elemental," in *The Phenomenon of Death,* ed. Edith Wyschogrod (London: Harper & Row, 1973).

23. For a survey of the opportunities of self-knowledge offered by play, see Hyland, *Philosophy of Sport*, pp. 70–87; for a Marxist critique of sport in capitalist society, see Jean-Marie Brohm, *Sport—A Prison of Measured Time*, trans. Ian Fraser (London: Ink Links, 1978).

24. A. Bartlett Giamatti, *Take Time for Paradise* (New York: Summit, 1989), p. 101.

25. Dennis Hemphill usefully reviews the pros, cons, and social history of the development of knowledgeable sports spectatorship in "Revisioning Sports Spectatorism," *Journal of the Philosophy of Sport* 22 (1995): 48–60.

26. Treating every pitch as a victory of pitcher over batter or vice versa, and every ball put in play as a victory for either the hitter or runner or the fielders handling it—in addition to game victories and all the categories (batting average, home runs, etc.) and domains (major league, league, club, All-Star game, League Championship Series, World Series) of statistical leadership.

27. I recall here Kant's formula for beauty, e.g., "what without a concept is cognized as the object of a *necessary* liking." *Critique of Judgment*, trans. Werner S. Pluhar (Indianapolis: Hackett, 1987), p. 90 (Ak. 241).
28. Paul Weiss, *Sport: A Philosophic Inquiry* (Carbondale: Southern Illinois University Press, 1969), p. 141.
29. On 6 September 1995, Cal Ripken Jr., the Baltimore Orioles shortstop, broke Lou Gehrig's record of 2,130 consecutive games played. Ripken's streak began in 1982.
30. Brohm, *Sports*, Allen Guttmann, *From Ritual to Record* (New York: Columbia University Press, 1978), chapter 3.
31. Quoted in Guttman, *From Ritual to Record*, p. 68.
32. A point of departure for my thinking about the "play self"–"real self" relation is Robert F. Neale's psychological account of a "play self" of inner harmony contrasted with a "work self" of inner conflict. *In Praise of Play* (New York: Harper & Row, 1969). If Neale's idea is to be applicable to play and work activities, however, a distinction must be drawn between psychological harmony and an in-principle harmony of human powers. As it stands, Neale's conception is almost at right angles to the phenomenology of playing and working, for players can respond tensely to challenges in the play realm and workers can calmly shoulder their burdens.
33. *Jackson Clarion-Ledger*, 19 July 1993.
34. Novak, *Joy of Sports*, p. 44.
35. Friedrich Nietzsche, *Philosophy in the Tragic Age of the Greeks*, trans. Marianne Cowan (Chicago: Gateway, 1962), p. 62.
36. Huizinga, *Homo Ludens*, p. 3.

Chapter Three

1. Jordan, in Emile Zola, *Work*, trans. Ernest Alfred Vizetelly (London: Chatto & Windus, 1901), p. 150.
2. Mark Twain, *The Adventures of Tom Sawyer* (New York: P. F. Collier & Son, 1920), p. 19.
3. Lawrence Hinman uses "intrinsic" and "extrinsic" in this problematic way, although the aim of his argument is probably convergent with mine, in "On Work and Play: Overcoming a Dichotomy," *Man and World* 8 (1975): 327–46, esp. 338–40.
4. I can't recall the source of this story. I think it was meant as a slander on Saxons.
5. Karl Marx, *Economic and Philosophical Manuscripts*, trans. T. B.

Bottomore, in Erich Fromm, *Marx's Concept of Man* (New York: Frederick Ungar, 1966), p. 102. Cf. Hannah Arendt, *The Human Condition* (Chicago: University of Chicago Press, 1958), p. 86 n. 14.

6. See, for instance, Frithjof Bergmann, "The Future of Work," in *Working in America*, ed. Robert Sessions and Jack Wortman (Notre Dame: University of Notre Dame Press, 1992), pp. 12–27.

7. Says my friend Liz Peel.

8. Arendt, *Human Condition*.

9. Ibid., chap. 3.

10. Jean-Paul Sartre, *Critique of Dialectical Reason*, trans. Alan Sheridan-Smith (London: Verso, 1976), pp. 80–83.

11. Leo Tolstoy, *Anna Karenina*, trans. David Magarshack (New York: Signet, 1961), pp. 261, 264–65.

12. Fletcher Cox, a woodworker-designer, points out another potentiality in this situation: "In most work, no matter how labor intensive, there is constant absorption in planning, in bringing forth the object, and in associated planning—disposing of the object, rounding up market, etc. It is a species of *alteración* [Ortega y Gasset's term for the decentering aspect of life] in that the object has command of the mind. But in lawn-mowing, I am free somehow just to the right extent of my planning mind. In such moments my best ideas come to me. A number of my colleagues have had the same experience. It is daydream central. The muse is invoked and answers the call, because the brain is not in the way." Private correspondence.

13. Gabriel García Márquez, *One Hundred Years of Solitude*, trans. Gregory Rabassa (New York: HarperPerennial, 1991), p. 340.

14. Arendt, pp. 107–8.

15. Frederick Taylor's "principles of scientific management" perfectly express that phase of the Industrial Revolution that entails the destruction of work's meaningfulness: rather than exercise any discretion whatsoever (over tasks or tools or even the dispositions of their bodies), workers must implement a rational "efficiency" plan in order to maximize output and profit. Taylor sincerely believed that all workers have a common interest in making work more productive. See his *The Principles of Scientific Management* (New York: Norton, 1947).

16. Simone Weil, *The Need for Roots*, trans. Arthur Wills (New York: Harper & Row, 1952), p. 295; cf. pp. 299–302.

17. Ibid., pp. 94–95.

18. Marx uses the example of a dozen masons constructing a building using much less than one day for every twelve days a mason working alone would take. *Capital*, trans. Samuel Moore and Edward Aveling

(New York: Modern Library, 1906), pp. 358–59. Arendt's assertion that "there can be hardly anything more alien or even more destructive to workmanship than teamwork, which actually is only a variety of the division of labor" is understandable, in the context of her critique of the rise of the *animal laborans* paradigm, but extreme. *The Human Condition*, p. 161.

19. Alexander Solzhenitsyn, *One Day in the Life of Ivan Denisovitch*, trans. Ralph Parker (New York: Signet, 1963), p. 105.

20. Arendt, *Human Condition*, chap. 4. My assumption about creation worth is that it primarily concerns enriching the world by novelty.

21. Criticizing the "job" conception as part of his advocacy of organic wholeness in work, Matthew Fox writes: "The very word *job* fits the Newtonian parts mentality. . . . In a mechanical view of the universe, a job is all one can hope for. Job denotes a discrete task, and one that is not very joyful. The Middle English word *gobbe*, from which *job* is derived, meant 'lump.' . . . Dr. Johnson defined *job* as: 'petty, piddling work; a piece of chance work.'" *The Reinvention of Work* (New York: HarperCollins, 1994), p. 6. I can accept this perspective on "jobs" as legitimate and complementary to the positive account I offer here—it is formulated going in the opposite direction, as it were—but I wonder whether too much fear or loathing of real work is expressed in it.

22. "Our word 'work' comes from the same root not only as the Greek *ergon*, from which 'energy' is derived, but as the Persian word for 'gain.'" Alasdair Clayre, *Work and Play* (New York: Harper & Row, 1974), p. 209.

23. The adding of things to the world is a hallmark of work proper stressed by Arendt, *Human Condition*, chap. 4.

24. Michelangelo starts complaining about what the pope owes him in letters of 5 and 7 November 1510, and is still licking the wound in a letter of 1524. Roberto Silvani, "Painting," in *The Complete Work of Michelangelo*, ed. Mario Salmi (New York: Reynal, n.d.), p. 198.

25. Arendt claims that the greater magnification of human power in work proper than in labor is associated with a kind of violence against nature and thus a separating wrench from nature (*Human Condition*, pp. 139–40). I am adding the point that our work-fabrications are wrenched away from ourselves too, and have to be reconciled with us by good work if they are to seem to belong to us—just as there must be ecological reconciliation if they are to be economically sustainable.

26. Joseph Conrad, *Heart of Darkness*, in *"Heart of Darkness" and "The Secret Sharer"* (New York: Signet, 1950), p. 97.

27. Rousseau worried about the corrupting potential of giving personal credit for craft: "Say of what is well made, 'This is well made.' But do

not add, 'Who made that?' If he himself says with a proud and self-satisfied air, 'I made it,' add coldly, 'You or another, it makes no difference; in any event it is work well done.'" *Emile*, trans. Allen Bloom (New York: Basic Books, 1979) p. 202. But of course Rousseau's concern *was* for the excellence of the person and not the product.

28. Aristotle, *Nicomachean Ethics* 1140a23–1145a12.
29. I borrow this formula from Eric Voegelin, *Israel and Revelation* (Baton Rouge: Louisiana State University Press, 1956), p. 13.
30. Clayre, *Work and Play*, p. 162.
31. Ibid., pp. 164, 166.
32. John Fortune, quoted in Studs Terkel, *Working* (New York: Pantheon, 1974), p. 73.
33. Karl Marx, *Grundrisse*, trans. Martin Nicolaus, in *The Marx-Engels Reader*, ed. Robert Tucker, 2d ed. (New York: Norton, 1978), pp. 240–41.
34. Alvin Toffler, *The Third Wave* (New York: Bantam, 1980), pp. 265–88.
35. Cliff Finch in Mississippi, 1975.
36. Miroslav Volf, *Work in the Spirit* (New York: Oxford University Press, 1991), pp. 88–122.
37. This example is inspired by the character Alvin Yark in E. Annie Proulx's *The Shipping News* (New York: Simon & Schuster, 1993).
38. Emile Durkheim, *The Division of Labor in Society*, trans. George Simpson (New York: Macmillan, 1933), pp. 398, 401.
39. Ibid., p. 403.
40. Karl Marx and Friedrich Engels, *The German Ideology*, trans. S. Ryazanskaya, in Tucker, *Marx-Engels Reader*, p. 160.
41. Edward Shils, quoted in Donald J. Treiman, *Occupational Prestige in Comparative Perspective* (New York: Academic, 1977), pp. 20–21.
42. Such charts can be found in Treiman based on cross-cultural data collected in the 1960's. 1989 data are available from the National Opinion Research Center.
43. Lee Braude, *Work and Workers* (New York: Praeger, 1975), pp. 105–106.
44. Interviewed in Terkel, *Working*, p. 297.
45. Compare the assembly-line worker's statement reported by Clayre: "I'm happy in my work. The point is, you've got to keep the home together, and you've got to keep going, so naturally you've got to work. And as long as I've got enough to keep my family going, I'm happy. I'd rather be working than, say, be on the dole. . . . Whether I'm happy in my work is . . . well, sometimes you'll get browned off, but there you are, you're happy to have a job and the money to go on, and

there's a lot of people that are not in that position." *Work and Play*, p. 173.

46. Pierre Sudreau, a French economic minister in the 1980s, said: "The justification for the reform of business must be sought less in the deficiencies of businesses' current results, than in the movement of society itself. It is because of the rapid mutations of industrial society that we must speed the mutation of enterprise." Quoted by Ted Mills in "Leadership from Abroad: European Developments in Industrial Democracy," in *A Matter of Dignity: Inquiries into the Humanization of Work*, ed. W. J. Heisler and John W. Houck (Notre Dame: University of Notre Dame Press, 1977), p. 118.

47. This is an original lesson of all cooperative activity, including play, and should not be credited to work alone, as Marxists tend to do. See e.g., Georg Lukács, *The Ontology of Social Being: Labor*, trans. David Fernbach (London: Merlin, 1980).

48. Buddhadāsa, *Toward the Truth*, ed. Donald Swearer (Philadelphia: Westminster, 1971), pp. 56–57, 62–63.

49. Ibid., p. 63.

50. Miroslav Volf discusses problems with the biblical warrant and logic of Luther's position in *Work in the Spirit*, pp. 105–10.

51. John Paul II, *Of Human Work* [*Laborem Exercens*] (Washington: United States Catholic Conference, 1981), p. 54.

52. Ibid.

53. Volf, *Work in the Spirit*, pp. 94–102.

54. "In the New Testament the injunction to wait eagerly for the kingdom is not opposed to the exhortation to *work diligently for the kingdom*. 'Kingdom participation' is not contrary, but complementary, to 'kingdom-expectation' and is its necessary consequence." Ibid., p. 100.

55. John Paul II, *Of Human Work*, pp. 9–10.

56. This connection was suggested to me by Søren Kierkegaard's analysis of love's "secret," "eternal" work of "upbuilding" in *Works of Love*, trans. Howard V. Hong and Edna H. Hong (Princeton: Princeton University Press, 1995), pp. 209–24.

57. John Paul II, *Of Human Work*, p. 54.

58. The Greek word here is ἐργάζομαι, meaning a worker's work more specifically.

59. David Reynolds, quoted by Patricia Ryan-Madson in "Reality's Work," in *Mindfulness and Meaningful Work*, ed. Claude Whitmyer (Berkeley: Parallax, 1994), p. 207.

60. Although Heidegger made important contributions to the phenomenology of work in *Being and Time* and "Building Dwelling Thinking,"

I'm not aware that he ever made a major theme of *arbeiten*. Of course, his program was to articulate an alternative to contemporary practical jargon, not to study it as sympathetically as I do.

Chapter Four

1. Hannah Arendt, *The Human Condition* (Chicago: University of Chicago Press, 1958).
2. Ibid., chaps. 2, 5.
3. Ibid., p. 205.
4. Thucydides, *The Peloponnesian War* 6.2, trans. Rex Warner (Harmondsworth: Penguin, 1954), pp. 376–77, 379.
5. The interpretation of Weil's last acts is controversial. See Simone Pétrement, *Simone Weil*, trans. Raymond Rosenthal (New York: Pantheon, 1976), chap. 17.
6. Simone Weil, "Last Thoughts" (letter of 26 May 1942 to Father Perrin), in *Waiting for God*, trans. Emma Craufurd (New York: Harper & Row, 1951), p. 99.
7. Lionel Trilling, introduction to George Orwell, *Homage to Catalonia* (New York: Harcourt Brace Jovanovich, 1952), p. x.
8. Arendt, *Human Condition*, pp. 197–98.
9. On evolved sex-linked psychic structures, I largely follow the thinking of Donald Symons, *The Evolution of Human Sexuality* (Oxford: Oxford University Press, 1979). I make no claim here, however, about how the sex-linking of personal attributes occurs. I discuss this issue in *Gender Thinking* (Philadelphia: Temple University Press, 1992), chap. 4.
10. Arendt, *Human Condition*, pp. 199–200.
11. Henry David Thoreau, *Walden* (Garden City: Dolphin, 1960), p. 68.
12. William James, "Is Life Worth Living?" in *The Will to Believe* (New York: Dover, 1956), p. 61.
13. William James, *The Principles of Psychology* (New York: Henry Holt, 1890), 2:449–67.
14. I thus seem to contest a thesis that Elaine Scarry says "is too self-evident and massive ever to be directly contested," namely that "the main purpose and outcome of war is injuring." *The Body in Pain* (Oxford: Oxford University Press, 1985), p. 63. But not really. War is at best a grossly impure form of fighting, although many of its more honorable participants try desperately to redeem it by interpreting it in that category. I hope to confirm the substantial warrants of Scarry's

critique of war even as I feature forms of worth that she represses. She is undoubtedly right that the cruelties of war are often disingenuously masked by appeal to or assumption of a fighting ethos.

15. Cf. Douglas Lackey on the issue of the accuracy of fame in "Fame as a Value Concept," *Philosophy Research Archives* 12 (March 1987): 543–46.

16. Thucydides, *Peloponnesian War*, p. 121 (2.4).

17. Aristotle, *Nicomachean Ethics*, trans. H. Rackham (Cambridge, MA: Harvard University Press, 1934), 1095b.

18. Robert Neville, "Value, Courage, and Leadership," *Review of Metaphysics* 43 (September 1989): 3–26. Another version is in chapter 11 of *The High Road around Modernism* (Albany: State University of New York Press, 1992).

19. Neville, "Value, Courage, and Leadership," p. 17.

20. Ibid., p. 18. There is an acknowledgement here of John Dewey, *The Public and Its Problems*, chapters 3–5.

21. Jack Henry Abbott, *In the Belly of the Beast* (New York: Vintage, 1982), p. 145.

22. Gen. 4:2–7.

23. Franco Fornari, *The Psychoanalysis of War*, trans. Alenka Pfeifer (Garden City: Anchor, 1974).

24. Carl von Clausewitz, *On War*, trans. J. J. Graham (Harmondsworth: Penguin, 1968), p. 101. Actually, the larger passage from which this line is taken categorizes war as a *duel*, that is, a fight; there is an implicit courtesy of opponent regard in "duel" violence that makes it less violent than the criminal's aggression.

25. "[War is] the only function in which peoples can employ all their powers at once and convergently. No victory is possible save as the resultant of a totality of virtues, no defeat for which some vice or weakness is not responsible." Thus Rudolf Steinmetz in his "Philosophy of War," according to William James in "The Moral Equivalent of War," in *Essays on Faith and Morals* (New York: Meridian, 1962), p. 319.

26. Michael Gelven, *War and Existence* (University Park: Pennsylvania State University Press, 1994), p. 256.

27. Ibid., p. 142. Gelven (pp. 141–42) interprets Kantian morality as founded existentially on *who* we are as rational beings.

28. Ibid., p. 216.

29. Ibid., p. 143.

30. Ibid., pp. 158–59.

31. Max Weber, "Religious Rejections of the World and Their Directions," in *From Max Weber: Essays in Sociology*, trans. H. H. Gerth and C.

Wright Mills (New York: Oxford University Press, 1946), p. 330. Weber could be seen to support Gelven insofar as he finds the key to a sense of universal brotherhood in a basically "acosmic" euphoria of communion with divinity. Meanwhile, the imperial project has never fulfilled that largest promise of overcoming all collective antagonisms.

32. *Iliad* bk. 8, lines 309–11.

33. On Paris's duel and destiny, see *Iliad* bk. 3, lines 325–65 and bk. 22, lines 355–60. I learn of Achilles' manner of death not from the *Iliad* but from "The Age of Fable," in *Bulfinch's Mythology* (New York: Modern Library, n.d.), pp. 183–84.

34. See, e.g., Exodus 32.9–14.

35. *Iliad* bk. 1, lines 348–430, 493–600.

36. Abraham Heschel elucidates this difference in terms of time vs. space orientation. See "A Religion of Time," in *God in Search of Man* (New York: Farrar, Straus & Giroux, 1955), pp. 200–212. Emmanuel Levinas contrasts a "kingdom" orientation with a "world" orientation (so that the "kingdom of God" is not a world at all, and the talmudic concept of "a share of the world to come" must be interpreted *utterly* nongeographically). *Otherwise than Being or Beyond Essence*, trans. Alphonso Lingis (The Hague: Martinus Nijhoff, 1981), p. 52.

37. Isaiah 42.1; see 42.1–4, 49.1–6, 50.4–11, and 52.13–53.12 for the increasingly grueling portrayal. (The Jewish Publication Society Bible is used for quotations throughout this section.)

38. In Genesis 3.8–10, the tip-off that Adam and Eve have gone wrong is that they miss their usual evening walk with God. For Noah, see Genesis 6.9. In between Adam and Noah the worthy Enoch walks with God (Genesis 5.22–24).

39. Genesis 6–9.

40. Genesis 11.

41. Genesis 17.1.

42. Leviticus 26.12; Deuteronomy 10.12.

43. Isaiah 42.6, 49.6.

44. Michael Wyschogrod, *The Body of Faith* (Minneapolis: Seabury, 1983), pp. 67–68.

45. In the passage Wyschogrod alludes to, Weil defines "the power of the social element" in this way: "Agreement between several men brings with it a feeling of reality. It brings with it also a sense of duty. Divergence, where this agreement is concerned, appears as a sin. . . . The state of conformity is an imitation of grace. . . . It is the social which throws the color of the absolute over the relative. The remedy is in the idea of relationship. Relationship breaks its way out of the social. It is the monopoly of the individual. . . . No crowd can conceive

relationship." *Gravity and Grace*, trans. Emma Craufurd (London: Routledge, 1983), pp. 147, 145.

46. This identification with the Hebrews in Egypt is made by Jews at the Passover seder. Compare the language of the Shechem covenant ceremony given in Joshua 24.16–18: "Far be it from us to forsake the Lord and serve other gods! For it was the Lord our God who brought us and our fathers up from the land of Egypt, the house of bondage, and who wrought those wondrous signs before our very eyes," etc.

47. Psalms 22.1, emphasis added. Jesus quotes this in Matthew 27.46 and Mark 15.34.

48. Emmanuel Levinas has developed this principle extensively in his ethically guided account of subjectivity. See especially *Otherwise than Being or Beyond Essence*.

49. Abraham J. Heschel, *Between God and Man* (New York: Free Press, 1959), pp. 61–63.

50. Heschel, *God in Search of Man*, p. 358.

51. Ibid., p. 359.

52. Psalms 38.16, emphasis added.

53. Psalms 124.2–3, 8.

54. Psalms 143.12.

55. Psalms 142.6 ("my portion" is from the Authorized and Revised Standard Versions [Protestant], translating *cheleq*); 115.16; 118.26.

56. Psalms 39.13.

57. Levinas has commented on this issue from his Jewish perspective in this wise: "Like Jews, Christians and Muslims know that if the beings of this world have the status of effects, humans go beyond this simple effect-existence and receive, in Aquinas' words, 'a dignity of cause' insofar as they undergo the action of the exterior cause par excellence, the divine cause. We all affirm that human autonomy rests on a supreme heteronomy and that the force that produces such marvelous effects, the force that institutes force, the force of civilization, is God. . . . [But] the rigorous affirmation of human independence, of its intelligent presence before an intelligible reality, the destruction of the numinous conception of the sacred, carries with it the risk of atheism. The risk must be run. . . . It is a great glory for the Creator to have set up a creature who affirms him after having challenged and denied the religious glamour of myth and enthusiasm." "Une religion d'adultes," in *Difficile Liberté*, 2d ed. (Paris: Albin Michel, 1976), pp. 25, 31, my translation.

58. See the ancient testimonies to the Mandate of Heaven idea in *The Book of Odes* and *The Book of History* selections in *Sources of Chinese*

Tradition, ed. William de Bary et al. (New York: Columbia University Press, 1960), pp. 10–15.

59. On *li*'s reference shifting from the supernatural to the (universally) human, see David Hall and Roger Ames, *Thinking Through Confucius* (Albany: State University of New York Press, 1987), p. 86.

60. *Mencius* 2.B.7, trans. D. C. Lau (Harmondsworth: Penguin, 1970).

61. *The Analects of Confucius*, trans. Arthur Waley (New York: Vintage, 1938), 3.7, 5.27.

62. "The Life of Confucius" [*Shiji* bk. 47], trans. Lin Yutang, in *The Wisdom of Confucius* (New York: Modern Library, 1938), p. 95.

63. *Analects* 4.9.

64. *Analects* 7.32.

65. *Analects* 8.13.

66. *Analects* 7.22.

67. "The Life of Confucius," p. 70.

68. *Mencius* 6.B.16.

69. Ronald Green writes of Kongzi's "relative neglect of the problem of personal moral reward" without, I think, recognizing the force of Kongzi's transworthy solution. *Religion and Moral Reason* (New York: Oxford University Press, 1988), p. 56.

70. *Basic Writings of Chuang Tzu* [*Zhuangzi*], trans. Burton Watson (New York: Columbia University Press, 1964), p. 104.

71. *Mencius* 6.A.17.

72. *Basic Writings of Chuang Tzu*, pp. 52–53.

73. De Bary et al., *Sources of Chinese Tradition*, p. 571.

74. Tu Weiming, *Centrality and Commonality* (Albany: State University of New York Press, 1989), p. 102.

75. Here are actions that impress Kongzi: "Hui is capable of occupying his whole mind for three months on end with no thought but that of Goodness" (*Analects* 6.5). "What action did [Shun] take? He merely placed himself gravely and reverently with his face due south, that was all" (15.4).

76. Hall and Ames, *Thinking Through Confucius*, p. 244, translating *Analects* 16.8 ("will of Heaven" borrowed from Waley for "*ming* of *tian*").

77. "If we strive to remain faithful to 'the distinction' of God from the world, we will realize that we are unable to find an image for the inter-action of creatures with their creator, since one of the terms is not an object in the world but the source of all that the other is. Yet it is this very fact which suggests a model for their interaction: that of lover and beloved . . . perhaps the manifest infelicity of causal models (like

'concurrence') forced [the Abrahamic] traditions to an interpersonal one, where the undeserved and utterly spontaneous character of a free creation would rule out any motive other than love." David Burrell, *Freedom and Creation in Three Traditions* (Notre Dame: University of Notre Dame Press, 1993), p. 128.

78. See Hall and Ames, *Thinking Through Confucius*, pp. 119–22, on *ai ren* in Kongzi. Wang Yangming moves to love later in the passage already quoted: "To manifest the clear character is to bring about the substance of the unity of Heaven, earth, and the myriad things, whereas loving the people is to put into universal operation the function of that unity. Hence manifesting the clear character must lie in loving the people. . . . Everything from ruler, minister, husband, wife, and friends to mountains, rivers, heavenly and earthly spirits, birds, animals, and plants, all should be truly loved in order to realize my humanity that forms a unity, and then my clear character will be completely manifested, and I will really form one body with Heaven, earth, and the myriad things." De Bary et al., *Sources of Chinese Tradition*, pp. 572–73.

79. Psalms 17.6–7.

80. Psalms 25.6.

81. Psalms 63.4.

Chapter Five

1. "[The lover] allows himself to be wounded, shocked, destroyed, to be used, debased, enslaved. He is engaged in that most important of efforts, the purging of himself, the freeing of himself from the encumbrances, the habits, the limitations that had been accreted over the course of his life. He abandons not so much himself as that which prevents that self from standing out and being itself, clearly, naked and pure." Paul Weiss, *Man's Freedom* (Carbondale: Southern Illinois University Press, 1950), p. 297.

2. C. S. Lewis, *The Four Loves* (New York: Harcourt Brace Jovanovich, 1960), p. 14 and passim.

3. My remarks are based on *Phaedrus* 244–57 and *Symposium* 201–12. It will strike the reader of the *Republic* that the "family" is the State.

4. Let it be said that in Plato's dialogues, a passionate concern for the beloved Socrates is in tension with the thesis that death cannot harm the good person whose soul is in continuity with impersonal forms. But it must also be said that the Platonic passion for Socrates is powerful

all along because that individual is interpreted as the glimmering of an ideal equally relevant to all.

5. Karl Jaspers produces an alternative formulation of Platonism on this point by bringing it into what he calls the "enthusiastic" attitude, an orientation to a process of real loving engagement in which (a) a concrete individual is deeply lovable to the degree that the relation with the Whole and Absolute is intended and achieved in it, and (b) the Whole and Absolute is real for a lover only in the relation with a concrete individual. *Psychologie der Weltanschauungen*, 3d ed. (Berlin: Julius Springer, 1925), pp. 117–36.

6. Lewis, *Four Loves*, pp. 53–54.

7. Ibid., pp. 58–59.

8. Cicero, *On Friendship*, in *On Old Age, On Friendship*, trans. Harry G. Edinger (Indianapolis: Bobbs-Merrill, 1967), pp. 22–23.

9. Ibid., p. 30.

10. Lewis, *Four Loves*, p. 96.

11. See Joseph Bédier, *The Romance of Tristan and Iseult*, trans. Hilaire Belloc and Paul Rosenfeld (New York: Vintage, 1994), pp. 104–5.

12. Cicero, *On Old Age. On Friendship*, p. 42; Lewis, *Four Loves*, pp. 114–15.

13. Hesiod, *Theogony* lines 121–22, trans. H. G. Evelyn-White.

14. I refer to the crystallization theory of Stendhal. See *On Love*, chap. 2 and passim. His analogy is the "Salzburg bough": a plain twig, stuck into a pool in the salt mines of Salzburg, will come out covered with beautiful crystals.

15. Lewis, *Four Loves*, pp. 156–58.

16. The sociologist Niklas Luhmann observes how a system of love thinking (or a "semantics of love") evolves precisely to code individualities and intimacies that differ from the socially common. *Love as Passion*, trans. Jeremy Gaines and Doris L. Jones (Cambridge, MA: Harvard University Press, 1986). The problems of justification or ideal meaning that I discuss overlap extensively with the problems of communicability that Luhmann is interested in. For instance, the love legalism I have called "inauthentic" is associated with an instability in the love code: a love expression has the job of marking something incommunicable, but here is meant to communicate all too definitely.

17. Paul, 1 Corinthians 13.7 NRSV.

18. Thus Lewis admits, at the painful conclusion of his argument in *The Four Loves*, that he does not know if he has ever tasted pure love of God, that if he thought he did he might only have imagined it, and that perhaps the best he can hope for in worldly life is to "practice the absence of God." *Four Loves*, pp. 191–92.

19. 1 Corinthians 13.7.
20. Matthew 6.3 (advice on how to give alms).
21. Lewis, *Four Loves*, pp. 81–82, 163.
22. In developing this case I have learned from Russell Vannoy's *Sex without Love* (Buffalo, N.Y.: Prometheus, 1980) and *The Lesbian Polyamory Reader: Open Relationships, Non-Monogamy, and Casual Sex*, ed. Marcia Munson and Judith Stelboum (Binghamton: Harrington Park, 1999).
23. Thus Dorothy Dinnerstein, among other feminists, has argued that women's general agency would be strengthened by cultivating this more "masculine" detachment of sex from love (and she takes into account further complications in the issue of female bodily self-rule caused by the maternal domination of everyone's infancy). *The Mermaid and the Minotaur* (New York: Harper & Row, 1976).
24. Erich Fromm, *The Art of Loving* (New York: Bantam, 1963), pp. 6–32.
25. Denis de Rougemont, *Love in the Western World*, trans. Montgomery Belgion (Princeton: Princeton University Press, 1983), pp. 307–8.
26. Immanuel Kant, *Groundwork of the Metaphysic of Morals*, trans. H. J. Paton (New York: Harper & Row, 1964), p. 67 (Ak. 399).
27. See the "Dialectic of Pure Practical Reason" in Kant's *Critique of Practical Reason*.
28. Kant, *Groundwork*, p. 67 (Ak. 399).
29. Such a case is suggested by Donald P. Verene in "Sexual Love and Moral Experience," in *Philosophy and Sex*, ed. Robert Baker and Frederick Elliston (Buffalo: Prometheus, 1975).
30. "[Brangien said:] 'In that cup, you have drunk not love alone, but love and death together.' The lovers held each other; life and desire trembled through their youth, and Tristan said, 'Well then, come Death.' And as evening fell, upon the bark that heeled and ran to King Mark's land, they gave themselves up utterly to love." Bédier, *Romance of Tristan and Iseult*, p. 45.
31. From the *Jackson Clarion-Ledger*, 27 November 1995.
32. Michael J. Hartwig, "Parenting Ethics and Reproductive Technologies," *Journal of Social Philosophy* 26 (spring 1995): 183–202. This criterion can accommodate both traditional family systems and contemporary alternatives, including gay and lesbian families.
33. Søren Kierkegaard, *Works of Love*, trans. Howard V. Hong and Edna H. Hong (Princeton: Princeton University Press, 1995), p. 349.
34. Ibid., p. 355.
35. For the Christian premise, see esp. 1 John 4.7–11. The strongest expression of a divine love ideal in Buddhism is found in the Mahayana

conception of the "undiscriminating" Bodhisattva: "When the Bodhisattvas face and perceive the happiness of the samadhi of perfect tranquilization, they are moved with the feeling of love and sympathy owing to their original vows . . . made for all beings, saying, 'So long as they do not attain Nirvana I will not attain it myself.' Thus they keep themselves away from Nirvana. But the fact is that they are already in Nirvana because in them there is no rising of discrimination [hence no sense of difference between the good and the evil as love objects]." Laṅkāvatāra Sūtra, quoted in *The Teachings of the Compassionate Buddha*, ed. E. A. Burtt (New York: Mentor, 1982), pp. 165–66.

36. Thomas Aquinas, *Summa Theologica* II–IIae, q. 25, art. 8, Dominican trans.

37. That ultimate reality is communion is argued, to pacifist effect, by James Douglass in *The Non-Violent Cross* (New York: Macmillan, 1966) and *Lightning East to West* (New York: Crossroad, 1980).

38. For a convenient overview of Augustine's relevant remarks see L. J. Swift, "Augustine on War and Killing: Another View," *Harvard Theological Review* 66 (July 1973): 369–83.

39. Mohandas Gandhi, *Non-Violent Resistance [Satyagraha]* (New York: Schocken, 1961).

40. In the *Bhagavad-Gita*, Krishna advises the warrior Arjuna that he can fight (in his just cause) with pure heart so long as he is not attached to the consequences of his actions. But Gandhi writes: "I have felt that in trying to enforce in one's life the central teaching of the *Gita*, one is bound to follow Truth and *ahimsa*. When there is no desire for fruit, there is no temptation for untruth or *himsa*. Take any instance of untruth or violence, and it will be found that at its back was the desire to attain the cherished end." Mohandas Gandhi, "A Vision of the Good Life," in *The Hindu Tradition*, ed. A. T. Embree (New York: Modern Library, 1966), p. 343.

41. See Richard Gregg, *The Power of Nonviolence*, 2d ed. (New York: Schocken, 1966).

42. Augustine: "It is clear that out of love God employs infirmity and sickness and even physical death itself as a means of correcting those whom He does not wish to condemn with the world." *Contra Adimantum* 17, in Swift, "Augustine on War and Killing," p. 382. I study the handling-dealing distinction in "Homicide and Love," *Philosophy and Theology* 5 (spring 1991): 259–76.

43. Susan Niditch finds in later biblical traditions (cf. 2 Chronicles 20) the seeds of an "ideology of nonparticipation" in war. *War in the Hebrew Bible* (Oxford: Oxford University Press, 1993), chap. 7.

44. The following is drawn from Bernard of Clairvaux, "On Loving God," in *Bernard of Clairvaux: Selected Works*, trans. Gillian Evans (New York: Paulist Press, 1987), pp. 192–97.
45. Augustine, *Enarrationes in Psalmos* 38.16, quoted in *An Augustine Synthesis*, ed. Erich Przywara (Gloucester: Peter Smith, 1966), p. 334.
46. Bernard of Clairvaux, "On Loving God," pp. 196–97.

Chapter Six

1. Josiah Royce, *The Philosophy of Loyalty*, lecture 4.4, in *The Philosophy of Josiah Royce*, ed. John K. Roth (Indianapolis: Hackett, 1982), p. 303; John Rawls, *A Theory of Justice* (Cambridge, MA: Harvard University Press, 1975), §63.
2. Harry Frankfurt, *The Importance of What We Care About* (Cambridge: Cambridge University Press, 1988).
3. I find this formula for love in Robert C. Solomon, *Love: Emotion, Myth, and Metaphor* (Buffalo: Prometheus, 1990), chap. 12.
4. Reviewing the debate between neo-Epicureans who hold that death cannot harm those who die (since it lies in a uniquely profound way outside their experience) and those opponents of "experiential ethics" who argue that death is analogous to other occasions of real though unexperienced harm (as in certain betrayals), John Martin Fischer remarks: "It is an interesting question *why* one might think that the difference between the examples adduced by the opponents of experiential ethics and the case of death should *make* a difference as to . . . the putative badness of death." "Recent Work on Death and the Meaning of Life," *Philosophical Books* 34 (April 1993): 66–68. What makes the difference, I submit, is the expansiveness of worth thinking, that is, its interest in a larger objective perspective on quality of life. For the debate, see John Martin Fischer, ed., *The Metaphysics of Death* (Stanford: Stanford University Press, 1993).
5. See Bernard Williams, "The Makropulos Case: Reflections on the Tedium of Immortality," in *Problems of the Self* (Cambridge: Cambridge University Press, 1973). Interestingly, Thomas Nagel, who has done so much to elucidate the interplay between subjective and objective views of life in ethical reasoning, and who argues against "experiential ethics" by taking seriously such issues as whether the terms of a person's will are carried out ("Death," in *Mortal Questions* [Cambridge: Cambridge University Press, 1979], p. 4), professes himself unable to offset the immediate subjective wish to continue existing:
   "Given the simple choice between living for another week and dying in

five minutes I would always choose to live for another week; and by a version of mathematical induction I conclude that I would be glad to live forever. Perhaps I shall eventually tire of life, but at the moment I can't imagine it." *The View from Nowhere* (Oxford: Oxford University Press, 1986), p. 224.

6. Williams, *Problems of the Self*, pp. 92–94. I fend off the difficulty as John Martin Fischer does in his introduction to *The Meaning of Death*, p. 12.

7. A good defense of the "death with dignity" ideal and discussion of the complexities in its application will be found in Richard Momeyer, *Confronting Death* (Bloomington: Indiana University Press, 1988), chap. 6.

8. Philippe Ariès, "The Reversal of Death," in *Death and Dying: Challenge and Change*, ed. Robert Fulton et al. (San Francisco: Boyd & Fraser, 1981), p. 53; cf. Momeyer, *Confronting Death*, pp. 66–68.

9. Thucydides, *The Peloponnesian War*, trans. Rex Warner (Harmondsworth: Penguin, 1954), 2.4, p. 120.

10. See the real case of Jinendra Varni reported in Purushottama Bilimoria, "The Jaina Ethic of Voluntary Death," *Bioethics* 6 (October 1992): 335–36.

11. As to the accuracy of saying this about Weil, which is hard to determine, see Simone Pétrement, *Simone Weil*, trans. Raymond Rosenthal (New York: Pantheon, 1976), p. 527.

12. *Plutarch's Lives*, trans. John Langhorne and William Langhorne (New York: William L. Allison, 1889), pp. 64–65.

13. Daniel Day Williams, *The Spirit and the Forms of Love* (New York: Harper & Row, 1968), p. 72.

14. One rich in spiritual merit may be able to cast "the credit for his good deeds onto the people he likes and the credit for his bad deeds onto the people he dislikes," which will certainly have consequences. *The Laws of Manu*, trans. Wendy Doniger and Brian K. Smith (London: Penguin, 1991), p. 125 (6.79).

15. Augustine, *The City of God*, bk. 1, chap. 23.

16. Arthur J. Droge and James D. Tabor, *A Noble Death* (San Francisco: HarperSanFrancisco, 1992), pp. 35 and 49 n. 76.

17. Diogenes Laërtius, 7.28 (cited in Droge and Tabor, *Noble Death*, p. 31).

18. Tacitus, *Annals* 15, 60–64. Seneca on freedom: "In any kind of slavery the way lies open to freedom. If the soul is sick and because of its own imperfection unhappy, a man may end its sorrows and at the same time himself. . . . In whatever direction you turn your eyes, there lies the means to end your woes. Do you see that cliff? Down there is the way to freedom. Do you see that ocean, that river, that well? There sits

freedom at the bottom [etc.] . . . Do you ask what is the path to freedom? Any vein in your body!" *On Anger* 3.15.3–4 (Droge and Tabor, *Noble Death*, p. 34).

19. Droge and Tabor, *Noble Death*, p. 6. The neck was rebound so that he would die.
20. Plato, *Phaedo* 61–62.
21. Epictetus, *Discourses*, trans. W. A. Oldfather, in *Epictetus* (Cambridge, MA: Harvard University Press, 1928), 2:367 (4.7.19).
22. Epictetus, *Discourses*, 3.24.99–102 (cited in Droge and Tabor, *Noble Death*, p. 38).
23. Emmanuel Levinas, *Existence and Existents*, trans. Alphonso Lingis (The Hague: Martinus Nijhoff, 1978), p. 67.
24. Martin Buber, *Tales of the Hasidim* (New York: Schocken, 1975), 1:252.
25. There appears to be a *form* of bath-taking that is much closer in meaning to a standard kind of intoxication experience, and that is sitting in a hot tub with friends. Consider, in the light of the present intoxication account, how immersion in warm, swirling water with other people dissolves old forms and obscurely nurtures a new personal/interpersonal reality. (So also do a number of counseling group procedures.) Consider how happiness is not merely restored but (sparked by good company) *bubbles forth* in this situation—a prospect about which one might be excited.
26. For a most suggestive reflection on the power of ruins to make new meaning available, see Robert Ginsberg, "The Aesthetics of Ruins," in *Aesthetic Experience and Aesthetic Quality*, ed. Michael Mitias (Amsterdam: Rodopi, 1988).
27. Friedrich Nietzsche, *Thus Spoke Zarathustra*, trans. Walter Kaufmann (New York: Penguin, 1966), pp. 317–24 (4.19).
28. Ibid., pp. 320–21 (4.19.4, 6).
29. Ibid., p. 322.
30. Ibid., p. 323.
31. Friedrich Nietzsche, *The Will to Power*, trans. Walter Kaufmann and R. J. Hollingdale (New York: Vintage, 1967), §§48, 29, 55. Yet he also affiliates intoxication with one of the two great types of power enhancement, the "Dionysian" dynamic of passionate love and bodily gesture as opposed to the "Apollonian" dynamic of lucid vision and poetry (*Will to Power*, §798). And he represents himself as a disciple or even reincarnation of Dionysus. See Walter Kaufmann, *Nietzsche* (Princeton: Princeton University Press, 1974), pp. 32–33, 67, 410–11.
32. "Suffering is in us as a seed: through it something enters into us, without us, in spite of us . . . the seed rots to become fertile. Suffering is like

this necessary decomposition for the birth of a work more full . . . the meaning of pain is to reveal to us what escapes egotistical knowledge and will; it is to be the way of effective love, because it detaches us from ourselves, in order to give us others and to solicit us to give ourselves to others." Maurice Blondel, *Action* [1893], trans. Olivia Blanchette (Notre Dame: University of Notre Dame Press, 1984), pp. 350–51.

33. Sonia Sikka's main point in "Nietzsche's Contribution to a Phenomenology of Intoxication," *Journal of Phenomenological Psychology* 31 (spring 2000), pp. 19–43, is that Zarathustra's conflicting moods and claims are not unified by a single intent or personality, and that this fragmentation, not some unveiling of a "deeper truth" of self, is the primary significance of intoxication in Nietzsche. She does recognize, however, that in Nietzsche's mind, at least, the fragmentation of *Thus Spoke Zarathustra* is related to the project of transformation toward an ideal "Übermensch" selfhood (pp. 40–41).

34. I am indebted to Stephen H. Webb's *Blessed Excess: Religion and the Hyperbolic Imagination* (Albany: State University of New York Press, 1993), chap. 3, for my introduction to this topic.

35. Georges Bataille, *Guilty*, trans. Bruce Boone (Venice: Lapis, 1988), p. 155, quoted in Webb, *Blessed Excess*, p. 84. Webb's interpretation highlights the theological stakes of Bataille's argument. While Bataille celebrates the crucifixion as God's experience of "*impossibility* right to the point of horror" (*Inner Experience*, trans. Leslie Anne Boldt [Albany: State University of New York Press, 1988], p. 35)—in accordance with the principle that "lucid holiness recognizes in itself the need to destroy, the necessity for a tragic outcome" (*Guilty*, p. 51)— what is crucial for a Christian theologian's dialogue with Bataille is that "absence, loss, and sacrifice have a power to heal that belies the void across which they venture" (Webb, *Blessed Excess*, p. 84).

36. This appears to be Plato's view in *Laws* 803b–c, reflecting the Greeks' profound confidence that their feasts and games are a crucial part of the recipe for their worldly success.

37. Al-Ghazālī, "Deliverance from Error," in *The Faith and Practice of Al-Ghazālī*, trans. W. Montgomery Watt (Chicago: Kazi, 1982), pp. 69–70.

38. Blaise Pascal, *Pensées*, trans. Honor Levi (Oxford: Oxford University Press, 1995), pp. 152–58. Pascal does not purport to speak for a realized piety here; the wager argument is "according to natural lights" only. But the wager argument does capture the self-hazarding aspect of piety and worship—not an uncertainty that the Holy is real, but a necessary uncertainty about what engagement with the Holy will finally mean for the self.

39. George Chryssides argues that worship can coherently be conceived without a God—that is, without a certain presuppositionally necessary cognitive referent—if such foci of worship as "Allah" and "Krishna" are interpreted as qualifications of worship in the same way that "foxtrot" and "tango" are qualifications of dance. "Subject and Object in Worship," *Religious Studies* 23 (September 1987), pp. 367–75. It is significant, though, that to save piety Chryssides has to put a transcendent "principle of order" in the place of that supremely Better to which worshipers mean to tie themselves. The reward of worship cannot be internal to the activity in the way that the reward of dance is normally internal to dancing.

40. On the early Confucians, see Robert Eno, *The Confucian Creation of Heaven* (Albany: State University of New York Press, 1990). Catherine Pickstock argues that a theologically regrettable shift took place in the understanding of medieval Western Christian liturgy, which went from being actually and ongoingly in touch with the divine source of life's goodness to "representing" a relationship with God. *After Writing: On the Liturgical Consummation of Philosophy* (Oxford: Blackwell, 1998).

41. For a fuller discussion of piety and faith, see my "Three Religious Attitudes," *Philosophy and Theology* 11 (1998): 3–24.

42. "[Rabbi Abraham said:] What is needed is not to strike straight at Evil but to withdraw to the source of divine power, and from there to circle around Evil, bend it, and transform it into its opposite." Buber, *Tales of the Hasidim*, 2:115.

43. Josephus describes Jews dying for refusing to fight on the sabbath in *Antiquities of the Jews* 12.6.2 (cf. 1 Maccabees 2.29–38) and *Wars of the Jews*, 1.7.3–5.

44. Meiho, sermon on zazen, in *World of the Buddha*, ed. Lucien Stryk (New York: Weidenfeld, 1968), p. 368.

45. Dōgen's word *shikantaza* can be translated "just sitting" or "single-minded sitting." Part of the idea is that one does nothing else and so is *devoted* to sitting; I am playing on the meaning that one is *merely* sitting. Dōgen, *Shōbōgenzō*, trans. Norman Waddell and Masao Abe, quoted by David Edward Shaner in *The Bodymind Experience in Japanese Buddhism* (Albany: State University of New York Press, 1985), p. 158.

46. From *Moon in a Dewdrop: Writings of Zen Master Dōgen*, ed. Kazuaki Tanahashi (San Francisco: North Point, 1985), p. 42, quoted by Newman Robert Glass, *Working Emptiness* (Atlanta: Scholars Press, 1995), p. 70.

47. David Bastow, "Becoming a Changed Person," *Philosophical Investigations* 18 (January 1995): 61–62, helpfully compares this Buddhist understanding of intention's intentional self-surrender with Christians' apprehensions of their relation to divine grace.

48. Glass's phrase in *Working Emptiness*. His interpretation of Dōgen stresses the two-part structure of enlightenment, not only a "cutting the roots of thinking" in meditation but a "dropping away of body and mind" in engagement with life (see esp. chaps. 4–5).

49. D. T. Suzuki (on Hyakujo), "The Meditation Hall and the Ideals of the Monkish Discipline," in *The Essentials of Zen Buddhism*, ed. Bernard Phillips (Westport: Greenwood, 1962), p. 254.

50. Rodger Kamenetz, *The Jew in the Lotus: A Poet's Rediscovery of Jewish Identity in Buddhist India* (San Francisco: HarperSanFrancisco, 1994).

51. Ibid., pp. 215–25. In the presentation by Blu Greenberg, the issue of women's status becomes prominent. The unworldliness of Buddhism, it appears, can be as disadvantageous for women (in *any* frame of reference) as involvement in a worldly marriage-and-family system. The question tacitly posed is how to combine Buddhist spirituality's way of cutting against sexism with the force that marriage and family life can exert against sexism.

52. Ibid., p. 97.

53. Michael Gelven, "Is Sacrifice a Virtue?" *Journal of Value Inquiry* 22 (1988): 235–52. Without denying that the meaning described by Gelven can obtain, I want to show that other meanings are dominant in religious thought.

54. *Encyclopedia Britannica*, 15th ed., s.v. "Sacrifice," by Robert Flaherty.

55. Maurice Bloch, *Prey into Hunter* (Cambridge: Cambridge University Press, 1992).

56. Cited from William Theodore de Bary, ed., *Sources of Indian Tradition* (New York: Columbia University Press, 1958) 1:26–27 (emphasis added).

57. *Bhagavad-Gita* 3.19; cf. 4.23–33.

58. Hebrews 11.4, 17; 13.15–16 [NRSV].

59. Judith Perkins, *The Suffering Self: Pain and Narrative Representation in the Early Christian Era* (London: Routledge, 1995). For historically close Jewish examples of leadership through suffering and death, see 2 Maccabees 14.37–46 (the death of Razis), 4 Maccabees, and the talmudic record of Rabbi Akiba.

60. I have taken my model of such a view from Paul Weiss, *Man's Freedom* (Carbondale: Southern Illinois University Press, 1950), chap. 19. Because Weiss wants to make sacrifice a central principle in rational

ethics and explicitly rejects certain well-known religious and statist interpretations of sacrifice, he well represents the sober element within religious and political reflection.

61. Robert Goss, *Jesus Acted Up: A Gay and Lesbian Manifesto* (San Francisco: HarperSanFrancisco, 1993).

62. On the church action, see Cindy J. Kistenberg, *AIDS, Social Change, and Theater* (New York: Garland, 1995), p. 144. The ashes demonstration was described on www.actupny.org/Campaign96/October Actions.html.

63. Judith Butler, "Imitation and Gender Insubordination," in *The Lesbian and Gay Studies Reader*, ed. Henry Abelove et al. (New York: Routledge, 1993), pp. 312–13.

64. Judith Butler, *Bodies that Matter* (New York: Routledge, 1993), p. 227.

65. Ibid., p. 228.

66. Ibid., chap. 4; cf. the useful discussion of Butler and her critics in Annamarie Jagose, *Queer Theory* (New York: New York University Press, 1994), pp. 83–93.

CHAPTER SEVEN

1. I have argued, however, that human-kind conceptions do have a questional aspect, in *Gender Thinking* (Philadelphia: Temple University Press, 1992), pp. 187–92, 303–5.

2. This restraint is a strength not only of liberal politics but of political or social, as distinct from moral, theory. The gap between these two kinds of theoretical program appears in Sen's resistance to Nussbaum's call for a more concrete account of human "functionings": "[T]his view of human nature (with a unique list of functionings for a good human life) may be tremendously overspecified." "Capability and Well-Being," in *The Quality of Life*, ed. Amartya Sen and Martha Nussbaum (Oxford: Oxford University Press, 1993), p. 47.

3. Beverly Guy-Sheftal, "Breaking the Silence: A Black Feminist Response to the Thomas/Hill Hearings," in *Court of Appeal: The Black Community Speaks Out on the Racial and Sexual Politics of Thomas vs. Hill*, ed. Robert Chrisman and Robert L. Allen (New York: Ballantine, 1992), p. 74.

4. Evelyn Hammonds, quoted in Guy-Sheftal, "Breaking the Silence," pp. 75–76.

5. The Thomas/Hill worth polarization was interpreted at the time in terms of class as well as race and sex. Priscilla Painton, "Woman Power," *Time* 138, no. 17 (28 October, 1991): 24.

6. Simone de Beauvoir, *The Second Sex*, trans. H. M. Parshley (New York: Vintage, 1974), introduction.

7. Ibid., chap. 23.

8. See Margaret Whitford's overview of Irigaray's scattered approaches to this matter in Whitford, *Luce Irigaray: Philosophy in the Feminine* (London: Routledge, 1991), pp. 140–47. Note that an empirical platform for Irigaray's speculation is her work on the sexist worth economy of the French language, in which women have inferior opportunities to speak and be spoken to. See, e.g., Irigaray et al., "Le Sexe Linguistique," *Languages* 21 (March 1987).

9. Immanuel Kant, *Critique of Practical Reason* 1.1.1, §§2–3.

10. See Russell E. Richey and Donald G. Jones, eds., *American Civil Religion* (New York: Harper & Row, 1974).

11. See, in ibid., Robert N. Bellah, "Civil Religion in America"; Sidney E. Mead, "The 'Nation with the Soul of a Church'"; Will Herberg, "America's Civil Religion: What It Is and Whence It Comes"; and W. Lloyd Warner, "An American Sacred Ceremony." But see also the mixed judgment of John L. Wilson, "An Historian's Approach to Civil Religion."

12. Bellah, "Civil Religion in America," p. 40.

13. Plato, *Apology*, trans. Harold North Fowler (Cambridge, MA: Harvard University Press, 1914), 34e–35b.

14. Plato, *Apology*, 20e–23b, 40a–c.

15. For example, Kongzi said: "I have listened in silence and noted what was said, I have never grown tired of learning nor wearied of teaching others what I have learned. These at least are merits which I can confidently claim. . . . The thought that 'I have left my moral power (*te*) untended, my learning unperfected, that I have heard of righteous men, but been unable to go to them; have heard of evil men, but been unable to reform them'—it is these thoughts that disquiet me." *The Analects of Confucius*, trans. Arthur Waley (New York: Vintage, 1938), p. 123, 7.1–3. The ultimate thrust of Confucianism with regard to transworth, however, like that of Stoicism, is to correlate the mandate of heaven with worldly reason as strictly as possible.

16. Herbert Richardson, "Civil Religion in Theological Perspective," in Richey and Jones, *American Civil Religion*, p. 175.

Index

Going Public

Going Public
New Strategies of Presidential Leadership

Second Edition

Samuel Kernell
University of California, San Diego

PRESS

A Division of Congressional Quarterly Inc.

Library of Congress Cataloging in Publication Data

Kernell, Samuel, 1945-
    Going public: new strategies of presidential leadership / Samuel
Kernell. — 2nd ed.
      p.   cm.
    Includes index.
    ISBN 0-87187-635-3 (hardback) — ISBN 0-87187-614-0 (softback)
    1. Presidents—United States.   2. Presidents—United States—Press
conferences.   3. Communication in politics—United States.
I. Title.
JK518.K46   1992
353.03'23—dc20   92-25581
                                                  CIP

Nothing is so unbelievable that oratory cannot make it acceptable.
                                                                —Cicero

One thought receiving wide expression [is] that the politician of tomorrow must become an "actor."
                                —Jack Gould, *New York Times,* June 25, 1951

Too many good people have been beaten because they tried to substitute substance for style.
                          —Adviser to Jimmy Carter, December 1976

Contents

Tables and Figures

Tables

Figures

Preface

Going public is a class of activities that presidents engage in as they promote themselves and their policies before the American public. Some examples of going public are a televised press conference, a special, prime-time address to the nation, a speech before a business convention on the West Coast, a visit to a day care center, and a White House ceremony to decorate a local hero that is broadcast via satellite to the hometown television station. What these various activities have in common is that they are intended principally to place presidents and their messages before the American people in a way that enhances their chances of success in Washington. Going public draws heavily upon techniques developed over the years in election campaigning; but in going public, the ultimate object of the president's designs is not the American voter, but fellow politicians in Washington.

The possibility that the president might at times appeal for the public's support in dealings with Congress occurred to James Madison. In *Federalist* No. 49 Madison argued against a constitutional provision that would allow any of the branches of the federal government to redress constitutional imbalance by appealing "to the people" for reform.

Citing recent occurrences in various state legislatures, Madison began by stipulating that if any branch were likely to be guilty of "aggrandizement," it would be the popular one, Congress. Though presidents "are generally the objects of jealousy; *and their administration is always liable to be discolored and rendered unpopular"* [emphasis added], members of Congress by virtue of being "more numerous," and having "connections of blood, of friendship, and of acquaintance, embrace a great proportion of the most influential part of society." Simply stated, Congress can trump any effort by the president to enlist public opinion.

Near the end of *Federalist* No. 49, Madison allowed the possibility that "the executive power might be in the hands of a peculiar favorite of the people." Against this he reverted to the distinction, common in his day, between the public's *passions* and its *reason.* Public appeals excite the passions so that the outcome, he concluded, "could never be expected to turn on the true merits of the question." In short, Madison had nothing much good to say about going public. Of course, his extraordinary precognition concerned political circumstances far different from those today that lead one to examine going public as a presidential strategy.

Today, over 200 years later, the matter warrants reassessment. No longer a subject only of speculation, modern presidents routinely appear before the American public on evening television on all kinds of issues ranging from national crises to the commemoration of a presidential library. Like Madison, I find the most interesting appeals to be those that involve the president's dealings with Congress. Because the president's success in publicly advancing his policies presupposes his own strong standing in the country, I also give considerable attention to the things presidents do to gain the public's favor.

The second edition further explores the use and effectiveness of going public, analyzing President Bush's media strategies, the link between opinion leadership and foreign affairs, and the rally phenomenon, in which presidents receive increased public support during times of international crisis, such as the Persian Gulf War.

The Plan of the Book

I begin by examining presidential power in the context of political relations in Washington. The president's influence with other, more or less autonomous politicians depends upon his ability to satisfy their needs and exploit their vulnerabilities. In the first chapter I develop a rationale for the rise of going public as a presidential strategy tailored to the ever-changing political relations in Washington. As other politicians' needs and expectations are changing, so too must the president's.

Alternative models of political relations in Washington that should be the most conducive to bargaining and going public are set forth in Chapter 2. It is not too surprising to find that different forms of influence thrive in quite different kinds of political communities. Paying special attention to changes in Congress and its relations with the presidency, I argue that within the past half century, political Washington has come to look less like institutionalized pluralism (which is conducive to bargaining) and more like individualized pluralism (which is conducive to going public). Presidents more freely go public nowadays because it is a strategy better adapted to modern politics.

In Chapter 3, I continue this analysis of presidential leadership as a function of evolving community relations, this time by chronicling presidential-press relations throughout the twentieth century. This inquiry reveals some of the specific political circumstances that gave rise to presidents adopting technologies of direct communications between the White House and the country—the *sine qua non* of going public.

Having established a rationale for the going public phenomenon, I next present the evidence that presidents do indeed increasingly rely upon public relations to build support for their policies in Washington. Chapter 4 presents 50-year trends that document the growing practice of going public, highlighting President Reagan's use of the televised address and President Bush's unprecedented number of domestic trips.

To appreciate the extent to which going public is altering the character of presidential leadership, one must examine firsthand the president's choice to go public or to bargain and its ramification on the choices of others. More than any other recent president, Reagan was ideally suited by experience, temperament, and ideology to capitalize on going public, and in Chapter 5, I analyze the strategies he employed in promoting his budgets in Congress during his first three years in office.

As presidents rely more heavily upon public strategies, their success in Washington will depend vitally upon the reactions of ordinary citizens. In Chapters 6 and 7, I shift the discussion from Washington relations to public opinion. We begin by considering the rally phenomenon, in which the public frequently responds to international crises by upgrading its assessment of the president's job performance. Typically, however, the president's public leadership rests on more than job performance ratings. Rather, it requires that the approval of the president's performance be transferred to support for his policies. In Chapter 6, I consider a model of this type of opinion change and then examine the effects of one specific presidential appeal—the Truman Doctrine speech of 1947. The way the American public did (and did not) respond to President Truman's appeal for emergency aid for Europe offers instruction to present-day presidents similarly interested in molding public opinion.

A president must not only be able to rally his supporters, he must also maintain the public's backing. Beyond the platitude "maintain peace and prosperity," the sizable literature on presidential popularity offers little strategic advice to presidents in this endeavor. In Chapter 7, I analyze the alternative ways a *strategic* president might seek to win and maintain the public's favor. Finally I conclude by considering some of the implications of going public on the continued evolution of community relations in Washington.

Because going public involves direct appeals to the American people, I think it is of value to be able to *see* and *hear* how presidential press conferences and direct communications from the White House have evolved from Franklin D. Roosevelt to present times. Drawing on historical newsreel and broadcast news footage, as well as interviews, I have prepared a half-hour videocassette for use in the classroom. Speeches and events of particular interest include Roosevelt's Fireside Chats, the Truman Doctrine speech, Nixon's "Silent Majority" speech, and Kennedy's first televised press conferences. This videotape is available from the publisher.

Acknowledgments

The proximate motivation to sit down and write the first edition of this book was Ronald Reagan. It was his success in 1981 that so confirmed and clarified my own views on the direction of presidential leadership. A fellowship at the Hoover Institution (and in particular the cookie hour banter there) gave me the needed time and additional inspiration to write *Going Public*. I am also grateful to the National Science Foundation, which supported the statistical analysis of public opinion in Chapter 7.

The revision of this text was prompted by the thoughtful comments and criticism generously offered by numerous colleagues over the past six years. In many respects, my conversations and correspondence with them have been as satisfying as writing the book.

Much of the text assumes the form of argument, but more of it is engaged in presenting statistical analysis and marshaling other kinds of evidence. Hardly any of these data originate with me. At various times I have called upon colleagues for assistance in obtaining hard-to-come-by facts and figures. The following individuals, some of whom I have never met, were most charitable in helping me obtain important material to sustain my argument: Roger Davidson, Denis Steven Rutkus, and Sula Richardson at the Congressional Research Service; Laura Kapnick at CBS News; Dianne Colonitas at Gallup; Teri Luke at A. C. Nielsen Company; and fellow scholars Richard Brody, Michael Baruch Grossman, Susan Webb Hammond, Martha Joynt Kumar, William Lammers, Richard W. Steele, and Jeffrey Tulis.

For the second edition, I'd like to acknowledge the contributions of Joe Foote, who gave me television ratings data he had employed in his fine book, *Television Access and Political Power*; Diane Buono at A. C. Nielsen Company, who updated Foote's series to include President Bush; and Gerald Rafshoon, who in interviews offered telling insights into President Carter's media strategy.

I'm grateful to Conrad, Herblock, and Jim Morin, whose cartoons of President Bush's public strategies are reproduced here. These cartoons aptly—and humorously—demonstrate that going public is a strategy fully appreciated by contemporary editorialists. Finally, students from my presidency class helped classify the public activities of President Bush in order to update the trends in public activities reported in Chapter 4.

Introduction: Going Public in Theory and Practice

1

When President Bush delivered his State of the Union address to the joint assembly of the mostly Democratic Congress in January 1992, he assumed what has become a familiar stance with Congress:

> I pride myself that I am a prudent man, and I believe that patience is a virtue. But I understand that politics is for some a game.... I submit my plan tomorrow. And I am asking you to pass it by March 20. And I ask the American people to let you know they want this action by March 20.
> From the day after that, if it must be: The battle is joined.
> And you know when principle is at stake, I relish a good fair fight.

Once upon a time, these might have been fighting words, but in this era of divided government, with the legislative and executive branches controlled by different parties, and presidents who therefore routinely enlist public support in their dealings with other Washington politicians, such rhetoric caused hardly a ripple in Congress.

By 1992, presidential appeals for public support had, in fact, become commonplace. Jimmy Carter delivered four major television addresses on the energy crisis alone and was about to give a fifth when his pollster convinced him that he would be wasting his time. Richard Nixon employed prime-time television so extensively to promote his policies on Vietnam that the Federal Communications Commission (FCC) took an unprecedented step when it applied the "fairness doctrine" to a presidential appeal and granted critics of the war response time on the networks.[1] (In the past, the FCC had occasionally invoked the "equal time" rule during presidential campaigns.) More than any other of Bush's predecessors, Ronald Reagan excelled in rallying public opinion behind presidential policies, but by the end of his second term, he had worn out his welcome with the networks, who stood to lose at least $200,000 in advertising each time he delivered one of his prime-time addresses. They instituted an independent assessment of the likely

1

newsworthiness of the president's address, thereby managing to pare down the frequency of Reagan's televised speeches.[2]

I call the approach to presidential leadership that has lately come into vogue at the White House "going public." It is a strategy whereby a president promotes himself and his policies in Washington by appealing to the American public for support. Forcing compliance from fellow Washingtonians by going over their heads to appeal to their constituents is a tactic not unknown during the first half of the century, but it was seldom attempted. Theodore Roosevelt probably first enunciated the strategic principle of going public when he described the presidency as the "bully pulpit." Moreover, he occasionally put theory into practice with public appeals for his Progressive reforms. During the next 30 years, other presidents also periodically summoned public support to help them in their dealings with Congress. Perhaps the most famous such instance is Woodrow Wilson's ill-fated whistle-stop tour of the country on behalf of his League of Nations treaty. Another historic example is Franklin D. Roosevelt's series of radio "fireside chats," which were designed less to subdue congressional opposition than to remind politicians throughout Washington of his continuing national mandate for the New Deal.

These historical instances are significant in large part because they were rare. Unlike President Nixon, who thought it important "to spread the White House around," [3] these earlier presidents were largely confined to Washington and obliged to speak to the country through the nation's newspapers. The concept and legitimizing precedents of going public may have been established during these years, but the emergence of presidents who *routinely* do so to promote their policies in Washington awaited the development of modern systems of transportation and mass communications. Going public should be appreciated as a strategic adaptation to the information age.

The regularity with which recent presidents have sought public backing for their Washington dealings has altered the way politicians both inside and outside the White House regard the office. The following chapters of this book present numerous instances of presidents preoccupied with public relations, as if these activities chiefly determined their success. Cases are recounted of other Washington politicians intently monitoring the president's popularity ratings and his addresses on television, as if his performance in these realms governed their own behavior. Also examined are testimonials of central institutional figures, such as the Speaker of the House of Representatives, citing the president's prestige and rhetoric as he explains Congress's actions. If the public ruminations of politicians are to be believed, the president's effectiveness in rallying public support has become a primary consideration for those who do business with him.

Presidential Theory

Going public merits study because presidents now appeal to the public routinely. But there is another reason as well. Compared with many other aspects of the modern presidency, going public has received scant attention in the scholarly literature. In part this can be attributed to its recent arrival in the president's repertoire, but by itself this explanation is inadequate. Although going public had not become a keystone of presidential leadership in the 1950s and 1960s when much of the influential scholarship on the subject was written, sufficient precedents were available for scholars to consider its potential for presidential leadership in the future.

Probably the main reason going public has received so little attention in the scholarly literature is its fundamental incompatibility with bargaining. Presidential power is the "power to bargain," as Richard E. Neustadt taught a generation of students of the presidency.[4] When Neustadt gave this theme its most evocative expression in 1960, the "bargaining president" had already become a centerpiece of pluralist theories of American politics. Nearly a decade earlier, Robert A. Dahl and Charles E. Lindblom had described the politician in America generically as "the human embodiment of a bargaining society." They made a special point to include the president in writing that despite his possessing "more hierarchical controls than any other single figure in the government ... like everyone else ... the President must bargain constantly." [5] Since Neustadt's landmark study, other major works in the field have reinforced and elaborated on the concept of the bargaining president.[6]

Going public violates bargaining in several ways. First, it rarely includes the kinds of exchanges necessary, in pluralist theory, for the American political system to function properly. At times, going public will be merely superfluous—fluff compared with the substance of traditional political exchange. Practiced in a dedicated way, however, it can threaten to displace bargaining.

Second, going public fails to extend benefits for compliance, but freely imposes costs for noncompliance. In appealing to the public to "tell your senators and representatives by phone, wire, and Mailgram that the future hangs in balance," the president seeks the aid of a third party—the public— to force other politicians to accept his preferences.[7] If targeted representatives are lucky, the president's success may cost them no more than an opportunity at the bargaining table to shape policy or to extract compensation. If unlucky, they may find themselves both capitulating to the president's wishes and suffering the reproach of constituents for having resisted him in the first place. By imposing costs and failing to offer benefits, going public is more akin to force than to bargaining. Nelson W. Polsby makes this point when he says that members of Congress may "find themselves ill disposed toward a president who prefers to deal indirectly with them [by going public] through what they may interpret as coercion rather than face-to-face in the spirit of mutual accommodation." [8] The following comment of one senator may well sum up commonly felt sentiments, if not the actions, of those on Capitol Hill who find themselves repeatedly pressured by the president's public appeals: "A lot of Democrats, even if they like the

President's proposal, will vote against him because of his radio address on Saturday." [9]

Third, going public entails public posturing. To the extent that it fixes the president's bargaining position, posturing makes subsequent compromise with other politicians more difficult. Because negotiators must be prepared to yield some of their clients' preferences to make a deal, bargaining proverbially proceeds best behind closed doors. Consider the difficulty Ronald Reagan's widely publicized challenge "My tax proposal is a line drawn in dirt" posed for subsequent budget negotiations in Washington.[10] Not only did the declaration threaten to cut away any middle ground on which a compromise might be constructed, it also probably stiffened the resolve of the president's adversaries, some of whom would later be needed to pass the administration's legislative program.

Finally, and possibly most injurious to bargaining, going public undermines the legitimacy of other politicians. It usurps their prerogatives of office, denies their role as representatives, and questions their claim to reflect the interests of their constituents. For a traditional bargaining stance with the president to be restored, these politicians would first have to reestablish parity, probably at a cost of conflict with the White House.[11]

Given these fundamental incompatibilities, one may further speculate that by spoiling the bargaining environment, going public renders the president's future influence ever more dependent upon his ability to generate popular support for himself and his policies. The degree to which a president draws upon public opinion determines the kind of leader he will be.

Presidential Practice

The distinction between bargaining and going public is a theme one hears more and more often from presidents and those who deal with them. No president has enlisted public strategies to better advantage than did Ronald Reagan. Throughout his tenure, he exhibited a full appreciation of bargaining and going public as the modern office's principal strategic alternatives. The following examples from a six-month survey of White House news coverage show how entrenched this bifurcated view of presidential strategy has become. The survey begins in late November 1984, when some members of the administration were pondering how the president might exploit his landslide victory and others were preparing a new round of budget cuts and a tax reform bill for the next Congress.

November 29, 1984. *Washington Post* columnist Lou Cannon reported the following prediction from a White House official: "We're going to have confrontation on spending and consultation on tax reform." The aide explained, "We have somebody to negotiate with us on tax reform, but may not on budget cuts." [12] By "confrontation" he was referring to the president's success in appealing to the public on national television, that is, in going public. By "consultation" he meant bargaining.

January 25, 1985. The above prediction proved accurate two months later when another staffer offered as pristine an evocation of going public as one is likely to find: "We have to look at it, in many ways, like a campaign. He [Reagan] wants to take his case to the people. You have a constituency of 535 legislators as opposed to 100 million voters. But the goal is the same—to get the majority of voters to support your position." [13]

February 10, 1985. In a nationally broadcast radio address, President Reagan extended an olive branch inviting members of Congress to "work with us in the spirit of cooperation and compromise" on the budget. This public statement probably did little to allay the frequently voiced suspicion of House Democratic leaders that such overtures were mainly intended for public consumption. One Reagan aide insisted, however, that the president simply sought to reassure legislators that "he would not 'go over their heads' and campaign across the country for his budget without trying first to reach a compromise." [14] In this statement the aide implicitly concedes the harm public pressure can create for bargaining but seeks to incorporate it advantageously into the strategic thinking of the politicians with whom the administration must deal by not foreswearing its use.

March 9, 1985. After some public sparring, the administration eventually settled down to intensive budget negotiations with the Republican-led Senate Finance Committee. Failing to do as well as he would like, however, Reagan sent a message to his party's senators through repeated unattributed statements to the press that, if necessary, he would "go to the people to carry our message forward." [15] Again, public appeals, though held in reserve, were threatened.

March 11, 1985. In an interview with a *New York Times* correspondent, a senior Reagan aide sized up his president: "He's liberated, he wants to get into a fight, he feels strongly and wants to push his program through himself. . . . Reagan never quite believed his popularity before the election, never believed the polls. Now he has it, and he's going to push . . . ahead with our agenda." [16]

May 16, 1985. To avoid entangling tax reform with budget deliberations in Congress, Reagan, at the request of Republican leaders, delayed unveiling his tax reform proposal until late May. A couple of weeks before Reagan's national television address on the subject, White House aides began priming the press with leaks on the proposal's content and promises that the president would follow it with a public relations blitz. In the words of one White House official, the plan was to force Congress to make a "binary choice between tax reform or no tax reform." [17] The administration rejected bargaining, as predicted nearly six months earlier by a White House aide, apparently for two strategic reasons. First, Reagan feared that in a quietly negotiated process, the tax reform package would unravel under the concerted pressure of the special interests. Second, by taking the high-profile approach of "standing up for the people against the special interests," in the words of one adviser, tax reform might do for Republicans what social security did for Democrats— make them the majority party.[18]

During these six months when bargaining held out promise—as it had during negotiations with the Senate Finance Committee—public appeals were held in reserve. The White House occasionally, however, threatened an appeal in trying to gain more favorable consideration. On other occasions, when opponents of the president's policies appeared capable of extracting major concessions—House Democrats on the budget and interest groups on tax reform, for example—the White House disengaged from negotiation and tried through public relations to force Congress to accept his policies. Although by 1985 news items such as the preceding excerpts seemed unexceptional as daily news, they are a recent phenomenon. One does not routinely find such stories in White House reporting 20 years earlier when, for example, John Kennedy's legislative agenda was stalled in Congress.

Clearly, going public appears to foster political relations that are quite at odds with those traditionally cultivated through bargaining. One may begin to examine this new phenomenon by asking, what is it about modern politics that would inspire presidents to go public in the first place?

Notes

1. Newton N. Minow, John Bartlow Martin, and Lee M. Mitchell, *Presidential Television* (New York: Basic Books, 1973), 84-87.
2. Peter J. Boyer, "Networks Refuse to Broadcast Reagan's Plea," *New York Times,* February 3, 1988.
3. Robert B. Semple, Jr., "Nixon Eludes Newsmen on Coast Trip," *New York Times,* August 3, 1970, 16.
4. Richard E. Neustadt, *Presidential Power* (New York: John Wiley and Sons, 1980).
5. Robert A. Dahl and Charles E. Lindblom, *Politics, Economics, and Welfare* (New York: Harper and Row, 1953), 333.
6. Among them are Aaron Wildavsky, *The Politics of the Budgetary Process* (Boston: Little, Brown, 1964); Graham Allison, *The Essence of Decision* (Boston: Little, Brown, 1971); Hugh Heclo, *The Government of Strangers* (Washington, D.C.: Brookings Institution, 1977); and Nelson W. Polsby, *Consequences of Party Reform* (New York: Oxford University Press, 1983).
7. From Ronald Reagan's address to the nation on his 1986 budget. Jack Nelson, "Reagan Calls for Public Support of Deficit Cuts," *Los Angeles Times,* April 25, 1985, 1.
8. Nelson W. Polsby, "Interest Groups and the Presidency: Trends in Political

Intermediation in America," in *American Politics and Public Policy,* ed. Walter Dean Burnham and Martha Wagner Weinbey (Cambridge: MIT Press, 1978), 52.

9. Hedrick Smith, "Bitterness on Capitol Hill," *New York Times,* April 24, 1985, 14.

10. Ed Magnuson, "A Line Drawn in Dirt," *Time,* February 22, 1982, 12-13.

11. See David S. Broder, "Diary of a Mad Majority Leader," *Washington Post,* December 13, 1981, C1, C5; David S. Broder, "Rostenkowski Knows It's His Turn," *Washington Post National Weekly Edition,* June 10, 1985, 13.

12. Lou Cannon, "Big Spending-Cut Bill Studied," *Washington Post,* November 29, 1984, A8.

13. Bernard Weinraub, "Reagan Sets Tour of Nation to Seek Economic Victory," *New York Times,* January 25, 1985, 43.

14. Bernard Weinraub, "Reagan Calls for 'Spirit of Cooperation' on Budget and Taxes," *New York Times,* February 10, 1985, 32. On Democratic suspicions of Reagan's motives see Hedrick Smith, "O'Neill Reflects Democratic Strategy on Budget Cuts and Tax Revisions," *New York Times,* December 6, 1984, B20; and Margaret Shapiro, "O'Neill's New Honeymoon with Reagan," *Washington Post National Weekly Edition,* February 11, 1985, 12.

15. Jonathan Fuerbringer, "Reagan Critical of Budget View of Senate Panel," *New York Times,* March 9, 1985, 1. Senate Majority Leader Robert Dole told reporters that if the president liked the Senate's final budget package he would campaign for it "very vigorously . . . going to television, whatever he needs to reduce federal spending." Karen Tumulty, "Reagan May Get Draft of Budget Accord Today," *Los Angeles Times,* April 4, 1985, 1.

16. Bernard Weinraub, "In His 2nd Term, He Is Reagan the Liberated," *New York Times,* March 11, 1985, 10.

17. David E. Rosenbaum, "Reagan Approves Primary Elements of Tax Overhaul," *New York Times,* May 16, 1985, 1.

18. Robert W. Merry and David Shribman, "G.O.P. Hopes Tax Bill Will Help It Become Majority Party Again," *Wall Street Journal,* May 23, 1985, 1. See also Rosenbaum, "Reagan Approves Primary Elements of Tax Overhaul," 14. Instances such as those reported here continued into summer. See, for example, Jonathan Fuerbringer, "Key Issues Impede Compromise on Cutting Deficit," *New York Times,* June 23, 1985, 22.

How Washington and Presidents Have Changed   2

The incompatibility of bargaining and going public presents a pressing theoretical question. Why should presidents come to favor a strategy of leadership that appears so incompatible with the principles of pluralist theory? Why, if other Washington elites legitimately and correctly represent the interests of their clients and constituents, would anything be gained by going over their heads? The answers to these questions are several and complex, having to do with the ways Washington and presidents have changed. All in all, bargaining has shown declining efficiency, and opportunities to go public have increased.

Some would account for the rise of going public by resorting to the imperative of technology as an explanation. Certainly, advances in transportation and communications have been indispensable to this process, but they have not been sufficient in themselves to alter political relations in such a contradictory way. Others who have noticed that recent presidents frequently prefer public relations to negotiation with members of Congress blame the presidential selection reforms of the late 1960s and the 1970s. The system of nominating presidential candidates through primaries (along with federal campaign financing) produces presidents with weak ties to core constituent groups within their parties and with little experience in Washington politics. They do, however, have a lot of experience in campaigning. Rather than negotiate with other institutional elites, these presidents are more inclined to pursue the same public strategies that placed them in the White House. Though this explanation has merit, it, too, is insufficient. If presidential selection reforms had simply been grafted onto traditional political arrangements, they might explain the inclination of recent presidents to go public, but they would not account for the success of that strategy. For traditional pluralist explanations of the presidency, Ronald Reagan's 1981 accomplishments—passing major cuts in social programs while cutting taxes and sharply increasing military spending—pose a serious anomaly.

There is another, more fundamental reason for the discrepancy between theory and current practice. Presidents have preferred to go public in recent years perhaps because the strategy offers a better prospect of success than it did in the past. Politicians in Washington may no longer be as tractable to bargaining as they once were. We are in an era of divided government, with Democrats in control of Congress and Republicans holding the presidency. Each side frequently finds political advantage in frustrating the other. On such occasions, posturing in preparation for the next election takes precedence over bargaining.

The decoupling of voters from political parties across the nation, which makes possible the occurrence of divided government, has also had more pervasive consequences for political relations among politicians in Washington. Weaker leaders, looser coalitions, more individualistic politicians, and stronger public pressure are among the developments reworking political relations in Washington that may inspire presidents to embrace a strategy of leadership antithetical to that prescribed by theory.

Institutionalized Pluralism: The Bargaining Community

In the early 1950s Dahl and Lindblom developed a theoretical rationale for America's particular brand of pluralism. In *Politics, Economics, and Welfare* they helped establish a framework for the study of American politics that would guide scholars for the next generation. They described the practice of politics in such a way as to make the appearance of a bargaining president inevitable.

> The politician is, above all, the man whose career depends upon the successful negotiation of bargains. To win office he must negotiate electoral alliances. To satisfy his electoral alliance he must negotiate alliances with other legislators and with administrators, for his control depends upon negotiation. Most of his time is consumed in bargaining. This is the skill he cultivates; it is the skill that distinguishes the master-politician from the political failure.[1]

For what structure of politics is bargaining ideally suited? It is one in which political elites, and for the most part only elites, matter. The citizenry is offered limited and occasional avenues of participation—through periodic elections and membership in such mediating associations as unions, voluntary societies, and churches. Politics need to be structured this way so that elites retain the flexibility to bargain and the certainty that once an accord is reached it will not be undone. The citizenry's interests are not ignored, however. Partitioned geographically, citizens participate vicariously through their elected representatives; partitioned functionally, they participate through interest groups and the agencies for whom they are clients.

In this pluralistic system each politician must be reckoned with not only according to the strength of his or her constituency but also according to the institutional resources provided by his or her office. Through intensive constitutionalism, the Founding Fathers sought to mitigate the plebiscitary tendency of democracy by giving officeholders legitimacy apart from their representative role. They succeeded and bestowed on Washington what has evolved into the pronounced institutional character of its politics.

In the absence of some overriding criterion, such as party fidelity, authority within institutions is generally distributed by seniority. Everywhere, senior partners matter more than junior partners, and transients for whom Washington is a way station to some private career count for little. These, in Hugh Heclo's words, are "the low credit risk in a high credit market." [2] From time to time some politicians will graduate to new roles as seniority rules are triggered to fill vacancies at the top. Others will try to rise to higher office by expanding their electoral constituency. Some of these, inevitably, will be defeated, along with others who merely sought reelection. And many of those forced off the career ladder will elect to leave Washington altogether.

Elections may be commended by democratic theory, but from the local vantage of a bargaining society they mostly pose disruptions. By generating turnover, they raise uncertainty for bargaining. A politician at risk in the next election will have greater interest in receiving credit than in extending it. But recognizing his precarious existence, his potential trading partners may see themselves giving something for nothing. This leaves, of course, little common ground for transacting business. Beyond this, campaigns and elections are unwanted distractions from the real business of politicians in Washington. Under the pressure of reelection, some community members may be tempted to hector or to make excessive demands of unaccommodating bargaining partners, or otherwise to behave in ways that make future negotiation and compromise more difficult.

The same disruptive tendencies are true of public opinion more generally. To function smoothly, a bargaining society must insulate itself against short-term swings in popular sentiment. Appreciating this, the Founding Fathers minimized the influence of the citizenry through staggered elections, which would require that "public passions" be sustained for a long time before they could influence the policies of each branch of government. And by differentiating constituencies into states and by delegating to these subdivisions specific constitutional prerogatives, they sought to give minorities a sufficient toehold to resist short-lived majorities.

A Washington ideally suited for bargaining should therefore be a stable and a somewhat insular community in which even a new president may be viewed as an interloper. It must be this way if the circumscribed avenues of mutual adjustment through negotiation are to work effectively. The system also needs to be this way to accommodate the local political economy. Negotiation occurs within a market where dissimilar goods and services are bartered. Identifying mutually attractive exchanges takes time, and once a transaction is opened it may not be consummated immediately. Indebtedness is commonplace; unspecified IOUs may not be called in for years.

I call this system "institutionalized pluralism" for several reasons. First, political exchange occurs within a dense institutional milieu that allocates resources among actors and identifies the relevant bargaining partners. Second, a stable bargaining society may be expected to institutionalize informal rules of the marketplace that regulate behavior and reduce uncertainty. Perhaps the most sacred commandment is "Honor one's commitments." Variants of this are tailored to each role. To the lobbyist it means never lie by knowingly giving legislators incorrect information on which they may base a vote or seek to persuade others. For the correspondent it means never publish material provided off the record or directly attribute background information to the source. Playing it straight with one's colleagues does not require that a participant reveal true preferences at the bargaining table, but it does require that once a bargain is agreed to, the politician strive to fulfill his or her part of it.

Another commandment is "Don't use force," for the simple reason that force usually will not work. Dahl and Lindblom noted, "The politician does not often give orders. He can rarely employ unilateral controls. Even as a chief executive or a cabinet officer he soon discovers that his control depends upon his skill in bargaining." [3] Even if politicians or bureaucrats enjoy hierarchical superiority over another or in some other way could unilaterally preempt another's choice, they should hesitate to use this advantage. That force begets counterforce is a law of political physics. A politician may be able to avoid compensation one day, but he cannot ensure himself against retribution the next.

Besides, collectively, a politician's peers in Washington have efficient ways of judging and punishing individuals who violate trust or fail to honor the standards of mutual accommodation. Each politician carries a reputation, a continuously updated record of all the qualities that are relevant to others as they contemplate doing business with him or her. Senator A may double-cross Senator B, but in doing so, he or she may be sure that some community members are watching and still others will soon learn about it. Depending upon the seriousness of the violation, concerted sanctions might be applied. Collective enforcement of community norms will generally be unnecessary, however. Other actors' pursuit of simple self-interest will suffice. The violator will naturally suffer ostracism proportionate to his or her transgression. What other senators, for instance, would be cheerfully willing to work with Senator A? If they were willing to deal with Senator A at all, it would be on their terms and with the requirement that his or her end of the bargain must first be fulfilled.

The local culture may also contain a variety of functional folkways and mores that restrain contravention of tacit rules. One such venerable understanding allows senators and representatives when back home to rail against Congress, the other party, and its leadership as much as they feel necessary to satisfy appetites of constituents; but in Washington, such displays are inappropriate. Having been exposed only to public rhetoric before arriving in Washington as a freshman in the 1950s, Clem Miller marveled at the "cocoon of good feeling" that enveloped Congress.[4]

Reciprocity is so vital to a bargaining society that it is deeply ingrained in the normative order. Writing about the Senate of the mid-1950s, Donald R. Matthews observed, "It is not an exaggeration to say that reciprocity is a way of life in the Senate." As a senator's administrative assistant told him, "My boss . . . will—if it doesn't mean anything to him—do a favor for any other Senator. It doesn't matter *who* he is. It's not a matter of friendship, it's just a matter of I won't be an S.O.B. if you won't be one." [5]

Trust and fellow-feeling will at times give rise to more focused and ambitious reciprocity arrangements. Whether because of shared goals or complementary resources or both, two politicians may come to recognize the mutual gain possible through a continuing relationship. The bargain may never be explicitly stated, much less negotiated, and no ledger of indebtedness kept. Instead, a simple understanding to work together exists until one party decides the relationship is too costly and ends it. Bargains in the form of relationships occur most naturally among proximate participants who share interests—among congressional committee members, for instance, or between an agency head and the representative of a clientele group the agency serves. The time-honored practice of "cue giving" between pairs of like-minded members of Congress during floor voting is a minor instance of this.

Protocoalitions

The president is doubtless the bargaining community's most prominent member. But even the consummate bargainer in this high office can participate in only a small fraction of the transactions that must occur daily in Washington to form governing coalitions. Exchange is thus a necessary and ubiquitous activity of Washington elites. It does not, however, proceed randomly.

Institutionalized pluralism promotes a two-tiered process of coalition building. The higher-level, presidential coalition can be distinguished by its greater size, the diversity of its membership, the specificity of its goals, and its fragility. Presidential coalitions are usually temporary associations, forming and dissolving around a single issue or bill. Arrived at in an ad hoc fashion, they rarely survive the resolution of the issue in question.

The building of lower-level coalitions, or protocoalitions, follows predictable lines by adhering to a couple of political principles. First, it spans the constitutionally mandated policy course from enactment to implementation. Because institutional barriers confine communication, exchange proceeds more easily and commonly within rather than between organizations.[6] Well-known examples of protocoalitions are Senate Majority Leader Lyndon Johnson's Democratic troops, Wilbur Mills's Ways and Means Committee, the Justice Department's civil rights lawyers under Nixon, even Eisenhower's military-industrial complex, if there was such a thing. Second, those building protocoalitions seek out mutual needs and complementary resources. The proverbial "iron triangles" among agencies, clienteles, and congressional committees are so called because they follow the policy course, spanning institutional boundaries as they do so and incorporating dissimilar yet compatible partners. These dense networks of political exchange form the subcommunities of institutionalized pluralism.

Many protocoalitions may be ad hoc and short lived, but those that matter most tend to be constructed more coherently and durably. They arise not from some fleeting issue but from kindred interest or the continuing need of proximate participants to work together. For example, the agency heads in the Department of Agriculture, subcommittee members of the House and Senate Agriculture committees, and the Washington representatives of the numerous farm groups must cooperate if they are to satisfy the interests of their common client—America's farmers. Rarely are these entities self-sufficient. Iron triangles notwithstanding, a protocoalition typically must join with others if its bill is to be passed or its policy implemented effectively. Leaders of protocoalitions arise if for no other reason than to conduct these external relations.

Activities and transactions among these groups may be far more consequential for the president's own success than any business he might conduct with them directly. Limits on his time, energy, and resources may prevent a president from intruding even when he recognizes the damage their transactions may have on his own designs. More often than not, the president must look on as an interested bystander. These protocoalitions define his options; they may prescribe particular combinations of coalition partners; they may even dictate the substance of exchange. Once the protocoalition pacts are concluded, they come to the president as givens from which he will try to stitch together a larger, more institutionally expansive coalition.

The President's Place in Institutionalized Pluralism

Constructing coalitions across the broad institutional landscape of Congress, the bureaucracy, interest groups, courts, and state governments requires a politician who possesses a panoramic view and commands the resources necessary to engage the disparate parochial interests of Washington's political elites. Only the president enjoys such vantage and resources. Traditional presidential scholarship leaves little doubt as to how they should be employed. Nowhere has Dahl and Lindblom's framework of the bargaining society been more forcefully employed than in Richard E. Neustadt's classic *Presidential Power,* published in 1960. Neustadt observes,

> Status and authority yield bargaining advantages. But in a government of "separated institutions sharing powers," they yield them to all sides. With the array of vantage points at his disposal, a President may be far more persuasive than his logic or his charm could make him. But outcomes are

not guaranteed by his advantages. There remain the counter pressures those whom he would influence can bring to bear on him from vantage points at their disposal. Command has limited utility; persuasion becomes give-and-take. . . .

The President's advantages are checked by the advantages of others. Continuing relationships will pull in both directions. These are relationships of mutual dependence. A President depends upon the men he would persuade; he has to reckon with his need or fear of them. They too will possess status, or authority, or both, else they would be of little use to him. Their vantage points confront his own; their power tempers his.[7]

Bargaining is thus the essence of presidential leadership, and pluralist theory explicitly rejects unilateral forms of influence as usually insufficient and ultimately costly. The ideal president is one who seizes the center of the Washington bazaar and actively barters with fellow politicians to build winning coalitions. He must do so, according to this theory, or he will forfeit any claim to leadership.

A president has the potential for symbiosis. Protocoalitions provide him with economy: he need not engage every coalition partner; talking to their leaders will do. In return the president provides protocoalitions with much needed coordination although, as Neustadt points out, presidential activity guarantees no more than that the president will be a "clerk." Clearly, however, institutionalized pluralism offers the virtuoso bargainer in the White House the opportunity for real leadership.

For years critics complained that autocratic committee chairmen, indifferent party leaders, and the conservative coalition of Republicans and Southern Democrats prevented Democratic presidents from achieving their ambitious policy goals. Yet institutionalized pluralism requires the president to keep company with these "obstacles" if he is to succeed. Leaders of lower-level coalitions may extract a steep price for cooperation, and at times they may defeat him outright. Still, as difficult as a Lyndon Johnson, a Wilbur Mills, a Wilbur Cohen at Social Security, or a J. Edgar Hoover might have been when he got his back up, each was indispensable as a trading partner. The reason is not difficult to see. Consider what these men had to offer: a majority leader who could strike a deal with the president on compromise legislation and then return to the chamber floor and deliver the critical votes necessary for its passage; a committee chairman who spoke so authoritatively for his committee that its markup sessions were spent detailing the language of an agreement reached earlier; or an agency head who, once persuaded, effectively redirected his organization's activities. A president simply has insufficient authority to command his way to success and insufficient time and energy to negotiate individually with everyone whose cooperation he needs.[8]

Bargaining Techniques

Perhaps the best way to specify more concretely how presidents behave under institutionalized pluralism is to list some of the things they have traditionally done when they have run into trouble with Congress. The doors of the Oval Office would fling open and scores of representatives and senators— some reluctantly, others with shopping lists in hand—would traipse through to hear the president's case. When large blocks of votes needed to be shifted, compromise positions were readied by White House aides with an eye toward giving the president the margin of victory at the least expense. As the vote date neared and the requisite number of converts shrank, fence-sitters would be singled out for special treatment. Outstanding IOUs would be called in and fresh ones tendered as the president courted ambivalent legislators with promises of goods and services for their constituencies.

These and many of the other tactics traditionally part of the presidential repertoire are essentially private transactions among elite negotiators. Beyond understanding the character of the game, the president must also sense the needs of the potential partners in the coalition and discover the most cost-effective exchange. What constitutes the "right stuff" for bargaining presidents has been a frequent subject of rich description. Douglass Cater's offering is typical:

> A President has to have an acute awareness of the resistances that exist to any step he takes. The elements of his essential knowledge can be picayune: that he must communicate with a certain committee chairman in the mornings because he is too drunk by afternoon—any afternoon—to be coherent; that a certain bureaucrat is so buttressed by interest-group support that he can regularly defy the occupant of the White House, Democrat or Republican; that a certain issue has grown so mired in lobbyist intrigue that it is irredeemable. If he is to be any good, a President must have a mental catalogue of the movers and shakers in the Washington community, their habits and habitats. He needs to know the crotchets of M. De Gaulle of France, Mr. Meany of AFL-CIO, Mr. Reston of the *New York Times,* and many, many others.[9]

Subtlety and fine tuning in bargaining are vital to conserve resources in such situations. The president's bargaining chips are limited, but demand for their expenditure is insatiable.

No president has understood the requirements of institutionalized pluralism better than Franklin Roosevelt. Occasionally there were lapses, but usually the congruence between the actions expected and Roosevelt's practice was remarkable—so much so that at times the model of the bargaining president appears to be little more than a generalization of Roosevelt's style. In his actions alone, every aspect of bargaining can be illustrated. I shall resist the temptation to add to the already voluminous Roosevelt hagiography, but not before considering an example of the paragon at work. In a memo dated September 16, 1941, Roosevelt instructs his aide Marvin McIntyre in the art of grooming congressmen:

> I have been disturbed about things I am hearing very frequently about "the Hill." You have probably heard the same. A large number of Senators and Congressmen, who should be and usually are our friends, have been saying

entirely too frequently that they get no cooperation from the White House; that no one in the White House will talk to them unless we want their votes. A new refrain is that the only way to get attention from the Administration is to vote against it a few times.

I do not think there is too much basis for these complaints. As you well know, a large portion of the favors they ask for we cannot give them. But I do think we should create a medium for them to register their complaints— and I want you to do that job.

I certainly do not mean that you should be a liaison man with the Hill.... But you should be the man in the White House whom Senators and Congressmen can talk to. It does not matter so much that they don't get what they want. If they can tell their colleagues and friends "I told Marvin McIntyre at the White House so and so" that will be a psychological advantage. If they can also say "Marvin McIntyre told me so and so", they will soon have a feeling their advice is being listened to.

I think the way to get this started is to do it in a very casual manner. If you could start telephoning two or three of your Congressional friends a day just to ask how they are and what they know, word will soon get around that Marvin McIntyre will listen to them. In a few weeks or so, the casual phone calls will soon develop into an iron-clad system. [Emphasis in original.][10]

The moral of Roosevelt's instruction to his aide was that the president's success rests upon satisfying others' needs.

Public Opinion and Institutionalized Pluralism

Public pressure has little place in the community I have described. To be effective it would generally need either to emanate from a dominant economic interest of the constituency or client, such as the tobacco industry in North Carolina, or to be an otherwise pervasive and strongly held value, such as anti-gun control sentiments among hunters in Montana. Presumably, representatives who know their districts, or agency heads or lobbyists who understand their clients, will represent the values of the constituency, thereby making grass-roots expression redundant. Writing about the Senate of the 1940s and 1950s, William S. White asserted, "Constituent pressure . . . is rarely the *cause* of any Senator's action." White recalled a conversation with Senator Theodore Francis Green of Rhode Island, who was at the time receiving hate mail from some of his state's McCarthyites. Pointing to "shoals of postcards," White asked, " 'What about all these, Senator?' 'Old disgusting little things, aren't they?' he said in a bored fastidious drawl, using the very end of his fingernail to flick his communications into the wastebasket. That closed the subject with him." [11]

Of interest group tactics during the same period, David Truman observed, "Skillful interest groups . . . make limited use of letters, telegrams, and petitions," and cited comments in a trade association publication that one or two personal contacts were "of far greater value than a hundred letters or telegrams from persons unknown to the legislator." [12]

Given such conditions, a president who goes public would only undercut the abilities of other Washington elites to act as representatives—and these are people with whom he must deal. Moreover, to the degree that the community is insulated, the strategy would not work. In denying elites their place at the bargaining table, the mobilization of public opinion becomes little more than an abrasive. One can see this in a 1944 survey of members of Congress that found them by and large resentful of the Roosevelt administration's occasional use of public opinion polls to buttress its case before Congress. One midwesterner responded, "A poll is supposed to represent the people; the Congressman represents them; he should know what the people think." He added, "Polls are in contradiction to representative government." Others interviewed concurred that polls were injurious.[13] Mobilizing public opinion might succeed occasionally, but in a setting of institutionalized pluralism, where reciprocity is normative and memory long, its regular use as a strategic device can sow only ill will and ultimately reap failure.

Public Opinion and Bargaining Presidents

Not all the tactics and resources available to bargaining presidents are private. Among Washington's political elites, the president is, after all, the only one chosen by the national electorate. Even some nineteenth-century presidents—the manufactured products of political machines who delivered their State of the Union messages to Congress via courier—found occasions between elections to solicit popular support.

Going public is sufficiently well precedented that statements of the pluralist theory of presidential leadership must take it into account. According to this view, however, if public pressure is to be applied, it must be insinuated into the bargaining process. Timely leaks of information—as age-old as they appear modern—have long made the president's bargaining posture more defensible to those outside Washington and hence more formidable to those inside. Trial balloons floated by presidents or their associates have also been a favorite technique to test the political winds before embarking on a new policy course. More direct public pressure has at times taken the form of personal overtures to sympathetic constituencies and organizations to voice their grievances to their representatives who would deny the president's policies. But in pluralist theory each of these public tactics is appropriate for the bargaining president only to the degree that it helps clarify the stakes and heighten others' appreciation of the need to bargain with him.

Consistent with the dictates of institutionalized pluralism, bargaining presidents of an earlier era rarely relied upon public strategies. With some, this shows up in their skepticism toward public opinion surveys. Harry Truman stated flatly, "I never paid any attention to the polls myself," arguing that they "did not represent facts but mere speculation." [14] Franklin Roosevelt, a president with a stronger public mandate to draw upon, showed more interest in surveys. Before scientific surveys were available, Roosevelt's staff monitored public opinion as best it could in other ways. The White House mail was continuously tallied, and the editorial stances of the nation's newspapers were routinely reported to Roosevelt in summary form.[15] Sometimes Roosevelt more actively sought out such information, as in late 1936 when he asked each state director of the National Emergency Council to assess public opinion toward an announced reallocation of jobs under the Works Progress Administration. The results of this canvass are displayed in Table 2-1. That the directors' reading of public opinion strongly correlated with the editorial positions of local papers is evidence of the poor state of knowledge about public opinion in the presurvey era.

After polling came into vogue, the Roosevelt administration occasionally commissioned official surveys. Except at elections, the president was usually more concerned with the views of specific publics who might be adversely affected by his policies than with any summary of national opinion.[16] According to Richard W. Steele,

> He saw public attitudes not as a mandate for initiatives generated outside the White House, but as potential obstacles to courses he had already decided upon. Since the President's interest in the public's views stemmed largely from his concern for preserving or strengthening Administration power, the information he sought was issue oriented, and especially attuned to the attitudes of those Americans whose opinions were most intense, and usually most negative, toward a given policy. Thus midwesterners came in for special attention in regard to their attitudes toward intervention; mothers, and women in general, concerning draft extension; farmers in regard to farm policy; Poles and Catholics in regard to relations with Russia, and so forth. This also helps explain Roosevelt's strong interest in the generally hostile views of the press and the business community. *The opposition of these publics could encourage obstructionism in Congress....If the President could get by these formidable groups without generating excessive criticism, he had a good chance of success....* Roosevelt's conception of the public's role tended to focus his attention on the opinions of the powerful and hostile. [Emphasis added.][17]

President Roosevelt occasionally went public to improve his position in Washington. Before World War II he delivered fireside chats directing public attention to his legislative agenda. Only once, however, did he succumb to the temptation to exhort the citizenry to pressure Congress. Using the ages of current Supreme Court members as an excuse, Roosevelt tried in 1937 to increase their number by six. This instance, the "court packing" proposal of 1937, ended in a fiasco.[18] Compared with today's presidents, Roosevelt enlisted public strategies sparingly. His game remained in Washington. His interest in public opinion was motivated by a need to anticipate and, when possible, to neutralize the representatives of interested publics who might oppose his programs.

Nowhere is the value of public opinion to a bargaining president more systematically explored than in Neustadt's study of presidential power. On the importance of public prestige, he writes:

Table 2-1   Presidential Survey of Public Opinion on Reallocation of
Jobs under the Works Progress Administration, 1936

States	Actual curtailment to Dec. 15, 1936[1] (%)	Possible further reductions for Jan., Feb., Mar. 1937[1] (%)	Reaction of Workers	Reaction of Public	Reaction of Press
Ala.	0	5	none	none	none
Ariz.	13	20	none	none	none
Ark.	8	0	none	favorable	favorable
Calif.	1	0	unfavorable	none	none
Colo.	20	14	unfavorable	none	favorable
Conn.	8	0	unfavorable	favorable	favorable
Fla.	2.25	10.6	none	favorable	none
Ga.	6.4	5	unfavorable	favorable	favorable
Idaho	0	0	unfavorable	none	favorable
Ill.	0	0	unfavorable	none	none
Ind.	5	0	unfavorable	unfavorable	none
Iowa	6	0	unfavorable	unfavorable	unfavorable
Kan.	10	0	unfavorable	unfavorable	unfavorable
Ky.	0	0	none	none	none
La.	7	0	none	none	none
Maine	0	0	favorable	favorable	favorable
Md.	8	0	unfavorable	none	none
Mass.	0	7	unfavorable	favorable	favorable
Mich.	9	0	unfavorable	favorable	favorable
Minn.	7	0	unfavorable	50-50	favorable
Miss.	9.04	6.9	unfavorable	favorable	favorable
Mo.	3	0	none	none	none
Mont.	20	0	unfavorable	unfavorable	unfavorable
Neb.	10	0	unfavorable	unfavorable	unfavorable
Nev.	0	0	none	none	none
N.H.	0	0	unfavorable	unfavorable	unfavorable
N.J.	4	0	unfavorable	favorable	favorable
N.M.	7.9	9.4	none	none	none
N.Y.	5.5	0	unfavorable	50-50	50-50
N.C.	0	12	none	favorable	favorable
N.D.	0	0	unfavorable	unfavorable	unfavorable
Ohio	8	0	unfavorable	none	none
Okla.	0	0	unfavorable	none	none
Ore.	0	0	none	none	none
Pa.	10	0	unfavorable	unfavorable	unfavorable
R.I.	5.4	0	unfavorable	favorable	favorable
S.C.	3	4	unfavorable	unfavorable	unfavorable
S.D.	49.5	0	unfavorable	unfavorable	unfavorable
Tenn.	13	0	unfavorable	none	none
Texas	1.9	2.8	unfavorable	favorable	favorable
Utah	10.3	0	unfavorable	none	none
Vt.	15	0	unfavorable	none	none
Va.	0	10	none	none	none
Wash.	0	0	none	none	none
W.Va.	1	7	none	none	none
Wis.	0	10	none	none	none
Wyo.	0	0	unfavorable	none	none

[1] Based on employment as of September 1, 1936.

SOURCE: Franklin D. Roosevelt Personal Collection, National Emergency Council box, Franklin Delano Roosevelt Library, Hyde Park, New York.

The Washingtonians who watch a President ... have to think about his standing with the public outside of Washington. They have to gauge his popular prestige. Because they think about it, public standing is a source of influence for him, another factor bearing upon their willingness to give him what he wants.

It works on power just as reputation does through the mechanism of anticipated reactions ... they anticipate reactions from the public. Most members of the Washington community depend upon outsiders to support them or their interests. The dependence may be as direct as votes, or it may be as indirect as passive toleration. Dependent men must take account of popular reaction to *their* actions. What their publics may think of them becomes a factor, therefore, in deciding how to deal with the desires of a President. His prestige enters into that decision; their publics are part of his. Their view from inside Washington of how outsiders view him thus affects their influence with them.[19]

Elsewhere Neustadt argues that presidents must husband their prestige just as they would their reputation and bargaining chips. Still, politics remains the exclusive domain of Washingtonians. Public opinion never does more than passively color the bargaining context. Within this intentionally confined role for public opinion, Neustadt concedes only that strong popular support purchases the president some leeway in his dealings with other elites.

Moreover, he does not consider that the president might abandon negotiation (or even threaten to) and take his case directly to the American people. But if Washington politicians are dependent on public opinion and so sensitive to a popular president's standing that some may recoil at being identified as his adversary, why should they not be all the more accommodating when the president summons public opinion to his side? If, as Neustadt suggests, elections allow the president's prestige to be insinuated into the bargaining society, why do they not also open the community to the president's active solicitation of popular support?

Neustadt offers two reasons. First, the public is normally inattentive. Only when events and conditions press upon the nation and the welfare of citizens does the president win an audience.[20] (Washington's insulation from short-term swings in public opinion is thus complemented by the country's inattention to elite relations.) Second, as a substitute for bargaining, going public amounts to little more than the application of force and necessarily violates the interdependence and reciprocity that make bargaining possible. It assumes a status akin to "command"—Neustadt's term for the unilateral application of authority—which he argues is usually costly and indicates previous failure to achieve one's goal through persuasion.[21]

Two Early Cases of Going Public

Dramatic, even heroic, instances of going public have tended historically to occur against a backdrop of prior failure. Consider briefly what are perhaps the two outstanding twentieth-century instances when presidents have gone public to pressure Congress.

The first is President Woodrow Wilson's attempt to force Senate ratification of his version of the League of Nations Treaty. Unwilling to accept any of the reservations to the treaty being promulgated by Republican Majority Leader Henry Cabot Lodge and a Foreign Relations Committee stacked with "irreconcilables and strong reservationists," President Wilson decided as "a last resort" to abandon Washington and take his case to the American public.[22] His travel schedule would have been grueling even for a healthy man, which Wilson was not. The trip began on September 3, 1919, and ended with his stroke on October 3. During the month he logged in over 8,000 miles, made 37 speeches, and endured countless hand-shaking gatherings. For all of his "resolve to overpower his opposition," his effort won him no new support in Washington, and by most accounts it stiffened opposition.[23] Going public broke Wilson politically as well as physically.

A second instance, though it too began in adversity, yielded a far different outcome. The Truman Doctrine speech is widely credited not only with securing President Truman his emergency aid legislation for Greece and Turkey but also with laying the groundwork for the more comprehensive Marshall Plan that shortly followed. In this instance the public appeal rested not on a prior failure of bargaining but on its remote chance of success before an isolationist, Republican-dominated Congress. Seeking counsel from Republican Senate leader Arthur Vandenberg, Truman reportedly was advised that he would first have to "scare hell out of the country" if he hoped to persuade Congress to pass his emergency aid program.[24]

Describing the new world order as comprising the forces of freedom on one side and those of totalitarianism on the other, the statement President Truman delivered to the joint session of Congress on March 12, 1947, was plainly hortatory.[25] Congress responded with an enthusiastic standing ovation. Although the ripples of elite and public opinion that followed over the next several weeks were less than uniformly supportive, it soon became apparent that most of the public and Congress were lining up behind the president's program. By early summer Truman's proposals for Greece and Turkey had become U.S. policy, and the more comprehensive Marshall Plan was headed toward enactment.

These two instances of going public differ in a way that helps to explain their dissimilar results. President Wilson sought through public pressure to force the Senate to accept his version of the League. Wilson's form of going public has become a familiar modern activity for which there are few historical examples. President Truman's effort was less confrontational. Only after conferring with congressional leaders and being warned to take a strong public stance did he begin to draft his address. President Truman and those members of Congress who counseled him perhaps foresaw potential opposition in the country that could be preempted only by an appeal that would generate a more favorable climate of public opinion. The speech identified no individuals or blocs of politicians in Washington as opponents. In strategic terms Truman's act of going public was part of a larger bargain in which he agreed to try to make this internationalist posture more palatable to the country and to shoulder responsibility for any adverse reactions in return for support from members of Congress who were rarely his allies. Wilson failed miserably; Truman succeeded brilliantly. Both men's standing in history has been heavily influenced by their performance in going public.

However much they differ, these two cases do share an important feature. In both instances negotiation alone had or would have failed. Historically, public strategies have been employed after other avenues proved insufficient. This still may be true.

The reciprocity of exchange and the complementarity of tasks between presidents and protocoalitions—especially when the latter equitably represents the interests of the nation—render institutionalized pluralism the look of a finely regulated clock. The synchronization of such a system of cogs and escapements would gratify those Newtonian mechanics whom we call our Founding Fathers. Of course, the American political system has never really achieved such clockwork performance. At best the model of institutionalized pluralism offers a rough approximation of reality, making recognizable some of its less obvious features. According to most students of American politics and not a few politicians, however, it illuminates even less about American politics today than at any time during the past half century. A consensus is emerging that at both levels—protocoalitional and presidential—leadership based on reciprocity and negotiation is in increasingly short supply.

Individualized Pluralism: The Emerging Community

If institutionalized pluralism depicts a society whose members are bound together by calculated fealty to a network of protocoalitions and a dense normative system for which bargaining is the prescribed behavior, for what kind of political community should going public be an appropriate strategy? It is one constituted of independent members who have few group or institutional loyalties and who are generally less interested in sacrificing short-run, private career goals for the longer-term benefits of bargaining. Social pluralism and institutional fragmentation guarantee that exchange will remain a ubiquitous activity, but egocentric traders will rarely subscribe to the kinds of commitments and tacit understandings that allow bargains to assume the form of relationships. Instead, these politicians will generally prefer immediate, explicit, and tangible exchanges.

A protocoalition's success in securing its members' collective interest is a function of its internal integration. When members agree on goals, or at least are prepared to subordinate their private interests, when they adhere to reciprocity agreements and endure personal apprenticeship, and when they invest in their leaders the authority and flexibility to negotiate with other leaders, the protocoalition achieves the internal coherence that makes it both a formidable and yet an attractive trading partner to others in Washington.

Conversely, protocoalitions containing egocentric members will suffer internally and will be less able to secure collective goals in the marketplace.

Weak protocoalitions reinforce the propensity of members toward independence. Unsustained by collective rewards, members must resort to their own devices to find their political fortunes. Unfettered by the commitments strong protocoalitions require, members are free to pursue private career goals. Because it is both burden and freedom, self-reliance creates uncertainty, which prompts many politicians to assume a continuous campaign footing. They spend proportionately more time cultivating clients and constituents than they do cementing relations with their Washington colleagues. Governing and campaigning lose their distinctiveness. This is as true for the ongoing polling and communications activities of the White House as it is for the same activities in a freshman representative's office. The result of this pervasive free agency is a more erratic community—one less well regulated by its internal mechanisms of exchange and less shock resistant to short-term perturbations of public opinion.

How might so different a system of political relations come to replace institutionalized pluralism? One can think of many possible reasons, any of them potentially sufficient and all of them probably true, which ensuing chapters will analyze as the appropriate data are introduced. For now, I will simply state the possible causes for the rise of individualized pluralism. First, the growth of the modern welfare state has both increased the size of the community and created large, interested constituencies outside of Washington. Second, modern communications and transportation have brought Washington prominently to the attention of the nation so that over-the-shoulder inspection by constituents and clients can easily contaminate the transactions of politicians. Third, and perhaps most important, the decay of institutionalized pluralism has been abetted by the decline of political parties in the country and in Washington. This decline has meant the erosion of affinity relations among political elites within and across institutions that made exchange easier and occasionally unnecessary.

Each of these possible causes has created opportunities for those in Washington to be more independent. How precisely they have affected strategic behavior will differ from one office to the next, but the expansion of federal services, the ability to send, as well as the probability of receiving, messages to and from targeted constituencies, and the fading of party feeling have thoroughly altered the way Washington politicians view their own and others' political options.[26] Nowhere should such self-awareness be more acute than in the White House.

For a president seeking to construct broad-based coalitions, the implications of individualized pluralism are profound. From his vantage, the leveled political topography offers fewer clues about where precisely his efforts at coalition building should begin. Instead of a subcommunity of leaders with solid reputations and convertible credits, the president finds himself surrounded by a larger number of weaker leaders who titularly preside over shaky protocoalitions. It is not that these people are uninterested in trading. To the contrary, success with the president should help them secure their position with their colleagues. The problem is that in the absence of local hierarchies where a few members authoritatively represent many others, the president quickly discovers that he needs to trade with many more participants, unsure as he does so which will or even can deliver on their promises. It is an unmanageable prospect, one that guarantees overload and multiplies the chances of failure. What is Neustadt's bargaining president to do in such a setting? It is conundrum without solution.

A president who feels effective in going public, however, will find frequent opportunities for leadership in a Washington of free agency and emaciated protocoalitions. The sensitivity of self-reliant politicians to public opinion is their vulnerability and the key to his influence. By campaigning around the country, the president can create uncertainty for them while offering refuge in their support for his policies. By giving up bargaining with individuals and instead working with politicians' preferences *en masse,* a president achieves comparative economy.

From Institutionalized to Individualized Pluralism

A change from institutionalized to individualized pluralism appears to be occurring rapidly on every front from the takeover of bureaucracies by issue specialists to the loss of leadership in Congress.[27] Appropriately, the causes are compound, some general, like those described above, and others specific to the institution. Articles and books on the subject, often carrying worried if not apocalyptic overtones, proliferate from think tanks and commercial presses. One is hard pressed to identify a recent development in Washington that someone has not credited with contributing to the decay of institutionalized pluralism. They may all be correct.

An anthology suggestively entitled *The New Congress*[28] examines several such developments, showing how pervasive the phenomenon is. Throughout the book, the case mounts against the hegemony of institutionalized pluralism. Thomas Mann singles out the heightened career concerns of members of Congress: "The forces fueling the individualistic tone of the present-day Congress remain strong. . . . Senators and representatives are in business for themselves." As a consequence, "they all are likely to view themselves first and foremost as individuals, not as members of a party or as part of a president's team." [29]

In the next contribution Michael Robinson offers a reason: "Compared with the class of 1958, the class of 1978 was three times more likely to make heavy use of the congressional recording studio, three times more likely to regard the House TV system as 'very useful,' three times more likely to have relied 'a lot' on TV in the last election." From these findings Robinson concludes that "although these figures pertain to campaign style more than legislative character, one may infer that the increasingly greater reliance on the media for nomination, election, status in the Congress, and reelection is one sign of a new congressional character—one more dynamic, egocentric, immoderate, and, perhaps, intemperate." [30] In short, many members of Congress today are themselves successfully going public.

Robinson's use of the class of 1958 nicely complements Douglass Cater's earlier observations. Writing in 1959, Cater was among the first to spot this new-style member of Congress. "There has *begun to emerge* in the halls of Congress a new type of politician conditioned to the age of mass media and more keenly aware of the uses of publicity. He is not apt to be a member of . . . the 'Inner Club,' where emphasis is still put on seniority and skill in negotiation" [emphasis added]. In fact, "usually he is lacking in direct influence among his colleagues." [31] One does not find such unfavorable judgments of the senator or representative who goes public today.

Roger Davidson begins his chapter in *The New Congress* by noting that the new, less cooperative, and certainly less submissive member of Congress described by Mann, Robinson, and Cater has created "persistent pressures . . . to expand the number of available workgroups and the overall number of seats and leadership posts." He then catalogues the proliferation of subcommittees and assignments, the growth of informal working groups, and the multiplication of staffs and budgets. Leadership posts were so numerous in the 96th Congress, Davidson points out, that "all but two Democratic senators and nearly half of all Democratic representatives chaired a committee or subcommittee." [32] Only a quarter of the Democratic members held these positions in the mid-1950s. Davidson notes that to accommodate the diffusion of power, additional institutional innovations, such as the practice of referring bills to several committees rather than only to one, have occurred to give more subcommittees an opportunity to get their hands on the president's program.

New Institutional Arrangements in Congress

In recent Congresses, new organizational forms have arisen to compete with the old. Two that give ample expression to the centrifugal forces at work are caucuses, or working groups, and political action committees (PACs). Each caucus and committee in its own way competes with the party leaders of Congress for influence and seeks to redirect its members' attention and loyalties beyond the institution to particular publics. I shall describe them not so much because they threaten to replace existing structures but because they show how Congress as an institution is adapting to the Washington community of individualized pluralism.

Today's venerable Democratic Study Group (DSG) was founded in 1959 by a cadre of liberal northern House Democrats who were frustrated with the dominance of southern conservatives in the chamber's leadership positions. By offering an alternative legislative program and by providing a mechanism for bloc voting that in turn leveraged liberals' negotiating positions with the leadership, the DSG has been credited with moving the legislative agenda in a liberal direction. Because of its large, diverse membership, its million-dollar annual budget, and the promotion of its liberal members to positions of House leadership, the Democratic Study Group has today lost much of its certitude as an alternative voice within the institution.[33] In recent years, however, a plethora of new caucuses has arisen to continue the legacy of the DSG.

With well over a hundred voluntary associations to choose from, members typically affiliate with a half dozen or so of these organizations. Many of these caucuses have achieved the status of legislative service organizations, which entitles them to staff and office space on Capitol Hill. Most of the caucuses created before 1971 concentrated on broad issues; those formed since then have assumed a decidedly parochial cast. According to some scholars, these caucuses provide many of the same services as their counterpart interest groups with whom they cooperate closely.[34] The Congressional Arts Caucus reveals how particularistic these would-be protocoalitions can be. Its single goal, passage of the National Heritage Resources Act, would make it possible for artists and authors to deduct from their taxes the full market value of any of their works they donate to charitable organizations.[35] Apparently, no interest or issue is too esoteric to deserve organizational embodiment.

Even were they so inclined, these organizations, founded upon affinity of interest rather than proximity of organizations in the policy-making process, are ill suited to negotiate agreement among competing interests. Whatever bargains a caucus may make will count for little unless its members are well placed on the relevant committees. To the degree the Arts Caucus, for instance, fails to include the members of the House Ways and Means and Senate Finance committees, it is deficient. Moreover, to the degree it includes members not on these committees, it is inefficient. Whatever their standing as functioning coalitions, committees remain the vital juncture of the legislative process.

Caucuses are also deficient as protocoalitions because they are casual, voluntary associations that lack the rewards or sanctions necessary to induce members to adhere to collective goals. Even when a consensus on policy and tactics emerges and the caucus negotiates as a bloc with other leaders or with the president, its effectiveness remains limited. Everyone recognizes that each member of the caucus retains independent judgment about the relative merits of whatever deals its leaders are able to achieve and that the consensus could unravel at any moment. Consequently, rather than serving as building blocks to coalitions, these caucuses commonly assume a less critical role as clearinghouses of position papers.

The rapid increase in the number of congressional caucuses has been more than matched by the rise of political action committees. In the six elections from 1974 through 1990, the number of PACs grew from 608 to 4,172. During this period their contributions to House and Senate races increased from $12 million to $150 million.[36]

Before the passage of the Federal Election Campaign Act in 1971, private groups participated openly in political campaigns at great risks. Some, such as unions and professional associations (the American Medical Association, for example), had flexed their financial muscle from time to time, but others, such as corporations, had shied away from overt participation for fear of running afoul of ambiguous election laws. The campaign finance reforms that began in 1971 have changed all that. All organizations, and particularly corporations, now have clear guidelines for participating in congressional elections.

The first PACs registered with the Federal Election Commission (FEC) were largely the traditional organized contributors, principally the unions. With each subsequent election, however, more and more businesses have joined. Many, if not most, corporate donations go to incumbents and are motivated more by defensive consideration than by any aspiration to alter the ideological disposition of Congress. A smaller share, but still a large amount, of PAC money goes to influence members, if not elections. Challengers and vulnerable incumbents are frequently invited to disclose their preferences on issues of concern to the PAC, and here is where the parochial character of this money leaves its greatest imprint. Rep. David Obey's assertion that "ten thousand dollars may come against you from one group because of a single vote" is supported by the experiences of many members of Congress.[37]

Contrary to the unflattering stereotype of the unctuous lobbyist, representatives of interest groups have traditionally spurned the unrefined tactics portrayed in Obey's remark. When some occasionally succumbed to the temptation to lubricate the legislative process with financial contributions, they were often caught and punished. One of the most frequently recounted instances occurred in 1956 when President Eisenhower, citing the natural gas industry's heavy-handed use of campaign funds, vetoed a gas deregulation bill that he was on record as favoring.[38] Memory was long, and such instances did not need to be repeated frequently. The opposite message was conveyed in 1982 when, after spreading nearly a million dollars among 300 candidates, the National Automobile Dealers Association easily won a congressional veto of the Federal Trade Commission's proposed "full disclosure" regulation for used cars.[39]

Under institutionalized pluralism the *modus operandi* of lobbyists was quiet diplomacy. "Never lie" and "don't threaten" were their operational codes. Quiet diplomacy has not disappeared, but increasingly it gives way to more direct, public strategies of influence. These include inspiring pressure from the constituency as well as targeting the group's PAC contributions.

One of the last groups to catch on to the opportunities of individualized pluralism was the national Chamber of Commerce. For years the chamber was one of the more staid, even stolid, inside players on Capitol Hill. After watching its legislative success rate drop with each successive Congress, however, it adopted an aggressive public relations strategy. Today, the chamber has its own public affairs television network called Biznet, which produces weekly programs that are fed from Washington to cable and independent broadcast stations around the country. These programs do not hesitate to advise viewers of what they need to do to protect their interests in Congress.[40]

Well-heeled corporate groups are not the only participants to take full advantage of the new opportunities for influence. One recent survey of 175 lobbying groups found that while the great majority said they were doing more of almost all kinds of lobbying activity, the greatest increases have occurred in the realm of going public. Of the 27 classes of lobbying identified in the study, "talking with people from the press and media" scored the greatest gains. A close second were reported increases in "mounting grass roots campaigns" and "inspiring letter-writing or telegram campaigns."[41] Savings and loan associations, environmentalists, anti-gun control organizations, and Mothers Against Drunk Driving have all won quick victories with grass-roots strategies of influence.

Judged against the requirements of institutionalized pluralism, political action committees and caucuses are functionally primitive entities. Serving only to articulate generally narrow positions on issues, these organizations are neither well designed for nor much interested in brokering the diverse interests brought into play by policy proposals. With them, the first-tier function of interest aggregation traditionally performed by protocoalitions is absent. From the vantage of the White House, caucuses and PACs threaten to "balkanize the political process."[42]

These new organizations will not replace congressional parties and standing committees, but they have weakened these traditional groups as protocoalitions. The "new Congress" has added a veneer, so that the typical representative and senator today are associated with more congressional organizations, both formal and informal, than ever before. Yet the paradoxical result has been a depreciation of institutions and an elevation of individual politicians as coalitional matter.

Going Public and Individualized Pluralism

The present-day susceptibility of relations within Washington to public opinion manifests itself in a variety of ways. The influence of single-issue constituencies has been abetted by the discovery that by defeating one targeted incumbent a clear message will be sent to others. Issues also blow into Washington more quickly and in less-filtered form. During the 97th Congress, for example, President Reagan's supply-side program, with its unprecedented deficits, was being enacted while a majority in each house appeared ready to endorse a constitutional amendment requiring a balanced budget. And off to the side, a large bipartisan huddle was forming to carry forward the recently arrived "flat tax" rate reform.[43]

In a recent appraisal of coalition politics within Congress during the past 30 years, Barbara Sinclair makes the same connection between internal organization and the effect of external forces: "Instead of a policy process dominated by powerful, conservative committee chairmen, one in which crucial decisions were made in secret and thus were relatively insulated from public influence, we now see a process characterized by extreme individualism, one in which open, public decision making often hinders compromise." [44] When asked by a reporter about changes in Congress, Reagan lobbyist Kenneth Duberstein echoed this conclusion and gave it recent origin: "It's not been like Lyndon Johnson's time, being able to work with 15 or 20 Congressmen and Senators to get something done. For most issues you have to lobby all 435 Congressmen and almost all 100 Senators." [45] As a result, "how Congress performs its legislative role," continues Sinclair, "depends much more upon the character of the environmental forces impinging upon its members than upon its internal organization." [46]

The President's Calculus

The limited goods and services available for barter to the bargaining president would be quickly exhausted in a leaderless setting where every coalition partner must be dealt with individually. When politicians are more subject to "environmental" forces, however, other avenues of presidential influence open up. No politician within Washington is better positioned than the president to go outside of the community and draw popular support. With protocoalitions in disarray and members more sensitive to influences from beyond Washington, the president's hand in mobilizing public opinion has been strengthened. For the new Congress—indeed, for the new Washington generally—going public may at times be the most effective course available.

Under these circumstances, the president's prestige assumes the currency of power. It is something to be spent when the coffers are full, to be conserved when low, and to be replenished when empty. As David Gergen remarked when he was President Reagan's communications director, "Everything here is built on the idea that the President's success depends on grassroots support." [47] Such a president must be attentive to the polls, but he will not be one who necessarily craves the affection of the public. His relationship with it may be purely instrumental, and however gratifying, popular support is a resource the expenditure of which must be coolly calculated.

Bargaining presidents require the sage advice of politicians familiar with the bargaining game; presidents who go public need pollsters. Compare the relish with which President Nixon was reported by one of his consultants to have approached the polls with the disdain Truman expressed. "Nixon had all kinds of polls all the time; he sometimes had a couple of pollsters doing the same kind of survey at the same time. He really studied them. He wanted to find the thing that would give him an advantage." [48] The confidant went on to observe that the president wanted poll data "on just about anything and everything" throughout his administration.

Indicative of current fashion, Carter, Reagan, and Bush have had in-house pollsters taking continuous—weekly, even daily—readings of public opinion.[49] They have vigilantly monitored the pulse of opinion to warn of slippage and to identify opportunities for gain. Before adopting a policy course, they have assessed its costs in public support. These advisers' regular and frequently unsolicited denials that they affected policy belie their self-effacement.

To see how the strategic prescriptions of going public differ from those of bargaining, consider the hypothetical case of a president requiring additional votes if he is to prevail in Congress. If a large number of votes is needed, the most obvious and direct course is to go on prime-time television to solicit the public's active support. Employed at the right moment by a popular president, the effect may be dramatic. This tactic, however, has considerable costs and risks. A real debit of lost public support may occur when a president takes a forthright position. There is also the possibility that the public will not respond, which damages the president's future credibility. Given this, a president understandably finds the *threat* to go public frequently more attractive than the *act*. To the degree such a threat is credible, the anticipated responses of some representatives and senators may suffice to achieve victory.

A more focused application of popular pressure becomes available as an election nears. Fence-sitting representatives and senators may be plied with promises of reelection support or threats of presidential opposition. This may be done privately and selectively, or it may be tendered openly to all who may vote on the president's program. Then there is the election itself. By campaigning, the president who goes public can seek to alter the partisan composition of Congress and thereby gain influence over that institution's decisions in the future.

All of these methods for generating publicity notwithstanding, going public offers fewer and simpler stratagems than does its pluralist alternative. At the heart of the latter lies bargaining, which above all else involves choice: choice among alternative coalitions, choice of specific partners, and choice of the goods and services to be bartered. The number and variety of choices place great demands upon strategic calculation, so much so that pluralist leadership must be understood as an art. In Neustadt's schema, the president's success ultimately reduces to intuition, an ability to sense "right choices."[50] Going public also requires choice, and it leaves ample room for the play of talent. (One need only compare the television performance of Carter and Reagan.) Nonetheless, public relations appears to be a less obscure matter. Going public promises a straightforward presidency—its options fewer, its strategy simpler, and consequently, its practitioner's behavior more predictable.

Thus there is a rationale for modern presidents to go public in the emerging character of Washington politics. As Washington comes to depend on looser, more individualistic political relations, presidents searching for strategies that work will increasingly go public. So far, I have said little about the individual in the White House or the personal character of leadership. To consider these ingredients important does not violate any of the assumptions made here. Rationality does not leave choice to be determined strictly by the environment. To the degree occupants of the Oval Office differ in their skills and conceptions of leadership, one may expect that similar circumstances will sometimes result in different presidential behavior.

Perhaps, as has frequently been suggested, presidents go public more today because of who they are. What did Jimmy Carter and Ronald Reagan have in common? The answer is their lack of interest in active negotiation with fellow politicians and their confidence in speaking directly to the voters.

The Calculus of Those Who Deal with the President

Those Washingtonians who conduct business with the president observe his behavior carefully. Their judgment about his leadership guides them in their dealings with him. Traditionally, the professional president watchers have asked themselves the following questions: What are his priorities? How much does he care whether he wins or loses on a particular issue? How will he weigh his options? Is he capable of winning?

Each person will answer these questions about the president's will and skill somewhat differently, of course, depending upon his or her institutional vantage. The chief lobbyist for the United Auto Workers, a network White House correspondent, and the mayor of New York City may size up the president differently depending upon what they need from him. Nonetheless, they arrive at their judgments about the president in similar ways. Each observes the same behavior, inspects the same personal qualities, evaluates the views of the same recognized opinion leaders—columnists and commentators, among others—and tests his or her own tentative opinions with those of fellow community members. Local opinion leaders promote a general agreement among Washingtonians in their assessments of the president. Their agreement is his reputation.[51]

A president with a strong reputation does better in his dealings largely because others expect fewer concessions from him. Accordingly, he finds them more compliant; an orderly marketplace prevails. Saddled with a weak reputation, conversely, a president must work harder. Because others expect him to be less effective, they press him harder in expectation of greater gain. Comity at the bargaining table may give way to contention as other politicians form unreasonable expectations of gain. Through such expectations, the president's reputation regulates community relations in ways that either facilitate or impede his success. In a world of institutionalized pluralism, bargaining presidents seldom actively traded upon their prestige, leaving it to influence Washington political elites only through their anticipation of the electorate's behavior. As a consequence, prestige remained largely irrelevant to other politicians' assessments of the president.[52] Once presidents began going public and interjecting prestige directly into their relations with fellow politicians, and once these politicians found their resistance to this pressure diminished because of their own altered circumstances, the president's ability to marshal public opinion soon became an important ingredient of his reputation. New questions were added to traditional ones. Does the president feel strongly enough about an issue to go public? Will he follow through on his threats to do so? Does his standing in the country run so deep that it will likely be converted into mail to members of Congress, or is it so shallow that it will expire as he attempts to use it?

In today's Washington, the answers to these questions contribute to the president's reputation. As a consequence, his prestige and reputation have lost much of their separateness. The community's estimates of Carter and Reagan rose and fell with the polls. Through reputation, prestige has begun to play a larger role in regulating the president's day-to-day transactions with other community members. Grappling with the unclear causes of Carter's failure in Washington, Neustadt arrived at the same conclusion:

> A President's capacity to draw and stir a television audience seems every bit as interesting to current Washingtonians as his ability to wield his formal powers. This interest is his opportunity. While national party organizations fall away, while congressional party discipline relaxes, while interest groups proliferate and issue networks rise, a President who wishes to compete for leadership in framing policy and shaping coalitions has to make the most he can out of his popular connection. Anticipating home reactions, Washingtonians . . . are vulnerable to any breeze from home that presidential words and sights can stir. If he is deemed effective on the tube they will anticipate. That is the essence of professional reputation.[53]

The record supports Neustadt's speculation. In late 1978 and early 1979, with his monthly approval rating dropping to less than 50 percent, President Carter complained that it was difficult to gain Congress's attention for his legislative proposals. As one congressional liaison official stated, "When you go up to the Hill and the latest polls show Carter isn't doing well, then there isn't much reason for a member to go along with him."[54] A member of Congress concurred: "The relationship between the President and Congress is partly the result of how well the President is doing politically. Congress is better behaved when he does well. . . . Right now, it's almost as if Congress is paying no attention to him."[55]

Presidential Selection Reforms: Outsiders in the White House

Campaigning and governing have always tended to draw upon the same conceptions of politics. Studying the former helps one comprehend the latter. In the nineteenth century, presidential candidates resulted from negotiations among political machines that came together at conventions to identify an acceptable candidate their state organizations could work for. Acceptability had something to do with electability and a lot to do with the perceived fairness of the candidate in distributing patronage to their locale. Frequently, aspiring politicians with established national reputations were ruled out because of their inevitable association with party organizations in one region of the country. This explains why conventions were commonly deadlocked, and unknowns, or dark horses, occasionally emerged with the nomination. In office these presidents were typically weak, which suited the needs of the state party organizations: they wanted someone at the patronage levers who would follow established protocol in distributing the federal largesse.

Twentieth-century bargaining presidents have been activists who were expected to lead their party to victory, rather than simply head the ticket, and to build coalitions in government. Just as in governing, these presidents succeeded as candidates by stitching together the disparate elements of their party. With state delegations to the convention handpicked by party leaders and bound to them by unit rules, aspiring presidential candidates sought the support of those who were, in the words of Thomas B. Reed, turn-of-the-century Speaker of the House and nemesis to reformers, "guided by the base desire to win." [56] Writing in 1968, Nelson W. Polsby and Aaron B. Wildavsky described this process of presidential nomination:

> Decision-making at conventions is ordinarily coordinated by a process of bargaining among party leaders. Each leader represents a state party or faction within a state which is independently organized and not subject to control by outsiders.... In order to mobilize enough nationwide support to elect a President, party leaders from a large number of constituencies must be satisfied with the nominee.[57]

During the middle decades of the twentieth century, a highly popular military hero was nominated, but presidential candidates mostly came from a class of politicians with established political careers—careers increasingly located in Washington, particularly in the Senate. Leadership through bargaining was the leitmotif of that era's presidents.

In these last decades of the twentieth century, these political arrangements appear to be giving way to those in which coalition building proceeds less through mediating organizations and elite negotiation and more through the direct mobilization of national constituencies. No aspect of the presidency has escaped this tendency. It is as true for how candidates seek the nomination and campaign in the general election as it is for how they behave once in the White House.

How the Reforms Changed Presidential Nominations

Until the 1972 Democratic convention adopted the proposed reforms of the McGovern-Fraser Commission, the convention system of nominating candidates had remained largely untouched during the twentieth century. Since then, reforming the presidential selection procedures has become a quadrennial political exercise as candidates have begun their campaigns by seeking to alter the rules under which they would compete for the nomination. The rules of the game have become an important part of the game itself.

The cumulative effect of these reforms has been to transfer the nomination of the party's candidate from party leaders at the convention to the mass electorate in primary elections and caucuses. One telltale indicator of this change can be found in the number of delegates who come to the convention already bound to a particular candidate. In 1960, committed delegates constituted 20 percent of all Democratic delegates and 35 percent of all Republican delegates. By 1980 these figures stood at 71 and 69 percent respectively.[58] This change reflects several specific reforms. The number of primaries was on the rise before the 1972 reforms, but increased sharply after state parties were required to open delegate selection procedures. From 1960 to 1992, the number of states holding primaries more than doubled to 39. Other reforms beefed up the primaries as the arena in which the nomination took place. Under the new rules, primary voters would choose candidates rather than anonymous slates of delegates, and delegates selected in primaries would be bound to their declared candidate at least for the first ballot at the convention. Finally, the winner-take-all primary was replaced with some form of proportional distribution of delegates according to the candidates' shares of the popular vote. This has inspired nationally unknown candidates to enter and stay in the race.[59]

In addition to these primary reforms, other reforms were also at work dismantling the convention system. State parties that did not opt for a primary were required to open their caucuses to all party members and to democratize delegate selection procedures. No longer could a state's delegation be selected well before election season, nor could it be led into the convention bound by a unit rule to some state party leader. As a result, delegates began showing up at the convention having little familiarity with, much less loyalty to, state party leaders. Instead, they gave their allegiance to a particular candidate or cause they wanted the convention to embrace.[60]

Further eroding the parties' presence were rules that, though falling short of strict quotas, insisted that more minorities, women, and young people be included in each state's delegation. Because most elected officeholders are white males over 30, this meant that many of them would no longer be attending the convention. From 1960 to 1980, the percentage of Democratic senators attending their party's convention fell from 68 to 17 percent, and for representatives, from 45 to 11 percent.[61]

Elected politicians were not the only losers under the reforms. Representatives of core constituency groups—most notably union leaders within the Democratic party—saw their influence dwindle piecemeal with reform. Their position further deteriorated with the enactment of new campaign finance laws that gave federal matching money to candidates for the nomination who could raise $5,000 in small contributions from each of 20 or more states and who agreed to abide by ceilings on campaign spending. This loosened the dependency of all candidates on the parties' core constituent groups for organizational and financial support.[62] More to the point, candidates who had little hope of winning endorsement from these groups could, nonetheless, raise and spend as much money as necessary to compete in the primaries.

Added together, these reforms ended any semblance of the nominating convention as a forum where the leaders of the party's constituencies came together to select the party's standard-bearer from the ranks of Washington-based politicians. In its place the reforms substituted a multiphased popularity contest with low entrance barriers. Many more candidates began showing up, few of whom would have stood a chance under the old convention arrangements. That some of these long-distance runners have won their party's nomination and the presidency and that others did well enough to ruin the chances of more conventionally styled candidates contribute independently to modern presidential leadership. Our presidents are, after all, the products of the system that selects them.

During the prereform era, the parties would occasionally find irresistible someone like Dwight Eisenhower whose fame and reputation rested on a nonpolitical career. More often, however, candidates were drawn from the mainstream of the party and frequently from among well-positioned members of the Washington political community. Others, "outsiders" even if technically Washington residents, stood not a chance. Having established national visibility in conducting televised hearings into organized crime in the early 1950s, Democratic Senator Estes Kefauver won virtually every presidential primary he entered in 1952, and yet largely because of a suspect reputation among the Washington elite, he managed to move no closer than his party's vice-presidential nomination.[63] Kefauver was clearly a man ahead of his time.

By the time Jimmy Carter and Ronald Reagan came to Washington, outsiders were no longer being shunted aside. Back-to-back, these two men were the first in memory to assume the Oval Office without any experience in Washington. Jimmy Carter's statement in his memoirs, "We came to Washington as outsiders . . . we left as outsiders," signifies how thoroughly the selection reforms have altered presidential recruitment.[64] Not even General Eisenhower had such impeccable credentials for boasting his nonpolitical rearing.

A candidate achieves his outsider status less by his non-Washington residency than by his standing within the party or governmental establishment. What precisely this establishment means is left to the candidate to define. It may be as specific as Eugene McCarthy's Lyndon Johnson or as general as Reagan's "bumbling bureaucrats" and "spendthrift politicians" who occupy the "puzzle palaces on the Potomac." For a Democrat to succeed as a credible outsider, organized labor must be included in the establishment. Generally, the strategy plays better when one is competing against a front-runner who occupies a credible "insider's" position. In 1972 George McGovern took apart Senator Edmund Muskie in the early primaries and Senator Hubert Humphrey in the later ones. Both appeared to have labor's support. In 1984 Gary Hart could not have campaigned nearly so well on the ambiguous platform of "new ideas" and being "less beholden" if his adversary had not been so conspicuously "more beholden" to the "old ideas" of the Democratic establishment.

The 1992 campaign for the Democratic nomination followed much the same script. Of the five candidates who competed in the first state primary in New Hampshire, only two then held public office in Washington. And two of the candidates—Paul Tsongas and Jerry Brown—held no office at all. Over the next six weeks, the two Washington-based politicians dropped out, then a former senator. Neither of the finalists—Bill Clinton or Jerry Brown—was tainted with having previously held public office in Washington.

The presidential selection system constitutes a strategic environment that enhances certain skills and resources while penalizing others. In addition to its direct effect on current candidates' fortunes, it shapes the kinds of presidents elected by influencing the career decisions and stylistic adaptations of potential candidates in the future. Politicians on the sideline go to school on the experiences of candidates in the arena. Eugene McCarthy's "victory" over President Johnson in the New Hampshire primary in 1968 instructed George McGovern and numerous other Democratic aspirants about the new opportunities provided by the expanding primary system. McGovern in turn demonstrated that a virtual unknown six months before the convention could capture the nomination. Jimmy Carter reinforced this lesson in 1976 and strengthened it by showing that such a candidate could also go on to win the general election in November. Similarly, in 1976 Ronald Reagan taught future candidates that in a world of primaries, incumbency no longer shields a sitting president from a primary challenge. When Patrick Buchanan, a former Reagan speechwriter and television commentator who had never run for elective office, announced his plans to enter the New Hampshire primary in 1992, Washington pundits carefully deliberated the damage his candidacy might inflict on Bush's reelection chances.

Outsiders as Presidents

Fresh from an extended and successful stint of campaigning, an outsider will enter the White House probably as uninterested in playing the bargaining game as he is ill prepared. For him, whether to promote his policies in Washington by attending to a great many transactions with other elites or by going over their heads to enlist popular support with a television appeal may be an easy choice.

Bargaining, however, is not dead. In the modern Washington characterized by individualized pluralism, presidents will continue to receive many invitations to the bargaining table. Beyond familiarity with the formal procedures and informal folkways that govern exchange even today, successful bargaining requires of the president a keen sense of the needs and preferences of those whom he seeks to influence. Bargaining may, however, surpass the capacities of the outsider president. Recognizing future bargaining partners and figuring out what a particular bargain might look like may seem trivial, but experience shows that both may escape White House occupants. When President Carter canceled 19 water projects without consulting fellow Democrats on Capitol Hill, did he appreciate the political costs he was inflicting upon others and eventually upon himself? Given the self-congratulatory aplomb with which he announced his decision, one suspects not. Several of these projects had been long-sought goals of Sen. Russell Long and Louisiana's House delegation. Senator Long was chair of the important Senate Finance Committee through which much of the White House's legislative program was destined to pass, and where in fact some of it came to rest.[65]

No less important and probably even more demanding for the outsider in the White House is awareness of an opportunity to bargain when it presents itself. At the least, the president must understand that his formal responsibilities and prerogatives are convertible in barter. In addition, he must know the customary routines of exchange that have grown up in Washington over the years to reduce the uncertainty of coalition building for all participants. Without such knowledge even an avid negotiator might quickly become overwhelmed.[66] The inability of outsiders in the White House to recognize these routines not only constitutes lost opportunity but also may assume real political costs.

President Carter, for example, repudiated the vestigial practice of replacing the other party's federal district attorneys with local partisans recommended by the district's Democratic members of Congress. The questionable legitimacy of such blatant partisanship muted the outcry among House and Senate Democrats, but those adversely affected by the decision no doubt recognized that they alone bore the costs of the president's unilateral action. Another political custom, seemingly costless to the president but invaluable to his party's members of Congress, has been that of allowing the local representative to claim some credit by announcing new federal programs in the district. The Carter administration, in contrast, issued periodic press releases from the White House that summarily listed new programs.[67]

I have dwelt on President Carter's shortcomings for a reason. Although other presidents have from time to time failed to enlist routine exchange systems, Carter did so more consistently and more flagrantly. Even taking into account the centrifugal forces at work in present-day Washington, the large Democratic majorities in Congress offered Carter the luxurious prospect that even uninspired, routine bargaining would reap great legislative rewards. As it was, his legislative accomplishments are generally judged to have been modest. Even his victories appeared grudgingly delivered by the Democratic congressional leaders. The explanation, of course, is his path to the White House.

One would be hard pressed to find a better illustration of the outsider's propensity for going public than the following colloquy between House

Speaker Thomas P. O'Neill, Jr., and President Carter during a pre-inauguration briefing in Plains, Georgia.

> O'Neill: Mr. President, I want you to understand something. Some of the brightest men in America are in this Congress of the United States. Don't make the mistake of underestimating them. . . . We want to work together, but I have a feeling you are underestimating the feeling of Congress and you could have some trouble.
>
> Carter: I'll handle them just as I handled the Georgia legislature. Whenever I had problems with the Georgia legislature I took the problems to the people of Georgia.[68]

Whatever the emerging job requirements or the partisan disposition of Washington, the style of presidential leadership will largely reflect the skills and experiences of the person in office. A president who developed his political skills in the chambers and corridors of Congress will understandably find it exasperating to deliver salutations to a television camera. Similarly, the outsider whose career success is founded largely upon the stylized public presentation of self will derive greater gratification and even stimulation from traveling around the country delivering speeches and appearing on television than in following the private, daily, all-too-mysterious rituals of cultivating support from other politicians. That today's Washington elites are less responsive to such methods only adds to modern presidents' distaste for them. Whenever the advantages of the recruitment process for outsiders prove decisive, going public will enjoy favored status within the White House.

The Politics of Divided Government

One of the most prominent, if underrecognized, political developments over the past several decades is the emergence of divided party control of government. The 1956 presidential election was the first in this century to result in split party control of the presidency and Congress. The pattern thus established of electing a Republican president and Democratic majorities in one or both houses of Congress has been repeated in five of the eight subsequent presidential elections, and since 1968 in five of six elections. The single exception occurred in 1976, an election that the Democratic nominee, Jimmy Carter, barely won against an unelected incumbent, Gerald Ford, and easily lost four years later.

Midterm congressional elections have always tended to go against the president's party. Occasionally during the first half of the century this midterm bias was strong enough to give the opposition party temporary control of one or both houses of Congress, but unified party control was restored in the next presidential election. In recent years, midterm elections have consistently reinforced divided government by increasing the opposition party's majority control of Congress.

In order to understand how divided government can influence a president's leadership strategies, we must first consider how it generally alters relations throughout the Washington community. With politicians increasingly loosened from the once dominant network of mutual dependency, political parties have not been portrayed here as prominent features of the Washington landscape. Nonetheless, every politician seeking reelection needs to provide constituents with two levels of products: local goods and services as well as information about his or her stand on national issues that concern them. Neither of these can easily be supplied alone. That a politician requires the ongoing cooperation of colleagues to provide goods and services is apparent. Less clear is the fact that communication is costly and may be just as difficult to achieve alone. Even a long-standing incumbent who has assiduously plied his or her constituency with goods and services may remain unknown to half or more of the electorate. And fewer still will be familiar with their representative's positions on national issues. Narrow self-interest therefore impels politicians to seek association with a party, through which information on their positions on public issues can be efficiently transmitted to voters. Evidence of the value of party as a cue to voters—even self-proclaimed independent voters—can be found in the minuscule number of unaffiliated candidates ever elected to Congress. Because the electoral fortunes of politicians are, at least in part, bound to the public's opinion of their party, they have a stake in its success. And because one party's gain at the ballot box is the other's loss, they have a comparable stake in the other party's failure.

When party control of Congress and the presidency is unified, leaders from both branches of government have a special incentive to resolve disagreements harmoniously. Whatever their policy differences, party members negotiate with one another, recognizing that each will be judged for the party's collective performance. If the governing party's leaders were to allow internal disagreements to erupt into public discord, they would be flirting with defeat in the next election. Instead, they engage in quiet diplomacy to reach the compromises necessary to unify the party and give it an attractive record for the next campaign. In this circumstance, going public will frequently be unnecessary and, as an application of force, might well upset party harmony. Members of the governing party team in the legislative and executive branches therefore have a strong incentive to resolve their differences discreetly.

But when party control of Congress and the presidency is divided, a much different dynamic arises, with public conflict frequently replacing cooperation. One problem has to do with reconciling the distant policy preferences that arise more between parties than within them. More importantly, under divided government opposing politicians can gain electoral advantage by frustrating and embarrassing the other side, even if this thwarts their own policy goals. During the 102d Congress, the majority Democrats rejected President Bush's overtures for concessions on bills expanding civil rights protection and extending unemployment benefits, preferring instead to send him repeatedly popular legislation he had publicly committed himself to veto.[69]

Conflict and confrontation can serve a party's electoral purposes even when its policy goals are the casualty. In 1985, as Richard Cheney, then House Republican whip, stated: "Polarization often has very beneficial results. If everything is handled through compromise and conciliation, if there are no real issues dividing us from the Democrats, why should the country change and make us the majority?"[70] Under divided government, the desire to achieve policy goals through give-and-take at the bargaining table yields to the strategic dictates of the next election.

The following two cases exemplify presidents contemplating bargaining with an opposition Congress. They are more than forty years apart and the presidents opted for different strategies, but the moral is the same.

Case 1: Truman Spurns Cooperation and Succeeds

After the 1946 midterm election in which the Republicans captured control of Congress for the first time since the 1920s, President Truman faced an outpouring of unsolicited advice from mostly Republican politicians and newspaper editorial writers urging him to cooperate with Congress. Some even championed novel institutional arrangements such as regularly scheduled "summit" meetings between the Democratic president and the Republican congressional leaders to hash out policy accords.

Observing from a distance the pressure being exerted on the uncertain president, James Rowe, a former White House assistant to Roosevelt, wrote Truman a lengthy, unsolicited memo entitled "Cooperation or Conflict?"[71] He sought to dissuade the president from agreeing to formal mechanisms of cooperation with the opposition Congress, arguing that they were just Republican schemes to ensnare the president. Truman found Rowe's argument persuasive and followed its advice in his relations with Congress.[72]

The premise of Rowe's argument was that the main business of an opposition Congress is to prepare for the next election. Investigations of administration decisions, contentious confirmation hearings, and passage of popular bills fashioned to elicit the president's veto were some of the devices available to an opposition Congress. With 11 of the last 12 Congresses laboring under divided government, these activities have become the familiar routines of politics. But at the time this memo was written, the country had not experienced divided government for 14 years (and then only briefly), so these were viewed as troubling prospects. There was not much the president could do, Rowe advised, but grin and bear it.

What the president could do—and this was the thrust of Rowe's argument—was to avoid being suckered into naively negotiating with Congress. With each side maneuvering the other into a position to be exploited, summit resolution becomes a sharp game in which the president plays with several distinct disadvantages stemming from the institutional characteristics of the legislature and the executive. First is the presidency's "extremely public nature," which "leaves no room whatever for the private give-and-take, the secrecy and anonymity of compromise, which is the essence of negotiation. . . . The presidency is rigid—when its incumbent speaks the world soon knows exactly what he said." Second, in agreeing to negotiate, "the president yields his one source of strength—the backing of public opinion for his point of view. He brings that opinion to his view only by means of public statements. But reaching agreement with [the opposition] . . . means sitting around the conference table with them and indulging in bargaining and negotiation with them. The agreements would be made public as a combined product and the people would not know which were the contributions—or the concessions—of the . . . President." Third, the president has the ability to deliver on his agreements, but congressional leaders do not or can easily claim not to. Once a compromise is reached, they can return to the bargaining table for more concessions to gain votes from members holding out. In the end, "cooperation is a one way street."

So what is the president to do? "Unlike majority presidents [in unified government] who are able to do business with their party . . . minority presidents are forced to fall back on their chief weapon—the marshalling of public opinion." Rowe identified two types of opportunity especially appropriate for going public: veto messages and press conferences. Today, in an era of jet transportation and television, these avenues of public persuasion seem rather timid and unimaginative, but they were the principal opportunities available to a president in the 1940s. He was being urged to confront the opposition Congress not because the prospects for going public were bright but rather because those for bargaining were bleak.

In his dealings with the Republican 80th Congress, President Truman followed Rowe's advice. He selectively vetoed legislation on which he could take forceful and politically attractive positions. Foremost, he refused to bow to pressure to engage in summit diplomacy. In public statements, he proposed popular social policies to Congress, daring it to reject them. And in 1948 he called the Republican Congress back into special session and presented it with popular social legislation, not in expectation of making policy but in order to create potent issues for his fall reelection campaign. Indeed, these activities laid the groundwork for the famous, come-from-behind victory in which he instructed future presidents on how to make an obstructionist Congress the campaign issue.

Case 2: President Bush Cooperates and Fails

In the fall of 1990, as President Bush sat staring at the teleprompter, waiting to deliver only his third prime-time appeal to the American people, he may well have wondered how he landed in his predicament. He was about to promote a deficit reduction budget package of increased taxes and reduced spending that more closely resembled the program of congressional Democrats

OPERATION CONGRESS STORM

Paul Conrad Copyright 1991, Los Angeles Times
Reprinted by permission

than his own. The legislation did not contain his long-sought reductions in capital gains taxes, but it did include a tax hike for wealthy, mostly Republican taxpayers. And yet here was the president about to shoulder responsibility for it with the American people.

An unpleasant irony for Bush was that he had worked hard to reach this uncomfortable moment. First, he had to sacrifice his earlier image of resoluteness in order to get budget negotiations moving. The Democrats had insisted that the president retract his 1988 campaign slogan, "Read my lips: no new taxes," before they would participate in any discussions that might result in new taxes. The president tried to minimize the political fallout by slipping the concession into a press release that buried "tax revenue increases" among a list of topics open to negotiation.

Throughout the summer of meetings, Bush had refrained from publicly criticizing the Democratic Congress, lest he drive its members away from the bargaining table. However, this necessitated surrendering his advantage on the public stage, which Rowe had advised Truman was the strongest card available to a president facing an opposition Congress.

One can therefore sympathize with Bush's predicament as he began his television address, feigning enthusiasm for the budget compromise. No wonder his appeal was brief and tepid, without impact in the country or Congress. This, his first solicitation of the public's support—"Tell your Congressmen and Senators you support this deficit reduction agreement"— did little to stem the "avalanche" of mail opposed to some feature of the legislation. The only indicator to register any movement after the speech was the further weakening of the president's job-performance rating in the opinion polls.

The less numerous and inflexible congressional Republicans had been largely ignored in developing the budget compromise. With little investment in the product, and fearing that, as members of the president's party, they would be tagged with responsibility for the tax increases in the upcoming congressional election, these Republicans were the first to bolt. Many congressional Democrats strategically followed the Republicans in highly public criticism of the budget compromise. Within 72 hours of the president's national appeal, the package of taxes and spending that had taken all summer to hammer out collapsed.

With congressional Republicans in open revolt, President Bush was stuck with a dilemma. He could allow the provisions of the current law to kick in and automatically reduce the deficit with severe, across-the-board cuts in discretionary spending or he could return to the negotiating table to develop a package that would attract stronger Democratic support. He opted for the latter, but not without a lot of bickering within the administration that spilled over into the press. The collective consternation was brought on by the realization that the bipartisan compromise no one in the White House was enthusiastic about would become the administration's new bargaining position from which an even less attractive, more Democratic policy would be fashioned.

As soon as the new package was signed, President Bush left town to repair his relations with congressional Republicans by helping in their reelection campaigns. He conjured up the image of himself as a Reaganesque outsider—"God, I'm glad to be out of Washington"—and painted congressional Democrats, his erstwhile trading partners, as "America's biggest and most entrenched special interest." And he adopted what his aides called a "Harry Truman style" by claiming the budget had been held "ransom" by Congress, and in the future he was "absolutely going to hold the line on taxes." [73]

There was little confidence among fellow partisans, however, that the president could switch from cooperation to confrontation so easily. A "senior Republican strategist" summed up the matter to one news correspondent this way: "They're going to sign off on the budget deal, then try to pin it on the Democrats, say George Bush didn't do it and expect the voters to believe this whole budget was an immaculate conception. . . . It's not going to be easy."

Republican congressional candidates also viewed this as a dubious strategy. Of the hundred or so who had made campaign commercials with Bush earlier in the fall, only a few chose to air them. Many canceled the president's visit to their district, and some of those who required his presence to raise campaign funds with the party faithful stayed in Washington on "pressing business." Sometimes matters did not improve even when the president succeeded in joining a candidate on stage. Surely the following introduction offered by a House Republican from Oklahoma was well intended: "George Bush on his worst day is a whole lot better than Michael Dukakis on his best day." The *coup de grace* came while the president was stumping in Vermont for another House Republican incumbent. Seeking maximum distance from the president, who was seated within a stone's throw, the candidate addressed the audience: "Ask yourselves, why did this President, last May, decide that the issue he had run on and won on now had to be laid on the table as a point of negotiations? We're talking about his pledge on taxes."

The Most Effective Strategy

Congress and the presidency are different kinds of institutions, mostly having to do with the number of principals involved. The modern institutional presidency has a staff of thousands, but only one individual is able to commit the institution. This gives that person special credibility and prominence when staking out policy positions either publicly or privately. When members of Congress take positions, they speak as one voice among many. Even when the institution's leaders take a position on an issue, which they do only infrequently, it assumes the form of a prediction or a reading of the unrevealed preferences of the collectivity. Especially in this era of individualized pluralism, congressional leaders cannot often commit their institution to a course of action.

While this difference gives the president a comparative advantage in going public, it becomes a disadvantage in negotiations between these institutions. Just as Rowe advised Truman, and as Bush had to learn for himself, only the president is obliged to honor his commitment. If he backs away from an agreement, he is reneging. If congressional leaders fail to deliver their members' votes, they can be faulted for ineffectiveness but not bad faith. In the politics of the 1990 budget accord, George Bush stumbled onto every mine field James Rowe had warned Truman about nearly half a century earlier. The moral of these two cases is clear. Under divided government, the president should engage Congress distantly, in full view of the public. In subsequent chapters we shall examine evidence showing that the arrival of divided party control of government has led incumbent presidents to increase their level of public activities, presumably aware of the implications of dealing with an opposition Congress.

Conclusion

We have considered several major developments in national politics as causes for the rise of going public as a presidential strategy: political relations in Washington that no longer permit a limited set of bargains to carry the day; presidential selection reforms that allow ordinary voters to determine nominations rather than state party organizations; and the rise of divided party control of government. Although on the surface these developments appear quite different and suggest a multiplicity of possible causes, they share a common root: the declining influence of political parties on the electorate. Since the 1960s, fewer voters identify with one of the two major parties. At times over the intervening years, the number of self-proclaimed "independents" has actually surpassed the number of party identifiers. But loyalties are fading even among partisans, who are more likely to defect at the ballot box than did their counterparts during the several decades when institutionalized pluralism reigned. As a result of weakening loyalty, local and state party organizations have atrophied and in many communities are extinct.

This attitude among the electorate has filtered into Washington. Politicians can no longer depend on their party's performance for their personal success and have made a strategic turn to self-reliant individualism. With voters' choices up for grabs, mobilization has been of less importance. State party organizations consequently have had less to offer and a weaker claim for control of party affairs. Since the 1940s the parties' national committees had been steadily weakening, and in the late 1960s the nominating convention was reformed to strip state organizations of the control they once had. Delegates were to be selected in primaries or highly public and open caucuses, and at the convention the majority of a state delegation could no longer control all of its delegates. Among those who benefited from parties' decline, of course, were those self-styled outsiders who would never have received their party's endorsement.

Many plausible explanations have been advanced for the rise of divided government, and a discussion of them would lead us far afield. However, the simple fact that divided government in Washington is the result of voters choosing candidates from both parties similarly ties this cause of going public to weakening of party loyalties.

From what has been said thus far, bargaining and going public appear to have little in common. Bargaining thrives when numerous protocoalitions represented by authoritative leaders are present and when the actors do not have to worry that deals will disintegrate because of short-term shifts in public opinion. Going public becomes the preferred course when protocoalitions are weak, when individual politicians are susceptible to public pressures, and when politicians in the White House appreciate the requirements of television better than the needs of committee chairs.

Institutionalized pluralism prescribes that presidents bargain, and individualized pluralism that they go public. But these settings are abstractions—their starkness intended to clarify the evolution of Washington politics during the past half century; presidents in the real world retain choice in their leadership. Bargaining continues to be a ubiquitous activity in today's Washington, just as going public was occasionally the choice of presidents of an earlier era. What has changed significantly is the balance of incentives and constraints that influences strategic choice and the kinds of politicians in the Oval Office who make them. After carefully considering their options in confronting opposition Congresses and less reliable coalition partners, contemporary presidents will choose going public over bargaining more often than did their predecessors.

The next chapter continues to explore presidential leadership as a reflection of the community within which the president works. Specifically, it examines the historical transformation of Washington from a community of institutionalized pluralism to one of individualized pluralism in the context of twentieth-century relations between the president and the press. The evolution of these relations, containing all the elements of old and new Washington, was instrumental in bringing about this alternative style of presidential leadership.

Notes

1. Robert A. Dahl and Charles E. Lindblom, *Politics, Economics, and Welfare* (New York: Harper and Row, 1953), 333.
2. Hugh Heclo, *The Government of Strangers* (Washington, D.C.: Brookings Institution, 1977), 194.
3. Dahl and Lindblom, *Politics, Economics, and Welfare,* 333.
4. Clem Miller, *Member of the House* (New York: Charles Scribner's Sons, 1962), 93.
5. Donald R. Matthews, *U.S. Senators and Their World* (Chapel Hill: University of North Carolina Press, 1960), 100-101.
6. From this perspective Richard F. Fenno has described the House Appropriations Committee as a coalition. Although the collective goals of the committee—to protect the Treasury and to preserve the House's influence—are rooted in institutional needs, its coalitional features are no less significant. Richard F. Fenno, *Power of the Purse* (Boston: Little, Brown, 1966), 191-264.
7. Richard E. Neustadt, *Presidential Power,* 28-29. Copyright © 1980. Reprinted by permission of John Wiley and Sons, Inc. Compare with Dahl and Lindblom's earlier observation: "The President possesses more hierarchical controls than any other single figure in the government; indeed, he is often described somewhat romantically and certainly ambiguously as the most powerful democratic executive in the world. Yet like everyone else in the American policy process, the President must bargain constantly—with Congressional leaders, individual Congressmen, his department heads, bureau chiefs, and leaders of nongovernmental organizations" (Dahl and Lindblom, *Politics, Economics, and Welfare,* 333).
8. Peter Sperlich questions whether the president has sufficient time, energy, and resources to bargain his way to coalitions even when authoritative leaders are available. Peter Sperlich, "Bargaining and Overload: An Essay on *Presidential Power,*" in *Perspectives on the Presidency,* ed. Aaron Wildavsky (Boston: Little, Brown, 1975), 406-430.
9. Douglass Cater, *Power in Washington* (New York: Vintage, 1964), 75.
10. Franklin Delano Roosevelt Library, Hyde Park, New York; PSF: McIntyre, 1-4. The memo continued:

> In this connection, there is something else I wish you would do. Up to now Jim Rowe [Justice Department official and Roosevelt confidant] has been clearing all nominations with the Democratic National Committee and on the Hill. For your very private information, there is too much friction between the Committee and the Senators on patronage. I want you to handle the Treasury and Justice nominations with Flynn and the Senators. I think I shall let Jim Rowe continue to handle the independent agencies. After you have cleared these nominations for

a while, perhaps you can be a mollifying influence and bring the Committee and the Senators more into harmony.

Let Jim Rowe know about this so he can shift over his arrangements with the Committee, Treasury and Justice to you.

11. William S. White, *The Citadel* (New York: Harper and Brothers, 1956), 135-153.

12. David B. Truman, *The Governmental Process* (New York: Alfred A. Knopf, 1951), 391.

13. Martin Kriesberg, "What Congressmen and Administrators Think of the Polls," *Public Opinion Quarterly* 9 (Fall 1945): 333-337. Concluding from this and other sources, historian Richard Jensen states, "The threat [of polls] was a short-circuiting of the representative form of government. It was one thing for Roosevelt, in his capacity as party leader and candidate to appeal for support. It was quite another to use the agencies of government to mold public opinion and thereby to force Congress to relinquish its authority to set policy" (Richard Jensen, "Public Opinion Polls: Early Problems of Method and Philosophy," Paper delivered at the Oxford Conference on History and Theory of the Social Sciences, Oxford, England, July 23, 1977, 14.)

14. *Memoirs by Harry S Truman: Years of Trial and Hope,* vol. 2 (Garden City, N.Y.: Doubleday and Co., 1956; reprint New York: New American Library, 1965), 207-208.

15. Leila A. Sussman, "FDR and the White House Mail," *Public Opinion Quarterly* 20 (Spring 1956): 5-15.

16. A case in point occurred in 1943 when farm organizations announced their opposition to the president's farm subsidy program. The White House responded by commissioning private surveys on farmers' views of his agricultural policies. On finding that by and large farmers had no idea what his policies were, Roosevelt used the results to refute farm group leaders' claims that their constituents opposed his program. Richard W. Steele, "The Pulse of the People: Franklin D. Roosevelt and the Gauging of American Public Opinion," *Journal of Contemporary History* 9 (October 1975): 210-212.

17. Ibid., 125. Newton N. Minow, John Bartlow Martin, and Lee M. Mitchell present Franklin Roosevelt as more actively mobilizing national opinion than argued by Steele. See their *Presidential Television* (New York: Basic Books, 1973), 29-32.

18. Befitting the lapse, the court packing case is one of the few instances when FDR failed to sound out congressional leadership before announcing his plan at a press conference. There are many good accounts of this event. One that does a good job conveying the surprise and consternation of Roosevelt's usual supporters at his "high handed" tactics is Joseph Alsop and Turner Catledge, *The 168 Days* (New York: Doubleday and Co., 1938).

19. Neustadt, *Presidential Power,* 64-65.

20. Ibid., 74-75.

21. Neustadt's use of the word "command" to mean the unilateral use of authority to alter others' behavior without compensation has entered the presidential literature as the chief alternative to bargaining as a mode of influence.

22. Alexander L. George and Juliette L. George, *Woodrow Wilson and Colonel House* (New York: J. Day Co., 1956), 290-292.

23. John Morton Blum, *Woodrow Wilson and the Politics of Morality* (Boston: Little, Brown, 1956), 189-191.

24. David S. McLellan and John W. Reuss, "Foreign and Military Policies," in *The Truman Period as a Research Field,* ed. Richard S. Kirkendall (Columbia: University of Missouri Press, 1967), 55-57. Curiously, this widely cited quotation is absent from Vandenberg's memoirs. It is ironic that Neustadt treats the Truman

Doctrine speech, which was perhaps the most successful use of public opinion in the postwar era to gain the president leverage vis-à-vis other political elites in Washington, as a prime example of pluralist exchange. He notes that Truman and others rallied the public to the subsequent Marshall Plan, but this was necessarily preceded, he argues, by elite exchange. Neustadt, *Presidential Power,* 36-40.

25. Truman in his memoirs vividly describes his rewriting of the "half hearted" draft from the State Department: "The key sentence, for instance, read, 'I believe that it should be the policy of the United States....' I took my pencil, scratched out 'should' and wrote in 'must'.... I wanted no hedging in this speech. This was America's answer to the surge of expansion of Communist tyranny. It had to be clear and free of hesitation or double talk" (Harry S Truman, *Memoirs,* vol. 2, 105-109). For further discussion of the writing of the Truman Doctrine speech, see Chapter 6.

26. See on each of these points, respectively, Morris P. Fiorina, *Congress: Keystone of the Washington Establishment* (New Haven: Yale University Press, 1977); Austin Ranney, *Channels of Power* (Washington, D.C.: American Enterprise Institute, 1983); and Martin P. Wattenberg, *The Decline of Political Parties* (Cambridge: Harvard University Press, 1984).

27. For similar treatment of the bureaucracy, see Hugh Heclo, "Issue Networks and the Executive Establishment," in *The New American Political System,* ed. Anthony King (Washington, D.C.: American Enterprise Institute, 1978), 87-124; and Nelson W. Polsby, *Consequences of Party Reform* (New York: Oxford University Press, 1983), 90-104.

28. Thomas E. Mann and Norman J. Ornstein, eds., *The New Congress* (Washington, D.C.: American Enterprise Institute, 1981). See also Eric L. Davis, "Legislative Reform and the Decline of Presidential Influence on Capitol Hill," *British Journal of Political Science* 9 (October 1979): 465-479; and Bruce I. Oppenheimer, "Policy Effects of U.S. House Reform: Decentralization and the Capacity to Resolve Energy Issues," *Legislative Studies Quarterly* 5 (February 1980): 5-30.

29. Thomas E. Mann, "Elections and Change in Congress," in *The New Congress,* ed. Mann and Ornstein, 53. On announcing his retirement from the Senate after 51 years in Congress, Sen. Jennings Randolph was asked what major changes in politics he had seen. Randolph responded, "There is a lack of discipline in the Senate—a deterioration every year I've been here. I just don't understand it" (Marjorie Hunter, "From Roosevelt's Outings to Reagan's Greetings," *New York Times,* October 5, 1984, B10). See also, Steven V. Roberts, "Senate's New Breed Shuns Novice Role," *New York Times,* November 26, 1984, 1; and Alan Ehrenhalt, "In the Senate of the '80s, Team Spirit Has Given Way to the Rule of Individuals," *Congressional Quarterly Weekly Report,* September 4, 1982, 2175-2182.

30. Michael Robinson, "Three Faces of Congressional Media," in *The New Congress,* ed. Mann and Ornstein, 93. For confirmation of Robinson's reference, see Julia Malone, "Party 'Whips' Lose Their Snap to TV and Voters Back Home," *Christian Science Monitor,* June 27, 1984, 16; and Bob Michel, "Politics in the Age of Television," *Washington Post,* June 4, 1984, 27.

31. Douglass Cater, *The Fourth Branch of Government* (Boston: Houghton Mifflin, 1959), 65.

32. Roger Davidson, "Subcommittee Government: New Channels for Policy Making," in *The New Congress,* ed. Mann and Ornstein, 109.

33. For the early history of the Democratic Study Group, see Mark F. Ferber, "The Formation of the Democratic Study Group," in *Congressional Behavior,* ed. Nelson W. Polsby (New York: Random House, 1971), 249-269. Dennis Farney

reports the DSG's efforts to overcome its recent complacency in "Democratic Study Unit in Ferment," *Wall Street Journal*, April 25, 1984, 54.

34. Susan Webb Hammond, Arthur G. Stevens, Jr., and Daniel P. Mulhollan, "Congressional Caucuses: Legislators As Lobbyists," in *Interest Group Politics*, ed. Allan J. Cigler and Burdett A. Loomis (Washington, D.C.: CQ Press, 1983), 285-287.

35. Michael Kinsley, "The Art of Deduction: Writer's Loophole," *Wall Street Journal*, March 11, 1983, 21.

36. Norman J. Ornstein et al., *Vital Statistics on Congress, 1984-1985 Edition* (Washington, D.C.: American Enterprise Institute, 1984), 86-87. Data for 1984 are from Federal Election Commission, "PAC Support of Incumbents Increases in '84 Elections" (May 19, 1985), 1-3.

37. Quoted in J. David Gopoian, "What Makes PACs Tick? An Analysis of the Allocation Patterns of Economic Interest Groups," *American Journal of Political Science* 28 (May 1984): 259-281.

38. For an account of this incident, see White, *The Citadel*, 144-146.

39. Defending the Senate's action Sen. Larry Pressler inadvertently made the critic's point: "We got 69 votes, and we might have been able to top out at 80. With that many votes I don't think you can attribute it to campaign contributions alone" (Albert R. Hunt, "Special-Interest Money Increasingly Influences What Congress Enacts," *Wall Street Journal*, July 26, 1982, 13).

40. In addition to contributing heavily to probusiness (almost exclusively Republican) candidates, the chamber has sought to coordinate the political donations of smaller business PACs. In 1982 it produced a closed-circuit show called "See How They Run," which reviewed 50 key races for 150 PAC managers around the country. Much of the information reported here on the Chamber of Commerce comes from the program titled "Congress and the Media" from the series "Congress: We the People," PBS network, 1984. See also "Running with the PACs," *Time*, October 25, 1982, 20-26.

41. Kay Lehman Schlozman and John T. Tierney, "More of the Same: Washington Press Group Activity in a Decade of Change," *Journal of Politics* 45 (May 1983): 351-377. Indicative of the growing fashion of enlisting public relations on Capitol Hill are executive seminars conducted by Congressional Quarterly with such unabashed titles as "Understanding Public Relations and the Washington News Media: Getting Your Message across to Congress" (from a conference listing in *Washington Post*, September 23, 1985, Business Calendar section, 19).

42. According to Stuart Eizenstat, Carter's domestic affairs adviser, "PACs balkanize the political process" ("Running with the PACs," 21).

43. Alvin Rabushka and Pauline Ryan, *The Tax Revolt* (Stanford: Hoover Institution, 1982); and Robert Hall and Alvin Rabushka, *Low Tax, Simple Tax, Flat Tax* (New York: McGraw-Hill, 1983). Another example is the unanimous House support in 1983 for legislation that would force absent parents to make child support payments. Earlier in the session Rep. Barbara Kennelly, the bill's sponsor, could attract little interest among her colleagues on the Ways and Means Committee. Once public opinion polls began showing that female voters across the country were sensitive to this issue, it did not take long for the bandwagon to fill up. "Members want to be able to go home and say, 'I've done something for women,'" stated Representative Kennelly (Steven V. Roberts, "Political Survival: It's Women and Children First," *New York Times*, December 6, 1983, 10).

44. Barbara Sinclair, "Coping with Uncertainty: Building Coalitions in the House and the Senate," in *The New Congress*, ed. Mann and Ornstein, 220. At the 1976 convention of the American Society for Public Administration, Dean Rusk

observed, "In the 1950s and 1960s we handled sensitive foreign affairs policy questions with the Congress by dealing with the 'whales'—Rayburn, Vinson, men like that. They could make commitments. Now it is as if we were dealing with 535 minnows in a bucket" (from a statement to the plenary session, Panel of Former Cabinet Officers, National Convention of the American Society for Public Administration, Washington, D.C., April 1976).

45. Steven R. Weisman, "No. 1, the President Is Very Result Oriented," *New York Times,* November 12, 1983, 10.

46. Sinclair, "Coping with Uncertainty," 220.

47. Sidney Blumenthal, "Marketing the President," *New York Times Magazine,* September 13, 1981, 110.

48. Cited in George C. Edwards III, *The Public Presidency* (New York: St. Martin's Press, 1983), 14.

49. B. Drummond Ayres, Jr., "G.O.P. Keeps Tabs on Nation's Mood," *New York Times,* November 16, 1981, 20.

50. Neustadt, *Presidential Power,* especially chap. 8; and Sperlich, "Bargaining and Overload."

51. This discussion of reputation follows closely that of Neustadt in *Presidential Power,* (New York: John Wiley and Sons, 1980), chap. 4.

52. Neustadt observed that President Truman's television appeal for tighter price controls in 1951 had little visible effect on how Washington politicians viewed the issue. This is the only mention of a president going public in the original eight chapters of the book. Neustadt, *Presidential Power,* 45.

53. Ibid., 238.

54. Cited in Gary C. Jacobson, *The Politics of Congressional Elections* (Boston: Little, Brown, 1983), 179-180. Jacobson goes on to note, "Carter did not enjoy broad public support during most of his presidency ... [and when] he was most popular early in his term ... he was unable to turn public support into political influence."

55. Statement by Rep. Richard B. Cheney cited in Charles O. Jones, "Congress and the Presidency," in *The New Congress,* eds. Thomas E. Mann and Norman J. Ornstein (Washington, D.C.: American Enterprise Institute, 1981), 241.

56. William A. Robinson, *Thomas B. Reed, Parliamentarian* (New York: Dodd, Mead, 1930), 100-101.

57. Nelson W. Polsby and Aaron B. Wildavsky, *Presidential Elections,* 2d ed. (New York: Charles Scribner's Sons, 1968), 80-81.

58. Polsby, *Consequences of Party Reform,* 64.

59. Polsby describes the reforms and convincingly argues their effects on the kinds of presidents elected in *Consequences of Party Reform.*

60. William Cavala, "Changing the Rules Changes the Game: Party Reform and the 1972 California Delegation to the Democratic National Convention," *American Political Science Review* 68 (March 1974): 27-42.

61. As a result of special rule changes that reserved at-large delegate seats for members of Congress, in 1984 these figures shot up to 63 percent for representatives and 62 percent for senators. "At Washington West, Clout and Compromise," *Congressional Quarterly Weekly Report,* July 21, 1984, 1745.

62. Richard B. Cheney, "The Law's Impact on Presidential and Congressional Election Campaigns," in *Parties, Interest Groups, and Campaign Finance Laws,* ed. Michael J. Malbin (Washington, D.C.: American Enterprise Institute, 1980), 238-248. On growing PAC participation in presidential elections, see Sara Fritz, "Changing Rules in Game of Politics Shaping Races," *Los Angeles Times,* December 22, 1983, 1.

63. Joseph Bruce Gorman, *Kefauver: A Political Biography* (New York: Oxford University Press, 1971), 80-106. For an account of the rise of Kefauver as an overnight television personality, see G. D. Wiebe, "Responses to the Televised Kefauver Hearings," *Public Opinion Quarterly* 16 (Summer 1952): 179-200.

64. Jimmy Carter, *Keeping the Faith* (New York: Bantam Books, 1982). For a more detailed treatment of the rise of outsiders, see Samuel Kernell, "Campaigning, Governing, and the Contemporary Presidency," in *The New Direction in American Politics,* ed. John E. Chubb and Paul E. Peterson (Washington, D.C.: Brookings Institution, 1985), 117-141.

65. Haynes Johnson, *The Absence of Power* (New York: Viking, 1980), 159-161.

66. Sperlich complains that Neustadt demands too much bargaining activity from the president and argues that more presidential influence comes from deference than Neustadt is willing to concede. Neither Neustadt nor Sperlich considers that bargaining is made more efficient by the routines of exchange and through political parties as protocoalitions. See Sperlich, "Bargaining and Overload."

67. Johnson, *Absence of Power,* 166-167.

68. Ibid., 22. Two months later they were having the same dialogue but in public. Hedrick Smith reports: " 'It upsets me when they say, "we'll bring it to the people," ' the stentorian white-haired speaker declared. 'That's the biggest mistake Carter could ever make' " ("Congress and Carter: An Uneasy Adjustment," *New York Times,* February 18, 1977, B16).

69. In both instances, the president eventually relented to mounting public pressure and signed essentially Democratic bills.

70. Walter J. Olezek, "The Context of Congressional Policy Making," in *Divided Democracy,* ed. James A. Thurber, (Washington, D.C.: CQ Press, 1991), 99.

71. James H. Rowe, Oral History Interview, 1969 and 1970, Harry S. Truman Library, Appendix.

72. "Oral History of the Truman White House" 1980, Harry S. Truman Library.

73. David E. Rosenbaum, "In Appeal for Support for Budget, President Calls Plan Best for Now," *New York Times,* October 3, 1990, A1.

74. Michael Oreskes, "Advantage: Democrats," *New York Times,* October 29, 1990, A14; and Maureen Dowd, "From President to Politician: Bush Attacks the Democrats," *New York Times,* October 30, 1990, A13.

The President and the Press 3

On May 18, 1937, with some 200 reporters packed around the president's desk in the Oval Office, Franklin Roosevelt opened his normal Tuesday press conference by saying,

> Off the record, wholly off the record. I wanted to tell you a story that I think you ought to know because it does affect the press of the country. . . . As you know, I have always encouraged, and am entirely in favor of, absolute freedom for all news writers. That should be and will continue to be the general rule in Washington.[1]

He then pulled out the latest pink sheet (the color signifying "not for publication") from the McClure Syndicate to approximately 270 member newspapers, and began to read:

> Unchecked. A New York specialist high in the medical field is authority for the following, which is given in the strictest confidence to editors: Toward the end of last month Mr. Roosevelt was found in a coma at his desk. Medical examination disclosed the neck rash which is typical of certain disturbing symptoms. Immediate treatment of the most skilled kind was indicated, with complete privacy and detachment from official duties. Hence the trip to southern waters, with no newspapermen on board and a naval convoy which cannot be penetrated.
>
> The unusual activities of Vice President Garner are believed to be in connection with the current situation and its possible developments. "Checking has been impossible."[2]

Then Roosevelt read another pink-sheet item that reported on a conversation at a private New York dinner party in which an official of American Cyanamid called the president "a paranoiac in the White House"; he declared that "a couple of well placed bullets would be the best thing for the country, and that he would buy a bottle of champagne as quick as he could get it to celebrate the news." In the ensuing conversation with reporters, the president revealed that the editor responsible for the stories was Richard Waldo. Waldo, who is better remembered for having originated the Good Housekeeping Seal of Approval, was not a Washingtonian and clearly must have felt he had little to lose by taking on the president.[3] After about 15 minutes, Roosevelt closed the discussion by reminding the reporters, "It is all off the record; all strictly in the family and nothing else." [4]

Institutionalized pluralism requires continuous face-to-face negotiations among partisan participants and inculcates strong norms of propriety. Cordial relations are functional. This incident reveals, however, that politics in this former era—especially when outsiders were involved—could be just as virulent as anything the egoism of individualized pluralism can produce. As startling as the episode must have been to the men and women gathered around the president's desk, it is, nonetheless, indicative of the FDR system of presidential-press relations, examined later in this chapter. It also shows how the normative order of the day dealt with deviant behavior.

Consider first that Roosevelt made his remarks "in confidence" to the regular assemblage of the Tuesday press conference. No effort was made to recruit sympathetic reporters. Nor did he have to resort to any hidden-hand strategies; the standard dictum "off the record" sufficed. Yet if Roosevelt did not wish his remarks to become news, why did he tell newspaper reporters? Two motives are possible. First, it is apparent on careful reading of his statement that FDR sought retribution against McClure's editor—not at his own hands, but at those of the Washington press corps. When asked, he did not hesitate to reveal the culprit's name. Roosevelt's fellow community members did not let him down.

Organically integrated societies commonly banish those guilty of serious violations of community norms, and Washington was no exception. The White House correspondents could not run Waldo out of town, but they could strip him of standing. Some tried to have him expelled from the National Press Club. When brought before the club's board of governors to answer charges, Waldo threatened to sue everyone present. According to one account, "The board members naturally hesitated." Although no formal action was taken, Waldo left the club.[5] The confidentiality of the president's remarks kept the story off the pages of the nation's newspapers and successfully summoned forth community sanctions.

A second, probably less immediate reason for giving this off-the-record information to reporters may have been to elicit the press corps' sympathy. Setting White House correspondents against this New York editor strengthened Roosevelt's ties with them and loosened theirs with distant editors. With most of the nation's newspapers and chains on record opposing his election in 1932 and again in 1936, Roosevelt made a special effort to generate good will among the working press in Washington. He largely succeeded. In consequence, Roosevelt enjoyed a more productive relationship with the press corps, over a longer time, than any president before or since.[6]

The Bargaining President and the Press

As traditionally conceived, presidential leadership flows through quiet diplomacy and is generally ill served by public pressure on bargaining partners. Why, then, should favorable press relations have been important to Roosevelt? The reason is that news contributes to pluralist leadership and affects the way elite relations are conducted. Close ties to the working press were, in fact, more highly valued in Roosevelt's time than they are today.

The universal "law of anticipated reactions" dictates that politicians in Washington will pay attention to their publics in deciding what stance to take with the president. Before scientific surveys were widely available, a politician's mail and the newspapers of the constituency substituted for public opinion. A favorable press may have only fostered an illusion of support, but frequently it sufficed. Also, prominent journalists serve as important opinion leaders in establishing the president's reputation. In Roosevelt's time the appraisals of David Lawrence, Walter Lippmann, Arthur Krock, and others were given close scrutiny by Washingtonians; others who would later take on this responsibility include James Reston, Richard Strout, Joseph Kraft, and David Broder.

The bargaining president can use press coverage in a variety of ways to improve his position. By making an issue newsworthy, he can force other negotiators to deal with it.[7] The president may selectively release information that enhances his position and diminishes the position of his bargaining partner. By assuming a firm public posture on an issue, he can stake out a negotiating stance that everyone recognizes cannot be easily abandoned. The president can float a trial balloon from which he may identify coalition partners and test potential avenues of compromise. Many of these activities have precedents reaching far back into the nineteenth century. Unlike purely public strategies of leadership, none requires a communications infrastructure that gives the president instant access to millions of citizens, and all are directed toward the bargaining table.

To appreciate why pluralist arts are sometimes publicly practiced, one must understand the rationale of the constitutional structure and how news serves the presidency. Montesquieu's proposition that unchecked power is inherently corrupt preoccupied the Founding Fathers as they deliberated a new constitutional order. Reasoning that in a democracy, tyranny requires collusion, they dispersed governmental authority wherever possible. The result was, and is, autonomous institutions with formal relations among them. On reading the Constitution, the capital's planner, Pierre L'Enfant, concluded, "No message to nor from the President is to be made without a sort of decorum." Accordingly, there was little reason to place the Capitol and the White House on the same hill.[8]

Despite continuous interaction today, the institutional distance created between Congress and the presidency 200 years ago has not been greatly shortened. Even as informal, face-to-face negotiation occurs, it is commonly preceded and facilitated by the preparatory public activities institutional distance encourages. As Douglass Cater has noted, "Unofficial communication between the executive and legislative branches of government—and within each branch—goes on regularly through the press, well in advance of official communications." [9] Woodrow Wilson was surely correct when, as president, he observed, "News is the atmosphere of politics." [10] This is why a devout bargainer like Franklin Roosevelt would be so attentive to the Washington press corps.

The conspicuous deficiency of professional good will between modern presidents and the Washington press has prompted some historians and journalists whose careers spanned the administrations of Franklin Roosevelt and Richard Nixon to reexamine the "secret" of Roosevelt's success. These chroniclers give the Great Depression and the New Deal much of the credit.[11] Never before during peacetime, they have written, had the country looked so intently to Washington to solve its problems.

For reporters, the rise of Washington as the center of the nation's politics meant that Washington by-lines suddenly commanded front-page space. For the president, the times posed unprecedented responsibilities and opportunities. Roosevelt sought the cooperation of more elites than any president since Lincoln. Beyond Capitol Hill, old-line agencies had to be made compliant, if not enthusiastic, about implementing the many New Deal programs. Interest groups had to be attracted to the programs. In a few instances, such as the formation of the Tennessee Valley Authority, altogether new constituencies had to be mobilized.[12] The federal courts—from those in the districts to the Supreme Court—had to be converted from the sanctity of the Constitution's contract clause that threatened to paralyze much of the administration's interventionist economic program.[13] Because the president needed to enlist so many persons dispersed throughout government, Washington correspondents could play a major role in helping Roosevelt sell the New Deal.

The urgency of the times explains what brought the presidency and the Washington press together, but it fails to account fully for the productive relationship that ensued. The rest of the explanation lies in the convergence of interests between a newly professional press corps and the presidency. The kind of relationship revealed in the news conference of May 18, 1937, served the emerging needs of both the president and the press.

From the late nineteenth century to Franklin Roosevelt's inauguration, Washington correspondents evolved from an amorphous collection of visiting editors, reporters on temporary assignment, and disguised job seekers to a stable community of professional journalists.[14] This professional development held consequences for a president seeking influence. Where Roosevelt excelled—and where his predecessors distinctly did not—was in recognizing correspondents' *professional* stake in a particular kind of news conveyed in a particular way. From his first day in office, Roosevelt understood this—better, one can add, than some of the correspondents' editors, who could not fathom why their reporters were toeing Roosevelt's line rather than that of their home paper.

To appreciate how the mutual interests of the president and the press formed a basis for reciprocity, one needs to understand the modern evolution of the Washington press corps. Because the institutional development of Congress has been well plotted in the political science literature,[15] it in large measure informs one's conception of the workings of institutionalized pluralism. What is largely unknown is that the development of the press corps since the late nineteenth century—a far less well documented story—follows a parallel course and similarly contributes to the transformation of Washington into a community of institutional actors.

This is also an ideal arena for examining the refinement of bargaining leadership because presidential exchange with the press appears thoroughly, though subtly, rooted in the institutional needs of each participant. When a president cuts a quick deal with the head of a powerful committee, one is afforded only a brief and superficial glimpse of the bargaining arts. Anyone anywhere can horse trade. By contrast, the workings of tacit, ongoing reciprocity agreements described below show how pluralist leadership is embedded in the institutional milieu.

Finally, this historical survey introduces key elements in the breakdown of institutionalized pluralism. Better than any other pairing in Washington, the modern evolution of presidential-press relations describes the recent transformation of the Washington community and the rise of presidents who routinely go public.

Emergence of the Washington Press as an Institution

Early Professionalization

Shortly after Henry Adams arrived in Washington in 1868 to pursue a career in journalism, he followed the established protocol of paying respects to the president. Adams's visit to the White House was uneventful, but that it happened at all reveals a lot about the size and pace of the Washington community in the late 1860s. "In four-and-twenty hours," reported Adams, a young man "could know everybody; in two days, everybody knew him." [16]

President Andrew Johnson could take an informal approach to press relations because there were fewer correspondents in those days and they were not so interested in him. Whereas about four-fifths of modern reporting of Congress and the presidency is devoted to the latter, the opposite pattern was the case throughout most of the nineteenth century. A study of Washington reporting in the newspapers of one midwestern city found closer scrutiny of congressional committees than of the presidency.[17] To discern the origins of the Washington press corps, one must therefore look to Capitol Hill.

The press corps had gained official recognition during the late 1850s when control over credentials to the House and Senate press galleries was turned over to a committee of correspondents, and registered journalists began to be listed in each year's official *Congressional Directory*. In 1868, 58 reporters were so listed. By Adams's death in 1918, the number had more than quadrupled.

Growth contributed to the professionalization of the Washington press corps, but as long as growth was accompanied by high turnover, the Washington assignment remained little more than a revolving door. Above all, professionalization required a stable membership. Though it is impossible to state definitively what increased stability and promoted professionalization at the turn of the century, biographical sketches and circumstantial evidence contained in gallery listings suggest several influences. One is that the number of papers that pulled out of the press gallery declined sharply after the turn of the century.[18] Also, one suspects that veteran correspondents were valued for their personal contacts with officials. These contacts increasingly became a resource that gave Washington correspondents an advantage over their would-be replacements.[19]

By the early 1900s, reporters viewed Washington as an attractive assignment. Correspondents were sent to Washington often after years of service on local and state political beats. When they returned home, they frequently did so to become their paper's managing editor. The Washington assignment had become an important step in career advancement.[20] The status of the Washington correspondent must have been secure by the 1920s when press chronicler Silas Bent remarked, "The corps of correspondents there represents the very flower of the American press." [21]

Another, more significant development that stabilized careers was the practice of writing for more than one paper. Begun as early as the 1870s, this custom resulted in consistently lower turnover rates for correspondents. Turnover declined sharply from the close of the Civil War to the election of Franklin Roosevelt (see Table 3-1). In 1864-1866, when all reporters worked for only one paper, 75 percent of the correspondents left Washington before the next session of Congress convened. By 1876, 15 percent of the gallery reporters listed in the *Congressional Directory* associated themselves with two or more papers, and turnover was down to 52 percent. By 1914, 35 percent of the listed reporters had multiple clients, and turnover was 34 percent. Turnover rates for correspondents between Congresses had been reduced to 22 percent by the early 1930s.

The trend toward working for multiple papers probably had a greater effect on career stability and professionalization than the numbers alone suggest. Many of the papers constituting multiple clients for a reporter came from smaller communities far from Washington and were only marginally interested in Washington coverage beyond that available from the wire services. Without being able to share the expenses of a correspondent with

Table 3-1 Turnover among Washington Correspondents, Selected
Years, 1864-1932

	1864-1866	1876-1878	1890-1892	1900-1902	1914-1916	1930-1932
Turnover (%)						
Departing	75	52	37	34	34	22
New[1]	70	59	36	34	35	26
Distribution of all correspondents, by clients (%)[2]						
Single paper	100	85	66	62	51	48
Syndicate	0	0	15	9	14	30
Multiple papers	0	15	19	29	35	22
Total number of correspondents	51	132	151	159	200	351
Percent leaving over two-year period, by client						
Single paper	75	56	41	40	44	22
Syndicate	—	—	26	29	38	25
Multiple papers	—	30	31	22	17	18

[1] New additions in gallery listings from first to second year.
[2] Calculated for first year of pair.

SOURCES: *Congressional Directory* for each year indicated.

other papers, they probably would not have long maintained a Washington bureau. Also, multiple papers were a form of diversification through which reporters were able to reduce uncertainty. The more papers reporters could sign on, the less their dependence upon any one of them. Newspapers became, then, a market for correspondents, and the relationship changed from employer to client.[22]

Diversification and the establishment of client relationships fostered professionalism and set it on a course that would in time shape presidential-press relations. One conspicuous consequence was the posture of journalists toward politicians. In the past when newspapers were as much party organs as they were business enterprises, correspondents served the party in the news they wrote. Absolute fidelity to the editorial position of the home paper was a prerequisite to assignment. Client relationships, however, required flexibility on the part of reporters. While they perhaps had to be willing to color reports with whatever slant a paper's editor wanted, correspondents could ill afford to be too partisan lest they lose their appeal to other current and potential clients. Too close an association with a particular party line reduced correspondents' marketability. The more neutral the stance reporters could maintain, the better their market position.

In the 1920s Washington correspondents began writing about them-selves—a self-absorption characteristic of blossoming professionalism. These articles and books are revealing in depicting correspondents largely shorn of personal partisanship. If they, as a class, held their subjects in any special regard, it was most likely one of cynicism. In 1927 Silas Bent wrote:

> Newspaper men are seldom men of strong convictions; their work seems somehow to militate against that. It is nothing unusual to see a Washington correspondent shift without the slightest jar from a newspaper of one political complexion to another of the opposite camp. . . . [H]ad it happened during the last century [it] would have provoked, almost certainly, cries of turncoat.[23]

All professions strive to legitimize practice with creed, and the Washing-ton press corps was no exception. At the same time that increasing numbers of Washington correspondents were working for multiple clients, growing syndi-cates, or neutral wire services, the concept of objective reporting came into vogue. The job of Washington correspondents, J. Frederick Essary explained in 1928, "demands of them scrupulous fairness and as near literal accuracy as may be possible, within human limitations, in the matter which is daily spread before their millions of readers." [24] Walter Lippmann was an early exponent of this "progressive" creed. In 1960 he served again as a bellwether for a new doctrine when he addressed the National Press Club and called for reporters to abandon mindless objectivity in favor of interpretation. From the 1920s through the 1950s, however, objective journalism reigned as the dominant ideology of the profession.[25]

Other trappings of professionalism, such as collegiality and collusive efforts to control the work environment, were also much in evidence during this era. There are many examples of the former, including the practice of "blacksheeting": reporters would informally divide up coverage of Washington events and share the carbon copies of their articles for others to rewrite for their home papers.[26] The formal expression of professional collegiality was the formation of professional societies, such as the Gridiron Club, the Press Gallery Correspondents Association, the National Press Club, and the White House Correspondents Association.

Creed, collegiality, and the recognition of collective goals all helped distinguish Washington correspondents as a separate and resourceful entity in the Washington community. Professional trappings would soon begin to alter the relations of these correspondents with the president.

Early Presidential-Press Relations

The nineteenth-century progenitor of the presidential press conference was the private interview, offered first by President Andrew Johnson (1865-1869) to selected reporters. Sensing that the public was reading published interviews more closely than his speeches, Johnson made it a practice during his impeachment trial to rebuke charges from Congress by summoning a sympathetic correspondent to the White House. Most of Johnson's nineteenth-century successors submitted to an occasional private interview.[27]

President William McKinley (1897-1901) attended to press relations more conscientiously than most of his predecessors. During important White House meetings reporters were frequently permitted to wait in an anteroom for interviews with the president's visitors. McKinley's staff also routinely gave reporters the president's speaking schedule and advance copies of his addresses. Personally, however, McKinley remained aloof, and any direct contact with the press was left largely to chance. Ida M. Tarbell describes White House coverage during the McKinley years.

> It is in "Newspaper Row," as the east side of the great portico is called, that the White House press correspondents flourish most vigorously. Here they gather by the score on exciting days and ... watch for opportunities to waylay important officials as they come and go. Nobody can get in or out of the Executive Mansion without their seeing him, and it is here most of the interviews, particularly with Cabinet officers, are held. ...
>
> It is part of the unwritten law of the White House that newspaper men shall never approach the President as he passes to and fro near their alcove or crosses the portico to his carriage, unless he himself stops and talks to them. This he occasionally does.[28]

McKinley left ample room for innovation in this realm to his successor—the man who called the presidency "the bully pulpit."

Theodore Roosevelt (1901-1909) was probably the first president to appreciate the value of public opinion in leading Washington. Certainly, he was the first to cultivate close ties with Washington correspondents and consequently was the first important transitional figure in presidential-press relations. In his age, before "direct communication" via radio and television, public relations and press relations were operationally largely the same. Roosevelt succeeded with the former because he was able to dictate such favorable terms with the latter.

According to David S. Barry, a prominent correspondent of the era and a Roosevelt favorite, the difference between Theodore Roosevelt and all the presidents who preceded him was that he read papers' treatment of the news more than their editorials. Roosevelt "knew the value and potent influence of a news paragraph written as he wanted it written and disseminated through the proper channels."[29]

On his first day in office, Roosevelt summoned several representatives of the wire services and enunciated a set of ground rules that would give the press unprecedented access to the White House but leave him with a large measure of control over what was printed. The president insisted that, above all, information given in confidence must remain confidential. "If you ever hint where you got [the story]," Roosevelt warned, "I'll say you are a damn liar."[30] Anyone who broke this rule would be banned from the White House and denied access to legitimate news. Historian George

Juergens describes how Roosevelt maintained this hierarchical relation with the press.

> He divided newsmen into distinct groups of insiders and outsiders, and was unforgiving in banishing those he felt, justifiably or not, had betrayed him. The fact that he could get away with such high-handedness goes far to explain why he received the favorable coverage he did. It did a journalist's career no good to be on the outside, not to know what was going on. The reporter had every reason to play along if that was the price for being informed. Of course the coercion only worked because of the unequal relationship between Roosevelt and a not yet fully mature press corps. Reporters in a later era, conscious of their own prerogatives, would not have tolerated a president telling them who could have access to the news and on what terms. But this was a different game played by different rules.[31]

Theodore Roosevelt's approach to press relations may have greatly increased accessibility to the White House, but it also posed serious problems for the rapidly professionalizing correspondents. By retaining control over which stories could be reported and how, the president preempted journalistic discretion, a prerogative Congress had surrendered by the mid-nineteenth century. Looking back on Roosevelt's administration a decade later, Washington correspondents found intolerable his division of the White House press into "insiders and outsiders." [32] This practice created uncertainty, obviously for the outsiders because they were missing the stories, but also for the insiders because they could so easily be demoted to the ranks of the outcasts. Among professionals whose careers depended upon their access to political news, this could, of course, be devastating, which is precisely why the stringent rules were seldom violated.

Finally, Roosevelt, who sported a strict and complex ethical code, excoriated reporters who wrote for papers that held distinctly different editorial positions. As far as he was concerned, these men had "sold their ethics." It could be cause for banishment.[33] Roosevelt may have been a fan of the news business, as his biographers attest, but his attitude reveals a fundamental lack of appreciation for the emerging professional requirements of the Washington correspondent. This stance appears all the more arbitrary (and hence revealing) since it served no apparent strategic purpose.

Roosevelt could dictate the rules because, as Juergens noted, he was working with a still poorly professionalized press. Washington correspondents had neither a strong sense of their rights nor any means for enforcing them. During the next two decades, both of these deficiencies would be corrected.

The other important transitional figure in the development of presidential-press relations was Woodrow Wilson (1913-1921).[34] Like Roosevelt, a Progressive facing a conservative Washington, he also recognized the value of public opinion and sedulously set out to establish favorable relations with the press. In this case, the talent was missing, and instead of substantive reciprocity, the result was procedural reform.

Wilson extended to the press most of the prerogatives that Roosevelt had held back. Continuing Roosevelt's practice of frequent meetings, he opened them to all correspondents. The response, he discovered somewhat to his chagrin, was overwhelming. At one of his early conferences more than 200 reporters—many of whom had never participated in a presidential interview—packed themselves into the Oval Office. This and his other meetings with the press proved to be unhappy affairs. Wilson considered reporters dullards, and they sensed his condescension. After two years of discomfort for all involved, Wilson quietly abandoned the weekly gatherings.

However unsatisfying for either party, those regular, open conferences yielded another significant advancement for the press corps. Roosevelt's small entourage of insiders, or "fair haired boys," as they would later be remembered, posed no problem for his rules of confidentiality, but Wilson's news conferences opened the door to violations. In 1913 a significant breach occurred. After Wilson had given his views "off the record" on current conditions in Mexico, the story appeared the next day on the front pages of several newspapers.[35] Recognizing the threat this incident posed to the future of the open conference, a group of reporters from the most respected papers and wire services met informally with the president's secretary, Joseph Tumulty, to rectify the situation. Out of their meeting came an agreement whereby the White House press corps would assume full responsibility for policing the president's news conference. Shortly thereafter, the White House Correspondents Association was formed with the mandate to establish standards of professional behavior and to regulate attendance at the conferences. Assuming collective responsibility, the profession gained control over its members and superseded White House regulation.

The next three presidents—Harding, Coolidge, and Hoover—experienced difficulties in the press relations they inherited from Roosevelt and Wilson. Each began well enough with a friendly announcement of frequent and open conferences. Within a few months, however, the press relations of each fell on hard times. Warren G. Harding (1921-1923) even caused some correspondents to voice concern over his incompetence with the freewheeling press conference format. When he finally made the anticipated egregious misstatement, which necessitated a White House retraction and a State Department disclaimer, Harding's aides decided the informal press conference was too risky. Subsequently, they insisted that all questions be written and submitted in advance. The correspondents complied, although privately many complained. With follow-up questions disallowed, spontaneity was lost, and the conferences became dull. Many reporters quit attending.

Calvin Coolidge (1923-1929) kept the written questions and added new stringencies. Correspondent Willis Sharp laid out the Coolidge ground rules.

The correspondents may not say that they saw the President. They may not quote the President. They may not say that an official spokesman said what the President said. The information or views he gives out are supposed to be

> presented to the public without any indication of official responsibility. The correspondents are supposed to present these views as if they had dropped from heaven, and are wholly unprotected when, as has happened, Mr. Coolidge finds it expedient to repudiate them. As a climax the correspondents are forbidden to mention that a question asked at the conferences was ignored.[36]

He went on to report "murmuring among the correspondents," who especially disliked the requirement that the president could not be directly quoted without permission. This rule had been in place since President Wilson's conferences, but no president hid behind the "White House spokesman" as frequently as Coolidge. Again, the White House press complied, but in magazine articles some correspondents began to ridicule the practice. "The White House spokesman" became "the Presidential Larynx" and "the Figure of Speech."[37] For the first time, the press began to impose costs on an unaccommodating president.

By the time Herbert Hoover (1929-1933) was inaugurated, the complaints of the press about Coolidge's rules were widely known and shared by other Washington elites who had to transact business with him.[38] So when Hoover announced at his first press conference that he would liberalize the attribution rules and consult with the White House Correspondents Association on ways to improve the news conference, his remarks evoked jubilation from the press. Their glee was short-lived, however. None of the reforms were instituted, none of the promised consultations held.

Instead, Hoover managed to strain press relations further when he failed to acknowledge the great majority of questions submitted by the press and began favoring sympathetic journalists with choice stories. Twenty-five years earlier Theodore Roosevelt had gotten away with this practice, but by this time the correspondents had a clear sense of their collective interests. They retaliated. Hoover's favorites were dubbed the "White House Pen Men's Association." According to James E. Pollard, "Other [than the favored] correspondents were affronted and they not only refrained from writing favorably about Mr. Hoover but were impelled to write things that hurt him."[39] Singling out the president's favorite insider, one journalist sniped, "If Hoover is defeated, a large share of his unpopularity can be attributed to Mark Sullivan."[40] Theodore Roosevelt and Woodrow Wilson were transitional figures in advancing presidential-press relations; Harding, Coolidge, and Hoover proved to be demonstration cases of the implications for a president's options of the developing professionalism of the press.

Early Competition and Collective Interests

As the market between papers and correspondents emerged, reporters competed tacitly with one another for choice clients, chiefly by competing for choice stories. Correspondents' growing independence from home editors increased their dependence on news sources—presidents included. Competition creates losers as well as winners, however, and unconstrained competition could be hazardous for budding careers.

The collective interests of the Washington press corps favored open news conferences over private presidential interviews. The reason was simple. Open news conferences gave no reporter undue advantage over another or permitted a president to divide and conquer. Within the first three decades of the century, the long-term, collective interests of the group achieved precedence over the short-term, competitive desires of its individual members, a mark of professionalization. In describing the professional needs of today's journalists, Anthony Smith explains how, once established, standardized outlets for news are perpetuated:

> The tensions within the news gathering process help to accentuate the dependence upon recognized channels and therefore the power of those channels over the shaping of news itself. Competition between reporters of different newspapers working at the same beat will ensure that they will not want to miss press conferences, announcements, or social functions at which principal makers of news or providers of information may be present. Competition will make them dissatisfied with the shared channels but will tend to entrench those channels in their importance.[41]

This explains why during Wilson's administration senior correspondents rushed in to protect the open conference when it appeared that a breach of confidentiality might end it; also why reporters chafed under Harding's "written questions" rule and Coolidge's refusal to allow attribution. Finally, it explains why Hoover was publicly derided when he showed favoritism in giving stories to correspondents. These professionals had a vested, collective interest in the integrity of the open press conference. The press conference became sacrosanct, not because it satisfied the competitive urges of journalists but precisely because it denied them.

As the Washington press corps evolved into a corporate entity, its members attained standing within the Washington community that few could have hoped to achieve acting alone. Writing about this era in 1937, Leo Rosten observed, "Their help is sought by persons and organizations trying to publicize an issue; their displeasure is avoided. They are aware by virtue of the deference paid to them and the importance attached to their dispatches, that they are factors of political consequence."[42]

The FDR System: Hard News, Openly Conveyed

This chapter opened with a press conference that took place in 1937, early in the second term of President Roosevelt's administration (1933-1945). By most estimates the honeymoon between the president and the press corps had long ended. Still, it was evident that the mutual respect and professional intimacy begun at Roosevelt's first press conference four years earlier remained firm. Years later, near the end of his presidency, reporters would still attribute their continuing amity to the relationship he spawned in 1933.[43] By the mid-1950s, they were writing about it nostalgically.

When Roosevelt began his first news conference in 1933, he, like Wilson 20 years earlier, was met by a throng of more than 200 reporters anxiously awaiting word as to how he planned to conduct business. Roosevelt began by announcing that he was dispensing with written questions. He then identified four classes of information that would be presented in these "delightful family conferences": (1) occasional direct quotations permitted only through written authorization from the White House; (2) press conference comments attributed to the president "without direct quotations"; (3) background information to be used in stories without a reference to the White House; and (4) "off the record" remarks not to be repeated to absent reporters. To administer the policy of authorized direct quotations and other relations with the press, Roosevelt appointed the White House office's first press secretary, Stephen Early.

When the conference ended, the correspondents applauded, the first time ever according to some veterans.[44] One seasoned reporter called it "the most amazing performance the White House has ever seen. The press barely restrained its whoopees ... the reportorial affection for the president is unprecedented. He has definitely captivated an unusually cynical battalion of correspondents." [45] *Editor and Publisher,* the semiofficial scribe and gossip of the profession, was unrestrained:

> Mr. Roosevelt is a great hit among newspapermen at Washington. I rubbed my ears and opened my eyes when I heard hard-boiled veterans, men who had lived through so many administrations and been so disillusioned that there are callouses in their brain, talk glibly about the merits of the White House incumbent. If Mr. Roosevelt fails the craft, by any false word or deed, he will break a hundred hearts that have not actually palpitated for any political figure in many a year.[46]

That first day Roosevelt gave them what they had sought for more than a decade: assurance of hard news, openly conveyed. The president had made his pact with the Washington press corps.

Roosevelt strengthened the press conference in other ways. He met with the press frequently and routinely; only rarely did he depart from his biweekly, Tuesday-Friday schedule. By the time of his death in April 1945, Roosevelt had invited correspondents into the Oval Office on 998 occasions. Equally important to White House reporters, he used these conferences as occasions to make significant announcements. Reporters came expecting hard news. "He never sent reporters away empty-handed ... [they] are all for a man who can give them several laughs and a couple of top-head dispatches in a twenty minute visit." [47] The White House correspondents not only appreciated the choice stories he saved for these gatherings, they also praised his "timing" and packaging in ways that enhanced an item's newsworthiness.[48] Frequently over the years, Roosevelt would go so far as to suggest how a story should be written, and rarely did the press find this spoon-feeding unpalatable.

For a talented pluralist president like Roosevelt, these delightful family conferences offered ample opportunity to employ his considerable interpersonal skills. The president was usually a model of cordiality. Even his harshest critics in the press corps freely conceded that they were treated fairly at these conferences.[49] Whenever Roosevelt complained about a particular article, he would frequently blame the paper's editor, who he tactfully asserted must have put the correspondent up to it.[50] This technique reduced tension and gave the reporter a convenient way of dissociating himself from his paper's editorial stance.

Even the editors who occasionally traveled to Washington to observe these conferences to see "what had gotten into" the reporters were defenseless against the president's charm. Writing on an incident that took place shortly before Roosevelt's death, Walter Davenport described how one group of editors responded to the Roosevelt treatment.

> Now they [the editors] had come to Washington to be the guests of their reporters at one of America's own peculiar institutions—a Presidential press conference. They were just that—visitors. Outside, they might shout until windows broke but here they were bound by rule and precedent to be silent. Only an accredited correspondent may ask questions or make comment. . . . They stood closely grouped, tight-lipped, skeptical, narrow-eyed, as though alerted against the widely advertised charm. That is, at first. Gradually they softened, relaxed. At one of the President's early sallies . . . they grinned. Before it was over, the grin had become a chuckle.
>
> Then came that sudden "Thank you, Mr. President," after a lull, and their Washington correspondents took them by the arms and presented them to Mr. Roosevelt. . . . He shook their hands with tremendous vigor—this Tired Old Man. He thanked them for their gladly given support of the bond drive. He rejoiced to hear they were feeling well and he told them that, given time (laughter), he'd make good reporters of their Washington men (laughter).
>
> Presently they were plodding across the White House park toward Pennsylvania Avenue. For a few moments they were silent. Then one of them observed that he'd be damned. Another said that in his opinion the President was a wonder. The third said that, anyway, Mr. Harold Ickes [FDR's secretary of interior and outspoken press critic] was an old fool. And then with one accord, they began tearing Mr. Ickes apart.[51]

Roosevelt also strengthened the press conference by relying upon it almost exclusively. With but one exception, he did not give private interviews. That exception is significant, however, because it reveals the entrenched character of the normative system prevailing in the palmy days of institutionalized pluralism. On February 27, 1937, the *New York Times* published a private interview with Roosevelt by Arthur Krock, perhaps Washington's most carefully read columnist. According to Krock's account of the incident, the next press conference was an angry one. The reporters accused Roosevelt of favoritism, which he had made all the more unacceptable by extending to a bureau chief rather than to a member of the working press. J. Frederick Essary, by then a senior Washington correspondent, asked the president pointedly whether he planned to repeat such favoritism. Roosevelt promptly confessed his blame. "My head is on the block. Steve's [press secretary Early] head is on the block. I promise to never do it again." [52] During the next eight years he kept his word.

Elevating the press conference to a place of primacy, Roosevelt offered the Washington press corps all that its profession required in its relations with the White House. As the Krock incident shows, however, this arrangement was not without cost. It ceded to the press corps control over the relationship to a degree that no president had done in the past or would do in the future. A few years later when Harry Truman was similarly cross-examined at a news conference about an exclusive interview, again with Krock, he retorted, "I'll give interviews to anybody I damn please." [53]

That the profession got its hard news, openly conveyed, is apparent. To appreciate what Roosevelt gained in return, one must largely trust the compliments of correspondents and the testimonials of disgruntled conservative editors. What they indicate is that Roosevelt succeeded in splitting off Washington correspondents from the editorial stance of their papers.

Evidence of this phenomenon is readily available in the election preferences of these two groups in 1936. In the spring of that year, Leo Rosten conducted an informal survey of Washington correspondents to determine their preferences. Of the 84 he questioned, 54 named Roosevelt as their first choice. Tying for second with 8 votes each were Republican preconvention front-runners Arthur Vandenberg and Alfred Landon. Altogether the Republican candidates had the support of 31 percent of the correspondents against Roosevelt's 65 percent.[54] By contrast, during the fall campaign 61 percent of the nation's major newspapers endorsed Republican opponent Landon.[55] Throughout his twelve years in office Franklin Roosevelt lived with a hostile newspaper industry and a friendly press corps.

Transition from the FDR System

The popular thesis that FDR's sympathetic treatment was a result of the times was presented earlier in this chapter. The Great Depression and the New Deal created a moment in history when the natural inclination of the government to retain information and of the press to extract it gave way to reciprocity. As never before, the president and the press needed each other to accomplish their respective tasks. Daniel Boorstin observed that Roosevelt's frequent conferences "bred intimacy, informality, and a set of institutionalized procedures; before long the spirit of those press conferences became on both sides much like that of any other responsible deliberative body." [56]

Figure 3-1 Growth of Washington Press Corps, 1864-1987

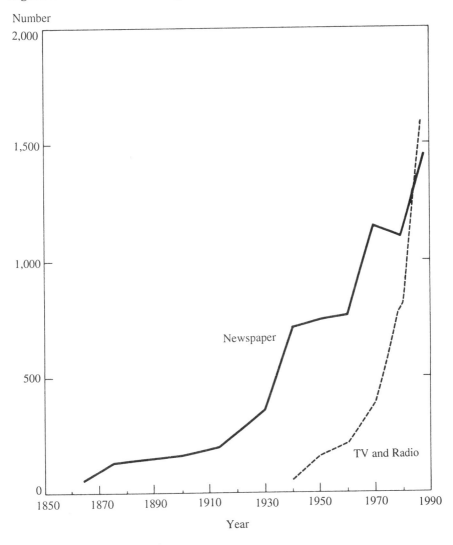

Number

SOURCE: Compiled by the author

The professional development of the Washington correspondent and the press practices Roosevelt established suggest, however, that systemic forces, unlike the crash of 1929, were also at work. Franklin Roosevelt succeeded with the press in the same way he succeeded with other Washingtonians. He founded a stable exchange relationship on the mutual professional needs of the participants.[57]

Given that the FDR system was rooted in the professional development of the Washington press, it seems ironic that these arrangements turned out to be fragile. Deterioration set in shortly after his departure not simply because Roosevelt's successors did not have his political acumen. The press conference declined because the needs of the participants changed. In different ways, advances in communications and transportation undermined the value of the FDR system for both the president and the press.

Radio, television, and air travel introduced the opportunity for presidents to engage in frequent, direct communication with the American public. No longer were they dependent upon the Washington press corps to convey their views to Washington and to the country. Going public would become a routine matter.

For the new breed of broadcast journalists who, as shown in Figure 3-1, grew rapidly in number and share of the press corps from 1940 on, Roosevelt's intimate family conferences held little attraction. As technology transformed the "press" into the "media," the press corps lost its corporate identity. "Hard news, openly conveyed" connoted something entirely different to broadcast journalists.

Press Relations under Truman and Eisenhower

For Harry S Truman (1945-1953) and Dwight D. Eisenhower (1953-1961), their styles and the needs of the press continued to shape presidential-press relations. Despite the manifold personal differences between Truman and Eisenhower, relations with the press retained a measure of continuity during the 16 years after Roosevelt largely because of the professional correspondents' attachment to the FDR system.

When Truman came into office he promptly announced that he would continue FDR's ground rules. Although Eisenhower during the transition period considered dropping scheduled press conferences altogether, he, too, ultimately made few changes in the Roosevelt format. Truman's directness and occasional irascibility at times reduced the news conference to verbal sparring matches; Eisenhower's famous syntactical convolutions left reporters scratching their heads and conferring among themselves after a conference to determine what the president had said. Under both presidents, news conferences displayed the structure if not the substance of the Roosevelt press conference. Moreover, neither Truman nor Eisenhower regularly went beyond the news conference to woo reporters with private interviews or with other practices that would become commonplace in the 1960s.

What these presidents did do during their combined 16-year tenure was to take small steps, more as concessions to the broadcast industry than as political strategies, that would make the dismantling of the FDR system under John Kennedy appear to be little more than the next step in an incremental progression. Midway through his second term, Truman permitted radio broadcasts of recorded excerpts of his news conferences. This meant that the president would normally be speaking for the record.[58] Transcription had begun earlier as a convenience to the press, but now with his comments being heard nationally, it was of little consequence when he permitted the press to publish a paraphrased transcript of his remarks. In 1950, with international events bringing the press to the president's door in greater numbers, the conference was moved from the Oval Office to a larger room in the State Department, then across the street from the White House. Added to the fact that Truman reduced the number of meetings from two to one a week, many reporters unhappily came to feel that the press conference had become a more formal affair. To them it lacked the spontaneity, and ultimately the newsworthiness, of the Roosevelt news conference with which it was invariably compared.

Eisenhower further eroded the intimacy of press conferences by holding them less frequently—only twice a month on average (see Table 3-2)—and by admitting television film crews in 1955. Neither practice was, it turned out, as disruptive as it might have been. When the president sought to gain the attention of the American public, he did so directly in a prepared address. Moreover, Eisenhower's press conference sputterings were hardly telegenic. After the novelty wore off, the networks rarely broadcast the entire conference.[59]

Robert Pierpoint, a veteran White House correspondent for CBS television, suggests also that in the 1950s television was not yet ready to make full use of presidential coverage. The news divisions of the networks were small, and until the middle of the next decade each network's evening news ran for only fifteen minutes.[60] Eisenhower's admission of filmed television altered presidential-press relations mostly by creating a precedent.

The Kennedy System: Press Relations in an Era of Direct Communication

The real break with the Roosevelt system came with John Kennedy. Everyone in Washington recognized the new president's rhetorical talents and expected him to use them. They had first been surprised when he won over Protestant voters in the West Virginia primary; they next had witnessed the way his addresses on college campuses ignited enthusiasm among students for the New Frontier; and they had judged his television performance favorably in the debates with Richard Nixon. Everyone, including the television networks, was primed for a publicly active president. They were not disappointed. Kennedy's innovations in presidential-press relations departed radically from the past and formed what may be called the Kennedy system. It remains in place today.

The Kennedy Press Conference

In early December 1960, at the behest of President-elect Kennedy, press secretary Pierre Salinger privately solicited reporters' views on the possibility of having live, nationwide televising of press conferences. We do not know their initial responses, but later in the month when Salinger announced the new policy to the regular White House correspondents, the reaction was clear. Salinger described the scene:

> I shall never forget this press conference. I went right into the live TV decision.... As I explained the ground rules, a storm of protest came from the assembled reporters.... I heard the gravelly voice of Bill Lawrence, then the White House correspondent of the *New York Times.* I do not remember his questions but the introductory phrase is sufficient: "Mr. Salinger, as you plunge deeper and deeper into matters about which you know absolutely nothing...." That did it. I didn't wait for the rest of the sentence. Now I was shouting back. It was the President's press conference—not theirs—and he would run it his own way. The decision was final. They could take it or leave it.[61]

New York Times correspondent James Reston called Salinger's plan for live television "the goofiest idea since the hoola hoop." [62] The president's transition team clearly had a different view. Kennedy aide Theodore Sorensen displayed a conveniently poor sense of history when he asserted that the press conference was a forum "to inform and impress the public more than the press." And television, he added, "provided a direct communication with the voters which no newspaper could alter by interpretation or omission." During the next several years, "direct communication" would become the leitmotif of those in the White House concerned with such matters.[63]

A significant factor motivating "direct communication" was Kennedy's awareness of its value in the event he were to lose favor with the press. This better explains the urge to go public, however, than the specific form adopted. He could have instituted, as James Hagerty proposed nearly a decade earlier, regularly scheduled television addresses or fireside chats from the Oval Office. Such a format would have provided this highly telegenic president with control over the program's message and exposed him to none of the vagaries of reporters' questions or his own misstatements. But such an innovation was unprecedented; there is no evidence that it or any similar alternative was ever seriously contemplated by Kennedy's transition team. The reason Pierre Salinger and others probably thought only in terms of the televised conference is that it required so little innovation. The precedent for television cameras was already well established by 1960; all that had to be done was substitute the networks' film cameras with live ones. In seeking to extricate himself from the confining Roosevelt system, Kennedy adapted existing arrangements to new purposes. The innovative use of live television in this important instance was as much a political adaptation as a technological one.

The first live telecast of a presidential press conference, in late January 1961, drew 418 correspondents to the new State Department auditorium and an estimated prime-time audience of 65 million viewers. Virtually everyone who expressed an opinion agreed that the new president had done well. There was little doubt that live television would be a fixture in Kennedy's press conferences. The networks' news offices were happy. Even some of the newspaper correspondents extolled this innovation. Lester Markel in a *New York Times Magazine* article advocated more public activities by the president and the creation of a Department of Public Opinion within the White House.[64]

By summer, however, many newspaper reporters began to complain on grounds readily understandable to those who appreciate the virtues of the "private" press conference of an earlier era. Peter Lisagor of the *Chicago Daily News* compared the Kennedy press conference to "making love in Carnegie Hall." "A mess ... disorderly, disorganized, almost chaotic" is the way he summed up the new press conference.[65] Others, like Clark Mollenhoff of the Des Moines *Register,* complained about the declining quality of the questions: "Too many of the questions are lobbed setups, and blooper balls, and there is too little effort to obtain any more than generalized information. I don't blame the President for knocking them out of the lot." He added, "Unless I have a specific question to ask, I rarely go any more." [66] A third correspondent offered the following summary assessment.

> In its new setting, blindingly lighted and amphitheatrical, ... each reporter [tries] unvaliantly to capture the eye of the President.
>
> Random, inevitably, is the selection of questioners and even more random is the nature of the questions. Few significant queries are put and when one is posed, a follow-through is almost impossible.[67]

According to print journalists, television reporters "hammed it up" with long-winded questions, "thus cheapening the conference." [68]

Almost a decade later newspaper reporters would still be voicing many of the same complaints. A survey of prominent Washington journalists found most of them dissatisfied with the modern press conference, and television received much of the blame.[69] The complaints were chronic because the problem is structural. As background briefings and sustained questioning on issues gave way to presidential position-taking and evasion, the print journalists lost their hard news. With television providing instantaneous transmission to the country, whatever fresh news came out of a press conference was stale by the time their stories were printed.

The press conference consequently matured into something quite different from the biweekly gatherings of Roosevelt. Robert Pierpoint's description of his preparation for the modern televised conference makes this clear:

> The presence of a vast audience magnifies the significance of any possible errors in questioning or in commentary afterward, and I always feel a slight sickness in the stomach and a sweatiness of the palms and forehead.
>
> After more than twenty years, I still go through a "psyching up" period, similar to that of a professional athlete before the big game. I read the morning newspapers and follow the news on radio and television, concentrating on the questions I will ask and the issues that could

Table 3-2   Presidential News Conferences with White House Correspondents, 1929-1984

President	Average per Month	Total Number
Hoover (1929-1933)	5.6	268
Roosevelt (1933-1945)	6.9	998
Truman (1945-1953)	3.4	334
Eisenhower (1953-1961)	2.0	193
Kennedy (1961-1963)	1.9	64
Johnson (1963-1969)	2.2	135
Nixon (1969-1974)	0.5	37
Ford (1974-1977)	1.3	39
Carter (1977-1981)	1.2	59
Reagan (1981-1984)	0.5	26

SOURCES: Data for Hoover, Carter, and Reagan are from *Public Papers of the President* series. Data for the others were taken from Michael Baruch Grossman and Martha Joynt Kumar, *Portraying the President* (Baltimore: Johns Hopkins University Press, 1981), 245.

emerge at that day's conference. This means writing down a half dozen questions which the President should answer that day. I try to anticipate how each might be answered, phrasing the question carefully so the President cannot evade it. At the same time, questions must be designed to elicit genuine information or reactions of national importance. And finally, the questions cannot be so obscure or so simple as to risk making me look foolish or to waste my colleagues' and the public's limited press-conference time.[70]

Expanded television coverage of the presidency has made celebrities of those who cover the White House for the networks. Many of these men and women come to Washington after being newscasters for local television. On arrival they commonly draw six-figure salaries. To them "professionalism" is as likely to mean free agency as any collective interests of correspondents. The advent of live television brought into the press conference new participants who promptly became stars.[71] They assumed front-rank positions at the conference and vied aggressively with one another as well as with the newspaper correspondents for recognition from the president. And since they were the conduit through which he gained a spot on the evening news, they generally got it.

Another change, which makes the modern press conference more eventful, is its relative infrequency. Since Roosevelt, presidents have wondered how often they could go before the public and retain its attention. This consideration led Salinger to move Kennedy's press conferences off prime time to a normal midafternoon schedule. More generally, it has meant that they are conducted less frequently. Table 3-2 shows that in employing the conference to speak directly to the American people, Kennedy conducted fewer conferences on average per month than Eisenhower, and, more to the point, less than a third as many as Roosevelt. Since Kennedy, the average number of conferences per month has further declined. Full realization of the diminished status of the press conference had occurred during the Nixon presidency. Initially, his failure to meet with the press on average no more than once every two months was widely viewed as being a result of the particular circumstances of his administration—an early, muted suspicion that matured into an ardent hostility between the president and the press. But the similarly low frequency rates of press conferences for Ford, Carter, and Reagan suggest that the reduced status of the press conference has resulted more from changes in the system of presidential-press relations than from personal styles or transient political conditions.

Once the news conference failed to provide a steady diet of hard news, it quickly lost standing among print correspondents. Over the years journalists have offered numerous proposals to resurrect aspects of the FDR system.[72] For their daily stories, however, they began to look elsewhere in the White House and in the agencies for presidential stories. Consequently, when the press conference became moribund for long stretches under Nixon and Reagan, who preferred political travel and nationally televised addresses, the complaints came most heavily from among network correspondents rather than print journalists.

The Local Press and the Private Interview

As the press conference became yet more formal under the glare of studio lights, Kennedy introduced other avenues of access to the press. For the most part, these innovations gave the president greater control over the content of information the press received. One such innovation was special, informal news conferences with publishers and reporters of papers from a particular state or region. With Kennedy these generally took the form of White House luncheons. Every subsequent president has adopted some variant of Kennedy's innovation.

Another innovation, if it may be called that, was the frequent use of the private interview. As senator, Kennedy was reputed to have had more friends in the press than in the Senate. As president, he continued his close personal associations with Charles Bartlett of the *Chattanooga Times* and Ben Bradlee, then with *Newsweek*. He also conducted private interviews with such notables as James Reston of the *New York Times* and columnist Joseph Alsop. A perquisite of friendship with Kennedy was special access to stories. According to one source, "Any of a dozen Washington hands have access to the President's Oval Office. . . . where, in the old days, an [Ernest K.] Lindley or an Arthur Krock could count on guidance 'at the highest level' only on the rarest occasions, the newsmen count on it almost weekly." [73] Network correspondents were not to be excluded. Before long, Kennedy opened the Oval Office to television crews for taped interviews.

Initially, this practice—a single instance of which had put FDR's "head on the block"—raised the ire of many members of the writing press more than did the televised press conference. Reston had personally warned the president-elect that private interviews might generate too much ill will. (Later, after becoming a favored insider, he recanted.)[74] Lisagor, whose distaste for the Kennedy system has already been recorded, called it "a baneful thing—a reporter ought to keep a public official at an arm's length." [75]

As Kennedy's sessions with the press neared the end of the first year, the expected question finally surfaced. Did not the president think it unfair to feed stories to the favored few? Obviously groping, Kennedy replied: "I think—yes, I will let them [his staff] know, and I think I ought to. I don't think there should be discrimination because of size or sex or another reason." [76] Spoken like lip service.

Routine use of the exclusive interview, cultivation of the press outside Washington, and live telecasts of news conferences constitute the Kennedy system. Each feature violates some ground rule of institutionalized pluralism upon which its predecessor, the FDR system, had been founded. Exclusive interviews with correspondents frustrate the profession's collective interests, at least as the Washington press corps was formerly constituted. Special attention to publishers and reporters from outside Washington denies the insularity of community relations and may arouse suspicion that the president is trying to replace negotiation with public pressure. From the perspective of institutionalized pluralism, the live telecast of news conferences is the most objectionable of all. Its antithetical nature was summed up earlier in Sorensen's naive remark that the forum was intended more to inform the public than the press. With television, the Kennedy system corrupted this centerpiece of the FDR system. And by introducing new—and, from the perspective of the White House, more manageable—avenues of contact with the press, the Kennedy system depreciated the status of the news conference.

The Kennedy System as a Model for Presidents Who Go Public

During the past quarter century, encompassing five presidents, the Kennedy system has remained the working model of presidential-press relations. To the degree it has changed at all, the system reflects more the forces it set in motion than any new ideas of Kennedy's successors. As the formal press conference has withered, Kennedy's alternative forms of press relations have thrived. Precise numbers for each administration are difficult to come by, but Ronald Reagan's 194 press interviews and 150 special White House briefings of the press from outside Washington during his first three years indicate sharply increased growth in the use of this news outlet since the Johnson administration.[77]

The development of satellite communications permitting instantaneous transmissions from the White House to local news stations around the country has created a booming market for White House communications beyond Washington. From 1981 to 1984, the number of local news stations with Washington bureaus grew from 15 to more than 50.[78] The business between local Washington television producers and stations throughout the country has been burgeoning as well. Local television news coverage offers several advantages over presidents' traditional news outlets. First, it allows the White House to segment the market—"to narrowcast its message to a very specific audience," in the words of one Reagan staffer.[79] Second, these newscasters are interested in presidential activities that the networks and even local press pay little attention to. The presidency is a ceremonial office. From it flows an endless stream of medals, commendations, and sometimes just salutations. Private citizens from all over the country come to the White House daily to receive the president's congratulations. For local television bureaus, these happy, often sentimental ceremonies offer wonderful local color. Of importance to the White House, the president is invariably cast as a sympathetic figure. The third advantage of local television coverage over traditional news outlets is that journalists for these bureaus, as recent arrivals with few prerogatives and an uncertain mandate, abide by White House instructions. The head of one of the largest local bureaus observed:

> The regular White House press corps is adversarial with the President in ways the locals are not. If the President is giving an award to a kid from Michigan for starting a community library, that is a good human-interest story for us. But if you get Sam Donaldson of ABC in on one of these things, he's going to ask the President . . . something. It becomes difficult for the President, and the White House doesn't like that.[80]

Many of the local bureaus began setting up shop during Jimmy Carter's administration. Given their special attraction, Carter was understandably quick to invite them to the White House. It was left to the Reagan administration, however, to incorporate local television reporters fully into the ongoing routines of White House media relations. This innovation, wholly consistent with the premises of the Kennedy system, has become one of the established routines of presidential-press relations under President Bush.

Presidents have adapted the Kennedy system to their personal styles in other ways as well, but none has altered the system's basic structure. As noted earlier, Lyndon Johnson constructed a television studio in the White House and obliged the networks to outfit it with cameras ready to broadcast on a moment's notice. Richard Nixon dismantled the studio, but to offset his numerous, rough dealings with the television networks and particularly the *Washington Post,* he dramatically expanded press relations outside Washington.[81] Jimmy Carter went to the public in his own way, with informal but well-orchestrated town meetings. Ronald Reagan showed a special fondness for the radio. His Saturday afternoon broadcasts from the Oval Office were frequently compared with Roosevelt's famous fireside chats. As important as these and other practices have been to a given president's overall public relations program, they amount to little more than personal and ultimately transient enhancements of the Kennedy system.

What was lost to the press when the news conference became a forum for the president's direct communications to the country was not fully realized as gains to the White House. With the adoption of the Kennedy system, presidents took more away from the traditional relationship than they contributed. It was up to the correspondents to establish a new equilibrium by withdrawing deference to the president's representation of events and policies. While the emergence of an adversarial press can be attributed in part to President Johnson's Vietnam "credibility gap" and Nixon's Watergate cover-up, it is important to understand that it inheres in presidents' strategic reformulation of press relations, and thus will not disappear as memories of these events fade into history. As late as the Eisenhower era, the president and the White House press corps generally followed the rule of institutionalized pluralism; each party sought reciprocity with the other to reduce uncertainty and to advance its own goals. Under the Kennedy system, however, this relationship broke down. Peter Lisagor hit upon this fundamental shift when he complained that the press was merely "one of the props" of the Kennedy press conference.[82]

Live television requires the president to be ever mindful of the public audience, and this setting necessarily gives rise to posturing. The correspondent's job consequently becomes one of "isolating fact from propaganda when a president seeks to use the press as a springboard to public opinion, as he does in a televised press conference.[83] Journalists no longer pay homage to unobtrusive, objective journalism. Instead, they speak of getting at the facts behind the president's statement or press release. Senior Washington correspondent James Deakin remarked: "The White House reporter has one accepted role—to report the news—and several self-appointed roles. . . . I feel I'm there, in part, to compel the government to explain and justify what it's doing. A lot of people don't like that, but I feel we're the permanent in-house critics of government."[84]

The adversarial aspect of presidential-press relations is an elusive quality, difficult to quantify, and the systematic evidence on the subject is inconclusive.[85] From the testimonials of the sparring partners, however, the adversarial relationship appears to be a well-established fact of life. The arrival of less deferential correspondents, some of whom were media stars in their own right, frequently has turned the conference into an occasion of irritation and embarrassment for the White House. Although no president has yet been willing to excuse himself altogether from these encounters, none has been reluctant to tamper with its format and schedule in an effort to produce more favorable results. Johnson, Nixon, and Reagan provide examples. As the Vietnam War heated up at home, Johnson sensed that reporters were lying in wait for him at press conferences with loaded questions. To throw them off balance, he switched to impromptu and short-notice press conferences that gave reporters little time to arm themselves. To stave off embarrassing issues, Nixon occasionally limited questions to specified policy areas. (This change, however, was generally well received by many newspaper correspondents because it gave them the opportunity to pursue newsworthy issues in depth.) In early 1982 some of Reagan's aides believed that their president was suffering from unflattering network "take-outs" of his noontime press conferences. They therefore rescheduled these conferences to later in the day, nearly doubling the television audience and reducing the time available to networks to edit the president's remarks. However the president's aides tweaked the schedule and format, it still failed to provide Reagan with a satisfactory arrangement. He conducted three such sessions in 1987 and four in 1988. By the end of his second term, the formal news conference had become an endangered species.

George Bush's Adaptation of the Kennedy System

Threatened with extinction, preservation of the press conference became a *cause célèbre* during Bush's first campaign for the presidency, if not with voters, certainly with the reporters and a number of organizations that study these matters. In response, Bush announced soon after his election that he would sharply increase the frequency of news conferences.

Frequency may "depressurize" the relationship, as one White House aide put it, but for Bush it introduced another problem. The president and those who work with him agree that he does not perform well on television. (Reflecting our media age, the disjointed phrases that constitute his rhetoric are commonly referred to as "sentence segments.") The White House solved the dilemma by giving the press conference its greatest overhauling since Kennedy's innovations. Instead of prearranged, frequently prime-time sessions, Bush called brief, impromptu morning sessions in which the networks were allowed a few minutes to assemble the cameras if they were interested in covering the conference. Frequently they were not; Cable News Network was the only network to broadcast many of these sessions. As no advance notice was given for these conferences, many correspondents were absent, but this in itself did not prove controversial, probably because the president rarely used the occasion to make newsworthy remarks. By the end of his first year in office, President Bush had conducted 38 such mini-conferences compared with only one that followed the formal, prime-time format. The consensus among Bush's aides that the latter was a "disaster" reinforced the administration's enthusiasm for this new approach to the press. So, up until the reelection campaign, he held only one more formal news conference.

The revamped format should be viewed not so much as a restoration of the press conference but rather as simply a strategy for pacifying the press. The conferences were scheduled at the president's convenience; correspondents had little time to prepare difficult questions, yet they could not complain that the president was inaccessible.[86] While these sessions may have satisfied White House correspondents accustomed to Reagan's sparse offerings, they provided little opportunity for the president to advance his policies. In assessing Bush's damage-control approach to the press conference, Reagan's media adviser, Michael Deaver, cautioned that the downside of this strategy would come when the president "will have to go over the heads of this town and go directly to the American people." [87]

The Modern Trajectory of Presidential-Press Relations

Whether by cutting back the number of Washington press conferences or minimizing their importance, modern presidents are clearly opting for more controllable means to communicate their views to the American public. Kennedy's innovations, private interviews and news conferences outside of Washington, remain prominent features of contemporary presidential media strategies. Presidents are also enlisting techniques that do not require the direct participation of reporters. Through television and speeches to gatherings of special constituencies, presidents can attract favorable news stories and direct press attention to particular issues and policies. These are venerable practices, of course, but whereas in the past they seemed to be desultorily planned outings from the White House, prompted as much by an invitation from some group as any tactic initiated by the president, they are now part of the chief executive's weekly, almost daily, routine. In the next chapter we shall document the extraordinary growth in these news-generating activities over the past 30 years.

Presidents and reporters still jointly produce news, but it is no longer a collaborative undertaking. Bush's frequent mini-conferences aside, the modern relationship is one in which each side anticipates and responds to distant actions of the other. The president's staff plans events and writes speeches with an eye to shaping the evening news story. Getting out "the line for the day" is, in fact, one of the principal activities of the contemporary White House staff; by one estimate more than a quarter of the staff is dedicated in some way to producing the president's public activities. Network news bureaus resist influence by aggressively editing presidential rhetoric and editorializing about its purposes. Reflecting this strategy is the amount of time allotted to the president on the evening network news. As late as 1968, he spoke on camera without interruption for an average of about 40 seconds. Over the years this figure has dwindled to about 9 seconds.[88]

At a recent conference of former presidential press secretaries I had occasion to raise the issue of the president's shrinking sound bite.[89] This led to an exchange between NBC Nightly News anchor John Chancellor and President Carter's press secretary, Jody Powell, which accurately characterizes the tension between modern presidents and the press. Compare the tenor of their remarks with that of Roosevelt's "family conference" with which we began our discussion:

Chancellor: The fact is—I think television reporters out in the field, when presented with pre-packaged, pre-digested, plastic coated phrases and with no opportunity to question a president, want to get something that isn't just pre-packaged and pre-digested, and that's why you are getting a more contentious kind of reporting in the twenty seconds at the end of the spot. I had an argument with Tom Pettit during the 1988 election, and I said, "Why is it that all of our correspondents end their pieces with some little snippy, nasty saying? Why don't they just say, 'And tomorrow the president goes to Cleveland.' And Pettit says, "It wouldn't come out that way. They would say, 'Tomorrow the president goes to Cleveland and no one knows why.'"

So that you set up a kind of contest of who controls and all of this is done in a piece of television that runs about a minute-and-a-half. So you compress the political propaganda on the one hand, you increase the reactive hostility on the other hand, and that's what a minute-and-a-half television spot is today. I think both sides are probably equally responsible for it, but I think that the politicians started it.

Powell: I will just raise a logical question. Assuming that there are other things to do in a White House and now and then something else comes along that might keep you busy, why would you go to all of the trouble to do all of these things that we are talking about [in packaging the president's message] if you did not find yourself faced with a situation in which it's the way to deal with it? Why would you go to all of this trouble?

Are we supposed to believe that one morning ten, fifteen years ago somebody in the Johnson White House or the Nixon White House or whatever woke up and said, "We don't need to do this, but just for the hell of it, why don't we create this whole structure here about going out on the road and doing that sort of thing," or rather perhaps it was a reaction—maybe intelligent, maybe unwise, maybe in the public interest, maybe not. It was a reaction to a set of circumstances which they saw and said, "We've got to do something."

With presidents increasingly going public and with a more assertive press, contention over control will remain a fixture of the modern system. Infrequent press conferences, cultivation of the press outside Washington, extensive private interviews, and adversarial relations are the new order. It is one in which pressure and competition have replaced professional reciprocity as the fabric of community relations.

Notes

1. Cited in Chalmers Roberts, "Franklin Delano Roosevelt," in *Ten Presidents and the Press,* ed. Kenneth W. Thompson (Washington, D.C.: University Press of America, 1983), 21.
2. Ibid. This incident is also reported in Olive Ewing Clapper, *Washington Tapestry* (New York: McGraw-Hill, 1946), 179-180.
3. Waldo continued as head of McClure until his death in 1943. "R. H. Waldo, Head of News Syndicate," *New York Times,* June 12, 1943, 13.
4. Roberts, "Franklin Delano Roosevelt," 22-23.
5. Clapper, *Washington Tapestry,* 180.
6. Roosevelt's relations with the press were not 12 years of uninterrupted bliss, however. Both the president and the press at times felt abused by the other. On one occasion, for example, the president went so far as to award an absent reporter the iron cross for a derogatory story on the newly formed Women's Army Corps.
7. It has been suggested that Roosevelt used his press conferences at times to complement his public strategies. Graham J. White notes that initiatives announced during Roosevelt's fireside chats were followed by background briefings for the press to sustain public interest and to prepare the ground for a formal message to Congress. See *FDR and the Press* (Chicago: University of Chicago Press, 1979), 20-22. Wilfred E. Binkley argues against the perception that all Roosevelt had to do was "glance toward a microphone" and a "congressional delegation would surrender." Instead, he credits much of Roosevelt's early success with Congress to the way he worked the Washington press corps. See *President and Congress,* 3rd ed. (New York: Vintage, 1962), 305.
8. Cited in James Sterling Young, *The Washington Community: 1800-1828* (New York: Columbia University Press, 1966), 6.
9. Douglass Cater, *Power in Washington* (New York: Vintage, 1964), 224.
10. Ibid., 226.
11. Typical is Daniel J. Boorstin's, "Selling the President to the People," *Commentary* (July 1955): 427.
12. See Philip Selznick, *TVA and the Grassroots* (Berkeley: University of California Press, 1948).
13. See Peter Irons, *The New Deal Lawyers* (Princeton, N.J.: Princeton University Press, 1982).
14. In 1918 the editors of *The Nation* used the obituary of a prominent correspondent as occasion to criticize this practice of political jobbing. "The pernicious habit of appointing Washington correspondents to political office has also had a good deal to do with the loss of prestige of the correspondents' corps" ("Washington Correspondents," *The Nation,* November 30, 1918, 638).
15. Nelson W. Polsby, "The Institutionalization of the U.S. House of Representatives," *American Political Science Review* 62 (March 1968): 144-168; and H. Douglas Price, "The Congressional Career—Then and Now," in *Congressional Behavior,* ed. Nelson W. Polsby (New York: Random House, 1971), 14-27.
16. *The Education of Henry Adams: An Autobiography* (Boston: Massachusetts Historical Society, 1918), 253.
17. For the modern era, see Alan P. Balutis, "The Presidency and the Press: The Expanding Presidential Image," *Presidential Studies Quarterly* 7 (1977): 244-251. The findings for the nineteenth century are reported in Samuel Kernell and Gary C. Jacobson, "Congress and the Presidency as News in the Nineteenth Century," *Journal of Politics* 49 (November 1987): 1016-1035.
18. Before 1880 well over half of the papers represented by correspondents listed in

the *Congressional Directory* closed their Washington offices within two years. Less than 10 percent did so in 1930.

19. By the 1930s when Franklin Roosevelt arrived on the scene, government contacts had become a critical underpinning of the correspondent's professional stature. Raymond P. Brandt noted,

> The good Washington reporter has news sources which he does not discuss by name, even with his own colleagues. They are the key men in the various departments who can be called on by telephone or met at lunch or on the golf course. They are the officials who give the real "off the record" information. They know the existence of a little known public document, or what their chief is about to do. They are the men who stay on in Washington regardless of whether the Democrats or Republicans are in power. Their cultivation is a matter of years. They must know their trust will not be betrayed.

"The Washington Correspondent," *Journalism Quarterly* 13 (June 1936): 176.

20. These generalizations come from the brief biographical sketches of members of the 1903 House gallery compiled by the Gridiron Club. Ralph M. McKenzie, *Washington Correspondents Past and Present* (New York: Newspaperdom, 1903).

21. Silas Bent, *Ballyhoo* (New York: Boni and Liveright, 1927), 85.

22. The trend toward multiple paper clients appears in Table 3-1 to have been arrested by the early 1930s. Although increased numbers of correspondents were writing simultaneously for two or more papers, they constituted a smaller share of the press corps. Two trends—one demographic, the other political—were at work. First, as America's cities continued to grow, more papers developed the circulation necessary to underwrite individual representatives in Washington. According to one study, the critical city size for Washington coverage during this era was 50,000 to 100,000. The number of cities in this population range increased sharply from the 1910 to the 1930 census. Second, with the nation's attention shifting to Washington in the late 1920s, more urban papers in all population classes began supplementing wire service news with individual coverage. Hence, over time the need for multiple clients to ensure job stability declined as well. On both points, see Malcolm M. Willey and Stuart A. Rice, *Communication Agencies and Social Life* (New York: McGraw-Hill, 1933), 168-170.

23. Bent, *Ballyhoo*, 87.

24. J. Frederick Essary, "President, Congress, and Press Correspondents," *American Political Science Review* 22 (November 1928): 903.

25. Walter Lippmann, "The Job of the Washington Correspondent," *Atlantic*, January 1960, 47-49. An excellent treatment of objective reporting as an ideology can be found in Michael Schudson, *Discovering the News* (Chicago: University of Chicago Press, 1978), 121-159.

26. The modern variant of this time-honored practice is described vividly by James Deakin in *Straight Stuff* (New York: William Morrow, 1983), 131-132.

27. One president who refused to submit to press interviews was Grover Cleveland (1885-1889, 1893-1897). Instead, he communicated to the press, and through it to the public, with routine Sunday evening press releases. James E. Pollard describes how awkward exclusive reliance on this form could at times be in *The Presidents and the Press* (New York: Macmillan, 1947), 528.

28. Ibid., 558.

29. David S. Barry, *Forty Years in Washington* (Boston: Little, Brown, 1924), 270.

30. George Juergens, *News from the White House* (Chicago: University of Chicago Press, 1981), 17.

31. Ibid.

32. George H. Manning, "Liberalizing of President's Contacts with Press Hoped for from Hoover," *Editor and Publisher*, January 12, 1929, 6.
33. Juergens offers individual accounts of this requirement in operation in *News from the White House*, 23.
34. This account of Wilson's presidency relies heavily on Juergens, *News from the White House*, 126-166; and Pollard, *Presidents and the Press*, 630-696.
35. Juergens, *News from the White House*, 151.
36. Willis Sharp, "President and Press," *Atlantic Monthly*, July 1927, 240.
37. Clapper, *Washington Tapestry*, 14-15.
38. See "Editor's Ire at Coolidge Innuendo," *Literary Digest* 96 (November 12, 1927): 12; "Covering Washington," *The Nation*, June 27, 1928, 714; David Lawrence, "President and the Press," *Saturday Evening Post*, August 27, 1927, 27; O. G. Villard, "Press and the President," *Century*, December 1925, 193-200; and S. Moley, "Trials of the White House Spokesman," *Illustrated Independent Weekly*, September 19, 1925, 317-319.
39. Pollard, *Presidents and the Press*, 743.
40. Ibid.
41. Anthony Smith, *Goodbye Gutenberg* (New York: Oxford University Press, 1980), 173.
42. Leo Rosten, *The Washington Correspondents* (New York: Harcourt, Brace, 1937), 4.
43. Journalist Walter Davenport wrote in "The President and the Press," *Colliers*, January 27, 1945, 12: "A most important contributing factor to the grip that Mr. Roosevelt has on the imaginations of the Washington correspondent corps and consequently on the quality of his press [is] the enthusiasm he generated in the beginning—in 1933—[that] is still visible and still vocal."
44. Roberts, "Franklin Delano Roosevelt," 24. He adds that they applauded "because the reporters knew they were going to have access to news, the meat and potatoes of their profession."
45. The reporter quoted here is Henry M. Hyde of the *Baltimore Evening Sun*. Cited in Rosten, *The Washington Correspondents*, 50.
46. Marlan E. Pew, "Shop Talk at Thirty," *Editor and Publisher*, April 8, 1933, 36.
47. Pollard, *Presidents and the Press*, 775.
48. Rosten, *The Washington Correspondents*, 50. Arthur Krock once remarked, "He [Roosevelt] could qualify as the chief of a great copy desk" (in Rosten, *The Washington Correspondents*, 53). Heywood Broun complimented Roosevelt as "the best newspaper man who has ever been President" (in Pollard, *Presidents and the Press*, 781).
49. Raymond Clapper is cited in Pollard, *Presidents and the Press*, 780, stating, "The President and his most indefatigable critic, Mark Sullivan, still exchange pleasantries at press conferences."
50. Ibid., 776.
51. Davenport, "The President and the Press," 11-12.
52. Arthur Krock, *The Consent of the Governed* (Boston: Little, Brown, 1971), 242.
53. Ibid., 243.
54. Rosten, *The Washington Correspondents*, 58-61.
55. Walter Davenport reported in *Editor and Publisher* that 45 percent of the nation's major newspapers supported Roosevelt in 1932, 34 percent in 1940, and 60 percent in 1944. "The President and the Press," *Collier's*, February 3, 1945, 16. White's *FDR and the Press* takes a revisionist stance, arguing that Roosevelt was far more hostile to the nation's publishers than they to him. See especially chaps. 3, 4, 5.
56. Boorstin, "Selling the President to the People," 425.

57. For another example of FDR striking a bargain by creating a relationship, see Richard Fenno's study of the appointment of Jesse Jones as Roosevelt's secretary of commerce in *The President's Cabinet* (New York: Vintage, 1959), 234-247.

58. A. L. Lorenz, Jr., "Truman and the Press Conference," *Journalism Quarterly* 43 (Winter 1966): 671-679, 708.

59. The standard procedure was for press secretary James Hagerty to give permission to the network for use of a given excerpt. This gave the White House the prerogative of censoring parts of the press conference. Reportedly, it was an option rarely invoked.

60. Robert Pierpoint, *At the White House* (New York: G. P. Putnam's Sons, 1981), 155-156.

61. Pierre Salinger, *With Kennedy* (New York: Doubleday, 1966), 57. In a conversation with James Rowe, President Kennedy said, "I am convinced that the press will turn against me sooner or later while I am President, and I must have a way to get to the American people. So, therefore, I have to use television to get there, to speak directly to them when the press is so hostile" (cited in Blaire Atherton French, *The Presidential Press Conference* [Washington, D.C.: University Press of America, 1982], 13).

62. Cited in Harry Sharp, Jr., "Live From Washington: The Telecasting of President Kennedy's News Conferences," *Journal of Broadcasting* 13 (Winter 1968-69): 25.

63. Cited in Newton N. Minow, John Bartlow Martin, and Lee M. Mitchell, *Presidential Television* (New York: Basic Books, 1973), 39. Similarly, Nixon remarked at a press conference, "I consider a press conference as going to the people" (*Public Papers of the Presidents of the United States, Richard Nixon, 1969* [Washington, D.C.: Government Printing Office, 1971], 301). And early in the Reagan administration, NBC executive Richard S. Salant sounded the same theme: "Presidents over the past 20 years have discovered that television provides them the means to go around and over print to talk directly and simultaneously to all the people, with no reporting filter in between" ("When the White House Cozies up to the Home Screen," *New York Times*, August 23, 1981, sec. 2, 25).

64. Lester Markel, "What We Don't Know *Will* Hurt Us," *New York Times Magazine*, April 9, 1961, 116-117.

65. Cited in Worth Bingham and Ward S. Just, "The President and the Press," *Reporter* 26 (April 12, 1962): 20.

66. Ibid.

67. Markel, "What We Don't Know," 116.

68. James E. Pollard, "The Kennedy Administration and the Press," *Journalism Quarterly* 41 (Winter 1964): 7. See also Alan L. Otten, "Whose Conference?" *Wall Street Journal*, August 5, 1970, 44.

69. Jules Witcover, "Salvaging the Presidential Press Conference," *Columbia Journalism Review* 9 (Fall 1970): 33.

70. Pierpoint, *At the White House,* 70-71. A similar account is offered by Alan L. Otten ("Whose Conference?" 44):

> With televised press conferences, every reporter sees himself as a television personality. Since he doesn't want to boot his moment in the camera's eye by stumbling over a spontaneously phrased question, he usually has his query prepared long in advance—often not so much a question as a long speech—and he asks it even if it is completely irrelevant to everything that's gone before and even if some earlier answer is crying for clarification.

71. Journalists writing about their profession appear compelled to mention the discrepancy in the salaries between broadcast and print correspondents. See, for

example, James Deakin on the "star system" of broadcast journalists, *Straight Stuff,* 107-109; and Stewart Alsop, *The Center* (New York: Harper and Row, 1968), 176-177.

72. Examples are Hedrick Smith, "When the President Meets the Press," *Atlantic,* August 1970, 65-67; and Witcover, "Salvaging the Presidential Press Conference," 28.

73. Bingham and Just, "The President and the Press," 18-20. In a blistering attack on the administration's press relations, Arthur Krock charged that Kennedy had done more to "manage the news" than any president in history. Krock, who was on the "outside," took special exception to the exclusive interview, though he had taken full advantage of this practice under both Roosevelt and Truman. "Mr. Kennedy's Management of the News," *Fortune,* March 1963, 82, 199-202.

74. Bingham and Just, "The President and the Press," 18.

75. Ibid., 20.

76. Pollard, "The Kennedy Administration," 6.

77. The figures for personal interviews come from Lou Cannon, "Phantom of the White House," *Washington Post,* December 24, 1984, 25. In Mark Hertsgaard, "How Reagan Seduced Us," *Village Voice,* September 18, 1984, 12, a White House aide offered the following description of a typical briefing:

> You'd bring in 80 or 90 [journalists], maybe from a certain part of the country . . . and invite anchormen or news directors from major markets and the editors of major newspapers. And this is how some press people from a little town in North Dakota or somewhere like that come to see things. And they're thrilled to come. We take them up to our main briefing room and have maybe 25 camera crews from local stations and then put on a real good program for them. . . . Then we take them over to the State Dining Room for a real good lunch with the president, and they are all very pleased to come to the White House, it's a nice trick.

78. Thomas B. Rosenstiel, " 'Local' News Bureaus Polish Reagan's Image," *Los Angeles Times,* July 14, 1984, 1.

79. Ibid., 18. In early 1985 the Reagan administration announced plans for a facility to allow direct television hookups from the White House to local stations around the country. Gerald M. Boyd, "White House Plans Direct TV Links," *New York Times,* January 8, 1985, 9.

80. Rosenstiel, " 'Local' News Bureaus," 18.

81. Richard Nixon's confrontations with the press have been amply documented in William E. Porter, *Assault on the Media: The Nixon Years* (Ann Arbor: University of Michigan Press, 1976); James Keogh, *President Nixon and the Press* (New York: Funk and Wagnalls, 1972); and George C. Edwards III, *The Public Presidency* (New York: St. Martin's Press, 1983), 104-133.

82. Pollard, "The Kennedy Administration," 7.

83. Witcover, "Salvaging the Presidential Press Conference," 28.

84. Cited in J. Anthony Lukas, "The White House Press 'Club,' " *New York Times Magazine,* May 15, 1977, 67. Fred Barnes, a senior editor of *The New Republic,* has described one of the "operating assumptions of the press" as being the view of many Washington reporters that "their job . . . [is] one of attacking, and if a president, say, retains high popularity, they take it as an affront" (cited in "Calling the Press on the Carpet," *Wall Street Journal,* August 21, 1985, 22).

85. Two studies that fail to find negative stories or hostile news conference questions are Michael Baruch Grossman and Martha Joynt Kumar, *Portraying the President* (Baltimore: Johns Hopkins University Press, 1981), chap. 10; and Jarol B. Mannheim, "The Honeymoon's Over: The News Conference and the Development

of Presidential Style," *Journal of Politics* 41 (February 1979): 55-74. Dan Hallin takes exception to the notion of an adversarial press in "The Myth of the Adversary Press," *Quill* 71 (November 1983): 31-36.

86. An incident occurred in early 1990 that reveals this purpose of the new-style press conference. After reading a spate of articles on White House secrecy and deception, President Bush lashed out at the small pool of reporters traveling with him on Air Force 1. "We've got a whole new relationship," he announced. Then he added, "I think we have had too many press conferences." Although the events resulting in critical reportage were completely unrelated to the format or to statements made at one of the president's press conferences, it was the conference that the president threatened to cut off. After all, his exceptional availability to White House correspondents was designed to shield him from this kind of press carping. Nonetheless, for the next two years the president continued to rely on these informal sessions. Andrew Rosenthal, "Bush's In-Flight Show: Pique, and a Bumpy Ride for the Press," *New York Times*, February 16, 1990.

87. Instead, Bush appears to have thought he could return to the golden years of Roosevelt's press relations. One morning he sought to enlist the help of White House correspondents in propelling his legislative program through the Democratic Congress. "I urge you people to join me in calling out for congressional action," he said, adding that the Democrats deserved an "editorial pounding . . . to support the President as he tries to move this country forward." Thomas B. Rosenstiel, "The Media: Bush Plays It Cozy," *Los Angeles Times*, December 9, 1989, 1.

88. Daniel C. Hallin, "Sound Bite News: Television Coverage of Elections, 1968-1988," Occasional Paper, Media Studies Project, Woodrow Wilson International Center for Scholars, Washington, D.C., 1991.

89. "The Presidency, the Press and the People," University of California, San Diego, January 5-6, 1990. Transcript reprinted in *APIP Report* 1 (January 1991): 4-5. John Anthony Maltese provides a history of the development of White House staffing for presidential communications in *Spin Control: The White House Office of Communications and the Management of Presidential News* (Chapel Hill: University of North Carolina Press, 1992).

The Growth of Going Public————— 4

The preceding chapters have presented the reasons modern presidents go public. Modern technology makes it possible. Outsiders in the White House find it attractive. And the many centrifugal forces at work in Washington frequently require it. The frequency with which presidents in the past half century have communicated directly with the American public shows that the more recent the president, the more often he goes public.

The most memorable such occasions occur when the president goes on national radio or television to solicit public support for his legislative program stalled in Congress or to define the U.S. position in an international crisis. Although these dramatic forms of going public have become more commonplace in recent years, they still constitute only a small share of the many kinds of public activities in which modern presidents daily engage. Going public usually involves quieter overtures to more select audiences. Just as bargaining presidents must continually nurture the good will of their trading partners, so, too, must public-styled presidents diligently cultivate public opinion. We commonly call the routines by which presidents do this "public relations." [1]

Like advertising generally, public relations perform the homeostatic function of maintaining public support of the president. Whenever the president's popularity begins to wane or press coverage appears unduly critical, the White House compensates with increased public relations. As much as the occasional dramatic moment when the president rallies the country behind his policies, these routines define the style of modern leadership from the White House.

The following two episodes illustrate the variety of resources available to the modern president seeking to promote himself and his policies with the American public. In February and March of 1971, Richard Nixon faced widespread criticism and protest of the U.S. invasion of Laos. To offset this opposition, the president took his case to the public. Biographers Rowland

Evans and Robert Novak leave little doubt that Nixon's public relations campaign was precipitated by a five-point drop in his popularity rating.

> Shortly after that Gallup finding, it was decided by Nixon's public relations experts to give the American people the largest concentrated dose of this president on television and in interviews with journalists. The purpose was to stimulate an immediate upward movement in the polls and thus prevent further deterioration of the president's position on Capitol Hill and in the nation.
>
> In quick succession, in the six weeks ending March 22, Nixon made these appearances: an interview on February 9 with conservative Peregrine Worsthorne of *the London Sunday Telegraph;* a non-televised press conference on February 17; a special televised press conference on March 4 limited to foreign policy questions; an interview on March 11 by Barbara Walters of NBC's Today show for broadcast on March 15; an interview on March 11 by nine women reporters for publication on March 13; a one-hour live televised interview on March 22 by ABC's Howard K. Smith—a rate of exposure to major media outlets of more than one a week.[2]

Ronald Reagan faced somewhat different circumstances in the spring of 1982. Falling as unemployment rose, his popularity had begun a gradual but cumulatively greater overall descent than Nixon's in 1971. Whereas Nixon could try to convince the public of the merits of his policy, there was little President Reagan could do to sell the country on unemployment. He could, however, shore up his softening support with appeals on other issues. After learning from in-house polls that he was losing the approval of blue-collar workers at an alarming rate—many of whom were Democrats who had crossed over to vote for him in 1980—Reagan decided to target special appeals to them.[3]

Along with other public activities directed to this constituency, President Reagan addressed a conference of Catholic lay organizations in Chicago in behalf of a proposal to have the federal government subsidize private school tuition. For the Catholic church, financially strapped by rising costs and declining enrollments in many communities, and for parents who send their children to these schools (or would like to), enactment of the president's proposal would be a godsend. Because of Reagan's penurious domestic budget and his heavy cutbacks in funds for education, the trip to Chicago was widely interpreted to have been inspired more by an immediate political need to shore up support with this constituency than by any expectation that this might give his stalled legislation on this issue a boost in Congress. It also promised an enthusiastic reception before a traditionally Democratic audience, one that would ensure prominent coverage on the networks' evening news programs.

Though the reasons for Nixon's and Reagan's difficulties in the polls were quite different, both men sought remedy in rhetoric. In neither instance did the loss of popular support prompt the president to reconsider those policies that displeased the public. The loss was sufficient in each case, however, to trigger concerted public relations. These cases also illustrate how public speaking, political travel, and appearances before special constituencies outside Washington constitute the repertoire of modern leadership.

Trends in Going Public

Going public can take a variety of forms. The most conspicuous is the formal, often ceremonial occasion, such as an inaugural address or a State of the Union message, when official duty places the president prominently before the nation. Going public may, however, involve no more than a pregnant aside to a news reporter. This sort of casual, impromptu activity eludes systematic analysis, but speeches, travel, and appearances—all of which take place in public view and therefore can be easily counted—form a good record of significant events with which to measure the rise of going public. Each of these nonexclusive activities can be further divided according to its locale or prominence.[4] (More detailed definitions of these categories can be found in the Appendix.)

Public Addresses

Appeals for support to constituencies outside Washington are the core activities of going public. Form, audience, and content make each appeal unique. Kennedy's October 1962 address to the nation, in which he announced a quarantine of Soviet ships laden with surface-to-surface missiles en route to Cuba, is different in each respect from Carter's trip to Iowa in 1977 to sell his agricultural policies before a gathering of farmers. With such diversity, one may reasonably wonder what any trends discerned from a large volume of public addresses could mean.

Without delving too deeply into form, audience, and content, I shall offer a general distinction by classifying public addresses as major and minor. Major addresses are those in which the president speaks directly to a national audience over radio or television. Minor addresses, by comparison, are those the president delivers to a special audience either in person or via some broadcast medium. By these definitions, Kennedy's statement on the Cuban missile crisis qualifies as a major address and Carter's farm speech as a minor address.[5]

The average yearly numbers of major and minor addresses for each elected president since Herbert Hoover are displayed in Figure 4-1.[6] Both forms of going public have been on the rise, although to far different degrees. Given the opportunity costs, as well as network resistance to presidents commandeering prime time television, it is not surprising that the use of major addresses has increased only slightly.

Ronald Reagan's major addresses in Figure 4-1 include only television broadcasts. In 1982 after becoming unhappy with press representation of his policies, he initiated a lengthy series of Saturday afternoon radio broadcasts. To include these addresses, which attracted small audiences, would misrepresent the frequency with which he issued dramatic national appeals. Nonethe-

Figure 4-1 Presidential Addresses, 1929-1990 (Yearly Averages for First Three Years of First Term)

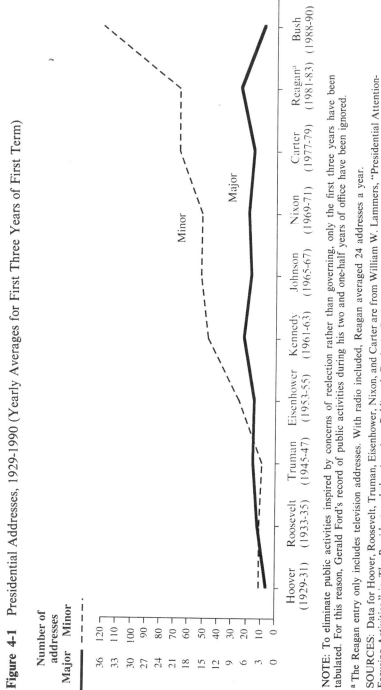

NOTE: To eliminate public activities inspired by concerns of reelection rather than governing, only the first three years have been tabulated. For this reason, Gerald Ford's record of public activities during his two and one-half years of office have been ignored.

[a] The Reagan entry only includes television addresses. With radio included, Reagan averaged 24 addresses a year.

SOURCES: Data for Hoover, Roosevelt, Truman, Eisenhower, Nixon, and Carter are from William W. Lammers, "Presidential Attention-Focusing Activities," in *The President and the American Public,* ed. Doris A. Graber (Philadelphia: Institute for the Study of Human Issues, 1982), Table 6-1, 152. Data for Kennedy, Johnson, Reagan, and Bush are from *Public Papers of the Presidents* series. See also Kernell, "Presidency and the People," 242.

less, the eight major televised addresses by President Reagan in 1981 (a month of which was spent convalescing from an assassination attempt) is a first-year record for any president. President Bush's major addresses, by contrast, have returned to the level of Reagan's predecessors.

Of the major addresses, the most dramatic and potentially the most effective are the special reports presented by the president on prime-time television to the nation. The subjects of these television talks, listed in Table 4-1, provide a calendar of the crises and national exigencies that have preoccupied presidents since 1953. Carter's appeals for energy conservation and for support of his legislative program and Reagan's regular appeals for support of his economic policies suggest that domestic issues are replacing international crises as the main occasion for prime-time addresses.[7]

Although major addresses may be the most dramatic and most effective approach for influencing public opinion, they also can be the most taxing. The public's attentiveness corresponds to the number of such appeals. If every presidential tribulation were taken to the country on prime-time television, people would soon lose interest. In private correspondence with a friend, Franklin Roosevelt said as much: "The public psychology ... [cannot] be attuned for long periods of time to the highest note on the scale ... people tire of seeing the same name, day after day, in the important headlines of the papers and the same voice, night after night, over the radio." [8] As noted earlier, John Kennedy and members of his staff had the same misgivings after his first, prime-time news conference and scheduled subsequent conferences for daytime television.[9] During the Carter presidency, Gerald Rafshoon, upon assuming his duties in the rejuvenated White House Office of Communications in the summer of 1978, sent a memorandum to the president that established his media strategy for the rest of his tenure. Rafshoon cautioned, "The power of presidential communication is great, but not unlimited. You may be able to talk to the people all day ... but the people can handle so much. *Investment of that power in too wide a range of issues will dissipate it. This has happened over the last eighteen months.*" After elaborating this theme, Rafshoon concluded, "Your involvement should always be weighed with an eye towards preventing the devaluation of presidential currency." [10] By potentially reducing the size and responsiveness of the audience for his next appeal, each prime-time address entails opportunity costs for the president.[11]

Although these concerns are still pondered in the White House, presidents in the past 25 years have continued to expand their prime-time exposure. Table 4-2 shows that Kennedy appeared on national television more frequently than did any president elected after him, but, with four exceptions, he limited himself to daytime exposure. By holding his press conferences in the early afternoon and delivering few direct television addresses—surprisingly few given the unsettled state of international affairs—Kennedy accumulated fewer than two hours of prime-time television during his first 19 months in office.

Table 4-1   Calendar of Presidential "Reports to the Nation" on National Television, Jan. 1953-Dec. 1991

	Jan.	Feb.	Mar.	Apr.	May	June	July	Aug.	Sept.	Oct.	Nov.	Dec.
Eisenhower 1953												
1954	Review			World affairs		Review		Congress				
1955							Geneva conference					
1956		Reelection announcement		Veto-agriculture	Mutual aid					Middle East		
1957		Middle East							Little Rock		Science, security	
1958			Berlin									
1959								Labor reform	Europe			International peace
Kennedy 1960		National defense	Latin America		Paris summit	Far East Europe meetings						
1961							Berlin					
1962			Nuclear tests					Taxes		Cuba	Cuba	
1963						Civil rights		Test ban	Tax cut			
Johnson 1964				Railroad labor dispute (2)				Tonkin Gulf		International affairs		

Year	Topics of televised addresses
1965	
1966	Bombing North Vietnam; Steel strike; Steel strike
1967	
1968	Pueblo; Vietnam; non-candidacy; Martin Luther King; Domini-can Rep.; Domini-can Rep.; Riots; Halt of bombing; Vietnam-ization; S.E. Asia
Nixon 1969	Veto-H.E.W.; Violence; Welfare
1970	Postal strike; Vietnam (2); S.E. Asia; Cambodia (2); Economy; Peace initiative
1971	Vietnam; SALT; Economy; Economy
1972	S.E. Asia; Busing; Vietnam; Vietnam; China trip; USSR trip (2); economy
1973	Vietnam; Economy; Watergate; Watergate; Energy crisis (2)
Ford 1974	Egypt-Israel; Watergate; Middle East crisis; Pardon of Nixon
1975	National issues; Tax cut; Mayaguez (2); energy; Tax cut
1976	
Carter 1977	Fireside chat; Panama Canal Treaty; Energy; Energy
1978	Inflation; China

Table 4-1 (Cont.)

	Jan.	Feb.	Mar.	Apr.	May	June	July	Aug.	Sept.	Oct.	Nov.	Dec.
1979	Farewell (Carter)	Economy				SALT II	Crisis of confidence		Soviet troops in Cuba			
1980			Economy	Energy								Poland
Reagan 1981												
1982				Budget			Tax bill		Economy; budget	Economy	Arms control	
1983			Defense-national security	Central America					Middle East (2); Korean airliner	Lebanon, Grenada		
1984					Central America							
1985		State of the Union; National security	Nicaragua	Budget	Tax reform						Soviet-U.S. Summit	
1986	Space Shuttle explosion						Independence Day		Drug abuse	Meetings with Gorbachev	Elections Iran and Contra aid	Iran arms and Contra aid
1987	State of the Union		Iran arms and Contra aid			Economic summit		Iran arms and Contra aid				
1988	State of the Union											Soviet-U.S. Summit
1989	Farewell to the nation											Panama

Bush 1989	Inauguration	Administration goals			Drug control strategy	Thanksgiving	
1990	State of the Union			Kuwait invasion	Persian Gulf; budget deficit	Budget agreement	
1991	Desert Storm; State of the Union	Persian Gulf; Iraqi withdrawal	Persian Gulf		Nuclear weapons reduction		Thanksgiving	Christmas

SOURCES: The entries from 1953 through November 1963 are from "Presidents on TV: Their Live Records," *Broadcasting*, November 8, 1965, 55-58; those from December 1963 through December 1975 are from Denis S. Rutkus, "A Report on Simultaneous Television Network Coverage of Presidential Addresses to the Nation" (Congressional Research Service, Washington, D.C., 1976, Mimeographed), appendix; entries since 1976 are from the *Public Papers of the Presidents* series and a tentative compilation by Denis Rutkus.

Table 4-2 Presidential Television from Kennedy to Bush, First 19 Months in Office

President	Number of Appearances in Prime Time	Time on Air in Prime Time (hours)	Total Number of Appearances	Total Time on Air (hours)
Kennedy	4	1.9	50	30.4
Johnson	7	3.3	33	12.5
Nixon	14	7.1	37	13.5
Carter	8	5.1	45	32.2
Reagan	12	8.9	39	26.5
Bush	7	3.7	56	22.3

NOTE: Gerald Ford has been omitted from analysis since his first 19 months in office cross into the reelection period.

SOURCES: For Kennedy, Johnson, and Nixon, data were supplied by the White House Press Office, quoted in *New York Times,* August 3, 1970, 16. For Carter, Reagan, and Bush, data are from program logs at CBS News, New York. Data are for speeches (including inauguration) and press conferences broadcast live on national television.

Richard Nixon surpassed this figure by nearly fourfold and in doing so raised the ire of network executives and their news departments. His mix of daytime and evening television was the reverse of Kennedy's. While holding fewer news conferences (hence, his low total number of hours), Nixon delivered more direct, prime-time addresses to the nation. With barely a third of Kennedy's overall television exposure, Nixon dominated the medium in a way none of his predecessors had come close to doing. He paved the way for Carter and Reagan, who relied upon equally heavy television schedules, but with a greater share of it during non-prime-time hours. Surprisingly, President Bush eclipsed all of his predecessors in the number of television appearances during his first nineteen months in office, but comparatively little of his network exposure occurred during prime time.

Going public is neither premised on nor does it promote a perception of America as a homogeneous society. Nor does it reduce politics to a plebiscite in which the president seeks continually to bring the weight of national opinion to bear in the resolution of policy questions.[12] Governance under individualized pluralism remains largely a process of assembling temporary coalitions from among diverse constituencies. For this purpose, minor presidential addresses directed toward special constituencies are particularly well suited. Not only are they less taxing on some future opportunity to gain the nation's attention, they may succeed where an undifferentiated national appeal may not. President Reagan's Chicago speech before Catholic organizations is a good illustration of why and how presidents cast appeals to particular publics.

Aside from being more focused and less obtrusive than major addresses (and therefore less taxing on future public appeals), minor addresses are attractive to presidents because the opportunities to give them are plentiful. The president is importuned daily to appear before graduation exercises, union conferences, and the conventions of trade and professional associations. With such advantages, minor addresses are understandably an integral component of a more general strategy of going public.

President Bush's calendar of speaking engagements for September 1991, presented in Table 4-3, illustrates how heavily presidents sometimes engage in these kinds of activities. During that month he delivered remarks and formal addresses on 19 occasions in 11 cities throughout the country. What makes this schedule even more impressive is that he also found time to deliver four national television and radio addresses, far exceeding any previous month of his tenure.

The real explosion in presidential talk has occurred in the class of minor addresses. Reagan, Carter, and Nixon on average surpassed Truman, Roosevelt, and Hoover by nearly fivefold in the use of such rhetoric. And President Bush managed to double these already high levels of targeted addresses. During his first three years in office he averaged a minor address nearly every other day. While this heavy schedule involved an unprecedented amount of travel to his audiences, he also addressed distant gatherings from the Oval Office by means of teleconferencing technology, which had been less available to his predecessors.[13]

If asked to name a president who could speak skillfully, one probably would think first of Franklin Roosevelt or perhaps John Kennedy, two men whose speeches have weathered time and relistening well. Nixon's pronouncements—such as his pre-presidential "Checkers" speech and later the Watergate denials—will be remembered mostly as objects of ridicule and, ultimately, of historical curiosity. Carter's and Bush's addresses will be recalled, if at all, as instructive examples of poor elocution and syntax. Of the recent class of presidents going public, only Ronald Reagan scores well as a thespian. The trends reported here reveal that it is not success but the type of politician recruited to the office and the strategic environment within which he operates that determine the volume of presidential rhetoric.

Public Appearances

Visual images can at times convey messages more effectively than talk. The audience to whom the president speaks and the location and circumstances of the event may contribute as much to his message's effectiveness as what he has to say. Jimmy Carter's inaugural stroll down Pennsylvania Avenue and the cardigan he wore at his first fireside chat on national television were gestures calculated to set the tenor of his administration in the

Table 4-3   President Bush's "Minor" Addresses, September, 1991

Date	Location	Audience	Subject
Sept. 3	Lewiston, Maine	High school faculty/students	Improvement of schools, education
Sept. 12	Philadelphia, Pennsylvania	Veterans' Hospital	Drug abuse
Sept. 17	Teleconference	School children	Education, NASA
Sept. 18	Grand Canyon, Arizona	Environmental-agreement signing ceremony	Environment policy
Sept. 18	Salt Lake City, Utah	Upon arrival	Education, volunteerism
Sept. 18	Salt Lake City, Utah	Children's Hospital staff	Infant mortality, Healthy Start
Sept. 18	Salt Lake City, Utah	Republican Party dinner	Choice in family affairs and education
Sept. 19	Portland, Oregon	Fundraising breakfast	Education, domestic policy
Sept. 19	Los Angeles, California	Construction workers	Transportation issues
Sept. 19	Los Angeles, California	Fundraising dinner	America 2000 (education), crime bill
Sept. 20	Chicago, Illinois	National convention of U.S. Hispanic Chamber of Commerce	North American free trade agreement, America 2000
Sept. 23	United Nations	General Assembly	Free trade, coup in U.S.S.R., Saddam Hussein, Zionism
Sept. 24	East Brunswick, New Jersey	Republican Party dinner	Energy, education, transportation
Sept. 25	Washington, D.C.	Blue Ribbon schools	Education reform, America 2000
Sept. 30	Orlando, Florida	575 Points of Light	Volunteering in community to help others
Sept. 30	Miami, Florida	Beacon Council annual meeting	Crime package, free trade agreement, education
Sept. 30	New Orleans, Louisiana	Fundraising dinner	Child care, civil rights, crime, transportation, capital gains, America 2000

SOURCES: Weekly Compilation of Presidential Documents, Office of the Federal Register, vol. 27, nos. 36-40, (Washington D.C.: Government Printing Office).

public's mind. Similarly, the image of President Nixon donning a hard hat and waving to cheering construction workers on the scaffolding above him made a strong pitch for support among his "silent majority."

Appearances are usually accompanied by public speaking, although, as in the Nixon example above, they need not be. Like minor addresses, appearances before select audiences offer the president an opportunity to target his appeals. In a preinaugural memo, Carter's pollster Patrick Caddell urged the president-elect to use "his personal leadership—through visits and political contacts—to maintain his base in the South." [14] As another example, President Reagan made some 25 appearances around the country in 1983 promoting his views on "excellence in education" (principally, merit pay for teachers and classroom discipline) after polls indicated a two-to-one public disapproval of his budget cutbacks in education. [15]

Appearances are distinguished in Figure 4-2 by locale, those in Washington from those throughout the rest of the United States. The number of public appearances outside the city generally reflects the president's non-Washington origins and divided party control of government. [16]

Political Travel

Generally, presidents travel in order to appear before particular constituencies or to find locations suitable for sounding a particular theme. Ronald Reagan kicked off his tax reform proposal in 1985 in Williamsburg, Virginia, to play up the plan's theme as "the new American Revolution." Days logged in domestic travel have no importance beyond the appearances or addresses before non-Washington audiences they reflect and the telegenic evening news spots they attract. As such, they offer another useful measure of the president's public activity.

When presidents travel abroad, however, they frequently do so in search of special opportunities to appear presidential. Meetings abroad with other heads of state are especially valuable in reminding the electorate of the weighty responsibilities of office and of the president's diligence in attending to them. Could future incumbents fail to notice the salutary effects of Kennedy's confrontation with Nikita Khrushchev in Vienna in 1961 and of Nixon's celebrated trip to China in 1972 on these presidents' images as national leaders? One may reasonably argue that affairs of state rather than voracious demands for publicity were the real reasons for these trips. Kennedy's biographers make clear his strongly felt need to impress the Soviet leader with America's commitments to its allies. And without the dramatic expression of national good will that Nixon's trip conveyed, the thaw in relations between the United States and China might not have been so complete. The considerable diplomatic merits of these trips notwithstanding, the fact is that both presidents thoroughly exploited their opportunities for publicity at home.

Kennedy's staff rushed film of the president with the Soviet leader to the Paris airport to give it the earliest possible airing on the networks' evening news.

Figure 4-2 Public Appearances by Presidents, 1929-1990 (Yearly Averages for First Three Years of First Term)

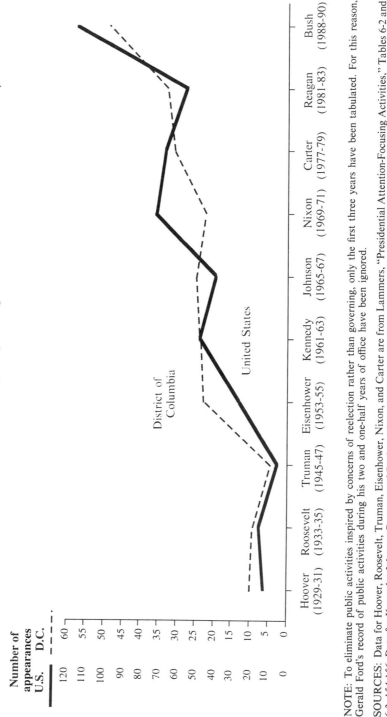

NOTE: To eliminate public activities inspired by concerns of reelection rather than governing, only the first three years have been tabulated. For this reason, Gerald Ford's record of public activities during his two and one-half years of office have been ignored.

SOURCES: Data for Hoover, Roosevelt, Truman, Eisenhower, Nixon, and Carter are from Lammers, "Presidential Attention-Focusing Activities," Tables 6-2 and 6-3, 154-156. Data for Kennedy, Johnson, Reagan, and Bush are from *Public Papers of the Presidents* series. See also Kernell, "Presidency and the People," 245.

Reprinted with special permission of King Features Syndicate, Inc.

By the time Nixon visited China, 11 years later, new technology had greatly expanded the opportunities for public relations. Hours of President Nixon's tour of famous sites and formal expressions of mutual friendship with China's leaders were televised by satellite. Air Force One landed in Peking during prime time at home; the president's tour of the Great Wall and ancient palaces and the state banquet in the Great Hall were broadcast live back to the United States; and for a finale, after a timely nine-hour layover in Anchorage, Air Force One touched down in Washington just in time to make the evening network news. All in all, the networks broadcast more than 41 hours of the seven-day trip. Afterwards, syndicated columnist Art Buchwald satirized the whole affair by reporting his wife's assumption that the television set must be broken because Nixon's program was not available on any channel.[17]

The logistical planning of the China trip remains an impressive example of making the most of the opportunities for favorable publicity at home. Advances in transportation and communications, of which the China trip took full advantage, have so reduced travel time and so enhanced its public relations value that modern presidents might contemplate trips abroad solely for this purpose. Insiders increasingly voice suspicion that, in fact, they already do.

In 1973, President Nixon went to Iceland for a special meeting with France's President Georges Pompidou. No major policy decisions were made, as those privy to the trip's preparations had predicted. The *New York Times* reported the comments of one foreign service officer: "All they cared about was how things would look on television. White House aides fussed about the lighting, about who would stand where, what the background would be, and the furniture. The entire time I was assigned to the detail, no one asked me a substantive question. I'm sure they didn't care. All they seemed to care about was television." [18]

Since Nixon's world travels during the Watergate investigation, in what turned out to be the last months of his presidency, White House correspondents have been especially mindful of the public relations value of trips abroad. During Reagan's first presidential trip to Europe, it was not surprising that network correspondents pointed out the publicity purposes of the visual images so carefully produced by Reagan's aides. What is remarkable, however, was the willingness of White House staffers to discuss openly the trip's value in just these terms. Taken together, their comments reveal the motive of the trip. Because the polls were showing a drop in the president's popularity—which made him vulnerable in Washington—his advisers decided that conferring on location with European heads of state would be good for his image as a leader. After assessing the poll results that shortly followed the trip, White House aides voiced delight that their goal had been achieved.[19]

In the age of television, every president may be suspected of, and perhaps forgiven for, engaging in strategic travel and posing for the continuous "photo opportunities." The president who rests his leadership on going public will be tempted to travel frequently, in search of sympathetic audiences and "presidential images."

Because foreign and domestic travel often have different political purposes, they are measured separately in Figure 4-3. Each increased significantly in the past half century. Domestic air travel for presidents began with Truman, but aside from brief vacation trips to his home in Independence, Missouri, he seldom took advantage of this new opportunity. Eisenhower was the first president to travel extensively around the country.[20] Not until Reagan and Bush, however, did presidents spend a total of a month away from Washington each year. Bush even challenged the two-month marker every year, and in 1991 he broke it, despite getting off to a late start because of the outbreak of the Gulf War in January of that year.

International political travel by presidents increased most sharply during the late 1960s. Eisenhower's 1959 "good-will" tour around the world is generally recognized as the first international presidential travel where favorable publicity appeared to all to be the primary consideration. As the figures for subsequent presidents suggest, it was an idea whose time had come. Both Presidents Carter and Bush, who enjoyed their major policy successes in foreign affairs, traveled extensively. By the close of his third year in office, Bush's overseas travels had become so conspicuous that his critics found a large segment of the public agreeing with them that the president wasn't

Figure 4-3 Days of Political Travel by Presidents, 1929-1990 (Yearly Averages for First Three Years of First Term)

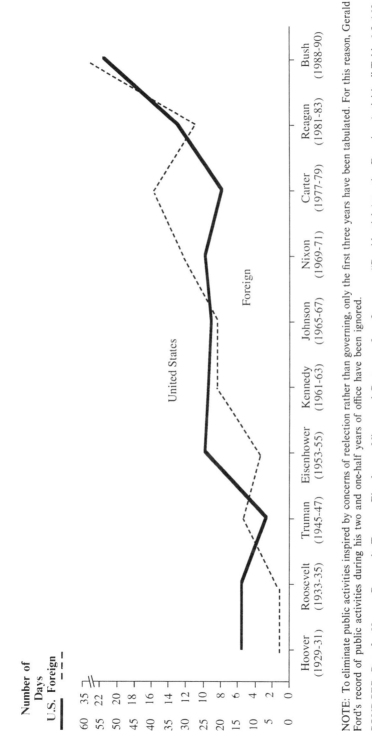

NOTE: To eliminate public activities inspired by concerns of reelection rather than governing, only the first three years have been tabulated. For this reason, Gerald Ford's record of public activities during his two and one-half years of office have been ignored.

SOURCES: Data for Hoover, Roosevelt, Truman, Eisenhower, Nixon, and Carter are from Lammers, "Presidential Attention-Focusing Activities," Table 6-5, 160. Data for Kennedy, Johnson, Reagan, and Bush are from *Public Papers of the Presidents* series. See also Kernell, "Presidency and the People," 244.

paying enough attention to the nation's troubles. Under pressure to focus more on domestic issues, Bush announced in November 1991 that he was postponing an Asian trip late that year, ostensibly to keep tabs on the Democratic Congress. Whatever the Bush presidency lacked in vision during its first three years, it certainly made up in motion.

During the past half century, trends in presidents going public—from political travel to public addresses and appearances—have moved steadily upward. There are some differences among them, however, in both the overall rate of growth and the timing of the sharpest increases. The number of minor public addresses, for example, has increased dramatically, even leaving aside Bush's exceptional level of activity. Political travel and public appearances also show differences in pace and timing. Cumulatively, these trends point toward a president today who is far more personally involved in public relations than were his predecessors 30 and 40 years ago.[21]

The Incremental Growth of Going Public

The rise of going public has proceeded more or less incrementally with each president taking advantage of the precedents and extensions of public activity offered by his predecessors. For the purpose of discussion, the various reasons for gradual change can be classified broadly as technological and political. The former have to do with opportunity, the latter with inspiration.

Incrementalism as a Function of Technology

Any explanation of the emergence of public strategies in the standard repertoire of presidents must take into account the continuous technological advances in transportation and mass communications during the past half century. Consider the difficulty a president 50 years ago would have encountered had he sought to rally the country behind his policies. By today's standards, the national transportation and communications systems of the early 1930s were primitive; barely 40 percent of all households owned radios. The president's potential audience was not only relatively small, one may assume that during the Great Depression it was also heavily skewed toward more affluent citizens. When Herbert Hoover defended his depression policies on national radio—and he did so regularly—he preached mainly to the converted.[22]

Transportation in the 1930s posed even greater difficulties. Air travel for presidents would not come for another two decades, and rail transportation was so slow and arduous that one did not undertake it casually. In the early 1920s, President Wilson suffered a stroke and President Harding a fatal heart attack during long political trips. Anxious to gain the legitimacy and the audience shares regular presidential appearances would provide, radio executives commonly cited these instances in promoting heavier presidential use of the new medium.[23] A decade later, a round trip from the east to the west coast still took about a week.[24] Obviously, slow transportation limited a president's appearances before and appeals to select audiences around the country.

International travel was even more time consuming and therefore infrequent. Woodrow Wilson's trip to Europe in 1919 to make the peace was a rare gesture befitting the historic moment. The first international flight by a president came in 1943 when Franklin Roosevelt secretly traveled to North Africa to meet with Winston Churchill. Compare the logistics of this trip with those described on page 101 for Nixon's trip to China 29 years later.

> The straight-line distance from Washington to Casablanca is 3,875 miles. A modern jet transport could have made the trip comfortably and without stopovers, in seven hours. But in 1943, the limited range, slower speeds, and lack of sophisticated navigational aids in the Boeing 314 and Douglas C-54 had required four legs of flying, three stopovers, a change of planes, and more than three days' travel time for the President—in each direction. The circuitous route required the President to touch three continents, cross the Equator four times, and spend approximately ninety hours in the air. When his train travel between Washington and Miami was included, Roosevelt had covered more than 17,000 miles before he was once more back home in the White House.[25]

The growth in presidential travel occurred piecemeal, with each new opportunity made possible by an advance in transportation technology. The 55 years shown in Figure 4-3 span the period in which travel shifted from rail to air and from prop to jet.

Technological breakthroughs in broadcast communications have had an even more profound effect on the opportunities for presidents to go public. Radio and television are, of course, the major developments, but smaller technological advances also had their effects. In 1955, for example, Kodak introduced its Tri-X film, which reduced the lighting requirements of television cameras; shortly thereafter Eisenhower admitted film crews into his news conferences.[26] The subsequent development of live satellite communications created a variety of new opportunities for live presidential television. Nixon's prime-time trip to China, Carter's town meetings at home and abroad, and Bush's teleconferences with national conventions in distant locales illustrate the kinds of public activities modern satellite communications make possible. The steady growth of going public during the past half century follows the sequence of technological advances in communication as well as transportation.

Going public increased incrementally not only with the introduction of new means of communication, but also with their dissemination. One may assume that the appeal to presidents of communicating via radio and television relates to the size of the audience. President Roosevelt's participation in an experimental television broadcast at the 1939 World's Fair had no real political significance if for no other reason than that only a minuscule audience could view the broadcast.[27] Figure 4-4 displays the rate with which

Figure 4-4 Households with Radios and Televisions, Cable TV and VCRs, 1930-1990 (Percent)

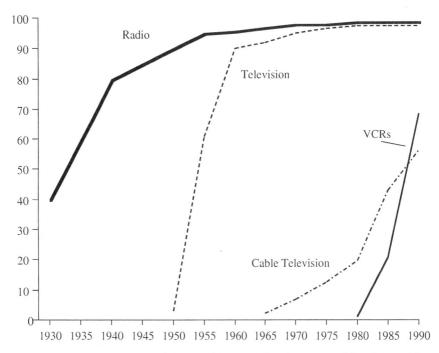

SOURCES: *Historical Statistics of the United States: Colonial Times to 1970,* vols. 1 and 2 (Washington, D.C.: Government Printing Office, 1975), series R104, R105, and A335. Data for 1975 through 1990 are from *Statistical Abstract of the United States* (Washington, D.C.: Government Printing Office, 1991), 556.

radio and television entered America's homes. By the early 1960s, the market was virtually saturated: more than 90 percent of households owned these appliances. During that decade presidents began more actively devising new ways to gain access to the nation's airwaves.

Although trends in going public follow the stepwise introduction and dissemination of technology, the correlation is not perfect. Presidents have adopted new technology cautiously.[28] In some instances this caution has resulted in a substantial time lag between a technology's availability and its political use. Harry Truman was the first president to go to the country on national television, but by modern standards he did so sparingly. Truman generally reserved television for moments of crisis, such as his announcement of the Korean War and seizure of the steel mills. On many pressing domestic issues of the day, he spoke to the country exclusively over radio and via newsreels. In the judgment of one observer, Truman failed "to use broadcasting consciously as a lever for increasing his influence on the Congress." [29]

Presidential television came of age in the 1952 election when Dwight Eisenhower became the first candidate for president to use television commercials heavily in his campaign.[30] In the postelection euphoria, press secretary James Hagerty referred to the advent of presidential television as a "new age" and raised the prospect of a regularly scheduled, monthly television program from the White House. Nothing came of this idea, however. During his eight years in office, Eisenhower instead continued Truman's practice of reserving television addresses mainly for international crises. Not until Lyndon Johnson and Richard Nixon did routine affairs of state become the subjects of presidential, prime-time television.

There is a similar time lag between technology and practice in presidential travel. Harry Truman valued the mobility offered by a plane designated for presidential use, but more for personal reasons (returning home to Missouri) than for possible political advantage. One might think that Truman, having assumed office on the death of FDR, would also have found good reason to travel around the country to gain national exposure and build support among local party organizations. But, as shown in Figure 4-3, Truman took few political trips. Eisenhower in turn was tardy in using jet transportation to travel abroad. It was left to his successors, principally Nixon, to make foreign travel a standard feature of the president's public repertoire and to discover, notably in the case of Bush, that the political limitations of extensive travel are more severe than the physical. These instances of a time lag between the availability of an innovation and its use suggest that something other than availability enters a president's decision to exploit new technology in going public.

Incrementalism as a Function of Politics

Going public is a strategic choice grounded as much in contemporary political relations as in available technology. The decline of party and institutional leadership in Congress and the rise of divided government have made the Washington community progressively more susceptible to public opinion throughout the past several decades. At the same time, the decay of protocoalitions has made bargaining at once both more difficult and less likely to suffice. Moreover, presidential selection reforms are sending people to the White House who are neither trained nor interested in learning the "ways" of Washington. These outsiders frequently prefer to go public rather than engage in quiet diplomacy. Technology has offered ever expanding opportunities, but changes within the political environment have provided the inspiration.

The decision to bargain or to go public is based upon a comparison of the relative costs and benefits of each strategy in a particular setting. Technology and evolving political relations have made the public approach increasingly attractive. But there are also costs that attend innovation and going public, which at times have applied a brake on the rapid expansion of public strategies. During an era of entrenched leaders, going public would generally be construed as an exercise in pressure politics and unless practiced delicately could easily backfire. Any public activity—but especially innovation—runs this risk of violating established expectations and triggering hostile reactions from other political elites in Washington.

Franklin Roosevelt's court-packing campaign illustrates this well. Fresh from a landslide reelection victory and perhaps suffering from euphoria, Roosevelt early in 1937 unveiled at a press conference his proposal for legislation to increase the number of Supreme Court justices and thereby gain more sympathetic treatment of New Deal programs.[31] In doing so, he broke with existing protocol by failing to brief key members of Congress before making a public announcement of a legislative initiative. In the opinion of many participants and commentators, this early mistake contributed to the proposal's eventual defeat. Even Roosevelt's staunchest supporters in Congress were taken aback; his detractors, predictably outraged. The court packing proposal was FDR's most stunning legislative failure in his 12 years in office. It was also the only time he used one of his famous fireside chats to ask the public to pressure Congress in behalf of his policies.[32] From the Senate, Harry Truman witnessed firsthand the ill will sowed by Roosevelt's innovative use of the press conference. Citing it a decade later, Truman as president would refuse to use the press conference for unveiling congressional initiatives.[33]

The court-packing episode is instructive in two ways. First, it shows that in the realm of public opinion, where politicians will understandably be quite sensitive, departures from established practices can easily backfire, even for someone as popular as Franklin Roosevelt. Second, Truman's response reveals how the experiences of one president become lessons for the next. Whether learned firsthand or observed from the sidelines, the negative reactions of other politicians serve to bring presidential strategy into conformity with expectations founded upon established practice. To the degree these forces impress themselves on political behavior, one president's activity will not much differ from that of his predecessor. Innovation occurs "at the margin." The results can be seen in the aggregate trends—both in the steady growth of direct communication and, as shown in Chapter 3, in the gradual decline of the traditional press conference.

Resistance to Innovation in Going Public

A president's decision to go public by enlisting a new technology or by employing an old one in a novel fashion brings forces of change into conflict with those of stability. New opportunities made possible by advances in technology and rising incentives brought on by changing political circumstances run up against the established prerogatives of other politicians. When the choice favors innovation, the president can try to minimize the political costs by having it conform to, or at least resemble, existing practices as much as possible. Two strategic devices are available to the president. First, he can summon precedents in introducing a new form of public activity. Second, he can expand a base by simply doing more of a familiar public activity. Both are venerable strategies of incremental politics.

In Chapter 3 we encountered an instance of the former in President Kennedy's introduction of the televised news conference. He adapted existing arrangements to a new purpose—direct communication with the public—and thereby managed to undo the old order even as he conformed to its expectations.

Examples of an incremental expanding of the base can be found in the gradually rising trends in going public presented in this chapter. Presidents have tended to increase their public activities only marginally beyond a base of accepted practice. As long as a president can credibly argue that his activity does not much differ from that of his predecessor, he should be able to blunt criticism from those who are adversely affected by his public activities. The greater the departure of current from past practice, of course, the less credible the president's claim becomes and the greater the likelihood of a negative response. This is precisely what happened after Nixon's first year in office when he began appearing on evening network television to an unprecedented degree. By one count Nixon appeared on national television 17 times within nine months beginning in late 1969. On 11 of these occasions, he preempted evening commercial television.[34]

The sudden surge in presidential television appearances generated complaints from various quarters and assumed the status of a prominent news story in its own right. During the summer of 1970, Washington correspondents began pressing Nixon at news conferences with pointed questions about his television strategy. The White House responded by arguing that the president was simply subscribing to the practices of past presidents. Aide John Ehrlichman compiled figures on the television appearances of Presidents Kennedy and Johnson, as well as Nixon, arguing that his president had been on television less than Kennedy and about as often as Johnson.

Ehrlichman's argument did little to allay criticism, however. A group of antiwar activists, citing repeated instances of Nixon's use of television to promote his Vietnam policies, had petitioned the Federal Communications Commission (FCC) for network time to respond to the president's remarks under the fairness doctrine. The Democratic National Committee appealed directly to the networks for a similar opportunity to rebut the president. In midsummer the FCC ruled for the first time that a president's repeated addresses on a subject had produced an imbalance in public debate and that those holding opposing views should be given network air time to respond.[35] Independent of the FCC ruling, the networks liberalized access of Democrats to answer the president's remarks.

The idea of granting air time to the president's opponents was not new. After Harry Truman blasted "greedy" steel company executives in announcing his seizure of the mills in 1951, the networks gave rebuttal time to the president of Inland Steel Company. During the mid-1960s, networks began the practice of granting air time to congressional opponents to answer the president's annual State of the Union message. According to archival research performed by the Library of Congress, opposition spokespersons—whether individuals, congressional leaders, or representatives of the opposition party—were allotted free response time on national television on only 4 occasions from 1961 to 1964. But from 1970 to 1974, during Nixon's administration, there were 14 such occasions; from 1975 to 1984, there were 34.[36]

Today, the right of opposition parties and congressional spokespersons to respond to presidential addresses remains a subject of some dispute and negotiation between politicians and network executives. Chief among the many issues yet to be resolved are which presidential statements warrant equal time, who is to respond, and when opposition responses will be aired.[37] Congressional and party opponents assert their right for equal time, the networks their prerogative to judge each request on its merits, and the FCC its intention to remain uninvolved. What is clear from the record, however, is that Nixon's heavy use of television helped establish strong precedents that will ensure opposition parties in the future their time on television.[38]

Opposition groups are not alone in complaining about the frequency of presidential rhetoric. After the heavy dose of prime-time television during President Nixon's first year, CBS head Frank Stanton publicly began to characterize the White House strategy as an attempt to monopolize the airwaves.[39] Given that a prime-time, thirty-second commercial can cost $200,000 or more, it is understandable why network executives might be concerned that the president was enjoying undue political advantage through his special access to national television. Granting the opposition party response time would seem to restore political parity, but this would, of course, result in an additional lost opportunity for the network to sell products.

In October 1975, the networks hit upon a less expensive way to rein in presidential television. Although the next election was over a year away, CBS and NBC refused to carry President Ford's address on tax reform on the dubious grounds that they would have to provide equal time to other announced candidates. (At that early date, there was apparently only one—an obscure, perennial candidate in Massachusetts.) Not until Reagan's second term did the networks enlist their prerogative to turn down a presidential request, but it is apparent that this first instance made gaining access to the airwaves an important factor as presidents and their aides considered their options. In late 1978, President Carter's communications director planned a media strategy involving unprecedented levels of national television. He advised the president to cultivate warm relations with the network heads, so that they would be less likely to balk at complying with his subsequent request for air time.[40]

From mid-1986 through the fall of 1987, one or more of the networks refused to give President Reagan air time on at least three occasions. Two of these involved appeals for public support for aid to the Nicaraguan *contras*;

the third concerned support for Judge Robert Bork, Reagan's nominee to the Supreme Court. During this nonelection period, the networks could not fall back on equal time for opponents as their rationale for denying the president's request. Instead, they used the criterion of newsworthiness, which would appear difficult to apply since little more than the topic of the address would have been known to those making the decision. One network comment struck directly at the strategy of going public: "Tonight's address is really directed at a small group of people on Capitol Hill, so my recommendation is not to interrupt our prime-time broadcast to carry that." [41]

The adverse reaction to presidential television from the opposition party in Congress and network executives pales in comparison to that from a third class of participants—the viewing public. Broadcast technology enabled the president to enter the homes of citizens, and the development of VCRs and cable technology, shown in Figure 4-4, is allowing these same citizens to usher him out.

In the 1960s and 1970s, when the three networks controlled 90 percent of the audience share in most markets, the president enjoyed a seemingly captive audience for his addresses to the nation. There is no evidence, based on audience size, that an appreciable number of viewers chose to turn off their televisions. [42] But with the rise of new technology providing alternative programming and tape formats, people have proven nimble at changing channels. However well they may be doing in the Gallup polls, recent presidents are clearly slipping in A. C. Nielsen's audience ratings. Figure 4-5 depicts a point-a-year decline on average in percentages of households with televisions that have tuned in to presidential addresses during the past five administrations. The high point is the first observation available in this series: President Nixon's statement of the Vietnam War in November 1969. Presidents Carter and Reagan nearly matched him once, in their first addresses to the nation, but Bush has not come close. His first address to the nation garnered only 38 percent of the households with televisions. [43] Despite a brief war and dramatic world events in which President Bush played a significant role, he managed no better than a 43 percent audience rating— that after the Gulf War in 1991.

Undoubtedly, many citizens who were unenthusiastic and hence inattentive viewers when they had few choices have now abandoned the president's audience. But since these were probably the least responsive members of the audience, their departure will not greatly affect the president's capacity to generate vocal support for his policies. Of greater strategic concern to a president is the fact that other viewers, as a result of the new technology, can now decide on each occasion whether to watch the president or turn their attention elsewhere. Their choice will rest on the comparative appeal of the president's message. In March 1986 when President Reagan spoke to the nation on increased U.S. support for the *contra* rebels in Nicaragua, an estimated 16 million households switched to alternative programming. Eight

Figure 4-5 The Declining Presidential Audience: 1969-1992

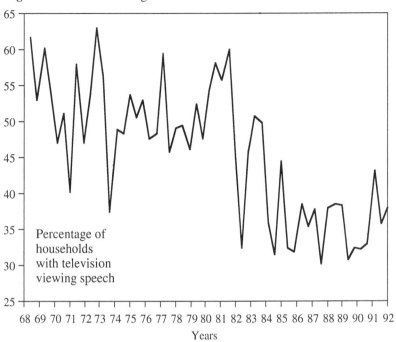

Percentage of households with television viewing speech

Years

SOURCE: Nielsen Media Research. Reprinted with permission.

months later during the Irangate scandal, the president defended himself at a nationally televised press conference. This time only 4 million households defected.[44] Today, with uncertainty about whether the networks will decide to broadcast the president's message and about whether viewers will opt to receive it, the availability of the audience becomes a serious consideration in planning the president's public strategies.

Conclusion

A proposition of this book is that the degree to which a president goes public determines the kind of leader he will be. With it I have argued that the style of leadership in the White House is changing. Modern presidents rely upon public opinion for their leadership in Washington to an extent unknown when Dahl and Lindblom in the early 1950s described the president as "an embodiment of a bargaining society," or later when Neustadt predicated presidential power on bargaining.[45]

The above proposition, claiming a change in the degree of going public and inferring a change in the character of leadership, is subject to rejoinder on two fronts. Because every president since Theodore Roosevelt has sought at some moment to rally public opinion to his side, and each in his public activity has drawn on the precedents and departed only marginally from the base lines of his immediate predecessor, one can easily miss the striking degree to which presidents today go public compared with the presidents of the 1930s, the 1940s, or even the 1950s.

Moreover, I suspect that the increasing quantity of public activity has tended to be obscured by the varying quality of public rhetoric, which is always more memorable than the quantity. To those who compared Ronald Reagan's rhetorical talents with those of Franklin Roosevelt, little appears to have changed in the past 50 years.

One misconception that results from incremental change is that in retrospect the past resembles the present. This, after all, is the purpose of the incremental strategy. A case in point is the story Arthur Schlesinger recounts of a phone call he received one morning from President Kennedy. The president asked how frequently FDR had held fireside chats. He said that *New York Times* correspondent Lester Markel was with him complaining that he ought to go before the American people more often. "Lester . . . seems to think that Roosevelt gave a fireside chat once a week." Schlesinger subsequently reported to Kennedy that before the war, Roosevelt averaged no more than two of these now famous radio addresses a year.[46] A couple of years later the issue was still current when Schlesinger passed along to Kennedy a letter from Samuel Beer, a prominent political scientist and former national chair of the Americans for Democratic Action, which said:

> I certainly do not agree, let alone sympathize, with my liberal friends who say that it is all the fault of the President; that if he would only resort to the magic of the "fire-side chat" he would create great waves of public opinion which would wash away Congressional obstruction. They simply don't remember the way FDR actually worked—e.g. the prolonged and tortured operation by which he got the Wage-Hour bill—and totally forget the political situation that gave him leverage.[47]

When it comes to collective memory of presidential performance, one seems as inclined to impose the present on the past as vice versa. Either way, the result is that nothing much *appears* to have happened.

Another counter-argument accepts the trends examined in this chapter but holds that they have little bearing on the character of presidential leadership. The president may be a more familiar face on television, and he may spend more time on the road, but his public relations have not reduced the role of bargaining in presidential leadership. Against this argument, quantitative indexes of public activity, no matter how dramatic the changes they depict, stand mute.

To conclude that the multitudinous public activities of modern presidents do matter—that they have altered the character of leadership in Washington—one needs to consider more qualitative evidence, such as the transactions between the president and those whom he seeks to influence. The next chapter examines the ways Ronald Reagan promoted his budget with Congress during his first three years in office. The budgetary politics of these years show how a president, who took pride in his skills as a communicator, enlisted public support in his dealings with congressional leaders and how these activities substituted for and at times interfered with bargaining.

Notes

1. In an early study of what has only recently become a prominent fact of presidential governance, Stanley Kelley, Jr., described the linkages between presidential activities (including campaigning) and professional public relations in *Professional Public Relations and Political Power* (Baltimore: Johns Hopkins University Press, 1956).
2. Rowland Evans and Robert Novak, *Nixon in the White House* (New York: Random House, 1971), 388-389.
3. Since fall 1981, Reagan's pollster, Richard Wirthlin, had been advising the president of his slipping popularity among blue-collar Democrats—many of whom are Catholic—who had supported him against Carter in 1980. See B. Drummond Ayres, Jr., "G.O.P. Keeps Tabs on Nation's Mood," *New York Times*, November 16, 1981, A20; and Howell Raines, "Reagan's Gamble: Bid for Popularity," *New York Times*, March 30, 1982, A27. Similar evidence of Reagan's decline in the polls is reported by Hedrick Smith in the CBS-*New York Times* survey in "Blue-Collar Workers' Support for Reagan Declines," *New York Times*, March 8, 1982, 1. The association between the president's decline in the polls and his tuition tax credit proposal is made by Dennis Williams, Lucy Howard, and Frank Marer, "Tax Credits for Tuition?" *Newsweek*, April 26, 1982, 86. See also Seymour Sudman, "The President and the Polls," *Public Opinion Quarterly* 46 (Fall 1982): 301-310; and Harrison Donnelly, "Little Hope Seen for Tuition Tax Credit Plan," *Congressional Quarterly Weekly Report*, April 24, 1982, 911-913.
4. These categories of going public correspond to those developed by William Lammers, who was the first to examine systematically trends in presidents' public activities. William W. Lammers, "Presidential Attention-Focusing Activities," in *The President and the American Public,* ed. Doris A. Graber (Philadelphia: Institute for the Study of Human Issues, 1982), 145-171.
5. Omitted from major addresses are presidential press conferences and purely ceremonial functions (for example, calls to astronauts and Christmas tree lighting ceremonies). See Table 3-2 for the decline in the use of press conferences. Lammers provides evidence that presidents adapt conference schedules to their strategic goals and to more direct means of communication in "Presidential Press Conference Schedules: Who Hides and When?" *Political Science Quarterly* 96 (Summer 1981): 261-267.
6. In Figures 4-1, 4-2, and 4-3, only the first three years have been tabulated in order to eliminate activities inspired by concerns for reelection rather than governing.

Since Gerald Ford's tenure does not include three nonelection years, his record of public activities has been ignored.

7. As a cautionary note, the sources used to compile this list of television addresses appear to provide a more inclusive definition in recent years.

8. Roosevelt continued, "If I had tried [in 1935] to keep up the pace of 1933 and 1934, the inevitable histrionics of the new actors, Long and Coughlin and Johnson, would have turned the eyes of the audience away from the main drama itself." Cited in Douglass Cater, "How a President Helps Form Public Opinion," *New York Times Magazine*, February 26, 1961, 12.

9. Pierre Salinger, *With Kennedy* (New York: Doubleday, 1966), 138-144. For a discussion of other presidents' concerns with overexposure, see Godfrey Hodgson, *All Things to All Men* (New York: Simon and Schuster, 1980), 188-189.

10. From a memorandum to President Carter, June 30, 1978, personal papers of Gerald Rafshoon.

11. Although systematic evidence on the size of the president's audience as a function of the number or recency of previous addresses is not now available, a cursory inspection of scattered audience rating data does not suggest a strong relationship. The series of Nielsen ratings below do show that the two largest television audiences came for Presidents Carter and Reagan in their first national address within weeks of their inauguration. Audience share and size have not otherwise varied significantly in the past 15 years.

       Figure 4-1   Yearly Average
                       Major Addresses: 9
                       Minor Addresses: 120

       Figure 4-2   Yearly Averages
                       Washington D.C. Appearances: 49
                       U.S. Appearances: 114

       Figure 4-3   Yearly Averages
                       U.S. Travel: 54 days
                       Foreign Travel: 33 days

12. Examples of such statements are Hodgson, *All Things to All Men*, and Arthur Schlesinger, Jr., *The Imperial Presidency* (Boston: Houghton Mifflin, 1973).

13. Enlisting a new technology and enlisting it well are, of course, different matters. On the problems Bush experienced in adapting to the teleconferencing format, see Michael Wines, "In Scripts for Bush, Questions on Images," *New York Times*, November 28, 1991.

14. James T. Wooten, "Pre-Inaugural Memo Urged Carter to Emphasize Style Over Substance," *New York Times*, May 4, 1977, 1.

15. Mark Hertsgaard adds that these efforts turned public opinion around on Reagan's education policies to a 2:1 favorable ratio. "How Reagan Seduced Us," *Village Voice*, September 18, 1984, 12.

16. An example of this genre is President Reagan's warm-up routine at a Jaycees convention in San Antonio the summer of 1981 while pressuring Democrats in Washington to accept his budget. To a roaring audience Reagan intoned, "Where on earth has he [Tip O'Neill] been for the last few years?" After a pause he continued, "The answer is, right in Washington, D.C." See "Reagan's Sweet Triumph," *Newsweek*, July 6, 1981, 18.

17. Newton N. Minow, John Bartlow Martin, and Lee M. Mitchell, *Presidential Television* (New York: Basic Books, 1973), 65-68.

18. Cited in George C. Edwards III, *The Public Presidency* (New York: St. Martin's Press, 1983), 75.

19. Another example of modern press treatment of presidential travel is Hedrick Smith's observation that Reagan's trip to China in the spring of 1984 was intended in part to "enhance his bid for reelection by casting himself as a negotiator for peace" ("The Road to Peking," *New York Times*, April 25, 1984, 6).

20. J. F. terHorst and Col. Ralph Albertazzie provide a lively chronology of presidential air travel in *The Flying White House* (New York: Coward, McCann, and Geoghegan, 1979).

21. Because the categories of public activity are not mutually exclusive, it is not possible to obtain comparable averages for other presidents by simply adding their appearances, travel days, and speeches.

22. "Hoover, with 37 Radio Talks in Past Year, Made a Record," *New York Times*, December 28, 1930, 1.

23. "Health of President Coolidge Conserved by Broadcasting," *New York Times*, February 24, 1924, 15.

24. Travel time during this era is nicely displayed in the isochronic map "Rates of Travel, 1930" in Charles O. Paullin, *Atlas of the Historical Geography of the United States* (Washington, D.C.: Carnegie Institution, 1932), plate 138D.

25. terHorst and Albertazzie, *Flying White House,* 33.

26. Douglass Cater, *The Fourth Branch of Government* (Boston: Houghton Mifflin, 1959), 40-42.

27. Roosevelt reportedly expressed to a friend his wish that the development of television would speed up. See Hodgson, *All Things to All Men*, 186.

28. See Samuel L. Becker, "Presidential Power: The Influence of Broadcasting," *Quarterly Journal of Speech* 47 (October 1961): 17.

29. Ibid.

30. Eisenhower spent $800,000 on television time compared with $77,000 spent by the Democratic candidate, Adlai Stevenson. See Kathleen Hall Jamieson, *Packaging the Presidency* (New York: Oxford University Press, 1984), 43.

31. Joseph Alsop and Turner Catledge, *The 168 Days* (New York: Doubleday and Co., 1938), 13-79.

32. Although as a *New York Times* commentary on earlier fireside addresses pointed out, the implications of the direct public approach in motivating Congress were clear. "His use of this new instrument of political discussion is a plain hint to Congress of a recourse which the president may employ if it proves necessary to rally support for legislation which he asks and which legislators might be reluctant to give him." Cited in Becker, "Presidential Power," 15.

33. *Memoirs by Harry S Truman: Years of Trial and Hope,* vol. 2 (Garden City, N.Y.: Doubleday and Co., 1956; reprint New York: New American Library, 1965).

34. Minow, Martin, and Mitchell, *Presidential Television,* 69-72.

35. Denis Steven Rutkus, "President Reagan, the Opposition and Access to Network Airtime" (Congressional Research Service, Washington, D.C., 1984, Mimeographed), 69-71.

36. The figures for the years 1961-1966 come from Robert Lee Baily, *An Examination of Prime Time Network Television Special Programs, 1948-1966* (New York: Arno Press, 1979), Appendix A; for the years 1967 and 1968, network program logs and secondary sources were used, and for the years 1969-1984, Denis Steven Rutkus, "President Reagan, the Opposition and Access to Network Airtime," Congressional Research Service, August 1984, Appendix C.

37. Rutkus, "President Reagan," 36-59.

38. More recently, Republicans claimed that President Jimmy Carter similarly violated established protocol. In an article in 1978, Ronald Reagan cited

Republican National Committee figures in calling for greater opportunities for opposition spokespersons. See Ronald Reagan, "Do the Networks Always Short-change the 'Loyal Opposition?' " *T.V. Guide*, March 11, 1978, 4-5.

39. Robert B. Semple, Jr., "Nixon Eludes Newsmen on Coast Trip," *New York Times*, August 3, 1970, 16.

40. Rafshoon to Carter, June 30, 1978.

41. Peter J. Boyer, "Networks Refuse to Broadcast Reagan's Plea," *New York Times*, February 3, 1988.

42. Nielsen estimates comparing audience size during presidential addresses and normal programming have found no significant differences. One study actually found that during President Ford's tenure, the audience grew slightly when he was on television. These findings are reported in Newton N. Minow and Lee M. Mitchell, "Incumbent Television: A Case of Indecent Exposure," *Annals of the American Academy of Political and Social Science* 425 (May 1976): 74-77.

43. While the 54 ratings graphed in Figure 4-5 do not represent all presidential prime-time addresses, they come close. I wish to thank Professor Joe Foote and Diane Buono at A. C. Nielsen for making available the data reported here. Various statistical tests of the change in the way Nielsen monitors viewers in the fall of 1987 did not turn up a significant effect on declining presidential audience shares.

44. This discussion is based on information provided in Joe S. Foote, *Television Access and Political Power* (New York: Praeger, 1990), 152-156.

45. See Robert A. Dahl and Charles E. Lindblom, *Politics, Economics, and Welfare* (New York: Harper and Row, 1960); and Richard E. Neustadt, *Presidential Power* (New York: John Wiley and Sons, 1980).

46. Arthur M. Schlesinger, Jr., *A Thousand Days* (Boston: Houghton Mifflin, 1965), 715. The following memorandum from Schlesinger to Kennedy, dated March 16, 1961, indicates that other members of the press were already forming similar expectations of the president.

> There is increasing concern among friends in the press about the alleged failure of the Administration to do as effective a job of public information and instruction as it should and must. Lippmann had a column about this last week. Joe Alsop has been haranguing me about this over the telephone and plans to do some columns about it soon. Lester Markel is going to do a long piece about it in the *Times Magazine*.

47. Cited in William E. Leuchtenburg, *In the Shadow of FDR* (Ithaca, N.Y.: Cornell University Press, 1985), 114.

President Reagan and His First Three Budgets ## 5

Try to imagine an individual better suited by experience, temperament, and ideology to lead by going public than Ronald Reagan. It is difficult to do so. Certainly not President Bush, who served eight years as his understudy but in office proved long on motion and short on vision. Reagan brought to the presidency ideal qualities for this new strategy of leadership, and his performance was not disappointing. When presented at critical moments with the choice to deal or to go public, he preferred to go public—sometimes exclusively, other times in combination with bargaining. The trends in direct public appeals surveyed in Chapter 4 culminated in Reagan's distinctive style of leadership, unimagined 30 years ago.

Contrary to some predictions, this outsider, this public president did not fall on his face. While his legacy is already being measured in terms of the volume of red ink it incurred, judged politically—that is, according to the accomplishment of his own programmatic goals—Reagan's record of going public proved fruitful. Political elites in Washington initially expressed surprise at the president's maneuvers—during the 97th Congress the words "shock" and "bewilderment" were recurrently attributed to Democrats in Congress—but more so at their profound effects on the behavior of fellow politicians than at the acts themselves. Nearly five years later, after the president had accumulated some political bruises that invariably come with time and his approach to leadership was no longer novel to Washington politicians, they were still paying him grudging respect. One Democratic member summed up congressional sentiment toward Reagan after five years in office: "He's still formidable, no question about that. We're still a bit afraid of him." [1]

Ronald Reagan's first three years contained all the variation in prestige and legislative accomplishment necessary to study the downside as well as the upside of public leadership. Success came early and in heaping portions, but it did not last. By the beginning of his third year, with his popularity spent, the president struggled to preserve the earlier budgetary achievements of real growth in defense expenditures, reductions in social programs, and a 25 percent cut in income taxes. Although the dollar amounts varied marginally from one budget to the next, President Reagan remained consistent, both in the substance of policies as well as the strategies he employed in their behalf. The politics that ensued in each of his first three budget seasons differed greatly, however. And yet they did so in a manner altogether consistent with the theory of individualized pluralism.

Not unlike various fairy tales with famous threesomes, "President Reagan and His First Three Budgets" is a didactic story, each episode instructive in itself as well as in its overall moral. It is worth telling here, for it fleshes out the emerging features of the modern office in a way that charts and tables cannot, however steep the trends they may depict. Before beginning, however, I need to introduce the main character.

Reagan as an Outsider

Ronald Reagan's previous career in movies, television, and public affairs groomed him well for the role of a president who goes public routinely. Movies brought him fame, a considerable resource employed by military heroes of earlier eras in transferring laterally to a public career. Reagan's early years in Hollywood contributed incidentally to his political maturation as he waged ideological war with liberals during his tenure as president of the Screen Actors Guild.[2] Later, a decade of television spent largely as spokesman first for Borax and then for General Electric gave him mastery of the requisite techniques. In his autobiography, *Where's the Rest of Me?*, Reagan described his duties for General Electric. "I know statistics are boring, but reducing eight years of tours, in which I reached all the 135 plants and personally met with 250,000 employees down to numbers, it turns out something like this: two of the years were spent traveling and with speeches sometimes running at 14 a day, I was on my feet in front of a 'mike' for about 250,000 minutes."[3] These ancillary public relations activities had him in training for the 32-round presidential primary campaign long before the reforms had been instituted. And they gave him ample opportunity to perfect his familiar criticisms of big government and his encomiums to private enterprise.[4]

In 1967, at the age of 55, Ronald Reagan embarked on a career in politics when he defeated Pat Brown for the governorship of California. Entering the public arena comparatively late in life and high on the rung of public offices also contributed to his style of leadership in the White House. If one considers a political career as a learning or developmental process where lower office not only promotes but also prepares a politician for higher office, Reagan's path to the presidency is clearly deficient. He skipped those formative experiences that take place mainly in legislatures—city councils, state assemblies, and Congress—and that expose a politician to bargaining and to compromise. Instead, as governor of California, Reagan's political tutelage occurred in peculiarly solitary yet visible environs for socialization. His tenure during years of campus unrest and Democratic legislatures gave him ample opportunity to hone his considerable rhetorical talents for the political arena. After eight years Reagan retired from office "to speak out on the issues," which meant to campaign full time for the presidency. Being a nationally syndicated columnist and radio commentator and one of the most sought-after speakers on the Republican circuit, Reagan was better positioned than anyone else to do so.

Finally, one must consider the extensive campaign experience any candidate for the presidency invariably accumulates. Ronald Reagan may have begun a public career late and held only one office before the presidency, but he nonetheless managed to contest more than 61 primary and general elections, amassing a record of 44 victories against 17 defeats. All of them were in the national limelight.[5]

Such experience prepared Reagan to be a public president as much by what it omitted as by what it included. Other twentieth-century presidents had won the office with the thinnest of claims of insight into the ways of Washington, much less of the presidency. But with the exception of Jimmy Carter, none was so bereft of such experience as Reagan. Eisenhower, avowedly apolitical, could and did point to his "invaluable," albeit brief, service in the War Department under George Marshall and subsequently as army chief of staff.[6] That Carter and Reagan should be so inexperienced is not, of course, mere coincidence. The reformed presidential nomination system coupled with lingering public memory of corruption and scandal in Washington allowed each man to convert his deprived political upbringing into a campaign asset.

Political ideology further distanced Ronald Reagan from Washington. Since his early and ardent conversion from the New Deal, Reagan has been an aggressive exponent of a traditional strain of Republican conservatism.[7] A favorite rhetorical device of his over the years was to decorate his attack of whatever Democratic policies were emanating from Washington at the moment with a simple, often folksy, statement of his own values and a caricature of Washington officials as "bureaucrats" and "spendthrift politicians." Reagan's insistent rhetoric helps to explain why on entering the White House he had accumulated an unusually large number of both intense followers and detractors.[8] As a conservative outsider moving to a city he perceived to be dominated by liberal insiders, Reagan was unsuited to be a pluralist president. Lou Cannon, a White House reporter and longtime Reagan watcher, attributes to him before he entered office a concept of the presidency that is consistent with his outsider status.

> Reagan is a modest man, but he did not object to the frequent descriptions of him as "the Great Communicator." He approvingly cited Theodore Roosevelt's description of the presidency as "a bully pulpit." With the forum of national television available to the President, Reagan was certain

that his own communicative skills were sufficient to persuade Congress and the country to do whatever it was that was asked of them.[9]

As president, a politician is subjected to a brief and intense stint of decision making. Little time is available for leisurely learning. Absent is any semblance of apprenticeship, a norm that pervades virtually all other work settings including those in Washington. Rather, the president enters office with great latitude to be the kind of politician he wants to be. His definition of the presidency derives from preconceptions grounded in experience, temperament, and ideology. In Franklin Roosevelt, a man who groomed himself to serve in the office, these qualities were so configured as to present a consummate bargainer. Roosevelt's self-concept was so pure that presidential scholars have been able to glean from his performance insights into this style of pluralist leadership. So it was with Ronald Reagan. His personal qualities combined to provide similarly pristine material for the study of going public as a strategy of leadership. What other president, can one imagine, would repeatedly insist to his Soviet counterpart that he be given television time to address the Russian people?[10]

Reagan's Three Budgets

Doonesbury's barbs about the president's laziness notwithstanding, Ronald Reagan's first three years in office were full ones. Contradicting skeptical predictions, he extracted from a Democratic House of Representatives and a narrowly Republican Senate the three major planks of his campaign platform: unprecedented budget reductions, increased military spending, and a massive three-year tax cut.[11] At the end of the first summer many observers were favorably comparing his legislative accomplishments with those of Franklin Roosevelt and the first New Deal and of Lyndon Johnson and the Great Society. The legacy of a massive national debt that this combination of policies would create was not yet fully realized.

As he accumulated an impressive string of victories during the summer of 1981, President Reagan increasingly appeared unbeatable. Liberal Democrats, at first stunned, gradually became more stoic. Many took solace in the rarely heard notion of letting the president have anything he wanted so he would be held responsible in the next election if the promised cornucopia of economic benefits failed to materialize.[12] Not until September 1981 when he proposed changes in social security benefits—which he quickly retracted—did the president's fortunes begin to turn. Even so, at the close of 1981, not even the most optimistic Democratic prognosis foresaw his political discomfiture the next year.

The second session of the 97th Congress, in 1982, gave President Reagan some legislative victories, but these pale against the triumphs of the preceding year. Real growth in military spending continued despite a swelling budget deficit and louder rumblings from Democrats.[13] Congress agreed to another round of budget reductions, but this time the administration was forced to make numerous concessions after its initial budget reconciliation resolution was defeated in the House (along with every Democratic alternative). The greatest alteration of the Reagan blueprint was the tax increase of $99 billion drafted not by House Democrats but by the Republican Senate Finance Committee. This, the largest election-year tax hike in history, triggered a curious coalitional realignment in Congress.

Because midterm elections were approaching and the economy was souring quickly, the president's control over political affairs began to slip badly. A balanced budget became an increasingly distant goal; only record deficits and double-digit unemployment were in immediate sight. The economy manifested itself politically in the president's steady decline in the polls and, in turn, in the diminished support of politicians about to stand for election. The president was no pariah, but he was no longer the local hero.

Democratic hopes and Republican fears about the changing fortunes were confirmed in the November 1982 elections; 26 House seats switched over to the Democratic column, about the margin of the president's recent floor victories. From the election until the president's State of the Union message in January 1983, the foremost question among Washington politicians and bureaucrats, including many of the White House staff, was, could the president adapt to the new, harsher political realities? The answer was no. Unwilling to compromise with the Republican Senate Budget Committee, President Reagan gave up on the budget resolution and announced his intention to veto any appropriations bills that violated his budget recommendations. The story of Reagan's first three budgets spans the peaks and valleys of leadership based on going public.

Budget Politics in 1981

The early history of President Reagan's budget and tax cuts largely comprises televised presidential addresses to the nation. The first occurred on February 5 when he announced that the country faced "the worst economic mess since the Great Depression" and presented the broad contours of an economic program that resembled the tax and budget cuts on which he had campaigned. On February 18, the president returned to prime-time television to fill in the details. Addressing a televised joint session of Congress, he unveiled a package of tax cuts totaling $53.9 billion for individuals and businesses and spending reductions of $41.4 billion for fiscal year 1982. The initial response was muted, and the popular wisdom in Washington was that success would be neither quick nor easy because of the many organized constituencies opposed to reduced spending.[14] Ten days later the White House announced that an additional $13 billion cut in expenditures would be necessary to keep the budget within the targeted deficit ceiling.

As the president's economic program began wending its way through Congress's budget labyrinth, it received critical scrutiny by the press and interested constituencies. By mid-March the president's rating in the Gallup Poll stood at 59 percent approving and 24 percent disapproving, the poorest approve-to-disapprove ratio the Gallup Poll has ever recorded for a president in his second month of office. Press Secretary James Brady explained, "The fat's gotten into the fire more quickly with this [economic] proposal than in normal administrations because of [its] comprehensive nature . . . and the fact it's changing the direction of government. There's resistance to change." [15] An independent pollster concurred: "He's spending his savings [in popularity] and he has less in the bank now, that's all." [16]

The assassination attempt in late March erased his early decline in the polls. In typical fashion the public immediately rallied to his side; Reagan's approval rating went up by 10 points or more in every national survey taken shortly after he was shot. More important, according to White House poll-watcher Richard Beal, the shooting and the president's unaided, almost nonchalant entry into the hospital, both of which were videotaped and reshown repeatedly on national television, "focussed uniquely on the President. It did a lot to endear the President to the people. . . . His personal attributes might never have come across without the assassination attempt." [17]

When Richard Wirthlin, the president's pollster, reported that the "resistance ratio" (a figure constructed from a battery of survey questions on the president's performance) to Reagan had improved from 2:1 to 3:1, presidential assistant Michael Deaver convened a strategy meeting to evaluate how this new "political capital" should be spent. Various options were aired, ranging from a radio address to a trip to Capitol Hill. Sensing the opportunity for high drama, they agreed on the latter course, a speech before a joint session of Congress. Journalist Sidney Blumenthal notes, "This decision was in keeping with overall strategy. To a greater extent than any other policy initiative, the President's economic program was being conducted as a national political campaign." [18]

To soften up potential allies before the president's appearance, Lyn Nofziger, the president's chief political aide, arranged for the Republican National Committee (RNC) to send party officials to the South over the Easter recess to stimulate grass-roots pressure on those Democratic representatives whose districts had gone heavily for Reagan in the November election.[19] By the time of his address to Congress on April 28, Reagan's surging popularity and the grass-roots campaign had created a vote deficit for the Democratic opposition. Democratic Whip Thomas Foley informed Speaker Thomas P. O'Neill, Jr., on his return from an Easter trip abroad that they were already down 50 to 60 votes. Then came the president's speech.

All news accounts depict President Reagan's reception from Congress as a love feast, which is ironic given that the audience was mostly Democrats who were well aware the president had come to advocate a starvation diet for many of the programs they had proudly enacted during the preceding decade. *Newsweek* reported, "His performance was a smash from the moment he entered the soaring House chamber, smiling and waving, to a three-minute thunderburst of whistles, huzzahs, and hand-clapping." [20] In the speech the president endorsed the Gramm-Latta budget reconciliation resolution (named for sponsors Phil Gramm and Delbert Latta), which carried the administration's proposals. He then attacked the Democratic alternative, calling it the "old and comfortable way." In closing his comments on the budget, President Reagan reminded the assembled legislators,

> When I took the oath of office, I pledged loyalty to only one special interest group—"We the people." Those people—neighbors and friends, shopkeepers and laborers, farmers and craftsmen—do not have infinite patience. As a matter of fact, some 80 years ago Teddy Roosevelt wrote these instructive words in his first message to the Congress: "The American people are slow to wrath, but when their wrath is once kindled, it burns like a consuming flame." [21]

A week after the speech and shortly before the budget's first major floor test, Speaker O'Neill could round up no more than 175 votes in opposition. A heated Democratic caucus followed in which O'Neill pleaded with fellow Democrats not to abandon the party and warned them: "The opinions of the man in the street change faster than anything in this world. Today, he does not know what is in this program, and he is influenced by a President with charisma and class [who] is a national hero. . . . But a year from now he will be saying, 'You shouldn't have voted that way.' " [22] For all his effort, O'Neill made but a single convert. Two days later, the House voted 253 to 176 to substitute Gramm-Latta for the Democratic bill and then promptly passed it by a wider margin. Fully a quarter of the House Democrats supported Reagan. "They say they're voting for it," reported Rep. Toby Moffett, a Connecticut liberal, "because they're afraid." [23]

It is one thing to support a general resolution that contains broad policy targets, and quite another to vote for the individual program cuts required to implement them. In mid-June, as the various House committees reported legislation implementing Gramm-Latta, the Reagan administration faced a difficult decision. With many of the spending measures departing sharply from the spending cuts mandated by the budget guidelines, should the president try to preserve his earlier victory through bargaining or going public? Each position was supported by a senior White House aide. Budget Director David Stockman urged the president to renew his public campaign to keep up the pressure on Democrats who had broken ranks with their party's leadership a month earlier. Chief of Staff James Baker and Communications Director David Gergen disagreed. Fearful of overtaxing public support, they advised the president to save his public strategy for his major tax initiative, Kemp-Roth, which was to come to a vote the next month. Stockman reports the argument this way: " 'We have to understand,' Baker warned Reagan, 'that we're running a very great risk here. If we throw down the challenge and lose, it'll sap our momentum.' " [24] The president was persuaded and instructed his aides to cut whatever deals were necessary to solidify his position with the boll weevils (southern Democrats) and gypsy moths (northern Republicans who did not favor cuts in social spending). Stockman recalls these transactions with disgust, blaming this decision for the failure of the Reagan revolution to cut back government while avoiding deficits: "[House Minority Leader Robert] Michel and I went straight from lunch to his office to preside over one of the most expensive sessions I have ever attended on Capitol Hill. I lost $20 billion in proposed three year budget savings in four hours.... Michel and I crammed . . . some of the worst features on the committee bills. Hour by hour I backpedaled." [25]

With mainstream House Democrats left out of the compromises, the party leadership and the House Rules Committee decided to induce second thoughts among the wayward Democrats by having the appropriations for individual programs voted on separately. By making their colleagues face up to these tough decisions, the Democratic leaders still appeared to have a chance to win.

On June 24, two days before the floor vote, President Reagan learned of this legislative maneuver while en route to San Antonio to deliver a speech. He responded with two quick public statements that made the networks' evening news on consecutive days, many phone calls to persuadable representatives, and private appeals for assistance from his business allies. According to one Reagan aide, the White House was amazed by the effectiveness of these lobbies. "Within 24 hours," he said, "one congressman had between 75 and 100 phone calls from businessmen in his district." [26] Again the president prevailed. This time by a narrow margin of 217 to 211, the full House overturned the Rules Committee's partitioning of the budget and substituted a single "up or down" vote. The House then promptly passed the president's budget by a comfortable margin of 232 to 193.

Understandably, the Democratic leaders who had just lost control over the chamber's procedures were shellshocked. Rules Committee chair Richard Bolling added Reagan to his list of "imperial presidents" along with Johnson and Nixon. Majority Leader James Wright complained bitterly that the administration was trying to "dictate every last scintilla, every last phrase" of legislation. Summing up the Democratic glum, Speaker O'Neill said, "I hope someday, this day is forgotten." [27]

Since early May, the taxation parts of the president's program had proceeded down a different institutional path. In late July, closely following his budget victory, President Reagan won his three-year, 25 percent income tax cut with the same coalition of Republicans and southern Democrats. His *modus operandi* was much the same and included a dramatic public appeal within a week of the House vote.

There were, however, some important differences in the budget and tax issues that made the president's task on the latter more difficult and, consequently, the need for a successful public strategy crucial. One problem clear to everyone was that the massive tax reductions contained in the Kemp-Roth bill (named for sponsors Jack Kemp and William Roth) would produce a huge shortfall in government revenues. Many of the southern Democrats who had favored reduced government expenditures were also committed to a balanced budget. Yet the president's plan moved the deficit in the opposite direction. Another difficulty was that as revenue legislation the tax bill had to pass through the House Ways and Means Committee chaired by Illinois Democrat Daniel Rostenkowski. Although this committee was no longer as formidable as it had once been under Wilbur Mills's leadership, it remained the chief fount of revenue legislation. Standing in the president's way was a committee run by northern Democrats who were unsympathetic to his economic philosophy and bent on protecting their prerogative to legislate tax policy.

In working with legislative sponsors to draft the Kemp-Roth bill, President Reagan agreed to the only compromise he would make during this budget session. He allowed the first-year tax cut to be reduced from 10 to 5 percent and to begin in October 1981 rather than to be retroactive to January. Both changes would reduce the growing deficit and in doing so would improve the bill's acceptability among the president's earlier congressional supporters. Unveiling the new tax package, the president announced that he would "compromise" no further.

His steadfastness was amply demonstrated in early June when he met at the White House with Democratic leaders who were clearly looking for a deal.[28] Rostenkowski began the meeting by offering Reagan the Democrats' support for a two-year tax cut. Reagan rejected it immediately stating that three years were "a matter of principle." Senate Minority Leader Robert Byrd then tried to sweeten the proposal with a full 10 percent cut the first year and a trigger clause allowing additional reductions later if economic conditions permitted. At this point the president reportedly glanced over to his counsel Edwin Meese, who shook his head, before replying with a simple "no." Next came House Majority Leader James Wright's turn. He tried a guaranteed three-year program of 5 percent tax cuts each year, but it drew hardly a response. Recognizing that a battle with the president was inevitable, Speaker O'Neill concluded the one-way negotiating session by telling him, "When you offer us a bill, we'll have an alternative. If you roll us, you roll us."[29]

The bravado with which the president rejected the Democrats' overtures is all the more impressive when one recognizes that all who attended the meeting knew that the administration did not then have sufficient votes to pass the Kemp-Roth bill. Confronted with this by a reporter after the meeting, Reagan responded, "If we don't have enough votes, we'll get them." Speaker O'Neill described the situation candidly in a nationally televised interview: "If the vote were tomorrow we could win it. Right now we have the votes. Can [Reagan] take them away from us? Let's wait and see."[30]

After the bargaining session with Reagan failed, the Democratic leadership tried to woo northern Republicans and southern Democrats with special tax concessions for constituencies in their districts. This approach, it was soon discovered, had two serious limitations. First, Rostenkowski was constrained by liberal Democrats on Ways and Means who preferred to let the president win and be held responsible. The second drawback, even more serious, was the president's willingness to match everything Rostenkowski offered. By the time the bidding ended, one embarrassed White House aide joked, "There's a good argument that we gave away the store." [31]

Advised by Wirthlin that "if push comes to shove" the public would easily side with him over Congress, President Reagan also embarked on a public strategy with several objectives.[32] Early in June, he played an important card when he told a group of southern Democrats, "I could not in good conscience campaign against any of you Democrats who have helped me." [33] This pledge quickly circulated on Capitol Hill, and within days it had received prominent press notice. With the president fully recuperated and able to be involved more personally in the campaign to pass the Kemp-Roth bill, the White House decided against another raid on southern districts. Besides, conceded a liberal Democrat, "They don't need to do it again. The point was made." [34]

In late June, Reagan traveled to Texas (the home state of a large Democratic House delegation whose support would be necessary for victory), Colorado, and California to speak for the Kemp-Roth bill and against the Democratic alternative. But these efforts proved to be only warm-up exercises. On July 27, two days before the floor vote in the House and the administration still short of victory, Reagan returned to national television. At first the network executives balked, arguing that the speech was too patently partisan, but after the Republican National Committee threatened to purchase air time, they relented and reserved rebuttal time for Democratic leaders O'Neill and Rostenkowski. With visual displays that represented the administration's savings in green and the Democrats' deficit in red, the president accused the Democrats of "sleight of hand." He conceded mockingly that a working person would fare better under the opposition's legislation but "if you're only planning to live two more years." Reagan then urged the American public to join him in lobbying Congress:

> I ask you now to put aside any feelings of frustration or helplessness about our political institutions and join me in this dramatic but responsible plan to reduce the enormous burden of federal taxation on you and your family.
> During recent months many of you have asked what can you do to help make America strong again. I urge you again to contact your senators and congressmen. Tell them of your support for this bipartisan proposal. Tell them you believe this is an unequaled opportunity to help return America to prosperity and make government again the servant of the people.[35]

Everyone in Washington who saw the speech knew that it was a blockbuster. Celebrating that evening, Treasury Secretary Donald Regan proclaimed it "a home run with the bases loaded." The only recorded reaction to be found from the normally garrulous O'Neill was one rueful word, "Devastating." These early reviews were correct; the public's reaction was swift and overwhelming. Ways and Means Democrat Richard Gephardt remarked, "The dam broke.... It fell apart." [36]

House Democrats who, before the president's speech, were either undecided or had announced support of the Democratic bill came under enormous pressure from constituents moved by Reagan's entreaty. The day after the speech, Caroll Hubbard of Kentucky received 516 calls from his district, and Norman Dicks of Washington received 400; each then changed his position and voted for the Kemp-Roth bill. Bo Ginn of Georgia was encouraged to maintain his support of the Democratic bill by Jimmy Carter, Andrew Young, and Coretta Scott King, but 600 appeals from "less famous constituents" swept him over to the president's side. Ralph Hall of Texas had made a deal with House Democratic leaders—a tax break for his district's oil industry in exchange for his support of their bill. But even Hall's pro-Reagan constituents held sway in the end, and he, too, voted in support of the president.[37]

The experiences of these Democrats appear typical. Within hours the issue was decided, as wavering representatives played it safe and went with the president. When the waters receded, Reagan had moved from an apparent defeat to a sizable victory. The closest of the key votes was 238-195. Forty-eight defections by Democrats made the difference.

Reviewing this extraordinary first session of the 97th Congress, reporter Steven V. Roberts found two basic reasons for Reagan's success: "Lawmakers believed their constituents supported that program and they were afraid that Mr. Reagan could galvanize that support through an adroit use of television and punish any dissidents at the polls." [38] Not without reason. The national polls showed strong support for Reagan as president, for increased defense spending, for elimination of waste, and for lower taxes. Supplementing these poll data in forms more compelling to representatives with close ties to their home district were the waves of mail, telegrams, and phone calls that overwhelmed Congress after each presidential address. Reagan's public appeals generated about 15 million more letters than normally flowed into congressional mailrooms each session.[39] What better testimony to the prowess of the president skilled at going public?

By the next budget season, in 1982, President Reagan's standing in Washington and the country had weakened considerably. His problems began in the fall of 1981 with a proposal to trim social security benefits that made even his own party's congressional leadership wince and stirred up an outpouring of protest from elderly voters. *Newsweek* announced in headlines, "The Runner Stumbles." [40] Quickly, President Reagan backtracked and agreed to await a report from a bipartisan commission reviewing social security. Shortly thereafter, in late September, he returned to the airwaves, this time calling for $24 billion in additional spending cuts. Sensing the president's vulnerability, Democrats were unsparing in their criticism. Many House Republicans were also annoyed—especially those who had reluctantly gone along with the deep reductions in domestic spending just two months earlier with the understanding that additional cuts would not be requested. Beyond Washington, the early responses were equally chilly. Bond prices fell sharply, and the Dow Jones industrial average plummeted 11 points to the lowest level since spring. Nor did representatives report a surge in their mail. On notice from his party's congressional leaders, the president quietly agreed to postpone the issue and reintroduce the cuts in his next year's budget.[41]

For many observers of the Reagan presidency, the social security and budget-cutting proposals of fall 1981 were the turning point. From then until after the Grenada invasion in late 1983, the president found himself dealing with Congress on its terms. An in-depth Gallup survey reveals, however, that Reagan retained much of his influence with the American public, who had served him so well in the summer.[42] Two weeks after Reagan's television address, a national survey asked, "In general are you in favor of budget cuts in addition to those approved earlier this year or are you opposed to more cuts?" More said they opposed (46 percent) further cuts than favored them (42 percent), an apparently unfavorable climate for the president's new initiative. Yet when asked specifically about the Reagan proposal three questions later, 74 percent answered that they approved the program, and only 20 percent expressed disapproval. Those who identified themselves as Democrats, a majority of whom by now were disapproving of his "job performance," gave his budget package an endorsement of 71 percent![43] Clearly, the president remained a persuasive force with a broad cross section of the American public.

There were other irritants for Congress as well. Late in the legislative year the president had surprised the leadership of both parties in Congress with a veto of a continuing appropriations bill that maintained current expenditures until the normal appropriations bills could be enacted. Of all the administration's pratfalls to occur in a season full of them, the most extraordinary was a long interview published in the *Atlantic* with David Stockman, director of the Office of Management and Budget. In it the president's chief architect of the budget laid bare and even caricatured the haphazard way the budget had been assembled.[44] Many within Congress felt betrayed; it seemed that they had been subjected to an ordeal for what appeared to be little more than a sham.

How much these incidents hurt the president and his policies in the polls is difficult to say.[45] In the fall his popularity began a descent that would continue through 1982. As for Reaganomics, Figure 5-1 shows that this neologism began to lose much of its appeal during this time. The index displayed in the figure registers the intensity as well as the direction of opinion by weighing emphatic responses twice as much. The mostly negative scores indicate that the public was never very optimistic about the personal financial rewards of Reaganomics, and by the close of 1981 was decidedly pessimistic.

Figure 5-1 Public Opinion on the Effects of Reaganomics on Personal Finances, March 1981-March 1983

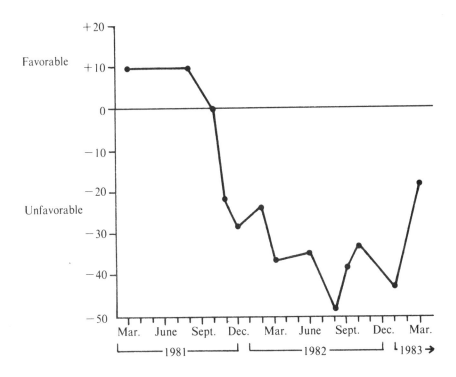

NOTE: Question: "Do you feel your financial situation will be much better, somewhat better, somewhat worse, or much worse as a result of Reagan's economic policies?" Responses are scored +2 for "much better," +1 for "somewhat better," 0 for no opinion or unsure, −1 for "somewhat worse," and −2 for "much worse." Polls were taken in March, August, October, and early and late November 1981; in February, March, June, August, September, and October 1982; and in January and March 1983.

SOURCE: *Gallup Report* 211 (April 1983): 14.

Whatever the cumulative effects of presidential retractions and subordinates' confessions, one need look no further than the economy to explain the beginning of the public's loss of confidence in Reagan and his policies. During the summer and fall of 1981 unemployment rose steadily. The projected budget deficits grew apace, in part because more unemployed workers were claiming benefits. The swelling deficits meant heavy federal borrowing in the financial markets, which contributed to historically high "real" interest rates. Completing what seemed to be a self-fueling spiral of economic deterioration, high interest rates prevented recovery in the credit-sensitive auto and construction industries, which were experiencing unemployment of nearly 20 percent. Even conservative economists joined in the growing speculation that a full-fledged depression was no longer unthinkable.[46]

Budget Politics in 1982

When the president unveiled his economic program in the spring of 1982 before the same lawmakers who had the previous year given him a rousing greeting, it was clear to everyone in the audience—if perhaps not to the man at the podium—that contrary forces of political economy were at work. All of the representatives and a third of the senators would have to stand for reelection in November; this made the president's audience all the more uneasy as he called for additional domestic spending cuts, continued growth in the defense budget, and reduced outlays for social security. Moreover, his proposal for a three-year, $55 billion increase in taxes seemed modest given the size of the deficit.

The president's budget found few takers. Republican Senator William Armstrong, a member of the Budget Committee and a Reagan supporter, declared unequivocally, "There is no chance that Reagan's budget will pass. Very few Republicans would vote for it. I know of no one." Senate Republican Whip Ted Stevens described himself in "sort of a state of shock" from the president's proposal. House Minority Leader Robert H. Michel, who would face the toughest reelection campaign of his career within six months, agreed that the proposed deficit was "mind boggling." [47] Democrats, needless to say, were just as critical and not nearly so restrained.

Because Republican unity was disintegrating, Reagan's parliamentary-like victories of the preceding session would not be repeated. As one representative said, "If anyone thinks that this is going to be a nice, neat package, with everyone jumping up and down and passing it in a few hours, well, that's not going to happen." [48] Whether President Reagan recognized this is unclear. Press reports of anxious hand wringing by the president's advisers over his blasé intransigence were mixed with those of kudos from among this same group for the astute manner with which he was preparing for future compromise.

The latter proved to be wishful thinking, for Reagan began the task of assembling a congressional coalition by following the straitlaced, strategic prescriptions of going public. In February he toured the Midwest where he employed tough language: "The budget we propose is a line drawn in dirt"; and he challenged "paid political complainers ... to put up or shut up." According to White House sources, these speeches were intended to shore up his crumbling congressional base.[49]

Although by early April several of his advisers were engaged in budget talks with party leaders of the House and Senate, the president continued to work Congress by going public. "He very much wants to regain the initiative," said a staffer. "The best way to do that in his estimation is to have him come directly to the people." [50] Accordingly, in mid-March the president planned two major television addresses for April; a switch from afternoon to evening press conferences, which he reasoned would double his television audience and prevent network newscasters from unfairly filtering his message; a series of live radio broadcasts on Saturdays in the vein of Franklin Roosevelt's fireside chats; and, finally, a heavy schedule of political travel.[51]

To White House political adviser Edward Rollins, the new offensive was necessary to get Republicans "back in line." He added, "It is imperative we put discipline back in this town." With the apparent blessing of the White House, Rollins initiated his own educational campaign. For those Republicans who expected difficulty in the fall elections and had begun "carping" at the president's policies, his message was simple: undermine the president and you will hurt yourself because "his strength and popularity will be a factor in [your] own elections." He went further. To make sure the association was appreciated, Rollins announced that neither President Reagan nor Vice-President Bush would assist any Republican who had been "blasting the hell out of the president." [52] Little did he realize that by fall, few Republican incumbents would be soliciting help from these men.

While Reagan was busy in public posturing, his lieutenants were quietly engaged in budget negotiations with the House Democratic and Senate Republican leadership. Whether the participation of the White House in the bargaining sessions indicated genuine flexibility on Reagan's part or simply reflected the stark certainty that his initial proposal did not stand a chance in Congress is difficult to say. Two conclusions, however, may be drawn from these negotiations. First, at risk of being wholly excluded from drafting the budget, the president did finally shift from his original hard-line stance. He agreed to smaller growth in defense spending, increases for social programs, and, most significant, a near doubling of new tax receipts from $55 billion to $99 billion during the next three years.

Second, though the extensive bargaining sessions failed to yield a compromise bill, they succeeded, according to White House estimates, as a public relations coup. On April 28 with reporters trailing behind, the president traveled down Pennsylvania Avenue for a summit meeting with Speaker O'Neill. As a bargaining session it went nowhere, but it did allow President Reagan to claim in an address on prime-time television the following evening that he had "gone the extra mile."

The president's speech followed a format by now familiar: black-white presentation of the issues, visual props, and an appeal for public support. Arguing that his and not the Democrats' budget was the one of moderation, Reagan departed from the standard script to describe in detail his efforts to reach a compromise.

> In yesterday afternoon's meeting on Capitol Hill, Speaker O'Neill, Senator Howard Baker, myself, and five of the Gang of 17 participated. As I say, the figures on which the group had found some agreement were far from those

we'd proposed in February. But I decided against trying to start the negotiations on the basis of that original budget.

Our original cuts totaled $101 billion. They—I can't make a big enough mark to show you [referring to a chart]—but they were rejected, believe me. Our own representatives from the Congress proposed compromising at $60 billion. Their counterparts from the Democratic side of the aisle proposed 35. In our meeting yesterday, which went on for more than 3 hours, our compromise of $60 billion was rejected—now my pen is working. And then I swallowed and had volunteered to split the difference between our 60 and their 35 and settle for 48, and that was rejected. The meeting was over.[53]

After viewing the president's address, Speaker O'Neill voiced suspicion that once again he had been set up in a public relations ploy. For a president who goes public, failure at the bargaining table may be rewarded with success in the public arena.

Once again, President Reagan closed his speech by exhorting the public to "make your voice heard." [54] Unlike the previous summer, however, this appeal was not followed by major tremors on Capitol Hill. Instead, a complex sequence of legislative maneuvers ensued over which few participants—foremost among them the president—appeared to exert much control. The Republican Senate proceeded to pass its own budget containing provisions substantially different from those Reagan had originally submitted. The president promptly endorsed it; he had little choice.[55]

In the House, Minority Leader Michel rejected the Senate version as unsalable to his Republican colleagues, many of whom were facing difficult reelections. Instead, he created a special panel to formulate a Republican alternative to the budget expected from the Budget Committee, which was controlled by Democrats. Again the president endorsed the Republican product, although this one differed significantly from the Senate version. By the time of the House floor vote, there were seven different budget proposals, none of them able to muster a majority. Two weeks later, with both parties agreeing that any budget resolution was better than none, the Republican proposal, more popular than any of the others, was passed without Democratic resistance; shortly thereafter it was reconciled with the Senate version in conference committee.

Through much of the remainder of the session, as the various committees in both chambers drafted appropriations and revenue legislation in rough accord with the provisions of the budget resolution, President Reagan kept a low profile. He traveled to Europe, vacationed on his Santa Barbara ranch, and spoke to Republican gatherings.[56] Only in late August, when it became apparent that his help would be required to line up reluctant House Republicans for a $99 billion tax hike, did President Reagan return to active duty.

By that time the tax provisions of the budget differed considerably from the president's February proposals, but Reagan embraced them as if they were his own. And well he should have. They raised substantial new revenues to close a yawning deficit while preserving his three-year, 25 percent tax cut.

Congress approached the largest election-year tax increase in history with caution befitting politicians whose jobs were in jeopardy. The posturing that resulted from calculations of political survival gave rise to an interesting configuration of alliances. Three blocs of representatives and senators were decisive to the outcome: loyal House Democrats, Senate Republicans, and House Republicans. The peculiar way in which political considerations aligned these groups in support for or in opposition to the tax increase gave President Reagan one last chance to win Congress by going public.

The Democratic leaders did not want their party blamed by the electorate for the tax hike, nor, having conceded so much to the president in the preceding 18 months, did they wish to leave themselves open for future accusations of undermining his policies. Consequently, they agreed to provide the administration the margin of victory on three conditions: (1) the legislation raising taxes would be drafted by the Republican-controlled Senate Finance Committee, and House Democrats would participate only at the conference stage; (2) a majority of House Republicans (about 100) would vote for it; and (3) indicative of the Democrats' queasiness, the president would write personal letters of appreciation to supportive Democrats, which could be used in the fall election to stave off criticism from Republican challengers.

As a group, Senate Republicans were unenthusiastic about the bill, but because of the swelling deficit, most realized they had little choice. They could vote higher taxes at that time—a year in which only 12 of their number were standing for reelection—or they could do so later, when more would be facing their constituents. Given the electoral calendar and the demand of House Democrats, the Republican Senate Finance Committee wrote the bill that the Republican Senate passed intact by a narrow margin.[57]

The political needs of the president, of Senate Republicans, and especially of House Democrats combined to create a serious dilemma for House Republicans. Because the Democrats were insisting that the Republicans be responsible for the tax increase, and because their Republican colleagues in the Senate and White House were willing to go along, many election-bound House Republicans felt they were being sacrificed to the deficit. Moreover, some of Washington's most fervent supply-siders came from the ranks of House Republicans. One was Rep. Jack Kemp, cosponsor of the Kemp-Roth bill, who immediately began to line up opposition to the unholy alliance. By late August, when the conference report was awaiting House ratification, Kemp could count on more Republican votes than could the White House. As the president began a public offensive to rally House Republicans, he had fewer than half the number of votes necessary to fulfill his end of the bargain with the Democrats. At this point Reagan's close friend Senator Paul Laxalt publicly observed, "This is the most difficult legislative challenge this President has had to face. It's tight as hell."[58]

One indicator of the difficulty facing a president who seeks to lead by going public is his popular standing across the country. Perhaps Laxalt had this fact in mind, for in mid-August a Gallup survey reported that the president's latest job performance rating stood at only 41 percent approving against 47 percent disapproving. Moreover, when questioned further about the president's economic performance, respondents were even more critical. Only 31 percent approved his handling of the economy overall, and because the unemployment rate was into double digits, only 23 percent were willing to endorse his handling of the unemployment problem.[59]

From such figures one might conclude that President Reagan's ratings were too thin to give him much chance of success. Had he been required to win substantial Democratic defections, as in the past session, such an assessment would be correct. In this instance, however, the political circumstances were tailored for victory. The president was simply trying to bring along fellow Republicans whose districts were generally believed to remain more favorably disposed to him and his policies than was the country overall. More important, because the Democrats had agreed to supply the rest, he had to pull only 100 Republican votes. The peculiar coalitional requirements of the tax bill gave the increasingly unpopular Reagan a last crack at success.

As the White House cranked up its public campaign to work its magic on the 97th Congress for the fourth time, the standard operating procedures were followed. Only the target differed. Once again the president embarked on political travel in search of telegenic and sympathetic audiences. Once again the numerous White House staffers assigned to public and congressional relations got busy. Speech writers prepared another national television address and a series of presidential commercials to be broadcast in select markets across the country by the Republican National Committee; Richard Wirthlin conducted briefings for Republican House members, explaining to them that the president's leadership image would be critical to their own success in November; and other staffers busied themselves contacting more than 5,000 business leaders across the country to stimulate yet another grass-roots campaign.[60] (More than 30,000 similar appeals were sent to local party leaders by the RNC.) To top it off, Rollins, posing threats as he had in the spring, spread the word that party campaign funds might be withheld from Republican representatives who bucked the president. After a congressional outcry, however, the White House retracted this form of coercion. By the time of the floor vote, more than 150 Republican House members had been escorted into the Oval Office or to Camp David for a friendly chat. All of these activities culminated with the president's prime-time address on August 16, in which he once again called on citizens to lobby Congress. Three days later the tax bill passed the House by a vote of 226 to 207. President Reagan had fulfilled his end of the bargain by bringing along 103 reluctant Republicans.

President Reagan exerted far less influence over the budget in 1982— both its substance and politics—than over the one in the preceding year. He gave concessions on taxes and expenditures, and by the end of the session he was championing a tax increase others had written that was nearly twice the figure he had proposed in February. In large part this change in fortune must be credited to his reduced political capital with Congress. The further he cut domestic spending, the fewer the number of natural allies that remained. Budget politics in 1982 reflected the president's decline in public opinion. High interest and unemployment rates and swelling projected deficits had sapped his popularity. All of these weaknesses were compounded in the minds of Washington politicians by the fall elections.

Still, the budgetary season was not as disastrous as these political conditions suggest. Reagan's fundamental economic policies survived. Real growth in the military budget continued, domestic spending was reduced further, and the tax increase did not touch his 25 percent cut in income taxes. In 1982 Ronald Reagan relinquished control of the legislative process to those with whom it properly belongs, but he was still able to set the agenda of Congress's budget deliberations. Although Reagan's weak popularity prevented him from producing the groundswells he had generated a year earlier, he did not shy away from publicly promoting his policies. The addition of his Saturday radio broadcasts gave him even greater occasion to go public than in 1981. On a more limited scale he continued to summon public support in his dealings with Congress. Judged by the budget politics of the next year, 1982 would appear successful indeed.

Budget Politics in 1983

The political context of any presidential action is defined by two realities: objective conditions and politicians' responses to those conditions. By the time President Reagan introduced his next budget, in 1983, both realities had become distinctly unfavorable for him. The reasons were that fewer Republicans would be returning to the 98th Congress, and the president's popularity was at a historic low.

Although the Democrats narrowly failed to improve their party's share of Senate seats, they gained a net of 26 seats in the House of Representatives, which exceeded preelection estimates of the number required to undo Reagan's coalition of Republicans and southern Democrats. A *New York Times* survey of newly elected members, including Republicans, confirmed the widespread suspicion that the new class would be decidedly less sympathetic to the president's economic policies than the members they had replaced.[61]

President Reagan's nearly continuous decline in the polls during the campaign season further aggravated the unfavorable election results. As shown in Table 5-1, Reagan had begun 1982 with almost a majority of respondents to a Gallup Poll approving his overall performance. Even then, however, there was the prospect of subsequent decline if the economy worsened. In the same survey only 41 percent endorsed Reagan's "handling of

Table 5-1   Performance Ratings of President Reagan, 1982-1983 (Percent)

Question	Jan. 1982		Aug. 1982		Nov. 1982		Dec. 1982		Jan. 1983	
	App.	Dis.	App.	Dis.	App.	Dis.	App.	Dis.	App.	Dis.
Do you approve of the way President Reagan is handling economic conditions in the country?	41	51	31	59	—	—	36	56	29	64
Do you approve or disapprove of the way Ronald Reagan is handling his job as president?										
National	49	40	41	47	43	47	41	50	37	54
East	43	46	40	49	42	51	36	57	35	55
Midwest	51	38	45	45	42	47	46	44	41	50
South	50	38	38	46	41	46	38	52	35	57
West	54	36	40	48	49	43	46	48	35	55

NOTE: App. = approve; Dis. = disapprove.

SOURCES: All data are from the Gallup Poll. Responses to the economic performance question as reported in *National Journal,* March 5, 1983, 524. Evaluations of President Reagan's overall job performance are from various issues of the *Gallup Report.*

economic conditions." During the year, unemployment climbed to a record post-depression high. Responses from a concerned public to Gallup's "most-important-problem" question shifted dramatically from inflation to unemployment.[62] At the opening of the 98th Congress, only 37 percent of the respondents registered overall approval, a figure lower than for any previous president at this stage of his first term.

Given the regional character of the president's Republican-southern Democrat coalition in the preceding Congress, the regional breakdown of his growing unpopularity is revealing. At the beginning of 1982, a majority of southerners and westerners approved his job performance; by the next year, respondents from these regions were no more supportive than respondents elsewhere. A national consensus appeared to be forming against the president.[63]

In a variety of ways, these harsh objective conditions were accentuated by politicians' strategic responses to them. During the fall congressional campaigns, Republican incumbents discovered on their own what can be seen in Figure 5-1; their association with Reaganomics was a political liability. With Democratic challengers everywhere taking up the issue, the president's Republican and boll weevil supporters found themselves forced to explain, excuse, apologize for, and in a few instances even recant their past association with these once popular policies.[64] Speaker O'Neill's prophecy of a year earlier about the fickleness of the typical voter had come to pass.

By Election Day 1982, so many Republican incumbents had become preoccupied with distancing themselves from Reagan and his economic policies that it was apparent before the first ballot was cast that the president's position in the next Congress would be weaker. Instead of the most active midterm campaign in recent history, as promised by political affairs aide Rollins in the spring of 1982, President Reagan stayed in Washington or on his Santa Barbara ranch as if sequestered there by Republican candidates. Mutual advantage dictated that he make cameo appearances in only the safest Republican districts.[65] Two weeks before the election, Rep. Guy Vander Jagt, the party's official booster and chair of the Republican National Campaign Committee, was steadfastly forecasting Republican gains in the House. Other more sober members, like House Republican Whip Trent Lott, had arrived at a different judgment. "Obviously, we won't have the same euphoria after this election we had two years ago," he told a reporter.[66]

Unfortunately, the press offers little insight into the all-important expectations of rank-and-file Republicans at the beginning of the 98th Congress. Rather, press accounts include only the comments of their leaders and of White House spokesmen about the administration's landslide victory, the better-than-expected victory, and the "moral" victory that had just occurred. Cutting through these traditional, self-serving post mortems, one may assume that instead of elation, those Republicans who were victorious sensed only relief. The 1982 midterm ended the 1980 mandate.

After the election, the boll weevils were on the move. These conservative southern Democrats who had provided President Reagan with the critical margin of victory began ambling back to the Democratic camp.[67] Rep. Buddy Roemer of Louisiana, a leader of the group and a former Reagan enthusiast, had a quick change of heart: "I don't think we need the President to write a budget," he told a reporter. Why the sudden turnaround? According to Rep. G. V. (Sonny) Montgomery of Mississippi, it was simply that the thrill of running around with the fast crowd uptown had faded.

> "There was a fascination about going to the White House," Mr. Montgomery recalled. "I was down there more in two years than in the whole 14 years I've been up here. But maybe the glamour and glitter has worn off a bit.
>
> "I think we might have gotten carried away with the White House," the Mississippian continued. "We weren't working enough with the Democratic leadership. That's the big change. We're trying to implement our philosophy through our party, not join somebody else." [68]

Although Montgomery's explanation reads more like a rationalization than a reason, it reveals that this boll weevil had returned to the ranks of his party.

The real reason, one suspects, these members gave up their apostasy can be found in the altered political circumstances. With the addition of 26 loyal Democratic members after the election, the conservative southerners no longer provided a swing vote. Even if this group voted solidly against their party, the Democratic leaders with their new 103-seat majority were generally assured victory. Consequently, confessed Representative Montgomery, "Nobody much talks to us." Another added, "Why get out there and take a bullet when you can't win anyway." [69]

Supporting the president not only was futile, and possibly injurious to their standing in the congressional party, it also had become risky at home. The midterm campaign appears to have conveyed the same messages to the boll weevils as it did to other politicians around the country. Rep. Charles Stenholm of Texas, a spokesman of the southern defectors, confessed, "We're having difficulty. There's a large amount of concern on the fairness question. The perception in the 17th District of Texas is that Reagan's program is basically unfair." [70] Testimony taken from these politicians led one reporter to conclude that the main reason for their return was "the declining support for President Reagan and his policies." [71]

It was evident early on to knowledgeable political elites in Washington that the election and the posturings of politicians had weakened President Reagan's hand with the 98th Congress. Whether it was as equally clear to the president, however, was anything but certain. As at the opening of the previous session Washington politicians were asking, did this outsider know the score? Could he adapt to the new political realities by becoming more flexible and more conciliatory toward the Democratic leadership? Such questions are appropriately asked about any president after his party has just suffered a setback; but with an outsider in the White House, especially one whose propensity to go public had been rewarded so handsomely during his first two years, these questions assumed a special poignancy.

Between the closing of the 97th Congress and the convening of the 98th, these questions were foremost among the concerns of the Washington press corps. Articles with such titles as "Midterm Malaise," "In the Event of a Presidential Power Vacuum . . . ," "The MX and Reagan's Receptivity to Compromise," and "At the Brink" proliferated in the news publications favored by those in power in Washington.[72] Nearly everyone was consulted on the matter, but nowhere did the press pry for answers more earnestly than at the White House.

The responses they received from White House insiders were as tentative and contradictory as elsewhere. No one knew how this president facing a novel situation would behave. One early prognosis, offered anonymously by a Reagan staffer, came as close to the mark as any: "He will submit a budget completely consistent with his program and philosophy, and it will probably get shot down pretty quickly." [73] Another gave a more moderate forecast that Reagan would happily agree to 75 percent of his request. A few were even more optimistic. Arguing that Reagan "has been willing to listen to people around him when they told him something would not work," one presidential adviser predicted that compromise would follow the tough proposals.[74]

With the exception of a conciliatory State of the Union address, the early signals were those of an uncompromising president who planned to spend more time in the country than at the bargaining table. The president's third budget was designed to "stay the course." Savings from additional reductions in domestic spending were to finance a 10 percent real growth in the Pentagon's budget. No major new taxes were called for, but if large deficits persisted beyond the 1985 fiscal year—and not coincidentally beyond the next election—contingency taxes were proposed.

Consistent with hanging tough on the budget, Reagan began a series of public relations maneuvers to enhance his public standing. John Herrington, an ardent Reaganite and assistant secretary of the Navy, was brought into the White House office to improve that organization's efforts in communicating his chief's positions to the American public. The president's travel budget was increased to permit more frequent trips to blue-collar constituencies with whom, his pollsters were telling him, he had experienced the greatest loss of support. Shorter, more narrowly focused news conferences were planned to give the press less opportunity to fish for negative stories.[75] A few of the president's strategists even urged him to declare his candidacy for renomination in January. This maneuver would put him on a campaign footing and "buttress his standing in current political struggles," they reasoned, adding that he could always choose not to run later.[76]

The Democratic response to the president's budget was swift and unequivocal. On March 15 after a single day of discussion, the House Budget Committee passed the Democratic leadership's budget without changing a cent. This plan differed from the president's in limiting growth of defense spending to 4 percent rather than the president's 10 percent figure, in mandating $30 billion in additional taxes during the next fiscal year, and in restoring many of the 1981-1982 cuts in social programs. Republican leader Michel labeled the Democratic bill the "Revenge on Ronald Reagan Act of 1983." [77]

With a 103-seat majority, the Democratic leadership was again firmly in control of procedures, and it exploited its prerogatives to the fullest. The Rules Committee refused a request from southern Democrats to allow amendments to the budget resolution on the floor. Rather, the House would be permitted a vote for a single Republican alternative—presumably the president's—if one were offered. Moreover, in an effort to head off intense lobbying from the White House that had preceded floor votes in the past, the leadership scheduled the vote within the week.

The president and his staff were given little time, but by all accounts they made the most of it. On March 19 at a televised, impromptu press briefing, Reagan denounced the Democratic resolution as a "dagger aimed straight at the heart of America's rebuilding program." Of the reduced growth in the Pentagon's budget, he added, "Nothing could bring greater joy to the Kremlin." He went on to characterize Democrats' domestic spending proposals as "a reckless return to the failed policies of the past." [78] And as for the resolution's provision for increased revenue, the president declared his readiness to veto any legislation that rescinded the third installment of his tax cut. The president served as the point man, while his staff got busy organizing constituent drives by the Chamber of Commerce and other business groups against targeted representatives. Though short on time, "our troops are fired up" and confident they could win, reported one White House staffer.[79]

The next day Speaker O'Neill fell under the grip of déjà vu. He told the press, "We thought we were in pretty good shape last week. Until this morning everybody was in accord." However, he continued, suddenly because the president and the Chamber of Commerce are out there beating the bushes, "the Democratic fissures were reopening." [80]

The Democratic majority, however, proved too great a hurdle for the administration. Three days later the House adopted the Budget Committee's resolution by a vote of 229 to 196. With Republicans in open disagreement among themselves over what an alternative budget should look like, none was offered. Despite a public invitation from the Rules Committee, the president's budget, remarkably, was never formally introduced in the House either in committee or in floor proceedings. Twenty-two of the conservative southern Democrats voted against the Democratic proposal, but this vote showed that their ranks had been thinned, and four northern Republicans further eroded their leverage by crossing over to support the Democratic resolution. For the first time since Ronald Reagan had entered office, the Democrats would take to conference a budget of their own making.

Undaunted, President Reagan returned to television within hours of the floor defeat. A national address had been scheduled to announce research into new forms of strategic weaponry. As forecast by aides, however, the president twice digressed from that subject to blast the Democratic budget. With an eye toward the Senate's upcoming markup of the legislation, he once again appealed to the public to demonstrate its continued support for his policies. "The choice is up to the men and women you have elected to Congress—and that means the choice is up to you." And later, "This is why I am speaking to you tonight—to urge you to tell your Senators and Congressmen that you know we must continue to restore our military strength." [81]

Indicative perhaps of the president's reduced status, the most noticeable response to the speech came not from the public but from congressional leaders. Even House Minority Leader Michel delivered a mild rebuke. Too much "overkill" and "macho image," he termed the performance. He further complained that since it deflected public attention away from House Republicans' criticisms of the Democratic budget, the speech "couldn't have come at a worse time." [82]

If the president expected more favorable treatment in the Senate, he was to be greatly disappointed. In a meeting with the Senate Budget Committee in early April, he was told by fellow Republicans that the projected deficit and continued military buildup were unacceptable. Reportedly, even the president's staff joined in urging him to compromise. He refused.

To give Reagan an opportunity to reconsider, Budget Committee chair Pete Domenici postponed his committee's markup for a week; and offering his president plenty of leeway, he told reporters that the president was simply assuming a "negotiation stance." [83] Meanwhile, Defense Secretary Caspar Weinberger was openly campaigning with President Reagan to ignore the budget process. In mid-April with no movement from the president, the Senate Budget Committee began the business of writing its own budget. What came out of markup was distinctly unfavorable to the White House: $30 billion in new taxes, an $11 billion increase in domestic spending over the president's figure, and a modest 5 percent growth in the defense budget.

As this resolution was presented on the floor, it remained unclear whether it or any budget bill could pass. In the absence of strong leadership from the White House, the Senate was divided into three distinct camps. On one side there were the Democrats who by and large were supporting the House bill; on the other side were the conservative Republicans who were prepared to stick with the uncompromising president. In the middle were the Republican moderates, including Majority Leader Howard Baker and most of the Republican members of the committee. Because the president was unable to unify his party "by rallying public support for his program ... the factions have grown bolder," reported one correspondent.[84] Pessimistic forecasts were fulfilled as the Senate rejected the committee's budget. A week later, Domenici returned with a fatter military budget and a substantial tax increase. Although Reagan was hardly enthusiastic and the Democrats were calling the new budget "rinky-dink," it passed by a single vote after 11 ballots.

As the conference committee negotiations were reported daily in the press, Reagan distanced himself ever farther from the budgetary process. When the brokered budget finally passed Congress in late June, the president had retreated to threats of a veto of any appropriations bills that violated his own earlier proposal. When questioned by a reporter on the wisdom of such a course, one senior White House official replied, "I just don't know what we have to gain from playing the budget game with Congress this year." He continued saying that having shown he could work with Congress over the past two years, President Reagan could now "afford to be more confrontational." Pressed further, the official conceded that the administration would likely get the "short end of the stick" on defense spending because opinion polls were not supportive. But on social spending and taxes, he insisted, "Those are the issues he [the President] can go to the people on every time." [85]

With the tax cut in place and the budget growing now from a smaller base, the president stepped back from the budget process. By the close of the 1983 budget season, President Reagan had assumed a defensive posture, threatening vetoes and promising public appeals at least on those issues where even an unpopular president might be able to elicit a favorable public response.

Going Public and Leadership: The Lessons of Reagan's Budgets

President Reagan may have radically altered the strategic routines of presidential leadership, but initially these changes did not disturb the routines of the Washington press in reporting on his performance. Accustomed to explaining presidential success by digging beneath the surface and ferreting out quiet compromises and discrete logrolling, the press was especially diligent in these activities in 1981. After all, a great deal needed to be explained. For their efforts they uncovered a few truffles. A story on Rep. Lawrence DeNardis's swap of budget support for renovation of the New Haven train depot was typical. Other commodities traded during the session included sugar price supports, restoration of some energy subsidies for the poor, more funds than originally budgeted for Medicaid, and a slowdown of the conversion of industrial boilers to coal in oil-producing states.[86] Even more heavily reported were various photo sessions at the White House and the liberal distribution of such patronage as theater tickets and special $4.40 cufflinks to representatives who voted with the president.[87] As indications of President Reagan's leadership strategy, however, all of these minor deals and presidential gifts pale in significance when placed next to the meeting in 1981 with Democratic leaders when he rejected their entreaties to compromise even while he was still short of votes.

Reagan's record as a president who preferred going public to bargaining remained virtually unblemished. On a few occasions, however, a public appeal would be accompanied with minor, face-saving concessions or side payments to fence-sitters. The bidding war with Rostenkowski for stray votes on the tax cut in 1981 offers the most prominent and substantial examples of such payments. When one considers that it was a game initiated by the Democrats and, as far as one can tell, was unanticipated by the White House, the bidding war appears more an unhappy outcome of failure to accept the generous overtures of the Democratic leaders than a planned strategy of coalition building.

One might even be tempted to find pluralist flexibility in Reagan's acceptance of the $99 billion tax hike the next year. However, the summer's sharply rising deficit projections that had so altered the fiscal environment and the public enthusiasm with which he ultimately embraced this legislation rather than try to split the difference with his original proposal suggest that the president's change of position was more a conversion than a political compromise. In accepting higher new taxes, more social spending, and less for defense than he had originally sought, President Reagan conducted himself less as a skilled bargainer than as a president who, having lost his leverage, was forced to accept more or less what others served up. Even in these episodes, he demonstrated a greater flair for going public than for negotiation.

He would continue to do so in his second term. After his huge victory over Walter Mondale in November 1984, a Reagan aide announced that the president would "take advantage" of his mandate and soon tour the country "to sell this budget package. . . . We have to look at it, in many ways, like a campaign. He wants to take his case to the people." [88]

Dependence of Policy on Popularity

Undeniably, going public rewarded the president handsomely in his dealings with Congress while he remained popular. During the first session of the 97th Congress the president achieved rare mastery over both policy and the legislative process, the likes of which had not occurred since Lyndon Johnson had enjoyed a surfeit of liberal Democrats in both chambers nearly two decades earlier. True to his campaign pledge, Reagan managed to slash domestic spending, boost the Pentagon's budget, and cut taxes.

The second budget, which sought to continue or to preserve the gains of the first, was not nearly as successful. In the spring of 1982 with his popularity in steep descent and the deficit and unemployment increasing with each new report, President Reagan found his messages less inspiring to Congress and the country. His leadership style precluded resorting to pluralist methods to continue his mastery of Congress; instead, he left Washington and budget policies to others. When called upon to cast a public appeal for a tax increase—one not of his making—President Reagan still managed to provide the margin of difference at a key moment.

Largely as a consequence of his diminished popularity, Reagan's majority coalition departed in the fall 1982 election. By the beginning of the third budget season, his popularity was still down. White House staffers were wondering aloud whether the president would even be allowed to participate in the game. His budget was delivered stillborn, never to be introduced on the floor of either chamber. When the Republican Senate insisted on reduced military spending and new taxes, Reagan gave up the budget fight and announced repeatedly that he would veto appropriations bills to defeat the "credit card Congress." Fearing a street fight with the president before public opinion, the House leadership reduced its spending bills to bring them more in line with the president's initial requests. Yet in 1983, the budget was made by Congress.

From late 1982 on, the White House gradually redirected its campaign from generating public support for the president's policies to support for the president himself. By the summer of 1983, many political elites subscribed to the view that Reagan was prepared to sacrifice his budget to gain an issue for the next election a full year and a half away.[89] The polls show little evidence that the concerted efforts to alter public evaluations of the president's performance met with much success. A resurgence in the polls did finally occur, but only after the economy began to rebound in the fall of 1983—too late to help him with the budget.

One lesson of Reagan's record, therefore, is that the public president may perform better in the "expenditure," or transference, of popular support than in its resupply. Individualized pluralism helps to explain why he performs well in using his public support, but as a model of Washington politics, it is silent on the subject of what an unpopular president should do to restore the public's confidence. The supply of popular support rests on opinion dynamics over which the president may exercise little direct control. This is not to say that the president will not try to improve the public's estimate of him. Given who public presidents are, one suspects the temptation for self-promotion will be irresistible.

Governing as Campaigning

Whether in exploiting favorable conditions to advance policy goals or in attempting to improve the incumbent's prestige, the strategic prescriptions of going public put the office on a campaign footing. Governing, according to a Reagan staffer, amounts to little more than an extension of the campaign that brought him into office. In early 1983 aides were urging him to announce his candidacy for reelection to strengthen his hand in Congress.

President Reagan's conduct of office closely resembled his campaign for it. Both entailed heavy political travel, numerous appearances before organized constituencies, and extensive use of television—even paid commercials during nonelection periods. Moreover, both campaigning and governing required systematic planning and extensive organizational coordination. Each major television appeal by President Reagan on the eve of a critical budget vote in Congress was preceded by weeks of preparatory work. Polls were taken; speeches incorporating the resulting insights were drafted; the press was briefed, either directly or via leaks. Meanwhile in the field, the ultimate recipients of the president's message, members of Congress, were softened up by presidential travel into their states and districts and by grass-roots lobbying campaigns, initiated and orchestrated by the White House but including the RNC and sympathetic business organizations. After describing some of these routines of Reagan's staff, Sidney Blumenthal draws the parallel between campaigning and governing.

> Once elected, candidates have to deal with shaky coalitions held together by momentary moods, not stable party structures. They then must try to govern through permanent campaigns. This is something more than the selling of the President—even of a telegenic President able to project an attractive image. It has become an inescapable necessity for Reagan, and probably for his successors.
>
> The President's strategists are at the center of the new political age. At the end of the day, they become spectators, seeing their performance tested by the contents of the television news programs. For the Reagan White House, every night is election night on television.[90]

As presidential governance has assumed the form of a campaign, the White House office has added trappings of a campaign organization. The available evidence indicates that Reagan's transition advisers appreciated the organizational imperatives of the public president. Although their fees were to be paid by the Republican National Committee, pollsters Richard Wirthlin and Robert Teeter were made proximate and frequent counselors to the president. Initially, the position of press secretary was downgraded to make room for an expanded Office of Communications, which was given a broad mandate to plan and coordinate all public affairs activities for the White House and executive agencies.[91]

With this office taking care of public relations, a smaller political affairs office transacted more partisan business. In addition to traditional White House political activities, such as monitoring gossip and polls and advising the president, its mandate was also to exercise the administration's political muscle. Patronage and campaign support from a variety of sources flowed to members of Congress through this office, headed for most of this period by Edward Rollins. Testimony to the office's integral role can be found in a comment by Rollins's deputy, Lee Atwater: "This shop is a new venture. I don't think the White House has ever had one before, but I think that every White House from now on will have one." [92]

Finally, as governing becomes campaigning, policy serves rhetoric. Rather than the substance of detailed scrutiny and negotiations, policy questions become overly simplified and stylized to satisfy the cognitive requirements of a largely inattentive national audience. Positions, publicly proclaimed, become fixed; intransigence among elites sets in. President Reagan's declaration before a midwestern audience that his 1982 budget was "a line drawn in dirt" is typical of what happens when partisan discussion flows through public channels.[93]

By any standard, Ronald Reagan and his three budgets constitute an extraordinary story. Extraordinary because no president in recent memory established such a presence as did Reagan vis-à-vis the 97th Congress. Extraordinary, moreover, because no president managed to exhaust his popular support so thoroughly by his first midterm election as did Reagan. And finally, extraordinary in retrospect because within a year of the budget vote in 1983, the president entered his reelection campaign generally conceded to be unbeatable and went on to amass one of the greatest landslides of this century.

These extraordinary swings in policy success and popularity reflect the volatility of a marketplace whose currency of exchange increasingly is public opinion. As exceptional as the Great Communicator's record appears today, there is good reason to suspect that it harbingers things to come. If individualized pluralism is indeed ascendant, an era of presidents who routinely go public is at hand. President Reagan's "peculiar" performance will cast a long shadow, not unlike that of Franklin Roosevelt's, against which the performance of future presidents will be judged.

Notes

1. Steven V. Roberts, "Reagan and Congress: Key Tests Ahead," *New York Times,* June 16, 1985. 14.

2. Lou Cannon, *Reagan* (New York: G. P. Putnam's Sons, 1982), 319.

3. Ronald Reagan, with Richard G. Hubler, *Where's the Rest of Me?* (New York: Duell, Sloan, and Pearce, 1965), 257.

4. Leslie H. Gelb, "The Mind of the President," *New York Times Magazine,* October 6, 1985, 4-5.

5. Reagan contested 4 gubernatorial primary and general elections and 57 presidential primaries in the 1976 and 1980 presidential elections. Richard M. Scammon and Alice V. McGillivray, *America Votes 14: A Handbook of Contemporary American Election Statistics* (Washington, D.C.: Congressional Quarterly Inc., 1980), 27-37.

6. Fred I. Greenstein attaches great significance to Eisenhower's Washington experience in arguing that his style in office, including his image among Washingtonians as a "bumbler," was actually an adroit strategic device to disarm potential adversaries and deflect responsibility. *The Hidden-Hand Presidency* (New York: Basic Books, 1982), chaps. 2, 3.

7. Reagan's rhetoric over the years portrays such consistency, as well as conviction, that his record refutes the "selling of the president" myth, which holds that television packaging requires plastic candidates whose issue positions can be molded by advertising executives guided by marketing surveys. A best-selling example of this genre is Joe McGinnis, *The Selling of the President* (New York: Trident Press, 1969).

8. "Reagan Popularity below Predecessors'," *Gallup Report* 186 (March 1981): 2-9.

9. Cannon, *Reagan*, 319.

10. Bernard Weinraub, "Reagan Wants to Voice Views on Russian TV," *New York Times,* September 4, 1985, A1.

11. There were other, equally impressive victories as well. When Reagan learned that a resolution vetoing the administration's planned sale of AWACS planes to Saudi Arabia had garnered a majority of the Senate as cosponsors, he went into action. In a brief flurry of phone calls, meetings in the Oval Office, and public pronouncements, he unraveled the coalition and salvaged the sale.

12. Peter Goldman, "The Reagan Steamroller," *Newsweek,* May 18, 1981, 40. Some became downright monastic. By summer, Mondale had publicly embarked on a retreat to contemplate the country's needs.

13. Notable among defense issues was the MX missile program, which was greatly scaled down yet spared from what at moments appeared to be its certain demise.

14. Lynn Rosellini, "Lobbyists' Row All Alert for Chance at the Budget," *New York Times,* February 26, 1981, 9.

15. George Skelton, "Reagan Dip in Poll Tied to Spending Cuts," *Los Angeles Times,* March 19, 1981, 6.

16. Ibid.

17. Sidney Blumenthal, "Marketing the President," *New York Times Magazine,* September 13, 1981, 111. Much of the subsequent material on the budget cut comes from Blumenthal and from Elizabeth Drew, "A Reporter in Washington," *New Yorker,* June 8, 1981, 138-142.

18. Blumenthal, "Marketing the President," 112.

19. Party officials were also sent to Ohio where Republican representatives were reportedly wavering. Drew, "Reporter in Washington," 138-142.

20. David M. Alpern, "The Second Hundred Days," *Newsweek,* May 11, 1981, 23.

Time reported that on "only a few occasions had a President enjoyed such a shouting, clapping, emotional reception from the assembled law-makers" (Ed Magnuson, "Reagan's Budget Battle," *Time,* May 11, 1981, 16).

21. "President Reagan's April Address on Economy," in *Reagan's First Year* (Washington, D.C.: Congressional Quarterly Inc., 1982), 118-119.

22. Goldman, "The Reagan Steamroller," 39.

23. Ibid. In an effort to downplay Reagan's public leadership, some scholars have searched for evidence of bargaining. And in fairness they have found important instances that went undetected in this book's first edition. However, on the passage of the Gramm-Latta budget resolution, signs of bargaining are quite thin. Some have said that agreeing to allow Phil Gramm, Democratic representative (soon to be Republican senator), to be the chief sponsor of the administration budget proposal was a major concession—a bargain if you will. But citing decisions that will give members of Congress credit for "carrying the president's water" strike me as dubious evidence of bargaining. The second "bargain" takes the form of President Reagan's assurances to individual members of Congress that some of the proposed cuts would later be reopened for discussion, and implicitly negotiation, if they supported the president's targets in the Gramm-Latta guidelines. Here, too, the president made no substantive concessions in return for a budget resolution vote. Such claims of bargaining demeans the concept. Marc A. Bodnick overstates the significance of these transactions in " 'Going Public' Reconsidered: Reagan's 1981 Tax and Budget Cuts, and Revisionist Theories of Presidential Power," *Congress and the Presidency* 17 (Spring 1990), 13-28.

24. David Stockman, *The Triumph of Politics* (New York: Avon, 1986), 211-212.

25. Ibid., 214.

26. Blumenthal, "Marketing the President," 112.

27. Peter Goldman, "Reagan's Sweet Triumph," *Newsweek,* July 6, 1981, 20.

28. This meeting between Reagan and five Democratic leaders is described in Peter Goldman, "Tax Cuts: Reagan Digs In," *Newsweek,* June 15, 1981, 26-27; and George J. Church, "He'll Do It His Way," *Time,* June 15, 1981, 10-12.

29. Goldman, "Tax Cuts," 25. Because reporters had gathered outside to receive the visibly glum Democrats, O'Neill may have been justified in his suspicions that they had been set up by the president for a media event.

30. Irwin B. Arieff, "Conservative Southerners Are Enjoying Their Wooing as Key to Tax Bill Success," *Congressional Quarterly Weekly Report,* June 13, 1981, 1024.

31. Peter Goldman, "Rest in Peace, New Deal," *Newsweek,* August 10, 1981, 17.

32. Wirthlin likely based such an assessment on poll results that gave the GOP almost as many identifiers as Democrats and that showed more than two-thirds of the respondents approving of Congress's earlier vote on the Gramm-Latta budget resolution. Elizabeth Wehr, "Reagan May Try to Block August Recess ... If Work Unfinished on Tax Cut Measure," *Congressional Quarterly Weekly Report,* June 27, 1981, 1134-1135.

33. Goldman, "Tax Cuts," 27.

34. Wehr, "Reagan May Try," 1135.

35. "Reagan's TV Address on Tax Bill," in *Reagan's First Year,* 122-124.

36. Goldman, "Rest in Peace," 16-20.

37. Ibid.

38. Steven V. Roberts, "President's Coalition," *New York Times,* October 27, 1982, 13. For another case study of the politics of the 1981 budget, see Allen Schick, "How the Budget Was Won and Lost," in *President and Congress,* ed. Norman J. Ornstein (Washington, D.C.: American Enterprise Institute, 1982), 14-43.

39. The 15 million figure was calculated by subtracting the total mailings (letter-sized

and larger envelopes) in 1980 from those in 1981. The source for these figures is Norman J. Ornstein et al., *Vital Statistics on Congress, 1982* (Washington, D.C.: American Enterprise Institute, 1982), 141. The 1984-1985 edition of *Vital Statistics* notes that mailings the next year returned to the 1980 levels, but fails to provide the data. Norman J. Ornstein et al., *Vital Statistics on Congress, 1984-1985 Edition* (Washington, D.C.: American Enterprise Institute, 1984), 142.

40. David M. Alpern, "The Runner Stumbles," *Newsweek*, September 28, 1982, 26-27.

41. For the standard journalistic treatment of this event, see Tom Morganthau, "Running to Stay in Place," *Newsweek*, October 5, 1981, 24; and Walter Isaacson, "Rough Waters Ahead," *Time*, October 5, 1981, 8-11.

42. The data used in the following analysis came from the American Institute of Public Opinion, Survey No. 183-G, October 2-5, 1981. The overall results are described in the *Gallup Opinion Index* (November 1981): 3-8. For a more detailed examination of this survey, see Samuel Kernell, "The Presidency and the People: The Modern Paradox," in *The Presidency and the Political System*, ed. Michael Nelson (Washington, D.C.: CQ Press, 1984), 250-253.

43. The question was worded: "To reduce the size of the 1982 budget deficiency, President Reagan has proposed cutting $13 billion in addition to the $35 billion in cuts approved earlier this year. About $11 billion of the new cuts would come from social programs and about $2 billion from defense programs. In general, would you say you approve or disapprove of the President's proposal?" (*Gallup Opinion Index*, 6).

44. William Greider, "The Education of David Stockman," *Atlantic*, December 1981, 32-43.

45. When a Gallup Poll in mid-November asked respondents if they had heard or read "about the situation in Washington involving David Stockman," 66 percent answered affirmatively. When these informed respondents were asked if it made them more or less confident in Reaganomics, 34 percent said less confident, 9 percent said more confident, and 53 percent said it had not changed their opinion. *Gallup Report* 194 (November 1981): 15.

46. Alan Greenspan, who chaired the Council of Economic Advisers under President Gerald Ford, was quoted as saying, "This scenario [of depression] still has a low probability, but it should no longer be put into the bizarre or kooky category" (George J. Church, "A Season of Scare Talk," *Time*, March 15, 1982, 12).

47. Ed Magnuson, "A Line Drawn in Dirt," *Time*, February 22, 1982, 12.

48. Ed Magnuson, "Stumbling to a Showdown," *Time*, April 26, 1982, 12.

49. Magnuson, "A Line Drawn in Dirt," 12.

50. Howell Raines, "Reagan's Gamble: Bid for Popularity," *New York Times*, March 31, 1982, A27.

51. Ibid.

52. Jack Nelson, "Administration Seeks to Stem GOP 'Potshots' against Reagan," *Los Angeles Times*, April 14, 1982, 14. Shortly thereafter, Rollins retracted the threat, but said such members of Congress would have low priority for White House assistance. Lee Atwater, Rollins's assistant, pedaled a softer line. "We'll never ask a member to vote against his own political interest, but we sure will . . . try to show them that it may be in their interest to support the President," he told reporter Dick Kirschten. See "Reagan's Political Chief Rollins," *National Journal*, June 12, 1982, 1054-1057. For congressional testimony to threats, see Jack Nelson, "President's 'Bad-Boy' List Aims for Republican Unity," *Los Angeles Times*, May 23, 1982, I1.

53. "Fiscal Year 1983 Federal Budget," *Weekly Compilation of Presidential Docu-*

ments 18 (May 3, 1982): 545-549. Speaker O'Neill and Rules Committee chair Richard Bolling disputed the president's rendition of the negotiating sessions; they claimed instead that both sets of figures used by the president were Republican in origin. "They rigged the sheet of paper we were working from," said Bolling. "This is a case where they split the difference between their figure and their figure" (Dale Tate, "Budget Battle Erupts on Hill as Compromise Talks Fizzle," *Congressional Quarterly Weekly Report,* May 1, 1982, 967-969).

54. He continued, "Let your representatives know that you support the kind of fair, effective approach I have outlined for you tonight. Let them know you stand behind our recovery program. You did it once, you can do it again. Thank you, and God bless you" ("Fiscal Year 1983 Federal Budget," 549).

55. Sen. Ernest Hollings and Sen. Daniel P. Moynihan, both Budget Committee Democrats, pressed Republican chair Pete Domenici for a vote on the president's original budget. He refused, responding, "We don't have to be subtle. The President's budget will not pass" (Tate, "Budget Battle Erupts on Hill," 968).

56. Shortly before the president's trip to Europe, two White House aides confided their anticipation to Elizabeth Drew. They "talked openly about the political fruits of the television spectacular, and the picture of the President as a leader." One said, "It's going to be great theater" (Elizabeth Drew, "A Reporter in Washington, D.C." *New Yorker,* June 21, 1982, 97). See also Karen Elliot House and Alan L. Otten, "White House Hopes Summit Will Enhance the President's Stature," *Wall Street Journal,* May 28, 1982, 1. Wirthlin would later claim that the trip improved Reagan's job performance rating the next month. "Pollster Finds a 'Pool of Patience' with Reagan Economics Program," *New York Times,* July 31, 1982, 8. See also Jack Nelson, "Public Still Patient with Reaganomics, Poll Finds," *Los Angeles Times,* July 31, 1982, 1.

57. Martin Tolchin anticipated the inherently conflicting budget considerations six months earlier in "G.O.P. Clocks Differ on Timing of Budget Moves," *New York Times,* November 12, 1981, 26.

58 Ed Magnuson, "Reagan Says All Aboard," *Time,* August 23, 1982, 7.

59. "Gallup Survey Finds Approval of Reagan at Its Lowest Point," *New York Times,* August 19, 1982, 14.

60. A defeat on the tax bill, he told them, "would make the President look weak and damage the party's candidates across the board." The record is unclear on the success of this argument with the House Republicans, but it certainly caught the attention of the press, which depicted Reagan's "leadership" on the line with this vote. For examples of the press buildup, see Howell Raines, "Leadership Image Risked," *New York Times,* August 17, 1982, 1; and Hedrick Smith, "Reagan's Big Victory," *New York Times,* August 20, 1982, D14. In an earlier article Howell Raines reported Wirthlin's lobbying activities, "Reagan Runs a Reverse, Collides with Right Wing," *New York Times,* August 15, 1982, E4.

61. Hedrick Smith, "New House to Back Reagan Less, Poll Shows," *New York Times,* November 4, 1982, E4.

62. The relative importance of unemployment and inflation as "the most important problem" is charted for the years 1977-1983 in *National Journal,* February 19, 1983, 401.

63. The CBS News/*New York Times* survey revealed an equally sharp decline in Reagan's support at the close of 1982. See Howell Raines, "Reagan's Policies Lose Favor in Poll," *New York Times,* January 25, 1983, 1.

64. Hedrick Smith, "Now Democrats Attacking President," *New York Times,* September 18, 1982; David S. Broder, "GOP Will Be Hurt, Both Parties Agree," *Washington Post,* October 19, 1982, A1.

65. This did not keep the president off national television, however. On October 14, 1982, he rejected Democratic criticisms and appealed to the American public to stay the course.

66. Roberts, "President's Coalition," 13. Even in the Senate where the Republicans staved off strong Democratic challenges, the message of the elections was clear. Because 19 Republican incumbents were facing reelection in 1984, Republican senator William Cohen of Maine predicted, "The Senate is going to be more independent next year" (Walter Isaacson, "Trimming the Sails," *Time,* November 15, 1982, 16). For an assessment of the reasons Republicans lost fewer House seats than widely predicted by various statistical models of the relation between economic conditions and the congressional vote, see Gary C. Jacobson and Samuel Kernell, *Strategy and Choice in Congressional Elections,* 2d ed. (New Haven: Yale University Press, 1983), 94-110.

67. All except one. The former head of the boll weevils, Rep. Phil Gramm of Texas, lost his committee assignment because of his collusion with Republicans and shortly thereafter changed parties.

68. Steven V. Roberts, "The Eclipse of the Boll Weevils," *New York Times,* March 26, 1983, 10.

69. Ibid.

70. Ibid. Montgomery's message from his Mississippi constituents parallels that of Stenholm: "People in my district used to say, 'support the President.' Now I'm not hearing that much."

71. Roberts, "President's Coalition," 13.

72. Rich Jaroslovsky, "Reagan's 'Revolution' Stalls as Policies Falter Both Here and Abroad," *Wall Street Journal,* December 23, 1983, 1; Leslie Gelb, "In the Event of a Power Vacuum . . . ," *New York Times,* February 23, 1983, 12; Hedrick Smith, "The MX and Reagan's Receptivity to Compromise," *New York Times,* December 16, 1982, B16; "At the Brink" is the front cover title of the *National Journal,* March 5, 1983.

73. Isaacson, "Trimming the Sails," 16.

74. Hedrick Smith, "Reagan at Midterm," *New York Times,* December 29, 1982, 1; and Smith, "The MX," B16.

75. Francis X. Clines, "An Outsider (Soon to Be an Insider) Stirs Concern," *New York Times,* February 4, 1983, 8; and Juan Williams, "Presidential Newsmaking," *Washington Post,* February 13, 1983, A18. Another tactic was to have President Reagan tape a brief statement for the nightly news whenever some economic index became favorable. See Jonathan Fuerbringer, "Good News Often Brings More News," *New York Times,* February 21, 1983, 10. See also Dick Kirschten, "Distributing Poll Data Prompting White House to Woo Alienated Voting Blocs," *National Journal,* March 5, 1983, 488-492.

76. *Wall Street Journal,* January 14, 1983, 1.

77. Edward Cowan, "Democratic Budget Is Adopted by House, 229-196," *New York Times,* March 24, 1983, 1. For a detailed breakdown of the differences between Reagan's and the Democrats' budgets, see "Two Budget Plans with Little in Common," *National Journal,* March 26, 1983, 670.

78. Juan Williams and Helen Dewar, "President Assails House Democrats' '84 Budget Plan," *Washington Post,* March 19, 1983, A1.

79. Ibid.

80. Dennis Farney, "House Democrats Waver on 1984 Budget, Leaders Concede, after Reagan Criticisms," *Wall Street Journal,* March 22, 1983, 2.

81. "President's Speech," *New York Times,* March 24, 1983, 8.

82. Steven V. Roberts, "Bill to Make Jobs Gets Final Assent," *New York Times,* March 25, 1983, 9.
83. Martin Tolchin, "Budget Process in Peril?" *New York Times,* April 16, 1983, 5.
84. Steven V. Roberts, "The Budget Victim: G.O.P. Senate Coalition Unravels," *New York Times,* May 7, 1983, 7.
85. Steven R. Weisman, "Turning Point on Budget," *New York Times,* June 22, 1983, D23.
86. In another instance cited in the press, some Florida lawmakers, disturbed by the rising crime rate in their state, sought and won an exemption of the 4 percent cut in federal law enforcement funds. Steven V. Roberts, "How Reagan Won in Congress," *New York Times,* December 30, 1982, 11; Hedrick Smith, "Taking Charge of Congress," *New York Times Magazine,* August 9, 1981, 17.
87. Taking a broader view of the marketplace, Alistair Cooke inferred meaning from the two-way traffic along Pennsylvania Avenue. By his counting, the president conducted 69 meetings with more than 400 members of Congress, which Cooke cites as indicative of a president who shed the uncompromising campaign rhetoric and quickly learned to behave like a "political veteran" reminiscent of Lyndon Johnson. Cooke even discerned parliamentary-like relations in these traffic patterns. "Getting the Hang of It," *New Yorker,* March 14, 1983, 148-153.
88. Bernard Weinraub, "Reagan Sets Tone of Nation to Seek Economic Victory," *New York Times,* January 25, 1985, 1. President Reagan hinted that he would pursue such a course the day after the election when he told reporters in Los Angeles that he would take his case "to the people" to force congressional cooperation. Jack Nelson, "Reagan Vows to Extend Conservative Agenda," *Los Angeles Times,* November 8, 1984, 1.
89. Hedrick Smith, "Budget Maneuvers: Prime Concern Is '84 Election," *New York Times,* May 11, 1983, 9; Steven R. Weisman, "Budget Tie-Up: Reagan at the Crossroads," *New York Times,* April 20, 1983, A21; and Steven V. Roberts, "Conferees and the Budget," *New York Times,* June 20, 1983, 9.
90. Blumenthal, "Marketing the President," 114.
91. Dick Kirschten, "Life in the White House Fish Bowl—Brady Takes Charge as Press Chief," *National Journal,* January 31, 1981, 180-183.
92. Dick Kirschten, "Reagan's Political Chief Rollins: 'We Will Help Our Friends First,'" *National Journal,* June 12, 1982, 1057. See also Francis X. Clines, "Propaganda, Propagation or Just Prop," *New York Times,* June 15, 1984, A16.
93. Magnuson, "A Line Drawn in Dirt." In early April 1984, President Reagan's difficulties with Congress reached a breaking point. At a nationally televised news conference the president attacked Congress on many fronts—from aid to El Salvador to Congressional Budget Office figures. With the exception of House Republican Whip Trent Lott, Democratic and Republican leaders of both chambers took umbrage. "I want to help him," House Minority Leader Michel said of the president, "but if in the process you get torpedoed without warning, I don't appreciate that. It's always one step forward and two steps backward." A Republican Senate aide summed up the common assessment: "The President is banking on the fact that the support he needs is there in the boonies. He ran against Congress in 1980, and I assume he'll run against this body again" (Steven V. Roberts, "Pointing Fingers: Lawmakers Reply to Reagan," *New York Times,* April 11, 1984, 10). For a report of President Reagan's speech, see Francis X. Clines, "Reagan Attacks Congress' Role on Many Fronts," *New York Times,* April 5, 1984, 1.

Opinion Leadership and Foreign Affairs 6

On the evening of September 17, 1991, a discouraged Secretary of State James Baker boarded a flight from Jerusalem to Cairo, the next leg of what was then his latest effort at shuttle diplomacy. Unusually blunt statements had been issued at the close of his meeting with Prime Minister Yitzhak Shamir. Baker had not only failed to alter Israel's program of new settlements in the disputed occupied territories but had also come under renewed pressure to provide Israel with $10 billion in U.S. loan guarantees for housing recent Soviet emigrants.

Shamir believed his position was just on both issues, as did the majority of Israeli citizens, who consistently endorsed his stance in national opinion polls. His bluntness with the American emissary was probably inspired to a greater extent by his similarly strong support in the United States. Close to a majority of members of Congress were committed to sponsoring the enabling legislation for the loan guarantees when President Bush announced that, despite the "1,000 lobbyists" supporting the guarantees on Capitol Hill, he would veto any such legislation so long as Israel refused to freeze new settlements.

No president since Eisenhower had publicly issued such an indelicate rebuke to Israel. Supporters of the aid package claimed that the intemperate character of the president's rhetoric alarmed them as much as the veto threat. Politicians everywhere started making political calculations. Jewish groups were quick to express outrage. California Senate candidate Diane Feinstein represented the class of 1992 Democratic hopefuls when she called a press conference to label the president's position "reprehensible." Republicans made a similar political assessment. "I'm catching hell from the party," President Bush told a friend. "They're afraid we could lose some Senate seats out of this." [1]

Next came the Israelis. Foreign Minister David Levy's remarks seemed more threatening than reassuring to Bush: "Israel would never want to defeat the president of the United States.... But we also don't want to be humiliated." Then it was Shamir's turn. He could hardly have been more direct in mobilizing the formidable pro-Israeli faction when he stated that Jews in America "have learned a lesson from the Holocaust" and are therefore "now united and very active, to the surprise of political circles in their country." [2] Although several key members of the House and Senate expressed some appreciation of the president's position, and viewed the outcome of a fight with Bush as uncertain, "an early count suggest[ed] they may win." [3] Secretary Baker departed Israel empty-handed because Prime Minister Shamir appeared to hold the strongest hand.

During the flight to Cairo, Baker vented his frustration to the traveling reporters. Whether by inadvertence or stratagem, he played what proved to be the administration's trump card. Baker told them he would recommend that the president go to the American people to make the administration's case, including a national television address "if that is what it takes." [4] As soon as reports of his comments filtered back to Washington, the political winds appeared to shift. The next day various unnamed aides informed correspondents that the White House staff was preparing for a national campaign that would include television. As one aide explained, "As long as this is an 'Inside-the-Beltway' issue, it plays to our disadvantage. 'Outside the Beltway,' the position that the president, not the Congress and not Israel, determines foreign policy seems eminently reasonable." [5]

During the next week, as President Bush defended his position and appeared to stiffen his resolve to use the veto, public opinion polls began recording strong support for his position. In an ABC News survey, 86 percent backed the president's position on loan guarantees, while another poll found 69 percent agreeing with the president that the decision should be postponed for six months. As shown in Figure 6-1, these same surveys reported strong approval for the president lingering nine months after the war with Iraq. The public's approbation had begun descending from the stratosphere, as it was bound to, but 70 percent of the American public still approved Bush's performance—well enough to make him look unbeatable in the next election a year away.

These impressive numbers spawned doubts among Israel's supporters in Congress. One Democratic senator remarked, "No one wants to belly up to this buzz saw," and a House member observed in a similar metaphoric vein, "There is very little stomach to confront the President on this." Even the normally resourceful lobbyists became stoic. "If the President of the United States goes to the American people and says 'Enough already,' the Israeli lobby can't counteract that," explained a senior pro-Israel lobbyist. A week after Baker's conversation with reporters, the Associated Press distributed a photograph of a smiling Baker shaking hands with Israel's foreign minister to symbolize their agreement to postpone the loan-guarantee issue as the White House desired.[6] The benign ripples of Desert Storm continued to benefit the administration's foreign policy.

Figure 6-1 President Bush's Popular Support As A Product of Rally Events

Percent
approving

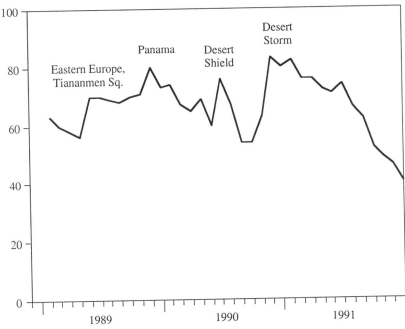

SOURCE: Various issues of *Gallup Opinion Report*

By any measure, Desert Storm was an extraordinary political event. The loan-guarantee case is but one instance of the great political leverage it gave President Bush as he formulated U.S. foreign policy at home and conducted it abroad. But it was extraordinary only in degree, as international crisis is normally associated with leadership. The Cold War era provided numerous instances of crisis leadership. One inventory recorded 65 rally events during the 40-year period from the Truman through the Reagan presidencies, or about one every eight months.[7] The job performance ratings of some presidents—Kennedy and Bush come to mind—appear to reflect little more than the accumulated surges and declines accompanying a succession of rally events that dominated their tenure.

Scholars sympathetic to the presidency have applauded this phenomenon. Just when the country most requires leadership, they assert, the public gives the president free, or at least a looser, rein to act. Others, however, regard it as an opportunity for perniciousness. In retrospect, the Tonkin Gulf incident appears far too ambiguous an event to have impelled Congress to officially launch the Vietnam War with a joint resolution supporting whatever actions

President Johnson deemed necessary. Storytellers with a conspiratorial bent find presidents going beyond opportunism to the actual manufacture of crises. A classic Oliver Stone-like tale, which refuses to die, has Franklin Roosevelt exposing our defenses to the attack on Pearl Harbor in 1941 because it was the only way he could persuade the country to declare an all-out war on the Axis powers.

Whatever one's view about the wisdom of the rally phenomenon, it is widely recognized that a president made suddenly popular by an international crisis enjoys improved prospects for going public.[8] This assumption of the literature will be tested later, but first we need to review what is known about why citizens rally.

Rally Events and Presidential Popularity

Most rally events arise as crises, although other dramatic and sharply focused foreign policy developments, such as treaties consummated at heads-of-state summits, may also trigger a rally response. The launching of the Soviet satellite Sputnik in 1957, the atmospheric test ban treaty in 1961, President Nixon's 1972 trip to China, and the 1991 war with Iraq were all attended by an upsurge in approval of the president.

Many occurrences that would appear to satisfy the necessary conditions for a rally response fail to do so. When the reconnaissance ship *Pueblo* was seized by North Korea in 1968, the American public, which had grown increasingly weary of the Vietnam War, was not distracted from its steady withdrawal of approval for Lyndon Johnson. Seven years later, however, in a strikingly similar incident, when the Cambodians seized another reconnaissance ship, the *Mayaguez,* President Ford's popular support shot up 11 percentage points.

Moreover, the success or wisdom of the president's action apparently has little bearing on the public's response. President Carter's failed attempt to rescue American hostages in Iran was greeted by a 4-percentage-point rise in his popularity. After the U.S.-sponsored invasion of Cuba ended disastrously at the Bay of Pigs in April 1961, President Kennedy's already high approval rating rose another 5 percentage points. This occasioned the bemused president's observation, "The worse I do, the more popular I get."

These and other peculiarities make generalizations about the rally events hazardous. Clearly, the specific details, context, and symbols enveloping these events greatly shape the public's response. If the particular aspects of each event were all that mattered, we would be left simply reporting and describing their occurrence without much likelihood of understanding why they arise.

Rally events may be less idiosyncratic, however, than they sometimes appear. Consider why an individual might upgrade his or her evaluation of the president's job performance as a reaction to news of the bombing of Marine barracks in Lebanon or the downing of a U-2 flight over the Soviet Union. Perhaps these respondents were simply expressing their patriotic fervor in the face of an external threat. The president, after all, does stand for the nation in our foreign relations. Supporting him during a crisis could well reflect the venerable American creed that "politics stops at the water's edge." While this explanation would account for the failure of domestic crises, such as riots in the cities during the late 1960s, to generate the same surge in presidential approval, it does not take us very far toward understanding why rally events sometimes fail to materialize during international crises.

Citing the variety of public responses to crises, Richard A. Brody has looked elsewhere for an explanation—specifically, in other politicians' responses and journalistic coverage of potential rally events. Rather than a case of reflexive patriotism, the public's assessment of the president's job performance during crises may be formed no differently than in normal times. What changes is the informational environment upon which public opinion is based. Coding stories from leading newspapers during both normal times and international crises, Brody does indeed find a strong bias toward favorable presidential coverage during crises. But this finding gives rise to the next question: why would news critical of the president's performance be temporarily suspended? To answer this, we need to understand how politicians assess uncertain situations and how journalists alter the way they gather the news.

During crises (or "staged" international summits), the president will enjoy near-monopoly control over information. His authority to respond decisively during international crises is unmatched by that of anyone else in government. Others who might normally challenge his policy and interpretation of events lack the opportunity to formulate a position. For example, when presidents address the nation on television to report on a crisis, response time is not made available to opposition party congressional leaders. Partisan opponents will hesitate to step into a potential mine field of quickly unfolding events. Reporters also suspend the normal practice of seeking opposing points of view, which they follow for the more partisan domestic issues. Citizens, following their normal routine of sampling the news and responding to cues, arrive at more favorable assessments of the president's performance.

The easiest way to detect the subtle political dynamics that contribute to the formation of a rally event is to examine carefully the strategic behavior of the president and other Washingtonians who shape public opinion. Neither of the two case studies presented below shows the president dominating the other participants in the news-making process. In the first case, members of the press immediately challenge the president's interpretation of the event. In the second case, the president appears pivotal in framing the responses of other politicians and the public.

Case 1.   On October 25, 1973, President Nixon summoned the network cameras to announce an alert of the armed forces for possible emergency action in the Middle East. With resolutions of impeachment referred to the House Judiciary Committee two days earlier and barely a third of the public endorsing his job performance, members of the press immediately began to suspect his motive. The next day they bluntly confronted Secretary of State Henry Kissinger at a news conference with the charge that the crisis had been fabricated to deflect public attention away from the president's Watergate troubles.[9]

Similarly, during the following June as President Nixon traveled abroad to meet with leaders from the Middle East and the Soviet Union, press suspicion followed him. One analysis of the stories about his diplomatic sojourns found half of them drawing an association between Nixon's travel and his domestic problems.[10] Modern White House correspondents, whose professional creed is to interpret as well as to report a president's actions, can more comfortably challenge an unpopular incumbent than one who enjoys the public's esteem.

Case 2. Shortly after the U.S. invasion of Grenada in the fall of 1983, all opinion indicators pointed to a confused and ambivalent public. Politicians within both parties were uncertain what posture they should assume toward President Reagan's action. Some Democratic spokespersons, including House Speaker O'Neill, began lobbing salvos at the White House, describing the invasion as "gunboat diplomacy."[11] Democratic senator Daniel P. Moynihan publicly declared the invasion to be "an act of war," adding, "I don't know that you restore democracy at the point of a bayonet."[12] One Democratic representative went so far as to announce a petition drive calling for the president's impeachment. For the most part, however, Democrats—including, prominently, those seeking their party's presidential nomination—and Republicans temporized.

With the military operation concluded and public opinion appearing increasingly to echo the president's critics, Reagan went on national television to account for his actions. The poll takers were poised; when they revealed the public's early, highly favorable response, the critics hushed up, and Reagan's previously silent partners became vocal.[13] One Democratic senator remarked, "Most people, once they saw the polls come out, went underground." Within two weeks after his initial criticism, Senator Moynihan conceded, "The move is popular and therefore there's no disposition in the Senate to be opposed to it."[14]

Events as novel as this one pose a special problem for politicians. Preexisting cues in public opinion are unserviceable. When the political winds blow at crosscurrents, most politicians tread lightly, neither embracing nor scoffing the president. Once clear signals from the country begin arriving in Washington, however, they swiftly assume an appropriate posture.

Clearly, context is critical. The Nixon episode suggests that the president's ability to define a crisis event rests with his credibility with the public. This may well explain why President Johnson failed to win the public's support at the time of the *Pueblo* seizure. The second case indicates a more complex interaction between political leaders and followers than either explanation presented above allows. During Grenada the citizenry did not reflexively rally. Only when they saw images of rescued American medical students joyfully returning home did the president effectively make his case, leading a significant number of respondents to upgrade their evaluation of his performance. Other elected politicians who participated in shaping the domestic context of the event were clearly looking over their shoulders for guidance from voters.

Thus far we have considered as context only the reactions of presidents, other Washington politicians, and those who report on their activities. But the context includes another critical feature: the state of public opinion entering the crisis. Since a rally event is defined by a surge in presidential support and measured by its magnitude, other things being equal, a president who already enjoys a strong public endorsement should experience smaller rallies than will be the case for one who is less popular. In early December 1979, with barely a third of the public registering its approval of him, President Carter faced a stiff challenge from Senator Edward Kennedy. More attention was focused on whether he could again win the nomination rather than his chances in the fall general election. However, the seizure of the hostages in Tehran changed his fortunes. Reinforced by the Soviet Union's invasion of Afghanistan in January, Carter's job performance ratings rose 23 points—the largest such surge ever—and it stayed high throughout the spring primary season.

Statistical evidence based on 25 rally events during the post-World War II era supports the conjecture that the level of prior approval predictably conditions the rally response. This relationship is not strong, however, which is not too surprising given the handicap of an unpopular president trying to frame an event.[15] Still, the statistical relationship is suggestive.

During normal times the public's evaluation of the president follows partisan lines. Democrats are consistently the least approving of President Bush, Republicans the most so, with independents somewhere in the middle. As a consequence, there were many more Democrats than Republicans available to rally during Desert Storm, and more in fact did so. Nearly a quarter of the Democrats switched from disapproval to approval compared with only 10 percent of the Republicans. Over half of all the changes to approval during the brief war with Iraq occurred among Democrats.[16] The partisan response during Desert Storm follows a more general pattern. For the rally events reported above, 8.5 percent of the opposition party's identifiers on average upgraded their evaluations of the president compared with 6 percent of those who identified with the president's party.

Ironically, the net result of these different partisan propensities is the emergence of a nonpartisan consensus in support of the president.[17] This introduces a distinctly different political setting for the exercise of presidential leadership. A compilation of approval ratings for Franklin Roosevelt before and after the bombing of Pearl Harbor illustrates this point (see Figure 6-2).

In those days party identification was not a well-recognized concept, so that the best available means for measuring the partisan composition of FDR's coalition was income. Prior to the attack on Pearl Harbor, evaluation of the president adhered to class lines. After the president's detractors massively rallied, his popular support was pervasive. Acutely sensitive to the mood of the public, and armed with reports of these approval ratings (which after U.S. entry into the war were not published but privately given to him), President Roosevelt restyled his leadership, in his own words, from "Dr. New Deal" to "Dr. Win the War."[18]

Rally Events and Opinion Leadership

Politicians will occasionally have the firsthand evidence of a recent national appeal as they assess the president's ability to go public. More commonly, however, they must judge the president's potential prowess with the circumstantial evidence of his approval ratings in the polls. The president's popularity helps them gauge his ability to use public strategies. Politicians are not alone in drawing a close association between the president's popularity and his ability to influence public opinion. During the past 20 years, this relation has been a standard hypothesis of research on the subject.

Past research has approached the relation between support for the president and support for his policies in a number of ways. One survey study, performed during the time of a popular incumbent, found that respondents were significantly more likely to endorse a hypothetical policy when they were told that it represented the president's position.[18] Another approach has been to examine public support for policies on which the president had actually staked out a clear position. The studies have generally found that respondents who approved of the president's performance were more enthusiastic about the policy than were those who disapproved.[19] Finally, a few studies have sought to gauge changes in aggregate public opinion on policy questions as a function of a president's intervention. They similarly report a relation between the president's popularity at the time of a public appeal and the magnitude of opinion change that followed.[20] Although alternative explanations to the transference of support from the president to his policies are available to explain each of these findings, the similar results generated by these different research designs present compelling circumstantial support for the importance of a president's prestige on his opinion leadership.

Of course, all one is really saying is that people tend to evaluate a message according to its source. One can easily develop a rationale for such a transference from traditional consistency theory in social psychology. This theory is premised on the fundamental assumption that individuals generally prefer consistent to inconsistent beliefs and opinions. An individual seeking to incorporate new information in a consistent fashion has a number of mechanisms available for doing so. One of particular relevance here is the congruence between source and message.[21] Following this principle, citizens

Figure 6-2 Support for FDR among Income Subgroups: 1937–1942

Percent Approving

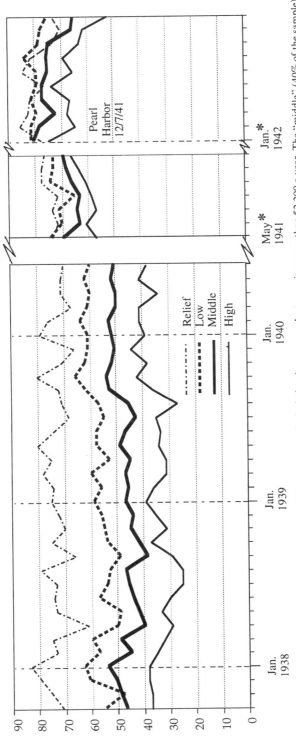

NOTE: For these surveys, "high," which averages 15% of the sample, includes those respondents earning more than $2,200 a year. The "middle" (40% of the sample) includes those earning greater than $1,285 a year but less than $2,200. The "low" (35%) includes those earning less than $1,285 a year. The "relief" (10%) includes those receiving direct relief, old age assistance, or those who are employed in a federal works program.

* No poll data are available June 1940–May 1941 and December 1941.

SOURCES: Data for 1936 through April 1940 from Westley C. Clarke, "Economic Aspects Of a President's Popularity," PhD dissertation, University of Pennsylvania, 1943. Figures for subsequent months obtained from the President's Personal Files at the Franklin Delano Roosevelt Library, Hyde Park, New York.

who are otherwise indifferent on a president's proposed policy will be inclined to adopt a position consistent with their evaluation of him as president. Approval inspires trust; disapproval, suspicion.

If going public is to succeed as a leadership strategy, presidential appeals must activate as well as persuade. Large numbers of citizens must be moved to contact their representatives. If the collective demonstration of support for the president's program impresses politicians, they will strategically align their public position on the policy in a way that is favorable to the president. The opinion dynamics required of going public, therefore, extend beyond mass persuasion, for which consistency between source and message is most appropriate. According to these dynamics, a national appeal will alter the preferences of sufficient numbers of politicians if the following four conditions are satisfied.

1. The president accurately communicates his preferences to the citizenry. The public recognizes the president's endorsement of a particular policy position. Past research on the public's familiarity with presidential appeals indicates that this is probably the least demanding condition.[22]

2. Citizens register favorable or unfavorable responses to a policy initiative according to their evaluation of the president. Moreover, the intensity as well as the direction of preference will be affected by the strength of the individual's position on an issue and of his or her evaluation of the president before learning of his position.

3. Citizens communicate support for the president's position to those politicians whom he hopes to influence. Ongoing communication is a commonly stipulated feature of representative democracy. Here, however, the principle takes on special emphasis, since the president will typically be trying to alter some specific behavior of politicians over a short time. For such a result, the more casual and leisurely forms of communication that arise from the representative's continuing contact with constituents will have to be supplemented by the direct effort of many citizens to contact their representatives.

4. To secure their own welfare, politicians strategically align their preferences with those of the president. Representatives do not have to decide that the president's position commands majority support among their constituents for such a posture to make political sense. A presidential appeal may succeed in creating a vocal, intense minority in support that will prevail over an indifferent or passive majority.

Facing these stringent conditions, a president might conclude that going public will not be worth the effort. Citing them, some observers have argued, in fact, that presidents should spurn going public as a substitute for bargaining. Here is what Nelson W. Polsby, a leading student of contemporary American politics, has said on the subject:

Efforts to ignore, bypass, or run roughshod over [national interest] groups by appealing over their heads to the people are doomed on at least two counts. First, the appeal to public opinion itself is likely to fail because of the ephemerality of mass public attitudes on most issues and because of the non-transferability of a president's popularity (when the president is popular) to the objects of a president's desires. Second, even if by some unusual combination of circumstances public opinion does for once yield to a president's entreaties, the effects may or may not reach Congress or influence congressional disposition of an issue.[23]

There are a number of ways to relax the four formal conditions above and to make the transference less dependent upon Polsby's "unusual combination of circumstances." First, the position of the president in the policy-making process allows him to choose from a large menu of policy proposals circulating around Washington at any moment. For those issues that are sufficiently advanced to merit the president's attention, much of the preparatory, coalition-building work will have been completed. Rather than being truly innovative and building winning coalitions from the ground up, presidents typically take up others' ideas and work at the margin of support that will make the difference in victory or defeat. An example of this tactic is President Reagan's use of national television and other public activities to swing 30 to 50 Republican House votes in the 1982 tax increase.

Further reducing the demands on the president's rhetoric, representatives also work at the margin of support within their constituencies. Even if a representative suspects that no more than 4 or 5 percent of the electorate will base its vote in the next election on his or her support of the president's program, it might still decisively alter his or her position on the issue.

The fact that marginal shifts of preferences, whether in Washington or in the rest of the country, often have major political consequences is what makes going public a viable strategy. The president makes an appeal; most citizens do not respond, but some do. A few of this latter group express their support actively. Most of the politicians who oppose the president's position will resist constituent pressure. A few whose positions are less fixed or who are electorally vulnerable will be persuaded that the president's course offers the least resistance. Frequently, this is all that is required for the president to appear to have worked his magic.

Moreover, the president possesses unusual institutional assets that may enhance his influence over public opinion well beyond that provided by his current popularity. The presidency's singular visibility allows its occupant to command the nation's attention; the office's broad constitutional mandate bestows upon him the authority to speak on any policy matter; and his acknowledged institutional expertise requires that his arguments be weighed and, even if opposed, dealt with.[24] In foreign policy, particularly, these resources will stand him in good stead.[25]

No president will ever persuade all of his admirers to support his cause. To the extent he fails, performance on condition 2 (transference of prestige to policy support) is weakened. But with the office's exceptional public standing, the incumbent president can also appeal to his detractors. His failure to persuade some of his admirers may be partly compensated by citizens who, while disapproving his current performance, nonetheless defer to his judgment. At times, consistency theory will be violated in ways that favor the president's efforts.

The remainder of this chapter tests the consistency model of opinion leadership on the Truman Doctrine speech of March 12, 1947. It is a single case, but a remarkable one. In the opinion of contemporaries and historians alike, President Truman faced a formidable task in preventing the country from settling comfortably into postwar isolationism and from failing to recognize the Soviet challenge. He certainly thought so. Some historians have argued that to achieve his goals Truman resorted to extraordinary rhetoric and other public activities that secured his program but also eventually unleashed an anticommunist phobia throughout the country. In this case, then, a president who set out to reshape public opinion on foreign affairs stands accused by some of having kicked off the Cold War at home.

The Truman Doctrine Speech: A Case Study

Delivered to Congress and broadcast across the nation on radio, this historic address has been widely credited not only with gaining the president his policy objectives but also with establishing the temper of U.S. foreign policy during the post-World War II era. Whether sympathetic to or critical of the Truman administration, historians agree that this speech more than any other single event marks the beginning of the Cold War between the United States and the Soviet Union. Moreover, its implications for the future did not require hindsight. Contemporaries in Washington and abroad grasped immediately that President Truman was advocating a fundamental change in the U.S. responsibility and posture toward the world. As Joseph Jones, a State Department participant in the formulation of the Truman Doctrine, recalled, "All who participated in the extraordinary developments of the period were aware that a major turning in American history was taking place." [26]

The Speech

Truman's speech to the country called for congressional authorization of $400 million in economic and military assistance to Greece and Turkey. Describing the deterioration of the Greek economy and the inability of its military to cope with Communist guerrilla activities, Truman starkly predicted that if the United States did not shortly replace the evacuating British forces, Greece would fall to the Communists. Turkey and the rest of the Middle East would succumb in turn. But he went beyond a simple request for aid. He described a bipolar world of democracy versus totalitarianism and called for the United States to assist "free people who are resisting attempted subjugation." Two major sections of the speech depicted the Communist threat and the American challenge. Midway through he turned his discussion from Greece and Turkey and spoke more generally:

> The peoples of a number of countries of the world have recently had totalitarian regimes forced upon them against their will. The Government of the United States has made frequent protests against coercion and intimidation, in violation of the Yalta agreement, in Poland, Rumania, and Bulgaria. I must also state that in a number of other countries there have been similar developments.
>
> At the present moment in world history nearly every nation must choose between alternative ways of life. The choice is too often not a free one.
>
> One way of life is based upon the will of the majority, and is distinguished by free institutions, representative government, free elections, guarantees of individual liberty, freedom of speech and religion, and freedom from political oppression.
>
> The second way of life is based upon the will of a minority forcibly imposed upon the majority. It relies upon terror and oppression, a controlled press and radio, fixed elections, and the suppression of personal freedoms.
>
> I believe that we must assist free people to work out their own destinies in their own way.
>
> I believe that our help should be primarily through economic and financial aid which is essential to economic stability and orderly political processes.

His peroration was even more graphic:

> The seeds of totalitarian regimes are nurtured by misery and want. They spread and grow in the evil soil of poverty and strife. They reach their full growth when the hope of a people for a better life has died.
>
> We must keep that hope alive.
>
> The free peoples of the world look to us for support in maintaining their freedoms.
>
> If we falter in our leadership, we may endanger the peace of the world and we shall surely endanger the welfare of our own nation.
>
> Greater responsibilities have been placed upon us by the swift movements of events.
>
> I am confident that the Congress will face these responsibilities squarely.[27]

At the close of the speech the assembled joint session responded with a standing ovation, and the immediate response of most columnists and editors around the country was favorable. There was some opposition, however, and it would be months before the aid authorization would pass Congress. Henry Wallace, who the next year would run for president against Truman as a third-party candidate, went on nationwide radio to lambast the speech and to characterize Truman, for his depiction of the gravity of the Soviet threat, "as the best salesman Communism ever had." [28] A number of prominent senators spanning the ideological spectrum from Robert Taft on the right to Claude Pepper on the left publicly expressed reservations.

After having experienced the Cold War rhetoric of the 1950s, one may not find much in Truman's statements that is particularly arousing or inflammatory. But it must be remembered that this was the first time a president had publicly identified the Soviet Union as an enemy and depicted so starkly the struggle between democracy and totalitarianism. Despite the disappointments after Yalta, Truman had repeatedly resisted making such public statements. Even now some of his closest advisers were disturbed by the speech's tenor. Secretary of State George C. Marshall en route to a Moscow conference was "somewhat startled to see the extent to which the anti-communist element ... was stressed." [29] James Byrnes, who had recently resigned as secretary of state, complained that the speech was too general in tone and commitment.[30] George Kennan, shortly to be head of the State Department's policy-planning staff, also objected to the "sweeping nature of the commitments." [31]

It is obvious from reading the memoirs of those who participated in drafting the speech that President Truman had intended it to be hortatory. Several days earlier at a White House briefing for a number of important senators and representatives, he had viewed the chilly response accorded Secretary Marshall's humanitarian reasons for giving assistance to Greece and Turkey. Only after Dean Acheson's presentation of the issue in strong anticommunist terms did the lawmakers warm to the proposal.[32] And as noted in Chapter 2, this is when Senator Arthur Vandenberg, the respected foreign policy expert, is reported to have advised the president that he would have to "scare hell out of the country" if he wanted to get authorization through Congress.[33] Moreover, other recent reconstruction programs proposed by the administration had received hostile responses from Congress and clearly would never be reported out of committee. Finally, Truman's vivid account of the speech writing reveals the dramatic rhetorical style he wanted infused into the text.

> The drafting of the actual message which I would deliver to the Congress had meanwhile been started in the State Department. The first version was not at all to my liking. The writers had filled the speech with all sorts of background data and statistical figures about Greece and made the whole thing sound like an investment prospectus. I returned this draft to Acheson with a note asking for more emphasis on a declaration of general policy. The department's draftsmen then rewrote the speech to include a general policy statement, but it seemed to me half-hearted. The key sentence, for instance, read, "I believe that it should be the policy of the United States. ..." I took my pencil, scratched out "should" and wrote in "must." ... I wanted no hedging in this speech. This was America's answer to the surge of expansion of Communist tyranny. It had to be clear and free of hesitation or double talk.[34]

As Richard M. Freeland has summed up the speech, President Truman committed himself and the nation to a "broad interpretative framework" of a "global assault of the 'totalitarian' forces against the forces of 'freedom'— calculated to command immediately the maximum public support." [35] When Marshall complained to the president that he had "overstated it a bit,"

Truman quickly replied that it had been necessary to receive favorable congressional treatment.[36]

After past wars the United States had withdrawn at least temporarily into an isolationist mood and policy. Despite the U.S. role in creating the United Nations, every indication from the recently elected Republican Congress was that U.S. economic and military commitments around the world would be sharply curtailed. Yet here was the president, only a year after the peace, attempting to commit a hostile Congress and an unconcerned nation to an activist, international posture.

Unlike President Reagan's use of national appeals as a bludgeon against his adversaries in Congress, President Truman's enterprise was more subtle. Working in an era where such force would have in all likelihood redoubled resistance, Truman sought to create an opinion climate that would make going along with his aid program for Greece and Turkey easier for members of Congress who might otherwise discern only the political costs to supporting such a policy. In going public, Truman sought not to circumvent bargaining. Indeed, by following Vandenberg's advice he tacitly agreed to shoulder responsibility for the policy and thereby remove a formidable obstacle to negotiation.[37] Truman's success, consequently, should be measured by the degree to which the speech generated a favorable opinion climate rather than by the volume of congressional mail it inspired. As such, it is an ideal case for testing at least the first two formal conditions of opinion leadership listed above.

I have hinted at another reason why the Truman Doctrine speech is of interest here. Since the late 1960s, a number of historians (whom I shall call revisionists) have been reevaluating the Truman presidency and concluding that the United States fomented the Cold War abroad and at home. Among them, Freeland identifies Truman's March 12 speech, as well as subsequent propaganda and "police" activities against subversion, as creating an opinion climate of anticommunism that made the McCarthyism of the early 1950s unavoidable.[38] Freeland's depiction of events, like that of other revisionist historians, is simple. He contends that President Truman raised the specter of Communist subversion to prompt Congress and the nation to embrace his foreign policy. Having succeeded in linking foreign and domestic threats and getting his program enacted, Truman found himself unable to turn off the pathological fear of Communism he promulgated. It is a parsimonious theory. It dismisses eventual passage of the Greco-Turkish aid program as well as the Marshall Plan; it explains away the president's pro-civil libertarian resistance to congressional investigations in the late 1940s and the early 1950s; and it accounts for the rise of McCarthyism. And finally there is a moral: we reap what we sow. During the 1952 presidential campaign, Truman and the Democrats were roasted for being soft on Communism.

This reinterpretation of foreign affairs in the late 1940s covers a broad range of occurrences in and out of government, and findings on the effect of a

Table 6-1 Public Concern over Foreign Policy before and after
Truman Doctrine Speech

Date	Percent Naming Foreign Problems as Most Important
Before Truman Doctrine Speech	
October 1945	7
February 1946	23
June 1946	11
September 1946	23
December 1946	22
After Truman Doctrine Speech	
March 1947	54
July 1947	47
September 1947	28
December 1947	30
February 1948	33

SOURCES: Gabriel Almond, *The American People and Foreign Policy* (New York: Praeger, 1960), 73; Samuel Kernell, "The Truman Doctrine Speech: A Case Study of the Dynamics of Presidential Opinion Leadership," *Social Science History* 1 (Fall 1976): 28.

single event no matter how dramatic can neither confirm nor deny revisionist history. Yet this history relies heavily upon the assumption that elites could easily manipulate public opinion. The Truman Doctrine speech is commonly regarded in revisionist statements as one of Truman's most prominent and successful efforts.[39] In investigating the public's response to Truman's address in a realm beyond policy support, one can test, in part, these revisionist claims and explore the limits of presidential opinion leadership.

Public Familiarity with the Speech

During the two-week interval between the March 12 address and the Gallup survey that queried the public about it, the president's remarks and proposal received continuous coverage in the nation's newspapers. As a result, an unusually large share of respondents, 84 percent, reported having heard or read about the speech. This compares with only 54 percent who would claim familiarity with the Marshall Plan in the summer at a later stage of that issue's development.[40]

Given the extent to which Truman's address reached its audience, it is not surprising that the speech coincided with heightened public awareness of international problems, as Table 6-1 shows. In March 1947 when a Gallup survey asked what was the nation's "most important problem," more than half of the respondents volunteered foreign affairs. Only three months earlier, barely a fifth had done so; and by late summer, pressing domestic issues would reemerge as the dominant public concerns. Although international events were

Table 6-2 Distribution of Public Support for Foreign Aid Requests in Truman Doctrine Speech (Percent)

	Aid for Greece	Aid for Turkey
Strongly oppose	20	22
Weakly oppose	18	23
Uncertain (don't know)	14	16
Weakly favor	29	22
Strongly favor	20	17

NOTE: Percentages may not total 100 because of rounding.

SOURCES: American Institute of Public Opinion, Survey No. 393, March 26-27, 1947; Kernell, "Truman Doctrine Speech," 34.

occurring quickly during this period, the Truman Doctrine speech appears to have been the most prominent one between the December and March surveys and probably accounts for the brief ascent of foreign affairs as the nation's "most important problem." Because the president's address to the joint session of Congress was an important event not only in Washington but in the rest of the country, one may consider the answers to the survey questions to be real opinions rather than merely obligatory responses.

Effects of the Speech on Public Opinion

Two aspects of the March 1947 survey indicate the success of the speech in achieving its primary goal, support for the administration's foreign aid package. First, respondents were asked whether they would like to see their representatives vote for or against Truman's aid requests of $250 million for Greece and $150 million for Turkey.[41] The distribution of opinions is displayed in Table 6-2. Given the novelty of the issue, it is somewhat surprising that 85 percent of the sample expressed a preference, and nearly half felt strongly either for or against the president's proposals. Aid for Greece was the more popular of the two requests. Among those registering an opinion, 57 percent favored aid for Greece compared with only 46 percent for Turkey. The president's speech, as well as subsequent daily news reports, clearly identified Greece as being in the more precarious position; Turkey was described as having a relatively healthy economy and being in no immediate danger unless Greece were to collapse. Although perhaps short of a mandate, Truman succeeded in quickly generating substantial public enthusiasm for his internationalist policy. If contemporaneous informal readings of public opinion were correct in portraying a pervasive isolationist mood throughout the country, these percentages represent a sizable turnaround in public opinion.

The second aspect of the March 1947 survey that reflects on the success of Truman's speech is the relation between source and message. Table 6-3 shows that the president's approvers were more supportive than his detractors

Table 6-3 Relationship between Approval of President Truman and Support for His Foreign Aid Requests (Percent)

	Aid for Greece		Aid for Turkey	
	Disapprove of Truman	Approve of Truman	Disapprove of Truman	Approve of Truman
Strongly oppose	38	13	41	16
Weakly oppose	21	16	26	21
Uncertain (don't know)	9	14	9	17
Weakly favor	24	32	14	26
Strongly favor	9	25	10	20

SOURCES: American Institute of Public Opinion, Survey No. 393; Kernell, "Truman Doctrine Speech," 38.

on both policy questions but that his opinion leadership was not limited to his admirers. A third of those respondents who disapproved of Truman's job performance nonetheless agreed to his aid program for Greece, and a fourth to his aid for Turkey. Because of the president's special credibility in foreign affairs, this finding is not unusual. Overall, approximately two-thirds of the respondents in Table 6-3 held opinions of the requests consistent with their evaluations of Truman's performance in office.

I enlisted consistency theory above to create a model of presidential opinion leadership that had the citizens' evaluations of Truman shaping their preferences about the president's policies. Of course, there is no intrinsic reason why consistent opinions could not arise from a reverse causal flow— that is, responses to the speech could have altered evaluations of the president. Causation is always a slippery problem in nonexperimental settings, and with a single survey, it is impossible to pin down the degree to which the president was leading public opinion or simply espousing what proved to be a popular policy. One must make educated guesses about the direction of causality from more circumstantial evidence. Since few citizens could have been so prescient as to have formed opinions on this issue before the speech, when even the State Department several weeks earlier had been caught unaware, one suspects that evaluations of the president's job performance probably heavily influenced opinions about his proposal.[42]

Although it is impossible to shed more light on the causal direction of opinion change with these data, one can tease out some of the probable dynamics of opinion change by learning more about who responded favorably to the president's appeal. Table 6-4 partitions respondents according to their 1944 presidential vote and their education. (Because the aid questions for Greece and Turkey yield highly similar relationships, I shall limit the remainder of the analysis to opinion on aid for Greece.) For only one subgroup—poorly educated Dewey voters—does the overall positive relationship between evaluations of Truman's job performance and support for military aid to Greece fail to turn up.

Within each educational class, the greatest support for Truman's proposal came from respondents who had both voted for Franklin Roosevelt in 1944 and approved of Truman's job performance at the time of the survey. The percentage endorsing aid to Greece varied from 60 to 86 percent depending upon educational class. The reinforcement of partisanship and approval contributes to this high approval rating.

The straightforward consistency model fails, however, to explain why Roosevelt voters who disapproved of Truman's performance consistently volunteered the least support for Truman's aid program. According to the consistency rationale, this distinction should belong to disapproving Dewey voters who had both partisanship and current opinions of Truman's performance to buttress a negative opinion. Yet controlling for education, these voters are consistently more supportive of Truman's policy than are their disapproving Democratic counterparts.

In the absence of better data, one can only speculate on the reason. Perhaps Truman's Democratic-voting detractors disproportionately belonged to some constituency for whom military aid to Greece and Turkey was objectionable. There are two difficulties with this argument, however. First, past research has identified no major segment of the Democratic constituency that was so positioned on these issues. Former Democratic vice-president Henry Wallace soon became an outspoken critic of the speech, but as he would demonstrate in garnering about 3 percent of the national vote as a third-party candidate in the next year's presidential election, the Wallace faction was too small—especially among voters with the least education—to produce the low support from Truman's detractors shown in Table 6-4. During these years, Republicans throughout the country as well as in Congress have been generally portrayed as more disposed to isolationism. Presumably, if any constituency's prior opinions would have led them to reject Truman's appeal, it should have been Republican voters. And yet roughly half of the Dewey voters who disapproved of Truman's job performance supported him on this issue.

Another possible explanation is the relative intensity with which Dewey and Roosevelt voters may have disapproved of Truman's performance. Many Dewey voters who disapproved of Truman may simply have been responding to partisan cues, and therefore their opinions had little intellectual basis or emotional investment. This cannot be said, however, of many Roosevelt voters who found reason to disapprove of Truman's job performance despite their shared partisanship.[43] Consequently, disapproving Dewey voters, on the whole, may have found it less disruptive to their prior opinions to go along with President Truman's foreign policy recommendations than would those Democratic voters who had a stronger, more substantive basis for their opinion.

Table 6-4 Relationship between Approval of President Truman and Support for Aid to Greece, Controlling for Education and Presidential Vote (Percent and Number Who Favor Aid to Greece Among Respondents Who Heard or Read about the President's Speech)

Evaluation of Truman	Low Education (0–8)				Moderate Education (9–12)				High Education (Some College +)			
	Voted for Dewey		Voted for FDR		Voted for Dewey		Voted for FDR		Voted for Dewey		Voted for FDR	
	%	(N)	%	(N)	%	(N)	%	(N)	%	(N)	%	(N)
Disapprove	48.1	(27)	23.9	(46)	46.2	(80)	33.8	(74)	57.7	(71)	35.3	(51)
Approve	47.8	(69)	59.9	(187)	64.4	(146)	64.9	(259)	74.7	(150)	86.0	(150)
Difference[1]	−0.3		+36.0		+18.2		+31.1		+17.0		+50.7	

[1] Positive percentage point differences indicate the beneficial effect of approval on favoring aid to Greece.

SOURCES: American Institute of Public Opinion, Survey No. 393; Kernell, "Truman Doctrine Speech," 39.

Table 6-5 Educational Differences in Support for the Truman Doctrine
(Percentage Points)

1944 Vote	Truman Evaluation	Difference between Respondents with Moderate and Low Education[1]	Differences between Respondents with High and Moderate Education[1]
Dewey	Disapprove	−1.9	+11.5
Dewey	Approve	+16.6	+10.3
FDR	Disapprove	+9.9	+1.5
FDR	Approve	+5.0	+21.1

[1] Based on responses in Table 6-4. Positive signs indicate that the higher educational category was more supportive of aid to Greece.

SOURCES: American Institute of Public Opinion, Survey No. 393; Kernell, "Truman Doctrine Speech," 40.

Such an explanation is rooted in the intensity of presidential performance evaluations rather than in the substance of the particular appeal. If correct, it should reappear in other issues with different presidents. Until such confirmation is available, however, only two general conclusions from the relationships in Table 6-4 are possible. First, the president's opinion leadership is associated with evaluations of his performance. Second, at least in the realm of foreign policy, the president may find a receptive audience among those citizens who would normally not number among his political allies. The findings offer empirical evidence of the familiar creed "Partisanship stops at the water's edge."

Another politically relevant finding is embedded in these relationships, namely, the effect of education on the public's receptivity to Truman's appeal. The subgroup differences in Table 6-4 have been rearranged in Table 6-5 to show the differences in support for aid to Greece according to education among groups who are otherwise similar. For example, where in Table 6-4, 46.2 percent of moderately well-educated and disapproving Dewey voters supported Truman's policy compared with 57.7 percent of their highly educated counterparts, in Table 6-5, this difference reappears as a difference of 11.5 percentage points in support. The positive signs indicate that in seven of the eight pairings, respondents in the higher educational category were more supportive.[44]

One might have supposed that education would have been correlated in the opposite direction, with poorly educated citizens being more susceptible to presidential appeals. Yet the finding shown here agrees with the results from other research. John E. Mueller, for example, discovered that public support for U.S. conduct of the Korean and Vietnam wars also came more heavily from the well-educated segments of the population.[45] In a somewhat different vein, another study found that politically attentive citizens, who also tend to be better educated, are the main source of shifts in American public opinion on emergent issues.[46]

Another basis of opinion leadership suggested earlier is that the president won support for his foreign policy by scaring the hell out of the country. In doing so, the argument continues, Truman nurtured an anticommunist phobia at home. Fortunately, questions in the Gallup survey of March 26-27, 1947, make it possible to test this claim.

Anticommunism as a Basis of Truman's Opinion Leadership

Revisionist historians emphasize the fear arousal aspects of Truman's rhetoric. They maintain that the president consciously sought to frighten the nation with the threat of Communist aggression and to mobilize this fear into public support for his policy. According to Walter LaFeber, "Insofar as public opinion was concerned this tactic worked well for the Administration." Arthur Theoharis argues that it "heightened public fears" and "contributed to a parochial, self-righteous nationalism." [47] But did it really have these effects? Could it account for the widespread endorsement of aid to Greece, especially among the president's detractors? To answer these questions, one must examine the anticommunist sentiment after the speech and the relation between these opinions and support for the Truman Doctrine program.

Although the Gallup survey did not query respondents directly about their fear of an external Communist threat, several questions did measure their concerns about domestic Communism. One can therefore test during this early period the presumed ultimate effects proposed by the "seeds of McCarthyism" thesis. Each survey item on the issue contains a prominent civil liberties component, and most of these items gained such a strong anticommunist endorsement, they contain too little variation with which to test the effect of Truman's message on opinion.[48] One item that did escape overendorsement asked the respondent simply, "Do you think the Communist Party in this country should be forbidden by law?" (I shall call this the "forbid-Communist-party" question.) Sixty percent agreed, 30 percent disagreed, and 10 percent held no opinion. Later this question would become a standard item of Gallup and the other national opinion surveys, but the March 26-27, 1947, survey appears to have been its first employment in a national poll.

Did the speech arouse anticommunism on the domestic front? The figures in Table 6-6 suggest not. Of all respondents, a slightly greater share of those who had heard or read about the Truman Doctrine speech did indeed register an anticommunist opinion. At the same time more of them also gave a pro-civil liberties response. These answers indicate only that citizens who are attentive to public affairs tend also to be more opinionated on political issues

Table 6-6 Relationship between Familiarity with Truman Doctrine Speech and Response to Forbid-Communist-Party Question (Percent and Number of Respondents)

Heard about Truman's Speech?	Forbid Communist Party?			
	Don't know	No	Yes	(N)
All responses				
No	24.8	18.3	56.8	(387)
Yes	8.3	31.4	60.4	(2,205)
Difference	−16.5	+13.1	+3.6	
Opinionated responses only				
No		24.4	75.6	(291)
Yes		34.2	65.8	(2,023)
Difference		+9.8	−9.8	

SOURCES: American Institute of Public Opinion, Survey No. 393; Kernell, "Truman Doctrine Speech," 35.

of the day. The direct effect of the speech is indicated by removing the replies of respondents who failed to offer an opinion to the forbid-Communist-party question. Table 6-6 shows that, contrary to the revisionist hypothesis, a greater percentage of those who were familiar with the speech opposed banning the Communist party than those who were not familiar with the speech.

The reason for this result again probably has more to do with a self-selection bias in respondents' exposure to the address than with any independent effects of the speech itself. This bias suggests the need for control variables to measure the direct effect of the speech. In an analysis of these data reported elsewhere, responses to both the forbid-Communist-party and "heard or read about the speech" questions were associated with education and past voting participation.[49] In Table 6-7, these variables are introduced as controls, but once again the predicted relationship between exposure to Truman's address and an anticommunist opinion fails to appear. For all but one instance (those with low education who did not vote in 1944), there was either no relationship or one opposite that predicted.[50]

Presidents, as well as scholars, should recognize that all segments of the public are not equally attentive to presidential messages. This may at times have important implications for the president's ability to rally public support. Before casually deriving or concluding mass attitude change from a president's appeal, one first needs to identify his audience. This should provide a clue as to how generally effective his message will be. There is some evidence in Table 6-3 that the effects suggested by revisionist

Table 6-7 Relationship between Familiarity with Truman Doctrine Speech and Anticommunist Opinion, Controlling for Education and Participation (Percent Who Favor Forbidding Communist Party)

| Familiarity with Speech | Low Education (0-8) | | | | Moderate Education (9-12) | | | | High Education (Some College +) | | | |
| | Did not vote in 1944 | | Voted in 1944 | | Did not vote in 1944 | | Voted in 1944 | | Did not vote in 1944 | | Voted in 1944 | |
	%	(N)	%	(N)	%	(N)	%	(N)	%	(N)	%	(N)
No	80.0	(60)	76.6	(94)	69.4	(36)	78.0	(82)	—[1]		53.8	(13)
Yes	85.0	(113)	76.5	(433)	68.5	(178)	69.8	(738)	41.5	(53)	48.2	(508)
Difference[2]	+5.0		−0.1		−0.9		−7.8		—[1]		−5.6	

NOTE: Percentaging based only on responses holding an opinion.

[1] Insufficient N for percentaging.
[2] Positive percentage point difference indicates that effects of hearing about speech are in the predicted direction.

SOURCES: American Institute of Public Opinion, Survey No. 393; Kernell, "Truman Doctrine Speech," 32.

historians may have been produced for the least-educated and nonparticipating segment of society. Familiarity with a speech depicting an external threat may have decreased this group's support of civil liberties for Communists. The president was talking disproportionately to other segments of the population, however, who were better equipped to differentiate their environment and therefore less likely to generalize in this fashion. Moreover, for highly educated and participating respondents, virtually all of whom said they were familiar with the president's address, to assume an antilibertarian stance would have probably required a significantly greater attitude change. Ample evidence has accumulated from past research to show that support for civil liberties in America is greatest among those citizens who, as found in these tables, were the most likely to have heard the speech and who offered the strongest endorsement of President Truman's proposal.[51]

There is some evidence and much argument that the public became less supportive of civil liberties from the late 1940s through the mid-1950s.[52] Although with these limited data one cannot wholly dismiss charges of Truman's culpability, one can conclude that his most forceful public expression of an anti-Soviet theme had little apparent effect on anticommunist sentiment in the country. To the extent that critics have employed this speech to indict Truman for the McCarthy era, the evidence presented here weakens the charge.

A second prediction of the revisionist model is that Truman traded upon anticommunism in mobilizing support for his foreign aid package. Although the Truman Doctrine speech does not appear to have stirred up greater anticommunist sentiment, it remains possible that such opinions could, nonetheless, have served as a useful resource. If Truman's support were found to have rested in large part on anticommunist sentiment, this finding would offer at least a partial confirmation of the revisionist's depiction of events. In Table 6-8 support for aid to Greece and Turkey turns out to be weakly associated with anticommunist opinion and quite possibly the result of measurement error.

This absence of a stronger relationship between these variables may strike some readers as surprising, but it corresponds well with the results of Mueller's analysis of public support for the Korean War. Examining responses to a Gallup survey of October 1950, he also found that opinions on the same forbid-Communist-party question were unrelated to support for the Korean War.[53] Although some attitude research during the mid-1950s found an empirical association in the public's perception of internal and external Communist threats on diffuse, generalized variables, the evidence reported here should caution one against imposing a simple opinion structure on the mass public.[54] Anticommunist sentiment at home did not necessarily strengthen the president's hand in fighting Communism abroad.

Table 6-8 Relationship between Response to Forbid-Communist-Party Question and Support for Aid to Greece and Turkey (Percent and Number of Respondents)

Truman's Foreign Aid Requests	Forbid Communist Party		
	No	Yes	Difference[1]
For Greece			
For	55.6	57.6	+2.0
Against	44.4	42.4	
(N)	(753)	(1,280)	
For Turkey			
For	44.5	48.1	+3.6
Against	55.5	51.9	
(N)	(730)	(1,249)	

[1] Neither percentage point difference is statistically significant. Positive differences are in the predicted direction.

SOURCES: American Institute of Public Opinion, Survey No. 393; Kernell, "Truman Doctrine Speech," 35.

Conclusion

The Truman Doctrine speech is an exceptional historic event, yet it has proved to be ordinary as an exercise of opinion leadership. It is historically exceptional because it has come to be widely viewed as ushering in the Cold War. It is exceptional also because contemporaries—at least those in Washington—sensed its profound significance. Finally, it is exceptional as a test case for studying opinion leadership because President Truman was so intent on reconstructing the nation's world view.

The Truman Doctrine speech has been found here to be typical, however, in the way it influenced public opinion. Although the overall extent of exposure to his declaration was indeed high, the president's message did not equally penetrate all segments of the citizenry. Better-educated citizens were on average both more familiar with the speech and, controlling the partisanship, more receptive to its content. And despite the highly charged rhetoric, President Truman's influence on public opinion remained specific to the issue.

Large numbers of citizens rallied behind the president's legislative proposals, but there is little evidence that the speech triggered a massive, domestic anticommunist phobia or exploited anticommunism already prevalent in the country at the time. Instead, opinion formation seems to have followed a normal pattern characterized by consistency in evaluations of source and message. The appeal of Truman's programs varied with respondents according to their evaluations of him as president. Also, approval of aid to Greece and Turkey came disproportionately from among the well-educated segments of the public, which perhaps helps to explain why anticommunism failed to materialize as an important factor.

The effects of President Truman's speech on public opinion are, therefore, consonant with the conventional wisdom of politicians rather than with history. Although the information on which these conclusions are based is, as noted, less than ideal, it is probably the best that will ever be available. Taken together, the findings portray a consistent and reasonable image of opinion leadership. Dramatic events may be able to generate a national phobia, but presidential rhetoric cannot. Instead, President Truman's capacity to lead the nation into a new, foreboding era of foreign affairs reflected in large part the citizenry's trust of him as its leader. How presidents go about maintaining this trust—their popular support—so that their public appeals will be received favorably is the subject of Chapter 7.

Notes

1. Doyle McManus, "Bush Prevailing in Battle With Israeli Lobby," *Los Angeles Times*, September 30, 1991, A16.
2. Jackson Diehl, "Israeli Minister Bars Concessions," *Washington Post*, September 20, 1991, A24; and Clyde Haberman, "Shamir Unmoved by Bush's Threat," *New York Times*, September 14, 1991.
3. Christopher Madison, "A Not-So-Sure Thing," *National Journal*, September 14, 1991, 2200.
4. Thomas L. Friedman, "U.S. Links Loan Guarantees to Freeze on Settlements as Baker's Israel Trip Fails," *New York Times*, September 18, 1991, 1.
5. John E. Yang, "Bush Tries to Ease Loan Crisis," *Washington Post*, September 20, 1991, A24.
6. Ibid., and McManus, A16.
7. Richard A. Brody, *Assessing the President* (Stanford, Calif.: Stanford University Press, 1991), 57-58.
8. The strongest case that presidents sometimes strategically confront crises is made by Ronald H. Hinckley, who documents instances of presidents consulting public opinion polls before deciding on a course of action. See *People, Polls, and Policy-Makers* (New York: Lexington Books, 1992).
9. This incident is described in Henry Kissinger, *Years of Upheaval* (Boston: Little, Brown, 1982), 587-589, 591. See also John Hebers, "Nixon's Motives in Alert Questioned and Defended," *New York Times,* October 26, 1973, 20; "Was the Alert Scare Necessary?" *Time,* November 5, 1973, 15; and "Transcript of Kissinger's News Conference on the Crisis in the Middle East," *New York Times,* October 26, 1973, 18-19.
10. Michael Baruch Grossman and Martha Joynt Kumar, *Portraying the President* (Baltimore: Johns Hopkins University Press, 1981), 237.
11. Hedrick Smith, "O'Neill Now Calls Grenada Invasion 'Justified' Action," *New York Times,* November 9, 1983, 1.
12. Stuart Taylor, Jr., "Experts Question the Legality of the Invasion of Grenada," *New York Times,* October 26, 1983, 7.

13. Barry Sussman reported that a *Washington Post*/ABC News survey the day after the speech showed a sharp rise in Reagan's support. The article provided figures from a November 3-7 survey, roughly a week after the speech. They show that from late September, approval of President Reagan's handling of foreign affairs increased from 42 to 55 percent, and during the same period he passed Mondale on a presidential preference question. "Reagan's Broad Gains in the Wake of Grenada," *Washington Post,* November 21, 1983, 10. See also James M. Perry, "Voters Strongly Back Invasion of Grenada but Waffle on Lebanon," *Wall Street Journal,* November 11, 1983, 1.

14. Republican senator Charles McC. Mathias also commented, "There's no question the President is on a high with Grenada" (Hedrick Smith, "Capitol Hill Clamor Softens as Public's Support Swells," *New York Times,* November 4, 1983, 11). See also Francis X. Clines, "The View from a Capitol Colored by Grenada," *New York Times,* November 4, 1983, 14; and Rudy Abramson, "Democrats Wary of Using Lebanon against Reagan," *Los Angeles Times,* December 10, 1983, 1.

15. The regression slope for the president's popularity in the month preceding the rally event is -.11 and not significant. The change score and prior approval are correlated at -.26.

16. Warren E. Miller, Donald R. Kinder, Steven J. Rosenstone, and the National Election Studies. AMERICAN NATIONAL ELECTION STUDY: 1990-1991 PANEL STUDY OF THE POLITICAL CONSEQUENCES OF WAR/1991 PILOT STUDY [computer file]. Ann Arbor, MI; University of Michigan, Center for Political Studies [producer], 1991. Ann Arbor, MI: Inter-University Consortium for Political and Social Research [distributor], 1991.

17. Brody, *Assessing the President,* pp. 70-71; and Lee Sigelman and Paula J. Conover, "The Dynamics of Presidential Support During International Conflict Situations," *Political Behavior* 3 (1981): 303-318.

18. Carey Rosen, "A Test of Presidential Leadership of Public Opinion: The Split Ballot Technique," *Polity* 6 (Winter 1973): 282-290. For a survey of this literature, see George C. Edwards III, *The Public Presidency* (New York: St. Martin's Press, 1983), 39-46. One experimental study in which the president's job performance is included in the analysis is Lee Sigelman and Carol K. Sigelman, "Presidential Leadership of Public Opinion: From 'Opinion Leader' to 'Kiss of Death'?" *Experimental Study of Politics* 7 (1981): 1022.

19. For analysis of the relation between performance evaluations and support for President Reagan's second round of budget cuts, see Samuel Kernell, "The Presidency and the People: The Modern Paradox," in *The Presidency and the Political System,* ed. Michael Nelson (Washington, D.C.: CQ Press, 1984), 250-253. See also Lee Sigelman, "The Commander in Chief and the Public: Mass Response to Johnson's March 31, 1968 Bombing Halt Speech," *Journal of Political and Military Sociology* 8 (Spring 1980): 1-14.

20. Examples of this research are Eugene J. Rossi, "Mass and Attentive Opinions on Nuclear Weapons Tests and Fallout, 1954-1963," *Public Opinion Quarterly* 29 (Summer 1965): 280-297; and John E. Mueller, *War, Presidents and Public Opinion* (New York: John Wiley and Sons, 1973). The most systematic and comprehensive study of this type to date is Benjamin I. Page and Robert Y. Shapiro, "Presidents as Opinion Leaders: Some New Evidence," *Policy Studies Journal* 12 (June 1984): 647-662.

21. An early exploration of the source-message relation in social psychology is C. I. Hovland and W. Weiss, "The Influence of Source Credibility on Communication Effectiveness," *Public Opinion Quarterly* 15 (1951): 635-650. An outstanding collection of conceptual and research articles on consistency theory is available in

Robert P. Abelson et al., *Theories of Cognitive Consistency: A Sourcebook* (Chicago: Rand McNally, 1968).

22. In a survey of the literature Donald R. Kinder and Susan T. Fiske conclude that for public opinion about the president, "Consistency appears to be a rather unimportant determinant of information-seeking." See "Presidents in the Public Mind," in *Handbook of Political Psychology,* vol. 2, ed. M. G. Hermann (San Francisco: Jossey-Bass, forthcoming).

23. Nelson W. Polsby, "Interest Groups and the Presidency: Trends in Political Intermediation in America," in *American Politics and Public Policy,* ed. Walter Dean Burnham and Martha Wagner Weinberg (Cambridge: MIT Press, 1978), 51.

24. In an earlier study on diffuse support for the presidency, my colleagues and I found strong endorsement for the president as the nation's leader. See Samuel Kernell, Peter W. Sperlich, and Aaron Wildavsky, "Public Support for Presidents," in *Perspectives on the Presidency,* ed. Aaron Wildavsky (Boston: Little, Brown, 1975), 148-183. See also Fred I. Greenstein, "Popular Images of the President," *American Journal of Psychiatry* 122 (November 1965): 523-529; Roberta S. Sigel, "Image of the American Presidency: Part II of an Exploration into Popular Views of Presidential Power," *Midwest Journal of Political Science* 10 (February 1966): 123-137. For a more recent and richly analytic statement, see Kinder and Fiske, "Presidents and the Public Mind."

25. Opinion leadership in foreign policy has long been acknowledged. As examples, see Aaron Wildavsky, "The Two Presidencies," in *The Presidency,* ed. Aaron Wildavsky (Boston: Little, Brown, 1969), 230-243; and Elmer E. Cornwell, Jr., *Presidential Leadership of Public Opinion* (Bloomington: Indiana University Press, 1965).

26. Joseph Jones, *The Fifteen Weeks* (New York: Vintage, 1955; reprint Corte Madera, Calif.: Harbinger, 1964), vii. Much of the subsequent account of political conditions in Washington at the time of the Truman Doctrine speech will be drawn from Jones.

27. *Public Papers of the Presidents of the United States, Harry S Truman, 1947* (Washington, D.C.: Government Printing Office, 1963), 176.

28. Jones, *The Fifteen Weeks,* 178.

29. Charles Bohlen, *The Transformation of American Foreign Policy* (New York: Norton, 1969), 86-87.

30. Richard M. Freeland, *The Truman Doctrine and the Origins of McCarthyism* (New York: Knopf, 1972), 100-101.

31. George F. Kennan, *Memoirs: 1925-1950* (Boston: Little, Brown, 1967), 319-322.

32. Dean Acheson, *Present at the Creation* (New York: Norton, 1969), 292-294.

33. Cited in David S. McLellan and John W. Reuss, "Foreign and Military Policies," in *The Truman Period as a Research Field,* ed. Richard S. Kirkendall (Columbia: University of Missouri Press, 1967), 55-57; and in Freeland, *The Truman Doctrine,* 89.

34. *Memoirs by Harry S Truman: Years of Trial and Hope,* vol. 2 (Garden City, N.Y.: Doubleday, 1956), 105-109.

35. Freeland, *The Truman Doctrine,* 114-118.

36. Bohlen, *Transformation of American Foreign Policy,* 87. This comment has received widespread circulation in revisionist accounts; see Joyce Kolko and Gabriel Kolko, *The Limits of Power* (New York: Harper and Row, 1972), 342; and Herbert Feis, *From Trust to Terror* (New York: Norton, 1970), 193.

37. Neustadt, *Presidential Power,* 39.

38. Three daily newspapers during the period were examined, and subsequent references to the news media reflect their coverage. These are the *New York*

Times, Chicago Daily Tribune, and the *San Francisco Chronicle.* There are as many revisionist interpretations as there are scholars writing on the subject. In some respects Freeland's thesis is among the bolder reinterpretations. All, however, tend to agree in emphasizing the effects of elite rhetoric on the formation of mass opinion.

39. Arthur G. Theoharis devotes five pages in his *Seeds of Repression* (Chicago: Quadrangle Books, 1971) to description of and excerpts from the speech. He concludes that the "oversimplified moralism of this [the speech's] rhetoric was to effectively reduce the administration's own political maneuverability" (56). See pages 47-49 and 51-53 for discussion of the speech. See also Theoharis's "The Rhetoric of Politics: Foreign Policy, Internal Security, and Domestic Politics in the Truman Era, 1945-1950," in *Politics and Policies of the Truman Administration,* ed. Barton Bernstein (Chicago: Quadrangle Books, 1970), 196-241. Walter LaFeber is more explicit in concluding the speech's effect on public opinion in *America, Russia, and the Cold War, 1945-1971,* 2d ed. (New York: John Wiley and Sons, 1972), 43-48. Kolko and Kolko give exhaustive attention to the speech's construction in *The Limits of Power,* 338-346. They suggest that the speech "manipulated" public opinion and "did not so much mirror the global facts as tend to transform and create them." Feis devotes two chapters (25 and 26) in *From Trust to Terror* to the Truman Doctrine speech and obliquely refers to its effect on public opinion in the following way: "Most Americans found temporary relief for their own exasperation and fears in Truman's blunt challenge to Communism and its agents in many lands" (198).

40. In May 1950, only 23 percent had heard of Truman's Point Four Program. Only 71 percent claimed familiarity with the Taft-Hartley legislation in mid-1948, although it was a major campaign issue. In 1963 the same percentage was familiar with the Peace Corps two years after it had been in operation. Only major international events and crises such as Sputnik, the U-2 incident, and the Berlin crisis in 1961 reached a higher plateau of public familiarity. David O. Sears, "Political Behavior," in *The Handbook of Social Psychology,* vol. 5, ed. Gardner Lindzey and Elliot Aronson, 2d ed. (Reading, Mass.: Addison-Wesley, 1969), 324-328.

41. LaFeber, *America, Russia,* 45; and Theoharis, "The Rhetoric of Politics," 206.

42. Another causal sequence might have individuals responding favorably or unfavorably to both the source and the message at the same time. Although such an occurrence poses no real problem for making a general case for presidential opinion leadership, it does describe a different process of opinion change that makes the policy or some other aspect of the appeal (such as acting presidential), rather than prior support, the primary basis of his success. If this is what explains the association of Truman's popularity with support for his aid program, it should show up in a surge of approval in the March 26-27, 1947, survey. From late January until this survey, Truman's job performance rating rose by 11 percentage points. This was part of a trend that had begun in October 1946 and would continue into the fall of 1947. It is impossible to know whether or how much the Truman Doctrine speech boosted the president's standing in the polls.

43. One can also argue that nonsupport among Democratic disapprovers reflected dissonance reduction. Because they had *decided* against the president earlier, opposition to President Truman's policies offered confirmation of their prior choice. See Leon Festinger, *A Theory of Cognitive Dissonance* (Stanford, Calif.: Stanford University Press, 1962).

44. The reason for this support could not have been the topic of the president's appeal; otherwise, Dewey voters would show similar levels of nonsupport. Note that the

exception is for a category that includes few members and is particularly susceptible to sampling error.

45. John E. Mueller, *War, Presidents and Public Opinion* (New York: John Wiley and Sons, 1983), 122-136.

46. Johannes Pederson, "Sources of Change in Public Opinion: A Probability Model with Application to Repeated Cross-sectional Surveys" (Paper delivered at the Annual Meeting of the American Political Science Association, Washington, D.C., September 5-9, 1972), 17-21.

47. LaFeber, *America, Russia,* 45; and Theoharis, "The Rhetoric of Politics," 206.

48. Although it is possible that President Truman's speech increased anticommunist sentiment on domestic affairs, the skewed responses are consistent with previously recorded anticommunism and may be in large part an artifact of question wording.

49. See Samuel Kernell, "The Truman Doctrine Speech: A Case Study of the Dynamics of Presidential Opinion Leadership," *Social Science History* 1 (Fall 1976): 20-45.

50. One might argue familiarity in itself is insufficient, and more direct exposure, such as having heard the address live over radio or having read the text in the newspaper, would have differentiated the public opinion on the civil liberties question in the predicted direction. Given the present findings, this appears unlikely. The 15 percent who claimed unfamiliarity represent a rather pure category, and the 85 percent who said they had heard or read about the speech include respondents who were directly exposed to the stimuli. Therefore, if there is an underlying relationship in the predicted direction, it may be weaker with the cruder operational measures, but there still should be some relationship. Yet there is none. Only if respondents in the middle range of familiarity are assumed to have responded in the opposite direction—which seems implausible—could this argument be maintained in the face of the slight inverse relationship for most of the subsamples.

51. Samuel Stouffer, *Communism, Conformity, and Civil Liberties: A Cross Section of the Nation Speaks Its Mind* (Gloucester, Mass.: P. Smith, 1955).

52. Herbert H. Hyman, "England and America: Climates of Tolerance and Intolerance," in *The Radical Right,* ed. Daniel Bell (Garden City, N.Y.: Doubleday, 1963), 268-306.

53. Mueller, *War, Presidents,* 161-163.

54. Daniel J. Levinson, "Authoritarian Personality and Foreign Policy," *Journal of Conflict Resolution* 1 (March 1957): 37-47. The scale is described and evaluated in *Measures of Political Attitudes,* eds. John P. Robinson, Jerrold G. Rusk, and Kendra B. Head (Ann Arbor: Michigan Survey Research for Social Research, 1968), 306-308.

The Politics of Popularity ══════ 7

So long as the citizenry remains attentive to matters of peace and prosperity, so must the president. Otherwise, his popular support will suffer and with it his ability to govern. In this chapter I shall marshal evidence that confirms this relationship between national conditions and evaluations of the president.[1] In our fragmented political system, holding the president accountable has the potential for injustice. The public will occasionally punish a hard-working president who is doing as good a job as one can reasonably expect under unfavorable circumstances, while on another occasion it will reward an underachiever who is blessed by good times.

So be it. Fairness to presidents is less important than motivating them to deal with the country's problems. The public must hold them responsible, even if at times it does so naively. To do less would encourage presidents to shirk their duties. A good example of the functional value of naive judgment by the public can be seen in the aggressive way recent presidents dealt with the energy crisis. No one would deny that events beyond their control caused the steep increases in energy prices during Nixon's and Carter's years in office. Nonetheless, rather than seek refuge behind the truth that the problem was not their fault, both presidents, to their credit, actively sought a solution even at the risk of promoting unpopular policies. The fact that energy-induced inflation ultimately took a heavy toll on the prestige of both men will undoubtedly provide future historians a basis for sympathetic revisions of their performance. But for the citizenry, such sentiments have little value.

One might expect that modern presidents, heavily dependent on popularity for their leadership, would be especially attuned to matters of peace and prosperity. If so, the emergence of such presidents would assure the public of politicians in the White House who will aggressively tackle the country's problems. Before resting easy, however, one must face two possible flaws in this conclusion. First, presidents who routinely go public might misinterpret weak approval ratings. Second, they might undertake activities other than problem solving to improve their standing in the polls. Either way they would be less than full-fledged problem solvers.

No matter how motivated they may be to satisfy the public, if presidents fail to appreciate the real sources of the nation's distress and their low ratings, their actions will probably miss the mark. Politicians who routinely engage in public relations to promote themselves and their policies may be especially prone to misperception. They must have abiding faith in the power of rhetoric. The way these politicians approach the electorate may well shape how they come to view it. Preceding chapters have recounted numerous instances of a modest downturn in a president's poll rating triggering a flurry of public relations activities from the White House. Moreover, the efficacy modern presidents assign to their own rhetoric they do not deny to others, especially members of the press. The readiness with which recent presidents have enlisted television and their attention to the nuance of public relations gives one cause to wonder whether they might fail to comprehend that the citizenry will ultimately judge them not on their rhetoric (or that of anyone else) but on their performance.

Even if a new-styled president realizes that his unpopularity is rooted in something more substantial than the rhetoric of others and that more is required of him than better public relations, the second flaw may come into play: what he is likely to do about it. How will he equate his unpopularity with the nation's problems? Strategic responsiveness and democratic responsibility can yield quite different outcomes, at moments at sharp odds with each other. The American system aspires toward the latter but is guaranteed only the former. A president whose leadership is heavily invested in public opinion offers no assurances. His preoccupation with public opinion guarantees no more than that as he pursues policies he will be acutely sensitive to his popularity ratings.

This condition may pose a problem akin to one raised by Henry Kissinger during the OPEC-induced inflation of the mid-1970s. Because industrial economies and, in turn, incumbent governments were suddenly becoming shaky, Kissinger voiced concern that public policy might become perversely driven by the requirements of political survival.

> There is the problem that as the pressures of their electoral process have increased, governments have become more and more tactically oriented. The more tactically oriented they are, the more short-term their policies. The more short-term their policies, the less successful they are. So we have the paradox that governments following public opinion polls begin to look more and more incompetent. As they look incompetent, confidence in government begins to disintegrate.[2]

The specific historical cause of Kissinger's pathology was a rapid and severe downturn in national economies. The cause of the myopia posed here is more endemic; it is the installation of politicians in the White House who soar or fall in Washington according to their popularity in the country. How to induce self-interested politicians to recognize the citizenry's concerns and to structure their incentives so that self-interest leads them to act in ways that promote the general welfare are related issues that have challenged political theory since the founding of the republic. They are no less relevant today as one ponders the emergence of presidents whose leadership rests heavily on the moods of the American public.

Popularity and Public Relations

If one could have asked Richard Nixon to assess the relative importance of rhetoric and performance as he orchestrated a multifaceted public relations campaign to offset his rising unpopularity after the Laos invasion, or similarly, if one could have posed the issue to Jimmy Carter when he hired public relations consultant Gerald Rafshoon to beef up the White House's media relations, both men, if candid, probably would have admitted they believed that rhetoric—public and press relations—was important in deflecting the full impact of unfavorable political circumstances. Moreover, they could have staked high ground by asserting that their official responsibilities included informing the public about national problems and the administration's policies. Does not the Constitution, after all, require the president to report to Congress on the state of the nation? They could also have argued that any marginal support for themselves generated by these activities would do no one any harm.[3] Public relations purchased for them the time necessary to solve tough problems, thereby allowing them to escape Kissinger's dilemma of strategic myopia. Finally, both men might have added as an afterthought that whatever the effect, it was far easier to turn on a media campaign than to turn off a war or inflation.

Public Relations as a Convenient and Satisfying Activity

The relative ease of public relations is no trivial matter. Without making any special claims for its efficacy, modern presidents may be tempted to resort to public relations for the simple reason that it is manageable. Chapter 4 showed that Presidents Nixon, Carter, and Reagan were preoccupied in their prime-time addresses with the Vietnam War, historically high inflation, and double-digit unemployment, respectively. None of these was in any way a trivial issue that rhetoric could gloss over. In going to the airwaves, these presidents sought the public's patience. However much they hoped to gain politically in their television addresses, their activities had the piquant quality of being doable.

Convenience alone is insufficient to explain the dedicated way in which presidents and many of their staff pursue public and press relations. Presidents do it because they believe it wins the public's sympathy. One need not make presidents into Frank Capra's arrogant manipulators of public opinion in his film *Meet John Doe* to have them believe that they can talk their way into the hearts of the citizenry. Well before they had the wherewithal to do so, presidents must have felt this way. Recall FDR's 1939 lament on the slow development of television.

The desire to explain one's actions and to respond to criticism springs from human nature. Probably every occupant of the White House has at some point blamed press treatment for his troubles in the country.[4] Probably each has also depreciated the public's current disfavor by stressing the proverbial "burdens of office" and "complexity of problems," neither of which the average citizen can appreciate. In the face of tough problems and a "bad press," presidents want to tell their side of the story. Books on the subject with such sinister titles as *The Selling of the President* and *On Bended Knee* miss the point.[5]

However phrased, the public's lack of expertise offers a comforting rationalization to a president who must otherwise confront the stark reality that he has failed. As self-serving as these sentiments are, one may assume they are sincere. The fine line between "bad news" and a "bad press" gives presidents ample opportunity to think this way. That these feelings are genuine helps to explain why modern presidents are quick to go public to defend their actions. Rationalizations that offered presidents of an earlier era a measure of solace today prescribe a course of action.

How Public Relations Matter

Thus far in this analysis I have treated going public to counter falling popular support as a form of therapy and the product of an interaction between human nature and advanced technology. There is, however, another reason, peculiar to the modern setting, why presidents will be especially inclined to resort to public relations to offset a decline in the polls. What fellow Washingtonians say publicly about the president's performance will, in fact, significantly influence the way people in the country judge him. What makes this explanation peculiar to the modern era is the extraordinary volume of messages transmitted from Washington to the country. One of the ways in which individualized pluralism is distinguished from institutionalized pluralism is precisely this attribute. Because present-day Washington is less insulated from outside pressures, politicians are both more sensitive to public opinion and more inclined to try to shape it as a way of controlling their own destiny and of influencing that of other politicians. One member of Congress, Senator Jesse Helms, went so far as to try to gain control of a major network for the stated purpose of altering its putative political slant in reporting public affairs.

An important result of the increased two-way communications is that the ordinary citizen has gained more information about the president and more varied opinions about his performance. Veteran Washington correspondent James Deakin concurs:

> The relationship between the president of the United States and the nation's news media is a subject of endless fascination. It exerts an irresistible attraction for presidents, members of the White House staff, reporters,

People were worried and fearful about a deep recession. They were trying to make ends meet—

They were short of money and heard about layoffs and unemployment WHEN

Suddenly they saw on TV, pictures of their leader in a store buying a pair of socks—

People were worried and fearful about a deep recession. They were trying to make ends meet—

©1991 HERBLOCK

© 1991 by Herblock in The Washington Post

editors and broadcasters, politicians, bureaucrats, political scientists, historians and an increasing number of ordinary citizens. For a long time, it was a local cottage industry in Washington, of no great interest to the rest of the country. Now it is a vast national enterprise whose tentacles spread into every village and shire.

How is the president getting along with the news media? Are they treating him well or badly? Is he a master of communications or an ineffective performer on the tube? Is he accessible to reporters and candid with them? Or is he secretive, misleading the press. . . ? Why doesn't he have more press conferences? Why have his press conferences become such increasingly meaningless spectacles? Why does he manipulate the press so brazenly to achieve his purposes? Why doesn't he use the press more effectively to achieve his purpose? Why is the press so subservient to the president? Why is the press so hostile to the president? The relationship between the president and the news media is a long-running soap. Drama. Suspense. Conflict. And a large, rapt audience.[6]

The recency with which the American public has become privy to political relations in Washington probably accounts for why presidential scholars have traditionally paid little attention to these events, compared, say, with the presidential pundits who look for great consequence from the most trivial pursuits. Conventional scholarship insists that presidents stand or fall on their performance in providing satisfactory conditions for the ordinary citizen. Richard E. Neustadt writes, "What a president should be is something most men see by light of what is happening to *them*. Their notions of the part a president should play, their satisfaction with the way he plays it, are affected by their private hopes and fears. Behind their judgments of performance lie the consequences in their lives. What threatens his prestige is their frustration." [7] Whatever slant the press may take, bad news will represent objectively unfavorable conditions and events—that is, poor performance. Stacked against paychecks and prices, a "bad press" and criticism from other politicians are inconsequential. So the argument goes. Maligned presidents may respond to the rhetoric of others, but they are just making noise as far as public opinion is concerned. Their performance is all that really matters.

With this in mind, Neustadt speculated that press revelations that Eisenhower's chief of staff, Sherman Adams, had improperly accepted gifts from an individual who transacted business with the government probably caused the White House more consternation than it should have.[8] President Eisenhower's approval rating remained stable as long as national conditions were static. It surged temporarily with the peace in Korea and briefly dipped below 50 percent approving during the recession of late 1957. President Johnson's popularity declined as U.S. casualties in Vietnam mounted; Nixon's and Carter's tracked inflation; Reagan's fell sharply in 1982 as unemployment skyrocketed. And the cushion of support provided President Bush in early 1991 by Desert Storm did not prevent his popularity ratings from dropping below 50 percent later in the year as the recession deepened. These are the kinds of experiences conventionally enlisted to explain past presidents' declining popular support.[9] They make eminent sense. If such experiences are *all* that matter, however, presidential self-promotion through intensive public relations makes no sense at all.

The public's reliance upon experience rather than news about Washington politics is consonant with the kind of political setting for which a bargaining president is ideally suited. Discounting the significance of public relations means all the more that presidents will succeed in the country only as they successfully negotiate coalitions that implement policies that work. Having the public monitor the outcomes of policies rather than the politics involved in their creation contributes to Washington's insularity and in large measure shields the bargaining society from intensive public posturing.

The analysis in preceding chapters provides reason to suspect that this traditional, exclusively experiential view of public opinion is deficient and that modern presidents may be smart in going public to check their adversaries and counter bad news. In Chapter 6, for example, presidents were found to be communicators whose messages are endorsed or rejected largely according to the citizen's regard for them as a source. In Chapter 5, strong circumstantial evidence of this appeared in the testimonies and behavior of other politicians in response to President Reagan's efforts at opinion leadership. Moreover, when the president's public standing changes from, say, 50 to 45 percent approving, relatively few citizens need to be monitoring politics in Washington for events there to generate prominent feedback in the monthly poll reports.

Recent survey and experimental research in public opinion also raises questions about the adequacy of relying exclusively upon direct, personal experiences to explain political judgments. Consider, for example, how the economy as an issue has been recently discovered to influence voting in congressional elections.[10] When survey respondents are asked general questions such as, "Do you think economic conditions in the country are getting better or worse?" their answers tend to be more closely aligned with their voting preferences than are their answers to other questions that deal exclusively with the respondent's personal financial well-being. Responses to "Are you personally better or worse off financially today than a year ago?" are at best only weakly related to voting preferences. Employing multivariate statistical procedures, researchers have found that these personal experiences influence political behavior largely to the degree that they filter into the more general sentiments, but there is no certainty that they will be so elevated.[11] This helps to explain why over the years polls have repeatedly found unemployed respondents holding political evaluations of the current president's performance similar to those of their employed counterparts.[12] "In evaluating the president," concluded Donald R. Kinder, "citizens seem to pay principal attention to the nation's economic predicament, and comparatively little to their own."[13]

Generalized evaluations of the current state of the economy and other politically relevant conditions reflect precisely the kinds of civic information citizens are likely to obtain in watching evening news programs and in reading their local newspapers. More direct evidence on the effect of news on presidential evaluations is available from an experimental study of opinions about then-president Jimmy Carter. Several groups of subjects attended six evening sessions in late 1980 and early 1981 in which they watched what was said to be a taped viewing of the previous evening's news broadcast. In fact, portions of each newscast had been altered to present a series of stories on one of several topics—American defense preparedness, inflation, or pollution of the environment. After viewing these messages over the course of a week, the subjects began assessing President Carter's overall performance by the issue to which they had been repeatedly exposed. The researchers concluded that "a president's overall reputation, and, to a lesser extent, his apparent competence, both depend upon the presentation of network news programs." [14]

The finding that generalized sentiments, based on the kind of civic data conveyed by news rather than personal experience, are consequential for political behavior is crucial to understanding how citizens in an information age evaluate their leaders. Later in this chapter I shall return to this finding in considering the kinds of policies for which the citizenry rewards and punishes the president in the polls. Here the implication for the effect of elite discourse on presidential approval is indirect but no less crucial. What the public learns from national news about the state of the country and from the president's competitors about his performance will frequently be more relevant than personal experience in their evaluations of him. If a president sometimes becomes exercised when the Commerce Department issues a high inflation rate, or when a commentator or another politician publicly questions the wisdom of his policy, or when members of the press appear to dwell upon his failures rather than his achievements, perhaps he is right to do so. Today, what others in Washington have to say about the president may shape what the rest of the country thinks of him.

Does this mean that the traditional observation that the president's standing in Washington bears little relation to his status in the country was wrong? Not at all. Washington has changed. What was true for Presidents Truman and Eisenhower may not be for Presidents Reagan and Bush. If the public now pays closer attention to politics in Washington than before, it is not because citizens today are somehow cognitively processing political information differently.[15] Nor has there been a national epidemic of "Potomac fever." Rather, the reason is simply that citizens are exposed to more—and more critical—information about the president than ever before. This is the argument. Now for some evidence.

News from the Capital: Then and Now

The record of White House coverage in the press during the past 30 years confirms the kind of change detected by Deakin and hypothesized here. One commonly employed indicator of the growing preponderance of presidential news is obtained by comparing it with news about Congress. Such comparisons are available for news coverage extending back to the mid-nineteenth century when, by one account, presidents received less press attention than congressional committees. During the twentieth century, the share of White House news has increased steadily to the point that today it attracts substantially more news stories than Congress.[16]

Behind the increased coverage of the presidency lie differences in how news was reported from one era to the next. Treatment by the Washington press of two presidential events 20 years apart illustrates this better. The first is a confrontation between President Eisenhower and the White House press corps; the second, the candid revelations of President Reagan's Budget Director David Stockman to a Washington journalist. Both events are purely political "news," generated by and about Washingtonians. To the extent they were communicated to the country, both stories were potentially damaging to the president's prestige. In the first instance, the message was not transmitted to the nation, the potential harm not realized. In the second instance, the story occupied front pages of the nation's newspapers and appeared prominently on the networks' evening news programs for nearly a week.

The first comes from an Eisenhower news conference in November 1953, shortly after Attorney General Herbert Brownell accused former president Truman of harboring a known "Communist spy" in his administration. As President Eisenhower responded to the regular assemblage of White House correspondents, he found himself quickly dogged with pointed questions about Brownell's statement.[17] When confronted with conflictual matters, especially those involving disagreement with other politicians, President Eisenhower typically obfuscated and temporized. He did so here, much to the chagrin of the correspondents. When challenged by a reporter's rhetorical question whether the Eisenhower administration had not, in fact, embraced McCarthyism, the president, stunned and flustered by the questioner's directness, replied that he would "take the verdict of the body on that." From the available accounts, it appears that at this point the president lost control of the conference. He stood watching, dumbfounded, as *New York Times* reporters Anthony H. Leviero and James Reston canvassed fellow correspondents. The verdict went against Eisenhower. That such an incident occurred is less remarkable today perhaps than that it failed to receive prominent coverage in the nation's press. Deakin relates this incident to illustrate the kinds of understandings that existed between the president and the press during this era.

> Very little of the atmosphere of Eisenhower's confrontations with reporters found its way into their stories. There was an occasional hint that the proceedings had been raucous, but overall the news accounts were bland. What had been a knock-down-drag-out at the press conference emerged in the news stories as a waltz-me-around-again-Willie. The press conferences

were essentially in-house encounters between the president and the reporters. The news, in the Eisenhower era, was objective. The flavor was lacking. So the public was not aroused. It slept easy.[18]

In vivid contrast, when David Stockman's book-length confessional was published in the September 1981 issue of the *Atlantic,* it was the gala political event of the season in Washington.[19] Everyone who had opposed President Reagan's budget program or whose clientele had suffered from it found in Stockman's "education" vindication for their differing view. And after months of imposed silence they now spoke up. Washingtonians had a field day predicting what President Reagan would do and, after he took Stockman "to the woodshed," forecasting when his by-now contrite young miscreant would reappear in public.

Unlike the preceding case, little about this incident was confidential, beginning with Stockman's ill-advised remarks and ending with his meeting with the president. To the contrary, much of what took place was designed to create publicity. The budget director lunched weekly with a well-known correspondent, revealing all kinds of damaging gossip with the full knowledge that by fall his comments would be published.

Dwight Eisenhower had a budget director, as had all of his predecessors back to President Harding; but unlike Reagan's and, before him, Carter's (Bert Lance), Eisenhower's assistant was a private officer whose sole mandate was to advise his president. Consequently, Joseph Dodge never became the "personality" outside Washington as did Stockman, who around the country became a favorite subject of political cartoonists and the object of such epithets as the "blow dried reaper." Had Dodge made similar observations about budget making under Eisenhower, they probably would not have attracted much press attention, much less become a major exposé.[20]

Eisenhower's run-in with the press corps did not alter public opinion because few, if any, of the participants in the news business reported it. This was certainly not the case with the Stockman story. Beyond the readership of the *Atlantic,* most of the country soon learned about the confessional from wire service and network news stories throughout the next week. The Gallup Poll felt it a public matter sufficiently familiar to warrant adding a battery of questions about the incident to one of its national surveys. Within two weeks of the appearance of the magazine article on newsstands, two-thirds of the respondents in a national survey reported "hearing or reading" about the "recent events of David Stockman." Among those familiar with the story, most felt that Budget Director Stockman's activities had hurt President Reagan's position politically and, by a narrow margin, that Stockman should leave office.[21] As discussed earlier, several unfavorable conditions were eroding the president's popular support in the fall of 1981—the most prominent among them, a rising unemployment rate. But the abundant adverse publicity Stockman generated hurt Reagan nationally in a fashion unknown to presidents of an earlier era.

Although both incidents were memorable in Washington, they differ in that the Eisenhower story was a nonevent in the country. Differences in the individual details of each story may have contributed to their dissimilar national coverage. Yet they illustrate in their respective extremes how differently present-day Washington elites conduct business from their not-so-distant predecessors and how these differences affect the way citizens judge their leaders.

These content analyses and case studies should be understood to offer no more than suggestive evidence of the hypothesis that presidents *must* pay closer attention to press and public relations today because they matter more. Rarely is the evidence of public opinion, such as that for Stockman, available for claiming more. The data necessary for citizens critically to judge the president's Washington performance is, however, increasingly easy to come by. It is safe, therefore, to assume that presidents will continue to engage in intensive public relations to counteract the probable effects of unfortunate news on public opinion.

Chapter 6 concluded that susceptibility of modern politicians to the president's public appeals is bringing the president's reputation in Washington and his prestige in the country into an alignment that did not exist in Truman's and Eisenhower's time. Another reason for this convergence is that events in Washington, which in an earlier era would have only pricked the attention of the small segment of the public who are politically attentive, today frequently hold the entire country enthralled. Peace and prosperity may remain the primary concerns of citizens as they judge the president, but president watchers both in Washington and throughout the country are sharing and comparing data as never before. The modern president who fails to rebut unfriendly remarks of Washington elites or to blunt criticism from the press may soon begin hearing echoes of these complaints emanating from the country.

The general strategy of going public, discussed in previous chapters, applies also to modern presidents who go public to help themselves. Technology makes it possible for them to satisfy the natural urge to answer their critics. Outsiders in the White House, who achieved their position by repeatedly winning presidential primaries, have a special faith in rhetoric. Channels of competing and at times unfavorable news from Washington have opened up as the president's adversaries also go public. And a less deferential news media more willingly transmit, if not actually stimulate, unfavorable stories about the White House. All this suggests that when a president goes public to counter his decline in the polls, he may be acting on more than rationalization. Indeed, he may be acting rationally.

Thinking Strategically about Popularity

Having considered the case for intensive public relations, one may have several questions about the modern president who often goes public. Does he recognize a world beyond communications and images? Will he retain the perspective that a bad press—even when it is that—feeds on bad news? Does he grasp that only by solving the nation's problems will he solve his own as president?

The anecdotal record for recent presidents cautions against alarmism. The convergent forces promoting public relations in the White House have not overwhelmed the capacity of presidents and their advisers to monitor accurately the concerns of the citizenry. Parts of the institutional apparatus that has grown up in the modern White House mitigate against such myopia. The president's pollsters and other staff who gather opinion data from a variety of sources continuously record the public's views on current issues. A president's heavy investment in public opinion should serve as a counterweight to whatever faith he places in rhetoric. Jimmy Carter's press secretary, Jody Powell, expressed a sentiment one commonly hears from the White House: "Communications and the management of them, the impact is marginal. The substance of what you do and what happens to you over the long haul is more important, particularly on the big things like the economy." [22]

Although presidents freely blame the news media for their difficulties in the polls, there is little evidence that they have lost sight of the real sources of the public's disillusionment with them. Lyndon Johnson and Jimmy Carter suffered both in the polls and with the press; against the latter, their spokesmen sometimes railed bitterly. Yet neither man had any difficulty appreciating the effects of major issues on his popular support. Johnson observed, "I think [my grandchildren] will be proud of two things. What I did for the Negro and seeing it through in Vietnam for all of Asia. The Negro cost me 15 points in the polls and Vietnam cost me 20." [23] Carter, too, was aware of the real reason for his low standing in the polls:

> I think the Roper poll shows that I was below 60 percent, the Gallup Poll about 60 percent. Of course, I would like to have higher than either one of those, but I think that the controversial nature of some of the things that we put forward inherently causes a concern about me and reduces my standing in the polls, although I didn't want the prediction to come true. When I announced that I would put forward an energy package, I predicted my poll rating would drop 15 percent.[24]

Reagan, despite his repeated complaints of unfair coverage throughout 1982, faced up to double-digit unemployment when he confided to a reporter in early 1983 that if his policies failed to produce a recovery it "obviously . . . would be a sign" that he should not seek reelection.[25] Meanwhile, White House Chief of Staff James Baker ranked for reporters the following reasons for President Reagan's decline in the polls: "the economy, the economy and the economy." [26] These are the kinds of excuses in which one should wish presidents to indulge.

The dependence of modern presidents on public support appears, therefore, to keep them attentive to "real world" problems, even as they engage in public relations. Because strict adherence to his fiduciary responsibility to promote the general welfare occasionally requires the president to adopt unpopular policies that undermine his public support, one may assume that he also behaves strategically. That is to say, as the president makes policy, his own political well-being will be a foremost concern.

A strategic president must answer for himself two kinds of questions. First, what does the public want? That is, what will it tolerate, and what will it not? A president may have hunches, but he can never be sure how the public will respond to an initiative. Those presidents who lead by going public will be especially dedicated to reducing uncertainty on this score. Staffed with professional pollsters, econometricians, and political analysts, modern presidents go to great lengths to improve their understanding of public opinion.[27]

The second question a strategic president must address is much like the first, except that he must ask it of himself. Having defined what he wants to accomplish, he must decide how much popular support he is willing to give up to secure his policy goals. This question arises because no president will be a strict popularity maximizer. Popularity is, after all, a resource that allows a president to go public, a means for achieving other ends. The decision to spend some of his support on a favored program, to husband what support remains, or to seek more is complex and fraught with risk. This introspective question is probably familiar to all twentieth-century presidents, but acutely so to those modern incumbents whose leadership is closely bound to their popularity. To appreciate better how presidents adapt policy to the requirements of popular support, one needs to understand how they go about answering these questions about the public and themselves. As E. E. Schattschneider exhorted the profession half a century ago, "What is now needed is a politician's theory of politics." [28]

Different presidents, similarly situated, may arrive at different answers. Strategic judgment will depend on the composition of the president's coalition of support, which is largely identified by his party label; on his own policy aspirations; on his view of the office and its responsibilities; and on his personal makeup, particularly his willingness to take risks. It is beyond the scope of this book to survey recent incumbents on these attributes, and to speculate on how they might be configured in some future president would be an exercise in fatuity. One can, however, learn more about how presidents think through the relation between their political options and their popular support by examining the common political circumstances that condition their choices.

How Much Popularity Is Enough?

Popularity is like ice cream in that the more of it one consumes, the less satisfying the next helping will be. Beyond some point, the value of additional increments of support will diminish sharply. The point at which diminishing return sets in will vary from one president to the next, depending on his leadership style and on his political circumstances in Washington. Harry

Truman disdained pandering to the polls (his euphemism for the public) and has been judged to have more freely spent his popular support than did others who have occupied the office since the time the president's popularity could be measured with any precision. Not surprisingly, Truman's tenure was marked by greater swings of popularity, an experience he once described as "like riding a tiger." [29]

His successor has often been depicted as a man who valued the public's approbation far more than most presidents. According to one recent portrait, President Eisenhower coveted the public's favor as if it were an end in itself. Fred I. Greenstein writes, "Eisenhower's seemingly effortless facility in weaning public confidence never stopped him from also working to find additional ways to enhance his support." [30] Eisenhower's failure to champion unpopular programs, his refusal to engage critics, incuding those within his administration, his pusillanimous defense of the State Department against McCarthy's witch hunt, and his willingness to delegate to subordinates responsibility for unhappy occurrences are all perfectly consistent with this view of a president intent on preserving his prestige as if it were an end rather than a means to other goals. Greenstein summarizes Eisenhower's style as "refusing to go public as a politician, looking carefully rather than leaping, and striving always to represent himself as President of all Americans." [31] In this both Eisenhower and Truman appear exceptional. For the others, the point at which a diminishing return in popularity sets in falls somewhere between the endpoints established by these two presidents.

Each president must answer for himself how much support is enough, but one may assume that none will have an insatiable appetite. Whatever equilibrium forces may be operating within the country to prevent the president from long remaining universally beloved, one such force operates within the White House itself—namely, that popular presidents will tend to spend surpluses of support. As discussed in Chapter 5, Reagan's polls began to show increasing public disapproval of his job performance before the attempted assassination in 1981. To a reporter's query about this early development, one Reagan aide observed matter-of-factly, "The job's gotten into the fire more quickly with this [budget] proposal than in normal administrations because of [its] comprehensive nature. There's resistance to change." A Republican pollster added, "He's spending his savings [popularity] and he has less in the bank now, that's all." [32]

Another principle governing the strategic expenditure of popular support is, the closer the next election, the farther away the point of diminishing return. Whatever the role going public plays in his leadership, every sitting president is aware that his popularity is critical to his reelection chances. Today, with party nomination decided by caucuses and primaries, unpopular incumbents are no longer even guaranteed renomination.

At what date on the electoral calendar presidents become transfixed on husbanding and where necessary rekindling the public's approbation depends upon how much of it they already have and how much of it they think they will require to win reelection. In the spring of 1983, with President Reagan the least popular of any president by the end of his first two years, many Republican senators who had been Reagan's cheerleaders just a year earlier began carping that the president was shying away from tough budget cuts in deference to an election nearly two years away. By summer, White House aides confirmed the president's election concerns while announcing an extensive itinerary of political travel that would include a visit to China. Reflecting his unprecedented weak popularity at midterm, President Reagan's fence-mending activities appropriately began earlier than most. Spring of the election year is the season one hears politicians voicing unfamiliar concerns, in some instances the same concerns they had turned a deaf ear to only a few months earlier.[33] Perhaps not coincidentally, presidents tend to become more popular during the six months preceding the beginning of the reelection campaign.[34]

In considering how much popularity is enough, Eisenhower's political adviser Bryce Harlow appeared conservative when he confided, "The trick is to get the president into the fourth year with an approval rating still over 50 percent."[35] In fact, his estimate accords well with the track record of the seven incumbents who have sought reelection since 1948. In Figure 7-1 each president's share of the vote is plotted against his job performance rating for the preceding June. The regression line crosses 50 percent of the vote precisely at 50 percent approving.[36] During the postwar era, no president lost who entered a reelection campaign with half or more of the public behind him. According to the estimate in Figure 7-1, any incumbent who fails to achieve this golden mean is destined to lose. Understandable was the panic that struck the Bush White House early in the 1992 election year when his approval rating dropped to 46 percent and failed to improve after his State of the Union address.

Strategic presidents balance their ongoing need for popular support against their desire to achieve policy goals important to them and to their party's core constituencies, and therefore they do not always automatically act to increase their popularity. When a president enjoys a surplus of popular support, he may be expected to try to convert some of it into support for his policy objectives. The pursuit of popularity will also be regulated by the proximity of the next election. As the election nears, a president will be tempted to husband even what he regards as surplus support. Accordingly, an unpopular president nearing reelection should come as close to resembling a single-minded popularity maximizer as one will find in the White House, and newly elected presidents basking in victory may be expected to be as programmatic as they will be for the remainder of their term. Franklin Roosevelt, Lyndon Johnson, and Ronald Reagan all exploited their early support to advance ideological policies dear to their core constituencies. Their failure to sustain their early accomplishments has frequently been blamed

Figure 7-1 Relationship between Vote Share and Popularity of Incumbent Presidents Seeking Reelection, 1948-1984 (Percent)

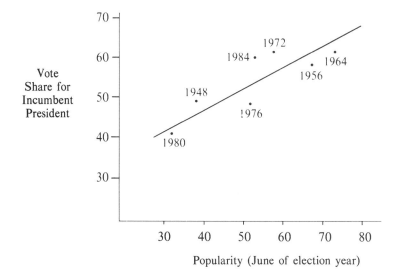

Popularity (June of election year)

NOTE: The estimated equation represented in the regression line in the figure is Vote = 30.4 + .44 × Popularity. This single variable explains 70 percent of the variance in the vote share of the incumbent president.

upon the intrusion of unfortunate events that made them lose their way, and the historical record provides numerous instances to support this argument. Fully cognizant of its potential damage for his domestic agenda, Lyndon Johnson initially resisted being sidetracked by Vietnam.[37] Even were no such events to intrude, the strategic considerations should, however, inspire presidents to pursue their preferred programs less and those that promise to enhance their popular support more. The advancing electoral calendar and the seemingly inexorable loss of their early support force them to respond to current events.[38]

Another more fundamental consideration is involved in weighing policy against popularity—the cost in public support of a particular policy venture. The severity of the trade-off will vary from one issue to the next. Some will impose little or no costs at all; a few may actually increase the president's popular base.[39] How presidents calculate this trade-off is the subject of the following sections.

Calculating Gains and Losses

This chapter so far has treated the president's approval rating as if it were a highly liquid commodity—something that can be spent and conserved in precise, calculated amounts. It is, of course, no such thing. Calling popular support a currency conveys its instrumental value, but once one tries to calculate the gains and losses resulting from a particular policy, the glint of this metaphor begins to fade. The exchange value of popularity will always be somewhat uncertain, depending upon the skill of the president in going public and upon only dimly understood dynamics of opinion change. At times a policy will provoke a particular constituency to withdraw its approval en masse—as in the farmers' reactions to President Carter's embargo of grain exports to the Soviet Union in 1980. At other times a policy will elicit no apparent response. There is perhaps no better example of the uncertain public reception to presidential actions than Gerald Ford's pardon of Richard Nixon. Could he, or for that matter could his pollsters, have foreseen that his brief televised announcement of the pardon would precipitate a 30-point drop in his approval rating or that nearly two years later voters would cite it as much as anything else as the reason for whatever unfavorable opinion they harbored toward him?[40] In a world where politicians strive for safe and certain outcomes, spending popularity can be a risky venture.

The downside risks and ease of miscalculation do not prevent presidents from entering the market, however. For presidents who are inclined to go public, popularity is, after all, their chief resource. Moreover, in that gains and losses of popular support inhere in presidential choice, strategic calculation is an activity that cannot be lightly ignored. President Reagan and his aides must have frequently pondered whether to fire James Watt, the controversial secretary of the interior. This issue arose recurrently because they knew that to do nothing might itself be costly. Strategic questions of this caliber confront every president. President Bush grappled with several issues. Should unemployment benefits be extended another 12 weeks? Should he sign or veto a new civil rights bill establishing new standards for combating discrimination in the workplace? How should the administration respond to the variety of health-care reform proposals circulating in Congress? These questions did not arise principally out of concern for Bush's popularity. They were policy matters that demanded a presidential position before other governmental actors would do their part. Yet they all contained important political stakes. One may assume that in none of these cases did the political ramifications escape President Bush or his staff. For a president to fail or to refuse to think about policy strategically is tantamount to a decision to spend his support inefficiently.

Presidents must associate policy with popularity. The reflections of Presidents Johnson and Carter show that they do, at least in retrospect. Although the question of how they calculate their gains and losses has no simple answer, presidents may be expected to consider the political consequences of their policy choices in one of two alternative ways.[41]

The first approach I shall call "general problem solving," or GPS. It offers a president a simple decision rule and promises not to lead him down too risky a path. In exchange, it limits the field of strategic policy choice and may require that the president produce outcomes that are beyond his capacity. The alternative approach can be stated largely as the converse of general problem solving. It requires the president to take a highly differentiated view of the public and to entertain a myriad of policy choices that would permit him to stitch together a national governing coalition from the particularistic and sometimes conflicting interests of diverse constituencies. This approach I shall call the "marginals" strategy.

These approaches will not always prescribe conflicting policies. In confronting a dominant national issue, the president may find that he is also making a strong bid to attract marginal constituencies into his coalition. Although the president's choice of strategies will depend in part on his own experiences as a politician, the approach he finds most attractive will sometimes have more to do with the character of the policy under consideration than with the character of the man making the choice.

To see how the substance of policy affects strategic considerations, it is helpful to classify the president's policy options. First, some policies will be national in scope, and their benefits broadly distributed. The most commonly cited example is national defense. Because of the president's national constituency, the visibility of his actions, and his position in national policy making, he more than anyone else will find his choices cloaked in a collective goods mantle. To continue the above example, as soon as the president's defense proposal reaches Congress and is parceled among the various committees and subcommittees, it will be disaggregated into a collection of decisions, each of which may have quite specific effects on particular constituencies. Which military installations and defense contractors should provide for the collective defense is historically how the president's defense proposals get restated. On its face, the general problem-solving strategy appears well suited to issues of this kind; for this reason it is a peculiarly presidential strategy.[42]

A second category of policies at the other extreme are those in which the president's choice will have highly specific, or particularistic, effects in the country. Here, specific localities and constituencies can be readily identified as the chief beneficiaries or victims of the president's policy. If there is a collective goods rationale for the policy, it will tend to be secondary to its particular effects in the way the public and Washington elites view the policy. Extension of unemployment benefits, an excise tax on the purchase of luxury yachts and expensive automobiles, start-up loans through the Small Business Administration, reregulation of the cable television industry, and duties on lumber imports from Canada are issues of this type that confronted Bush from 1989 through 1992. A policy's political ramifications may be assumed to be as specific as its effects on particular constituencies; consequently, policies of this kind invite presidents to take a highly differentiated view of the public in assessing potential gains and losses.

Sometimes a third kind of policy arises in which both its national and particular effects are prominent. The general welfare is at issue, but at the same time some constituencies will be asked to suffer more than others.[43] The most persistent policy question of this type is the economy. The general welfare component can be seen in widespread agreement over what an ideal economy should be, but since few ever expect this ideal to be fully realized, ample room remains for disagreement. Which economic problems of the moment should the White House address, and who should be asked to make the necessary sacrifice to correct the economy's course? Differing opinions arise in large part because economic conditions have disproportionate effects on the labor force. Blue-collar workers, for example, are hurt more by increases in unemployment than are white-collar workers. Conversely, some economists have argued that upper-income groups suffer relatively greater losses from inflation.

These economic effects take on special political significance because they correspond to the party cleavages of the electorate. Given their respective constituencies, Democrats and their core support group, organized labor, have emphasized employment policies, and Republicans and their allies in the business community have traditionally shown greater concern with inflation. Since the ideal economy is unrealizable, politicians as purveyors of their party's creed will frequently find cause to dispute the priorities contained in any administration's current economic program.

There is another aspect of economic relations that pushes policy discussion in this realm toward the particular distribution of benefits rather than the general welfare. "It turns out that good economic policies that bring you better growth, better employment, lower inflation and higher levels of prosperity usually have short-run cost," observed Beryl Sprinkel, who as chair of Reagan's Council of Economic Advisers was in a good position to appreciate the political dilemmas attending economic policy. He elaborated, "You go through the pain first, and get the goodies later. If I could change something, I would certainly get the goodies up front because it would solve a lot of political problems." [44] Fellow economist Lester Thurow similarly argues that these up-front costs to particular constituencies prevent good economic planning in the United States.[45] Economists may provide politicians with any number of economic proposals that would eventually move the economy to some better state for everyone, he argues, but because each imposes immediate cost to specific groups, presidents will be reluctant or unable to implement them.[46]

That the costs precede the gains is less significant in evaluating the relative attractiveness of GPS and the marginals strategies than that the short-run costs tend to be distributed unevenly. To improve one aspect of the economy, politicians must tamper with another; one group will be asked to pay for another's gain. The Phillips curve trade-off between inflation and unemployment is the most prominent example of the distributional consequences of alternative economic policies. The country is threatened with "runaway" inflation, and the administration responds by trying to reduce economic expansion by trimming federal spending and tightening credit to consumers and producers.[47] The predictable consequence is an increase in unemployment. When unemployment is high, conversely, presidents have typically sought to stimulate the economy by increasing government spending, cutting taxes, or lobbying the Federal Reserve to loosen credit. As presidents evaluate different doses of economic medicine, they must—to economists' lament—weigh the requirements of politics against those of economic theory.[48]

Within the past half century, managing the economy has joined "maintaining the peace" as one of the president's chief responsibilities. A president's success has been closely linked with his ability to maintain balanced growth. Because economic policy involves both the broad and the specific distribution of benefits, it affords an opportunity to study the implications for public support of these alternative approaches to calculating the political gains and losses embedded in policy alternatives.

General Problem Solving. Edward R. Tufte has offered a straightforward statement of the general problem-solving approach to popular support: "If there is a single, highly visible economic problem that is very important to the electorate, [the president should] seek preelection improvements on that problem regardless of the economic priorities of the party program." [49] Tufte's prescription applies to preelection economic policy, but one can readily extend it to other times and issues. Essentially, what GPS asks of the president is programmatic flexibility. The president who succeeds will be the one who neither slavishly serves the preferences of his political party and its core constituency nor panders to the special claims of narrow constituencies on the periphery of his coalition for maximum short-run payoff. Rather, he must address whatever economic problem threatens to throw the economy out of balance. If the unemployment rate had risen, say, by three percentage points in the past year, the president, regardless of his political party, should generate employment.

When more than one economic malady is present, especially when they appear to require contradictory policy responses as in the Phillips trade-off, Tufte has the president follow the preferences of his political party. Facing both high unemployment and inflation, a Republican in the White House would tackle inflation; a Democrat, unemployment. To be consistent with the spirit of GPS, however, the president would continue to address whichever problem appeared to be most severe. In the abstract, this kind of problem-solving politician cuts an attractive figure—a rare instance where the requirements of the general welfare are congruent with those of political ambition.

Immediately, however, GPS raises the question, could a president succeed by being seemingly indifferent to the particular distributional effects of his policy? Earlier I offered a rationale for an affirmative answer in the survey findings that individuals evaluate the president's performance more according to their assessment of general economic conditions than on the basis of their current financial well-being. This allows the distinct possibility that the president will not be exposed to the political costs—at least in public opinion—of policies that more greatly hurt some groups than others. That the public behaves this way is, of course, critical if GPS is to be a viable strategy. Otherwise, by failing to include the real costs of policy options in his deliberations, the president would probably choose a politically less attractive course.

More direct evidence of how the public assesses economic conditions is mixed. One study found that when survey respondents are presented with the Phillips curve trade-off between unemployment and inflation, those who by their occupation were more exposed to unemployment consistently selected it as the greater evil; those less threatened by unemployment chose inflation.[50] According to these findings, citizens do not appear to be indifferent to the particular effects of macroeconomic policy.

More consistent with the findings presented earlier in this chapter, however, is evidence showing that these occupational cleavages largely disappear when respondents are not presented with the stark choice between unemployment and inflation. When asked simply to identify the "most important problem facing the country today," Gallup Poll respondents over the years have typically named unemployment or inflation to about the same degree regardless of their positions in the labor force. These similarities are shown for manual and professional workers since 1974 in Table 7-1. Only during periods of high unemployment do the responses of these groups differ significantly; at these times, manual workers do become somewhat more sensitive to unemployment. With this occasional divergence, however, the occupational differences are neither statistically significant nor, one may assume, politically consequential. From this evidence, general problem solving does not appear to entail a sizable, hidden trade-off in the president's public support.[51]

Table 7-1 also presents answers to the most-important-problem question according to respondents' party identification. Consistent with the political parties' traditional constituencies, marginal differences in the preferences between Democrats and Republicans resemble those between the occupational classes. These preferences contribute to the political incentives facing Democratic and Republican presidents as they calculate the effects of alternative economic policies on their popularity.

Evidence of GPS in Presidential Economic Policy. Circumstantial evidence suggests that in setting overall economic policy, presidents have usually followed the dictates of general problem solving. For the period 1947 to 1976, Tufte found that when unemployment or inflation was a serious problem during the year preceding a presidential election, it tended to improve during the election year, regardless of which party controlled the White House.[52] Evidence that presidents routinely engaged in general problem solving during nonelection years can be found in another of Tufte's exercises. Using the number of mentions of "unemployment" and "inflation" in the annual

Table 7-1   Group Preferences in Selection of Unemployment and . . .

| | Preferences by Working Group | | | | | |
| | Actual Rates | | Manual | | Professional | |
Date	U	I	U	I	U	I
Oct. 1974	6.0	0.9	3	81	2	84
Mar. 1975	8.7	0.3	21	61	19	66
July 1975	8.4	1.0	22	51	20	52
Oct. 1975	8.6	0.6	23	56	21	60
Jan. 1976	7.8	0.4	25	45	20	54
Oct. 1976	7.9	0.3	35	45	26	54
Mar. 1977	7.3	0.6	43	58	36	60
Oct. 1977	6.8	0.3	23	35	24	33
Apr. 1978	6.0	0.9	23	50	10	62
Oct. 1978	5.8	0.8	11	76	5	76
May 1979	5.8	1.1	6	53	3	59
Oct. 1979	6.0	1.0	8	61	6	67
Jan. 1980	6.2	1.4	3	39	4	40
Mar. 1980	6.3	1.4	5	75	3	76
Nov. 1980	7.5	1.1	13	50	7	57
Feb. 1981	7.4	1.0	10	72	5	71
Jan. 1982	8.5	0.3	33	49	23	54
Aug. 1982	9.9	0.3	48	27	40	22
Oct. 1982	10.5	0.4	66	19	54	18
Apr. 1983	10.2	0.6	55	20	52	17
Nov. 1983	8.4	0.0	38	11	22	9
Feb. 1984	7.8	0.2	33	10	20	9
June 1984	7.1	0.3	33	13	23	14
Jan. 1985	7.3	2.4	28	12	15	8
Nov. 1985	7.1	2.4	30	7	17	5
July 1986	7.0	1.0	26	5	16	4
Apr. 1987	6.3	4.2	18	5	9	6

NOTE: Respondents were permitted more than one choice. U = Unemployment; I = Inflation.

Economic Report of the President from 1962 to 1977 to determine the president's priority, he tested the numbers against variations in economic conditions and the political party controlling the White House. Table 7-2 contains the data necessary to extend Tufte's original analysis through 1992. A casual inspection of these data reveals that mentions of unemployment (*UM*) and of inflation (*IM*) rise and fall with changes in the respective economic indexes and with the party in the White House.

To test these relationships more precisely, I shall follow Tufte's procedure of combining and converting the unemployment and inflation indexes into ratios. This results in two new variables: *UM/IM*, indicating the president's relative priority, and *U/I*, measuring the severity of unemployment relative to

... Inflation as the Most Important Problem, 1974-1987 (Percent)

| | Preferences by Party Identification | | | | | |
| | Democrats | | Independents | | Republicans | |
Date	U	I	U	I	U	I
Oct. 1974	2	81	3	78	3	82
Mar. 1975	23	63	19	61	17	60
July 1975	22	52	17	51	23	50
Oct. 1975	25	61	19	54	18	56
Jan. 1976	25	47	19	50	26	45
Oct. 1976	40	46	24	45	22	51
Mar. 1977	44	62	35	52	33	59
Oct. 1977	26	33	26	35	20	40
Apr. 1978	21	52	17	57	14	56
Oct. 1978	12	79	12	58	7	79
May 1979	7	58	4	52	3	62
Oct. 1979	8	62	5	63	6	65
Jan. 1980	5	43	3	37	2	38
Mar. 1980	5	71	3	78	3	75
Nov. 1980	12	51	10	56	6	54
Feb. 1981	11	68	8	77	3	76
Jan. 1982	31	46	29	50	21	56
Aug. 1982	55	22	40	22	36	25
Oct. 1982	68	15	58	19	54	19
Apr. 1983	57	19	49	16	49	16
Nov. 1983	39	11	28	10	22	10
Feb. 1984	36	10	25	11	22	7
June 1984	35	14	21	13	18	16
Jan. 1985	27	13	15	12	16	7
Nov. 1985	35	8	18	4	15	7
July 1986	30	3	18	4	20	3
Apr. 1987	16	7	12	4	8	4

SOURCE: Various issues of *Gallup Report.*

inflation. These indexes are correlated with each other at .61, and the ratios of mentions at .46 with a dummy variable for political party (*PP*, where 1 = Democratic president and 0 = Republican). The regression estimates presented in the following equation show the relative importance of these two variables on this measure of the president's economic priority.[53]

$$UM/IM = -.04 + .36 \ U/I + .77 \ PP$$
$$(4.2) \quad + \quad (3.3)$$

The *t*-statistic figures in parentheses indicate that both the ratio of the economic indicators and the party of the administration are significantly related to the ratio of presidential references to unemployment and inflation. The coefficients in the equation cannot be readily compared since they are based on variables with different metrics. One way to solve this problem is with the elasticity coefficient, which standardizes a regression coefficient against the mean values of the dependent and independent variables. A comparison of elasticities in the equation shows that the ratio of presidential references is roughly twice as sensitive to changes in the economic variable as to party turnover.[54]

The equation and Table 7-2 reveal a general agreement in the way the public and presidents assess economic priorities. While presidents are, by these indicators, more partisan than their followers, both place greater emphasis on those economic conditions that are widely recognized to be problems. These findings offer compelling circumstantial evidence on behalf of general problem solving as a representation of the way presidents make strategic presidential policy, at least in the realm of managing the economy.

The Marginals Strategy.   "Support thy friends and woo thine enemies" is a long-practiced political maxim. It would appear as valid for a president seeking to improve his standing in the polls as it would for a local alderman trying to put together a victory on Election Day. At various points, this study has examined presidents putting this maxim into practice. President Reagan's school reform and tax credit proposals were designed more to strengthen wavering support among certain traditionally Democratic constituencies than to serve as blueprints for policy. If this simple maxim does not fully capture the range of alternatives offered by the marginals strategy, it does, nevertheless, establish the important analytic principle that politicians should differentiate their constituencies.

The maxim is too limited because frequently it will be contradictory. After all, one's friends and one's enemies have found some compelling reason for disagreeing with each other. Also, as discussed earlier, presidents might decide to pursue unpopular goals. Presidents enter office with policy objectives, which one may assume will generally be consistent with the traditional commitments of their political party. A popular president for whom additional increments of support will have little value may well prefer to forfeit these marginal gains in favor of his policy objectives. In effect, he would be practicing the less venerable but equally ancient strategy of "support thy friends and screw thine enemies," more commonly known as majority rule.[55] Although, as the initial maxim suggests, the pursuit of core objectives need not always jeopardize support from more distant constituencies, there are good structural reasons in the class composition of the parties and the economic trade-offs that confront policymakers for believing this will frequently, perhaps generally, be the case.

With the help of a class of citizens I shall call "captive approvers," the marginals approach of differentiating constituencies can even be found to

Table 7-2 Relative Importance of Unemployment and Inflation in the
Annual *Economic Report of the President,* 1962-1992

Date of Report	President's Party (PP)[1]	Mentions in President's Report[2]		Economic Conditions[3] (percent)	
		Unemploy- ment (UM)	Inflation (IM)	Unemploy- ment (U)	Inflation (I)
1962	D	13.0	3.2	6.7	0.9
1963	D	9.2	3.6	5.5	1.8
1964	D	9.4	6.3	5.7	1.5
1965	D	4.8	5.4	5.2	1.6
1966	D	7.7	5.5	4.5	2.3
1967	D	6.0	3.0	3.8	3.3
1968	D	5.6	2.0	3.8	2.9
1969	D	5.7	3.8	3.6	4.5
1970	R	10.3	21.7	3.5	5.0
1971	R	20.0	38.5	4.9	5.4
1972	R	18.8	29.2	5.9	5.1
1973	R	12.8	34.0	5.6	4.1
1974	R	7.0	18.3	4.9	5.8
1975	R	9.3	16.7	5.6	10.0
1976	R	16.1	26.8	8.5	9.3
1977	R	4.9	23.2	7.7	5.1
1978	D	15.2	21.3	7.1	5.8
1979	D	5.3	32.0	6.1	7.4
1980	D	12.0	28.7	5.8	8.6
1981	D	3.7	22.1	7.1	9.2
1982	R	3.8	20.0	7.6	9.4
1983	R	12.5	10.0	9.7	6.0
1984	R	11.1	18.9	9.6	3.2
1985	R	8.6	18.5	7.4	4.3
1986	R	1.8	13.6	7.2	3.6
1987	R	1.25	13.75	7.0	2.8
1988	R	5.0	11.0	6.2	3.6
1989	R	2.7	6.4	5.5	4.1
1990	R	3.8	7.5	5.3	4.8
1991	R	1.0	7.0	5.5	5.4
1992	R	2.0	4.0	6.6	4.2

[1] Reports are filed in January and February. Note that after election years with party turnover, the former administration issues the first report of the new administration's term, as in 1969, 1977, and 1981.

[2] Number of mentions of root word per 10 pages of text.

[3] Unemployment and inflation rates during the preceding year.

SOURCES: The data for 1962 through 1977 are from Edward R. Tufte, *Political Control of the Economy* (Princeton: Princeton University Press, 1978), 79-81. The data for 1978 through 1992 are from yearly issues of the *Economic Report of the President.*

prescribe that rational presidents pursue the opposite strategy of "screw thy friends and woo thine enemies." If the president is so popular among his own party's identifiers that he believes an unpopular policy would not be greeted by a mass exodus, he might seek to expand his coalition by enticing marginal constituencies with policies they favor.[56]

Clearly this strategy appears too risky for the elected politician to be as commonly practiced as either of the above variants. One can, nevertheless, easily turn up instances of politicians putatively practicing it. Justifiably or not, black civil rights leaders have long complained that Democratic politicians have inadequately addressed their needs because they know that black voters are locked into the Democratic column on Election Day. More recently, the same theme was sounded by the conservative right under Bush. They have charged repeatedly that to maintain a broad popular base, President Bush has sacrificed his predecessor's supply-side economics and paid only lip service to the social agenda of his party's conservatives. Both of these charges became the bread-and-butter issues of his insurgent challenger, Patrick Buchanan, in the 1992 Republican presidential primaries. At least one study has investigated the possibility that presidents might strategically enlist economic policy in this manner. The results were mixed, but they do indicate that from 1947 to 1977, real income of major occupational groups tended to rise faster when the political party associated with a group's opposition (Republicans for blue-collar workers, for example) controlled the White House.[57]

This last variant of the marginals approach to strategic economic policy is most interesting here for two reasons. Since economic policies generally involve an unequal distribution of short-term costs and frequently entail trade-offs, the first maxim of taking care of everyone will generally be unavailable. (And when it is available, it will be so obvious as to be uninteresting for the study of strategic calculation.) The second maxim of playing a majority rule game is more strategic. In it, the president has consciously decided to spend his popular support, even at the risk of shortening his time in office. Only when a president is unpopular within his party will such a policy course also give him a chance to improve his standing in the polls. Since this circumstance rarely arises, the third strategic course of "woo thine enemies" will normally be the one that extends the greatest potential rewards to a president bent on improving his standing in the polls. For such a strategy to be attractive, the president must already enjoy strong support among his own party's identifiers. This situation both encourages him to look elsewhere for new supporters and frees him to pursue policies that are more attractive to marginal constituencies than to his core. As shown in the average popularity ratings of presidents by party in Table 7-3, this condition has frequently been satisfied. Only Jimmy Carter failed to average approval from two-thirds or more of his party's members. Considering that these figures include respondents who offered no opinion, Presidents

Table 7-3 Average Popularity Rating of Presidents by Partisan Group

President	President's Partisans		Independents		Opposition Partisans	
	Mean	S.D.	Mean	S.D.	Mean	S.D.
Eisenhower	87	4.0	67	7.4	49	8.3
Kennedy	84	5.4	66	7.5	49	10.3
Johnson	69	10.7	49	13.2	39	13.8
Nixon	76	12.4	50	13.6	35	12.5
Ford	66	6.0	46	7.5	35	6.5
Carter	57	12.2	44	11.7	32	10.4
Reagan	84	5.5	54	7.4	31	8.2
Bush (Jan. '89-Jan. '92)	85	7.1	64	10.9	52	12.1

NOTE: S.D. = standard deviation.

SOURCES: Various issues of *Gallup Report* and the International Survey Library Association.

Eisenhower, Kennedy, Reagan, and Nixon (until Watergate) found few within their ranks who needed conversion. The search for new support required them to look elsewhere.

Evidence of a Marginals Strategy under Reagan and Carter. Because of the way the public evaluates the economy, a marginals strategy may be less suited for macroeconomic policy than for issues less national in scope. Nonetheless, one can catch glimpses of it in the strategic planning of the Carter and Reagan administrations.

In late August 1981, with all of Reagan's major budget requests having sailed through Congress, the president's pollster and adviser, Richard Wirthlin, reflected on the future. Despite the president's continued strong popular support (about 60 percent approving) throughout the summer, Wirthlin's prognosis was guarded: "Political allegiances are deeply rooted. We are going to have to be very effective in order to keep the Reagan coalition together because the *natural tendency* will be for groups to go back to their original base" [emphasis added.][58] Among these groups, he singled out Catholics, certain blue-collar workers, and southern Protestants—all traditionally Democratic voters who had swung heavily to Reagan in 1980 and who were still behind him nearly a year later. Considering future developments, Wirthlin identified one potential problem area: blue-collar workers on the margin. "If unemployment increased to 10 percent next year that probably would have a more serious consequence on our new coalition than if inflation stayed at 15 percent." [59]

By the end of the next year, Wirthlin's dire scenario had come to pass. With it, Reagan's popular support plummeted to the 30 to 35 percent approval range, dropping even more sharply among Democrats and independents. Echoing his adviser's earlier prognosis, Reagan told a reporter that if he could not get unemployment down, it might indicate that he should not seek a second term.[60] When in late 1983 the economy turned up sharply and with it his popular support, this septuagenarian's talk of early retirement was replaced by renewed rhetoric about leading the way to an ascendant Republican party. In the 1984 presidential election, these marginal constituencies supported Reagan even more strongly than they had in 1980.

Jimmy Carter was not so fortunate at the marginals game. In the end, his failure to contain inflation may be judged to have cost him reelection. The irony is that throughout his term, this president, who came to the White House with weak ties to his party's core constituent groups, appears to have appreciated the political risks of inflation more than most Democrats in Washington. This can be seen in his posture toward the Humphrey-Hawkins full employment bill. Despite a ringing endorsement of this legislation early in his term, President Carter quietly insisted on an amendment that would allow him to suspend the program if inflation became a problem. And later, as increasing consumer prices, fed by spiraling energy prices, spread throughout the economy and Carter's popular support dissipated, there was little doubt that he preferred to deal with inflation rather than the by-now chronic 7 percent unemployment rate. By 1979, according to one White House planner, although the administration recognized that "the [unemployment/inflation] tradeoff is worse than it used to be," it would tackle inflation anyway, even at the risk of appearing "callous" to the unemployment problem. Another White House aide said candidly, "What Carter needs to get reelected is a policy that's pro-investment, maybe even pro-business." [61]

In this instance, inflation fighting conformed to the prescriptions of both the marginals and the GPS strategies, yet it remained highly risky. No president in Table 7-3 suffered weaker support among his own party's identifiers than did Carter. By turning away from the unemployment problem, Carter ran the risk of further alienating the party faithful, many of whom openly preferred Senator Edward Kennedy as their party's nominee in the next election.

Shortly after Carter's November defeat, former secretary of the Treasury Michael Blumenthal reflected upon the reasons for the failure of the administration's economic policies. In his opinion, failure resulted from "a basic schizophrenia within the Administration." The president was committed to an anti-inflation effort "if for no other reason than they know [inflation] is politically damaging." He then added, however, "the liberals [in the White House] believe that high interest rates are bad, that fighting inflation hurts poor people, and that we have to be very careful how we fight inflation in order not to hit 'the natural constituency of the Democratic Party.' " The net result was a policy of "fighting inflation but not too hard. It was tighten the belt, but don't cut out any important programs, cut down on government regulation but don't offend any special interest groups." [62]

The vacillation of the Carter administration reveals how presidents are sometimes pulled in opposite directions as they formulate economic policy. This is consistent with an earlier finding of independent effects of party and economic conditions on mentions of unemployment and inflation in the president's annual economic report. Although in the above cases the language of the marginals strategy appears to have dominated policy discussion, it remains unclear more generally whether presidents in deviating from their party's economic priorities are playing a marginals game at the expense of their supporters or are engaged in general problem solving. Under certain economic conditions each will yield similar results. In the absence of detailed, even intimate, information about the way individual presidents have examined their options, the question of which approach comes closest to representing strategic policy making must remain open.

Short of this, however, one can obtain from the study of public opinion suggestive information about incentives that inform the strategic thinking of presidents. If, for example, party groups similarly evaluated the president's performance as suggested by responses to Gallup's most-important-problem question, there would be little reason for presidents to calculate the relative gains and losses among different groups required by the marginals strategy. The following section presents direct evidence that the public judges the president as a national problem solver.

Presidential Popularity and Economic Performance

To assess their relative merits as strategies of presidential policy making, general problem solving and the marginals strategy need to be stated more precisely as predictions about public opinion, which one can then test. GPS holds that citizens, whatever their party or position in the labor force, will judge the economy on the basis of general conditions. Two specific predictions spin off from this statement. First, whatever economic condition is widely regarded to be a problem will be the one citizens will use to evaluate the president's performance. Second, Democrats, independents, and Republicans will not significantly differ in the relative importance they attach to this issue as they judge the president's performance. If these predictions are borne out in the public opinion data, it will mean that the president is on solid ground when he takes on national economic problems even when his policies impose costs on particular constituencies.

The marginals strategy views public opinion differently. Reflecting the class composition of the political parties, Democrats and Republicans will tend to pay greater attention to different features of the economy in evaluating the president's performance. The first prediction, therefore, is that Democrats' support of the president will be more closely associated with unemployment; and Republicans' support, with inflation. Under certain conditions, the marginals strategy also holds out the prospect that the president can gain new support among opposition identifiers. For this strategy to succeed, the president's identifiers would need to be less responsive to changes in the economy than independents or supporters of the opposition party.[63] Although this is not in itself a prediction that derives from the marginals strategy, it is a necessary condition for this strategy to be opportune. In sum, the marginals approach to strategic policy will be best suited for a setting in which party groups differ in their economic assessments and support among the president's partisans is less affected by changes in the economy.

To test these predictions on the monthly popularity ratings for each president beginning with Eisenhower, I have disaggregated the president's approval rating for the 368 national polls that make up the overall time series. Altogether, the hypothesized relationships require an examination of 24 different time series—the monthly ratings of Democrats, independents, and Republicans for eight presidents.

In estimating the effects of the economy on presidential popularity, one must address several critical methodological issues. These include identifying exogenous variables in addition to the economy so that the results for the economic conditions will not be biased; operationally measuring these variables in a way that makes good theoretical sense and allows their true effects to be best represented; and specifying the functional form of their relationship with presidential popularity. None of these issues has simple answers, a fact fully supported by the great variety of preferences on these matters that can be found in the burgeoning scholarship on presidential popularity.[64] These methodological issues are only tangentially related to the substantive questions here, and so I have reserved a full discussion of them for the Appendix. Because the way the analysis is performed greatly affects the results reported below, the reader is urged to consult this discussion.

In Table 7-4 the statistics necessary for testing the competing predictions have been collected from the analysis of the different time series. (See Tables A-1, A-2, A-3, and A-4 in the Appendix for a full presentation of the regression estimates.) The coefficients for unemployment and inflation have been adjusted by their variables' mean values so that their actual effects on popularity are broadly comparable. Because inflation failed to produce the correct sign for any of the partisan groups during the Kennedy or Reagan administrations, they were omitted from the analysis.[65] Only one other coefficient—that, ironically, for unemployment for Democrats under Carter— fails to show the correct negative sign, signifying an inverse relation between the economic indicator and the president's approval rating. Finally, the deleterious effects of rising unemployment on President Bush's public approval was delayed by Desert Storm. As a result, the unemployment rate rather than its change was used for this administration.

On the whole, the evidence presented in Table 7-4 offers impressive evidence on behalf of the general problem-solving approach to strategic

Table 7-4 Relative Effects of Unemployment and Inflation on Presidential Popularity among Party Groups

President	Unemployment			Inflation		
	Same party	Indepen- dents	Opposition party	Same party	Indepen- dents	Opposition party
Eisenhower (N=86)	−.67	−.53	−.70	−1.8	−2.8	−3.5
Kennedy (N=32)	−9.8	−16.7	−8.0	—	—	—
Johnson (N=50)	−6.8	−11.4	−5.6	−4.0	−9.1	−7.7
Nixon (N=61)	−1.74	−1.0	−5.5	−5.2	−3.8	−.1
Ford (N=21)	−.26	−2.4	−1.1	−6.9	−4.7	−6.3
Carter (N=40)	+1.34	−3.3	−4.4	−19.2	−18.3	−8.7
Reagan (first term) (N=41)	−3.1	−4.3	−2.8	—	—	—
Bush (N=36)	−22.4	−57.8	−61.4	−9.4	−6.0	−3.9

NOTE: Coefficients are the long-term, mean effects of variable on the president's monthly Gallup rating. Unemployment is the annualized percentage change in the unemployment rate during the preceding six months. For the Bush estimates, the unemployment rate is used. (See the Appendix for discussion and full specification of the model.)

SOURCE: From Tables A-3 and A-4.

economic policy. There are differences in the relative strengths of the relationships across partisan groups, reflecting for the most part the random error yielded by the generally small number of observations on which the calculations are based. Except for the rankings for Johnson and Nixon, the relationships thoroughly support the GPS predictions. Partisan groups similarly weigh unemployment and inflation in evaluating the president's job performance.

Although they are not nearly so impressive as to dissuade a strategic president from general problem solving, traces of support can also be found for the marginals strategy. Neither unemployment nor inflation had much effect on Eisenhower's popularity, which is appropriate given the general unimportance of these issues during the 1950s; but the relationships do satisfy the critical conditions of the marginals strategy in being stronger for opposition identifiers than for the president's partisans. Only on this occasion, however, does this ranking appear for both economic indexes. Stronger evidence of different economic priorities for Democrats and Republicans can be seen in the relationships during the Johnson and Nixon years. Consistent with the marginals prediction, in both instances, unemployment is a stronger determinant of approval for Democrats, and inflation is stronger for Republicans.[66]

Conclusion

This chapter opened by asking whether rhetoric or performance governs the president's standing with the American public. The testimony and behavior of presidents and their lieutenants suggest both do. The evidence assembled here agrees.

What presidents say to the public, and what others say to the public about them, matters more today than ever before in part because of the emerging political relations I have called individualized pluralism. These relations have created a community that inspires, as it facilitates, every member to go public.

The president, of course, enjoys special legitimacy as well as other, more tangible resources for engaging in such activities, but others in more modest ways do so as well. The circular letters of early nineteenth-century congressmen are today live satellite feeds to local news stations back in the district. Agency heads collaborate with clientele groups to campaign publicly for some policies and against others. From all accounts, interest groups, braced with well-heeled political action committees, are more dedicated and systematic in mobilizing constituent pressure on Congress than ever before. Cumulatively, these activities provide a significant counterbalance to the public relations that flow from the White House. News from Washington abounds, and it shapes opinions in the country more so today for the simple reason that there is more of it.

The role of the press in the politics of popularity has undergone a more subtle transformation than has the Washington political community as a whole. Its mission has always been to communicate news from Washington to the country, but for the effects of individualized pluralism to be fully realized, the Washington press has had to be willing to accommodate the increased efforts of politicians to go public. The evidence presented here indicates that the press has indeed opened itself as a conduit for the greater flow of news from and about Washington—particularly news of a critical tenor.

Whether one abhors or applauds these developments depends upon one's view of presidents as public men. They are either being saddled with certain criticism or being exposed to the sunlight of truth. The public's continuing expectations of the president's performance should prevent these changes from distracting the chief executive from his primary duties of the office. Quite simply, the American public holds the president responsible for promoting the general welfare. Although presidents may be expected to engage in public relations, and, depending upon one's disposition, even forgiven for doing so, they will succeed neither in the country nor in Washington if they pursue their public image to the neglect of active problem solving.

Notes

1. Further evidence that the public acts this way, and that this behavior is politically consequential, can be found in the significant relationship between the success of congressional candidates of the president's party and the current state of the economy. This relationship persists even when the president's party does not control Congress. Gerald H. Kramer, "Short-Term Fluctuations in U.S. Voting Behavior, 1896-1964," *American Political Science Review* 65 (March 1971): 131-143; Edward R. Tufte, *Political Control of the Economy* (Princeton, N.J.: Princeton University Press, 1978).
2. From interview in "Is There a Crisis of Spirit in the West?" *Public Opinion* 1 (May/June 1978): 3-8.
3. Jody Powell's characterization of presidential public relations is apt: it cannot "turn a sow's ear into a silk purse . . . but just a silkier sow's ear." Cited in Michael Baruch Grossman and Martha Joynt Kumar, "Carter, Reagan, and the Media: Have the Rules Changed on the Poles of the Spectrum of Success?" (Paper delivered at the Annual Meeting of the American Political Science Association, New York, September 1981), 18. On the marginal effects of presidential rhetoric, see Lyn Ragsdale, "The Politics of Presidential Speechmaking, 1949-1980," *American Political Science Review* 78 (December 1984): 971-984.
4. Harvy G. Zeidenstein, "White House Perceptions of News Media Bias," *Presidential Studies Quarterly* 13 (Summer 1983): 345-356.
5. Joe McGinnis, *The Selling of the President* (New York: Trident Press, 1969); and Mark Hertsgaard, *On Bended Knee* (New York: Farrar Straus Giroux, 1988).
6. James Deakin, *Straight Stuff* (New York: William Morrow, 1984), 44.
7. Richard E. Neustadt, *Presidential Power* (New York: John Wiley and Sons, 1980), 70.
8. Ibid., 22.
9. Lest the reader believe that I am chastising scholars for their work on the subject, I offer as an example of this literature my "Explaining Presidential Popularity," *American Political Science Review* 72 (June 1978): 506-522.
10. M. Stephen Weatherford, "Economic Conditions and Electoral Outcomes: Class Differences in the Political Response to Inflation," *American Journal of Political Science* 22 (November 1978): 917-938; D. Roderick Kiewiet, *Macroeconomics and Micropolitics* (Chicago: University of Chicago Press, 1985); Donald R. Kinder and Roderick Kiewiet, "Sociotropic Politics: The American Case," *British Journal of Political Science* 11 (April 1981): 129-161; Donald R. Kinder, "Presidents, Prosperity, and Public Opinion," *Public Opinion Quarterly* 45 (Spring 1981): 1-21; Richard Lau and David O. Sears, "Cognitive Links between Economic Grievances and Political Responses," *Political Behavior* 3, no. 4 (1981): 279-302.
11. M. Stephen Weatherford, "Evaluating Economic Policy: A Contextual Model of the Opinion Formation Process," *Journal of Politics* 45 (November 1983): 867-888.
12. Kay L. Schlozman and Sidney Verba, *Injury to Insult: Unemployment, Class and Political Response* (Cambridge: Harvard University Press, 1979).
13. Kinder, "Presidents, Prosperity," 17. See also Mark Peffley and J. T. Williams,

"Attributing Presidential Responsibility for National Economic Problems," *American Politics Quarterly* 13 (1985): 393-425.

14. Shanto Iyengar, Mark D. Peters, and Donald R. Kinder, "Experimental Demonstrations of the 'Not-So-Minimal' Consequences of Television News Programs," *American Political Science Review* 76 (December 1982): 853. This line of research is developed further in Shanto Iyengar, *Is Anyone Responsible? How Television Frames Political Issues* (University of Chicago Press, 1991). Using a less elaborate research design, Michael T. Robinson concluded that exposure to negatively biased stories led to more cynical views of politics. See his "Public Affairs Television and the Growth of Political Malaise: The Case of 'The Selling of the Pentagon,' " *American Political Science Review* 70 (June 1976): 409-432.

15. On this issue of how personal and interpersonal variables mediate the way citizens process mass communications, see Michael MacKuen, "Exposure to Information, Belief Integration and Individual Responsiveness to Agenda Change," *American Political Science Review* 78 (June 1984): 372-391; and Lutz Ebring, Edie N. Goldenberg, and Arthur H. Miller, "Front-Page News and Real-World Cues: A New Look at Agenda-Setting by the Media," *American Journal of Political Science* 24 (February 1980): 16-49.

16. Relative press attention to the president and Congress has been examined systematically for different historical eras. Findings showing the preponderance of congressional news during the middle half of the nineteenth century are reported in Samuel Kernell and Gary C. Jacobson, "Congress and the Presidency as News in the Nineteenth Century: The Cleveland Press, 1820-1876" (Paper delivered to the Annual Meeting of the Southern Political Science Association, Savannah, Ga., November 1-3, 1984). The rise of presidential news from 1885 to 1957 is recorded in Elmer E. Cornwell, Jr., "Presidential News: The Expanding Public Image," *Journalism Quarterly* 36 (Summer 1959): 175-283. Continued expansion of presidential news relative to that of Congress for the years 1958 to 1974 is presented in Alan P. Balutis, "The Presidency and the Press: The Expanding Presidential Image," *Presidential Studies Quarterly* 7 (Fall 1977): 244-251.

17. This case study draws heavily from an account by Deakin, *Straight Stuff*, 159-162.

18. Ibid., 161. A sample of newspaper reports on these press conferences confirms Deakin's recollection: James Reston, "Patriotism Backed," *New York Times,* November 12, 1953, 1; Robert W. Richards, "Velde to Press Quiz of Truman on Spies," *San Diego Union,* November 12, 1953, 1. Some reporters complained that their criticisms of Eisenhower were being muted by Republican editors and publishers. A year later, TRB (Richard Strout) offered the following instances of insufficient questioning of administration policies: "The Administration's security risk 'numbers game'; the phony unleashing of Chiang Kai-shek; the President's personal order directing the Atomic Energy Commission to write the Dixon-Yates contract" (TRB, "Washington Wire," *New Republic,* December 27, 1954, 2).

19. Republished in book form: William Greider, *The Education of David Stockman and Other Americans* (New York: E. P. Dutton, 1981).

20. Perhaps the closest thing to the Stockman episode during Eisenhower's tenure was the Treasury secretary's denunciation of the administration's annual budget as he unveiled it to the press. Though the event aroused much comment in Washington, there is little evidence it had much effect on public opinion. See Neustadt, *Presidential Power,* 80-84.

21. "Public Leans to View Stockman Should Remain As OMB Director," *Gallup Opinion Index* 194 (November 1981): 14-16.

22. Quoted in George C. Edwards III, *The Public Presidency* (New York: St. Martin's

Press, 1983), 88.

23. Quoted in Daniel Wise, "The Twilight of a President," *New York Times Magazine,* November 3, 1968, 131.

24. Jimmy Carter, "The President's News Conference of October 27, 1977," *Public Papers of the Presidents, Jimmy Carter, 1977* (Washington, D.C.: Government Printing Office, 1978), 1914.

25. Rich Jaroslovsky, "Economic Upturn Aids President's Popularity, but It Is Not Panacea," *Wall Street Journal,* April 28, 1983, 1.

26. Ibid.

27. Based on correspondence with one of Nixon's economic advisers, Edward R. Tufte relates the following story:

> Gearing up for the 1972 campaign, staff members of the Office of Management and Budget under the direction of the Assistant Director for Evaluation developed statistical models and ran multiple regressions assessing the influence of economic conditions on the outcomes of presidential elections. The OMB studies concluded that between-election increases in real net national product per capita had a strong impact on the electoral support won by the presidential candidate of the incumbent party. These findings were then reported to George Shultz and John Ehrlichman in the fall of 1971.

In *Political Control,* 136.

28. E. E. Schattschneider, *Party Government* (New York: Holt, Rinehart and Winston, 1942), 16.

29. Nelson Polsby offers such an assessment in Nelson W. Polsby, ed., *The Modern Presidency* (New York: Random House, 1973), 37-38.

30. Fred I. Greenstein, *The Hidden-Hand Presidency* (New York: Basic Books, 1982), 98-99.

31. Fred I. Greenstein, "Ike and Reagan," *New York Times,* January 29, 1983, 19.

32. George Skelton, "Reagan Dip in Poll Tied to Spending Cuts," *Los Angeles Times,* March 19, 1984, 6.

33. For examples of Reagan's efforts to restore lost support among women in preparation for the election, see Barbara Bosler, "G.O.P. Starting Campaign to Show 'Reagan Is Terrific on Women's Issues,'" *New York Times,* April 6, 1984, 11; and "Reagan on Women's Issues," *New York Times,* April 6, 1984, 11.

34. This was first examined systematically by James Stimson, "Public Support for American Presidents," *Public Opinion Quarterly* 40 (1976): 1-21.

35. Bryce Harlow, in a private interview with Professor John H. Kessel; Kessel, letter to author, October 16, 1985.

36. This analysis follows the procedures employed by Michael S. Lewis-Beck and Tom W. Rice, "Presidential Popularity and the Presidential Vote," *Public Opinion Quarterly* 46 (Winter 1982): 534-537.

37. The result in the view of many who have retraced U.S. steps into the Vietnam War was a "muddling through" policy that was incapable of achieving military victory and that virtually guaranteed the high costs of the protracted conflict. See David Halberstam, *The Making of a Quagmire* (New York: Random House, 1965). How Johnson's concern for his domestic programs contributed to an incrementalist strategy is well documented in Larry D. Berman, *Planning a Tragedy: The Americanization of the War in Vietnam.* (New York: Norton, 1983).

38. Elsewhere, I have systematically examined the tendency for presidents to lose support during their first 18 months in office. See "The Presidency and the People: The Modern Paradox," in *The Presidency and the Political System,* ed. Michael Nelson (Washington, D.C.: CQ Press, 1984), 253-256.

39. The reason the happy coincidence of popular and preferred policy infrequently occurs has to do with the inherently imbalanced distributional consequences of policies that serve the interests of core constituencies. This line of argument is developed more fully below.

40. The effects of the pardon on President Ford's defeat in 1976 is documented in Arthur H. Miller and Warren E. Miller, "Partisanship and Performance: 'Rational' Choice in the 1976 Presidential Election" (Paper delivered at the Annual Meeting of the American Political Science Association, Washington, D.C., September 1-4, 1977).

41. These alternative approaches to strategic calculation are not presented as exhaustive, but as elaborated versions of underlying notions about public opinion that will probably be found in other conceptualizations of the president's strategic calculus.

42. On the extraordinary ability of members of Congress to particularize policy, see David R. Mayhew, *Congress: The Electoral Connection* (New Haven: Yale University Press, 1974).

43. The critical distinction between policy issues in the second and third categories may be little more than that the distribution of costs in the third category are "apparent," and in the second they are not.

44. Peter T. Kilborn, "Alive and Thinking in Economic Advice," *New York Times,* August 9, 1985, A12.

45. Lester C. Thurow, *The Zero-Sum Society* (New York: Basic Books, 1980).

46. After briefly reviewing the pluralistic features of American politics that have long troubled reformers, Thurow finally gives up hope for economic reforms in the present system. The book ends with a proposal to reform the political order along the lines of British politics so that the executive could better withstand the unpopularity that often attends good economic policy.

47. For the purposes of this analysis, it is less important whether there is anything more than a short-term trade-off between unemployment and inflation than that most politicians and those who advise them on these matters act as though there is. Since the early 1960s, the Phillips trade-off has come in and out of vogue in policy discourse. For a review of its varying fashionableness, see Leonard Silk, "Phillips Curve Back in Business," *New York Times,* May 18, 1978. See also John M. Barry, "Inflation and Unemployment," *Washington Post,* August 27, 1984, 19.

48. Political considerations intrude when economists cannot agree what policy to prescribe. Moreover, presidents generally have little trouble finding the prescriptive economic advice to satisfy their political goals. Leonard S. Silk, "Truth vs. Partisan Political Purpose," *American Economic Review* 62 (May 1972): 376-378.

49. Tufte, *Political Control,* 101.

50. Douglas A. Hibbs, Jr., "The Mass Public and Macroeconomic Performance: The Dynamics of Public Opinion toward Unemployment and Inflation," *American Journal of Political Science* 23 (November 1979): 705-731.

51. For a thorough treatment of the perception of inflation as a problem for different economic groups, see Paul Peretz, *The Political Economy of Inflation in the United States* (Chicago: University of Chicago Press, 1983), 71-105.

52. Tufte, *Political Control,* 76-83.

53. The logarithms of the economic and mentions ratios are used so that changes in either the numerator or denominator receive equal weight. The estimation procedure differs from Tufte's analysis in using the previous year's unemployment and inflation figures rather than a three-year average. For this longer series the latter procedure proved unnecessary to avoid the serious collinearity problem he encountered.

54. An alternative interpretation arises when one examines these variables' "mean"

effects. Multiplying each by its mean value reveals that over the 24-year period, alternations of party control of the presidency had a slightly greater effect on presidential references than did changes in the economic ratios. This procedure is explained in Christopher H. Achen, *Interpreting and Using Regression* (Beverly Hills, Calif.: Sage Publications, 1982).

55. One strategic rationale for this approach is the dilution of rewards to the core necessary to maintain high popular support. It is a variant of William H. Riker's theory of minimum winning coalitions. See his *The Theory of Political Coalitions* (New Haven: Yale University Press, 1962).

56. One catches a glimpse of such regard for the core constituency in Richard Wirthlin's observation that during Reagan's first year the president's "governing" decisions had generally been accepted by "the political coalition that elected him" (Dick Kirschten, "The 'Revolution' at the White House: Have the People Caught Up with the Man?" *National Journal,* August 29, 1981, 1532). See also Robert Pear, "Making Old Constituency a New One for Reagan," *New York Times,* March 14, 1984, 12.

57. Paul Peretz, "Who Gets What, How and Why: The Economic Effects of Party Change" (Paper prepared for delivery to the Annual Meeting of the American Political Science Association, New York, September 1978).

58. Kirschten, "The 'Revolution,' " 1532.

59. Ibid., 1536.

60. Jaroslovsky, "Economic Upturn Aids President's Popularity," 1.

61. Edward Cowan, "Carter's Policy: Storm Clouds Grow," *New York Times,* June 7, 1979, D1. Referring to the captive voter concept introduced by Anthony Downs, one Carter adviser confided in the spring of 1980 that "Jimmy Carter has become a thoroughly Downsian president" (private conversation).

62. Hobart Rowen, "Blumenthal Tells Where Carter Erred," *Los Angeles Times,* October 10, 1979, 1, sec. 4.

63. This does not mean that if the president's remedy is so draconian as to replace one dominant problem with another the public will remain supportive. President Reagan's precipitous decline in the polls when his and the Federal Reserve's anti-inflation policies pushed the unemployment rate toward double digits attests to the public's willingness to switch problems. (Note the most-important-problem trends in Table 7-1.)

64. For samples of the variety of models developed to explain presidential popularity, see the following: John E. Mueller, "Presidential Popularity from Truman to Johnson," *American Political Science Review* 64 (1970): 18-34; Timothy Haight and Richard Brody, "The Mass Media and Presidential Popularity," *Communications Research* (January 1977): 41-60; Samuel Kernell, "Explaining Presidential Popularity," *American Political Science Review* 72 (1978): 506-522; Douglas A. Hibbs, Jr., "The Dynamics of Political Support for American Presidents among Occupational and Partisan Groups," *American Journal of Political Science* 26 (1982): 312-332; David G. Golden and James M. Poterba, "The Price of Popularity: The Political Business Cycle Reexamined," *American Journal of Political Science* 24 (November 1980): 696-714; Michael MacKuen, "Political Drama, Economic Conditions, and the Dynamics of Presidential Popularity," *American Journal of Political Science* 27 (1983): 165-192; and Charles W. Ostrom, Jr., and Dennis M. Simon, "Promise and Performance: A Dynamic Model of Presidential Popularity," *American Political Science Review* 79 (June 1985): 334-358.

65. Rao and Miller recommend that wrong-signed coefficients be left in the equation unless one can justify their exclusion. I have omitted these variables in Table 7-4 because the resulting equations behave better on a variety of criteria. Serial

correlation, according to Durbin's *h*-statistic, becomes less severe in each case. Moreover, the commentary of pollsters and White House advisers in these administrations fails to mention inflation—even the declining one for Reagan—as a major source of the president's public support. For a discussion of the risk of omitting theoretically indicated variables because of wrong signs, see Potluri Rao and Roger LeRoy Miller, *Applied Econometrics* (Belmont, Calif.: Wadsworth Publishing Co., 1971), 32-40.

66. This finding for Nixon corresponds to the unusually consistent ranking of the correlates of unemployment and inflation on Nixon's popularity by income classes reported by Friedrich Schneider. The exceptional character of this pattern presented here is consistent with the failure of Schneider's results to be repeated in subsequent research. See Friedrich Schneider, "Presidential Popularity Functions of Different Classes: A Theoretical and Empirical Approach" (1977, Mimeographed). See also Kristen R. Monroe, *Presidential Popularity and the Economy* (New York: Praeger, 1984).

Conclusion: The Prospects for Leadership   8

It is traditional, if not quite obligatory, for studies that argue change as their central thesis to conclude with a speculation about the future. What is in store? With events daily yielding new insights into going public as a strategy for presidential leadership, it is appropriate to entertain this question here. Before considering the future, however, one should be aware of the opportunities and pitfalls presented by the current vantage.

Perhaps the most conspicuous limitation to projecting the future is the recency of the developments I have described. Reading current events to theorize about even the present state of presidential leadership is like walking a tightrope; one's footing is still more unsure for predicting the behavior of presidents throughout the next decade. No matter whether one arbitrarily designates Richard Nixon or Jimmy Carter as the president who initiated the *routine* practice of going public for his leadership in Washington, data are still insufficient to delineate fully the implications of going public for future politics. And yet, since Nixon was in the White House, regularities in presidential behavior and in others' responses to it, which are at odds with past practices, have begun to reveal how the new order might look. These emerging patterns appear all the more indicative since they are consistent with the model of today's Washington, which has been described as individualized pluralism.

Aside from the caution that must attend instant history, the personal character of the office also limits speculation about the future. The presidency affords each occupant the latitude to define the job for himself. In the absence of apprenticeship, the incumbent must lean heavily upon his experience in public life. In important respects, then, presidential leadership will be as varied as the political careers and talents of the politicians who occupy the Oval Office. Ronald Reagan eclipsed all of his predecessors in the quantity of national appeals and outdid most of them as well in the quality of presentation. George Bush took his public leadership in a different direction. Spurning ambitious policy departures, he sought instead to shore up public support for himself and his party through unprecedented levels of travel and personal appearances.

One is not completely adrift, however, in trying to chart the future. Some presidents leave their mark on the office. Occasionally a figure enters the White House whose political intuition eclipses the perspicuity of those who are currently studying the office. His success educates scholars and future presidents alike. Franklin Roosevelt was just such a president. Within a short time after his departure, Roosevelt emerged a paragon, clarifying for many the techniques of bargaining, for others the exercise of charisma, and for still others the inner bearings necessary for success at the job. Because Roosevelt established new standards, his successors have been saddled with comparisons of their performance against his.[1]

Will Ronald Reagan cut such a figure? Will his shadow loom over the next generation of White House occupants? Quite possibly. This is more than idle speculation, for Ronald Reagan relied on going public for his influence in Washington more heavily and more profitably than did his predecessors. His success has forced others in Washington to reevaluate the way they assess the office. How they adapt to these new assessments will permit, and even encourage, future presidents similarly to go public.

As instructive as Reagan's example may have been for Bush and future presidents, the accuracy of the prognosis for future leadership does not depend wholly on the length of his shadow. Going public is a leadership style consistent with the requirements of a political community that is increasingly susceptible to the centrifugal forces of public opinion. The choice to go public will be inspired less by Reagan's example than by the circumstances of the moment encountered by future presidents. The evolving structure of political relations along the lines described by individualized pluralism will continue to make going public a favored approach to leadership.

Other tendencies are emerging in Washington relations that reflect but also complement, accentuate, and reinforce the strategy of going public. Together they may shortly move community politics to a state even less recognizable to those steeped in the traditions of institutionalized pluralism. Future evolution can be classified into two broad types: the behavior of politicians and the effects on policy.

Adaptive Responses to Presidents Going Public

Expectations of going public routinely become incorporated into relations between presidents and other politicians, especially in this era of divided party control of government. Politicians from the opposition party plan their strategies to minimize the president's potential damage to their designs, and they look for opportunities to exploit for their own purposes his capacity to go public. Adaptive responses occur at a variety of levels—from the competing parties posturing on issues to individuals planning their careers. Examples of each abound.

Issue Posturing

When a president goes to the country, he is counting on his prestige to persuade sufficient numbers of citizens to communicate their support of his position to their representatives. Success depends neither on building majority support in the country nor on buffaloing other politicians into believing that he has. All the president need do is convince a sufficient number of politicians that the political cost of resisting his policy is greater than any potential gain.

Intense minorities scare politicians more than inattentive majorities for the good reason that the former will act on their beliefs and the latter will not. Presidents who exhort viewers to contact their members of Congress are trading upon the caution with which politicians greet intense preferences. At times, even when representatives know that their position and not the president's represents majority opinion, they will shy away from openly breaking with him for fear that he may take his case to the people. Such an instance occurred in the spring of 1985 when many House and Senate Democrats expressed reluctance to legislate an end to the financial aid for rebel forces in Nicaragua on the suspicion, as one Democratic leader explained, that President Reagan might make it a major public issue later in the summer. Fearful of being caught on the wrong side of the issue, as they had with Reagan in the past on budget cuts and defense spending, the Democrats ceded to the president greater latitude than they otherwise might have. The ability to go public presents presidents with the opportunity to control policy discussion to an extent unavailable to those who would rely exclusively upon elite negotiation for their leadership.

Strategic Planning

At a more advanced level of strategic calculation, politicians anticipate the president's option to go public as they engage in coalition building. On no subject is this calculation more precise than on taxes. Increasing taxes is always painful for politicians, especially during an election year when they must ask for taxpayers' votes shortly after taking their money. This accounts for the unusual wariness with which President Bush and the Democratic congressional leadership approached one another on a tax increase during the summer of 1990, at a time when a ballooning deficit was about to cause severe and politically unacceptable reductions in federal programs. Members of Congress were, if anything, even more squeamish about an election-year tax increase. Unlike Bush, whose first term still had two years left, all of the members of the House and a substantial part of the Senate Democrats faced reelection in November. The Democrats had been evading any association with taxes ever since George Bush had trumped Democratic candidate Michael Dukakis in the 1986 presidential election with the words "Read my lips: 'No new taxes.' "

The Democratic solution to their dilemma was to turn the president's capacity to go public to their advantage. Bush and by association his party's congressional candidates would bear principal responsibility for justifying the tax increase to the public. (Speaker of the House O'Neill, as noted in Chapter 4, had followed much the same course in successfully negotiating an election-year tax increase in 1982.) First, the Democrats demanded a *mea culpa* from Bush for his "no new taxes" pledge before they would enter into serious negotiations. In early summer the president tried to avoid political fallout by burying in a press release, in a list of possible revisions of the tax code, the phrase "tax revenue increases." Despite his best effort, this reference, stripped of its circumlocution, won banner headlines in the nation's newspapers and was the lead story on each network's evening national news program. Second, at the conclusion of negotiations in early October, the president agreed to present the proposed tax increase to the American people in a national broadcast. One can sympathize with the president's predicament and explain his tepid performance as he unveiled a budget compromise at odds with his campaign pledge and outspokenly opposed by his party's members of Congress. In the end, the Democratic Congress got an even more attractive tax package; the president's job performance rating went into a nosedive, and the Democrats picked up nine House seats in the November election.

Redefining the Strategic Repertoire

A third level of strategic planning, which derives at least in part from the president's demonstrated ability to go public, is the way other Washington politicians view their own strategic opportunities at public relations. Increasingly, whether learned independently or from observing the president, politicians throughout Washington are coming to adopt aspects of going public as part of their own repertoire.

One of the most striking examples occurred in late May 1985 when House Ways and Means Committee Chair Daniel Rostenkowski followed President Reagan's prime-time appeal for public support for tax reform with a national television appeal of his own. What an incongruous sight it must have been for the men and women who served with former Ways and Means Chair Wilbur Mills to watch a successor telling the country that with its active support his committee would beat back the "special interests" that would be hard at work to frustrate tax reform.

In adopting much of Reagan's script, Rostenkowski sought to neutralize the president's mandate as well as siphon off a share of whatever credit might be forthcoming if a popular tax reform measure were to be enacted. Those close to Rostenkowski offered another reason for his rousing appeal. Speaker O'Neill had announced his retirement and sealed it with a million-dollar contract for his memoirs, and Rostenkowski was planning "an outside" bid for the post. To stand a chance against fellow Democrat James Wright, whose job as majority leader made him heir apparent to the speakership, Rostenkowski was building a record of his ability to represent Congress in its dealings with presidents who go public.[2] This quintessential institutional actor appealed to the country to "write Rosty" not only to promote the Democrats' commitment to tax reform but also to advance his own claim later for the highest leadership position within the House of Representatives.

Rostenkowski's insight was not altogether lost on the man he hoped to succeed. In 1981 Speaker O'Neill hired a new, more publicly active press secretary. Although public relations cut against O'Neill's grain, he faced the dilemma, as observed by one congressional reporter, that "if he had not gone public, there would have been nobody at all to tell the Democratic story." [3] Strategic adaptation of this kind is increasingly common on Capitol Hill. Though on most occasions it does not arise directly in response to the president's initiative, his example nonetheless inspires others to try their hand at going public. House leaders, for example, have complained that junior members no longer toe the party line in hope of favorable committee assignments that might help them get reelected. Instead, according to one of O'Neill's senior staffers, they "go directly to voters via television." [4] Senate Majority Leader Howard Baker agreed: "If you don't let them do anything on the floor, they do it on the steps [of the Capitol]. And somehow there's always a TV camera out there." [5]

As politicians at every level routinely go public, the president's public activities become normal behavior to which others respond when they must but to which they no longer take exception. Furthermore, as other politicians similarly engage in public relations to pursue their own political objectives, public posturing will tend to displace quiet diplomacy as the normal means by which fellow Washingtonians communicate with one another across the institutional boundaries that separate them.[6]

Career Adaptations: Washington Correspondents and Presidential Aspirants

The rise of this new style of presidential leadership appears to have profoundly altered the careers of two groups in Washington: correspondents and presidential aspirants. I examined both in earlier chapters; I return to them here to clarify the ways in which political careers adapt to the altered circumstances posed by going public as a routine of the modern White House.

During the 1960s and 1970s, the reporting style of Washington correspondents evolved from objective to interpretive journalism. Various reasons have been offered for this reorientation. Certainly, any reporter whose Washington career spanned Johnson's Vietnam credibility gap and Nixon's Watergate would likely say that these events conclusively exposed the deficiencies of objective journalism.

As significant as these events were, other, more structural features of political relations in Washington had begun reworking the professional creed of Washington correspondents by the onset of the Vietnam War. With growing opportunities for news analysis provided by increasing network coverage of the White House, longer evening news programs, and televised news conferences, objective journalism made a hasty retreat. Reporters found themselves describing events their readers had already viewed for themselves. For traditional correspondents whose job it was to report on events in Washington for the readers back home, expanded network television coverage of the White House threatened to leave them without a purpose.

As politicians increasingly employed national media to market policies as well as themselves, objective journalism encountered another problem. Because this creed offers the reporter little latitude for evaluation and interpretation, it is better suited for covering what politicians do than what they say. Reporters found themselves serving as vehicles for the propaganda activities of politicians. Even in reporting what they privately regarded to be partial truths and outright falsehoods, objective journalism required them to play the role of neutral scribes. For some, the credibility gap of Vietnam and the coverage of Watergate posed this dilemma.

Perhaps at no time, however, was the dilemma more sharply felt by the working press in Washington than during Senator Joseph McCarthy's witch hunt in the State Department and the Army in the early 1950s. However outlandish were McCarthy's charges in the opinion of many correspondents, they felt obliged to report them in a straightforward manner as news. When privately pressed by these reporters to substantiate his claims, McCarthy would dissimulate and at times as much as admit that he had no proof.[7] Yet because these encounters were "off the record," many correspondents were obliged not to report this information to their readers. Some reporters did over time switch to a more evaluative, critical reporting of McCarthy's shenanigans, but one study of press coverage found that efforts to rebut false statements rarely appeared in the wire services and that the other critical stories were significantly less likely to be picked up by other papers around the country.[8] During the early 1950s, various internal and external mechanisms of the newspaper business were enforcing objective journalism. In the judgment of historians and journalists looking back on the era, the result was that the practice of objective journalism served to broadcast McCarthy's campaign.[9]

In mobilizing public opinion to sway events in Washington, McCarthy along with Senator Estes Kefauver, who conducted televised hearings into wrong-doing within the drug industry, were precursors of the modern politician who goes public. Confronted with going public as a political strategy, objective journalism neither supplies reporters with good copy nor permits them to assess rhetoric against reality. The creed of analysis and interpretation solves both problems.

Because going public is only one part of a broader transformation of community relations, one cannot state precisely the degree to which trends in presidents' public activities, such as those presented in Chapter 4, contributed to the professional reorientation of Washington correspondents in the 1960s.

There is little doubt, however, that this new style of journalism has correspondents balancing presidential rhetoric with independent analysis. One sees it in the insistent questioning at news conferences, in the television and newspaper commentary that follows presidential addresses, and in the coverage of presidents on the evening news. On this last score, one study of network news found that by 1985 the average taped segment of the president speaking lasted only 9 seconds, compared with 44 seconds during the years 1965 to 1972.[10]

The other group whose careers are being redirected in ways that reflect and reinforce the prospects of going public as presidential strategy is the men and women who aspire to hold that office. Reflecting the rise of the national government in public life at home and abroad, during the early post-World War II era the U.S. Senate replaced the states' governorships as the chief source of presidential timber. Senators enjoy resources that few other officeholders can match. Unlike their House colleagues, who are forced to specialize by their districts' narrower concerns and their chamber's greater number, senators find that their varied committee responsibilities and the relaxed floor procedures permit them to be reputable and vocal dilettantes on any number of domestic and foreign issues that arise from day to day. The Senate serves as a megaphone with which its members champion policies before a national constituency. Moreover, the Senate is a school for the pluralist arts. When elected to the White House, Lyndon Johnson and John Kennedy—but not Richard Nixon, who served in the Senate only briefly before entering the isolation booth of the vice-presidency—were familiar with, if not expert in, the requirements of a bargaining president.[11]

Since the presidential selection reforms and the entry of strong "outsider" contenders for the nomination, the Senate has lost some of its standing as the home of future presidents. This does not mean that it will go the way of the cabinet, which served briefly as the presidency's penultimate office in the early nineteenth century, but it does mean that aspiring politicians will no longer need to find their way to the Senate—or for that matter to Washington—to make a serious run for the White House.

The strategic effects of the biases of the reformed selection system on the 1988 election were already apparent by 1985, winnowing and tailoring candidates to generate party nominees who if elected might well seek to emulate Ronald Reagan's style of leadership. Observers caught a glimpse of these processes in late 1984 when Howard Baker retired early from the Senate after finding his duties as majority leader, and perhaps the "insider" status that comes with it, an encumbrance during his brief and uneventful bid for the Republican presidential nomination in 1980.[12] For much of 1985, three years before the election, private citizen Baker could be found on the circuit of New Hampshire's civic lunches and coffee klatches, which quadrennially provide citizens of that state with their special form of entertainment. While Baker was laying the groundwork for a bid in New Hampshire's early primary, his former Senate Republican colleagues, some of whom also aspire to the presidency, were stuck in Washington grousing with their president and struggling with such unpleasant subjects as the budget deficit, import quotas, and the multiple problems of the American farmer. The same consideration can be seen in the decisions of Arizona Governor Bruce Babbitt and incumbent Colorado Senator Gary Hart to forego promising races for the Senate in 1986 in order to free themselves to seek the Democratic party's presidential nomination in 1988. Their strategic preference to make an office-less bid for the White House was repeated in 1992 when two of the five principal Democrats competing in the presidential primaries did so as former officeholders. By having voluntarily stepped off the political career ladder, former California Governor Jerry Brown and former Senator Paul Tsongas were able to stake out the moral high ground over their officeholding rivals.

Finally, individuals who have never held public office, but who do possess the requisite resources—ample television exposure, political action committees, and an established fundraising list—will in the future be considered serious contenders for this pinnacle office of the political career structure. When television evangelist Pat Robertson declared his presidential candidacy in 1987, his announcement was greeted in Washington not with derision but with an invitation to speak at the National Press Club. Four years later, another never-elected television personality, Patrick Buchanan, undertook the apparently quixotic task of winning the Republican party's nomination away from its sitting president. That he turned in a credible performance in the early presidential primaries strengthens the prospect of future candidacies from nonofficeholding politicians. Neither Robertson nor Buchanan, however, enjoyed the status of a serious contender that H. Ross Perot's vast personal fortune conferred on him.

Throughout this book going public has been presented as a product of the new Washington and its new breed of presidents. Because the political marketplace is regulated in no small part by anticipation of and adaptation to others' choices, going public has become incorporated generally into the expectations and behavior of Washingtonians. In this way it reinforces and accentuates the community's continued evolution.

Public Policy and Going Public

The implication of public strategies of leadership for policy has been a subject of recurrent interest in this study. Thus far I have concentrated mostly upon the deleterious side effects of public activity on bargaining to show that rather than complement, public strategies, when frequently engaged, damage and displace bargaining. Public discussion requires issues to be stylized in ways that frequently reduce choices to black-and-white alternatives and to principles that are difficult to modify. In part this reflects the rigidifying effect of declaring one's preferences publicly, but it also results from the stylization of issues required to accommodate the limited attention span of the public audience and the brief time spots available on national television.

Perhaps more damaging, public discussion tends to harden negotiating positions as both sides posture as much to rally support as to impress the other side. Bargaining and compromise suffer. Even when a stalemate is avoided, the adopted policy may not enjoy the same firm foundation of support had it been enacted by a negotiated consensus. These are some of the unfortunate consequences of making policy in the public arena. Other consequences strike more deeply to the foundation of democratic politics, if not shaking it, at least altering the structure of political relations it supports.

Supply-side Politics

At first glance the perforated borders of individualized pluralism would appear to bode well for democratic politics. After all, should the citzenry's demands not flow more freely into Washington? Weakened leadership and the deterioration of other mechanisms of conformity to the requirements of protocoalitions have made institutions more easily penetrable and have weakened their resistance to poaching by others who compete for the same jurisdiction. As a result, outsiders today are provided with a porous governmental apparatus that contains numerous access points for those who seek to influence policy. Moreover, the increased sensitivity of politicians to public pressure, which follows from these relaxed internal constraints, improves the chances that outsiders will find the necessary institutional sponsorship for their views. A fair reading of these developments might lead one to assume a closer alignment between policies favored in the country and those deliberated in Washington. If so, whatever its ill effects on partisan discussion, individualized pluralism's corruption of the traditionally insular political relations would be a boon to democracy.

The swiftness with which some new issues sweep into present-day Washington and traverse its policy course appears to confirm this assessment. The "flat tax" drive of the late 1970s found eager congressional sponsorship, and under Reagan it emerged in altered form as the core concept of the administration's comprehensive tax reform proposal. An even more impressive example is the alacrity with which Mothers Against Drunk Driving (MADD) won federal legislation in a policy realm that had traditionally been reserved to the states. In 1980, just two years before its legislative triumph, MADD was created by two mothers who had lost children in automobile accidents involving drunken drivers. Enjoying continuous television and press coverage, by 1982 MADD had formed 230 chapters in 42 states with a quarter of a million members. Because of its inspired grass-roots campaign, the federal government today insists that states have tough drunk driving laws on their books.[13]

In 1983 the savings and loan industry staved off an imminent Internal Revenue Service (IRS) regulation that would have required banks and savings associations to withhold a portion of depositors' interest for taxes. The similar quick success of these bankers is less impressive only because they needed a simple resolution of Congress and did not require the president's signature to accomplish their goal.[14]

These cases and others like them succeeded by short-circuiting the slow and arduous process by which policy issues have traditionally attracted majority coalitions in Washington. The traditional method consisted of continuous discussions with representatives of those constituencies who would be most affected by the policy and with key governmental participants—most frequently committee and subcommittee chairs and agency heads who would be chiefly responsible for enacting and implementing the program. This involved ongoing reformulation to broaden the policy's political support and to make it administratively feasible. Ultimately, if in this incubation phase the issue succeeded in attracting the right sponsors and sufficient support to give it a reasonable prospect of success (and few did), it would then typically wait in queue for a presidential endorsement, which might provide the necessary impetus to get it enacted.

What allowed the issues described above to circumvent the traditional process was the massive grass-roots campaign generated outside Washington; by the time representatives of these campaigns approached potential legislative sponsors, many politicians had already begun lining up to support the policy. The savings and loan industry's campaign quickly generated millions of letters and post cards. One senator alone counted 769,000 pieces of constituent mail—almost all of it supporting the industry.[15] By so thoroughly stirring the opinion that flows to members of Congress, many of those promoting special causes find that they can frequently prevail even when their efforts fail to win the endorsement of the president, the relevant agency heads, or committee chairs. The most senior Republican the savings and loan industry could recruit to sponsor its cause was first-term Senator Robert Kasten of Wisconsin. A generation earlier, this member's status would have earned him little more than an opportunity to be seen but not heard. By 1983, of course, the Senate had changed, and the opportunities available to a junior member had greatly expanded. Over the opposition of his party's committee and floor leaders, his president, and the Internal Revenue Service, Kasten promoted the cause of the savings and loan industry to a resounding victory on the Senate floor.[16]

Even in the altered circumstances of present-day Washington, Senator Kasten's feat surprised the local cognoscenti. It demonstrated that great external pressure can be sufficient to induce congressional compliance even without engaging traditional avenues of influence. This is a far cry from the lobbyist's code of "never pressure" under institutionalized pluralism.

Pressure is the essence of public strategies, whether they are engaged in by presidents or outside groups. Going public succeeds not by adjusting policy to the mix of preferences represented in Washington but rather by trading on the strategic concerns of elected politicians and, thereby, changing those preferences. When success or failure is decided in the country, institutional leaders are less necessary; even a junior senator can do a splendid job.

If by now the activities of the savings and loan industry and MADD look familiar, they should, because they follow much the same strategic formula President Reagan employed so successfully in 1981 to push massive tax and social spending cuts through Congress. The difference is one only of scale. Whether undertaken by a president seeking to redirect the priorities of the federal government or by two mothers wanting tougher drunk-driving laws, going public has become a frequently preferred approach to coalition building in Washington. On their face, these cases appear to support the improved responsiveness of national political institutions to the citizenry's demands under individualized pluralism.

But is this really what is going on? Are demands flowing more freely into Washington and shaping policy, or rather, are they being created by politicians through inspired mass advertising? One might argue that the distinction does not much matter because the appeals must still strike a responsive chord, or they will be quickly deflated by the public's inattention or even its antipathy. One can support this argument by pointing to the dismal performance of grass-roots lobbying by the Natural Gas Supply Association in 1983. Seeking to decontrol natural gas prices, this organization created a $1-million front called Alliance for Energy Security to drum up a national letter campaign to Congress. A consultant who specializes in targeted mail was retained to mount special pressure on 15 members of Congress whom the gas lobby had designated as vulnerable. Despite enlisting sophisticated technology and an appeal for energy security, the effort failed to generate the desired groundswell of support.[17]

The distinction between the citizenry's continuing demands rooted in life experiences and those of a more ephemeral quality generated by issue entrepreneurs is critical for appreciating the working of modern democracy in a communications age. Do the fixed preferences of the public motivate and direct the strategic activities of politicians, or, conversely, do politicians shape the preferences of the public, at least those that are effectively communicated to Washington? To use an analogy from economics, the distinction is between demand-side and supply-side politics. At one time, before the media had begun to replace work-related, ethnic, religious, and other voluntary associations as the chief source of civic information, and before political entrepreneurs had the technological wherewithal to mass market ideas through such diverse and specialized media as television and targeted mail, it would have been easy to say that the citizenry's demands are the autonomous force of American politics. Today, however, the answer is less clear. The emergence of mass communications technology gives voice to politicians and organizations who enjoy the financial resources to broadcast commercials to millions of citizens or who have the legitimacy to command similar access via the news media. The president has both.

Except perhaps for the concerted efforts of the Framers to draft a Constitution that would mitigate transient, "inflamed popular passions," one seldom finds American political thought directed to this matter of supply-side politics. In early democratic theory, representatives served as passive receptacles with whom the citizens could deposit their demands. Later, when under Edmund Burke's influence, students of politics began to view representatives less as delegates and more as fiduciary agents, or trustees, who were to exercise independent judgment, little attention was given to marketing, except as an officeholder defended his policies in a reelection campaign. Even in twentieth-century discussions of party democracy, political parties formulate their programs through close association with mediating organizations that articulate constituency demands, and they adjust their programs to match the preferences of as broad a cross section of the electorate as they can.[18] The idea of campaigning to mobilize public opinion for issues currently before Congress has not so much been condemned by theory as ignored. Such campaigns and the continuing public relations of modern presidents suggest that traditional thinking about the relationship between the representative and the represented needs revision.

Consider the evidence of supply-side politics available in the cases introduced above. Before the efforts of MADD, the savings and loan industry, or the Alliance for Energy Security, one would have had difficulty finding instances of ordinary citizens importuning members of Congress to do something about drunk drivers, to rescind the IRS's plan to withhold interest, or to decontrol natural gas prices. Similarly, recall from Figure 5-1 that President Reagan's budget cuts enjoyed majority endorsement only briefly, and that moment came well before he initiated the public campaign for the policy's enactment. On none of those subjects does the issue's sponsor appear to have merely given expression to pent-up or nascent demands. Instead, they (the president included) acted as entrepreneurs creating demands and channeling their expression to Washington. These instances lend support to the recent observation by one member of Congress that "grass-roots lobbying today is a highly sophisticated effort. Just by the sheer mechanics of modern technology, they can often generate what [appears to be] a groundswell of public opinion, when in fact that groundswell does not really exist." [19]

A Variable Agenda and Volatile Outcomes

Individualized pluralism liberates politicians from institutional and party bonds. This has two effects on policy: politicians are freer to choose which issues they wish to sponsor, and the success of those issues depends more heavily upon the talents and fortunes of their sponsors. The first means greater variability in the issues that rise, albeit perhaps temporarily, to the top of the agenda in Washington. The second means that coalition building will be subject to new, extraneous forces and, hence, will be more volatile.

As presidents and aspirants to the office have traditionally tried to expand their electoral support beyond their party's core constituency, a number of political forces have kept them tethered fairly near home. The large role of state parties and mediating organizations in selecting presidential candidates at the party convention meant that these politicians could ill afford to advocate policies too distant from the priorities of the party's base. In Congress, the party supplied institutional leadership, which meant that its legislative agenda already enjoyed substantial progress toward the development of a winning coalition. Consequently, policies associated with political parties and their core groups resided comfortably atop the national agenda. Since the early 1970s, however, presidential selection reforms and the reduced role of the party in coalition building have relaxed the parties' influence on presidential policy.

Today's presidents, more likely to be outsiders, are freer to choose their issues than typically were their predecessors. As a consequence, the policy agenda will vary with the incumbent and will do so in ways that cannot be easily predicted by the president's party affiliation.[20] This does not mean that presidents will sponsor issues randomly. As individualized pluralism has loosened bonds to party and institution, it has tightened others. Attentiveness to public opinion, of course, has always been a chief occupational requirement for those who serve in elective office, but today's politicians are displaying exceptional sensitivity to the breezes that blow into Washington. Sometimes it shows up in the president's conformity to the perceived moods of the public, but more often it manifests itself in White House behavior in the way presidents seek to influence other politicians who are equally subject to public opinion and who have fewer resources at hand with which to mold opinion to their liking.

There is a compelling rationale for suspecting that the more presidents rest their leadership on going public, the more volatile policy outcomes in Washington will be. The public can be assumed to be more fickle in its assessments of politicians and policies than will be a stable community of Washington elites, whose business it is to make informed judgments. As the former becomes more important and the latter less, political relations will be more easily disrupted. Moreover, the effect of the president's own public standing on his ability to rally public opinion behind his policies exposes policy to extraneous and wholly unrelated events. Whatever affects the president's standing with the public will alter the prospects for those policies he sponsors. Sometimes the result may be altogether salutary, as in the boost President Reagan's 1981 budget proposals received after the assassination attempt. But if the president falters, so, too, will those policies that depend upon him for their sustenance.[21]

A president who is unable to generate a groundswell of popular support for his program may soon find others sharply escalating their demands on him in return for their cooperation. Unlike bargaining, where failure at one negotiating session can be repaired at the next, going public does not appear to offer similarly easy avenues for remedying failure. Also, one may assume that public opinion will be more volatile than elites' expectations for exchange. So too, then, will be a style of leadership that relies more heavily upon popular support.[22]

By virtue of going public, a president may actually contribute to unfavorable swings of opinion in the country. Casting himself as the fount from which the answers to the nation's problems flow, such a president may raise public expectations to unrealistic heights.[23] If so, he will be setting himself up for a fall in the polls, which will be closely followed by a decline in his fortunes in Washington. No modern occupant of the White House may be able to repeat President Truman's performance in maintaining a large measure of his influence in Washington while barely a quarter of the country approved his job performance. Going public may allow a popular president to soar, but even as he does so, he creates the risk of an eventual collapse.

The volatility of modern politics is plainly conveyed in the interpretations Washington politicians and the press give to presidential events. Two occurrences within a six-week period during the summer of 1985 illustrate the heavy dependence of policy on the public fortunes of its sponsor. After recouping much of his sagging popularity during late spring with a forceful national appeal for tax reform, President Reagan entered June with tax reform the number one issue on Congress's agenda. Other less politically favorable developments during these weeks, such as the controversial U.S. support for the contras in Nicaragua, had failed to register in the news and the public utterances of politicians to the same degree they might have had tax reform not grabbed the headlines. On June 14, however, terrorists hijacked an international airliner and took more than 50 American passengers to Lebanon as hostages. Tax reform faded quickly. During the next weeks, some aides contended that Reagan's presidency hung in the balance.[24] Would this crisis paralyze the administration the way the Iranian hostage crisis had Carter's? Early on, one senior White House official confided to *Washington Post* columnist Lou Cannon that it was fortunate that tax reform would not come up for a vote in Congress until fall. Aside from whatever potential damage the hostage crisis might have on the president's public standing, tax reform had suddenly fallen from public view; and without active public support, it would face tough going in Congress. Then, nearly two weeks into the crisis, as those close to the negotiations realized that the hostages might be released soon, White House aides began voicing brighter prognostications for tax reform. One Reagan aide told Cannon that if the president "were successful in winning the release of the hostages, he would gain in public standing and use his increased popularity to become a more activist president." [25] The next day, before an audience in Illinois, President Reagan returned to the tax issue, stating with renewed enthusiasm that after Congress returned from the summer recess, "I'm heading out to the country—I'm going to campaign all across the nation throughout the fall for tax fairness." [26]

The promise of a "fall offensive" of public appeals was repeated frequently during the next few weeks. But it was turned off again when on

July 12 the president was admitted to Bethesda Naval Medical Center to remove a growth from his colon. Next to the president's health, the foremost political question was, if the president is unable to take to the hustings, what becomes of tax reform? Reagan pollster Richard B. Wirthlin cautiously answered one reporter's query by saying that the effect on tax reform depended upon "the speed and completeness of the recovery." [27] Meanwhile, *New York Times* columnist Tom Wicker was speculating that the public sympathy the president's illness could be expected to engender would give his legislative program a new boost.[28] Senator Pete Wilson sounded a cautionary note on tax reform, however, when during the president's convalescence he told a reporter that the "tax reform is losing rather than gaining momentum [in the country]." [29]

The president gives a prime-time address on tax reform, and it immediately soars to the top of the legislative agenda. Within moments, the chair of the House Ways and Means Committee in his own televised address promises action and exhorts the public for demonstrations of support. But when hostages are seized a couple of weeks later, the prospects of tax reform dim. Just as quickly, they brighten when the hostages are released. Then comes the president's operation and his speedy recuperation, tax reform once again waning and waxing in a two-week period. In a system such as ours where governing coalitions are formed by independent officeholders rather than by party teams, the personal skills and fortunes of the sponsor have always been a key ingredient in an issue's chances of success, but with the injection of public opinion into policy deliberation through grass-roots campaigns and the president's popularity, policy making promises to become more volatile.

The President's Agenda

Whatever their differences in personality—and they were considerable—Theodore Roosevelt and Woodrow Wilson shared one attribute that shaped their approach to leadership style as much as any other. Both men were Progressives. This meant that each envisioned a responsive federal government led by an energetic president actively promoting the collective interests of the country over the particular concerns of its political, geographical and economic subdivisions. Strategically, both men solicited demonstrations of public support for their program. They had to, since many of their Progressive reforms would strip power and its usufructs from those politicians who would be asked to enact them.

Compared with the access of modern presidents to the airwaves and to jet transportation, their opportunities to go public were truly modest. However handicapped, this strategy sometimes held more promise than did negotiations. When Wilson, as New Jersey's newly elected governor, was once pressed by reporters to explain how he could possibly hope to win political reforms from a state legislature dominated by solons loyal to their party organizations, he replied, "I can talk, can't I?" [30]

Neither president enlisted public strategies casually. The idea of continuous forays into the country to generate public support for their initiatives before Congress was plainly impractical. In their day, the imbalance between costs imposed by confining technology and benefits limited by firm institutional resistance would have made frequent public campaigns foolhardy. Roosevelt and Wilson regarded going public as a strategy appropriate for a limited set of issues. These issues were ones in which traditional bargaining could be expected to fail and for which the president could legitimately play the role of the national tribune against "the special interests" entrenched in Congress. By and large, these issues constituted the Progressive agenda. When these presidents expatiated on political reform, on the regulation of big business, and, for Roosevelt especially, on conservation, they spoke to the country as well as for it. On more fractious national issues—such as tariff reform, a bloated embodiment of Congress's particularistic urges—they refrained from enlisting public strategies. One Roosevelt biographer writes: "Significantly, Roosevelt reserved nearly all his opportunities as president for public persuasion—'a bully pulpit,' he called the office—for appeals to transcendent national interests and higher standards of personal conduct, rather than redress or justice to particular people or groups." [31] Woodrow Wilson recognized the necessary symbolic distinction when on the subject of regulation he asserted, "The present conflict in this country is not between capital and labor. It is a contest between those few men in whose hands the wealth of the land is concentrated, and the rest of us." [32]

The practices of Roosevelt and Wilson suggest that going public is more serviceable for some issues than for others. A president will enjoy his strongest claim to the public's attention and support when he can present his policies as uprooting unsavory particularism. This theme must be played off a backdrop of an unassailable public interest. For good measure, these appeals should, when possible, exploit Americans' deeply ingrained distrust of politicians. On these rhetorical criteria, the Progressive agenda was a motherlode to Roosevelt and Wilson.

With so many avenues for going public available to modern presidents, one finds them frequently appealing for public support more casually and frequently before the same "special interests" many Progressives held in open contempt. Nonetheless, the president's special legitimacy in going to the people to defend the public interest from private greed remains a powerful force today. Nor have the strategic implications been lost on the White House's recent occupants. Presidents Carter, Reagan, and, to a lesser degree, Bush couched their major legislative proposals as a struggle between public and private interests. When, early in his term, Jimmy Carter began a series of prime-time television addresses in behalf of his comprehensive energy program currently before Congress, he did not hesitate to conjure up the threat of rapacious special interests: "We can be sure that all the special interest groups in the country will attack . . . this plan. . . . If they succeed with this approach, then the burden on the ordinary citizen, who is not organized into an interest group, would be crushing. There should be only one test for this plan—whether it will help our country." [33]

President Reagan also cloaked his major legislative proposals in the public interest. Although his program differed diametrically from Progressivism in advocating the reduction of federal responsibilities to provide social services and to regulate industry, the imagery fit comfortably in that tradition. Chapter 5 examined Reagan's rhetorical style in his promotion of the budget and tax cuts of 1981. The following is an excerpt from his presentation of his tax reform proposal to a national television audience on May 28, 1985:

> The proposal I am putting forth tonight for America's future will free us from the grip of special interests and create a binding commitment to the only special interest that counts, you, the people who pay America's bills. It will create millions of new jobs for working people and it will replace the politics of envy with a spirit of partnership.[34]

For the rest of the year, Reagan would continue to sound this theme.[35]

The earlier two presidents engaged in public leadership to the degree they could because, despite their different party affiliations, each sought to enact a Progressive agenda over formidable opposition in Congress. What did Presidents Carter and Reagan have in common that led them to enlist similar rhetorical devices? Certainly, it was not Progressivism. I earlier noted their outsider status, which enhanced the credibility of their attacks on special interests. Presidents of this era portray special interests as being entrenched in the bureaucracy that doles out government funds ("puzzle palaces on the Potomac" administering the "social pork barrel") rather than in the party machines that extorted graft and dispensed patronage.

Even more important than their outsider status, these presidents share the modern facility to go public. For its first practitioners, going public was an invention inspired by a policy agenda that would fail if left to the traditional political process. The ends dictated the means. Today the situation may well be reversed. As modern presidents seek to exploit their strategic advantage in public opinion, they gravitate toward issues that endow them with the strongest claim to represent the "public interest." By its very nature, the policy program of the president's core constituency will be ill-suited for the kinds of appeals public strategies require. But no matter; presidents are no longer much beholden to these constituencies. Nor, in the setting of supply-side politics, are their policy options sharply circumscribed by the once great need to choose among policy ideas that had over time already attracted a sizable number of supporters in Washington. The profusion of think tanks, new-styled interest groups, and even the congressional caucuses offer presidents an ample supply of policy ideas from which to choose.[36]

When President Reagan mentioned in his 1984 State of the Union message that he would ask the Treasury Department to examine tax reform, his remark elicited tepid applause befitting its apparent insignificance. Little did the assembled members of Congress and other president watchers realize that by year's end, tax reform would emerge as the centerpiece of his second administration. With it he hoped to establish the Republican party as the new majority party of the country. That one of the principal authors of the Treasury bill had been a colleague of some of the early proponents of the "flat tax" proposal at the Hoover Institution illustrates the new, alternative sources of policy available to modern presidents.

As one looks to the future, the prospect for the continued use of going public as presidential strategy shines bright. The forces of technology and of an evolving political environment that set public campaigning from the White House on its current trajectory have not abated. Moreover, professional self-interest dictates that all participants in Washington's politics take going public into account as they plan their strategies. The president must as he decides which policies he wishes to promote. Would-be presidents must as they groom themselves and tailor their policy appeals for a future bid for the White House. So must White House correspondents as they evaluate the president's performance and as they weigh his rhetoric against their own and others' notions of reality. And so must all who do business with the president and are thereby vulnerable to his public appeals. The strategic adaptations these men and women are making will, as much as its original causes, guarantee that going public will occupy a prominent place in the strategic repertoire of future presidents.

Notes

1. The standards of performance Franklin Roosevelt established for his successors is the subject of William E. Leuchtenburg, *In the Shadow of FDR* (Ithaca, N.Y.: Cornell University Press, 1985).
2. Peter T. Kilborn, "The Key Democrat," *New York Times*, May 30, 1985, 15; and Hedrick Smith, "Analysis of Democrats' Strategy on Tax Reform? Yes—With Three Conditions," *Washington Post National Weekly Edition,* February 18, 1985, 28; and Steven V. Roberts, "A Most Important Man on Capitol Hill," *New York Times Magazine,* September 22, 1985, 44.
3. Alan Ehrenhalt, "Speaker's Job Transformed under O'Neill," *Congressional Quarterly Weekly Report,* June 22, 1985, 1247.
4. Julia Malone, "Party 'Whips' Lose Their Snap to TV and Voters Back Home," *Christian Science Monitor,* July 27, 1984, 16.
5. Steven V. Roberts, "Senate's New Breed Shuns Novice Role," *New York Times,* November 26, 1984, 15.
6. A recent example is the Department of Agriculture's grass-roots campaign to persuade Congress to adopt farm legislation it drafted. Ward Sinclair, "USDA's Farm Bill Lobbying Hit," *Washington Post,* October 1, 1985, A5.
7. Incidents such as this one are recounted in Edwin R. Bayley, *Joe McCarthy and the Press* (Madison: University of Wisconsin Press, 1981).

8. Ibid., 216-219; and Richard H. Rovere, *Senator Joe McCarthy* (New York: Harcourt, Brace, 1959).

9. Rovere, *Senator Joe McCarthy*.

10. Daniel C. Hallin, "Changing Conventions in Television Coverage of the Presidency, 1969-1985" (Paper delivered at the Annual Meeting of the Southern Political Science Association, Nashville, Tenn., November 1985). Technological advances—especially the introduction of the digital video effects machine—have had a hand in this change. Rather than an anchorperson editorializing during a video segment that may wander away from the subject, modern editing technology allows broadcast journalists to harness video footage to reinforce their message. For a discussion of the effects of modern broadcast technology, see Joan Bieder, "Television Reporting," in *The Communications Revolution in Politics,* ed. Gerald Benjamin (New York: Academy of Political Science, 1982), 36-48.

11. For a discussion of the Senate's special role in spawning presidential candidates and in the process incubating new policy issues, see Nelson W. Polsby, *Political Innovation in America* (New Haven: Yale University Press, 1984).

12. Martin Tolchin, "Baker Reported Planning to Quit Senate After '84," *New York Times*, January 11, 1983, Al.

13. Cited in Samuel Kernell and Dianne Kernell, *Congress: We the People* (Washington, D.C.: American Political Science Association, 1984), 90-91.

14. Timothy B. Clark, "Bankers' Opposition to Withholding May Leave a Bitter Legislative Aftertaste," *National Journal*, April 2, 1983, 700-703. Similarly, on the speedy passage of legislation providing federal incentive payments to states to strengthen enforcement of garnishing the wages of parents who are delinquent in child support payments, see Steven V. Roberts, "Political Survival: It's Women and Children First," *New York Times,* December 6, 1983, 10.

15. Ann Cooper, "Middleman Mail," *National Journal*, September 14, 1985, 2038.

16. For the background of this issue and a description of Kasten's floor maneuvers, see Clark, "Bankers' Opposition," 700-703.

17. One member targeted by the campaign, Philip Sharp of Indiana, calculated that he should have gotten 27,500 post cards according to the number of volunteer kits the Natural Gas Supply Association had distributed to his district. Instead, he received 1,125 post cards, and 200 of those had antidecontrol messages scribbled over the printed message. Cooper, "Middleman Mail," 2041. See also Milton R. Benjamin, "Natural Gas Lobby Organizes 'Grass-Roots' Decontrol Move," *Washington Post*, August 13, 1983, Al.

18. Two statements that arrive at much the same conclusion on this matter via quite different intellectual exercises are E. E. Schattschneider, *Party Government* (New York: Holt, Rinehart and Winston, 1942), 1-17, passim; and Anthony Downs, *An Economic Theory of Democracy* (New York: Harper and Row, 1957), 114-141.

19. Cooper, "Middleman Mail," 2037.

20. Nathaniel Beck makes precisely this point in his statistical analysis of recent administrations' macroeconomics policies. See his "Parties, Administrations, and American Macroeconomic Outcomes," *American Political Science Review* 76 (March 1982): 83-93.

21. Recent presidents have faltered in their popularity ratings more quickly and more seriously than their predecessors of the 1950s and 1960s. For evidence of this, see Samuel Kernell, "The Presidency and the People: The Modern Paradox," in *The Presidency and the Political System*, ed. Michael Nelson (Washington, D.C.: CQ Press, 1984), 253-256.

22. The volatility of popularity ratings is examined in detail in Chapter 7. See also Samuel Kernell, "The Presidency and the People: The Modern Paradox," in *The*

Presidency and the Political System, ed. Michael Nelson (Washington, D.C.: CQ Press, 1984), 223-263.

23. Godfrey Hodgson so argues in *All Things to All Men* (New York: Simon and Schuster, 1980), 209-260.

24. Lou Cannon, "The Wait It Out Pitfall," *Washington Post,* June 23, 1985, A26.

25. Lou Cannon, "Reagan Agenda May Get a Lift," *Washington Post,* July 1, 1985, A19. For a more general treatment of the relation between the president's popularity and programmatic support, see Barry Sussman, "How Public Opinion Surveys May Bring Us a Fairer Tax System," *Washington Post National Weekly Edition,* June 24, 1985, 37.

26. Cannon, "Reagan Agenda," A19.

27. Jack Nelson, "Illness May Dim Outlook for President's Programs," *Los Angeles Times,* July 21, 1985, 1.

28. Tom Wicker, "After Surgery, What?" *New York Times,* July 23, 1985, 27.

29. Nelson, "Illness May Dim Outlook," 12. Senator Wilson's impressions were confirmed in Lou Cannon and Helen Dewar, "Tax Overhaul Hit in Poll, GOP Caucus," *Washington Post,* September 25, 1985, A3.

30. John Milton Cooper, Jr., *The Warrior and the Priest* (Cambridge: Harvard University Press, 1983), 173.

31. Ibid., 86.

32. Ibid., 126.

33. Jimmy Carter, "The Energy Problem" (address to the nation, April 18, 1977), *Public Papers of the Presidents of the United States, Jimmy Carter, 1977* (Washington, D.C.: Government Printing Office, 1978), 661-662. A year later when he kicked off his "three martini lunch" tax reform, he argued, "Average Americans foot the bill for the rich and others who mark off from their tax payments high-priced meals, high-priced theater tickets, ballgame tickets, first-class air travel, even country club dues.... And the ones who pay are the quiet, average American working family members" (Jimmy Carter, "Tax Reduction and Reform" [remarks concerning proposals submitted to the Congress, April 17, 1978], *Public Papers of the Presidents, 1978,* 755).

34. "Text of Speech by President on Overhauling the Tax System," *New York Times,* May 29, 1985, A18.

35. David E. Rosenbaum reports, "President Reagan has often succeeded in establishing himself as champion of the people and his political opponents as tools of 'special interest' " ("Momentum and the Tax Bill," *New York Times,* October 19, 1985, 8).

36. On the role of "think tanks" as the origin of ideas for the Reagan administration, see Dom Bonafede, "Issue-Oriented Heritage Foundation Hitches Its Wagon to Reagan's Star," *National Journal,* March 20, 1982, 502-507; Al Kamen and Howard Kurtz, "Theorists on Right Find Fertile Ground," *Washington Post,* August 9, 1985, A1; and Sidney Blumenthal, "Outside Foundation Recruited the Inside Troops," *Washington Post,* September 10, 1985, A1. On presidential-caucus relations, see Susan Webb Hammond, "Congressional Caucuses and Party Leaders" (Paper prepared for delivery at the Annual Meeting of the American Political Science Association, Washington, D.C., August 30-September 2, 1984).

Appendix

Chapter 4

To incorporate the research of William W. Lammers on the public activities of modern presidents, I adopted his coding scheme. I also consulted with Professor Lammers at the early stages of this study for his advice on how to code difficult cases. The present analysis, therefore, benefits from both his considerable research and good judgment.[1]

The three general categories of public activities presented in Figures 4-1, 4-2, and 4-3 are intended to be neither mutually exclusive nor together an exhaustive classification of all public behavior. Press conferences (examined in Table 3-2), purely ceremonial functions such as lighting the White House Christmas tree, vacation travel, and minor public activities such as White House receptions and brief remarks have been excluded from the analysis.

Addresses

Major addresses are those generally delivered in Washington, broadcast on television or radio, and focused on more than a narrow potential audience. Inaugural and State of the Union speeches are included in this group. Note that because of the extensive number of nationally broadcast radio addresses by President Reagan, I have separated his radio from his television addresses in Figure 4-1. Minor addresses are all nonmajor statements made outside the White House in which the president spoke more than 1,000 words. Question and answer sessions, even if conducted outside a formal press conference setting, are excluded.

Political Travel

To distinguish purely vacation travel from work-related travel, only those travel days that involved public political activity are included in Figure 4-2. Moreover, to be coded as domestic political travel, the president must do more than engage in brief conversation with reporters. To be coded as political foreign travel, the travel day must include comments exceeding 200 words, a meeting with a head of state, or attendance at an international conference, even if the president does not engage in public activity.

Appearances

Washington appearances take place away from the White House and the Executive Office Building and include all appearances in Washington and its surrounding suburbs. Brief comments with reporters are excluded from both Washington and U.S. appearances, but prepared remarks on arrival are included in the coding. Unlike Professor Lammers, who excluded President Carter's town meetings, I have coded them as constituting both days of travel and appearances.

Chapter 7

The coefficients reported in Table 7-4 are the products of an elaborate procedure to estimate well-specified models of partisan popularity for the seven presidents from Eisenhower through Reagan. Each stage of the statistical analysis of the popularity time-series presents choices that indirectly contribute to the strengths of the economic variables reported in Table 7-4. These choices concern variable specification and the implicit model of opinion change employed in the statistical analysis.

Specification of Variables

Deciding which variables should be included in the statistical analysis and how each should be operationally defined has important implications for the results. The omission or misspecification of noneconomic variables can bias the estimates of the economic variables. Generally, this phase of the analysis closely follows the procedures employed in earlier published research on presidential popularity. The reader is referred to those sources for a fuller discussion of the issues presented below.[2]

The dependent variables in the regression equations reported in Tables A-1, A-2, A-3, and A-4 are the percentages among respondents in each of the partisan subgroups who answered the monthly Gallup query "Do you approve or disapprove of the way ____ is handling his job as president?" with approval. If the president's popularity rating were to drop below 25 percent or rise above 75 percent, the "ceiling and floor effects" of variables expressed as proportions might bias the results. The president's overall popularity rating rarely exceeds these extremes, however, so that transforming them to adjust for ceiling and floor effects is normally unnecessary.[3] Estimating popular support for partisans, however, is a different matter. As indicated in Table 7-3, among those who identify with the president's party, support infrequently drops below 75 percent approving. And although the mean support levels of the opposition party's identifiers indicate that their support typically resides above 25 percent approving, the standard deviations indicate that it has sometimes declined below this threshold. To adjust for this potential bias, the regression equations in Tables A-1 and A-2 were also estimated with a logistical transformation of the popularity ratings. Since the relative strengths of the economic variables were unaffected by this procedure and the untransformed values are more readily interpretable, the results presented below and in Chapter 7 use the untransformed percentages.

The independent variables of principal interest in Chapter 7 are unemployment and inflation. A variety of statistical evidence suggests that citizens pay greater attention to *changes* in political conditions during a relatively brief time period than either to changes since the beginning of the president's term or to absolute conditions. As one of Reagan's political consultants averred, "It's far better to come into an election with a 9% unemployment rate that's falling than a 6% rate that is rising."[4] Accordingly, unemployment and inflation are defined as the percentage change in the unemployment rate and consumer price index over the preceding six months.[5] Finally, I have assumed that the public does not hold the president responsible for changing economic conditions during his first six months in office. The economic variables for this period were set at their respective mean values over the incumbent's term.

A number of dummy and real-value exogenous variables also appear in the four Appendix tables. Since presidents frequently begin their terms with a surfeit of popular support, an early-term variable was constructed by setting its initial value at 6 and decreasing it one unit each month until it reached a value of 0. A similar variable was constructed for those international events, typically crises, during which the president's overall rating appeared to surge temporarily beyond its normal level. Here, the dummy variable was set at 5 for the first observation after the onset of the rally event and decreased one unit per month until reaching 0. The following events were designated as rally events in Tables A-1, A-2, A-3, and A-4.[6]

Two long-lasting events that had a substantial negative effect on the public standing of Presidents Johnson and Nixon were the Vietnam War and Watergate, respectively. The first is measured with two indicators: the monthly figures of U.S. war dead and the log of the number of bombing missions over North Vietnam. Each measures a different aspect of the war's intensity, and Tables A-1 and A-3 show each to have been independently related to President Johnson's popularity. Watergate is represented by a simple dummy variable that assumes a value of 0 before the Senate Watergate Committee convened and a value of 1 thereafter.[7] Since political events and conditions are argued here to shape political evaluations to the degree they become political issues, I have weighted the Vietnam and Watergate variables by the percentage of Gallup Poll respondents who named this issue as "one of the most important problems facing the country

	Rally 1	Rally 2	Rally 3	Rally 4
Eisenhower	Korean truce	Sputnik	Lebanon	Khrushchev visit
Kennedy	Bay of Pigs	Berlin wall	Berlin crisis	Cuban missile crisis
Johnson	Dominican Republic	Bombing of North Vietnam	Glassboro summit	Tet offensive
Nixon	Vietnam peace agreement	—	—	—
Ford	Mayaquez	—	—	—
Carter	Camp David summit	Iran-Afghanistan	—	—
Reagan	Korean airliner	Grenada	—	—
Bush	Panama	Desert Shield	Gulf War	—

today." [8] A similar procedure was applied to the economic variables. Despite the variability of inflation and unemployment as major public concerns in recent years, this procedure had little effect on the coefficients. Therefore, to facilitate interpretation, I have retained the unweighted values for unemployment and inflation.

A Dynamic Model of Opinion Change

One may reasonably assume that events such as those presented above continue to have a residual effect on the president's popular support beyond the month in which they occur. This information must be incorporated into the analysis to obtain properly specified equations. How one estimates the residual effects of incremental opinion change depends upon the model of opinion formation under consideration. In recent years many specifications for the lagged effects of past events have been suggested in the literature.[9] Several approaches were tested before settling on an exponential decay function of past events on subsequent popularity ratings. By including the approval rating for the previous month on the right-hand side of the regression equation, I am stipulating that past events continue to have a lingering effect on the president's current popularity, and that they decay at the same rate for each exogenous variable.[10]

Inclusion of the president's popularity for the preceding month in the equation means that the coefficients for the other variables state their immediate effect on popularity. This explains why many of the coefficients in Tables A-1 and A-2 may appear to be unduly small and statistically

Table A-1 Effects of Political Conditions on Presidential Popularity among Party Groups: Eisenhower, Kennedy, and Johnson

	Eisenhower (N = 86)			Kennedy (N = 32)			Johnson (N = 50)		
	Same party	Independents	Opposition party	Same party	Independents	Opposition party	Same party	Independents	Opposition party
Intercept	27.9	23.8	20.3	37.1	21.8	17.2	58.5	43.1	22.9
Early-term	.4	1.2	1.8	.8	1.5	3.3	1.0	.8	−.1
Rally 1	.4	.4	1.0	1.3	1.2	1.2	.9	1.0	.4
Rally 2	.8	1.3	1.5	1.0	1.5	2.4	.7	2.0	1.5
Rally 3	.3	.1	.5	.1	1.9	−.2	.7	−.2	1.0
Rally 4	.4	.5	1.0	2.1	2.0	2.5	−.6	.5	−.5
VN bombings	—	—	—	—	—	—	−.001	−.005	−.0013
U.S. killed in VN	—	—	—	—	—	—	−.008	−.008	−.006
Unemployment	−3.1	−2.8	−4.2	−99.3	−137.8	−77.3	−523.6	−841.2	−247.1
Inflation	−290.2	−498.2	−715.6	—	—	—	−1,012.8	−2,225.1	−1,111.2
Lag of popularity	.68	.64	.59	.52	.61	.54	.23	.26	.56
Adjusted r^2	.61	.61	.64	.75	.76	.75	.87	.87	.92
Durbin's h	2.57	2.29	1.65	1.25	2.8	.82	−3.8	2.3	.90

Table A-2 Effects of Political Conditions on Presidential Popularity among Party Groups: Nixon, Ford, Carter, and Reagan

	Nixon (N = 6)			Ford (N = 21)			Carter (N = 40)			Reagan (N = 40)		
	Same party	Independents	Opposition party	Same party	Independents	Opposition party	Same party	Independents	Opposition party	Same party	Independents	Opposition party
Intercept	19.9	10.0	11.4	46.8	40.7	22.7	26.0	31.1	16.7	43.7	22.2	8.9
Early-term	.8	1.0	.7	-.5	-.1	.1	3.2	4.9	4.0	.8	1.3	1.2
Rally 1	.5	.8	.4	1.3	1.7	1.0	2.0	1.9	1.1	.9	1.2	1.6
Rally 2	—	—	—	—	—	—	3.1	3.2	3.0	.8	.4	.6
Watergate	-36.6	-35.1	-66.0	—	—	—	—	—	—	—	—	—
Unemployment	-46.4	-20.2	-175.9	-2.2	-19.0	-5.4	-26.8	-28.5	-37.6	-10.1	-16.6	-10.3
Inflation	-82.8	-48.3	-1.1	-132.6	-111.4	-101.2	-120.9	-199.1	-69.9	—	—	—
Lag of Popularity	.76	.81	.71	.34	.18	.42	.62	.44	.50	.46	.55	.65
Adjusted r^2	.92	.91	.91	.39	.33	.38	.81	.80	.76	.51	.72	.88
Durbin's h	3.38	3.30	1.40	2.77	.68	1.51	-1.04	-1.84	-1.40	-1.13	-1.21	-2.16

Table A-3 Long-term and Mean Effects of Political Conditions on Presidential Popularity among Party Groups: Eisenhower, Kennedy, and Johnson

	Eisenhower			Kennedy			Johnson		
	Same party	Independents	Opposition party	Same party	Independents	Opposition party	Same party	Independents	Opposition party
Early-term	1.3	.43	4.39	1.67	3.85	7.17	1.29	1.08	−.23
Rally 1	1.25	1.11	2.44	2.7	3.08	2.61	1.17	1.35	.91
Rally 2	2.5	3.61	3.66	2.1	3.85	5.22	.91	2.7	3.41
Rally 3	.94	.28	1.22	.32	.04	4.13	−.26	.94	2.27
Rally 4	1.25	1.39	2.44	4.38	5.13	5.43	−.78	−.68	1.14
Total rally (R1–R4)	5.94	6.39	9.76	9.6	12.1	17.39	1.04	4.31	7.73
VN bombings	—	—	—	—	—	—	−.0013	−.0007	−.003
U.S. killed in VN	—	—	—	—	—	—	−.010	−.011	−.014
Unemployment	−9.7	−7.8	−10.2	−206.9	−353.3	−168.0	−680.0	−1,136.8	−561.6
Inflation	−906.9	−1,388.9	−1,745.4	—	—	—	−1,315.32	−3,006.9	−2,525.5

Table A-4 Long-term and Mean Effects of Political Conditions on Presidential Popularity among Party Groups: Nixon, Ford, Carter, Reagan, and Bush

	Nixon			Ford			Carter		
	Same party	Independents	Opposition party	Same party	Independents	Opposition party	Same party	Independents	Opposition party
Early-term	3.33	5.26	2.41	−.76	−.12	−.17	8.42	8.75	8.0
Rally 1	2.08	4.21	1.38	1.97	2.07	1.72	5.26	3.39	2.2
Rally 2	—	—	—	—	—	—	8.15	5.71	6.0
Rally 3	—	—	—	—	—	—	—	—	—
Total rally	2.08	4.21	1.38	1.97	2.07	1.72	13.41	9.1	8.2
Watergate	—	—	—	—	—	—	—	—	—
Unemployment	−193.3	−106.3	−606.6	−3.33	−23.2	−9.3	17.9	−50.9	−75.2
Inflation	−345.0	−254.2	−3.79	−200.9	−135.9	−174.5	−318.16	−355.54	−137.8

Table A-4 Continued

	Reagan			Bush		
	Same party	Independents	Opposition party	Same party	Independents	Opposition party
Early-term	1.48	2.90	3.43	2.1	−2.1	−1.9
Rally 1	1.67	2.67	4.57	2.5	2.5	2.8
Rally 2	1.48	.89	1.71	1.6	2.6	1.4
Rally 3	—	—	—	3.6	7.4	6.5
Total rally	3.15	3.56	6.28	7.7	12.5	10.7
Watergate	—	—	—	—	—	—
Unemployment	−18.7	−36.89	−29.43	3.8	−9.8	10.4
Inflation	—	—	—	−253.0	−461.0	−297.0

NOTE: The main entries state the cumulative effects of the variables on the presidents' current popularity.

insignificant. A variable's long-term effect on popularity can be obtained with the following formula:[11]

$$\text{long-term effect of } X = \frac{bX_t}{1-cY_{t-1}}$$

where X_t is an exogenous variable and Y_{t-1} is the lag term of the dependent variable. The estimates presented in Tables A-3 and A-4 have been transformed to represent the long-term effects of the variables on popularity.

The coefficients have been transformed in another way as well. To compare the actual effects of variables that are based on different units of measurement, the coefficients have been multiplied by their mean values.[12] The relationships reported, therefore, in parentheses in Tables A-3 and A-4, and in Table 7-4, represent the long-term, "level" effects of the variables on the president's approval rating.

Notes

1. For the most comprehensive presentation of Lammers's work, see William W. Lammers, "Presidential Attention-Focusing Activities," in *The President and the American Public*, ed. Doris A. Graber (Philadelphia: Institute for the Study of Human Issues, 1982), 145-171.

2. Samuel Kernell, "Explaining Presidential Popularity," *American Political Science Review* 72 (June 1978): 506-522; and Samuel Kernell and Douglas A. Hibbs, Jr., "A Critical Threshold Model of Presidential Popularity," in *Contemporary Political Economy*, ed. Douglas A. Hibbs, Jr., and Heino Fassbender (New York: North-Holland, 1981), 49-72.

3. John E. Mueller was among the first to test for and dismiss these effects on the estimation of presidential popularity. See his "Presidential Popularity from Truman to Johnson," *American Political Science Review* 64 (March 1970): 18-34.

4. Rich Jaroslovsky, "Economic Upturn Aids President's Popularity, but It Is Not Panacea," *Wall Street Journal*, April 28, 1983, 1.

5. The unemployment and inflation variables have been annualized. The evidence for this specification is discussed fully in Kernell, "Explaining Presidential Popularity."

6. These events were identified by using criteria developed in Samuel Kernell, "Presidential Popularity and Electoral Preference" (Ph.D. diss., University of California, Berkeley, 1975); and in Richard A. Brody, "That Special Moment: The Public Response to International Crisis" (Paper delivered at the Annual Meeting of the Western Political Science Association, Seattle, Wash., March 24, 1983).

7. Kernell, "Explaining Presidential Popularity."

8. This procedure is suggested in the work of Charles W. Ostrom, Jr., and Dennis M. Simon, "Promise and Performance: A Dynamic Model of Presidential Popularity," *American Political Science Review* 79 (June 1985): 334-358.

9. Among others is the distributed lag approach of Douglas A. Hibbs, Jr., "On the Reward for Economic Outcomes: Macroeconomic Performance and Mass Political Support in the United States, Great Britain, and Germany," *Journal of Politics* 44 (May 1982): 426-461. For shortcomings of this procedure, see Samuel Kernell, "Strategy and Ideology: The Politics of Unemployment and Inflation in Modern Capitalist Democracies" (Paper delivered at the Annual Meeting of the American Political Science Association, Washington, D.C., August 28-31, 1980). Kristen R. Monroe employs an Almon model of lagged effects of the economy in *Presidential Popularity and the Economy* (New York: Praeger, 1984). For a different (and somewhat iconoclastic) approach to this issue, see Helmut Norpoth and Thom Yantek, "Macroeconomic Conditions and Fluctuations of Presidential Popularity: The Question of Lagged Effects," *American Journal of Political Science* 27 (November 1983): 785-807.

10. After several tests, a standard exponential decay function for all independent variables appeared to be a reasonable one.

11. For a discussion of this procedure, see Potluri Rao and Roger LeRoy Miller, *Applied Econometrics* (Belmont, Calif.: Wadsworth Publishing Co., 1971), 45-46. Rao and Miller also provide a useful discussion (pp. 123-125) of Durbin's h, a statistic for testing serial correlation of the error terms in autoregressive models. Eleven of the 21 entries equal or exceed the values ± 1.645 indicating that the errors are serially correlated. An analysis (not shown) of the residuals suggested first-order autocorrelation. Reestimating the equations with an instrumental variable substituted for the lagged term eliminated the serial correlation. While the overall relationships are weaker than those reported in Tables A-3 and A-4, the relative strengths of unemployment and inflation with each other and across party groups were unaffected by this procedure.

12. This approach to causal interpretation of regression estimates is persuasively advocated by Christopher H. Achen in *Interpreting and Using Regression* (Beverly Hills, Calif.: Sage Publications, 1982), 68-77.

Index